ÆSTHETICS

A Reader in Philosophy of the Arts

Second Edition

■ David Goldblatt ■
Denison University

■ Lee B. Brown ■
The Ohio State University

PEARSON
Prentice
Hall

Upper Saddle River, New Jersey 07458

Library of Congress Cataloging-in-Publication Data
Aesthetics : a reader in philosophy of the arts / [edited by] David Goldblatt, Lee B. Brown.—2nd ed.
    p. cm.
    ISBN 0-13-112144-8
  1. Aesthetics.   2. Art—Philosophy.   I. Goldblatt, David   II. Brown, Lee

    BH39.A287 2005
    111'.85—dc22

                                                                                    2004004851

Editorial Director: Charlyce Jones-Owen
Senior Acquisitions Editor: Ross Miller
Assistant Editor: Wendy Yurash
Editorial Assistant: Carla Worner
Production Liaison: Fran Russello
Director of Marketing: Beth Mejia
Marketing Manager: Kara Kindstrom
Marketing Assistant: Jennifer Lang
Manufacturing Buyer: Christina Helder
Cover Design: Bruce Kenselaar
Composition/Full-Service Project Management: Patty Donovan/Pine Tree Composition
Printer/Binder: Courier Companies, Inc.
Cover Printer: Coral Graphics, Inc.

Credits and acknowledgments borrowed from other sources and reproduced,
with permission, in this textbook.

Pearson Education, Ltd., London   Pearson Educación de Mexico,
Pearson Education Singapore Pte. Ltd.   S.A. de C.V.
Pearson Education Canada, Ltd.   Pearson Education Malaysia, Pte. Ltd.
Pearson Education—Japan   Pearson Education, Upper Saddle River,
Pearson Education Australia Pty. Limited   New Jersey
Pearson Education North Asia Ltd.

10 9 8 7 6 5 4 3
ISBN 0-13-112144-8

For Sarah, Wes, and Emily

CONTENTS

PART IV ■ MUSIC ■ 181

PART V ■ DANCE ■ 235

PART VI ■ LITERATURE ■ 265

PART VII ■ PERFORMANCE ■ 315

SPECIAL
ACKNOWLEDGMENTS

■|■

A book with this many readings is an undertaking by many people. The editors are grateful for their contributions. We would like to thank every author and publishing house for the essays contained in this volume. Authors deserving special mention here include David Antin, Sally Banes, Peg Brand, David Carrier, Noël Carroll, Ted Cohen, Edmund Burke Feldman, Theodore Gracyk, Fredric Jameson, Laura Mulvey, Albert Mawere Opoku, Diana Raffman, Sara K. Schneider, and Robert Venturi. Donald Kuspit has helped us track down several sources. We must single out Philip Alperson, the editor of *The Journal of Aesthetics and Art Criticism,* for his prompt assistance with permissions from that publication. For some early advice on our selections and organization, we acknowledge the help of Peter Kivy and Richard Shusterman. At Prentice Hall we very much appreciated our dealings with an enthusiastic editor, Angie Stone, who saw to it that we were not neglected and who made it a point of staying in touch with our project. In preparing the final copy for Prentice Hall, we also benefited from the experience and advice of Harriet Tellem.

Much of our scattered and sometimes overwhelming paperwork took place at the offices of the Department of Philosophy at Denison University and we are grateful for the patience and tolerance of its departmental members, Barbara Fultner, Tony Lisska, Mark Moller, Ronald E. Santoni, and Steven Vogel. Also, Pat Davis, the philosophy department administrative assistant, was there when we needed her. Jennifer Seeds spent a good part of a summer completing many of the tasks we dreaded doing ourselves and she deserves a very special nod of thanks for all her work in putting together this book.

We would like to thank the following for their help in reviewing our manuscript: Fraser Snowden, Scholars' College; Perry Weddle, California State University, Sacramento; Orville Clark, University of Wisconsin, Green Bay; Cynthia A. Freeland, University of Houston; Carl R. Hausman, Pennsylvania State University; Richard Shusterman, Temple University; Peter Kivy, Rutgers University; and Terry H. Foreman, Murray State University.

SPECIAL
ACKNOWLEDGMENTS
FOR THE SECOND EDITION

Our second edition contains many new readings. Some of the selections appear in this edition because of friendly and not-so-friendly advice concerning gaps that needed to be filled in the first edition. We have also added excerpts in order to update issues and controversies in the expanding field of aesthetics. While preserving the fundamental purpose of the book, we revised some sections and replaced others with ones we felt were more appropriate. In addition, we have moderately expanded our offerings in non-European art and aesthetics. We have revised introductions and added some useful illustrations. Also, we have attempted to correct as many errors as we could find.

For their advice and for their generous support and written contributions we would like to thank the following friends and colleagues for help in the second edition: Philip Auslander, Richard Bodman, Peg Zeglin Brand, Allen Carlson, Ted Cohen, Anne Eaton, Peter Eisenman, Ted Gracyk, Garry L. Hagberg, Greg Hayman, Paul Mattick, Henry John Pratt, Diana Raffman, and Anita Waters. We thank Barbara Fultner, Tony Lisska, Jonathan Maskit, Mark Moller, Ron Santoni, Robert Venturi, and Steve Vogel, members of the Department of Philosophy at Denison University. Also, Kenneth Wahl, an American artist living in Paris, has been a help and an inspiration. In addition, we thank Robert Kraut, Tom Leddy, and David Mitchell.

We would like to thank our philosophy editor Ross Miller, the Senior Acquisitions Editor for philosophy and religion at Prentice Hall, and Carla Worner, the Editorial Assistant for Philosophy and Religion at Prentice Hall, who have helped get us many of things we requested for this edition. Patty Donovan, our Project Coordinator at Pine Tree Composition, has been generously responsive to every request and question.

GENERAL
INTRODUCTION

The philosophy of the arts, like art itself, is a far-reaching and fascinating area of inquiry and investigation. It is often as microscopic as it is macroscopic, as devious as it is sometimes straightforward. We hope we have put together a collection of readings that represent the scope and detail that is the philosophy of the arts and one that is as exciting and instigating as art itself.

It was the Scottish philosopher David Hume (1711–1776) who recognized a human tendency to give simple identities through language to complex and changing entities. Hume thought that yielding to this tendency might mislead us into thinking of very diverse and changing phenomena as if they were unified and stable wholes.

Our perspective on the philosophy of the arts heeds Hume's warning. We believe this reader reflects a tendency to resist thinking of art as one seamless whole. We believe that one way to acknowledge the diverse character of philosophical thinking about the arts is by organizing our readings in terms of areas of art. Another is to offer a great many readings that display the panoramic and complex field that aesthetics actually is.

Consider these remarks by Peter Kivy, found in a presidential address delivered before the American Society for Aesthetics:

> We may be wise, then to take as a temporary heuristic principle, if not a timeless truth . . . "There is no art, there are only arts". . . . We can no longer hover above our subject matter like Gods from machines, bestowing theory upon practice in sublime and even boastful ignorance of what takes place in the dirt and mess of the workshop.

Traditional categories of art, even when they are not explicitly addressed, often function as paradigms that initiate general claims about art, frequently extending their domains to areas where former insights are sometimes vitiated. So it may be, for example, that what an *audience* is for music might be very different from what it is for film or painting. By constructing our text in a way that encourages learning aesthetics in context, we hope to represent philosophical writing in its most beneficial form. We also feel that students will come to understand art and the philosophical study of it simultaneously—something like learning a foreign language in a foreign restaurant instead of in a domestic classroom.

By its organization, we hope this book of readings will introduce a reader at any level of sophistication to philosophical problems as they pertain to *specific* arts. So it is that the book is divided into sections for Painting, Architecture, Music, Literature, and so forth. The sheer complexity of the topic should not take anything away from the fact that the philosophy of the arts constitutes an intriguing and inviting network of human activities. Rather, it should add to it.

Of course, many philosophers have argued that all the arts, no matter how diverse in form and function, really do have something fundamental in common. The foregoing remarks should not discourage those who want to engage in gradual generalization about the arts from doing so. The anthology includes essays—particularly in the final two sections of the collection—that address the feasibility of a single philosophy of *all* the arts or of aesthetic experience. Many classic texts, as well as key contemporary sources, can be found there.

Two further points about the volume should be stressed. First, we try to recognize the growing merge, especially at artistic intersections, of the analytical and continental schools of philosophy. Second, we try to direct more attention than has been customary to the popular arts and to the issues that occupy the borders between the so-called high and low arts. In short, we believe that it is time for a more open and inclusive approach to the philosophy of the arts.

The volume is a large one. While not pretending to be a definitive source book, it will provide instructors and students with a wide range of choices from which they can compose their own list of readings. We like to think of this book not merely as the textual basis for a philosophical regimen, but as the kind of book anyone interested in the arts might take along were they to be stranded on the proverbial desert island. And we hope it will help whet an exile's desire to get back to the artworks left behind.

David Goldblatt
Lee B. Brown

PART I

PAINTING

Before the advent of modern painting it was widely assumed that art was *essentially* a species of imitation. While the theory came in many forms, the most straightforward version assumed that such art as painting and drawing aimed at making faithful *copies* of their subject matter. Beginning with this assumption about the nature of art, Plato developed his elaborate critique of the arts. For Plato, the construction of visual copies of things is not a noble activity. Indeed, quite the opposite.

On several grounds, the art historian Ernst Gombrich casts doubt on the assumption with which Plato begins, namely that the idea of making a copy of something is a coherent one. *Can* artists really make copies of things? Graphic artists of antiquity did not represent things differently than we moderns do simply because they were less skillful or less intelligent. For one thing, Gombrich says a painting in a given style reflects the temperament of its artist. Second, the techniques by which artists learn how to convey information about a subject matter—which Gombrich does not regard as identical with *copying*—are developed slowly over time. The style of an artist's representation is, in part, a function of the technology available to him or her. For instance, consider graphic arts in an age in which modern paintbrushes did not yet exist.

Nelson Goodman builds on Gombrich's idea that the truth in a painting is a function both of the *kind* of information it is expected to yield and of our understanding of how to extract information from paintings in that style. In Goodman's opinion, a judgment that a painting is realistic is not a function of any absolute relationship it has to the world, but of what kinds of paintings with which one is familiar.

Elsewhere in his main study of philosophical aesthetics, Goodman poses interesting questions about *forgeries*. In fact, he suggests, only members of a certain category of artworks—which he terms *autographic*—are even capable of being forged. Members of the other main category—the *allographic*—are not. Musical compositions, for example, are cases of the latter.

Pressing on the foregoing question, Denis Dutton asks just what is wrong with a forged painting if no one could tell it apart from the original. His answer is that such artworks, in misrepresenting their true origins, may misrepresent the degree and character of their *achievement*. Dutton turns our attention from the object of painting to the act or *performance* of painting for his discussion of artistic "crimes."

In an era of modernist art, the idea that what is important about painting is its ability to represent reality was seriously challenged. Clive Bell, for instance, argued in the early decades of this century that what makes a painting art is not its imitative power or content, but what he called its "significant form." Without committing himself to Bell's formalism, the art historian Edmund Burke Feldman illustrates, with the example of Pablo Picasso's *Les Demoiselles d'Avignon* (1907), what a formalist analysis of a painting might be like. The formalistic approach to painting was further developed by the American art critic, Clement Greenberg, in order to make it specifically relevant to abstract expressionism. Greenberg considered works of painters such as Jackson Pollock to be attempts at testing the limits of painting. Just as the German philosopher Immanuel Kant used philosophy to critique the limits of philosophy, so too does modernist painting use painting to critique itself. One might say that, for Greenberg, the subject of modernist painting is painting itself.

Michael Baxandall addresses the question of what it means when we say that one painter, such as Cézanne, *influenced* another, such as Picasso. He argues that this simplistic way of describing the situation ignores the fact that our concept of Paul Cézanne's contribution to painting is dependent upon Picasso's special way of understanding Cézanne. In short, influence can also work backwards in time.

What is the difference between the artwork Andy Warhol made and titled *Brillo Boxes* (1964) and a perceptually indistinguishable stack of commonplace Brillo containers? An analogous puzzle could be posed about two artworks—for example, originals and copies—that are perceptually indistinguishable. His answer, developed in several essays and reprised in the present selection, is that an entity is an artwork in virtue of its place in an elaborate tissue of discourse Arthur Danto termed "the artworld." In particular, the identity and meaning of a work of a specific artwork can only be understood in light of its place in art history. An even more fundamental contrast emerges from the overall discussion.

Being beautiful, for Danto, is not definitive of being an artwork. Paintings, like emeralds or diamonds, can be beautiful. However, to be an artwork, any object, beautiful or otherwise, demands *interpretation*. According to Danto, commonplace objects—no matter how beautiful—may not be *about* anything.

Martin Heidegger, like Danto, is concerned with the difference between the artwork as mere *thing* and as *artwork*. But he moves in a very different direction. He suggests that art "unconceals" certain truths that "happen" in a work by "setting up" a world. For Heidegger, although artworks are also things, they are a peculiar kind of "equipment." In the course of considering the idea of equipment, Heidegger uses an example of a pair of peasant shoes, which happens to be the subject of a famous painting by Vincent Van Gogh.

Like Danto, Linda Nochlin gives great importance to art history in her essay "Why Are There No Great Women Artists?" She believes that many feminist criticisms of a male-dominated art history are misdirected. It isn't just that great women artists have been excluded from art histories, but rather that women painters were completely blocked by social and political handicaps from being able to paint at all.

Continuing the theme of meaning in art, Garry Hagberg calls our attention to the concept of *artistic expression.* He sets forth certain paradoxes we encounter when we assume that what an artwork expresses is something *hidden* in the mind of the artist. What an artwork expresses, he suggests, is either nothing at all or something "out there," in the public space.

Paintings are not persons, and so it would seem confused to make moral judgments, either for or against them. Anne Eaton, however, outlines various reasons why we might, without confusion, introduce ethical considerations into the seemingly pure sphere of artworks and the aesthetic experience they provide.

Against Imitation

■ Plato ■

[Socrates speaks] Of the many excellences which I perceive in the order of our State, there is none which upon reflection pleases me better than the rule about poetry.

[Glaucon speaks] To what do you refer?

To the rejection of imitative poetry, which certainly ought not to be received; as I see far more clearly now that the parts of the soul have been distinguished.

What do you mean?

Speaking in confidence, for I should not like to have my words repeated to the tragedians and the rest of the imitative tribe—but I do not mind saying to you, that all poetical imitations are ruinous to the understanding of the hearers, and that the knowledge of their true nature is the only antidote to them.

Explain the purport of your remark.

Well, I will tell you, although I have always from my earliest youth had an awe and love of Homer, which even now makes the words falter on my lips, for he is the great captain and teacher of the whole of that charming tragic company; but a man is not to be reverenced more than the truth, and therefore I will speak out.

Very good, he said.

Listen to me then, or rather, answer me.

Put your question.

Can you tell me what imitation is? for I really do not know.

A likely thing, then, that I should know.

Why not? for the duller eye may often see a thing sooner than the keener.

Very true, he said; but in your presence, even if I had any faint notion, I could not muster courage to utter it. Will you enquire yourself?

Well then, shall we begin the enquiry in our usual manner: Whenever a number of individuals have a common name, we assume them to have also a corresponding idea or form—do you understand me?

I do.

Let us take any common instance; there are beds and tables in the world—plenty of them, are there not?

Yes.

But there are only two ideas or forms of them—one the idea of a bed, the other of a table.

True.

"Against Imitation" by Plato has been excerpted from "The Republic," in *The Dialogues of Plato,* Volume I, Benjamin Jowett, trans., Random House, Inc. (1937), pages 852–857.

And the maker of either of them makes a bed or he makes a table for our use, in accordance with the idea—that is our way of speaking in this and similar instances—but no artificer makes the ideas themselves: how could he?

Impossible.

And there is another artist—I should like to know what you would say of him.

Who is he?

One who is the maker of all the works of all other workmen.

What an extraordinary man!

Wait a little, and there will be more reason for your saying so. For this is he who is able to make not only vessels of every kind, but plants and animals, himself and all other things—the earth and heaven, and the things which are in heaven or under the earth; he makes the gods also.

He must be a wizard and no mistake.

Oh! you are incredulous, are you? Do you mean that there is no such maker or creator, or that in one sense there might be a maker of all these things but in another not? Do you see that there is a way in which you could make them all yourself?

What way?

An easy way enough; or rather, there are many ways in which the feat might be quickly and easily accomplished, none quicker than that of turning a mirror round and round—you would soon enough make the sun and the heavens, and the earth and yourself, and other animals and plants, and all the other things of which we were just now speaking, in the mirror.

Yes, he said; but they would be appearances only.

Very good, I said, you are coming to the point now. And the painter too is, as I conceive, just such another—a creator of appearances, is he not?

Of course.

But then I suppose you will say that what he creates is untrue. And yet there is a sense in which the painter also creates a bed?

Yes, he said, but not a real bed.

And what of the maker of the bed? were you not saying that he too makes, not the idea which, according to our view, is the essence of the bed, but only a particular bed?

Yes, I did.

Then if he does not make that which exists he cannot make true existence, but only some semblance of existence; and if any one were to say that the work of the maker of the bed, or of any other workman, has real existence, he could hardly be supposed to be speaking the truth.

At any rate, he replied, philosophers would say that he was not speaking the truth.

No wonder, then, that his work too is an indistinct expression of truth.

No wonder.

Suppose now that by the light of the examples just offered we enquire who this imitator is?

If you please.

Well then, here are three beds: one existing in nature, which is made by God, as I think that we may say—for no one else can be the maker?

No.

There is another which is the work of the carpenter?

Yes.

And the work of the painter is a third?

Yes.

Beds, then, are of three kinds, and there are three artists who superintend them: God, the maker of the bed, and the painter?

Yes, there are three of them.

God, whether from choice or from necessity, made one bed in nature and one only; two or more such ideal beds neither ever have been nor ever will be made by God.

Why is that?

Because even if He had made but two, a third would still appear behind them which both of them would have for their idea, and that would be the ideal bed and not the two others.

Very true, he said.

God knew this, and He desired to be the real maker of a real bed, not a particular maker of a particular bed, and therefore He created a bed which is essentially and by nature one only.

So we believe.

Shall we, then, speak of Him as the natural author or maker of the bed?

Yes, he replied; inasmuch as by the natural process of creation He is the author of this and of all other things.

And what shall we say of the carpenter—is not he also the maker of the bed?

Yes.

But would you call the painter a creator and maker?

Certainly not.

Yet if he is not the maker, what is he in relation to the bed?

I think, he said, that we may fairly designate him as the imitator of that which the others make.

Good, I said; then you call him who is third in the descent from nature an imitator?

Certainly, he said.

And the tragic poet is an imitator, and therefore, like all other imitators, he is thrice removed from the king and from the truth?

That appears to be so.

Then about the imitator we are agreed. And what about the painter?—I would like to know whether he may be thought to imitate that which originally exists in nature, or only the creations of artists?

The latter.

As they are or as they appear? you have still to determine this.

What do you mean?

I mean, that you may look at a bed from different points of view, obliquely or directly or from any other point of view, and the bed will appear different, but there is no difference in reality. And the same of all things.

Yes, he said, the difference is only apparent.

Now let me ask you another question: Which is the art of painting designed to be—an imitation of things as they are, or as they appear—of appearance or of reality?

Of appearance.

Then the imitator, I said, is a long way off the truth, and can do all things because he lightly touches on a small part of them, and that part an image. For example: A painter will paint a cobbler, carpenter, or any other artist, though he knows nothing of their arts; and, if he is a good artist, he may deceive children or simple persons, when he shows them his picture of a carpenter from a distance, and they will fancy that they are looking at a real carpenter.

Certainly.

And whenever any one informs us that he has found a man who knows all the arts, and all things else that anybody knows, and every single thing with a higher degree of accuracy than any other man—whoever tells us this, I think that we can only imagine him to be a simple creature who is likely to have been deceived by some wizard or actor whom he met, and whom he thought all-knowing, because he himself was unable to analyse the nature of knowledge and ignorance and imitation.

Most true.

And so, when we hear persons saying that the tragedians, and Homer, who is at their head, know all the arts and all things human, virtue as well as vice, and divine things too, for that the good poet cannot compose well unless he knows his subject, and that he who has not this knowledge can never be a poet, we ought to consider whether here also there may not be a similar illusion. Perhaps they may have come across imitators and been deceived by them; they may not have remembered when they saw their works that these were but imitations thrice removed from the truth, and could easily be made without any knowledge of the truth, because they are appearances only and not realities? Or, after all, they may be in the right, and poets do really know the things about which they seem to the many to speak so well?

The question, he said, should by all means be considered.

Now do you suppose that if a person were able to make the original as well as the image, he would seriously devote himself to the image-making branch? Would he allow imitation to be the ruling principle of his life, as if he had nothing higher in him?

I should say not.

The real artist, who knew what he was imitating, would be interested in realities and not in imitations; and would desire to leave as memorials of himself works many and fair; and, instead of being the author of encomiums, he would prefer to be the theme of them.

Yes, he said, that would be to him a source of much greater honour and profit.

Then, I said, we must put a question to Homer; not about medicine, or any of the arts to which his poems only incidentally refer: we are not going to ask him, or any other poet, whether he has cured patients like Asclepius, or left behind him a school of medicine such as the Asclepiads were, or whether he only talks about medicine and other arts at second-hand; but we have a right to know respecting military tactics, politics, education, which are the chiefest and noblest subjects of his poems, and we may fairly ask him about them. 'Friend Homer,' then we say to him, 'if you are only in the second remove from truth in what you say of virtue, and not in the third—not an image maker or imitator—and if you are able to discern what pursuits make men better or worse in private or public life, tell us what State was ever better governed by your help? The good order of Lacedaemon is due to Lycurgus, and many other cities great and small have been similarly benefited by others; but who says that you have been a good legislator to them and have done them any good? Italy and Sicily boast of Charondas, and there is Solon who is renowned among us; but what city has anything to say about you?' Is there any city which he might name?

I think not, said Glaucon; not even the Homerids themselves pretend that he was a legislator.

Well, but is there any war on record which was carried on successfully by him, or aided by his counsels, when he was alive?

There is not.

Or is there any invention of his, applicable to the arts or to human life, such as Thales the Milesian or Anacharsis the Scythian, and other ingenious men have conceived, which is attributed to him?

There is absolutely nothing of the kind.

The Limits of Likeness
■ Ernst Gombrich ■

In his charming autobiography, the German illustrator Ludwig Richter relates how he and his friends, all young art students in Rome in the 1820s, visited the famous beauty spot of Tivoli and sat down to draw. They looked with surprise, but hardly with approval, at a group of French artists who approached the place with enormous baggage, carrying large quantities of paint which they applied to the canvas with big, coarse brushes. The Germans, perhaps roused by this self-confident artiness, were determined on the opposite approach. They selected the hardest, best-

"The Limits of Likeness" by Ernst Gombrich has been excerpted from *Art and Illusion,* Princeton University Press (1956), pages 63–74, 84–90, and is reprinted by permission of the publisher.

pointed pencils, which could render the motif firmly and minutely to its finest detail, and each bent down over his small piece of paper, trying to transcribe what he saw with the utmost fidelity. "We fell in love with every blade of grass, every tiny twig, and refused to let anything escape us. Every one tried to render the motif as objectively as possible."

Nevertheless, when they then compared the fruits of their efforts in the evening, their transcripts differed to a surprising extent. The mood, the color, even the outline of the motif had undergone a subtle transformation in each of them. Richter goes on to describe how these different versions reflected the different dispositions of the four friends, for instance, how the melancholy painter had straightened the exuberant contours and emphasized the blue tinges. We might say he gives an illustration of the famous definition by Emile Zola, who called a work of art "a corner of nature seen through a temperament."

It is precisely because we are interested in this definition that we must probe it a little further. The "temperament" or "personality" of the artist, his selective preferences, may be one of the reasons for the transformation which the motif undergoes under the artist's hands, but there must be others—everything, in fact, which we bundle together into the word "style," the style of the period and the style of the artist. . . .

The very point of Richter's story, after all, is that style rules even where the artist wishes to reproduce nature faithfully, and trying to analyze these limits to objectivity may help us get nearer to the riddle of style. One of these limits we know from the last chapter; it is indicated in Richter's story by the contrast between coarse brush and fine pencil. The artist, clearly, can render only what his tool and his medium are capable of rendering. His technique restricts his freedom of choice. The features and relationships the pencil picks out will differ from those the brush can indicate. Sitting in front of his motif, pencil in hand, the artist will, therefore, look out for those aspects which can be rendered in lines—as we say in a pardonable abbreviation, he will tend to see his motif in terms of lines, while, brush in hand, he sees it in terms of masses.

The question of why style should impose similar limitations is less easily answered, least of all when we do not know whether the artist's intentions were the same as those of Richter and his friends.

Historians of art have explored the regions where Cézanne and van Gogh set up their easels and have photographed their motifs. Such comparisons will always retain their fascination since they almost allow us to look over the artist's shoulder—and who does not wish he had this privilege? But however instructive such confrontations may be when handled with care, we must clearly beware of the fallacy of "stylization." Should we believe the photograph represents the "objective truth" while the painting records the artist's subjective vision—the way he transformed "what he saw"? Can we here compare "the image on the retina" with the "image in the mind"? Such speculations easily lead into a morass of unprovables. Take the image on the artist's retina. It sounds scientific enough, but actually there never was *one* such image which we could single out for comparison with either photograph or painting. What there was was an endless succession of innumerable images as the painter scanned the landscape in front of him, and these images sent a complex pattern of impulses through the optic nerves to his brain. Even the artist knew nothing of these events, and we know even less. How far the picture that formed in his mind corresponded to or deviated from the photograph it is even less profitable to ask. What we do know is that these artists went out into nature to look for material for a picture and their artistic wisdom led them to organize the elements of the landscape into works of art of marvelous complexity that bear as much relationship to a surveyor's record as a poem bears to a police report.

Does this mean, then, that we are altogether on a useless quest? That artistic truth differs so much from prosaic truth that the question of objectivity must never be asked? I do not think so. We must only be a little more circumspect in our formulation of the question. . . .

Now the historian knows that the information pictures were expected to provide differed widely in different periods. Not only were images scarce in the past, but so were the public's opportunities to check their captions. How many people ever saw their ruler in the flesh at sufficiently close quarters to recognize his likeness? How many traveled widely enough to tell one city from another? It is hardly surprising, therefore, that pictures of people and places changed their captions with sovereign disregard for truth. The print sold on the market as a portrait of a king would be altered to represent his successor or enemy.

There is a famous example of this indifference to truthful captions in one of the most ambitious publishing projects of the early printing press, Hartmann Schedel's so-called "Nuremberg Chronicle" with woodcuts by Dürer's teacher Wolgemut. What an opportunity such a volume should give the historian to see what the world was like at the time of Columbus! But as we turn the pages of this big folio, we find the same woodcut of a medieval city recurring with different captions as Damascus, Ferrara, Milan, and Mantua. Unless we are prepared to believe these cities were as indistinguishable from one another as their suburbs may be today, we must conclude that neither the publisher nor the public minded whether the captions told the truth. All they were expected to do was to bring home to the reader that these names stood for cities. . . .

In our culture, where pictures exist in such profusion, it is difficult to demonstrate this basic fact. There are freshmen in art schools who have facility in the objective rendering of motifs that would appear to belie this assumption. But those who have given art classes in other cultural settings tell a different story. James Cheng, who taught painting to a group of Chinese trained in different conventions, once told me of a sketching expedition he made with his students to a famous beauty spot, one of Peking's old city gates. The task baffled them. In the end, one of the students asked to be given at least a picture post card of the building so that they would have something to copy. It is stories such as these, stories of breakdowns, that explain why art has a history and artists need a style adapted to a task.

I cannot illustrate this revealing incident. But luck allows us to study the next stage, as it were—the adjustment of the traditional vocabulary of Chinese art to the unfamiliar task of topographical portrayal in the Western sense. For some decades Chiang Yee, a Chinese writer and painter of great gifts and charm, has delighted us with contemplative records of the Silent Traveller, books in which he tells of his encounters with scenes and people of the English and Irish countryside and elsewhere. I take an illustration from the volume on the English Lakeland.

It is a view of Derwentwater. Here we have crossed the line that separates documentation from art. Mr. Chiang Yee certainly enjoys the adaptation of the Chinese idiom to a new purpose; he wants us to see the English scenery for once "through Chinese eyes." But it is precisely for this reason that it is so instructive to compare his view with a typical "picturesque" rendering from the Romantic period. We see how the relatively rigid vocabulary of the Chinese tradition acts as a selective screen which admits only the features for which schemata exist. The artist will be attracted by motifs which can be rendered in his idiom. As he scans the landscape, the sights which can be matched successfully with the schemata he has learned to handle will leap forward as centers of attention. The style, like the medium, creates a mental set which makes the artist look for certain aspects in the scene around him that he can render. Painting is an activity, and the artist will therefore tend to see what he paints rather than to paint what he sees.

It is this interaction between style and preference which Nietzsche summed up in his mordant comment on the claims of realism:

"All Nature faithfully"—But by what feint
Can Nature be subdued to art's constraint?
Her smallest fragment is still infinite!
And so he paints but what he likes in it.
What does he like? He likes, what he can paint!

There is more in this observation than just a cool reminder of the limitations of artistic means. We catch a glimpse of the reasons why these limitations will never obtrude themselves within the domain of art itself. Art presupposes mastery, and the greater the artist the more surely will he instinctively avoid a task where his mastery would fail to serve him. The layman may wonder whether Giotto could have painted a view of Fiesole in sunshine, but the historian will suspect that, lacking the means, he would not have wanted to, or rather that he could not have wanted to. We like to assume, somehow, that where there is a will there is also a way, but in matters of art the maxim should read that only where there is a way is there also a will. The individual can enrich the ways and means that his culture offers him; he can hardly wish for something that he has never known is possible. . . .

Need we infer from this fact that there is no such thing as an objective likeness? That it makes no sense to ask, for instance, whether Chiang Yee's view of Derwentwater is more or less correct than the nineteenth-century lithograph in which the formulas of classical landscapes were applied to the same task? It is a tempting conclusion and one which recommends itself to the teacher of art appreciation because it brings home to the layman how much of what we call "seeing" is

Wolgemut, Woodcuts from the *Nuremberg Chronicle* (1493).

Chang Yee, *Cows in Derwentwater* (1936).

Anonymous: Derwentwater, looking toward Borrowdale (1826).

Source: Reproduced through courtesy of Princeton University Press.

conditioned by habits and expectations. It is all the more important to clarify how far this relativism will take us. . . .

From the point of view of information there is surely no difficulty in discussing portrayal. To say of a drawing that it is a correct view of Tivoli does not mean, of course, that Tivoli is bounded by wiry lines. It means that those who understand the notation will derive *no false information* from the drawing—whether it gives the contour in a few lines or picks out "every blade of grass" as Richter's friends wanted to do. The complete portrayal might be the one which gives as much correct information about the spot as we would obtain if we looked at it from the very spot where the artist stood.

Styles, like languages, differ in the sequence of articulation and in the number of questions they allow the artist to ask; and so complex is the information that reaches us from the visible world that no picture will ever embody it all. This is not due to the subjectivity of vision but to its richness. Where the artist has to copy a human product he can, of course, produce a facsimile which is indistinguishable from the original. The forger of banknotes succeeds only too well in effacing his personality and the limitations of a period style.

But what matters to us is that the correct portrait, like the useful map, is an end product on a long road through schema and correction. It is not a faithful record of a visual experience but the faithful construction of a relational model.

Neither the subjectivity of vision nor the sway of conventions need lead us to deny that such a model can be constructed to any required degree of accuracy. What is decisive here is clearly the word "required." The form of a representation cannot be divorced from its purpose and the requirements of the society in which the given visual language gains currency.

Languages of Art
■ Nelson Goodman ■

1. Reality Remade

Realism is relative, determined by the system of representation standard for a given culture or person at a given time. Newer or older or alien systems are accounted artificial or unskilled. For a Fifth-Dynasty Egyptian the straightforward way of representing something is not the same as for an eighteenth-century Japanese; and neither way is the same as for an early twentieth-century Englishman.

"Languages of Art" by Nelson Goodman has been excerpted from *Languages of Art*, Bobbs-Merrill (1968), pages 37–39, 113–114, and is reprinted by permission of Hackett Publishing.

Each would to some extent have to learn how to read a picture in either of the other styles. This relativity is obscured by our tendency to omit specifying a frame of reference when it is our own. "Realism" thus often comes to be used as the name for a particular style or system of representation. Just as on this planet we usually think of objects as fixed if they are at a constant position in relation to the earth, so in this period and place we usually think of paintings as literal or realistic if they are in a traditional European style of representation. But such egocentric ellipsis must not tempt us to infer that these objects (or any others) are absolutely fixed, or that such pictures (or any others) are absolutely realistic.

Shifts in standard can occur rather rapidly. The very effectiveness that may attend judicious departure from a traditional system of representation sometimes inclines us at least temporarily to install the newer mode as standard. We then speak of an artist's having achieved a new degree of realism, or having found new means for the realistic rendering of (say) light or motion. What happens here is something like the 'discovery' that not the earth but the sun is 'really fixed.' Advantages of a new frame of reference, partly because of their novelty, encourage its enthronement on some occasions in place of the customary frame. Nevertheless, whether an object is 'really fixed' or a picture is realistic depends at any time entirely upon what frame or mode is then standard. Realism is a matter not of any constant or absolute relationship between a picture and its object but of a relationship between the system of representation employed in the picture and the standard system. Most of the time, of course, the traditional system is taken as standard; and the literal or realistic or naturalistic system of representation is simply the customary one.

Realistic representation, in brief, depends not upon imitation or illusion or information . . . but upon inculcation. Almost any picture may represent almost anything; that is, given picture and object there is usually a system of representation, a plan of correlation, under which the picture represents the object. . . .

Indeed, there are usually many such systems. A picture that under one (unfamiliar) system is a correct but highly unrealistic representation of an object may under another (the standard) system be a realistic but very incorrect representation of the same object. Only if accurate information is yielded under the standard system will the picture represent the object both correctly and literally. . . .

How correct the picture is under that system depends upon how accurate is the information about the object that is obtained by reading the picture according to that system. But how literal or realistic the picture is depends upon how standard the system is. If representation is a matter of choice and correctness a matter of information, realism is a matter of habit.

Our addiction, in the face of overwhelming counterevidence, to thinking of resemblance as the measure of realism is easily understood in these terms. Representational customs, which govern realism, also tend to generate resemblance. That a picture looks like nature often means only that it looks the way nature is usually painted. Again, what will deceive me into supposing that an object of a given kind is before me depends upon what I have noticed about such objects, and this in turn is affected by the way I am used to seeing them depicted. Resemblance and deceptiveness, far from being constant and independent sources and criteria of representational practice, are in some degree products of it . . .

Neither here nor elsewhere have I argued that there is no constant relation of resemblance; judgments of similarity in selected and familiar respects are, even though rough and fallible, as objective and categorical as any that are made in describing the world. But judgments of complex overall resemblance are another matter. In the first place, they depend upon the aspects or factors in terms of which the objects in question are compared; and this depends heavily on conceptual and perceptual habit. In the second place, even with these factors determined, similarities along the several axes are not immediately commensurate, and the degree of total resemblance will depend upon how the several factors are weighted. Normally, for example, nearness in geographical location has little to do with our judgment of resemblance among buildings but much to do with our judgment of resemblance among building lots. The assessment of total resemblance is subject to influences galore, and our representational customs are not least among these. In sum, I have sought to show that insofar as resemblance is a constant and objective relation, resemblance between a picture and what is represents does not coincide with realism; and that insofar as resemblance does coincide with realism, the criteria of resemblance vary with changes in representational practice.

2. The Forgeable and the Unforgeable

Let us speak of a work of art as autographic if and only if the distinction between original and forgery of it is significant; or better, if and only if even the most exact duplication of it does not thereby count as genuine. If a work of art is autographic, we may also call that art autographic. Thus painting is autographic, music nonautographic, or allographic. These terms are introduced purely for convenience; nothing is implied concerning the relative individuality of expression demanded by or attainable in these arts. Now the problem before us is to account for the fact that some arts but not others are autographic.

One notable difference between painting and music is that the composer's work is done when he has written the score, even though the performances are the end-products, while the painter has to finish the picture. No matter how many studies or revisions are made in either case, painting is in this sense a one-stage and music a two-stage art. Is an art autographic, then, if and only if it is one-stage? Counterexamples come readily to mind. In the first place, literature is not autographic though it is one-stage. There is no such thing as a forgery of Gray's *Elegy*. Any accurate copy of the text of a poem or novel is as much the original work as any other. Yet what the writer produces is ultimate; the text is not merely a means to oral readings as a score is a means to performances in music. An unrecited poem is not so forlorn as an unsung song; and most literary works are never read aloud at all. We might try to make literature into a two-stage art by considering the silent readings to be the end-products, or the instances of a work; but then the lookings at a picture and the listenings to a performance would qualify equally as end-products or instances, so that painting as well as literature would be two-stage and music three-stage. In the second place, printmaking is two-stage and yet autographic. The etcher, for example, makes a plate from which impressions are then taken on paper. These prints are the end-products; and although they may differ appreciably from one another, all are instances of the original work. But even the most exact copy produced otherwise than by printing from that plate counts not as an original but as an imitation or forgery.

Artistic Crimes
■ Denis Dutton ■

The concept of forgery is a touchstone of criticism. If the existence of forgeries—and their occasional acceptance as authentic works of art—has been too often dismissed or ignored in the theory of criticism, it may be because of the forger's special power to make the critic look ridiculous. Awkward as it is, critics have heaped the most lavish praise on art objects that have turned out to be forged. The suspicion this arouses is, of course, that the critics were led to praise the forgery for the wrong reasons in the first place. Since the aesthetic object as perceived is no different after the revelation that it is forged, the implication to be drawn is that it had previously been critically valued not for its intrinsic aesthetic properties, but because it was believed to be the work of an esteemed artist.

As natural as this suspicion is, it represents a point of view I shall seek to discredit in the following discussion. Everyone recognizes that the proper identification of an art object as genuine or forged is crucial as regards monetary value, that forgery has moral implications, that there are important historical reasons for wanting to distinguish the genuine from the faked art object. . . .

Consider for a moment Smith and Jones, who have just finished listening to a new recording of Liszt's *Transcendental Études*. Smith is transfixed. He says, "What beautiful artistry! The pianist's tone is superb, his control absolute, his speed and accuracy dazzling. Truly an electric performance!" Jones responds with a sigh. "Yeah, it was electric all right. Or to be more precise, it was electronic. He recorded the music at practice tempo and the engineers speeded it up on a rotating head recorder." Poor Smith—his enthusiasm evaporates. . . .

"Artistic Crimes" by Denis Dutton has been excerpted from *The Forger's Art*, Denis Dutton, ed., University of California Press (1983), pages 172, 174–175, 180–187, and is reprinted by permission of the author.

The distinction between so-called creative and performing arts has certain obvious uses: We would not wish to confuse the actor and the playwright, the conductor and the composer, the dancer and the choreographer. And yet this distinction (often employed invidiously against the performer) can cause us to lose sight of the fact that in certain respects all arts are creative, and correlatively, all arts are performing. It is this latter fact which is of particular relevance to understanding what is wrong with forgeries. For it can be argued that every work of art—every painting, statue, novel, symphony, ballet, as well as every interpretation or rendition of a piece of music, every reading of a poem or production of a play—involves the element of performance.

When we speak of a performance we usually have in mind a human activity which stands in some sense complete in itself: We talk of the President's performance at a press conference, or a student's performance on an examination, with the intention of marking off these particular activities from the whole of a presidential administration or the quality of the student's work done throughout a course. Moreover, as these examples also indicate, performances are said to involve some sense of accomplishment, of achievement. As objects of contemplation, artworks stand in differing relations to the performances of artists, depending on the art form in question. On the one hand, we have such arts as the dance, where the human activity involved in creating the object of contemplation and the object itself are one and the same thing. In such a case it would be odd to say that the object somehow represents the performance of the artist, because to perceive the object is to perceive the performance. On the other hand, we have painting, where we normally perceive the work of art without perceiving those actions which have brought it into being. Nevertheless, in cases such as the latter what we see is the end-product of human activity; the object of our perception can be understood as representative of a human performance. That arts differ with respect to how or whether we actually perceive at the moment of creation the artist's performance makes no difference to the relevance of the concept to understanding all of the arts. In fact, the concept of performance is internal to our whole notion of art. . . .

In the most obvious sense, a forgery is an artifact of one person which is intentionally attributed to another, usually with the purpose of turning a profit. But what is wrong with forgeries—and forgeries of painting would stand merely as the most famous examples—is that they not only misattribute origin: Because they misattribute origin, they *misrepresent achievement.* It is essential that forgeries be understood as a subset of a wider class of misrepresented artistic performances. Since all art can be seen under the aspect of performance, whether or not the art in question is conventionally called "performing," there exists always the possibility that the nature of the achievement involved in the performance may be misrepresented or misunderstood. In my example of the piano recording, Smith brings to his experience certain expectations regarding what is to count as achievement in the art in question, and these expectations are not met. The point is that Smith's experience cannot be understood as an experience of sound, such that the faster and more brilliant the sounds the better; Smith's experience of sound implies the experience of a performance, of something done in a certain way by a human being.

The fundamental question, then, is, What has the artist done, what has he achieved? The question is fundamental, moreover, not because of any contingent facts about the psychology of aesthetic perception, but because of the nature of the concept of art itself. As I have noted, Smith's initial disappointment in the piano recording may later be replaced by admiration for the skill and sensitivity with which the engineer has varied the tempi of the recording. This does not indicate that Smith's response can be understood as merely conditioned by his beliefs about what he perceives. To the contrary, Smith's beliefs are about what he takes to be a work of art, and hence are centered on what he understands to be the achievement implicit in what he perceives. Technological advances in the arts in general, the inventions of airbrushes, electric stage lighting, sound synthesizers, and so forth, have tended progressively to alter what counts as achievement in the arts; these advances have in no way altered the relevance of the concept of achievement in art or criticism and hence have not changed to that extent the concept of art *überhaupt*. Smith's mistake about the nature of the achievement before him, or the experts' mistakes about the van Meergeren* Vermeers, simply requires that the question of what the achievement is be recast: Indeed, the achievement of the engineer may be worthy of admiration, just as the achievement of Hans van Meergeren was considerable. Still, the achievement of an engineer is not the achievement of a pianist, and the achievement of van Meergeren, however notable it may be, cannot be identical with that of Vermeer. . . .

Thus the concept of art is constituted a priori of certain essential properties. I do not propose to enumerate those features (the question of the contents of any such list lies at the heart of the philosophy of art); but I do insist that reference to origins and achievement must be included among these properties. This whole issue is what gives the problem of forgery such central philosophical importance: Theorists who claim that it ought to make no difference to appreciation whether a work is forged or not do not merely challenge a few dearly held cultural beliefs about what is important in art. To the contrary, they attack the very idea of art itself.

Let us take stock of what I have so far argued. I have claimed that in certain respects, differing according to the type of art in question, the concept of performance is intrinsic to our understanding of art; that works of art of whatever sort can be seen under the aspect of performance. In emphasizing the importance of the notion of performance in understanding art, I have centered attention on the extent to which works of art are the end-products of human activities, on the degree to which they represent things done by human agents. In this way, part of what constitutes our understanding of works of art involves grasping what sort of achievement the work itself represents. This takes us, then, to the question of the origins of the work: We cannot understand the work of art without some notion of its origins, who created it, the context in which the creator worked, and so forth. But now it

*Hans van Meergeren, forger of paintings in the style of Vermeer.

must be stressed that our interest in origins, in the possibility or actuality of human achievement, always goes hand-in-hand with our interest in the work of art as visual, verbal, or aural surface. In it extreme forms, contextualism in critical theory has tended to emphasize the origins of the work, its status as human achievement, at the expense of attention to the purely formal properties; in its exclusive concentration on formal properties, isolationism, or formalism, has (by definition) tended to slight the importance of the human context, the human origins, of art. Both of these positions in their more extreme and dogmatic forms constitute a kind of philistinism. The more familiar sort of philistinism has it that if a work of art is a forgery, then it must somehow be without value: Once we are told that these are van Meergerens before us, and not Vermeers, we reject them, though their formal properties remain unchanged. The opposed sort of philistinism, which could well be called *aestheticist philistinism,* claims that formal properties are the only significant properties of works of art; that since questions of origins are not important, it ought to make no difference to us at all whether we are confronted with Vermeers or van Meergerens. Both positions are properly called philistine because both fail to acknowledge a fundamental element of artistic value. . . .

The significant opposition I find then is not between "forged" and "original," but between correctly represented artistic performance and misrepresented artistic performance. Originality remains a highly relevant concept here, however, insofar as it shows us that some notion of the origins of a work is always germane to appreciation. Without such concern, we cannot understand the full nature of the achievement a work represents, and such understanding is intrinsic to a proper grasp of the work of art. The predictable challenge to this involves the insistence that while I have been directing attention to human performances, what is really in question in appreciating works of art is aesthetic experience. On this account, aesthetic experience is said to refer to the visual or auditory experience of the sensuous surface of the work of art. Yet who is it who ever has these curious "aesthetic experiences"? In fact, I would suppose they are never had, except by infants perhaps—surely never by serious lovers of painting, music, or literature (the latter always a difficult case for aestheticians who like talking about "sensuous surface"). The encounter with a work of art does not consist in merely hearing a succession of pretty sounds or seeing an assemblage of pleasing shapes and colors. It is as much a matter of hearing a virtuoso perform a dazzling and original interpretation of a difficult piece of music or of experiencing a new vision of a familiar subject provided by a painter. Admittedly, there is an attraction in wanting to look past these thorny complexities to concentrate on the sensuous surface, and it is the same attraction that formalism in all its various guises has always had. It is a marvelously simple view, but (alas!) art itself is even more marvelously complex. Against those who insist that an object's status as forged is irrelevant to its artistic merit, I would hold that when we learn that the kind of achievement an art object involves has been radically misrepresented to us, it is not as though we have learned a new fact about some familiar object of aesthetic attention. To the contrary, insofar as its position as a work of art is concerned, it is no longer the same object.

Form in Modern Painting
■ Clive Bell ■

The starting-point for all systems of aesthetics must be the personal experience of a peculiar emotion. The objects that provoke this emotion we call works of art. All sensitive people agree that there is a peculiar emotion provoked by works of art. I do not mean, of course, that all works provoke the same emotion. On the contrary, every work produces a different emotion. But all these emotions are recognisably the same in kind; so far, at any rate, the best opinion is on my side. That there is a particular kind of emotion provoked by works of visual art, and that this emotion is provoked by every kind of visual art, by pictures, sculptures, buildings, pots, carvings, textiles, &c., &c., is not disputed, I think, by anyone capable of feeling it. This emotion is called the aesthetic emotion; and if we can discover some quality common and peculiar to all the objects that provoke it, we shall have solved what I take to be the central problem of aesthetics. We shall have discovered the essential quality in a work of art, the quality that distinguishes works of art from all other classes of objects.

For either all works of visual art have some common quality, or when we speak of "works of art" we gibber. Everyone speaks of "art," making a mental classification by which he distinguishes the class "works of art" from all other classes. What is the justification of this classification? What is the quality common and peculiar to all members of this class? Whatever it be, no doubt it is often found in company with other qualities; but they are adventitious—it is essential. There must be some one quality without which a work of art cannot exist; possessing which, in the least degree, no work is altogether worthless. What is this quality? What quality is shared by all objects that provoke our aesthetic emotions? What quality is common to Sta. Sophia and the windows at Chartres, Mexican sculpture, a Persian bowl, Chinese carpets, Giotto's frescoes at Padua, and the masterpieces of Poussin, Piero della Francesca, and Cézanne? Only one answer seems possible—significant form. In each, lines and colours combined in a particular way, certain forms and relations of forms, stir our aesthetic emotions. These relations and combinations of lines and colours, these aesthetically moving forms, I call "Significant Form"; and "Significant Form" is the one quality common to all works of visual art.

At this point it may be objected that I am making aesthetics a purely subjective business, since my only data are personal experiences of a particular emotion. It will be said that the objects that provoke this emotion vary with each individual, and that therefore a system of aesthetics can have no objective validity. It must be replied that any system of aesthetics which pretends to be based on some objective

"Form in Modern Painting" by Clive Bell has been excerpted from *Art*, Putnam Publishing Group (1958), pages 17–22, 28, 30.

truth is so palpably ridiculous as not to be worth discussing. We have no other means of recognising a work of art than our feeling for it. The objects that provoke aesthetic emotion vary with each individual. Aesthetic judgments are, as the saying goes, matters of taste; and about tastes, as everyone is proud to admit, there is no disputing. A good critic may be able to make me see in a picture that had left me cold things that I had overlooked, till at last, receiving the aesthetic emotion, I recognise it as a work of art. To be continually pointing out those parts, the sum, or rather the combination, of which unite to produce significant form, is the function of criticism. But it is useless for a critic to tell me that something is a work of art; he must make me feel it for myself. This he can do only by making me see; he must get at my emotions through my eyes. Unless he can make me see something that moves me, he cannot force my emotions. I have no right to consider anything a work of art to which I cannot react emotionally; and I have no right to look for the essential quality in anything that I have not *felt* to be a work of art. The critic can affect my aesthetic theories only by affecting my aesthetic experience. All systems of aesthetics must be based on personal experience—that is to say, they must be subjective.

Yet, though all aesthetic theories must be based on aesthetic judgments, and ultimately all aesthetic judgments must be matters of personal taste, it would be rash to assert that no theory of aesthetics can have general validity. For, though A, B, C, D are the works that move me, and A, D, E, F the works that move you, it may well be that x is the only quality believed by either of us to be common to all the works in his list. We may all agree about aesthetics, and yet differ about particular works of art. We may differ as to the presence or absence of the quality x. My immediate object will be to show that significant form is the only quality common and peculiar to all the works of visual art that move me; and I will ask those whose aesthetic experience does not tally with mine to see whether this quality is not also, in their judgment, common to all works that move them, and whether they can discover any other quality of which the same can be said.

Also at this point a query arises, irrelevant indeed, but hardly to be suppressed: "Why are we so profoundly moved by forms related in a particular way?" The question is extremely interesting, but irrelevant to aesthetics. In pure aesthetics we have only to consider our emotion and its object: For the purposes of aesthetics we have no right, neither is there any necessity, to pry behind the object into the state of mind of him who made it. Later, I shall attempt to answer the question; for by so doing I may be able to develop my theory of the relation of art to life. I shall not, however, be under the delusion that I am rounding off my theory of aesthetics. For a discussion of aesthetics, it need be agreed only that forms arranged and combined according to certain unknown and mysterious laws do move us in a particular way, and that it is the business of an artist so to combine and arrange them that they shall move us. These moving combinations and arrangements I have called, for the sake of convenience and for a reason that will appear later, "Significant Form."

A third interruption has to be met.

"Are you forgetting about colour?" someone inquires. Certainly not; my term "significant form" included combinations of lines and of colours. The distinction between form and colour is an unreal one; you cannot conceive a colourless line or a colourless space; neither can you conceive a formless relation of colours. In a black and white drawing the spaces are all white and all are bounded by black lines; in most oil paintings the spaces are multi-coloured and so are the boundaries; you cannot imagine a boundary line without any content, or a content without a boundary line. Therefore, when I speak of significant form, I mean a combination of lines and colours (counting white and black as colours) that moves me aesthetically. . . .

The hypothesis that significant form is the essential quality in a work of art has at least one merit denied to many more famous and more striking—it does help to explain things. We are all familiar with pictures that interest us and excite our admiration, but do not move us as works of art. To this class belongs what I call "Descriptive Painting"—that is, painting in which forms are used not as objects of emotion, but as means of suggesting emotion or conveying information. Portraits of psychological and historical value, topographical works, pictures that tell stories and suggest situations, illustrations of all sorts, belong to this class. That we all recognize the distinction is clear, for who has not said that such and such a drawing was excellent as illustration, but as a work of art worthless? Of course many descriptive pictures possess, amongst other qualities, formal significance, and are therefore works of art; but many more do not. They interest us; they may move us too in a hundred different ways, but they do not move us aesthetically. According to my hypothesis they are not works of art. They leave untouched our aesthetic emotions because it is not their forms but the ideas or information suggested or conveyed by their forms that affect us. . . .

To appreciate a work of art we need bring with us nothing but a sense of form and colour and a knowledge of three-dimensional space. That bit of knowledge, I admit, is essential to the appreciation of many great works, since many of the most moving forms ever created are in three dimensions. To see a cube or a rhomboid as a flat pattern is to lower its significance, and a sense of three-dimensional space is essential to the full appreciation of most architectural forms. Pictures which would be insignificant if we saw them as flat patterns are profoundly moving because, in fact, we see them as related planes. If the representation of three-dimensional space is to be called "representation," then I agree that there is one kind of representation which is not irrelevant. Also, I agree that along with our feeling for line and colour we must bring with us our knowledge of space if we are to make the most of every kind of form. Nevertheless, there are magnificent designs to an appreciation of which this knowledge is not necessary: so, though it is not irrelevant to the appreciation of some works of art it is not essential to the appreciation of all. What we must say is that the representation of three-dimensional space is neither irrelevant nor essential to all art, and that every other sort of representation is irrelevant. . . .

I do not understand music well. I find musical form exceedingly difficult to apprehend, and I am sure that the profounder subtleties of harmony and rhythm more often than not escape me. The form of a musical composition must be simple indeed if I am to grasp it honestly. My opinion about music is not worth having. Yet, sometimes, at a concert, though my appreciation of the music is limited and humble, it is pure. Sometimes, though I have a poor understanding, I have a clean palate. Consequently, when I am feeling bright and clear and intent, at the beginning of a concert for instance, when something that I can grasp is being played, I get from music that pure aesthetic emotion that I get from visual art. It is less intense, and the rapture is evanescent; I understand music too ill for music to transport me far into the world of pure aesthetic ecstasy. But at moments I do appreciate music as pure musical form, as sounds combined according to the laws of a mysterious necessity, as pure art with a tremendous significance of its own and no relation whatever to the significance of life; and in those moments I lose myself in that infinitely sublime state of mind to which pure visual form transports me.

A Formal Analysis
■ Edmund Burke Feldman ■

In formal analysis, we try to go "behind" a descriptive inventory to discover the relations among the things we have named. We may have identified five female figures in *Les Demoiselles* but now we want to know how they have been organized as shapes, areas of color, and forms with particular contours, textures, and locations in space.

In *Les Demoiselles,* some of the figures are made of angular, flat planes of color, whereas the two central figures are more curvilinear, have gentler transitions of color, and seem less distorted. One of the central figures has white lines to delineate its shapes. Strangely, the outer figures, have heads which are in marked contrast to their bodies. The central figures, while frontally posed, present the nose in profile; and one figure seems insecure, like a statue which might fall from its pedestal. Her torso is erect, but her feet are too far to the left to support her body.

My notion that the figure seems to be falling illustrates one of the sources of inferences about form: the erectness of man's posture and the influence of gravity. No matter what style of art we examine, certain physical and biological assumptions about man are shared by artist *and* viewer. We cannot view a tilted representation of the human figure without feeling that it may fall. The expectation of collapse may be an important perception about the work.

Although the color in *Les Demoiselles* seems to be modeling forms, we have very little impression of depth. Instead there is a shallow space implied by the

"A Formal Analysis" by Edmund Burke Feldman has been excerpted from *Varieties of Visual Experience,* Prentice Hall (1967), pages 469–472, and is reprinted by permission of the publisher.

Pablo Picasso, *Les Demoiselles d'Avignon* (1907).
Source: Pablo Picasso, "Les Demoiselles d'Avignon," Paris (June–July 1907). Oil on Canvas, 8′ × 7′8″ (243.9 × 233.7 cm). The Museum of Modern Art/ Licensed by Scala-Art Resource, NY. Acquired through the Lillie P. Bliss Bequest. Photograph (c) 2001. The Museum of Modern Art. © 2002 Estate of Pablo Picasso / Artist Rights Society (ARS), New York

overlapping of the forms. There are no perspective devices, no changes in size, focus, color intensity, or sharpness of edge to suggest a representation of space deeper than the picture plane.

Notice that the drawing of the hand in the central figure involves some skill in foreshortening; it is more or less believable, but the other two hands in the painting are crudely drawn; one is childlike, while the other is schematic and stiff—part of an arm which resembles a carved substance more than flesh. But that arm, at the left of the canvas, is painted in the typical pink tones of European figurative art. Thus, there is a conflict, within the arm, between the drawing and the color and paint quality. Is this the type of conflict [sometimes noted in] architectural critique[s], or is it an *intended conflict* which has relevance to an interpretation of the work?

We should also notice that there are three kinds of distortion in the heads of the three outer figures. In the head at the left, color shifts from pink to brown, the eye is much enlarged, and the planes of the nose are simplified as in African wood sculpture. The *shape* of the head remains naturalistic, however; it is conventionally illuminated. Moving to the upper-right head, we depart from logical representation. Very pronounced harsh green lines are used to indicate the nose plane in shadow; a rough, unfinished kind of execution characterizes the head. The breast has a squarish shape. At this point the painting begins to depart from the simple imitation of appearances as the goal of painting.

Nevertheless, the upper-right head has a normal attachment to the body. The head on the seated figure, however, is uncertain in its relation to the body. The nose has been flattened out; the convention of a shadow plane has been employed as a decorative element, or an element of pure form in what might be called a synthetic composition based on the head. The alignment of the eyes is illogical. A collection of forms based on different views of the head has been assembled and located where the head would be. From this head alone, we cannot deduce the sex, race, age, or any other distinguishing characteristic of the figure. Only the hips and thighs, plus the title, confirm that the figure is a woman.

At the extreme left position of the canvas is a brown area which seems to be a close-up of a female figure, employing forms typical of African art. It is not one of the *demoiselles* but seems to be an echo of a woman's back carried out in the brown color of carved wood sculpture. Perhaps it is an announcement of the *leitmotif* of the painting, or an enlarged rear view of the figure at the left.

The idea of the viewer's expectation is very important in formal analysis. And the artist is usually aware of the viewer's conditioning. Picasso knows how to use linear perspective and he knows that viewers in the Western world expect perspectivist illusions to create the space for the *demoiselles*. Nevertheless, he deliberately breaks up any possibility of deep space. The still life in the bottom of the painting provides the merest hint of a plane leading *into* the picture space. But the artist does not follow through on that spatial representation. Indeed, he locates the foot of the figure on the left in the same plane and at the same height as the still life. The foot must be on the floor, yet the floor cannot be at the same level as the table top on which the still life rests. Obviously, the expected logic of spatial representation is destroyed in this painting.

It is plain that in making a formal analysis, we have been accumulating evidence for an interpretation of the work and a judgment of its excellence. The breakdown of spatial logic might justify a conclusion that the work is unsuccessful. However, we must first ascertain whether a different logic has been created. Or perhaps a logic of spatial representation is irrelevant here. In the case of *Les Demoiselles,* it is enough to say that the activity of the forms takes place in a shallow space parallel to the plane of the picture. The linear and coloristic clues keep us close to the surface. As soon as our eyes begin to penetrate inward, they are turned to one side. Picasso makes the viewer feel he must move to make sense of the profile view of the nose. A fixed position for the viewer will not let him deal with a front view of the face and a profile of the nose in the same head. *We must move imaginatively from left to right as we view the two central figures.* And this imaginative movement is in the same direction as the "falling" central figure. We encounter a reinforcement of our tendency to "read" everything in a clockwise direction. But there are numerous violations of our other expectations. By the time we reach the seated figure at the right, we are willing to accept the joining of the shoulder, arm, forearm, and hip in a single continuous form, with emphasis shifted from the limbs to the *shape of the openings* they form.

Our formal analysis has begun to move from an objective description of forms to statements about the way we perceive them. We appear to be groping for a principle of organization, an idea or set of ideas which can account for the way the work is structured. As observations of the work increase, as information accumulates, it becomes increasingly difficult to defer the work of interpretation. However, we can undertake the task with certain modest feelings of security: We have *tried* to be objective in our description, we have tried *not* to overlook evidence, and we have endeavored to make assertions which would not in themselves be the subject of disagreement.

By interpretation in art criticism, I mean the process of expressing the meanings of a work the critic has analyzed. I do not mean that the critic finds verbal equivalents for the art object. Neither does he evaluate the work. Obviously, we are not in a position to judge a work until we have decided what it means, what its themes are, what problems it has succeeded in solving.

Interpretation is tremendously challenging; it is certainly the most important part of the critical enterprise. Indeed, if we have thoroughly interpreted a work, the business of evaluation can often be omitted. Explaining a work of art involves discovering its meanings *and also* stating the relevance of these meanings to our lives and to the human situation in general.

Certain assumptions underlie critical interpretation. We assume that an art object, being a human product, cannot escape some aspect of the value system of the artist. Just as a human being cannot go through life without consciously or unconsciously forming a set of values, an art object cannot avoid being a vehicle of ideas. As critics, we are not particularly interested in whether these ideas are faithful to the artist's views. That is, we are not interested in using art to find out what an artist thinks. However, an art object somehow becomes charged with ideas— ideas which may be significant in more than a technical sense. They may be present in the work without the conscious knowledge of the artist. But it is our function as critics to discover what they are.

An important principle of criticism is that *the artist is not necessarily the best authority on the meaning of his work.* As critics, we are interested in what the artist thinks about his work; we are interested in anything he can tell us about it. But we regard his views as material which requires confirmation by our own methods of analysis and interpretation.

It may be felt that interpretation violates the qualities of art which are not readily verbalized. How can one talk about colors and textures and shapes except in very imprecise terms? My reply is that art criticism is not intended to be a substitute for aesthetic experience. I realize that if the content of a work of art could be expressed verbally, it would not be necessary to make it in the first place. In critical interpretation we deal with sensuous and formal qualities of the art object by examining their *impact* upon our vision. As we perceive the work, its qualities seem to organize themselves into a kind of unity, and it is this unity which becomes the meaning of the work, the meaning we wish, however badly, to verbalize.

During description and analysis we *direct the attention* of viewers to *actual* colors and shapes in the art object, not to our language about them. Now variation in perception becomes troublesome because we are faced with the problem of making statements about art which others can accept without surrendering their individuality.

On Modernist Painting
■ Clement Greenberg ■

Modernism includes more than just art and literature. By now it includes almost the whole of what is truly alive in our culture. It happens, also, to be very much of a historical novelty. Western civilization is not the first to turn around and question its own foundations, but it is the civilization that has gone furthest in doing so. I identify Modernism with the intensification, almost the exacerbation, of this self-critical tendency that began with the philosopher [Immanuel] Kant. Because he was the first to criticize the means itself of criticism, I conceive of Kant as the first real Modernist.

The essence of Modernism lies, as I see it, in the use of the characteristic methods of a discipline to criticize the discipline itself—not in order to subvert it, but to entrench it more firmly in its area of competence. Kant used logic to establish the limits of logic, and while he withdrew much from its old jurisdiction, logic was left in all the more secure possession of what remained to it.

The self-criticism of Modernism grows out of but is not the same thing as the criticism of the Enlightenment. The Enlightenment criticized from the outside, the way criticism in its more accepted sense does; Modernism criticizes from the inside, through the procedures themselves of that which is being criticized. It seems natural that this new kind of criticism should have appeared first in philosophy, which is critical by definition, but as the nineteenth century wore on it made itself felt in many other fields. A more rational justification had begun to be demanded of every formal social activity, and Kantian self-criticism was called on eventually to meet and interpret this demand in areas that lay far from philosophy.

We know what has happened to an activity like religion that has not been able to avail itself of 'Kantian' immanent criticism in order to justify itself. At first glance the arts might seem to have been in a situation like religion's. Having been

"On Modernist Painting" by Clement Greenberg is from *Arts Yearbook,* No. 1 (1961), and is reprinted by permission of Janice Greenberg.

denied by the Enlightenment all tasks they could take seriously, they looked as though they were going to be assimilated to entertainment pure and simple, and entertainment itself looked as though it was going to be assimilated, like religion, to therapy. The arts could save themselves from this leveling down only by demonstrating that the kind of experience they provided was valuable in its own right and not to be obtained from any other kind of activity.

Each art, it turned out, had to effect this demonstration on its own account. What had to be exhibited and made explicit was that which was unique and irreducible not only in art in general, but also in each particular art. Each art had to determine, through the operations peculiar to itself, the effects peculiar and exclusive to itself. By doing this each art would, to be sure, narrow its area of competence, but at the same time it would make its possession of this area all the more secure.

It quickly emerged that the unique and proper area of competence of each art coincided with all that was unique to the nature of its medium. The task of self-criticism became to eliminate from the effects of each art any and every effect that might conceivably be borrowed from or by the medium of any other art. Thereby each art would be rendered 'pure,' and in its 'purity' find the guarantee of its standards of quality as well as of its independence. 'Purity' meant self-definition, and the enterprise of self-criticism in the arts became one of self-definition with a vengeance.

Realistic, illusionist art had dissembled the medium, using art to conceal art. Modernism used art to call attention to art. The limitations that constitute the medium of painting—the flat surface, the shape of the support, the properties of pigment—were treated by the Old Masters as negative factors that could be acknowledged only implicitly or indirectly. Modernist painting has come to regard these same limitations as positive factors that are to be acknowledged openly. Manet's paintings became the first Modernist ones by virtue of the frankness with which they declared the surfaces on which they were painted. The Impressionists, in Manet's wake, abjured underpainting and glazing, to leave the eye under no doubt as to the fact that the colors used were made of real paint that came from pots or tubes. Cézanne sacrificed verisimilitude, or correctness, in order to fit drawings and design more explicitly to the rectangular shape of the canvas.

It was the stressing, however, of the ineluctable flatness of the support that remained most fundamental in the processes by which pictorial art criticized and defined itself under Modernism. Flatness alone was unique and exclusive to that art. The enclosing shape of the support was a limiting condition, or norm, that was shared with the art of the theater; color was a norm or means shared with sculpture as well as the theater. Flatness, two-dimensionality, was the only condition painting shared with no other art, and so Modernist painting oriented itself to flatness as it did to nothing else.

The Old Masters had sensed that it was necessary to preserve what is called the integrity of the picture plane: that is, to signify the enduring presence of flatness under the most vivid illusion of three-dimensional space. The apparent contradiction involved—the dialectical tension, to use a fashionable but apt phrase—was essential to the success of their art, as it is indeed to the success of all pictorial art.

The Modernists have neither avoided nor resolved this contradiction; rather, they have reversed its terms. One is made aware of the flatness of their pictures before, instead of after, being made aware of what the flatness contains. Whereas one tends to see what is *in* an Old Master before seeing it as a picture, one sees a Modernist painting as a picture first. This is, of course, the best way of seeing any kind of picture, Old Master or Modernist, but Modernism imposes it as the only and necessary way, and Modernism's success in doing so is a success of self-criticism.

It is not in principle that Modernist painting in its latest phase has abandoned the representation of recognizable objects. What it has abandoned in principle is the representation of the kind of space that recognizable, three-dimensional objects can inhabit. Abstractness, or the non-figurative, has in itself still not proved to be an altogether necessary moment in the self-criticism of pictorial art, even though artists as eminent as [Wassily] Kandinsky and [Piet] Mondrian have thought so. Representation, or illustration, as such does not abate the uniqueness of pictorial art; what does do so are the associations of the things represented. All recognizable entities (including pictures themselves) exist in three-dimensional space, and the barest suggestion of a recognizable entity suffices to call up associations of that kind of space. The fragmentary silhouette of a human figure, or of a teacup, will do so, and by doing so alienate pictorial space from the two-dimensionality which is the guarantee of painting's independence as an art. Three-dimensionality is the province of sculpture, and for the sake of its own autonomy painting has had above all to divest itself of everything it might share with sculpture. And it is in the course of its effort to do this, and not so much—I repeat—to exclude the representational or the 'literary,' that painting has made itself abstract.

At the same time Modernist painting demonstrates, precisely in its resistance to the sculptural, that it continues tradition and the themes of tradition, despite all appearances to the contrary. For the resistance to the sculptural begins long before the advent of Modernism. Western painting, insofar as it strives for realistic illusion, owes an enormous debt to sculpture, which taught it in the beginning how to shade and model towards an illusion of relief, and even how to dispose that illusion in a complementary illusion of deep space. Yet some of the greatest feats of Western painting came as part of the effort it has made in the last four centuries to suppress and dispel the sculptural. Starting in Venice in the sixteenth century and continuing in Spain, Belgium, and Holland in the seventeenth, that effort was carried on at first in the name of color. When [Jacques-Louis] David, in the eighteenth century, sought to revive sculptural painting, it was in part to save pictorial art from the decorative flattening-out that the emphasis on color seemed to induce. Nevertheless, the strength of David's own best pictures (which are predominantly portraits) often lies as much in their color as in anything else. And Ingres, his pupil, though subordinating color far more consistently, executed pictures that were among the flattest, least sculptural done in the West by a sophisticated artist since the fourteenth century. Thus by the middle of the nineteenth century all ambitious tendencies in painting were converging (beneath their differences) in an anti-sculptural direction.

Modernism, in continuing this direction, made it more conscious of itself. With Manet and the Impressionists, the question ceased to be defined as one of color versus drawing, and became instead a question of purely optical experience as against optical experience modified or revised by tactile associations. It was in the name of the purely and literally optical, not in that of color, that the Impressionists set themselves to undermining shading and modeling and everything else that seemed to connote the sculptural. And in a way like that in which David had reacted against Fragonard in the name of the sculptural, Cézanne, and the Cubists after him, reacted against Impressionism. But once again, just as David's and Ingres' reaction had culminated in a kind of painting even less sculptural than before, so the Cubist counter-revolution eventuated in a kind of painting flatter than anything Western art had seen since before Cimabue—so flat indeed that it could hardly contain recognizable images.

In the meantime the other cardinal norms of the art of painting were undergoing an equally searching inquiry, though the results may not have been equally conspicuous. It would take me more space than is at my disposal to tell how the norm of the picture's enclosing shape or frame was loosened, then tightened, then loosened once again, and then isolated and tightened once more by successive generations of Modernist painters; or how the norms of finish, of paint texture, and of value and color contrast, were tested and retested. Risks have been taken with all these, not only for the sake of new expression, but also in order to exhibit them more clearly as norms. By being exhibited and made explicit they are tested for their indispensability. This testing is by no means finished, and the fact that it becomes more searching as it proceeds accounts for the radical simplifications, as well as radical complications, in which the very latest abstract art abounds.

Neither the simplifications nor the complications are matters of license. On the contrary, the more closely and essentially the norms of a discipline become defined the less apt they are to permit liberties ('liberation' has become a much abused word in connection with avant-garde and Modernist art). The essential norms or conventions of painting are also the limiting conditions with which a marked-up surface must comply in order to be experienced as a picture. Modernism has found that these limiting conditions can be pushed back indefinitely before a picture stops being a picture and turns into an arbitrary object; but it has also found that the further back these limits are pushed the more explicitly they have to be observed. The intersecting black lines and colored rectangles of a Mondrian may seem hardly enough to make a picture out of, yet by echoing the picture's enclosing shape so self-evidently they impose that shape as a regulating norm with a new force and a new completeness. Far from incurring the danger of arbitrariness in the absence of a model in nature, Mondrian's art proves, with the passing of time, almost too disciplined, too convention-bound in certain respects; once we have become used to its utter abstractness we realize that it is more traditional in its color, as well as in its subservience to the frame, than the last paintings of Monet are.

It is understood, I hope, that in plotting the rationale of Modernist art I have had to simplify and exaggerate. The flatness towards which Modernist painting orients itself can never be an utter flatness. The heightened sensitivity of the picture plane may no longer permit sculptural illusion, or *trompe-l'oeil,* but it does and must permit optical illusion. The first mark made on a surface destroys its virtual flatness, and the configurations of a Mondrian still suggest a kind of illusion of a kind of third dimension. Only now it is a strictly pictorial, strictly optical third dimension. Where the Old Masters created an illusion of space into which one could imagine oneself walking, the illusion created by a Modernist is one into which one can only look, can travel through only with the eye.

One begins to realize that the Neo-Impressionists were not altogether misguided when they flirted with science. Kantian self-criticism finds its perfect expression in science rather than in philosophy, and when this kind of self-criticism was applied in art the latter was brought closer in spirit to scientific method than ever before—closer than in the early Renaissance. That visual art should confine itself exclusively to what is given in visual experience, and make no reference to anything given in other orders of experience, is a notion whose only justification lies, notionally, in scientific consistency. Scientific method alone asks that a situation be resolved in exactly the same kind of terms as that in which it is presented—a problem in physiology is solved in terms of physiology, not in those of psychology; to be solved in terms of psychology, it has to be presented in, or translated into, these terms first. Analogously, Modernist painting asks that a literary theme be translated into strictly optical, two-dimensional terms before becoming the subject of pictorial art—which means its being translated in such a way that it entirely loses its literary character. Actually, such consistency promises nothing in the way of aesthetic quality or aesthetic results, and the fact that the best art of the past seventy or eighty years increasingly approaches such consistency does not change this; now as before, the only consistency which counts in art is aesthetic consistency, which shows itself only in results and never in methods or means. From the point of view of art itself its convergence of spirit with science happens to be a mere accident, and neither art nor science gives or assures the other of anything more than it ever did. What their convergence does show, however, is the degree to which Modernist art belongs to the same historical and cultural tendency as modern science.

It should also be understood that the self-criticism of Modernist art has never been carried on in any but a spontaneous and subliminal way. It has been altogether a question of practice, immanent to practice and never a topic of theory. Much has been heard about programs in connection with Modernist art, but there has really been far less of the programmatic in Modernist art than in Renaissance or Academic art. With a few untypical exceptions, the masters of Modernism have betrayed no more of an appetite for fixed ideas about art than Corot did. Certain inclinations and emphases, certain refusals and abstinences seem to become necessary simply because the way to stronger, more expressive art seems to lie through them. The immediate aims of Modernist artists remain individual before anything else, and the truth and success of their work is individual before it is anything else. To the extent that it succeeds as art Modernist art partakes in no way of the character of a demonstration. It has needed the accumulation over decades of a good deal of individual achievement to reveal the self-critical tendency of Modernist painting. No one artist was, or is yet, consciously aware of this tendency, nor could any artist work successfully in conscious awareness of it. To this extent—which is by far the largest—art gets carried on under Modernism in the same way as before.

And I cannot insist enough that Modernism has never meant anything like a break with the past. It may mean a devolution, an unraveling of anterior tradition, but it also means its continuation. Modernist art develops out of the past without gap or break, and wherever it ends up it will never stop being intelligible in terms of the continuity of art. The making of pictures has been governed, since pictures first began to be made, by all the norms I have mentioned. The Paleolithic painter or engraver could disregard the norm of the frame and treat the surface in both a literally and a virtually sculptural way because he made images rather than pictures, and worked on a support whose limits could be disregarded because (except in the case of small objects like a bone or horn) nature gave them to the artist in an unmanageable way. But the making of pictures, as against images in the flat, means the deliberate choice and creation of limits. This deliberateness is what Modernism harps on: That is, it spells out the fact that the limiting conditions of art have to be made altogether human limits.

I repeat that Modernist art does not offer theoretical demonstrations. It could be said, rather, that it converts all theoretical possibilities into empirical ones, and in doing so tests, inadvertently, all theories about art for their relevance to the actual practice and experience of art. Modernism is subversive in this respect alone. Ever so many factors thought to be essential to the making and experiencing of art have been shown not to be so by the fact that Modernist art has been able to dispense with them and yet continue to provide the experience of art in all its essentials. That this 'demonstration' has left most of our old *value* judgments intact only makes it the more conclusive. Modernism may have had something to do with the revival of the reputations of Uccello, Piero, El Greco, Georges de la Tour, and even Vermeer, and it certainly confirmed if it did not start other revivals like that of Giotto; but Modernism has not lowered thereby the standing of Leonardo, Raphael, Titian, Rubens, Rembrandt or Watteau. What Modernism has made clear is that, though the past did appreciate masters like these justly, it often gave wrong or irrelevant reasons for doing so.

Still, in some ways this situation has hardly changed. Art criticism lags behind Modernist as it lagged behind pre-Modernist art. Most of the things that get written about contemporary art belong to journalism rather than criticism properly speaking. It belongs to journalism—and to the millennial complex from which so many journalists suffer in our day—that each new phase of Modernism should be hailed as the start of a whole new epoch of art making a decisive break with all the customs and conventions of the past. Each time, a kind of art is expected that will be so unlike previous kinds of art and so 'liberated' from norms of practice or taste, that everybody, regardless of how informed or uninformed, will be able to have his say about it. And each time, this expectation is disappointed, as the phase of Modernism in question takes its place, finally, in the intelligible continuity of taste and tradition, and as it becomes clear that the same demands as before are made on artist and spectator.

Nothing could be further from the authentic art of our time than the idea of a rupture of continuity. Art is, among many other things, continuity. Without the past of art, and without the need and compulsion to maintain past standards of excellence, such a thing as Modernist art would be impossible.

Intentional Visual Interest
■ Michael Baxandall ■

Don't talk to the driver!

(Picasso, to Metzinger)

A word must be said about 'intention,' I suppose. I have declared an interest in addressing pictures partly by making inferences about their causes, this both because it is pleasurable and because a disposition towards casual inference seems to penetrate our thought and language too deeply to be excised, at least without doing oneself a quite disabling mischief. But since pictures are human productions, one element in the causal field behind a picture will be volition, and this overlaps with what we call 'intention.'

I am not aligned or equipped to offer anything useful on the matter of whether it is necessary to appeal to an author's historical intention in interpreting a picture (or, of course, a poem). The arguments for doing so—that it is necessary if there is to be any determinate meaning in a work, that the relation between intention and actual accomplishment is necessary to evaluation, and so on—are often attractive, but they sometimes seem to refer to a slightly different sort of intention (a complex word) or to intention seen from a slightly different angle from what I feel committed to. The intention to which I am committed is not an actual, particular psychological state or even a historical set of mental events inside the heads of Benjamin Baker or Picasso, in the light of which—if I knew them—I would interpret the Forth Bridge or the *Portrait of Kahnweiler*. Rather, it is primarily a general condition of rational human action which I posit in the course of arranging my circumstantial facts or moving about on the triangle of re-enactment. This can be referred to as 'intentionality' no doubt. One assumes purposefulness—or intent or, as it were, 'intentiveness'—in the historical actor but even more in the historical ob-

"Intentional Visual Interest" by Michael Baxandall has been excepted from *Patterns of Intention.* Yale University Press (1985), pages 41–45, 58–62, and is reprinted by permission of the publisher.

jects themselves. Intentionality in this sense is taken to be characteristic of both. Intention is the forward-leaning look of things.

It is not a reconstituted historical state of mind, then, but a relation between the object and its circumstances. Some of the voluntary causes I adduce may have been implicit in institutions to which the actor unreflectively acquiesced: Others may have been dispositions acquired through a history of behaviour in which reflection once but no longer had a part.

Genres are often a case of the first and skills are often a case of the second. In either case I may well want to expand the 'intention' to take in the rationality of the institution or of the behaviour that led to the disposition: This may not have been active in the man's mind at the time of making the particular object. Even his own descriptions of his own state of mind—like Baker's of his aesthetic intention and, most certainly, Picasso's later remarks about his—have very limited authority for an account of intention of the object: They are matched with the relation between the object and its circumstances, and retouched or obliquely deployed or even discounted if they are inconsistent with it.

So 'intention' here is referred to pictures rather more than to painters. In particular cases it will be a construct descriptive of a relationship between a picture and its circumstances. In general, intentionality is also a pattern posited in behaviour, and it is used to give circumstantial facts and descriptive concepts a basic structure. In fact, 'intention' is a word I shall use as little as possible, but when I do use it I do not know what other word I could use instead. 'Purpose' and 'function' and the rest present their own difficulties and anyway their force is different.

The issue is now whether the pattern of intention derived from Benjamin Baker's Forth Bridge can be adapted to meet the demands of Picasso's *Portrait of Kahnweiler*. . . . [A]t Queensferry Benjamin Baker was seen as being possessed of a general Charge—'Bridge!' or 'Span!'—and a specific Brief that included such matters as strong side winds, silt, and shiproom. He selected and deployed resources to meet these. In the case of Picasso's *Kahnweiler* it was less clear what Charge and Brief were, and also who delivered them.

A painter's Charge is indeed more elusive than a bridge-builder's. By definition, the bridge-builder's role has been to span: The manner in which he has done so has varied within his circumstances, the character of the site and of the material and intellectual resources of his culture. To find anything like as long-running a role for the painter it is necessary, temporarily, to be rather general. (The need to do so at all will shortly disappear.) In a quite arbitrary and stipulative way I shall say for the moment that the painter's role has been to make marks on a plane surface in such a way that their visual interest is directed to an end. This is less a definition of painting than a specification of the sort of painting I wish to cover. We can all think of pictures that we would say lacked visual interest, or in which the visual interest does not seem directed to an identifiable end. In saying this we would often be making a negative value judgement. In either case this would not be the sort of picture I shall be concerned with. Further, the specification—'intentional visual interest' for short—involves a sort of demarcation against such historical objects as the

Forth Bridge. The Forth Bridge is visually interesting, but is not so capitally: It does not meet its Charge, attain its end, primarily by being visually interesting. Visual interest is secondary and, even though not excluded, incidental.

This may seem an unduly exclusive stipulation, ruling out whole historical episodes in painting, but that is not so. Take, for example, the medieval religious image. To say that it is a thing of intentional visual interest may seem an antihistorical superimposition of a modern aestheticizing point of view. But while our own culture is obviously involved in putting it in this way, in describing its role in these particular terms, the terms do not produce something untrue, just something very general that fails to describe the particular qualities of the medieval image. Medieval religious pictures—and for that matter such Renaissance religious images as Piero della Francesca's *Baptism of Christ*—were produced with a degree of conformity to a general rubric with a history of argument behind it. The thinking took its stand on the fact that, of the five senses, vision is the most precise and the most powerful in the mind, more precise and vivid than hearing, the sense which brings us the Word. Because it was the most precise and vivid faculty given us by God, it was to be used to a pastoral purpose, and its special quality directed to three specified ends. First, it was to expound religious matter clearly: Its precision equipped it and the painter's medium for this task. Secondly, it was to expound the matter in such a way as to move the soul: The vividness in the mind of seen things gave it great power here, more power (it was felt) than the word, a heard thing. Thirdly, it was to expound the matter memorably: Vision is more retentive than hearing, and things seen stick in the mind better than things heard. Thus the painter's general rubric—made more particular, of course, in particular circumstances—was determined by a recognition that vision was the first sense and gave him a peculiar potentiality: He could use his medium to do things other mediums could not. If we rewrite this as 'intentional visual interest,' we are generalizing it, not excluding it.

But 'intentional visual interest' is too general to be useful in the particular case. Its usefulness is purely as a nondescript base—nondescript enough to accommodate as much of the last five hundred years of European painting as I want to—on which to hang the specific qualifications involved in particular cases. The Charge is featureless. Character begins with the Brief. And since things are becoming unpleasantly abstract I shall propose at this point three elements in Picasso's Brief of 1910—equivalents, as it were, of silt, side winds and shiproom—without attempting to substantiate them. They are, in fact, simply adapted from Kahnweiler's account of Picasso and Braque in his book *Der Weg zum Kubismus,* written about 1915 and published in 1920, which seems to me the most plausible of the near-contemporary descriptions of early Cubism. What the status of such assertions is, what they are describing, who can be considered as having set Picasso's Brief, and (eventually) how one assesses such claims about intention, are problems I shall return to once we have something concrete to think around.

One element in the Brief would come out of the fact that representational painters like Picasso represent a three-dimensional reality on a two-dimensional surface, this being a very old issue indeed. How is one both to represent things and persons, tables and art-dealers, recalcitrantly three-dimensional, and yet also positively to acknowledge the two-dimensional plane of the canvas? How does one make a virtue of this curious relation rather than play at what can be seen as a mountebank's game of creating on the plane an illusion of depth? The issue was involved in much recent painting. Impressionism had offered canvases that played on a tension between an openly dabbed-on plane surface and a rendering of sense-impressions of seen objects that put emphasis on their hues. Matisse and others had subsequently dabbed less and played with an oscillation between perception of flatter patterns of hues on the picture surface and our inference about the patterning of the object of representation. There was a problem here.

A second element is a question about the relative importance of form and of colour, again an ancient issue in painting and in thinking about painting. Impressionist painting and some Post-Impressionist painting had made much, both pictorially and verbally, of the overriding importance to us of colour, in the sense of hues. But colour is an accident of vision, a function of the beholder not an intrinsic quality of real objects; whereas form is not only real but offers the security of perception through more than one sense, since we can apprehend form not only with vision but also with touch. How then can a grown-up spend time playing about with colour when the form of the objective world is available to him?

A third element is a question about the fictive instantaneousness of much painting. The convention (if that is what it is; I am not sure) that the painter is offering a moment of experience was in question, partly because of unease about the programme of Impressionism. Matisse, for one, raised it in an essay of 1908. The point is, of course, that in fact it takes a painter much longer than a moment to paint a picture: It takes hours or months. Might there be a case for the painter acknowledging *in the character of his depiction* the fact that this is a record of sustained perceptual and intellectual engagement with the object of representation? Should one not make a virtue, again, of the truth, which is that we do not just have a single sense-impression of an object important enough to us to paint? We have thought about it, analytically about its parts and synthetically about their constitution. We have studied it in different lights, very probably, and from different angles. And—an important point entailed in a remark of Braque's in 1908—our emotions are less about the object itself than about the history of our minds' engagement with the object. . . .

'Influence' is a curse of art criticism primarily because of its wrong-headed grammatical prejudice about who is the agent and who the patient: It seems to reverse the active/passive relation which the historical actor experiences and the inferential beholder will wish to take into account. If one says that X influenced Y, it does seem that one is saying that X did something to Y rather than that Y did something to X. But in the consideration of good pictures and painters the second is always the more lively reality. It is very strange that a term with such an incongruous astral background has come to play such a role, because it is right against the real energy of the lexicon. If we think of Y rather than X as the agent, the vocabulary is much richer and more attractively diversified: draw on, resort to, avail oneself of, appropriate from, have recourse to, adapt, misunderstand, refer to, pick up, take on, engage with, react to, quote, differentiate oneself from, assimilate oneself to, assimilate, align oneself with, copy, address, paraphrase, absorb, make a variation on, revive, continue, remodel, ape, emulate, travesty, parody, extract from, distort, attend to, resist, simplify, reconstitute, elaborate on, develop, face up to, master, subvert, perpetuate, reduce, promote, respond to, transform, tackle . . .—everyone will be able to think of others. Most of these relations just cannot be stated the other way round—in terms of X acting on Y rather than Y acting on X. To think in terms of influence blunts thought by impoverishing the means of differentiation.

Worse, it is shifty. To say that X influenced Y in some matter is to beg the question of cause without quite appearing to do so. After all, if X is the sort of fact that acts on people, there seems no pressing need to ask why Y was acted on: The implication is that X simply is that kind of fact—'influential.' Yet when Y has recourse to or assimilates himself to or otherwise refers to X there are causes: Responding to circumstances Y makes an intentional selection from an array of resources in the history of his craft. Of course, circumstances can be fairly peremptory. If Y is apprentice in the fifteenth-century workshop of X, they will urge him to refer to X for a time, and X will dominate the array of resources that presents itself to Y at that moment; dispositions acquired in this early situation may well stay with Y, even if in odd or inverted forms. Also there are cultures—most obviously various medieval cultures—in which adherence to existing types and styles is very well thought of. But then in both cases there are questions to be asked about the institutional or ideological frameworks in which these things were so: These are causes of Y referring to X, part of his Charge or Brief.

The classic Humean image of causality that seems to colour many accounts of influence is one billiard ball, X, hitting another, Y. An image that might work better for the case would be not two billiard balls but the field offered by a billiard table. On this table would be very many balls—the game is not billiards but snooker or pool—and the table is an Italian one without pockets. Above all, the cue ball, that which hits another, is *not* X, but Y. What happens in the field, each time Y refers to an X, is a rearrangement. Y has moved purposefully, impelled by the cue of intention, and X has been repositioned too: Each ends up in a new relation to the array of all the other balls. Some of these have become more or less accessible or masked, more or less available to Y in his stance after reference to X. Arts are positional games, and each time an artist is influenced, he rewrites his art's history a little.

Let X be Cézanne and Y Picasso. In the autumn of 1906 Cézanne died and Picasso started working towards *Les Demoiselles d'Avignon*. For some time Picasso had been able to see pictures by Cézanne: In particular, his dealer Vollard had large holdings and there were large Cézanne exhibits at the Autumn Salon in 1904 and also in 1907, when there was besides an exhibition of Cézanne watercolours at the Galerie Bernheim Jeune. Many of the new painters were drawing on one or another aspect of Cézanne, never quite the same. For instance, Matisse, who had bought a *Trois Baigneuses* by Cézanne with his wife's dowry in 1899, read in

Cézanne a reductive registration of the local structures of the human figure. This reading Matisse put to distinctive use around 1900 as a means to a form both energetically decorative on the picture-plane and suggestive of a toughly colossal sort of object of representation. In time this reading of Cézanne was absorbed into complex modes in which readings of other painters were also active for Matisse, who was an eclectic referrer.

In 1906–10 Picasso (one infers) saw Cézanne in various ways. In the first place Cézanne was for him part of the history of interesting painting he chose to be aware of and which constituted his Charge. But then, by attending to him, he made him more than that. There were various rather general Cézannian things Picasso accepted *en troc* from the culture, as part of his Brief: One would be Cézanne as an epic model of the determined individual who saw his own sense of the problem of painting as larger than any immediate formulation urged on him by the market; another might be some of Cézanne's verbalizations about painting—'deal with nature in terms of the cylinder, the sphere, the cone . . .' and so on—which, in the form of letters to Emile Bernard, were published in 1907. But then, too, Cézanne was part of the problem Picasso elected to address: There are indications in the composition and in some of the poses of *Les Demoiselles d'Avignon* that one of the elements Picasso was tackling here was a sense of problems left by Cézanne's pictures of bathers, a sense that these were something to tackle. But again, and very obviously, Picasso also went to Cézanne's pictures as an actual resource, somewhere he could find means to an end, varied tools for solving problems. The matter of Cézannian *passage*—of representing a relation between two separate planes by registering them as one continuous superplane—I have already mentioned, but there are other things too Picasso is considered to have adapted from Cézanne: for instance, high and sometimes shifting view-points that flatten out on the picture-plane arrays of objects phenomenally receding in depth. To Picasso, different aspects of Cézanne were what 'Span!' and side winds and the cantilever principle and Siemens steel were to Benjamin Baker—or as, in what is emerging as my grossly oversimplified and over-schematic account, I described them as being to Baker.

To sum all this up as Cézanne influencing Picasso would be false: It would blur the differences in type of reference, and it would take the actively purposeful element out of Picasso's behaviour to Cézanne. Picasso acted on Cézanne quite sharply. For one thing, he rewrote art history by making Cézanne a that much larger and more central historical fact in 1910 than he had been in 1906: He shifted him further into the main tradition of European painting. Then again, his reference to Cézanne was tendentious. His angle on Cézanne—to revert to the billiard-table image—was a particular one, affected among other things by his having referred also to such other art as African sculpture. He saw and extracted this rather than that in Cézanne and modified it, towards his own intention and into his own universe of representation. And then again, by doing this he changed forever the way we can see Cézanne (and African sculpture), whom we must see partly diffracted through Picasso's idiosyncratic reading: We will never see Cézanne undistorted by what, in Cézanne, painting after Cézanne has made productive in our tradition.

'Tradition,' by the way, I take to be not some aesthetical sort of cultural gene but a specifically discriminating view of the past in an active and reciprocal relation with a developing set of dispositions and skills acquirable in the culture that possesses this view. But influence I do not want to talk about.

Works of Art and Mere Real Things
■ Arthur C. Danto ■

Let us consider a painting once described by the Danish wit, Sören Kierkegaard. It was a painting of the Israelites crossing the Red Sea. Looking at it, one would have seen something very different from what a painting with that subject would have led one to expect, were one to imagine, for example, what an artist like Poussin or Altdoerfer would have painted: troops of people, in various postures of panic, bearing the burdens of their dislocated lives, and in the distance the horsed might of the Egyptian forces bearing down. Here, instead, was a square of red paint, the artist explaining that "The Israelites had already crossed over, and the Egyptians were drowned." Kierkegaard comments that the result of his life is like that painting. All the spiritual turmoil, the father cursing God on the heath, the rupture with Regina Olsen, the inner search for Christian meaning, the sustained polemics of an agonized soul, meld in the end, as in the echoes of the Marabar Caves, into "a mood, a single color."

So next to Kierkegaard's described painting let us place another, exactly like it, this one, let us suppose, by a Danish portraitist who, with immense psychological penetration, has produced a work called *St Kierkegaard's Mood.* And let us, in this vein, imagine a whole set of red rectangles, one next to the other. Beside these two, and resembling each as much as they resemble one another (exactly), we shall place *Red Square,* a clever bit of Moscow landscape. Our next work is a minimalist exemplar of geometrical art which, as it happens, has the same title, *Red Square.* Now comes *Nirvana.* It is a metaphysical painting based on the artist's knowledge that the Nirvanic and Samsara orders are identical, and that the Samsara world is fondly called the Red Dust by its deprecators. Now we must have a still-life executed by an embittered disciple of Matisse, called *Red Table Cloth;* we may allow the paint to be somewhat more thinly applied in this case. Our next object is not really an artwork, merely a canvas grounded in red lead, upon which, had he lived to execute it, Giorgione would have painted his unrealized masterwork *Conversazione Sacra.* It is a red surface which, though hardly an artwork, is not without art-historical

"Works of Art and Mere Real Things" Arthur C. Danto has been excerpted from *The Transfiguration of the Commonplace,* Harvard University Press (1981), pages 1–3, 44, 105–107, 135, 164, and is reprinted by permission of the publisher.

interest, since Giorgione himself laid the ground on it. Finally, I shall place a surface painted, though not *grounded,* in red lead: a mere artifact I exhibit as something whose philosophical interest consists solely in the fact that it is not a work of
art, and that its only art-historical interest is the fact that we are considering it at
all: It is just a thing, with paint upon it.

This completes my exhibition. The catalogue for it, which is in full color,
would be monotonous, since everything illustrated looks the same as everything
else, even though the reproductions are of paintings that belong to such diverse
genres as historical painting, psychological portraiture, landscape, geometrical abstraction, religious art, and still-life. It also contains pictures of something from the
workshop of Giorgione, as well as of something that is a mere thing, with no pretense whatsoever to the exalted status of art.

It is what he terms the "rank injustice" in according the classy term *work of
art* to most of the displayed items in my exhibit, while withholding it from an object that resembles them in every visible particular, which outrages a visitor, a
sullen young artist with egalitarian attitudes, whom I shall call J. Seething with a
kind of political rage, J paints up a work that resembles my mere rectangle of red
paint and, insisting that his is a work of art, demands that I include it in my show,
which I am happy enough to do. It is not one of J's major efforts, but I hang it nevertheless. It is, I tell him, rather empty, as indeed it is, compared with the narrative
richness of *The St Israelites Crossing the Red Sea* or the impressive depth of
Nirvana, not to mention *The Legend of the True Cross* by Piero della Francesca or
Giorgione's *La Tempesta.* Much the same epithet would characterize another of J's
works, what he regards as a piece of sculpture and which consists, as I recall it, in a
box of undistinguished carpentry, coated with beige latex paint applied casually
with a roller. Yet the painting is not empty in anything like the way that mere expanse of red-painted canvas is, which is not even empty as a blank page might be,
for it is not plain that it awaits an inscription, any more than a wall of mine might
were I to paint *it* red. Nor is his sculpture empty in the way a crate would be, after
its cargo is taken out or unloaded. For "empty" as applied to his works represents
an aesthetic judgment and a critical appraisal, and presupposes that what it applies
to is an artwork already, however inscrutable may be the differences between it and
mere objects that are logically unsusceptible to such predications as a class. His
works are literally empty, as are the works in the rest of my show: But literalness is
not what I have in mind in saying, in effect, that J's achievements lack richness.

I ask J what is the title of his new work, and predictably he tells me that *St Untitled* will serve as well as anything. This *is* a title of sorts rather than a mere statement of fact, as it sometimes is when an artist neglects to give his work a title or if
we happen not to know what title he gave it or would have given it. I may observe
that the mere thing in whose political cause J created his work also lacks a title, but
this is by dint of an ontological classification: Mere things are unentitled to titles. A
title is more than a name; frequently it is a direction for interpretation or reading,
which may not always be helpful, as when someone perversely gives the title *The*

Annunciation to a painting of some apples. J is somewhat less fantastic than this: His title is directive in at least the sense that the thing to which it is given is meant not to be interpreted. So predictably too, when I ask J what his work is about, I am told that it is about nothing. I am certain this is not a description of its content (chapter two of *Being and Nothingness* is *about* nothing, *about* absence). For that matter, *Nirvana* may be said to be about nothing in the sense that nothing is what it is about, a picture of the void. His work, J points out, is void of picture, less a case of the mimesis of vacuity than the vacuity of mimesis: So he repeats, about nothing. But neither, I point out, is that red expanse in defense of which he painted *Untitled* about anything, but *that* is because it is a thing, and things, as a class, lack aboutness just because they are things. *Untitled,* by contrast, is an artwork, and artworks are, as the description of my exhibition shows, typically about something. So the absence of content appears to be something rather willed in J's instance.

Meanwhile, I can only observe that though he has produced a (pretty minimal) artwork, not to be told by naked inspection from a bare red expanse of paint, he has not yet made an artwork out of that bare red expanse. It remains what it always was, a stranger to the community of artworks, even though that community contains so many members indiscernible from it. So it was a nice but pointless gesture on J's part: He has augmented my little collection of artworks while leaving unbreached the boundaries between them and the world of just things. This puzzles J as it puzzles me. It cannot be simply because J is an artist, for not everything touched by an artist turns to art. Witness Giorgione's primed canvas, supposing the paint to have been laid on by him: A fence painted by J is only a painted fence. This leaves then only the option, now realized by J, of *declaring* that contested red expanse a work of art. Why not? Duchamp declared a snowshovel to be one, and it was one; a bottlerack to be one, and it was one. I allow that J has much the same right, whereupon he declares the red expanse a work of art, carrying it triumphantly across the boundary as if he had rescued something rare. Now everything in my collection is a work of art, but nothing has been clarified as to what has been achieved. The nature of the boundary is philosophically dark, despite the success of J's raid. . . .

There are doubtless works of art, even great works of art, which have material counterparts that are beautiful, and they are beautiful in ways in which certain natural objects would be counted as beautiful—gemstones, birds, sunsets—things to which persons of any degree of aesthetic sensitivity might spontaneously respond. Perhaps this is dangerous to suppose: Sailors might respond to sunsets only in terms of what they foretell of coming weather; farmers might be indifferent to the flowers they tramp on; there may be no objects to which everyone must respond that can be offered as paradigm cases. Nevertheless, let us suppose a group of people who do in fact respond to just the things we would in fact offer as paradigms: to fields of daffodils, to minerals, to peacocks, to glowing irridescent things that appear to house their own light and elicit from these people, as they might from us, the almost involuntary expression "How beautiful!" They would partition off beautiful things just as we would. Except these people happen to be "barbarians," lacking a concept of art. Now we may suppose these barbarians would respond to certain works of art as well as to natural objects just as we would—but they would do so only to those works of art whose material counterparts are beautiful, simply because they see works of art as we would see those material counterparts, as *beautiful things:* such as the rose-windows of Chartres, or thirteenth-century stained glass generally; certain works in enamel; confections wrought by grecian goldsmiths; the saltcellar of Cellini; the sorts of things collected by the Medici and the later Habsburgs—cameos, ornaments, precious and semiprecious stones, things in lace and filagree; things luminous and airy, possession of which would be like possessing a piece of the moon when that was thought to be a pure radiance rather than a ranch of rocks. There is some deep reason, I am certain, why these things attract, but I shall forgo any Jungian rhapsodizing. . . .

Imagine now our sensitive barbarians sweeping across the civilized world, conquering and destroying like Huns. As barbarians reserve the fairest maidens for their violent beds, we may imagine these sparing for their curious delectation just those works of art which happen to have beautiful material counterparts. Some paintings, certainly, will survive. Those with lots of goldleaf will certainly do so, and certain icons with highly ornamented frames. Or paintings where the colors have a kind of hard mineral brilliance, as in Crivelli or perhaps Mantegna. But how many Rembrandts would make it through under this criterion, how many Watteaus or Chardins or Picassos? Appreciation of these require them to be perceived first as artworks, and hence presupposes availability of the concept we are disallowing the subjects of this *Gedanken* experiment. It is not that aesthetics is irrelevant to art, but that the relationship between the artwork and its material counterpart must be gotten right for aesthetics to have any bearing, and though there may be an innate aesthetic sense, the cognitive apparatus required for it to come into play cannot itself be considered innate. . . .

There was a certain sense of unfairness felt at the time when [Andy] Warhol piled the Stable Gallery full of his Brillo boxes; for the commonplace Brillo container was actually *designed* by an artist, an Abstract Expressionist driven by need into commercial art; and the question was why Warhol's boxes should have been worth $200 when that man's products were not worth a dime. Whatever explains this explains, as well, why the primed canvas of Giorgione, in our first example, fails to be an artwork though resembling in every respect the red expanses which are such.

In part, the answer to the question has to be historical. Not everything is possible at every time, as Heinrich Wölflin has written, meaning that certain artworks simply could not be inserted as artworks into certain periods of art history, though it is possible that objects identical to artworks could have been made at that period. . . .

Duchamp's snowshovel was pretty banal in the early twentieth century, simply because chosen from the set of indiscernible industrial products from a shovel factory, with its peers to be found in garages throughout the bourgeois world. But the identical object—a curved sheet of metal attached to a wooden stick at the

Andy Warhol, *Brillo Box* (1964).
Source: The Andy Warhol Foundation, Inc. Art Resource, NY.

other terminus of which was a shape like today's snowshovel handle—would have been, I should think, a deeply mysterious object in the thirteenth century; but it is doubtful that it could have been absorbed into the artworld of that period and place. And it is not difficult to conceive of objects which, though they would not have been works of art at the time they were made, can have in a later period objects precisely like them which are works of art. . . .

To see something as art at all demands nothing less than this, an atmosphere of artistic theory, a knowledge of the history of art. Art is the kind of thing that depends for its existence upon theories; without theories of art, black paint *is* just black paint and nothing more. Perhaps one *can* speak of what the world is like independently of any theories we may have regarding the world, though I am not sure that it is even meaningful to raise such a question, since our divisions and articulations of things into orbits and constellations presupposes a theory of some sort. But it is plain that there could not be an artworld without theory, for the artworld is logically dependant upon theory. So it is essential to our study that we understand the nature of an art theory, which is so powerful a thing as to detach objects from the real world and make them part of a different world, an *art* world, a world of *interpreted things*. What these considerations show is that there is an internal connection between the status of an artwork and the language with which artworks are identified as such, inasmuch as nothing is an artwork without an interpretation that constitutes it as such.

The Origin of the Work of Art
■ Martin Heidegger ■

Origin here means that from and by which something is what it is and as it is. What something is, as it is, we call its essence or nature. The origin of something is the source of its nature. The question concerning the origin of the work of art asks about the source of its nature. On the usual view, the work arises out of and by means of the activity of the artist. But by what and whence is the artist what he is? By the work; for to say that the work does credit to the master means that it is the work that first lets the artist emerge as a master of his art. The artist is the origin of the work. The work is the origin of the artist. Neither is without the other. Nevertheless, neither is the sole support of the other. In themselves and in their interrelations artist and work *are* each of them by virtue of a third thing which is prior to both, namely that which also gives artist and work of art their names—art.

As necessarily as the artist is the origin of the work in a different way than the work is the origin of the artist, so it is equally certain that, in a still different way, art is the origin of both artist and work. But can art be an origin at all? Where and how does art occur? Art—this is nothing more than a word to which nothing real any longer corresponds. It may pass for a collective idea under which we find a place for that which alone is real in art: works and artists. Even if the word art were taken to signify more than a collective notion, what is meant by the word could exist only on the basis of the actuality of works and artists. Or is the converse the case? Do works and artists exist only because art exists as their origin?

Whatever the decision may be, the question of the origin of the work of art becomes a question about the nature of art. Since the question whether and how art in general exists must still remain open, we shall attempt to discover the nature of art in the place where art undoubtedly prevails in a real way. Art is present in the art work. But what and how is a work of art?

What art is should be inferable from the work. What the work of art is we can come to know only from the nature of art. Anyone can easily see that we are moving in a circle. Ordinary understanding demands that this circle be avoided because it violates logic. What art is can be gathered from a comparative examination of actual art works. But how are we to be certain that we are indeed basing such an examination on art works if we do not know beforehand what art is? And the nature of art can no more be arrived at by a derivation from higher concepts than by a collection of characteristics of actual art works. For such a derivation, too, already has in view the characteristics that must suffice to establish that what we take in advance

"The Origin of the Work of Art" by Martin Heidegger has been excerpted from *Poetry, Language and Thought,* Albert Hofstadter, trans., Harper Collins (1971), pages 17–21, 32–37, and is reprinted by permission of the publisher.

to be an art work is one in fact. But selecting works from among given objects, and deriving concepts from principles, are equally impossible here, and where these procedures are practiced they are a self-deception.

Thus we are compelled to follow the circle. This is neither a makeshift nor a defect. To enter upon this path is the strength of thought, to continue on it is the feast of thought, assuming that thinking is a craft. Not only is the main step from work to art a circle like the step from art to work, but every separate step that we attempt circles in this circle.

In order to discover the nature of the art that really prevails in the work, let us go to the actual work and ask the work what and how it is.

Works of art are familiar to everyone. Architectural and sculptural works can be seen installed in public places, in churches, and in dwellings. Art works of the most diverse periods and peoples are housed in collections and exhibitions. If we consider the works in their untouched actuality and do not deceive ourselves, the result is that the works are as naturally present as are things. The picture hangs on the wall like a rifle or a hat. A painting, e.g., the one by Van Gogh that represents a pair of peasant shoes, travels from one exhibition to another. Works of art are shipped like coal from the Ruhr and logs from the Black Forest. During the First World War Hölderlin's hymns were packed in the soldier's knapsack together with cleaning gear. Beethoven's quartets lie in the storerooms of the publishing house like potatoes in a cellar.

All works have this thingly character. What would they be without it? But perhaps this rather crude and external view of the work is objectionable to us. Shippers or charwomen in museums may operate with such conceptions of the work of art. We, however, have to take works as they are encountered by those who experience and enjoy them. But even the much-vaunted aesthetic experience cannot get around the thingly aspect of the art work. There is something stony in a work of architecture, wooden in a carving, colored in a painting, spoken in a linguistic work, sonorous in a musical composition. The thingly element is so irremovably present in the art work that we are compelled rather to say conversely that the architectural work is in stone, the carving is in wood, the painting in color, the linguistic work in speech, the musical composition in sound. "Obviously," it will be replied. No doubt. But what is this self-evident thingly element in the work of art?

Presumably it becomes superfluous and confusing to inquire into this feature, since the art work is something else over and above the thingly element. This something else in the work constitutes its artistic nature. The art work is, to be sure, a thing that is made, but it says something other than the mere thing itself is, *allo agoreuei*. The work makes public something other than itself; it manifests something other; it is an allegory. In the work of art something other is brought together with the thing that is made. To bring together is, in Greek, *sumballein*. The work is a symbol.

Allegory and symbol provide the conceptual frame within whose channel of vision the art work has for a long time been characterized. But this one element in a work that manifests another, this one element that joins with another, is the

Vincent van Gogh, *Old Shoes with Laces* (1886).
Source: Reproduced courtesy of Art Resource, N.Y.

thingly feature in the art work. It seems almost as though the thingly element in the art work is like the substructure into and upon which the other, authentic element is built. And is it not this thingly feature in the work that the artist really makes by his handicraft?

Our aim is to arrive at the immediate and full reality of the work of art, for only in this way shall we discover real art also within it. Hence we must first bring to view the thingly element of the work. To this end it is necessary that we should know with sufficient clarity what a thing is. Only then can we say whether the art work is a thing, but a thing to which something else adheres; only then can we decide whether the work is at bottom something else and not a thing at all.

What in truth is the thing, so far as it is a thing? When we inquire in this way, our aim is to come to know the thing-being (thingness) of the thing. The point is to discover the thingly character of the thing. To this end we have to be acquainted with the sphere to which all those entities belong which we have long called by the name of thing.

The stone in the road is a thing, as is the clod in the field. A jug is a thing, as is the well beside the road. But what about the milk in the jug and the water in the well? These too are things if the cloud in the sky and the thistle in the field, the leaf in the autumn breeze and the hawk over the wood, are rightly called by the name of thing. All these must indeed be called things, if the name is applied even to that which does not, like those just enumerated, show itself, i.e., that which does not appear. According to Kant, the whole of the world, for example, and even God himself, is a thing of this sort, a thing that does not itself appear, namely, a "thing-in-itself." In the language of philosophy both things-in-themselves and things that appear, all beings that in any way are, are called things.

Airplanes and radio sets are nowadays among the things closest to us, but when we have ultimate things in mind we think of something altogether different. Death and judgment—these are ultimate things. On the whole the word "thing" here designates whatever is not simply nothing. In this sense the work of art is also a thing, so far as it is not simply nothing. Yet this concept is of no use to us, at least immediately, in our attempt to delimit entities that have the mode of being of a thing, as against those having the mode of being of a work. And besides, we hesitate to call God a thing. In the same way we hesitate to consider the peasant in the field, the stoker at the boiler, the teacher in the school as things. A man is not a thing. It is true that we speak of a young girl who is faced with a task too difficult for her as being a young thing, still too young for it, but only because we feel that being human is in a certain way missing here and think that instead we have to do here with the factor that constitutes the thingly character of things. We hesitate even to call the deer in the forest clearing, the beetle in the grass, the blade of grass a thing. We would sooner think of a hammer as a thing, or a shoe, or an ax, or a clock. But even these are not mere things. Only a stone, a clod of earth, a piece of wood are for us such mere things. Lifeless beings of nature and objects of use. Natural things and utensils are the things commonly so called. . . .

That the thingness of the thing is particularly difficult to express and only seldom expressible is infallibly documented by the history of its interpretation indicated above. This history coincides with the destiny in accordance with which Western thought has hitherto thought the Being of beings. However, not only do we now establish this point; at the same time we discover a clue in this history. Is it an accident that in the interpretation of the thing the view that takes matter and form as guide attains to special dominance? This definition of the thing derives from an interpretation of the equipmental being of equipment. And equipment, having come into being through human making, is particularly familiar to human thinking. At the same time, this familiar being has a peculiar intermediate position between thing and work. We shall follow this clue and search first for the equipmental character of equipment. Perhaps this will suggest something to us about the thingly character of the thing and the workly character of the work. We must only avoid making thing and work prematurely into subspecies of equipment. We are disregarding the possibility, however, that differences relating to the history of Being may yet also be present in the way equipment *is*.

But what path leads to the equipmental quality of equipment? How shall we discover what a piece of equipment truly is? The procedure necessary at present must plainly avoid any attempts that again immediately entail the encroachments of the usual interpretations. We are most easily insured against this if we simply describe some equipment without any philosophical theory.

We choose an example a common sort of equipment—a pair of peasant shoes. We do not even need to exhibit actual pieces of this sort of useful article in order to describe them. Everyone is acquainted with them. But since it is a matter here of direct description, it may be well to facilitate the visual realization of them. For this purpose a pictorial representation suffices. We shall choose a well-known painting by Van Gogh, who painted such shoes several times. But what is there to see here? Everyone knows what shoes consist of. If they are not wooden or bast shoes, there will be leather soles and uppers, joined together by thread and nails. Such gear serves to clothe the feet. Depending on the use to which the shoes are to be put, whether for work in the field or for dancing, matter and form will differ.

Such statements, no doubt correct, only explicate what we already know. The equipmental quality of equipment consists in its usefulness. But what about this usefulness itself? In conceiving it, do we already conceive along with it the equip-mental character of equipment? In order to succeed in doing this, must we not look out for useful equipment in its use? The peasant woman wears her shoes in the field. Only here are they what they are. They are all the more genuinely so, the less the peasant woman thinks about the shoes while she is at work, or looks at them at all, or is even aware of them. She stands and walks in them. That is how shoes actu-ally serve. It is in this process of the use of equipment that we must actually en-counter the character of equipment.

As long as we only imagine a pair of shoes in general, or simply look at the empty, unused shoes as they merely stand there in the picture, we shall never dis-cover what the equipmental being of the equipment in truth is. From Van Gogh's painting we cannot even tell where these shoes stand. There is nothing surrounding this pair of peasant shoes in or to which they might belong—only an undefined space. There are not even clods of soil from the field or the field-path sticking to them, which would at least hint at their use. A pair of peasant shoes and nothing more. And yet—

From the dark opening of the worn insides of the shoes the toilsome tread of the worker stares forth. In the stiffly rugged heaviness of the shoes there is the accu-mulated tenacity of her slow trudge through the far-spreading and ever-uniform fur-rows of the field swept by a raw wind. On the leather lie the dampness and richness of the soil. Under the soles slides the loneliness of the field-path as evening falls. In the shoes vibrates the silent call of the earth, its quiet gift of the ripening grain and its unexplained self-refusal in the fallow desolation of the wintry field. This equip-ment is pervaded by uncomplaining anxiety as to the certainty of bread, the word-less joy of having once more withstood want, the trembling before the impending childbed and shivering at the surrounding menace of death. This equipment belongs to the *earth,* and it is protected in the *world* of the peasant woman. From out of this protected belonging the equipment itself rises to its resting-within-itself.

But perhaps it is only in the picture that we notice all this about the shoes. The peasant woman, on the other hand, simply wears them. If only this simple wearing were so simple. When she takes off her shoes late in the evening, in deep but healthy fatigue, and reaches out for them again in the still dim dawn, or passes them by on the day of rest, she knows all this without noticing or reflecting. The equipmental quality of the equipment consists indeed in its usefulness. But this usefulness itself rests in the abundance of an essential being of the equipment. We call it reliability. By virtue of this reliability the peasant woman is made privy to the silent call of the earth; by virtue of the reliability of the equipment she is sure of her world. World and earth exist for her, and for those who are with her in her mode of being, only thus—in the equipment. We say "only" and therewith fall into error; for the reliability of the equipment first gives to the simple world its security and assures to the earth the freedom of its steady thrust.

The equipmental being of equipment, reliability, keeps gathered within itself all things according to their manner and extent. The usefulness of equipment is nevertheless only the essential consequence of reliability. The former vibrates in the latter and would be nothing without it. A single piece of equipment is worn out and used up; but at the same time the use itself also falls into disuse, wears away, and becomes usual. Thus equipmentality wastes away, sinks into mere stuff. In such wasting, reliability vanishes. This dwindling, however, to which use-things owe their boringly obtrusive usualness, is only one more testimony to the original nature of equipmental being. The worn-out usualness of the equipment then obtrudes itself as the sole mode of being, apparently peculiar to it exclusively. Only blank usefulness now remains visible. It awakens the impression that the origin of equipment lies in a mere fabricating that impresses a form upon some matter. Nevertheless, in its genuinely equipmental being, equipment stems from a more distant source. Matter and form and their distinction have a deeper origin.

The repose of equipment resting within itself consists in its reliability. Only in this reliability do we discern what equipment in truth is. But we still know nothing of what we first sought: the thing's thingly character. And we know nothing at all of what we really and solely seek: the workly character of the work in the sense of the work of art.

Or have we already learned something unwittingly, in passing so to speak, about the work-being of the work?

The equipmental quality of equipment was discovered. But how? Not by a description and explanation of a pair of shoes actually present; not by a report about the process of making shoes; and also not by the observation of the actual use of shoes occurring here and there; but only by bringing ourselves before Van Gogh's painting. This painting spoke. In the vicinity of the work we were suddenly somewhere else than we usually tend to be.

The art work let us know what shoes are in truth. It would be the worst self-deception to think that our description, as a subjective action, had first depicted everything thus and then projected it into the painting. If anything is questionable here, it is rather that we experienced too little in the neighborhood of the work and that we expressed the experience too crudely and too literally. But above all, the work did not, as it might seem at first, serve merely for a better visualizing of what a piece of equipment is. Rather, the equipmentality of equipment first genuinely arrives at its appearance through the work and only in the work.

What happens here? What is at work in the work? Van Gogh's painting is the disclosure of what the equipment, the pair of peasant shoes, *is* in truth. This entity emerges into the unconcealedness of its being. The Greeks called the unconcealedness of beings *aletheia*. We say "truth" and think little enough in using this word. If there occurs in the work a disclosure of a particular being, disclosing what and how it is, then there is here an occurring, a happening of truth at work.

In the work of art the truth of an entity has set itself to work. "To set" means here: to bring to a stand. Some particular entity, a pair of peasant shoes, comes in the work to stand in the light of its being. The being of the being comes into the steadiness of its shining.

The nature of art would then be this: the truth of beings setting itself to work. But until now art presumably has had to do with the beautiful and beauty, and not with truth. The arts that produce such works are called the beautiful or fine arts, in contrast with the applied or industrial arts that manufacture equipment. In fine art the art itself is not beautiful, but is called so because it produces the beautiful. Truth, in contrast, belongs to logic. Beauty, however, is reserved for aesthetics.

But perhaps the proposition that art is truth setting itself to work intends to revive the fortunately obsolete view that art is an imitation and depiction of reality? The reproduction of what exists requires, to be sure, agreement with the actual being, adaptation to it; the Middle Ages called it *adaequatio;* Aristotle already spoke of *homoiosis*. Agreement with what *is* has long been taken to be the essence of truth. But then, is it our opinion that this painting by Van Gogh depicts a pair of actually existing peasant shoes, and is a work of art because it does so successfully? Is it our opinion that the painting draws a likeness from something actual and transposes it into a product of artistic—production? By no means.

The work, therefore, is not the reproduction of some particular entity that happens to be present at any given time; it is, on the contrary, the reproduction of the thing's general essence.

Why Are There No Great Women Artists?
■ Linda Nochlin ■

"Why are there no great women artists?" This question tolls reproachfully in the background of discussions of the so-called woman problem, causing men to shake their heads regretfully and women to grind their teeth in frustration. Like so many other questions involved in the red-hot feminist controversy, it falsifies the nature

"Why Are There No Great Women Artists?" by Linda Nochlin is excerpted from *Women in Sexist Society,* V. Gornick and B. K. Moran, eds., Harper Collins (1971), pages 344–346, 350–354, and is reprinted by permission of the author.

of the issue at the same time that it insidiously supplies its own answer: "There are no great women artists because women are incapable of greatness." The assumptions lying behind such a question are varied in range and sophistication, running anywhere from "scientifically" proven demonstrations of the inability of human beings with wombs rather than penises to create anything significant, to relatively open-minded wonderment that women, despite so many years of near-equality—and after all, a lot of men have had their disadvantages too—have still not achieved anything of major significance in the visual arts.

The feminist's first reaction is to swallow the bait, hook, line and sinker and to attempt to answer the question as it is put: that is, to dig up examples of worthy or insufficiently appreciated women artists throughout history; to rehabilitate rather modest, if interesting and productive careers; to rediscover forgotten flower painters or David-followers and make out a case for them; to demonstrate that Berthe Morisot was really less dependent upon Manet than one had been led to think—in other words, to engage in activity not too different from that of the average scholar, man or woman, making out a case for the importance of his own neglected or minor master. Whether undertaken from a feminist point of view, such attempts, like the ambitious article on women artists which appeared in the 1858 *Westminster Review,* or more recent scholarly studies and reevaluations of individual woman artists like Angelica Kauffmann or Artemisia Gentilesch, are certainly well worth the effort, adding to our knowledge both of women's achievement and of art history generally; and a great deal still remains to be done in this area. Unfortunately, such efforts, if written from an uncritically feminist viewpoint, do nothing to question the assumptions lying behind the question "Why are there no great women artists?"; on the contrary, by attempting to answer it and by doing so inadequately, they merely reinforce its negative implications.

At the same time that champions of women's equality may feel called upon to falsify the testimony of their own judgment by scraping up neglected female artistic geniuses or puffing up the endeavors of genuinely excellent but decidedly minor women painters and sculptors into major contributions, they may resort to the easily refuted ploy of accusing the questioner of using "male" standards as the criterion of greatness or excellence. This attempt to answer the question involves shifting the ground slightly; by asserting, as many contemporary feminists do, that there is actually a different kind of greatness for women's art than for men's, one tacitly assumes the existence of a distinctive and recognizable feminine style, differing in both its formal and its expressive qualities from that of male artists and positing the unique character of women's situation and experience.

This, on the surface of it, seems reasonable enough: In general, women's experience and situation in society, and hence as artists, is different from men's; certainly, the art produced by a group of consciously united and purposefully articulate women intent on bodying forth a group consciousness of feminine experience might be stylistically identifiable as feminist, if not feminine art. Unfortunately, this remains within the realm of possibility; so far, it has not occurred. While the Danube School, Caravaggio's followers, the painters gathered around Gauguin at

Pont Aven, the Blue Rider, or the Cubists may be recognized by certain clearly defined stylistic or expressive qualities, no such common qualities of femininity would seem to link the styles of women artists generally, any more than such qualities can be said to link all women writers—a case brilliantly argued, against the most devastating, and mutually contradictory, masculine critical clichés, by Mary Ellmann in her *Thinking About Women*. No subtle essence of femininity would seem to link the work of Artemesia Gentileschi, Elisabeth Vigée-Lebrun, Angelica Kauffmann, Rosa Bonheur, Berthe Morisot, Suzanne Valadon, Käthe Kollwitz, Barbara Hepworth, Georgia O'Keeffe, Sophie Taeuber-Arp, Helen Frankenthaler, Bridget Riley, Lee Bontecou, and Louise Nevelson, any more than one can find some essential similarity in the work of Sappho, Marie de France, Jane Austen, Emily Brontë, George Sand, George Eliot, Virginia Woolf, Gertrude Stein, Anaïs Nin, Emily Dickinson, Sylvia Plath, and Susan Sontag. In every instance women artists and writers would seem to be closer to other artists and writers of their own period and outlook than they are to each other.

Women artists are more inward-looking, more delicate and nuanced in their treatment of their medium, it may be asserted. But which of the women artists cited above is more inward turning than Redon, more subtle and nuanced in the handling of pigment than Corot at his best? Is Fragonard more or less feminine than Elisabeth Vigée-Lebrun? Or is it not more a question of the whole rococo style of eighteenth-century France being "feminine," if judged in terms of a two-valued scale of masculinity versus femininity? Certainly, though, if daintiness, delicacy, and preciousness are to be counted as earmarks of a feminine style, there is nothing very fragile about Rosa Bonheur's *Horse Fair,* or dainty and introverted about Helen Frankenthaler's giant canvases. If women have indeed at times turned to scenes of domestic life or of children, so did men painters like the Dutch Little Masters, Chardin, and the impressionists—Renoir and Monet as well as Berthe Morisot and Mary Cassatt. In any case, the mere choice of a certain realm of subject matter, or the restriction to certain subjects, is not to be equated with a style, much less with some sort of quintessentially feminine style.

The problem here lies not so much with the feminists' concept of what femininity is, but rather with their misconception of what art is: with the naive idea that art is the direct, personal expression of individual emotional experience, a translation of personal life into visual terms. Art is almost never that, great art certainly never. The making of art involves a self-consistent language of form, more or less dependent upon, or free from, given temporally defined conventions, schemata, or systems of notation, which have to be learned or worked out, either through teaching, apprenticeship, or a long period of individual experimentation. The language of art is, more materially, embodied in paint and line on canvas or paper, in stone or clay or plastic or metal—it is neither a sob story nor a hoarse, confidential whisper. The fact of the matter is that there have been no great women artists, as far as we know—although there have been many interesting and good ones who have not been sufficiently investigated or appreciated—or any great Lithuanian jazz pianists, or Eskimo tennis players, no matter how much we might wish there had been. That this should be the case is regrettable, but no amount of manipulating the historical or critical evidence will alter the situation; neither will accusations of male-chauvinist distortions of history and obfuscation of actual achievements of women artists (or black physicists or Lithuanian jazz musicians). The fact is that there *are* no women equivalents for Michelangelo or Rembrandt, Delacroix or Cézanne, Picasso or Matisse, or even, in very recent times, for de Kooning or Warhol, any more than there are any black American equivalents for the same. If there actually were large numbers of "hidden" great women artists, or if there really should be different standards for women's art as opposed to men's—and logically, one cannot have it both ways—then what would feminists be fighting for? If women have in fact achieved the same status as men in the arts, then the status quo is fine as it is. . . .

Just as a very little power may corrupt one's actions, so a relatively minor degree of false consciousness may contaminate one's intellectual position. The question "Why are there no great women artists?" is simply the top tenth of an iceberg of misinterpretation and misconception revealed above the surface; beneath lies a vast dark bulk of shaky *idées reçues* about the nature of art and its situational concomitants, about the nature of human abilities in general and of human excellence in particular, and the role that the social order plays in all of this. While the woman problem as such may be a pseudoissue, the misconceptions involved in the question "Why are there no great women artists?" point to major areas of intellectual obfuscation beyond the specific political issues involved in the subjection of women and its ideological justifications.

Beneath the question lie naive, distorted, uncritical assumptions about the making of art in general, much less the making of great art. These assumptions, conscious or unconscious, link together such unlikely super-stars as Michelangelo and Van Gogh. Raphael and Jackson Pollock under the rubric of Great Artist—an honorific attested to by the number of scholarly monographs devoted to the artist in question—and the Great Artist is conceived of as one who has genius; genius, in turn, is thought to be an atemporal and mysterious power somehow embedded in the person of the Great Artist. Thus, the conceptual structure underlying the question "Why are there no great women artists?" rests upon unquestioned, often unconscious, metahistorical premises that make Hippolyte Taine's race-milieumoment formulation of the dimensions of historical thought seem like a model of sophistication. Such, unfortunately, are the assumptions lying behind a great deal of art history writing. It is no accident that the whole crucial question of the conditions *generally* productive of great art has so rarely been investigated, or that attempts to investigate such general problems have, until fairly recently, been dismissed as unscholarly, too broad, or the province of some other discipline like sociology. To encourage such a dispassionate, impersonal, sociological, and institutionally oriented approach would reveal the entire romantic, elitist, individual-glorifying, and monograph-producing substructure upon which the profession of art history is based, and which has only recently been called into question by a group of younger dissidents within the discipline.

Underlying the question about woman as artist, then, we find the whole myth of the Great Artist—unique, godlike subject of a hundred monographs—bearing within his person since birth a mysterious essence, rather like the golden nugget in Mrs. Grass's chicken soup, called genius or talent, which must always out, no matter how unlikely or unpromising the circumstances.

The magical aura surrounding the representational arts and their creators has given birth to myths since earliest times. Interestingly enough, the same magical abilities attributed by Pliny to the Greek painter Lysippos in antiquity—the mysterious inner call in early youth, the lack of any teacher but nature herself—is repeated as late as the nineteenth century by Max Buchon in his biography of the realist painter Courbet. The supernatural powers of the artist as imitator, his control of strong, possibly dangerous powers, have functioned historically to set him off from others as a godlike creator, one who creates being out of nothing like the demiurge. The fairy tale of the boy wonder, discovered by an older artist or discerning patron, usually in the guise of a lowly shepherd boy, has been a stock in trade of artistic mythology ever since Vasari immortalized the young Giotto, whom the great Cimabue discovered drawing sheep on a stone, while the lad was guarding his flocks; Cimabue, overcome with admiration for the realism of the drawing, immediately invited the humble youth to be his pupil. Through some mysterious coincidence, later artists like Beccafumi, Andrea Sansovino, Andrea del Castagno, Mantegna, Zurbaran, and Goya were all discovered in similar pastoral circumstances. Even when the Great Artist was not fortunate enough to come equipped with a flock of sheep as a lad, his talent always seems to have manifested itself very early, independent of any external encouragement: Filippo Lippi, Poussin, Courbet, and Monet are all reported to have drawn caricatures in the margins of their schoolbooks, instead of studying the required subjects—we never, of course, hear about the myriad youths who neglected their studies and scribbled in the margins of their notebooks without ever becoming anything more elevated than department store clerks or shoe salesmen—and the great Michelangelo himself, according to his biographer and pupil, Vasari, did more drawing than studying as a child. So pronounced was the young Michelangelo's talent as an art student, reports Vasari, that when his master, Ghirlandaio, absented himself momentarily from his work in Santa Maria Novella and the young Michelangelo took the opportunity to draw "the scaffolding, trestles, pots of paint, brushes, and the apprentices at their tasks," he did so so skillfully that upon his return his master exclaimed: "This boy knows more than I do."

As is so often the case, such stories, which may indeed have a grain of truth in them, tend both to reflect and to perpetuate the attitudes they subsume. Despite the actual basis in fact of these myths about the early manifestations of genius, the tenor of the tales is itself misleading. It is no doubt true, for example, that the young Picasso passed all the examinations for entrance to the Barcelona, and later to the Madrid, Academy of Art at the age of fifteen in a single day, a feat of such difficulty that most candidates required a month of preparation; however, one would like to find out more about similar precocious qualifiers for art academies, who then went on to achieve nothing but mediocrity or failure—in whom, of course, art historians are uninterested—or to study in greater detail the role played by Picasso's art professor father in the pictorial precocity of his son. What if Picasso had been born a girl? Would Señor Ruiz have paid as much attention or stimulated as much ambition for achievement in a little Pablita?

What is stressed in all these stories is the apparently miraculous, non-determined, and asocial nature of artistic achievement this gratuitous, semireligious conception of the artist's role was elevated into a true hagiography in the nineteenth century, when both art historians, critics, and, not least, some of the artists themselves tended to erect the making of art into a substitute religion, the last bulwark of higher values in a materialistic world. The artist in the nineteenth-century Saints' Legend struggles onward against the most determined parental and social opposition, suffering the slings and arrows of social opprobrium like any Christian martyr, and ultimately succeeds against all odds—generally, alas, after his death—because from deep within himself radiates that mysterious, holy effulgence: genius. Here we have the mad Van Gogh, spinning out sunflowers despite epileptic seizures and near-starvation, or perhaps because of them; Cezanne, braving paternal rejection and public scorn in order to revolutionize painting; Gauguin, throwing away respectability and financial security with a single existential gesture to pursue his calling in the tropics, unrecognized by crass philistines on the home front; or Toulouse-Lautrec, dwarfed, crippled, and alcoholic, sacrificing his aristocratic birthright in favor of the squalid surroundings that provided him with inspiration.

Of course, no serious contemporary art historian ever takes such obvious fairy tales at their face value. Yet it is all too often this sort of mythology about artistic achievement and its concomitants that forms the unconscious or unquestioned assumptions of art scholars, no matter how many crumbs are thrown to social influences, ideas of the times, economic crises, and so on. Behind the most sophisticated investigations of great artists, more specifically, the art history monograph, which accepts the notion of the Great Artist as primary, and the social and institutional structures within which he lived and worked as mere secondary "influences" or "background," lurks the golden nugget theory of genius and the free enterprise conception of individual achievement. On this basis, women's lack of major achievement in art may be formulated as a syllogism: If women had the golden nugget of artistic genius, then it would reveal itself. But it has never revealed itself. Q.E.D. Women do not have the golden nugget of artistic genius. If Giotto, the obscure shepherd boy, and Van Gogh, the epileptic, could make it, why not women?

Yet as soon as one leaves behind the world of fairy tale and self-fulfilling prophecy and instead casts a dispassionate eye on the actual situations in which important art has been produced, in the total range of its social and institutional structures throughout history, one finds that the very questions that are fruitful or relevant for the historian to ask shape up rather differently. One would like to ask, for instance, from what social classes, from what castes and subgroups, artists were most likely to come at different periods of art history? What proportion of painters and sculptors, or more specifically, of major painters and sculptors, had fathers or other close relatives engaged in painting, sculpture, or related professions? As Nikolaus Pevsner points out in his discussion of the French Academy in the seventeenth and eighteenth centuries, the transmission of the artistic profession from father to son was considered a matter of course (as in fact it was with the Coypels, the Coustous, the Van Loos, and so forth); indeed, sons of academicians were exempted from the customary fees for lessons. Despite the noteworthy and dramatically satisfying cases of the great father-rejecting révoltés of the nineteenth century, a large proportion of artists, great and not-so-great, had artist fathers. In the rank of major artists, the names of Holbein and Dürer, Raphael and Bernini immediately spring to mind; even in our more recent, rebellious times, one can cite the names of Picasso, Calder, Giacometti and Wyeth as members of artist families.

As far as the relationship of artistic occupation and social class is concerned, an interesting parallel to "why are there no great women artists?" might well be: "why have there been no great artists from the aristocracy?" One can scarcely think, before the antitraditional nineteenth century at least, of any artist who sprang from the ranks of any more elevated class than the upper bourgeoisie; even in the nineteenth century, Degas came from the lower nobility—more like the *haute bourgeoisie,* in fact—and only Toulouse-Lautrec, metamorphosed into the ranks of the marginal by accidental deformity, could be said to have come from the loftier reaches of the upper classes. While the aristocracy has always provided the lion's share of the patronage and the audience for art—as indeed, the aristocracy of wealth does even in our more democratic days, it has rarely contributed anything but a few amateurish efforts to the actual creation of art itself, although aristocrats, like many women, have had far more than their share of educational advantage and leisure, and, indeed, like women, might often be encouraged to dabble in the arts or even develop into respectable amateurs. Napoleon III's cousin, the Princess Mathilde, exhibited at the official salons; Queen Victoria and Prince Albert studied art with no less a figure than Landseer himself. Could it be possible that the little golden nugget—genius—is as absent from the aristocratic make-up as from the feminine psyche? Or is it not rather that the demands and expectations placed on both aristocrats and women—the amount of time necessarily devoted to social functions, the very kinds of activities demanded—simply made total devotion to professional art production out of the question and unthinkable?

When the right questions are finally asked about the conditions for producing art (of which the production of great art is a subtopic), some discussion of the situational concomitants of intelligence and talent generally, not merely of artistic genius, has to be included. As Piaget and others have stressed in their studies of the development of reason and the unfolding of imagination in young children, intelligence—or, by implication, what we choose to call genius—is a dynamic activity, rather than a static essence, and an activity of a subject *in a situation.* As further investigations in the field of child development reveal, these abilities or this intelligence are built up minutely, step by step, from infancy onward, although the patterns of adaptation-accommodation may be established so early within the subject-in-an-environment that they may indeed *appear* to be innate to the unsophisticated observer. Such investigations imply that, even aside from metahistorical reasons, scholars will have to abandon the notion, consciously articulated or not, of individual genius as innate and primary to the creation of art.

The question "Why are there no great women artists?" has so far led to the conclusion that art is not a free, autonomous activity of a superendowed individual, "influenced" by previous artists, and, more vaguely and superficially, by "social forces," but rather, that art making, both in terms of the development of the art maker and the nature and quality of the work of art itself, occurs in a social situation, is an integral element of the social structure, and is mediated and determined by specific and definable social institutions, be they art academies, systems of patronage, mythologies of the divine creator and artist as he-man or social outcast.

The Paradox of Expression
▪ Garry L. Hagberg ▪

In the criticism of art and its attendant search for meaning, many are inclined to attribute a distinctively metaphysical priority to the artist, a priority that quickly engages us with implicit theories of the ontological nature of artworks, the nature of artistic meaning itself, and the proper function of criticism. The progression of thought is as follows. Beginning with a critically problematic or conceptually troublesome artwork, we look for the meaning *behind* the work and ask, "What did Kandinsky, Pollock, Joyce, Cage, or Stockhausen, *mean* by that?" The metaphysical assumptions implied by this question are, of course, that (1) the artwork is one thing—a physical artifact—and (2) its meaning—a mental object or conceptual entity—is another, and that (3) because of our aesthetic puzzlement we need criticism that will lead us from the enigmatic outward object back to the clarifying—but hidden—significance. This metaphysical priority granted the artist is a natural analogue to the priority we grant within language, the primary residence of meaning. If someone utters a phrase we do not initially understand or which in various ways puzzles us, for example, "What we cannot speak about we must pass over in silence," we often ask, in the linguistic case, for an explication of verbal meaning that stands exactly parallel to the criticism we invite in the above artistic case. Thus we stand here at yet another point of intersection between the philosophies of art and of language, where a conception of meaning in art is given shape by a prior, if implicitly held, conception of linguistic meaning. To summarize the themes intersecting here: The word stands parallel to the work; the linguistic meaning in the

"The Paradox of Expression" by Garry L. Hagberg is excerpted from *Art as Language,* Cornell University Press (1995), pages 118–124, 131–132, 135, and is reprinted by permission of the publisher and the author.

mind of the speaker stands parallel to the artistic meaning in the mind of the artist; and the critic in art stands parallel to the translator or expositor in language.

It is true, of course, that this entire metaphysical construction in the art world, built on the now shaky conceptual foundations of a Cartesian dualism separating mind and matter, is shrouded in suspicion, and it is widely understood that the pall was cast over this construction of art and its criticism in some indirect way by [Ludwig] Wittgenstein. It is not clear, however, that his *argument,* carried out not in aesthetics but in the philosophy of language, has been assimilated by the wider art-theoretical community. Indeed, one often encounters the conviction that Wittgenstein certainly did something of the first importance for our conception of meaning in the arts, and that in the postmodern critical and theoretical atmosphere, with its emphasis on artistic languages, a grasp of this contribution is essential to theoretical progress, but along with this conviction comes an uncomfortable feeling of uncertainty—of knowing that the old conceptions of meaning are unacceptable but still not quite knowing why. To clarify Wittgenstein's contribution we must briefly return to the fundamental problem of twentieth-century aesthetic theory already familiar from the first three chapters above, the problem of expression.

The problem of expression in art can be succinctly described as something of a paradox; the shroud of mystery covering the word "expression" in the philosophy of art comes from the following conceptual collision:

1. Emotions are private, phenomenologically internal objects that are logically beyond the reach of others; they are not a part of the public, observable physical world to which others have access. They are, in a sense, secrets inviolably kept by ontology.

2. Artworks are physical objects (albeit of a curious sort), objects located in the public, observable, external world. Their existence, we might say, is physical rather than phenomenological, and their existence does not depend—unlike emotions—on the mind that perceives them.

3. Artistic expression is nothing short of the apparently impossible process of merging (1) and (2). Expressive artworks cannot, as ontological impossibilities, exist—and yet they most assuredly, as the empirical fact of the case, do exist.

The problem is a function, of course, of the obvious metaphysical incompatibility of inward emotions and outward objects. We believe on the one hand that there must be an insurmountable ontological barrier separating the two, and yet we know on the evidence of actual expressive works of art that such a barrier, if it exists, has in fact been crossed. Every philosopher (including those we discussed above) who has espoused a version of the expression theory, i.e., that the essential unity of the arts comes from the fact that they serve as outward expressive vehicles for inner emotional states, has puzzled over this paradoxical situation of thinking that it must be one way and seeing that it is in fact the other. This incompatibility, this sense of theoretical impossibility in the face of museums and concert halls full of evidence to the contrary, has provided the universal point of departure for the "classical" expression theorists of philosophical aesthetics. Bernard Bosanquet writes, "How can the feeling be got into the object?" Similarly, Louis Arnaud Reid asks, "How does a body, a nonmental object, come to 'embody' or 'express,' for our aesthetic imagination, values which it does not literally contain? Why should colors and shapes and patterns, sounds and harmonies and rhythms, come to *mean* so very much more than they are?" This mysterious move from the private to the public is also what Eugene Veron has in mind when he says that "art is the manifestation of emotion, obtaining external interpretation." [George] Santayana, propelled by the same conceptual tension, refers to the "two terms," of "private and public." He writes, "In all expression we may thus distinguish two terms: The first is the object actually presented, the word, the image, the expressive thing; the second is the object suggested, the further thought, emotion, or image evoked, the thing expressed."

Tolstoy states that in the aesthetic experience people "experience . . . a mental condition," which is produced "by means of certain external signs." [Monroe] Beardsley, in reference to the statement, "This Moorish interior by Matisse is cheerful," writes that what the speaker must mean is, "It makes me cheerful" because "only *people* can be cheerful, strictly speaking." Beardsley is here being strict about the *kinds* of things that can, and the kinds of things that cannot, experience emotions.

Thus the ontological problem itself, as the paradoxical source of philosophical mystery surrounding artistic expression and as the governing question beneath expression theories of art, is clear, as is an underlying dependence upon the metaphysical dualism dividing mind and matter. To begin to assess the damage to this way of thinking carried out by Wittgenstein in his work on privacy or "private language," we must turn to his diary-keeping genius who invents (or, rather, does *not* invent) a private language. First, however, we must move one step closer to clarity about the connection between that work in the philosophy of mind and language and our initial intuitions concerning the artist's priority and its art-theoretical corollaries.

Picasso's *Guernica* provides a classic case that directly contradicts our theoretical prohibition: It indisputably expresses Picasso's rage at, and the horror of, Franco's inhuman experiment in saturation bombing. The form of explanation, despite its apparently paradoxical content, is quite simply "A expresses X," where A is a public physical object—the painting—and X is a private emotion—rage. Thus the more general puzzlement of the expression theorist is here refined into a particular problem concerning the creative process: How did Picasso put the emotion into the object? A crude explanation, surely ranking among the most theory-driven conclusions imaginable in aesthetics, states that Picasso *felt* rage at the moment of execution, and that it was through the presence of this powerful emotion that he was enabled, in some way still unspecified, to paint *Guernica*. This view, of course, stands as the aesthetic analogue to the conception of natural linguistic expressivity, wherein cries, shrieks, and howls are naturally occurring outward expressions of inner states and other slightly more refined linguistic performances are parasitic on these.

But can this suggestion, in aesthetic form, be taken seriously? Can we imagine that Picasso remained full of rage through all the preliminary sketches, all the intermediate designing, and the final detailing? Did he not feel a momentary delight at a certain stroke, or frustration at a technical limitation, or elation at the progress of the work—or anguish in the course of producing it? Any and all of these are possible. The problem may be brought into clearer focus by returning to the linguistic analogue: If the troglodyte is howling at the moon with the wolves but inwardly is optimistically contemplating evolutionary theory, then the outward expression—the howling—is not natural and immediate, but rather mediate and deliberate. Thus this emotion-to-utterance causal chain is broken, and the frustration that an art theorist feels upon realizing that any realistic scenario disturbs the rage-into-paint picture quickly generates a partial refinement of the theory; Picasso was able to recall to mind, or recollect in tranquillity, the rage he initially felt at the bombing. This is the dual-model theory of artistic expression in another form. Here the artist has both an outward and inward model, i.e., Picasso works from both the scene depicted and the feeling generated by that scene.

We know that this view of the inner model has taken a number of forms in aesthetic theory—the "feeling-image" of [C.J.] Ducasse, the "given emotion" of R. G. Collingwood, [Suzanne] Langer's "envisagement of feeling" yielding the "vital import" of the work, and so on. The crucial point, however, is to see that these various formulations of inner models stand as the artistic analogues to the "private objects," or inner private emotions which, through acts of introspection and related acts of naming, constitute the alleged private meaning of emotion terms. . . .

Our fundamental concern here is with the view that the artist is in all essentials like a speaker of a language and that the meaning of an artwork is thus like the meaning of a word. The ways in which this analogy can be given detail, however, differ considerably. In Collingwood's theory the work of art was defined in terms of an inner mental entity private to the artist. It was only in virtue of this inner mental work that the artist was called an artist at all, and on that view it is possible that the artist, although perfectly capable and perhaps even accomplished, never produced an external public instantiation of this inner content. We must here ask, in spelling out the precise details of the analogy, whether the artist is to be seen as the analogue to the speaker who is only speaking to herself inwardly, or rather as the analogue to a speaker who has thoughts but no language, no vocabulary in which to express them? On the weaker analogy, the logic of the expression theorist is *not* parallel to that of the privacy theorist, because the artist, like the speaker, has already acquired a "language"—she already thinks in terms of, or elaborates her inner images in terms of, the given materials of her art, and in this case the entire issue of linguistic privacy would be irrelevant because disanalogous. The expression theory in aesthetics does in fact itself dictate that the analogy be spelled out in the stronger case, where the artist stands parallel to the "speaker" with thoughts but no language. The two-term explanatory schema, where work A expresses feeling X,

Pablo Picasso, Guernica (1937).
Source: Photo (c) 1999 by John Bigelow Taylor, N.Y.C. Art Resource, N.Y.

requires that the inner object expressed be separable from the outer thing that expresses it. The object must be separable in the same way that a cause, in order to be understood as a cause, must be isolable from and prior to its effect. This essentially dualistic schema demands the separability of the "cause" of the work of art, the inner object, from the physical work itself. Most important, it requires that the "cause" of the outward expressive object *precede* that outward work, be it object of art or verbal utterance. Thus these two essential conditions—separability and priority—dictate that the art-language analogy be spelled out, at least within the domain of expression theory, in the stronger terms. The artist here stands parallel to the speaker who has the thought or feeling before he has the word or sign that attaches to it. The meaning of the word must, to make this view good, come first, just as the meaning of the work must precede its expression. . . .

Wittgenstein invites us to think of a group of people, each of whom has a box with something in it, an object which each calls "beetle." Each person can only see his private beetle, but they all share the common word, the meaning of which they learn from consulting the contents of their own boxes. Now it is "quite possible for everyone to have something different in his box." The point here is that the supposed relation between the object and its sign, i.e. referent and sign, could not be that which is envisaged by the privacy theorist, because all of these people do in fact have the word in common. Of course, we cannot object by skeptically saying that they do not really know what it means, because each learns it from his own case, which, as a perfect specimen of immediate ostensive definition, allegedly guarantees referential certainty. Wittgenstein further suggests that the object in the box could be a sort of chameleon object, constantly changing, and curiously, this fact would have no effect whatsoever on this word, "beetle," which has "a use in these people's language." For the aesthetic parallel, we might imagine a group of painters in a studio, all of whom agree to use a bright red stroke on their canvases as the sign for a particular feeling; the inward feeling could constantly change without the change being detected and yet the red stroke would continue to operate within the "language" defined by the studio's practices. "If [the word "beetle" had such a use] it would not be used as the name of a thing. The thing in the box has no place in the language-game at all; not even as a *something;* for the box might even be empty." Similarly, although publicly used in the studio, the red stroke would not be used as the "name" or sign of an emotion. Thus, although it would undeniably have a meaning—or a range of meanings—within the studio, it would *not* acquire this meaning through reference to an inner object.

Wittgenstein's last point is the final blow to the account of inward emotion naming. The problem is not only that the "beetle" users all have *something* there, which may differ and change but to which the word "beetle" still refers and in virtue of which it still possesses meaning as a sign. Nor is the problem merely that they may indeed have *nothing* there and yet still use the sign. The deeper problem is that the categories in terms of which the entire explanation is constructed are misleading and insufficient; the sign is not what the privacy theorist presumed it to be—a dead linguistic sign given life by the inner object to which it refers—precisely because the inner object is not relevant as the sole determinant of meaning in the way predicted. It may have, in fact, as we have seen in the "beetle" case, no position at all; thus it becomes clear that the supposition concerning the central relevance for meaning of the private object was erroneous. "No, one can 'divide through' by the thing in the box; it cancels out, whatever it is." One may similarly "divide through" by the emotive significance believed to be private to each of the artists in our imaginary studio. Clearly, the categories of inner object and outward designation within which this explanation of emotive-linguistic meaning is given are insufficient. . . . Indeed, these categories *must* be theoretically otiose if not pernicious, for "if we construe the grammar of the expression of sensation on the model of 'object and designation' the object drops out of consideration as irrelevant." . . .

Picasso's rage is, I believe, perfectly visible in *Guernica,* and it would be deeply misguided to deny that brute aesthetic fact. To claim that the emotion is metaphysically private, that it is only contingently associated as the mental meaning behind a physical artwork, and that the proper function of criticism is to provide guidance from the visible artifact to an hypothesis concerning the immaterial emotional state hidden behind it, is to revert to the dualistic categories from which Wittgenstein's arguments provide a much needed escape.

Painting and Ethics
■ Anne Eaton ■

Paintings can be valuable in a variety of ways. They can have economic value, instrumental value, historical value, religious value, sentimental value, therapeutic value, or educational value—to name only a few. They can also be valuable simply as works of art. One problem for the philosopher of art is to explain what this peculiar kind of value is and how, if at all, it relates to the other kinds of value that a painting might possess. This problem is particularly pressing and difficult in the case of the relationship between a painting's ethical value and its artistic value. Can a painting be worse artistically speaking because it is ethically flawed, or artistically better due to its ethical merits? That is, can a painting's ethical character affect its value as art? And if so, how much?

Before we can answer these questions, we need to decide whether a painting can be the object of an ethical judgment at all, for this is far from obvious. Ethical judgments, after all, are about people and actions. Depending on the ethical theory to which one subscribes, ethical judgments evaluate motives, reasons, intentions, actions, consequences, character traits, institutions, principles of distribution, laws, social systems, or even sentiments and feelings. But paintings are inanimate objects that neither act nor possess mental states, and so one can reasonably doubt their candidacy for ethical judgment. Judging a painting ethically might seem as inappropriate as passing ethical judgment on chairs or suitcases or toasters. How can a mere *thing* be good or bad in an ethical sense? To begin to answer this question, let us consider the different ways in which ethical concerns might arise with respect to paintings.

Consider a recently discovered group of watercolor landscapes that bear the signature "Adolf Hitler." These paintings have been deemed so morally reprehensible that they have been hidden in a secret location protected by the U.S. Army. Does this sort of case shed light on the candidacy of paintings for ethical judgments? It seems not, for in such cases the ethical judgment regards the *painter* rather than the painting itself.

Another kind of ethical concern about painting might pertain to the act or process of painting. Imagine, for instance, a painting produced under unjust conditions such as slavery, or a painting made from the blood of someone who had been murdered for that very purpose. Couldn't we legitimately deem such paintings unethical? It seems not, for although one should concede that painting is, or involves, an ethically assessable act, this still does not tell us anything about the ethical character of the *product* of that action, namely the painting itself. The painting and the

"Painting and Ethics" by Anne Eaton is published here by permission of the author.

act that produced it are ontologically distinct and an ethical judgment about one implies nothing about the other.

Perhaps the right way to explain how paintings can be candidates for ethical judgment is to focus on that which distinguishes them from chairs, toasters, suitcases, and other inanimate objects. This will be easiest in the case of representational paintings—that is, paintings, no matter how abstract, that have some identifiable subject matter. Unlike toasters or suitcases, representational paintings can depict actions or events that are *themselves* clearly ethically assessable. Imagine for instance, a painting that represents some atrocious act such as rape or unjust war. We have recently seen this kind of ethical judgment emerge repeatedly in public discourse in the United States. Think, for instance, of Senator Jesse Helms' indictment of Robert Mapplethorpe's homoerotic photographs that represent acts and lifestyles that he deems immoral. One might condemn a painting, then, simply because it represents something unethical. Is this the proper way to construe paintings as the objects of ethical assessment? Again it seems not, for in such cases the judgments are aimed at the things (actions, events, etc.) represented, not at the representation itself. Although Picasso's *Guernica* depicts an act of terror and cruelty, namely the 1937 German bombing of a nonmilitary town in Basque country, we shouldn't thereby conclude that the painting itself is unethical; one ought not confuse the ethical character of the thing represented in the work with that of the representation itself. We shall return to this point shortly.

So far our attempts to explain how ethical judgments can be about paintings have revealed only judgments that are in fact aimed at something else instead (the painter, the process of painting, or the things represented in the painting). But at least one explanation of how artworks can be judged ethically appears to tie the purported ethical feature more closely to a painting itself by focusing on its effects in the world. According to this view, a painting would be ethically meritorious insofar as it produces good actions, states of affairs, attitudes, and the like, and bad insofar as it promotes ethically bad ones. Consider, for instance, Titian's *Rape of Europa,* which shows the god Jupiter disguised as a bull dragging off the helpless maiden Europa in order to have intercourse with and impregnate her. Now imagine that this painting has a morally corrupting effect by encouraging its audience to have erotic feelings toward rape, even inciting some to go so far as to commit acts of non-consensual sexual violence. Shouldn't we say that the painting is unethical?

If it could be shown that Titian's painting did have such effects, a consequentialist—one who holds that ethical properties depend only on consequences—should deem the painting unethical. But this understanding of a painting's candidacy for ethical judgment seems unpromising for several reasons. First, it is likely that one's encounter with a painting serves as a mere provocation for the expression of a person's already-formed dispositions toward ethical or unethical behavior or attitudes. It is highly unlikely that Titian's painting, to return to our example, would turn a virtuous, gentle person with deep commitments to gender equality into a sexist, much less a rapist. The true cause of any such unethical action would be due to pre-established proclivities toward sexism or non-consensual sexual violence; the painting should not be blamed. A consequentialist understanding of how

Titian, Rape of Europa (1559–62)
Source: The Isabella Stewart Gardner Museum.

paintings can be objects of ethical judgment, then, is saddled with the burden of isolating a painting as the cause of a person's ethical or unethical behavior or attitudes, and this seems a very difficult thing to prove.

But let us imagine that the consequentialist can somehow handle this problem. It *still* remains to be shown that the action in question results from a correct interpretation of the painting. That is, the consequentialist has to contend with the fact that many paintings have layers of subtle, indeterminate, and sometimes contradictory meanings. This hermeneutic complexity means that many paintings readily lend themselves to misinterpretation. If a painting consistently incites unethical actions or attitudes, but does so because of the audience's failure to properly understand the work, it would be unreasonable to judge the painting unethical; that is, the consequentialist would hold a painting accountable for far too much. Only when the audience's unethical response is appropriate—that is, only when it accords with what is called for—should the painting be judged unethical. But this suggests that it is the response that the painting *invites,* and not the audience's *actual* response, that makes the painting a candidate for ethical judgment. When a painting calls upon the audience to respond in ways that are either problematic or commendable, this would seem to make it a candidate for ethical judgment.

The question is, what does it mean to say that a painting *invites* or *calls for* a response? After all, the question of the candidacy of paintings for ethical judgment was motivated by the fact that paintings are mere inanimate things. And although they are unlike other inanimate objects such as toasters in that they often represent, it may seem a stretch to say that paintings invite or call for responses, ethical or otherwise. However, before we give up on this understanding of how paintings might legitimately be objects of ethical judgment, let us return to our two examples, the Titian and the Picasso.

Both paintings depict acts of cruelty—one rape and the other an unjustified bombing of a civilian town—and, as we have seen, although we can make negative ethical judgments about these acts, this licenses no conclusions about the ethical character of the paintings themselves. If it is possible to judge the paintings ethically, one needs to consider not simply what the paintings depict, but *how* these events are depicted. Put another way, we have to consider what attitudes the paintings take toward their subject matter. Whereas Picasso's painting *condemns* the bombing of the Basque town, Titian's painting *celebrates* and *eroticizes* Jupiter's sexual violation of Europa. This is to say that Picasso's picture calls upon the audience to be horrified by the massacre of the innocent inhabitants of Guernica, whereas Titian's picture calls upon the audience to be erotically titillated by and celebrate Europa's rape. It would be a gross misunderstanding of either painting to think otherwise. This is not to say that everyone who encounters Picasso's painting is in fact horrified by its scene of violence and mayhem, nor that everyone who encounters Titian's painting is sexually titillated by rape; this is not an empirical statement about actual audience responses. Rather, I mean to make a normative claim about how one *should* respond to these paintings: such are the responses that proper engagement with the pictures requires.

But how can one tell what responses a painting invites? Not only are paintings inanimate, and so unable to make overt demand of their audience, but they also differ from other art forms such as novels and films in that they lack narrators to guide audiences' responses. By what means does a painting call upon a viewer to say, affirm or celebrate the event it depicts?

The answer to this question is complicated and I can only offer a brief sketch here. Learning to look at paintings is in many respects like learning another language. It involves not simply understanding paintings, subject matter (what is typically called their iconography), but also coming to see just *how* that subject matter is presented. The latter means discerning and correctly interpreting a variety of formal elements such as color, line, volume, space, value (light and dark), texture and brushstrokes, pattern, and overall composition, to name only a few. These are the means by which paintings order and hierarchize the elements of their represented world, indicate their spatial and temporal relations, and lend these elements an emotional character. Learning to look at paintings means learning to respond to these elements in the right sort of way. To see this more clearly, let us briefly consider our two examples.

Titian's painting, I have said, celebrates and eroticizes rape. Where do we see evidence of this attitude and by what means does the painting call upon its audience to partake in it? Notice, for instance, Europa's firm grip on the bull's phallic horn, her bare breast, her navel revealed by clinging drapery, and the generous folds of wet drapery evoking genitalia between her bare and fleshy thighs. Also notice the way that the picture draws attention to these erogenous elements by placing them along the strongest diagonal in the painting, by positioning Europa so that her legs open toward the viewer, and through the gaze of two *putti* or cherubs (one in the lower left of the painting and the other directly above Europa) who stare directly at her crotch. The glowing colors of sunrise (or sunset) that seem to emanate from Europa in conjunction with her triumphal wave of the pink scarf also lend the picture a celebratory air. By attending to these and other visual elements of the painting, we can see that it clearly aims to kindle the viewer's carnal appetites and respond to Europa's rape with festive feelings.

Now compare this to Picasso's painting.

Whereas Titian's painting offers a panoply of gay colors, flowing lines, and sensual textures (flesh, frothy sea foam, and a variety of fabrics), *Guernica* presents a flat, austere landscape that is colorless, with only stark contrasts between light and dark. This joyless world is packed with jagged edges, sharp angles, and a chaotic pile-up of figures that lead the eye irregularly in every direction. This unruly composition lends the painting an unsettling mood of disorder, confusion, and turmoil. Adding to this, the figures themselves suggest extreme suffering and misery. Consider, for instance, the grief-stricken mother at the left of the canvas, her face, itself a disorderly assemblage of eyes and nostrils and razor-like tongue, turned upward in anguish as she cradles her dead (or perhaps unconscious) child. Or notice the figure at the far right with mouth agape in horror and arms outstretched in a gesture that is at once painfully convulsive and imploring. Unlike Titian's painting, this is a scene of misery and pain, one that offers little to please the viewer's eye. We are not encouraged to take sensual delight in the scene presented to us, but instead are faced with a turmoil aimed to provoke feelings of distress and discomfort. Picasso's painting aims to unsettle and disturb.

There is of course much more to say about these paintings, but our brief examination of some key visual components reveals the very different ways in which each encourages the viewer to respond to acts of violence: whereas the Picasso calls upon us to condemn the bombing of Guernica as an atrocity, the Titian calls upon us to eroticize and celebrate rape. And it is this solicitation of responses, which as we have seen derives from formal and contentful features of the paintings themselves, that is ethically assessable. For whereas one ought to condemn the unjustified bombing of a civilian town as a crime, one ought not respond to rape with erotic and celebratory feelings. So although both paintings depict events that are ethically reprehensible, the Picasso solicits feelings that are ethically appropriate to such a crime whereas the Titian solicits responses that are ethically inappropriate. This is a more promising way of understanding paintings as legitimate candidates of ethical judgment since it allows us to describe the Titian as ethically flawed and the Picasso as ethically commendable without relying on empirical claims about the paintings, capacity to morally corrupt or improve their audiences. The question is, do these ethical features bear on the paintings' artistic value?

I do not have space to fully address the very complex problem of the relationship between ethical and artistic value, so I shall just briefly sketch major positions on the topic. One view, let us call it *separatism,* holds that ethical and artistic values are utterly distinct and have no bearing upon one another. This view requires a crisp distinction between a painting's artistic properties and its ethical ones, but as we have seen in the cases of both Picasso and Titian, such a rigid separation does not always obtain. If the ethical feature of a painting is understood as its call for a given response to its subject matter, then the ethical dimension will likely be woven into the artistic nuts and bolts—that is, into both the form and the content—of the painting itself. The best paintings do not lend themselves to being carved up into discrete compartments.

At the other end of the spectrum is a view often called *moralism* which holds that an artwork, in this case a painting, is artistically excellent insofar as it is ethically good, and no features other than those pertaining to the painting's ethical value are relevant to appreciating it artistically. As we have seen in the recent reemergence of this view in the Mapplethorpe and Brooklyn museum controversies, this reduction of artistic value to ethical value is unsatisfactory because it effectively ignores artistic value altogether. If a painting's artistic value is simply a matter of whether the painting promotes the good, there seems no point in speaking of *artistic* value at all.

Between the poles of separatism and moralism lies the moderate position often called *ethicism.* (Although ethicism is a view about artworks in general, I limit myself here to paintings since this is the topic of our inquiry.) Ethicism holds that a painting can be artistically improved or diminished by its ethical properties. Two distinguishing features of this view are that it does not hold that (1) ethical features diminish or augment paintings artistically in each and every case, nor that (2) ethical features of paintings *determine* their artistic value, that artistic value is *simply* a matter of whether a painting promotes the good. Rather, ethicism holds that in certain instances a painting's ethical failings can make it less good as a work of art and its ethical merits can make it a better work of art.

I propose that the two paintings we have been discussing are just such cases, for in both paintings the call for a certain response to the events depicted is a central artistic feature of the work. But in Titian's case, the artistically relevant response is one that we ought not have, whereas in Picasso's case the artistically relevant response is both appropriate and commendable. We ought to join Picasso in his sensitive and engaging exploration of the horrors of war, whereas we ought not join Titian in his eroticizing and celebratory fantasy of rape. The ethical dimension interferes with our appreciation of the artistic features of Titian's painting whereas it facilitates our appreciation of the artistic features of the Picasso. This is a promising way of understanding how a painting's ethical character can affect, without necessarily determining, its value as a work of art. But any such assessment must ultimately rest on scrupulous attention to the visual details of a painting.

PART II

PHOTOGRAPHY AND FILM

The *camera obscura* (literally, dark chamber) is a centuries-old device in which an image is received through a small opening and "screened" in natural color on a facing surface. At least since the Renaissance, the history of the *camera obscura* has been linked to artistic pursuits as an aid for tracing images. The problem for the birth of photography (literally, "writing with light") was with "fixing" the projected virtual scene. The competition was fierce as to who would do it first, and credit is usually given to Louis-Jacques-Mandé Daguerre and Joseph-Nicéphore Niepce as long ago as 1822. But the cultural world still has not assimilated the full implications of the invention of photography, and philosophical writing has often reflected the consequences of its entry into the world of pictures.

There is a tendency to think of artworks as one-of-a-kind entities, not entirely unlike the way we think of persons. However, in his classic 1936 essay Walter Benjamin argues that, because of its peculiar capacity to produce a plurality of copies, photography has undermined our assumptions about the uniqueness of a work of art. Benjamin reflects upon the way this technology of mechanical reproduction negatively affects what he calls the traditional *aura* we attribute to artworks. He says, "That which withers in the age of mechanical reproduction is the aura of the work of art." Mechanical reproduction put objects in the presence of the masses on a scale that was impossible before the extended use of technology, particularly the use of the printed photograph.

Recognizing the peculiar fascination that photographs have for us, Kendall Walton suggests that we think of photographs the way we think of telescopes or mirrors, as aids to or instruments for seeing. He claims that through photographs, we can actually see things and persons in situations that no longer exist—that, for example, we are presently seeing our dead ancestors when we look at photographs of them. In Walton's view, photographs, like telescopes or mirrors, are aids to or instruments for seeing. Rather than explaining the realism we attribute to photographs by their resemblance to the world they depict, Walton attributes their realism to this transparency.

Cohen suggests that Walton's interesting view at least requires qualification. If Walton is right, he is only right about those photographs where the light source that caused them really was the presumed subject of the photo. Cohen also takes issue with theorists—Roger Scruton is an example—who have argued that the purely mechanical nature of photography prevents it from being a genuine art form at all. Cohen believes that the "merely" mechanical nature of the camera has been exaggerated. Although it is easy to obtain what Cohen terms "gross depiction" by simply "pointing and shooting," photographic artists face problems that are analogous to those faced by other artists. Nevertheless, Cohen does think there is something special about photography. The picture you took of your sister ten years ago, for example, has a personal power that should not be underestimated.

The scenario in Plato's famous allegory from the *Republic* about prisoners in a cave strikes us as an uncanny "anticipation" of the medium of cinema, which some have thought of as part of the prehistory of cinema. Not only are its dark interior and projected wall shadows analogous to a movie theater; the prisoners, set in their face-to-the-front position, is comparable to the cine-subject or moviegoer. (It seems natural that Orson Welles, a large figure in U.S. movie history, actually narrated an animated film version of Plato's tale.) The allegory has many interpretations. It is sometimes seen as marking a distinction between appearance and reality, something like the movies, or as displaying an educational turnaround from false belief to knowledge, from darkness to light. And it is sometimes understood as Plato's illustration of the philosopher's situation relative to his or her alienated and disbelieving peers.

As an analogy to the way we experience film, Plato's allegory conveys the impression of one's being in the *grip* of a movie's power. In his essay, Noël Carroll asks how we are to explain this peculiar power. He argues that films possess, first, a general accessibility that is quite different from the way information is accessed, for example, in written texts. The reason for this, Carroll claims, is the purely pictorial character of the filmic image. Unlike the action in a staged drama, film can direct the eye to the exact topic in the visual field required for the purpose at hand. Chief among the techniques for doing this, Carroll says, are *scaling, bracketing,* and *indexing,* terms he explains in his essay. But complementing these visual techniques are the special narrative potentialities of film. The movies are able, by visual means, to unfold a series of questions to which subsequent scenes continuously supply answers: "Why is that woman on this train?" "Will the hero defuse the bomb before it explodes?" This he calls *erotetic model of narrative,* according to which a well-made film has the capacity to pose and then answer virtually every question posed by the unfolding action.

Laura Mulvey is also concerned with cinematic power. Situating her theory within a psychoanalytic background, Mulvey expands upon the theme of the peculiar visual pleasure we get from films by identifying the *voyeuristic* potency of this medium. However, the gaze that generates pleasure in the movie theater, like the "look" of the camera itself, on her view, is a fundamentally male gaze—one that typically puts women on display, thus eroticizing them and maintaining a power over them. Stanley Cavell also uses the concept of the gaze in order to distinguish between actors in general from film *stars*. Unlike stage actors, film stars play themselves. It is always Clark Gable, for example, wearing different hats, who is the object of our gaze in the films in which he starred.

Leni Riefenstahl was one of the great geniuses of moving pictures. However, her film *Triumph of the Will* poses a complex problem about the interface between aesthetic and moral judgments. Viewed formally, the film is clearly a masterpiece. However, at the same time, it was a forceful and successful piece of Nazi propaganda. How can we manage to give credit to Riefenstahl as an artist, given the morally repugnant context in which the film was made? Mary Devereaux offers a subtle resolution of this conundrum.

The Work of Art in the
Age of Mechanical Reproduction
■ Walter Benjamin ■

In principle a work of art has always been reproducible. Man-made artifacts could always be imitated by men. Replicas were made by pupils in practice of their craft, by masters for diffusing their works, and, finally, by third parties in the pursuit of gain. Mechanical reproduction of a work of art, however, represents something new. Historically, it advanced intermittently and in leaps at long intervals, but with accelerated intensity. The Greeks knew only two procedures of technically reproducing works of art: founding and stamping. Bronzes, terra cottas, and coins were the only art works which they could produce in quantity. All others were unique and could not be mechanically reproduced. With the woodcut graphic art became mechanically reproducible for the first time, long before script became reproducible by print. The enormous changes which printing, the mechanical reproduction of writing, has brought about in literature are a familiar story. However, within the phenomenon which we are examining from the perspective of world history, print is merely a special, though particularly important, case. During the Middle Ages engraving and etching were added to the woodcut; at the beginning of the nineteenth century lithography made its appearance.

With lithography the technique of reproduction reached an essentially new stage. This much more direct process was distinguished by the tracing of the design on a stone rather than its incision on a block of wood or its etching on a copperplate and permitted graphic art for the first time to put its products on the market, not only in large numbers as hitherto, but also in daily changing forms. Lithography enabled graphic art to illustrate everyday life, and it began to keep pace with printing. But only a few decades after its invention, lithography was surpassed by photography. For the first time in the process of pictorial reproduction, photography freed the hand of the most important artistic functions which henceforth devolved only upon the eye looking into a lens. Since the eye perceives more swiftly than the hand can draw, the process of pictorial reproduction was accelerated so enormously that it could keep pace with speech. A film operator shooting a scene in the studio captures the images at the speed of an actor's speech. Just as lithography virtually implied the illustrated newspaper, so did photography foreshadow the sound film. The technical reproduction of sound was tackled at the end of the last century. These convergent endeavors made predictable a situation which Paul Valéry pointed up in this sentence: "Just as water,

"The Work of Art in the Age of Mechanical Reproduction" by Walter Benjamin has been excerpted from *Illuminations,* Schocken Books (1955), pages 218–224, copyright 1955 by Suhrkamp Verlag, Harry Zohn, trans., Frankfurt, A. M., and is reprinted by permission of Harcourt Brace and Co.

gas, and electricity are brought into our houses from far off to satisfy our needs in response to a minimal effort, so we shall be supplied with visual or auditory images, which will appear and disappear at a simple movement of the hand, hardly more than a sign." Around 1900 technical reproduction had reached a standard that not only permitted it to reproduce all transmitted works of art and thus to cause the most profound change in their impact upon the public; it also had captured a place of its own among the artistic processes. For the study of this standard nothing is more revealing than the nature of the repercussions that these two different manifestations—the reproduction of works of art and the art of the film—have had on art in its traditional form.

Even the most perfect reproduction of a work of art is lacking in one element: its presence in time and space, its unique existence at the place where it happens to be. This unique existence of the work of art determined the history to which it was subject throughout the time of its existence. This includes the changes which it may have suffered in physical condition over the years as well as the various changes in its ownership. The traces of the first can be revealed only by chemical or physical analyses which it is impossible to perform on a reproduction; changes of ownership are subject to a tradition which must be traced from the situation of the original.

The presence of the original is the prerequisite to the concept of authenticity. Chemical analyses of the patina of a bronze can help to establish this, as does the proof that a given manuscript of the Middle Ages stems from an archive of the fifteenth century. The whole sphere of authenticity is outside technical—and, of course, not only technical—reproducibility. Confronted with its manual reproduction, which was usually branded as a forgery, the original preserved all its authority; not so vis à vis technical reproduction. The reason is twofold. First, process reproduction is more independent of the original than manual reproduction. For example, in photography, process reproduction can bring out those aspects of the original that are unattainable to the naked eye yet accessible to the lens, which is adjustable and chooses its angle at will. And photographic reproduction, with the aid of certain processes, such as enlargement or slow motion, can capture images which escape natural vision. Secondly, technical reproduction can put the copy of the original into situations which would be out of reach for the original itself. Above all, it enables the original to meet the beholder halfway, be it in the form of a photograph or a phonograph record. The cathedral leaves its locale to be received in the studio of a lover of art; the choral production, performed in an auditorium or in the open air, resounds in the drawing room.

The situations into which the product of mechanical reproduction can be brought may not touch the actual work of art, yet the quality of its presence is always depreciated. This holds not only for the art work but also, for instance, for a landscape which passes in review before the spectator in a movie. In the case of the art object, a most sensitive nucleus—namely, its authenticity—is interfered with whereas no natural object is vulnerable on that score. The authenticity of a thing is the essence of all that is transmissible from its beginning, ranging from its substantive

duration to its testimony to the history which it has experienced. Since the historical testimony rests on the authenticity, the former, too, is jeopardized by reproduction when substantive duration ceases to matter. And what is really jeopardized
when the historical testimony is affected is the authority of the object.

One might subsume the eliminated element in the term "aura" and go on to
say: *That which withers in the age of mechanical reproduction is the aura of the
work of art.* This is a symptomatic process whose significance points beyond the
realm of art. One might generalize by saying: The technique of reproduction de-
taches the reproduced object from the domain of tradition. By making many reproductions it substitutes a plurality of copies for a unique existence. And in permitting the reproduction to meet the beholder or listener in his own particular
situation, it reactivates the object reproduced. These two processes lead to a
tremendous shattering of tradition which is the obverse of the contemporary crisis
and renewal of mankind. Both processes are intimately connected with the contemporary mass movements. Their most powerful agent is the film. Its social significance, particularly in its most positive form, is inconceivable without its destructive, cathartic aspect, that is, the liquidation of the traditional value of the cultural
heritage. This phenomenon is most palpable in the great historical films. It extends
to ever new positions. In 1927 Abel Gance exclaimed enthusiastically: "Shakespeare, Rembrandt, Beethoven will make films . . . all legends, all mythologies
and all myths, all founders of religion, and the very religions . . . await their exposed resurrection, and the heroes crowd each other at the gate." Presumably without intending it, he issued an invitation to a far-reaching liquidation.

During long periods of history, the mode of human sense perception changes
with humanity's entire mode of existence. The manner in which human sense perception is organized, the medium in which it is accomplished, is determined not
only by nature but by historical circumstances as well. The fifth century, with its
great shifts of population, saw the birth of the late Roman art industry and the Vienna Genesis, and there developed not only an art different from that of antiquity
but also a new kind of perception. The scholars of the Viennese school, [Alois]
Riegl and [Franz] Wickhoff, who resisted the weight of classical tradition under
which these later art forms has been buried, were the first to draw conclusions from
them concerning the organization of perception at the time. However far-reaching
their insight, these scholars limited themselves to showing the significant, formal
hallmark which characterized perception in late Roman times. They did not attempt—and, perhaps, saw no way—to show the social transformations expressed
by these changes of perception. The conditions for an analogous insight are more
favorable in the present. And if changes in the medium of contemporary perception
can be comprehended as decay of the aura, it is possible to show its social causes.

The concept of aura which was proposed above with reference to historical
objects may usefully be illustrated with reference to the aura of natural ones. We
define the aura of the latter as the unique phenomenon of a distance, however close
it may be. If, while resting on a summer afternoon, you follow with your eyes a
mountain range on the horizon or a branch which casts its shadow over you, you

experience the aura of those mountains, of that branch. This image makes it easy to comprehend the social bases of the contemporary decay of the aura. It rests on two circumstances, both of which are related to the increasing significance of the masses in contemporary life. Namely, the desire of contemporary masses to bring things "closer" spatially and humanly, which is just as ardent as their bent toward overcoming the uniqueness of every reality by accepting its reproduction. Every day the urge grows stronger to get hold of an object at very close range by way of its likeness, its reproduction. Unmistakably, reproduction as offered by picture magazines and newsreels differs from the image seen by the unarmed eye. Uniqueness and permanence are as closely linked in the latter as are transitoriness and reproducibility in the former. To pry an object from its shell, to destroy its aura, is the mark of a perception whose "sense of the universal equality of things" has increased to such a degree that it extracts it even from a unique object by means of reproduction. Thus is manifested in the field of perception what in the theoretical sphere is noticeable in the increasing importance of statistics. The adjustment of reality to the masses and of the masses to reality is a process of unlimited scope, as much for thinking as for perception.

The uniqueness of a work of art is inseparable from its being imbedded in the fabric of tradition. This tradition itself is thoroughly alive and extremely changeable. An ancient statue of Venus, for example, stood in a different traditional context with the Greeks, who made it an object of veneration, than with the clerics of the Middle Ages, who viewed it as an ominous idol. Both of them, however, were equally confronted with its uniqueness, that is, its aura. Originally the contextual integration of art in tradition found its expression in the cult. We know that the earliest art works originated in the service of a ritual—first the magical, then the religious kind. It is significant that the existence of the work of art with reference to its aura is never entirely separated from its ritual function. In other words, the unique value of the "authentic" work of art has its basis in ritual, the location of its original use value. This ritualistic basis, however remote, is still recognizable as secularized ritual even in the most profane forms of the cult of beauty. The secular cult of beauty, developed during the Renaissance and prevailing for three centuries, clearly showed that ritualistic basis in its decline and the first deep crisis which befell it. With the advent of the first truly revolutionary means of reproduction, photography, simultaneously with the rise of socialism, art sensed the approaching crisis which has become evident a century later. At the time, art reacted with the doctrine of *l'art pour l'art,* that is, with a theology of art. This gave rise to what might be called a negative theology in the form of the idea of "pure" art, which not only denied any social function of art but also any categorizing by subject matter. (In poetry [Stephane] Mallarme was the first to take this position.)

An analysis of art in the age of mechanical reproduction must do justice to these relationships, for they lead us to an all-important insight: For the first time in world history, mechanical reproduction emancipates the work of art from its parasitical dependence on ritual. To an ever greater degree the work of art reproduced becomes the work of art designed for reproducibility. From a photographic negative, for example, one can make any number of prints; to ask for the "authentic" print makes no sense. But the instant the criterion of authenticity ceases to be applicable to artistic production, the total function of art is reversed. Instead of being based on ritual, it begins to be based on another practice—politics.

Transparent Pictures
■ Kendall L. Walton ■

Those who find photographs especially realistic sometimes think of photography as a further advance in a direction which many picture makers have taken during the last several centuries, as a continuation or culmination of the post-Renaissance quest for realism. There is some truth in this. Such earlier advances toward realism include the development of perspective and modeling techniques, the portrayal of ordinary and incidental details, attention to the effects of light, and so on. From its very beginning, photography mastered perspective (*a* system of perspective that works, anyway, if not the only one). Subtleties of shading, gradations of brightness nearly impossible to achieve with the brush, became commonplace. Photographs include as a matter of course the most mundane details of the scenes they portray—stray chickens, facial warts, clutters of dirty dishes. Photographic images easily can seem to be what painters striving for realism have always been after.

But "photographic realism" is not very special if this is all there is to it: Photographs merely enjoy *more* of something which other pictures possess in smaller quantities. These differences of degree, moreover, are not differences between photographs *as such* and paintings and drawings *as such*. Paintings *can* be as realistic as the most realistic photographs, if realism resides in subtleties of shading, skillful perspective, and so forth; some indeed are virtually indistinguishable from photographs. When a painter fails to achieve such realism up to photographic standards, the difficulty is merely technological, one which, in principle, can be overcome—by more attention to details, more skill with the brush, a better grasp of the "rules of perspective." Likewise, photographs aren't necessarily very realistic in these sort of ways. Some are blurred and badly exposed. Perspective "distortions" can be introduced and subtleties of shading eliminated by choice of lens or manipulation of contrast. Photographic realism is not essentially unavailable to the painter, it seems, nor are photographs automatically endowed with it. It is just easier to achieve with the camera than with the brush.

"Transparent Pictures" by Kendall L. Walton has been excerpted from *Critical Inquiry*, University of Chicago Press (December 1984), pages 246–247, 250–255, 258–259, and is reprinted by permission of the publisher.

[André] Bazin and others see a much deeper gap between photographs and pictures of other kinds. This is evident from the marvelously exotic pronouncements they have sometimes resorted to in attempting to characterize the difference. Bazin's claim that the photographic image is identical with the object photographed is no isolated anomaly. He elaborates it at considerable length; it is echoed by Christian Metz; and it has resonances in the writings of many others.

Such wild allegations might well be dismissed out of hand. It is simply and obviously false that a photographic image of Half Dome, for example, *is* Half Dome. Perhaps we shouldn't interpret Bazin's words literally. But there is no readily apparent nonliteral reading of them on which they are even plausible. Is Bazin describing what seems to the viewer to be the case rather than what actually is the case? Is he saying that, in looking at photographs, one has the impression, is under an illusion, of actually seeing the world, that a photographic image of Half Dome appears to be Half Dome?

There is no such illusion. Only in the most exotic circumstances would one mistake a photograph for the objects photographed. The flatness of photographs, their frames, the walls on which they are hung are virtually always obvious and unmistakable. Still photographs of moving objects are motionless. Many photographs are black-and-white. Even photographic motion pictures in "living color" are manifestly mere projections on a flat surface and easily distinguished from "reality." Photographs look like what they are: *photographs.*

Does our experience of a photograph *approach* that of having an illusion more closely than our experiences of painting do, even though not closely enough to qualify as an illusion? Possibly. But this is not what Bazin means. If it were, theater would qualify as even more realistic than photography. Theater comes as close or closer to providing genuine illusions than film does, it would seem. There are real flesh-and-blood persons on stage, and they look more like the people portrayed than do plays of light and dark on a flat screen. But Bazin regards the fact that photographs are produced "mechanically" as crucial to their special realism— and theatrical portrayals are not produced "mechanically." . . . (Erwin Panofsky explicitly contrasts film with theater, as well as with painting.)

Bazin seems to hold that photographs enjoy their special status just by virtue of being photographs, by virtue of their mechanical origins, regardless of what they look like. "No matter how fuzzy, distorted, or discolored, no matter how lacking in documentary value the [photographic] image may be, it shares, by virtue of the very process of its becoming, the being of the model of which it is the reproduction; it is the model." . . .

To add to the confusion, let us note that claims strikingly similar to Bazin's observations about photography, and equally paradoxical, have been made concerning painting and other "handmade" representations, the very things Bazin and others mean to be distinguishing photography from!

When we point to [a painted] image and say 'this is a man' [s]trictly speaking that statement may be interpreted to mean that the image itself is a member of the class 'man.' . . . [A stick which a child calls a horse] becomes a horse in its own right, it belongs in the class of 'gee-gees' and may even merit a proper name of its own. [E. H. Gombrich]

[A wooden robin poised on a bird-feeding station] does not say: Such is a robin! It *is* a robin, although a somewhat incomplete one. It adds a robin to the inventory of nature, just as in Madame Tussaud's Exhibition the uniformed guards, made of wax, are . . . intended . . . to weirdly increase the staff of the institution. [R. Arnheim]

What, then, is special about photography?

There is one clear difference between photography and painting. A photograph is always a photograph of something which actually exists. Even when photographs portray such nonentities as werewolves and Martians, they are nonetheless photographs of actual things: actors, stage sets, costumes. Paintings needn't picture actual things. A painting of Aphrodite, executed without the use of a model, depicts nothing real. But this is by no means the whole story. Those who see a sharp contrast between photographs and paintings clearly think that it obtains no less when paintings depict actual things than when they do not, and even when viewers fully realize that they do. Let's limit our examples to pictures of this kind. The claim before us is that photographs of Abraham Lincoln, for instance, are in some fundamental manner more realistic than painted portraits of him.

I shall argue that there is indeed a fundamental difference between photographs and painted portraits of Lincoln, that photography is indeed special, and that it deserves to be called a supremely realistic medium. But the kind of realism most distinctive of photography is not an ordinary one. It has little to do either with the post-Renaissance quest for realism in painting or with standard theoretical accounts of realism. It is enormously important, however. Without a clear understanding of it, we cannot hope to explain the power and effectiveness of photography.

Painting and drawing are techniques for producing pictures. So is photography. But the special nature of photography will remain obscure unless we think of it in another way as well—as a contribution to the enterprise of seeing. The invention of the camera gave us not just a new method of making pictures and not just pictures of a new kind: It gave us a new way of seeing.

Amidst Bazin's assorted declarations about photography is a comparison of the cinema to mirrors. This points in the right direction. Mirrors are aids to vision, allowing us to see things in circumstances in which we would not otherwise be able to; with their help we can see around corners. Telescopes and microscopes extend our visual powers in other ways, enabling us to see things that are too far away or too small to be seen with the naked eye. Photography is an aid to vision also, and an especially versatile one. With the assistance of the camera, we can see not only around corners and what is distant or small; we can also see into the past. We see long deceased ancestors when we look at dusty snapshots of them. To view a screening of Frederic Wiseman's *Titicut Follies* (1967) in San Francisco in 1984 is to watch events which occurred in 1967 at the Bridgewater State Hospital for the Criminally Insane. Photographs are *transparent.* We see the world *through* them.

I must warn against watering down this suggestion, against taking it to be a colorful, or exaggerated, or not quite literal way of making a relatively mundane point. I am not saying that the person looking at the dusty photographs has the *impression* of seeing his ancestors—in fact, he doesn't have the impression of seeing them "in the flesh," with the unaided eye. I am not saying that photography *supplements* vision by helping us to discover things that we can't discover by seeing. Painted portraits and linguistic reports also supplement vision in this way. Nor is my point that what we see—photographs—are *duplicates* or *doubles* or *reproductions* of objects, or *substitutes* or *surrogates* for them. My claim is that we *see,* quite literally, our dead relatives themselves when we look at photographs of them.

Does this constitute an extension of the ordinary English sense of the word "see"? I don't know; the evidence is mixed. But if it is an extension, it is a very natural one. Our theory needs, in any case, a term which applies both to my "seeing" my great-grandfather when I look at his snapshot and to my seeing my father when he is in front of me. What is important is that we recognize a fundamental commonality between the two cases, a single natural kind to which both belong. We could say that I *perceive* my great-grandfather but do not *see* him, recognizing a mode of perception ("seeing-through-photographs") distinct from vision—if the idea that I do perceive my great-grandfather is taken seriously. Or one might make the point in some other way. I prefer the bold formulation: The viewer of a photograph sees, literally, the scene that was photographed.

Slippery slope considerations give this claim an initial plausibility. No one will deny that we see through eyeglasses, mirrors, and telescopes. How, then, would one justify denying that a security guard sees via a closed circuit television monitor a burglar breaking a window or that fans watch athletic events when they watch live television broadcasts of them? And after going this far, why not speak of watching athletic events via delayed broadcasts or of seeing the Bridgewater inmates via Wiseman's film? These last examples do introduce a new element: They have us seeing past events. But its importance isn't obvious. We also find ourselves speaking of observing through a telescope the explosion of a star which occurred millions of years ago. We encounter various other differences also, of course, as we slide down the slope. The question is whether any of them is significant enough to justify digging in our heels and recognizing a basic theoretical distinction, one which we might describe as the difference between "seeing" (or "perceiving") things and not doing so.

Mechanical aids to vision don't necessarily involve *pictures* at all. Eyeglasses, mirrors, and telescopes don't give us pictures. To think of the camera as another tool of vision is to de-emphasize its role in producing pictures. Photographs are pictures, to be sure, but not ordinary ones. They are pictures through which we see the world.

To be transparent is not necessarily to be invisible. We see photographs them-selves when we see through them; indeed it is by looking at *Titicut Follies* that we see the Bridgewater inmates. There is nothing strange about this: One hears both a bell and the sounds that it makes, and one hears the one by hearing the other. (Bazin's remarkable identity claim might derive from failure to recognize that we can be seeing both the photograph and the object: *What we see* are photographs, but we do see the photographed objects; so the photographs and the objects must be somehow identical.)

I don't mind allowing that we see photographed objects only *indirectly,* though one could maintain that perception is equally indirect in many other cases as well: We see objects by seeing mirror images of them, or images produced by lenses, or light reflected or emitted from them; we hear things and events by hear-ing the sounds that they make. One is reminded of the familiar claim that we see *directly* only our own sense-data or images on our retinas. What I would object to is the suggestion that indirect seeing, in any of these cases, is not really *seeing,* that *all* we actually see are sense-data or images or photographs.

One can see through sense-data or mirror images without specifically notic-ing them (even if, in the latter case, one notices the mirror); in this sense they *can* be invisible. One may pay no attention to photographic images themselves, con-centrating instead on the things photographed. But even if one does attend espe-cially to the photographic image, one may at the same time be seeing, and attend-ing to, the objects photographed.

Seeing is often a way of finding out about the world. This is as true of seeing through photographs as it is of seeing in other ways. But sometimes we learn little if anything about what we see, and sometimes we value the seeing quite apart from what we might learn. This is so, frequently, when we see departed loved ones through photographs. We can't expect to acquire any particularly important infor-mation by looking at photographs which we have studied many times before. But we can *see* our loved ones again, and *that* is important to us.

What about paintings? They are not transparent. We do not see Henry VIII when we look at his portrait; we see only a representation of him. There is a sharp break, a difference of kind, between painting and photography.

Granted, it is perfectly natural to say of a person contemplating the portrait that he "sees" Henry VIII. But this is not to be taken literally. It is *fictional,* not true, that the viewer sees Henry VIII. It is equally natural to say that spectators of the Unicorn Tapestries see unicorns. But there are no unicorns; so they aren't really seeing any. Our use of the word "see," by itself, proves nothing.

A photograph purporting to be of the Loch Ness monster was widely pub-lished some years ago. If we think the monster really exists and was captured by the photograph, we will speak comfortably of seeing it when we look at the photo-graph. But the photograph turned out not to be of the monster but (as I recall) of a model, dredged up from the bottom of the lake, which was once used in making a movie about it. With this information we change our tune: What we see when we look at the photograph is not the monster but the model. This sort of seeing is like the ordinary variety in that only what exists can be seen.

What about viewers of the movie (which, let us assume, was a straightforward work of fiction)? They may speak of seeing the monster, even if they don't believe for a moment that there is such a beast. It is fictional that they see it; they actually see, with photographic assistance, the model used in the making of the film. It is fictional also that they see Loch Ness, the lake. And since the movie was made on location at Loch Ness, they really do see it as well.

Even when one looks at photographs which are not straightforward works of fiction, it can be fictional that one sees. On seeing a photograph of a long forgotten family reunion, I might remark that Aunt Mabel is grimacing. She is not grimacing *now* of course; perhaps she is long deceased. My use of the present tense suggests that it is *fictional* that she is grimacing (now). And it is fictional that I see her grimacing. In addition, I actually see, through the photograph, the grimace that she effected on the long past occasion of the reunion.

We should add that it is fictional that I see Aunt Mabel *directly,* without photographic assistance. Apart from very special cases, when in looking at a picture it is fictional that one sees something, it is fictional that one sees it not through a photograph or a mirror or a telescope but with the naked eye. Fictionally one is in the presence of what one sees.

One such special case is Richard Shirley's beautiful film *Resonant* (1969), which was made by filming still photographs (of an elderly woman, her house, her belongings). Sometimes this is obvious: Sometimes, for example, we see the edges of the filmed photographs. When we do, it is fictional that we see the house or whatever through the photographs. But much of *Resonant* is fascinatingly ambiguous. The photographs are not always apparent. Sometimes when they are not, it is probably best to say that fictionally we see things directly. Sometimes we have the impression of fictionally seeing things directly, only to realize later that fictionally we saw them via still photographs. Sometimes, probably, there is no fact of the matter. Throughout, the viewer *actually* sees still photographs, via the film, whether or not he realizes that he does. And he actually sees the woman and the house through the photographs which he sees through the film.

We now have uncovered a major source of the confusion which infects writings about photography and film: failure to recognize and distinguish clearly between the special kind of seeing which actually occurs and the ordinary kind of seeing which only fictionally takes place, between a viewer's *really* seeing something *through a photograph* and his *fictionally* seeing something *directly.* A vague awareness of both, stirred together in a witches' cauldron, could conceivably tempt one toward the absurdity that the viewer is really in the presence of the object.

Let's look now at some familiar challenges to the idea that photography differs essentially from painting and that there is something especially realistic about photographs. Some have merit when directed against some versions of the thesis. They are irrelevant when the thesis is cashed out in terms of transparency.

The objection that a photograph doesn't look much like the actual scene, and that the experience of looking at a photograph is not much like the experience of observing the scene in ordinary circumstances, is easily dismissed. Seeing directly and seeing with photographic assistance are different modes of perception. There is no reason to expect the experiences of seeing in the two ways to be similar. Seeing something through a microscope, or through a distorting mirror, or under water, or in peculiar lighting conditions, is not much like seeing it directly or in normal circumstances—but that is no reason to deny that seeing in these other ways is *seeing*. The point is not that "a photograph shows us . . . 'what we would have seen if we had been there ourselves.' " Joel Snyder and Neil Allen's objections to *this* view are well taken but beside the point. . . . It may be *fictional* not that viewers of the photographs are shown what they *would* have seen but that they are actually there and see for themselves. Here, again, the confusion is caused by not distinguishing this from the fact that they actually do see via the photograph.

If the point concerned how photographs look, there would be no essential difference between photographs and paintings. For paintings can be virtually indistinguishable from photographs. Suppose we see Chuck Close's superrealist *Self-Portrait* thinking it is a photograph and learn later that it is a painting. The discovery jolts us. Our experience of the picture and our attitude toward it undergo a profound transformation, one which is much deeper and more significant than the change which occurs when we discover that what we first took to be an etching, for example, is actually a pen-and-ink drawing. It is more like discovering a guard in a wax museum to be just another wax figure. We feel somehow less "in contact with" Close when we learn that the portrayal of him is not photographic. If the painting is of a nude and if we find nudity embarrassing, our embarrassment may be relieved somewhat by realizing that the nudity was captured in paint rather than on film. My theory accounts for the jolt. At first we think we are (really) seeing the person portrayed; then we realize that we are not, that it is only fictional that we see him. However, even after this realization it may well continue to *seem* to us as though we are really seeing the person (with photographic assistance), if the picture continues to look to us to be a photograph. (In the case of the nude, this may account for the continuation of some of our original feelings of embarrassment.)

We have here a case of *genuine* illusion. It really does look to us as though we are seeing someone via the medium of photography, and at first we are fooled. This is not the sort of illusion which so often is attributed to viewers despite overwhelming evidence that it almost never occurs. It does not appear to us that we see a person directly, one standing right in front of us.

We have genuine illusions also when we do see through a photograph but what we see through it is not what it seems to be. . . . Illusions of this kind are commonplace in film, and they contribute importantly to viewers' experiences. A detective in a movie surprises two thugs, pulls a gun, fires, and they drop. The viewer seems to be seeing these events via the film. He *does* see one man, an actor, approach two others, draw a gun, and pull the trigger. But he doesn't see the one *kill* the others, since what was photographed was not an actual killing—the bullets were blanks, and the blood, ketchup, Still, the scene *looks* as though it were an actual killing which was filmed. The obvious considerations against the idea that a killing occurs *in the viewer's presence* are irrelevant to the illusion I have described. The sharp edges of the illuminated rectangle, the obvious flatness of the screen, the fuzziness of some images, the lack of color do nothing to keep it from seeming to the viewer that he is seeing an actual killing *via a photographic film* of it.

There are some superrealist paintings—Douglas Bond's *Ace I* for instance—which have distinctly photographic stylistic traits but are rather obviously not photographs. Their photographic character is more pretense than illusion. It doesn't seem to the viewer that he sees through the photographs, but it may be fictional that he does. It may be fictional that *Ace I* is a photograph through which one sees a group of men walking in front of Pasadena City Hall.

The debate about whether photography is special sometimes revolves around the question of whether photographs are especially *accurate.* Some contend that photographs regularly falsify colors and distort spatial relationships, that a photograph of a running horse will portray it either as a blur, which it is not, or as frozen, which it also is not—and of course there is the possibility of retouching in the darkroom. It remains to be seen in what sense photographs can be inaccurate. Yet misleading they certainly can be, especially to viewers unfamiliar with them or with photographs of a given kind.

But why should this matter? We can be deceived when we see things directly. If cameras can lie, so can our eyes. To see something through a distorting mirror is still to see it, even if we are misled about it. We also see through fog, through tinted windshields, and through out-of-focus microscopes. The "distortions" or "inaccuracies" of photographs are no reason to deny that we see through them.

To underscore the independence of accuracy and transparency, consider a theatrical portrayal of actual events, an acting out in a courtroom of events that led to a crime, for example. The portrayal might be perfectly accurate. Jurors might gain from it much correct information and no misinformation. Yet they certainly do not see the incident via the portrayal.

Is the difference between photographs and other pictures simply that photographs are *generally* more accurate (or less misleading), despite occasional lapses, that the photographic process is a "more reliable mechanism" than that of drawing or painting, and that therefore there is a better prima facie reason to trust photographs? I doubt it. Consider a world in which mirrors are so flexible that their shapes change constantly and drastically and unpredictably. There seems no reason to deny that people see through these mirrors, notwithstanding the unreliability of the mechanism. Perhaps the mechanism is not a *knowledge*-producing one. If a person looks into a mirror and forms beliefs, on the basis of what he sees, about the things reflected in it and if those beliefs happen to be true, perhaps his beliefs do not constitute *knowledge.* But this does not mean that he does not *see* the reflected things.

What's Special about Photography?
■ Ted Cohen ■

The single most pervasive conviction about photographs is that they stand in some peculiar relation to the world, a relation not shared by other pictures. We might try to put this by saying that a photograph must be *of* something. That is not clear enough, however, even for getting started, because it is ambiguous. If 'being a photograph of' means being a picture of, and any picture of *I* guarantees the existence of *I*, then the statement that every photograph must be of something is false. On the other hand, if 'being a photograph of' means being a causal sequel to something's reflection or emission of light, then the statement that every photograph must be of something is true—but this is an odd sense of 'photograph of' which is not congruent with the normal sense of 'picture of' or of 'photograph of.' A photograph certainly guarantees the existence of a light source, but that much follows trivially from the meaning of the word 'photograph.'

The conviction that photographs hold a special relation to the world seems most often to amount to the idea that a photograph is a *fossil*. Perhaps this idea is defensible, but fossils are not, in general, pictures. The amplified idea, perhaps, is that a photograph is a picture of whatever it is a fossil of. I would not like to defend this formulation, because of cases like this:

> You have a family photograph showing several people on the beach. In the upper right there is dark speck. As a matter of fact, although no one could determine this by looking at the photograph, that speck is there because Uncle Fritz was frolicking in the waves far off shore at the instant the shutter snapped (and, as another matter of fact, the photographer didn't even notice him).

Do you think this photograph is a *picture* of Uncle Fritz? I am not sure, and I'm not entirely comfortable even with the assertion that it is, or contains, a *photograph* of him. What makes me uncomfortable is the knowledge that this photograph might look exactly the same if Uncle Fritz had been out to lunch but a piece of dirt had been on the camera lens or if a speck of lint had been on the enlarger's lens or if a stray shaft of light had struck the undeveloped photographic paper. And yet in the photograph as we are imagining it, there is no doubt that the speck is a fossil of Fritz; as a matter of relatively simple causation, it is there in the photograph because Uncle Fritz was there in the waves.

We need a better idea than that a photograph is a picture of whatever it is a fossil of. A promising idea is that it is a fossil of whatever it happens to be a picture of. There is no doubt that the speck is a fossil of Fritz. Whether it is a photograph of

"What's Special About Photography?" by Ted Cohen has been excerpted from *The Monist* (April 1988), pages 293–303, and is reprinted by permission of the publisher.

him now depends upon whether it is a picture of him, and that is a question to be decided independently, and in any case this example and ones like it cease to be troublesome. It is an idea like this, I believe, which has led Kendall Walton to assert that photographs are "transparent," by which he means that in them we see— literally—what they depict. In a photograph of Ken you see Ken. I see less in this idea than Walton does but I am not sure that he is wrong. . . .

Perhaps a photograph is like a natural child, while other pictures are like adopted children. An adopted child may resemble a parent, and to some extent this may be due to its acquisition of mannerisms, posture, etc. which do come from the adoptive parents. And a natural child may not resemble the parent, or it may resemble it only with regard to this set of acquired, environmental features. But if it does resemble the parent, then we think that the resemblance is the result of genetic influence—a kind of basic, direct causation. So with photographs. A photograph may not resemble its subject, and a non-photographic picture may resemble its subject; but when a photograph does resemble its subject we think that the resemblance is the result of some basic, direct causation.

We look for parents in their children. We look for subjects in their photographs. If we find parents in their adopted children, or subjects in non-photographic pictures, we attribute this to artifice. If we find them in natural children or photographs, we attribute this to nature. I do not doubt that we do this. I wonder whether we are sensible to do it. Some cases, and they are not atypical, are mixed and complex. When I was a child, people remarked that I looked like my father when seen walking down the street, and the same thing has been said about my son and me. The noted similarity has many components. There are size, shape of body, relative length of limbs, for instance, but there are also posture and manner of walking. This manner incorporates speed, gait, placement of heel and toe, and motion of arms, while the posture includes the angle of head and torso. Some of these characteristics would be shared by my son, probably, if he were adopted and had spent as many years walking with me, but some would not. And some would be partial. For instance if my son's neck and torso were larger—if, say, I had adopted the child of a football player, a defensive lineman—then he would likely acquire a semblance of my walking posture but not a complete one. As things stand, some of my son's walking similarity seems due to genetics and some to habits acquired in his association with me. To these two constituents, the first apparently more directly and simply natural than the other, although the other is not "unnatural," might have been added characteristics developed in him by my explicit artifice. I might, for instance, have ordered him to walk in a certain way or suggested that he assume an erect posture. In the end, if you say that he looks like me, you will not have an easy time analyzing the similarity into discrete, simple parts, some natural and some not.

You will not have a much easier time explaining the resemblance of a photograph to its subject. The fact that the photograph shows a man with close-set, brooding eyes may be due to the fact that the subject has such eyes, but it may also be due to the angle from which the photographer shot, the play of light around the forehead, nose, and eyes—and this light display may have been wrought largely in the darkroom. Certainly a photographer can shoot a picture of me which resembles me so little that you won't pick me out. Why deny, then, that when his picture does resemble me, at least some measure of the resemblance is due to how he made the picture?

Then let us not deny it; let us suppose that all characteristics of the photograph, including those which have to do with its status as a representation and a resembler, are there, at least in part—and probably in very large part—because of the efforts of the photographer.

We should, however, note another thing as well. Earlier I said that I do not doubt that when we find parents in their children or subjects in their photographs, we attribute this to something more or other than artifice—call it 'nature.' I also said that I do not know just why we make this attribution. My remarks about parents and children were meant to show that when we do it we do it rather clumsily and out of a kind of prejudice, and that it is unclear what we are saying when we credit nature with my daughter's resemblance to her mother. But we do say it, we do do it. I do it. I admit it. I want to find the implicit content when I say it.

I am looking at a photograph. In it I see my son and his bicycle, among other things. This fact, that I see my son and his Motobecane in there, is due to the fact that *he and the bike were there* when the shot was taken. This is not *a priori*. The fact needn't have been a fact. There are other ways in which a photographic picture which looks much like this one might have been made. And my boy and his bike might have been there, and a photograph have been made which looked so little like this one that you couldn't see the boy and bike in it. So the fact of their being there is not an *a priori* fact, not a necessary fact, and certainly not a fact you could discern with certainty merely by gazing at this photograph. But it is a fact. And the knowledge that it is a fact informs my view of this photograph every instant. It is this quality, this flavor, this phenomenology of viewing photographs which leads people to say that when we look at photographs we look—really look—into the world's past. It may be one of the things that lead Ken Walton to say that we look at the things themselves. It leads us, at least some of us, some times, to prefer to look at a photograph than any other kind of picture.

This may sound like voodoo. (This may *be* voodoo.) But try to keep this epistemology out of it. Maybe I am wrong about the photograph. Maybe it wasn't taken in the summer of 1984. Maybe it's not Amos: It's his twin or a robot or a picture of him. Can I prove that it's him? No. So what? When I look at my daughter, sometimes, it makes all the difference that I know she is my daughter. I know she is my natural daughter, in fact. Can I prove it? Maybe she's the milkman's. Maybe, as she is wont to insist when she is disgusted, she was stolen at birth from a better family and brought to us, and maybe I don't know this. So I look at her as my natural daughter and I am wrong to do so. I can't prove that she is my daughter. So what?

One has faith in photographs, so to speak. It can be misplaced. When photographs are introduced in court, competent attorneys insist on documentation of the provenance of the pictures. They know that a photograph itself, alone, doesn't prove anything. And sometimes, in court and elsewhere, a man might have to try to prove, as they say, beyond a reasonable doubt, that a girl is his daughter. The fact that the man and the girl look alike and have been together virtually all her life—those things themselves, alone, don't prove fatherhood.

Fatherhood is not carried out in court, however, nor are photographs characteristically appreciated there. To see this photograph, of my son and his wheels, as if it were merely contingently, incidentally, insignificantly connected to the fact that once he and it were there, on Dorchester Avenue, is a possible achievement, I suppose. It is, however, an arch aestheticization, a diminution, I think.

Another kind of diminution is achieved by those who view this as the only relevant fact, as if it were trivial that the film was Kodak's MP 5247, ASA 200, that the f stop was 8 and the shutter speed 1/250 of a second, and the rest of those things. Drop those things out and you are practicing voodoo. If those things weren't as they were, you wouldn't see him in the photograph as you do.

What follows from this? Nothing, I think, in this sense: Nothing follows about the character of photography or its aesthetics. There is nothing in this to suggest that photographs are devoid of art; but there is nothing to suggest that their capacity to support nostalgia and their use as a tool against skepticism are illegitimate. The relation of photographs to the world is in some respects more natural than the comparable relation of other pictures. I have said what I can about those respects, and I conclude this section by observing that nothing whatever is implied about whether photographs are art, or have style or can be expressive, or are in those respects different from other pictures.

The alleged special relation of photographs to the world is, allegedly, related to the alleged mechanical or automatic character of photography. What about this machinery? The machine in question, I suppose, is the camera, although the not infrequent reference to things like "optical and chemical" properties suggests that darkroom apparatus involved in developing and printing is to be included. There are two, separate points, and I will take them quickly in turn. The first concerns the fact that there is a machine in the works, the second has to do with the fact that this machine is somehow automatic.

The first point, despite the extent to which it dominates much thinking about photography, has remarkably little substance. It often seems to amount to an obsession with the fact of the camera, with the fact that it is a *machine*. This fact cannot by itself be especially pertinent, because machines are parts of a number of arts. When my son is cleaning and repairing his French horn, the parts of this incredible apparatus cover the dining room floor. He plays the horn well, and he has a commendable knowledge of how the thing works. I would guess that his knowledge is comparable in scope to a photographer's knowledge of how his machine works. The difference, some would say, is that the camera is an *automatic* kind of machine and the horn is not that kind of machine. What does that mean? That cameras work all by themselves? They can be made to work by themselves, after a fashion; but if you outfitted the horn with an altered mouthpiece and set it out in a blizzard, then it would work by itself. Responding to praise of his performance at the organ, Bach is reported to have said this:

> There is nothing remarkable about it. All one has to do is hit the right notes at the right time, and the instrument plays itself.

A charming remark, but not meant to be taken seriously; and the idea of setting up the French horn in a blizzard is just foolish. Still, I don't see exactly how it is more foolish than the idea that the camera is automatic—when this automatism is cited as an inherently unartistic or uncreative core in photography. With a camera, I suppose one might say, all one has to do is set the aperture and shutter mechanisms, point the thing the right way, hit the shutter button at the right time, and the instrument will play itself, just like Bach's organ.

The significant difference has to do with the results: The camera delivers a picture (at least sometimes), and it might do this, as it were, almost "by chance." Neither a pipe organ nor a French horn is likely to deliver a tune by chance. Let us try to get a grip on this idea that a camera is an automatic picture-making machine. Then we can try to understand why this fact about the camera seems to some to diminish the artistic capacities of photography, and finally I can say why this fact does not do this but does render photographs a special kind of picture.

It is undeniable that photography is automatically in possession of a capacity for a kind of gross, generic representation. By that I mean that with a camera virtually anyone can make easily detected likenesses of things and people. Not many of us can do this without a camera, especially when the task is to make a likeness of a person. In this respect one might say that photographs are infinitely "easier" to make than are other kinds of pictures. But it is only in this respect, and negative consequences for the artistic potential of photographs would follow, if at all, only if they were easier in all other respects. Some people write as if they were.

One way to make a picture which looks like a tall man is to turn your camera on a tall man (and pay some attention to what else shows up in your picture). One way to make a picture which looks like a tall, sad man is to turn your camera on a tall man looking sad. Some writers write as if they thought that were the only way to get sadness into a photograph, indeed as if the only way any of the oft-cited, little-understood values of plastic art—the expression of feeling and emotion, the celebration of life or God or whatever—as if the only way any of that could get into a photograph is by way of the photographer's finding those expressions, celebrations, etc. in the world and turning his camera on them. That idea is so misguided and so wrong that the only interest it yields is wonder at how it can arise. I personally believe it arises either from (1) an abysmal ignorance of the most elementary facts concerning how photographs are made, or (2) a steady diet of examples in each of which something like a family-album snapshot is compared with something like a Velazquez or a Rembrandt. Or it arises from the ignorance plus the stacked examples, perhaps because the ignorance leads one to choose just such pairs of examples.

A photograph might be profoundly sad and yet show a happy-looking person, or the other way round. A photograph might be "about" the isolation of a person from others, the insignificance of people, the triumph of the will, the eternal new-ness of America, the impossibility of the marriage contract. Of course it might, it could be about any of those things. And the photographer's problem in making such a photograph would be exactly the same as any picture-maker's, except, of course, that he has to address the problem in terms of the resources of photography, which are not the same as those of oil painting, but they do not make his task eas-ier, nor do they make it impossible.

The picture we seem to be stuck with is this. Suppose M [a maker] makes something, X. Suppose L [a looker] looks at X. The question is, how does the relation of M to X compare with the relation of L to X? There seem to be two extreme cases, one in which the relations have to be the same, and one in which they cannot be the same. We are tempted to believe that photography is an instance of the first case, and painting an example of the second. In the second case M must have had a pre-conception of X in order to make X, and therefore his relation to it is different from that of L, who has no conception of X until he sees it. (This pre-conception is what, in the *Critique of Judgement*, Kant calls a *Zweck*.) That is to say, for instance, that the painter has to know what he's going to do before he does it. This contrasts with the first case, where photography is supposed to belong, in which M needs no prior conceptualizing but makes do with a camera, something to point it at, and some light to reflect off whatever he's pointing at. He need have no efficacious conception, and so his photograph can be his occasion for the conception just as it is L's. (This is why it seems unremarkable when a photographer *discovers* what is in his own picture.)

This way of thinking of things leaves very little room for artistry on the part of the photographer. There certainly are photographs like this, ones about which, had you noticed where the camera was aimed, you would have as good an idea as the photographer how the picture would look. But if the photographer is able, and especially if he is very good, you won't know how his picture will look, not even if you look through the viewfinder. Or, to put it better, the things you do know are precisely not the things that will matter most.

The things you do know about what the photograph is likely to look like are, on the whole, exactly those things that will appear because of photography's auto-matic capacity for what I am calling gross depiction—the achievement of easily recognized likenesses. My idea is that this achievement dislocates the value of rep-resentation, especially relative to its value in other kinds of pictures. It is an old idea that photography freed painting from the burden of representing. I think this old idea is backwards. It is photography which is freed of this burden, just because it is no *burden* in photography. Contrary to Susan Sontag, for instance, I think that one's informed attention when looking at photographs tends to go elsewhere than to what is (grossly) depicted. . . .

Neither the intimate relation of photographs to reality (such as that relation may be), nor the mechanical character of the camera is a bar to art in photography. It follows that there is no need for those who find photography artistic to deny ei-ther of these things. And it would be a mistake to do so. In the fist place, as diffi-cult as it is to describe the intimate relation, and as annoying as it is to be forced to say what's different in photography's automatism that would distinguish it from any other art's machinery, these are special, unique features of photography. In the second place, these features endow photographs with specials interest which may or may not have to do with *Art*. . . .

Take my photograph of my son. . . . [T]his picture is no work of art, or at least it is not one of consequence. It is, however, of considerable value to me; and I dearly hope that someday it will touch him as what it is, or was meant to be, my attempt to make sense for him and me of the day of a city boy and his bike in the summer—an attempt to create his day.

Only a photograph could do this for us, because, unlike a painting, it signals that he was there and I was there and we were together making this photograph. Photographs can do such things for us. They can also be art. Perhaps in some cases their artistry incorporates this value of intimacy in the past preserved, this sense of the object and the photographer united in this picture. I think this of some things by [Eugène] Atget and some by Walker Evans. In those pictures I sense the choice of the photographer, the selection of something with which to unite. But this is all very flighty (as my friendly critic Joel Snyder would say, I have left the ground). Let me conclude, therefore, by concluding that there is nothing whatever in the nature of photography which disqualifies it as art, and by speculating that there are things in its nature which make it—some of the time—one of the kinds of art it can be.

Allegory of the Cave
■ Plato ■

[Socrates speaks] And now, I said, let me show in a figure how far our nature is enlightened or unenlightened:—Behold! human beings living in an underground den, which has a mouth open towards the light and reaching all along the den; here they have been from their childhood, and have their legs and necks chained so that they cannot move, and can only see before them, being prevented by the chains from turning round their heads. Above and behind them a fire is blazing at a distance, and between the fire and the prisoners there is a raised way; and you will see, if you look, a low wall built along the way, like the screen which marionette players have in front of them, over which they show the puppets.

[Glaucon speaks] I see.

And do you see, I said, men passing along the wall carrying all sorts of vessels, and statues and figures of animals made of wood and stone and various materials, which appear over the wall? Some of them are talking, others silent.

"Allegory of the Cave" by Plato has been excerpted from "The Republic," in *The Dialogues of Plato*, Volume I, Benjamin Jowett, trans., Random House Inc. (1937), pages 773–776.

You have shown me a strange image, and they are strange prisoners.

Like ourselves, I replied; and they see only their own shadows, or the shadows of one another, which the fire throws in the opposite wall of the cave?

True, he said; how could they see anything but the shadows if they were never allowed to move their heads?

And of the objects which are being carried in like manner they would only see the shadows?

Yes, he said.

And if they were able to converse with one another, would they not suppose that they were naming what was actually before them?

Very true.

And suppose further that the prison had an echo which came from the other side, would they not be sure to fancy when one of the passers-by spoke that the voice which they heard came from the passing shadow?

No question, he replied.

To them, I said, the truth would be literally nothing but the shadows of the images.

That is certain.

And now look again, and see what will naturally follow if the prisoners are released and disabused of their error. At first, when any of them is liberated and compelled suddenly to stand up and turn his neck round and walk and look towards the light, he will suffer sharp pains; the glare will distress him, and he will be unable to see the realities of which in his former state he had seen the shadows; and then conceive some one saying to him, that what he saw before was an illusion, but that now, when he is approaching nearer to being and his eye is turned towards more real existence, he has a clearer vision—what will be his reply? And you may further imagine that his instructor is pointing to the objects as they pass and requiring him to name them—will he not be perplexed? Will he not fancy that the shadows which he formerly saw are truer than the objects which are now shown to him?

Far truer.

And if he is compelled to look straight at the light, will he not have a pain in his eyes which will make him turn away to take refuge in the objects of vision which he can see, and which he will conceive to be in reality clearer than the things which are now being shown to him?

True, he said.

And suppose once more, that he is reluctantly dragged up a steep and rugged ascent, and held fast until he is forced into the presence of the sun himself, is he not likely to be pained and irritated? When he approaches the light his eyes will be dazzled, and he will not be able to see anything at all of what are now called realities.

Not all in a moment, he said.

He will require to grow accustomed to the sight of the upper world. And first he will see the shadows best, next the reflections of men and other objects in the water, and then the objects themselves; then he will gaze upon the light of the moon and the stars and the spangled heaven; and he will see the sky and the stars by night better than the sun or the light of the sun by day?

Certainly.

Last of all he will be able to see the sun, and not mere reflections of him in the water, but he will see him in his own proper place, and not in another; and he will contemplate him as he is.

Certainly.

He will then proceed to argue that this is he who gives the season and the years, and is the guardian of all that is in the visible world, and in a certain way the cause of all things which he and his fellows have been accustomed to behold?

Clearly, he said, he would first see the sun and then reason about him.

And when he remembered his old habitation, and the wisdom of the den and his fellow-prisoners, do you not suppose that he would felicitate himself on the change, and pity them?

Certainly, he would.

And if they were in the habit of conferring honours among themselves on those who were quickest to observe the passing shadows and to remark which of them went before, and which followed after, and which were together; and who were therefore best able to draw conclusions as to the future, do you think that he would care for such honours and glories, or envy the possessors of them? Would he not say with Homer,

'Better to be the poor servant of a poor master,' and to endure anything, rather than think as they do and live after their manner?

Yes, he said, I think that he would rather suffer anything than entertain these false notions and live in this miserable manner.

Imagine once more, I said, such an one coming suddenly out of the sun to be replaced in his old situation; would he not be certain to have his eyes full of darkness?

To be sure, he said.

And if there were a contest, and he had to compete in measuring the shadows with the prisoners who had never moved out of the den, while his sight was still weak, and before his eyes had become steady (and the time which would be needed to acquire this new habit of sight might be very considerable), would he not be ridiculous? Men would say of him that up he went and down he came without his eyes; and that it was better not even to think of ascending; and if any one tried to loose another and lead him up to the light, let them only catch the offender, and they would put him to death.

No question, he said.

This entire allegory, I said, you may now append, dear Glaucon, to the previous argument; the prison-house is the world of sight, the light of the fire is the sun, and you will not misapprehend me if you interpret the journey upwards to be the ascent of the soul into the intellectual world according to my poor belief, which, at your desire, I have expressed—whether rightly or wrongly God knows. But, whether true or false, my opinion is that in the world of knowledge the idea of good appears last of all, and is seen only with an effort; and, when seen, is also inferred to be the universal author of all things beautiful and right, parent of light and of the lord of light in this visible world, and the immediate source of reason and truth in the intellectual; and that this is the power upon which he who would act rationally either in public or private life must have his eye fixed.

The Power of Movies
■ Noël Carroll ■

Given that the typical movie image is a pictorial representation, what has this to do with accessibility? Well, a picture is a very special sort of symbol. Psychological evidence strongly supports the contention that we learn to recognize what a picture stands for as soon as we have become able to recognize the objects, or kinds of objects, that serve as the models for that picture. Picture recognition is not a skill acquired over and above object recognition. Whatever features or cues we come to employ in object recognition, we also mobilize to recognize what pictures depict. A child raised without pictorial representations will, after being shown a couple of pictures, be able to identify the referent of any picture of an object with which he or she is familiar. The rapid development of this picture-recognition capacity contrasts strongly with the acquisition of a symbol system such as language. Upon mastering a couple of words, the child is nowhere near mastering the entire language. Similarly, when an adult is exposed to one or two representational *pictures* in an alien pictorial idiom, say a Westerner confronting a Japanese image in the floating-point-of-view style, he will be able to identify the referent of any picture in that format after studying one or two representations of that sort for a few moments. But no Westerner, upon learning one or two linguistic symbols of the Japanese language, could go on to identify the reference of all, or even merely a few more, Japanese words. Moreover, historically the Japanese were eminently able to catch on to and replicate the Western system of perspectival picturing by examining a selection of book illustrations; but they could never have acquired any European language by learning the meanings of just a few words or phrases. . . .

We have explained why movies are more accessible than genres like novels. But what features of movies account for their presumably superior accessibility and intensity in comparison with media and genres like drama, ballet, and opera, in which recognition of what the representations refer to is, like movies, typically not mediated by learned processes of decoding, reading, or inference? What standard features of movies differentiate them from the standard features of the presentation

"The Power of Movies" by Noël Carroll has been excerpted from *Daedalus* 114, number 4 (1985), pages 79–80, 82–83, 87–88, 89–91, 95–99, and is reprinted by permission of the publisher.

of plays, for example, in a way that make typical movies more accessible than typical theatrical performances? . . .

Of course, movies and standard theatrical productions share many of the
same devices for directing the audience's attention. Both in the medium-long shot
and on the proscenium stage, the audience's attention can be guided by: the central
positioning of an important character; movement in stasis; stasis in movement;
characters' eyelines; light colors on dark fields; dark colors on light fields; sound,
notably dialogue; spotlighting and variable illumination of the array; placement of
important objects or characters along arresting diagonals; economy of set details;
makeup and costume; commentary; gestures; and so on. But movies appear to have
further devices and perhaps more effective devices for directing attention than does
theater as it is presently practiced. The variability of focus in film, for example, is a
more reliable means of making sure that the audience is looking where the spectator "ought" to be looking than is theatrical lighting. Even more important is the use
in movies of variable framing. Through cutting and camera movement, the filmmaker can rest assured that the spectator is perceiving exactly what she should be
perceiving at the precise moment she should be perceiving it. When the camera
comes in for a close-up, for example, there is no possibility that the spectator can
be distracted by some detail stage-left. Everything extraneous to the story at that
point is deleted. Nor does the spectator have to find the significant detail; it is delivered to her. The viewer also gets as close or as far-off a view of the significant
objects of the story—be they heroines, butcher knives, mobs, fortresses, or planets—as is useful for her to have a concrete sense of what is going on. Whereas in a
theater the eye constantly tracks the action—often at a felt distance, often amidst a
vaulting space—in movies much of that work is done by shifting camera positions,
which at the same time also assures that the average viewer has not gotten lost in
the space but is looking precisely at that which she is supposed to see. Movies are
therefore easier to follow than typical stage productions, because the shifting camera positions make it practically impossible for the movie viewer *not* to be attending where she is meant to attend.

Variable framing in film is achieved by moving the camera closer or farther
away from the objects being filmed. Cutting and camera movement are the two
major processes for shifting framing: In the former, the actual process of the camera's change of position is not included in the shot; we jump from medium-range
views, to close views, to far-off views with the traversal of the space between excised; in camera movement, as the name suggests, the passage of the camera from a
long view to a close view is recording within the shot. Reframing can also be
achieved optically through devices such as zooming-in and changing lenses. These
mechanical means for changing the framing of an on-screen object or event give
rise to three formal devices for directing the movie audience's attention: indexing,
bracketing, and scaling. Indexing occurs when a camera is moved toward an object.
The motion toward the object functions ostensively, like the gesture of pointing. It
indicates that the viewer ought to be looking in the direction the camera is moving,

if the camera's movement is being recorded, or in the direction toward which the camera is aimed or pointing, if we have been presented with the shot via a cut.

When a camera is moved towards an array, it screens out everything beyond the frame. To move a camera toward an object either by cutting or camera movement generally has the force of indicating that what is important at this moment is what is on screen, what is in the perimeter of the frame. That which is not inside the frame has been *bracketed,* excluded. It should not, and in fact it literally cannot, at the moment it is bracketed, be attended to. At the same time, bracketing has an inclusionary dimension, indicating that what is inside the frame or bracket is important. A standard camera position will mobilize both the exclusionary and inclusionary dimensions of the bracket to control attention, though the relative degree may vary as to whether a given bracketing is more important for what it excludes, rather than what it includes, and vice-versa.

There is also a standard deviation from this use of bracketing. Often the important element of a scene is placed outside the frame so that it is not visible on-screen, e.g., the child-killer in the early part of Fritz Lang's *M.* Such scenes derive a great deal of their expressive power just because they subvert the standard function of bracketing.

As the camera is moved forward, it not only indexes and places brackets around the objects in front of it; it also changes their scale. Whether by cutting or camera movement, as the camera nears the gun on the table, the gun simultaneously appears larger and occupies more screen space. When the camera is pulled away from the table, the gun occupies less screen space. This capacity to change the scale of objects through camera positioning—a process called "scaling"—can be exploited for expressive or magical effects. Scaling is also a lever for directing attention. Enlarging the screen size of an object generally has the force of stating that this object, or gestalt of objects, is the important item to attend to at this moment in the movie.

Scaling, bracketing, and indexing are three different ways of directing the movie spectator's attention through camera positioning. In general, a standard camera positioning, whether executed by cutting or camera movement, will employ all three of these means. . . .

So far, our speculations about the sources of the power of movies have been restricted to what would have classically been considered the medium's "cinematic features": pictorial representation and variable framing. This, of course, does not reflect a belief that these elements are uniquely cinematic, but only that they are features that help account for movies' power, the capacity to engender what appears to be an unprecedentedly widespread and intense level of engagement. There is another core defining features of what we are calling movies that needs to be treated: This is that they are fictional narratives. The question naturally arises to what degree this fact about movies can help explain their power.

The fact that movies tend to be narrative, concerned primarily with depictions of human actions, immediately suggests one of the reasons they are accessible. For narrative is, in all probability, our most pervasive and familiar means of explaining human action. . . .

A story film will portray a sequence of scenes or events, some appearing earlier, some later. A practical problem that confronts the filmmaker is the way in which these scenes are to be connected, i.e., what sort of relation the earlier scenes should bear to the later ones. [V.I.] Pudovkin* recommends—as a primary, though not exclusive, solution—that earlier scenes be related to later scenes as questions are to answers. If a giant shark appears offshore, unbeknownst to the local authorities, and begins to ravage lonely swimmers, this scene or series of scenes (or this event or series of events) raises the question of whether the shark will ever be detected. This question is likely to be answered in some later scene when someone figures out why all those swimmers are missing. At that point, when it is learnt that the shark is very, very powerful and nasty to boot, the question arises about whether it can be destroyed or driven away. The ensuing events in the film serve to answer that question. Or, if some atomic bombs are sky-jacked in the opening scenes, this generates questions about who stole them and for what purposes. Once the generally nefarious purposes of the hijacking are established, the question arises concerning whether these treacherous intents can be thwarted. Or, for a slightly more complicated scenario, shortly after a jumbo jet takes off, we learn that the entire crew has just died from food poisoning while also learning that the couple in first class is estranged. These scenes raise the questions of whether the plane will crash and whether the couple in first class will be reconciled by their common ordeal. Maybe we also ask whether the alcoholic priest in coach will find God again. It is the function of the later scenes in the film to answer these questions. . . .

Thus, to narrate by generating questions internal to the film that subsequent scenes answer is a distinctive form of narration. Admittedly, this is not a form unique to films or movies, for it is also exploited in mystery novels, adventure stories, Harlequin romances, Marvel comics, and so on. Nevertheless, it is the most characteristic narrative approach in movies.

How can this be proven? The best suggestion one can make here is to embrace the question/answer model of movie narration—what I call the *erotetic* model of narrative—and then turn on your TV, watch old movies and new ones, TV adventure series and romances, domestic films and foreign popular films. Ask yourself why the later scenes in the films make sense in the context of the earlier scenes. My prediction is that you will be surprised by the extent to which later scenes are answering questions raised earlier, or are at least providing information that will contribute to such answers. In adopting the hypothesis that the narrative structure of a randomly selected movie is fundamentally a system of internally generated questions that the movie goes on to answer, you will find that you have

---

*Russian film director

hold of a relationship that enables you to explain what makes certain scenes especially key: They either raise questions or answer them, or perform related functions including sustaining questions already raised, or incompletely answering a previous question, or answering one question but then introducing a new one. . . .

A successful erotetic narrative tells you, literally, everything you want to know about the action being depicted, i.e., it answers every question, or virtually every question, that it has chosen to pose saliently. (I say "virtually" in order to accommodate endings such as that in the original *Invasion of the Body Snatchers,* where the audience is left with one last pregnant question.) But even countenancing these cases, an erotetic movie narrative has an extraordinary degree of neatness and intellectually appealing compactness. It answers all the questions that it assertively presents to the audience, and the largest portion of its actions is organized by a small number of macro-questions, with little remainder. The flow of action approaches an ideal of uncluttered clarity. This clarity contrasts vividly with the quality of the fragments of actions and events we typically observe in everyday life. Unlike those in real life, the actions observed in movies have a level of intelligibility, due to the role they play in the erotetic narrative's system of questions and answers. Because of the question/answer structure, the audience is left with the impression that it has learned everything important to know concerning the action depicted. How is this achieved? By assertively introducing a selected set of pressing questions and then answering them—by controlling expectation by the manner in which questions are posed. This imbues the film with an aura of clarity while also affording an intense satisfaction concerning our cognitive expectations and our propensity for intelligibility. . . .

We began by addressing the issue of the power of movies, which was understood as a question concerning the ways in which movies have engaged the widespread, intense response of untutored audiences throughout the century. We have dealt with the issue of the widespread response to movies by pointing to those features of movies that make them particularly accessible. We have also dealt with our intense engagement with movies in terms of the impression of coherence they impart, i.e., their easily grasped, indeed, their almost unavoidable, clarity. The accessibility of movies is at least attributable to their use of pictorial representation, variable framing, and narrative, the latter being the most pervasive form of explaining human actions. Their clarity is at least a function of variable framing in coordination with the erotetic narrative, especially where erotetic narration and variable framing are coordinated by the principle that the first item or gestalt of items the audience apprehends be that which, out of alternative framings, is most important to the narration. In short, this thesis holds that the power of movies—their capacity to evoke unrivaled widespread and intense response—is, first and foremost, at least a result of their deployment of pictorial representation, variable framing, and the erotetic narrative.

Woman as Image, Man as Bearer of the Look
■ Laura Mulvey ■

In a world ordered by sexual imbalance, pleasure in looking has been split between active / male and passive / female. The determining male gaze projects its phantasy on to the female figure which is styled accordingly. In their traditional exhibitionist role women are simultaneously looked at and displayed, with their appearance coded for strong visual and erotic impact so that they can be said to connote *to-be-looked-at-ness*. Woman displayed as sexual object is the leit-motif of erotic spectacle: From pin-ups to strip-tease, from Ziegfeld to Busby Berkeley, she holds the look, plays to and signifies male desire. Mainstream film neatly combined spectacle and narrative. (Note, however, how in the musical song-and-dance numbers break the flow of the diegesis.) The presence of woman is an indispensable element of spectacle in normal narrative film, yet her visual presence tends to work against the development of a story line, to freeze the flow of action in moments of erotic contemplation. This alien presence then has to be integrated into cohesion with the narrative. As Budd Boetticher has put it:

> What counts is what the heroine provokes, or rather what she represents. She is the one, or rather the love or fear she inspires in the hero, or else the concern he feels for her, who makes him act the way he does. In herself the woman has not the slightest importance.

(A recent tendency in narrative film has been to dispense with this problem altogether; hence the development of what Molly Haskell has called the "buddy movie," in which the active homosexual eroticism of the central male figures can carry the story without distraction.) Traditionally, the woman displayed has functioned on two levels: as erotic object for the characters within the screen story, and as erotic object for the spectator within the auditorium, with a shifting tension between the looks on either side of the screen. For instance, the device of the show-girl allows the two looks to be unified technically without any apparent break in the diegesis. A woman performs within the narrative, the gaze of the spectator and that of the male characters in the film are neatly combined without breaking narrative verisimilitude. For a moment the sexual impact of the performing women takes the film into a no-man's-land outside its own time and space. Thus Marilyn Monroe's first appearance in *The River of No Return* and Lauren Bacall's songs in *To Have and Have Not*. Similarly, conventional close-ups of legs (Dietrich, for instance) or a face (Garbo) integrate into the narrative a different mode of eroticism. One part of a fragmented body destroys the Renaissance space, the illusion of

"Women as Image, Man as Bearer of the Look" by Laura Mulvey has been excerpted from *Visual and Other Pleasures,* University of Indiana Press (1984), pages 19–26, and is reprinted by permission of the author.

depth demanded by the narrative, it gives flatness, the quality of a cut-out or icon rather than verisimilitude to the screen.

An active / passive heterosexual division of labor has similarly controlled narrative structure. According to the principles of the ruling ideology and the physical structures that back it up, the male figure cannot bear the burden of sexual objectification. Man is reluctant to gaze at his exhibitionist like. Hence the split between spectacle and narrative supports the man's role as the active one of forwarding the story, making things happen. The man controls the film phantasy and also emerges as the representative of power in a further sense: as the bearer of the look of the spectator, transferring it behind the screen to neutralize the extradiegetic tendencies represented by woman as spectacle. This is made possible through the processes set in motion by structuring the film around a main controlling figure with whom the spectator can identify. As the spectator identifies with the main male protagonist, he projects his look on to that of his like, his screen surrogate, so that the power of the male protagonist as he controls events coincides with the active power of the erotic look, both giving a satisfying sense of omnipotence. A male movie star's glamorous characteristics are thus not those of the erotic object of the gaze, but those of the more perfect, more complete, more powerful ideal ego conceived in the original moment of recognition in front of the mirror. The character in the story can make things happen and control events better than the subject/spectator, just as the image in the mirror was more in control of motor coordination. In contrast to woman as icon, the active male figure (the ego ideal of the identification process) demands a three-dimensional space corresponding to that of the mirror-recognition in which the alienated subject internalized his own representation of this imaginary existence. He is a figure in a landscape. Here the function of film is to reproduce as accurately as possible the so-called natural conditions of human perception. Camera technology (as exemplified by deep focus in particular) and camera movements (determined by the action of the protagonist), combined with invisible editing (demanded by realism) all tend to blur the limits of screen space. The male protagonist is free to command the stage, a stage of spatial illusion in which he articulates the look and creates the action.

[Previous] sections have set out a tension between a mode of representation of woman in film and conventions surrounding the diegesis. Each is associated with a look: that of the spectator in direct scopophilic contact with the female form displayed for his enjoyment (connoting male phantasy) and that of the spectator fascinated with the image of his like set in an illusion of natural space, and through him gaining control and possession of the woman within the diegesis. (This tension and the shift from one pole to the other can structure a single text. Thus both in *Only Angels Have Wings* and in *To Have and Have Not,* the film opens with the woman as object of the combined gaze of spectator and all the male protagonists in the film. She is isolated, glamorous, on display, sexualized. But as the narrative progresses she falls in love with the main male protagonist and becomes his property, losing her outward glamorous characteristics, her generalized sexuality, her show-girl connotations; her eroticism is subjected to the male star alone. By means of identification with him, through participation in his power, the spectator can indirectly possess her too.)

But in psychoanalytic terms, the female figure poses a deeper problem. She also connotes something that the look continually circles around but disavows: her lack of a penis, implying a threat of castration and hence unpleasure. Ultimately, the meaning of woman is sexual difference, the absence of the penis as visually ascertainable, the material evidence on which is based the castration complex essential for the organization of entrance to the symbolic order and the law of the father. Thus the woman as icon, displayed for the gaze and enjoyment of men, the active controllers of the look, always threatens to evoke the anxiety it originally signified. The male unconscious has two avenues of escape from this castration anxiety: preoccupation with the re-enactment of the original trauma (investigating the woman, demystifying her mystery), counterbalanced by the devaluation, punishment or saving of the guilty object (an avenue typified by the concerns of the *film noir*); or else complete disavowal of castration by the substitution of a fetish object or turning the represented figure itself into a fetish so that it becomes reassuring rather than dangerous (hence overvaluation, the cult of the female star). This second avenue, fetishistic scopophilia, builds up the physical beauty of the object, transforming it into something satisfying in itself. The first avenue, voyeurism, on the contrary, has associations with sadism, pleasure lies in ascertaining guilt (immediately associated with castration), asserting control, and subjecting the guilty person through punishment or forgiveness. This sadistic side fits well with narrative. Sadism demands a story, depends on making something happen, forcing a change in another person, a battle of will and strength, victory/defeat, all occuring in a linear time with a beginning and an end. Fetishistic scopophilia, on the other hand, can exist outside linear time as the erotic instinct is focused on the look alone. These contradictions and ambiguities can be illustrated more simply by using works by Hitchcock and Sternberg, both of whom take the look almost as the content of subject matter of many of their films. Hitchcock is the more complex, as he uses both mechanisms. Sternberg's work, on the other hand, provides many pure examples of fetishistic scopophilia.

It is well known that Sternberg once said he would welcome his films being projected upside down so that story and character involvement would not interfere with the spectator's undiluted appreciation of the screen image. This statement is revealing but ingenuous. Ingenuous in that his films do demand that the figure of the woman (Dietrich, in the cycle of films with her, as the ultimate example) should be identifiable. But revealing in that it emphasizes the fact that for him the pictorial space enclosed by the frame is paramount rather than narrative or identification processes. While Hitchcock goes into the investigative side of voyeurism, Sternberg produces the ultimate fetish, taking it to the point where the powerful look of the male protagonist (characteristic of traditional narrative film) is broken in favor of the image in direct erotic rapport with the spectator. The beauty of the woman as object and the screen space coalesce; she is no longer the bearer of guilt but a perfect product, whose body, stylized and fragmented by close-ups, is the content of the film and the direct recipient of the spectator's look. Sternberg plays down the illusion of screen depth; his screen tends to be one-dimensional, as light and shade, lace, steam, foliage, net, streamers, etc., reduce the visual field. There is little or no mediation of the look through the eyes of the main male protagonist. On the contrary, shadowy presences like La Bessière in *Morocco* act as surrogates for the director, detached as they are from audience identification. Despite Sternberg's insistence that his stories are irrelevant, it is significant that they are concerned with situation, not suspense, and cyclical rather than linear time, while plot complications revolve around misunderstanding rather than conflict. The most important absence is that of the controlling male gaze within the screen scene. The high point of emotional drama in the most typical Dietrich films, her supreme moments of erotic meaning, take place in the absence of the man she loves in the fiction. There are other witnesses, other spectators watching her on the screen, their gaze is one with, not standing in for, that of the audience. At the end of *Morocco,* Tom Brown has already disappeared into the desert when Amy Jolly kicks off her gold sandals and walks after him. At the end of *Dishonored,* Kranau is indifferent to the fate of Magda. In both cases, the erotic impact, sanctified by death, is displayed as a spectacle for the audience. The male hero misunderstands and, above all, does not see.

In Hitchcock, by contrast, the male hero does see precisely what the audience sees. However, in the films I shall discuss here, he takes fascination with an image through scopophilic eroticism as the subject of the film. Moreover, in these cases the hero portrays the contradictions and tensions experienced by the spectator. In *Vertigo* in particular, but also in *Marnie* and *Rear Window,* the look is central to the plot, oscillating between voyeurism and fetishistic fascination. As a twist, a further manipulation of the normal viewing process which in some sense reveals it, Hitchcock uses the process of identification normally associated with ideological correctness and the recognition of established morality and shows up its perverted side. Hitchcock has never concealed his interest in voyeurism, cinematic and noncinematic. His heroes are exemplary of the symbolic order and the law—a policeman (*Vertigo*), a dominant male possessing money and power (*Marnie*)—but their erotic drives lead them into compromised situations. The power to subject another person to the will sadistically or to the gaze voyeuristically is turned on to the woman as the object of both. Power is backed by a certainty of legal right and the established guilt of the woman (evoking castration, psychoanalytically speaking). True perversion is barely concealed under a shallow mask of ideological correctness—the man is on the right side of the law, the woman on the wrong. Hitchcock's skillful use of identification processes and liberal use of subjective camera from the point of view of the male protagonist draw the spectators deeply into his position, making them share his uneasy gaze. The audience is absorbed into a voyeuristic situation within the screen scene and diegesis which parodies his own in the cinema. In his analysis of *Rear Window,* Douchet takes the film as a metaphor for the cinema. Jeffries is the audience, the events in the apartment block opposite correspond to the screen. As he watches, an erotic dimension is added to his look, a central image to the drama. His girl-friend Lisa had been of little sexual interest to him, more or less a drag, so long as she remained on the spectator side. When she crosses the barrier between his room and the block opposite, their relationship is re-born erotically. He does not merely watch her through his lens, as a distant meaningful image, he also sees her as a guilty intruder exposed by a dangerous man threatening her with punishment, and thus finally saves her. Lisa's exhibition-ism has already been established by her obsessive interest in dress and style, in be-ing a passive image of visual perfection; Jeffries's voyeurism and activity have also been established through his work as a photo-journalist, a maker of stories and cap-tor of images. However, his enforced inactivity, binding him to his seat as a specta-tor, puts him squarely in the phantasy position of the cinema audience.

In *Vertigo,* subjective camera predominates. Apart from one flashback from Judy's point of view, the narrative is woven around what Scottie sees or fails to see. The audience follows the growth of his erotic obsession and subsequent despair precisely from his point of view. Scottie's voyeurism is blatant: He falls in love with a woman he follows and spies on without speaking to. Its sadistic side is equally blatant: He has chosen (and freely chosen, for he had been a successful lawyer) to be a policeman, with all the attendant possibilities of pursuit and investi-gation. As a result, he follows, watches and falls in love with a perfect image of fe-male beauty and mystery. Once he actually confronts her, his erotic drive is to break her down and force her to tell by persistent cross-questioning. Then, in the second part of the film, he re-enacts his obsessive involvement with the image he loved to watch secretly. He reconstructs Judy as Madeleine, forces her to conform in every detail to the actual physical appearance of his fetish. Her exhibitionism, her masochism, make her an ideal passive counterpart to Scottie's active sadistic voyeurism. She knows her part is to perform, and only by playing it through and then replaying it can she keep Scottie's erotic interest. But in the repetition he does break her down and succeeds in exposing her guilt. Her curiosity wins through and she is punished. In *Vertigo,* erotic involvement with the look is disorientating: the spectator's fascination is turned against him as the narrative carries him through and entwines him with the processes that he is himself exercising. The Hitchcock hero here is firmly placed within the symbolic order, in narrative terms. He has all the attributes of the patriarchal super-ego. Hence the spectator, lulled into a false sense of security by the apparent legality of his surrogate, sees through his look and finds himself exposed as complicit, caught in the moral ambiguity of looking. Far from being simply an aside on the perversion of the police, *Vertigo* focuses on the implications of the active/looking, passive/looked-at split in terms of sexual difference and the power of the male symbolic encapsulated in the hero. Marnie, too, performs for Mark Rutland's gaze and masquerades as the perfect to-be-looked-at image. He, too, is on the side of the law until, drawn in by obsession with her guilt, her secret, he longs to see her in the act of committing a crime, make her confess and thus save her. So he, too, becomes complicit as he acts out the implica-tions of his power. He controls money and words, he can have his cake and eat it.

Summary

The psychoanalytic background that has been discussed in this article is relevant to the pleasure and unpleasure offered by traditional narrative film. The scopophilic instinct (pleasure in looking at another person as an erotic object), and, in con-tradistinction, ego libido (forming identification processes) act as formations, mechanisms, which this cinema has played on. The image of woman as (passive) raw material for the (active) gaze of man takes the argument a step further into the structure of representation, adding a further layer demanded by the ideology of the patriarchal order as it is worked out in its favorite cinematic form—illusionistic narrative film. The argument returns again to the psychoanalytic background in that woman as representation signifies castration, inducing voyeuristic or fetishis-tic mechanisms to circumvent her threat. None of these interacting layers is intrin-sic to film, but it is only in the film form that they can reach a perfect and beautiful contradiction, thanks to the possibility in the cinema of shifting the emphasis of the look. It is the place of the look that defines cinema, the possibility of varying it and exposing it. This is what makes cinema quite different in its voyeuristic potential from, say, strip-tease, theater, shows, etc. Going far beyond highlighting a woman's to-be-looked-at-ness, cinema builds the way she is to be looked at into the specta-cle itself. Playing on the tension between film as controlling the dimension of time (editing, narrative) and film as controlling the dimension of space (changes in dis-tance, editing), cinematic codes create a gaze, a world, and an object, thereby pro-ducing an illusion cut to the measure of desire. It is these cinematic codes and their relationship to formative external structures that must be broken down before mainstream film and the pleasure it provides can be challenged.

To begin with (as an ending), the voyeuristic-scopophilic look that is a crucial part of traditional filmic pleasure can itself be broken down. There are three differ-ent looks associated with cinema: that of the camera as it records the pro-filmic event, that of the audience as it watches the final product, and that of the characters at each other within the screen illusion. The conventions of narrative film deny the first two and subordinate them to the third, the conscious aim being always to elimi-nate intrusive camera presence and prevent a distancing awareness in the audience. Without these two absences (the material existence of the recording process, the critical reading of the spectator), fictional drama cannot achieve reality, obvious-ness and truth. Nevertheless, as this article has argued, the structure of looking in narrative fiction film contains a contradiction in its own premises: the female image as a castration threat constantly endangers the unity of the diegesis and bursts through the world of illusion as an intrusive, static, one-dimensional fetish. Thus the two looks materially present in time and space are obsessively subordinated to the neurotic needs of the male ego. The camera becomes the mechanism for producing an illusion of Renaissance space, flowing movements compatible with the human eye, an ideology of representation that revolves around the perception of the sub-ject; the camera's look is disavowed in order to create a convincing world in which the spectator's surrogate can perform with verisimilitude. Simultaneously, the look of the audience is denied an intrinsic force: As soon as fetishistic representation of the female image threatens to break the spell of illusion, and the erotic image on the screen appears directly (without mediation) to the spectator, the fact of fetishization, concealing as it does castration fear, freezes the look, fixates the spectator and prevents him from achieving any distance from the image in front of him.

This complex interaction of looks is specific to film. The first blow against the monolithic accumulation of traditional film conventions (already undertaken by radical film-makers) is to free the look of the camera into its materiality in time and space and the look of the audience into dialectics, passionate detachment. There is no doubt that this destroys the satisfaction, pleasure and privilege of the "invisible guest," and highlights how film has depended on voyeuristic active/passive mechanisms. Women, whose image has continually been stolen and used for this end, cannot view the decline of the traditional film form with anything much more than sentimental regret.

Audience, Actor, and Star
■ Stanley Cavell ■

The depth of the automatism of photography is to be read not alone in its mechanical production of an image of reality, but in its mechanical defeat of our presence to that reality. The audience in a theater can be defined as those to whom the actors are present while they are not present to the actors. But movies allow the audience to be mechanically absent. The fact that I am invisible and inaudible to the actors, and fixed in position, no longer needs accounting for; it is not part of a convention I have to comply with; the proceedings do not have to make good the fact that I do nothing in the face of tragedy, or that I laugh at the follies of others. In viewing a movie my helplessness is mechanically assured: I am present not at something happening, which I must confirm, but at something that has happened, which I absorb (like a memory). In this, movies resemble novels, a fact mirrored in the sound of narration itself, whose tense in the past.

It might be said: "But surely there is the obvious difference between a movie house and a theater that is not recorded by what has so far been said and that outweighs all this fiddle of differences. The obvious difference is that in a theater we are in the presence of an actor, in a movie house we are not. You have said that in both places the actor is in our presence and in neither are we in his, the difference lying in the mode of our absence. But there is also the plain fact that in a theater a real

---

"Audience, Actor, and Star" by Stanley Cavell has been excerpted from *The World Viewed*, Harvard University Press (1971), pages 25–29, and is reprinted by permission of the publisher.

man is *there*, and in a movie no real man is there. That is obviously essential to the differences between our responses to a play and to a film." What that means must not be denied; but the fact remains to be understood [André] Bazin meets it head on by simply denying that "the screen is incapable of putting us 'in the presence of' the actor"; it, so to speak, relays his presence to us, as by mirrors. Bazin's idea here really fits the facts of live television, in which the thing we are presented with is happening simultaneously with its presentation. But in live television, what is present to us while it is happening is not the world, but an event standing out from the world. Its point is not to reveal, but to cover (as with a gun), to keep something on view.

It is an incontestable fact that in a motion picture no live human being is up there. But a human *something* is, and something unlike anything else we know. We can stick to our plain description of that human something as "in our presence while we are not in his" (present *at* him, because looking at him, but not present *to* him) and still account for the difference between his live presence and his photographed presence to us. We need to consider what is present or, rather, since the topic is the human being, *who* is present.

One's first impulse may be to say that in a play the character is present, whereas in a film the actor is. That sounds phony or false: One wants to say that both are present in both. But there is more to it, ontologically more. Here I think of a fine passage of [Erwin] Panofsky's:

> Othello or Nora are definite, substantial figures created by the playwright. They can be played well or badly, and they can be "interpreted" in one way or another; but they most definitely exist, no matter who plays them or even whether they are played at all. The character in a film, however, lives and dies with the actor. It is not the entity "Othello" interpreted by Robeson or the entity "Nora" interpreted by Duse, it is the entity "Greta Garbo" incarnate in a figure called Anna Christie or the entity "Robert Montgomery" incarnate in a murderer who, for all we know or care to know, may forever remain anonymous but will never cease to haunt our memories.

If the character lives and dies with the actor, that ought to mean that the actor lives and dies with the character. I think that is correct, but it needs clarification. Let us develop it slightly.

For the stage, an actor works himself into a role; for the screen, a performer takes the role onto himself. The stage actor explores his potentialities and the possibilities of his role simultaneously; in performance these meet at a point in spiritual space—the better the performance, the deeper the point. In this respect, a role in a play is like a position in a game, say, third base: Various people can play it, but the great third baseman is a man who has accepted and trained his skills and instincts most perfectly and matches them most intimately with his discoveries of the possibilities and necessities of third base. The screen performer explores his role like an attic and takes stock of his physical and temperamental endowment; he lends his being to the role and accepts only what fits; the rest is nonexistent. On the stage there are two beings, and the being of the character assaults the being of the actor; the actor survives only by yielding. A screen performance requires not so much training as planning. Of course, both the actor and the performer require, or can make use of, experience. The actor's role is his subject for study, and there is no end to it. But the screen performer is essentially not an actor at all: He *is* the subject of study, and a study not his own. (That is what the content of a photograph is—its subject.) On a screen the study is projected; on a stage the actor is the projector. An exemplary stage performance is one which, for a time, most fully creates a character. After Paul Scofield's performance in *King Lear,* we know who King Lear is, we have seen him in flesh. An exemplary screen performance is one in which, at a time, a star is born. After *The Maltese Falcon* we know a new star, only distantly a person. "Bogart" *means* "the figure created in a given set of films." His presence in those films is who he is, not merely in the sense in which a photograph of an event is that event; but in the sense that if those films did not exist, Bogart would not exist, the name "Bogart" would not mean what it does. The figure it names is not only in our presence, we are in his, in the only sense we could ever be. That is all the "presence" he has.

But it is complicated. A full development of all this would require us to place such facts as these: Humphrey Bogart was a man, and he appeared in movies both before and after the ones that created "Bogart." Some of them did not create a new star (say, the stable groom in *Dark Victory*), some of them defined stars—anyway meteors—that may be incompatible with Bogart (e.g., Duke Mantee and Fred C. Dobbs) but that are related to that figure and may enter into our later experience of it. And Humphrey Bogart was both an accomplished actor and a vivid subject for a camera. Some people are, just as some people are both good pitchers and good hitters; but there are so few that it is surprising that the word "actor" keeps on being used in place of the more beautiful and more accurate word "star"; the stars are only to gaze at, after the fact, and their actions divine our projects. Finally, we must note the sense in which the creation of a (screen) performer is also the creation of a character—not the kind of character an author creates, but the kind that certain real people are: a type.

Beauty and Evil: the Case of Leni Riefenstahl
■ Mary Devereaux ■

Leni Riefenstahl's documentary of the 1934 Nuremberg rally of the National Socialist German Workers' Party, *Triumph of the Will,* is perhaps the most controversial film ever made. At once masterful and morally repugnant, this deeply troubling film epitomizes a general problem that arises with art. It is both beautiful and

"Beauty and Evil: The Case of Leni Riefenstahl" by Mary Devereaux has been excerpted from *Aesthetics and Ethics: Essays at the Intersection,* Jerrold Levinson, ed., Cambridge University Press (1998), pages 227, 231, 234–238, 240–247, and is reprinted by permission of the publisher.

evil. I shall argue that it is this conjunction of beauty and evil that explains why the film is so disturbing. . . .

Much has been written on the formal features of Riefenstahl's art. What has not been generally appreciated is that the film's artistic achievement is not merely structural or formal. Equally important is Riefenstahl's masterful command of traditional narrative means: theme and characterization, the use of symbolism, and the handling of point of view. It is the use of these devices to tell a *story*—the story of the New Germany—that, combined with the structural techniques already surveyed, creates the vision of Hitler and National Socialism that makes *Triumph of the Will* so powerful.

That vision is one in which the military values of loyalty and courage, unity, discipline, and obedience are wedded to a heroic conception of life and elements of German *völkisch* mythology. In Riefenstahl's hands, an annual political rally is transformed into a larger historical and symbolic event. *Triumph of the Will* presents the Nazi world as a kind of Valhalla, "a place apart, surrounded by clouds and mist, peopled by heroes and ruled from above by the gods." Seen from the perspective of the film, Hitler is the hero of a grand narrative. He is both leader and savior, a new Siegfried come to restore a defeated Germany to its ancient splendor. . . .

Riefenstahl weaves the narrative and thematic elements of her film around the central National Socialist slogan *Ein Führer. Ein Volk. Ein Reich* as tightly as she weaves the visual elements of eagle and swastika. As she tells it, the tale of Hitler—stalwart and alone, heroic—is the tale of the German people. His will is their will. His power their future. It is all this and more that makes *Triumph of the Will* the powerful film it is. . . .

Clearly, *Triumph of the Will* is a troubling film. My claim is that it is so because of its conjunction of beauty and evil, because it presents as beautiful a vision of Hitler and the New Germany that is morally repugnant. But might not there be a simpler, more straightforward explanation of the film's disturbing nature? Can't it be wholly explained by the fact that the film is a documentary?

As a *documentary* film, *Triumph of the Will* is disquieting because the events it portrays are themselves disquieting. As a documentary *film, Triumph of the Will* conveys the sheer immediacy of these events. We view Hitler's speeches, the flag ceremonies, the spotlighted evening assemblies as if they were happening *now.* And our knowledge that what we are seeing stands in a causal chain of events that led to the Second World War and the Holocaust makes this immediacy chilling. It is as if we were watching the buds of these horrors unfold before our eyes.

But Riefenstahl's film does more than document historical events. And it is more than an ordinary documentary. *Triumph of the Will* is also troubling because it is a work of Nazi propaganda. The word 'propaganda' originated in the celebrated papal society for "propagating the faith" established in 1622. In modern contexts, the term has taken on more specifically political connotations. In claiming that *Triumph of the Will* is a work of propaganda, I mean that it is designed to propagate the Nazi faith—and mobilize the German people. *Triumph of the Will* thus unites the older religious connotations of 'propaganda' with the modern political connotations, presenting National Socialism as a political religion. Its images, ideas, and narrative all aim at establishing the tenets of that religion: Hitler is a messianic leader, Germany is one *Volk,* and the Third Reich will endure for a thousand years.

It may come as some surprise, then, to learn that the film's status as propaganda is controversial. Amazingly, Riefenstahl and her supporters deny that *Triumph of the Will* is a work of propaganda. And because there is a controversy—in fact, a rather heated one—we need to pause briefly to take up this issue. Riefenstahl and her supporters contend that her concerns in *Triumph of the Will*—as in all her films—were aesthetic, not political: that it was the cult of beauty, not the cult of the *Führer,* that Riefenstahl worshiped. The claim is that stylistic devices like the cloud motif in the film's opening sequence, the rhythmic montage of faces in the Labor Services sequence, and so on were *just* that: stylistic devices meant to avoid newsreel reportage, enrich the film artistically, and nothing more.

Certainly Riefenstahl *was* preoccupied with beauty in *Triumph of the Will.* Her films of the 1936 Berlin Olympics, her photographs of the Nuba, indeed the whole of her artistic corpus, make clear that visual beauty was one of her central artistic preoccupations. But the claim that a concern for beauty and stylistic innovation is the only thing going on in *Triumph of the Will* is undermined by the film itself. As we have seen, the film is aimed not simply at stylistic innovation and formally beautiful images, but at using these means to create a particular vision of Hitler and National Socialism.

The pure-aestheticism defense is also belied by the historical record. Riefenstahl was, as she willingly admits, a great admirer of Hitler. Attending a political rally for the first time in her life in February 1932, she was "paralyzed," "fascinated," "deeply affected" by the appearance of Hitler and the crowd's "bondage to this man." Even at the end of the war, by which point she, like many Nazi sympathizers, claims to have harbored doubts about Hitler's plans for Germany, Riefenstahl, by her own admission, "wept all night" at the news of his suicide. To this day, Riefenstahl has never distanced herself from the political content of *Triumph of the Will* or any of the other films she made for Hitler. Nor, despite years of ostracism and public controversy, has she shown—or even feigned—remorse for her artistic and personal association with many members of the Nazi Party.

It might be added that Riefenstahl agreed to film the 1934 Nuremberg rally only on condition that she be given complete artistic control over the project, a condition to which Hitler apparently agreed. She demanded, and got, final cut. Thus, we can assume that the film Riefenstahl made—the film organized around the ideas of *Ein Führer. Ein Volk. Ein Reich* that presents Hitler as savior to the German people, and that describes the Nazi future as full of promise—is the film she chose to make. . . .

In any case, the debate about Leni Riefenstahl's intentions (what was going on "in her head") is largely beside the point. For the question whether *Triumph of the Will* is a work of propaganda is a question about the *film,* not a question about (the historical person) Leni Riefenstahl. And as we have seen, the answer to this question is plainly yes.

So *Triumph of the Will* is a work of Nazi propaganda. And that is clearly part of what makes the film so troubling. But Riefenstahl is not the first or last artist to make fascist art. Hundreds of propaganda films were made in German between 1933 and 1945. Many, like the feature film *Jud Süss,* had much wider popular success. And some, like the virulently anti-Semitic "documentary" *Der ewige Jude* (The Eternal Jew, 1940), had arguably as harmful an effect on German thought and behavior.

Triumph of the Will is distinguished from these and other Nazi propaganda films in two ways. First, it is extremely well made. (And the fact that it is an excellent work of propaganda is part of what makes it so disturbing.) But the film is more than first-class propaganda. It is also a work of art. A work of creative imagination, stylistically and formally innovative, its every detail contributes to its central vision and overall effect. The film is also very, very beautiful. *Triumph of the Will* can be properly called a work of art because it offers a beautiful, sensuous presentation—a vision—of the German people, leader, and empire in a recognized artistic genre (documentary) of a recognized artistic medium (film). It is the fact that *Triumph of the Will* is an excellent work of propaganda *and* a work of art that explains why Riefenstahl's film has more than historical interest and why it has a place in film and not just history classes. . . .

If this is right, it raises a question about how we are to respond to this film. Its every detail is designed to advance a morally repugnant vision of Hitler, a vision that, as history was to prove, falsified the true character of Hitler and National Socialism. Enjoying *this film*—recognizing that we may be caught up, if only slightly, in its pomp and pageantry or be stirred by its beauty—is likely to make us ask, "What kind of person am I to enjoy or be moved by this film?" Isn't there something wrong with responding in this way to a Nazi film? . . .

The concern is not only that if I enjoy such a film. I may be led to act badly (e.g., to support neo-Nazi movements), but also that certain kinds of enjoyment, regardless of their effects, may themselves be problematic. Pleasure in this work of art (like pleasure in a work of art that celebrates sadism or pedophilia) might lead one to ask not just about what one may *become,* but about who one is *now.* The point is an Aristotelian one. If virtue consists (in part) in taking pleasure in the right things and not in the wrong things, then what is my character now such that I can take pleasure in these things? . . .

These questions merely highlight the long-standing general problem of beauty and evil: that aesthetic and moral considerations may pull in different directions. The problem emerges not only with *Triumph of the Will* and the other cases mentioned earlier but with, for example, the literary works of the Marquis de Sade and T. S. Eliot. The problem posed by the conflict between the demands of art and the demands of morality is familiar. What are we to make of it?

For much of the twentieth century, the standard solution to this conflict has been to recommend that we look at art from an "aesthetic distance." As originally described by Edward Bullough in 1912, an attitude of aesthetic distance allows us to set aside the practical concerns of everyday life, including questions of a work's origins, its moral effects, and so on, and concentrate exclusively on the work of art itself. By "the work itself" Bullough means, of course, the work's "formal" (i.e., its structural and stylistic) features. Bracketing all nonformal features frees us, at least temporarily, "to elaborate experience on a new basis," much as we do in appreciating the beauty of a fog at sea despite its danger.

The basic strategy here is simple: When approaching a work of art that raises moral issues, sever aesthetic evaluation from moral evaluation and evaluate the work in aesthetic (i.e., formal) terms alone. This is the formalist response to the problem of beauty and evil. Formalism treats the aesthetic and the moral as wholly independent domains. It allows us to say that, evaluated morally, *Triumph of the Will* is bad but, evaluated aesthetically, it is good. . . .

But in the case of *Triumph of the Will,* the formalist strategy fails. It won't work here, not because we're too obsessed by the moral issues to assume a properly distanced standpoint, or because when we assume a posture of aesthetic distance we forget about the historical realities associated with the film, or because adopting an attitude of aesthetic distance toward a film like *Triumph of the Will* is itself an immoral position (though some may wish to argue that it is). Nor does adopting an attitude of aesthetic distance require that we literally forget about the historical realities. Aesthetic distance is, after all, only a shift in perspective, and a temporary one at that.

The reason the formalist strategy fails in the case of *Triumph of the Will* is that distancing ourselves from the morally objectionable elements of the film—its deification of Hitler, the story it tells about him, the party, and the German people, and so on—means distancing ourselves from the features that make it the work of art it is. If we distance ourselves from these features of the film, we will not be in a position to understand its artistic value—that is, why this lengthy film of political speeches and endless marching is correctly regarded as a cinematic masterpiece. We will also miss the beauty (horrifying though it is) of its vision of Hitler. . . .

Now, defenders of formalism can opt for a more complex understanding of aesthetic distance, one that does not require us to bracket an artwork's content. According to this view (call it "sophisticated formalism"), understanding a work of art consists in grasping and appreciating the relationship between its form and content, that is, the connection between the message and the means used to convey it. Artistic success consists in expressing a particular message in an effective way. Sophisticated formalism thus allows—indeed requires—us to pay attention to the particular content of the work. On this subtler view, we can't just ignore the content of art or its message. We must attend to the relation between a work's form and content, if we are to appreciate the work itself. . . .

Note that sophisticated formalism doesn't require abandoning the distinction between aesthetic and moral evaluation. As with the simpler version, with sophisticated formalism, aesthetic evaluation belongs to one domain, moral evaluation to another. Sophisticated formalism tells us to judge not the message but its expression. In this respect, the approach we are meant to take toward the National Socialist elements of Riefenstahl's documentary is no different from the approach we are meant to take toward the Christianity of *The Divine Comedy* or *Paradise Lost*. Our finding the message conveyed by *Triumph of the Will* repulsive (or attractive) should not therefore affect our aesthetic judgment. Nor should it affect our aesthetic response to the film.

Indeed, according to sophisticated formalism, *Triumph of the Will* and works of art like it shouldn't (from an aesthetic point of view) cause any problem at all. We can distance ourselves from—that is, set aside—the moral dimension of the work's content while still *paying attention to* that content—that is, the way in which the film's content figures in its expressive task.

Is this broader, more inclusive understanding of aesthetic distance satisfactory? The answer, I think, is no. Even sophisticated formalism, with its richer concept of the aesthetic, makes it impossible to talk about the political meaning of *Triumph of the Will,* the truth or falsity of its picture of Hitler, whether it is good or evil, right or wrong—*while doing aesthetics.* These cognitive and moral matters are ones we are meant to distance ourselves from when engaged in the business of aesthetic evaluation. Sophisticated formalism doesn't ignore content, but it does *aestheticize* it. When we follow its recommendations, we adopt an aesthetic attitude toward the Christianity of *The Divine Comedy* and an aesthetic attitude toward the National Socialism of *Triumph of the Will* . . .

At this point there are two ways to go. We can say that there is more to art than aesthetics or that there is more to aesthetics than beauty and form. The first option allows us to keep the historically important, eighteenth-century conception of the aesthetic intact. (It is in effect the conception of the aesthetic introduced by sophisticated formalism.) This conception has the advantage of keeping the boundaries of the aesthetic relatively narrow and clearly defined. And it keeps aesthetic evaluation relatively simple. Questions of political meaning, of truth and falsity, good and evil, right and wrong fall outside the category of the aesthetic. One implication of adopting this option is that, since there are works of art that raise these issues, the category of the artistic outstrips the category of the aesthetic.

The second option broadens the concept of the aesthetic beyond its traditional boundaries. It says that we are responding to a work of art "aesthetically" not only when we respond to its formal elements or to the relationship between its formal elements and its content, but also whenever we respond to a feature that makes a work the work of art it is. (These features may include substantive as well as formal features.) On this second option, the aesthetic is understood in such a way as to track the artistic, however broadly or narrowly that is to be understood.

It is this second route that I recommend. Let me at least briefly say why. The first option remains wedded to a conception of the aesthetic that preserves the eighteenth-century preoccupation with beauty. This is a rich and important tradition, but it focuses—and keeps us focused—on a feature of art that is no longer so important to us. Indeed, one of the significant and widely noted facts about the development of modern art is that beauty is no longer central to art. The price of regarding this conception of the aesthetic as the only legitimate one is to marginalize aesthetics—isolating it from much of the philosophy of art—and, indeed, from much of our experience of art.

Opting for this broader conception of the aesthetic gives us a more inclusive category, one more adequate to what art is in all of its historical and cultural manifestations and to the full range of its values. It sets much of what we humanly care about back into the aesthetic arena and offers a much more complete view of the value of art.

My claim, which employs this richer conception of the aesthetic, is, then, that in order to get things aesthetically right about *Triumph of the Will,* we have to engage with its vision. And this means that we have to engage with the moral issues it raises. This nonformalist notion of the aesthetic rides piggyback on a nonformalist conception of art. It doesn't require wholesale abandonment of the distinction between aesthetic and moral value. We can, for example, still distinguish between the formal beauty of *Triumph of the Will*'s stylistic devices and its moral status as a work of National Socialist propaganda. Nor does it require denying that art and morality belong to different domains. But it does require recognizing that there are areas where these domains overlap and that certain works of art, especially works of religious and political art, fall within this overlapping area.

PART III

‖

ARCHITECTURE AND THE THIRD DIMENSION

We live in and around architecture. We use buildings for sheltering families and for watching hockey games. We gather for funerals and baptisms in sacred places, shop in malls, and spend time in casinos and classrooms. Architecture is also a place for the contemplation of other arts. However, we contemplate architecture itself. The misleading saying "There is no such thing as paper architecture" draws attention to the large sums of money necessary to turn even a modest architectural drawing into a finished project.

However, despite the fact that we make many practical demands upon architecture, architecture, like other art forms, is of enormous theoretical interest. Roger Scruton makes this clear in his essay "The Problem of Architecture." In obvious ways, other art forms such as music or painting have detached themselves from many practical constraints. Scruton claims, however, that since buildings are functional, certain constraints are imposed upon them from the outset. In addressing this issue, he sketches important implications for a general aesthetics of architecture. For instance, architecture, Scruton argues, cannot be personally *expressive* in the way that poems or paintings can be.

Taking a divergent position, Suzanne Langer argues that functionalism is not essential to our understanding of architecture as an art. In this respect, architecture is like sculpture. This does not mean, however, that there is no essential difference between architecture and sculpture, in spite of their shared three-dimensionality. Langer claims, for example, that the Washington Monument is not a work of sculpture, even if it superficially resembles one; conversely, the Statue of Liberty is not a work of architecture even if people can occupy its interior. The paradigm of sculpture, she argues, is always the image of a living thing while, by contrast, architecture always establishes an image of a place of human habitation—whether actually inhabited or not.

As the nineteenth century drew to a close, the capitals of Europe began to witness a new kind of excess. In the growing urban centers, privileged classes invented new forms of ostentatious expression. Partly as a reaction to this excess, modern architecture embraced a policy of severe economy. Its minimalist "look" was also connected with an important paradigm for a new form of architectural thinking: the machine. One of the most conspicuous effects of the new architectural thinking was the prohibition against ornamentation in modern buildings. The decorative/anti-decorative argument would eventually become one of the central issues in the modernist/postmodernist debate about the arts.

One of the early proponents of a minimalist or modern approach to building was the Viennese architect Adolf Loos. In his famous essay, "Ornament and Crime," Loos writes about the relationship between the criminality and *tattooing,* which Loos sees as a form of decadent bodily ornament. Likewise—so the comparison goes—ornamentation in architecture has criminal qualities. Thus, Loos arrives at his prescription to remove ornament from objects in daily use, including buildings.

A few years later, Loos' point of view was to have strong influence on the work of the distinguished architect, Le Corbusier (Charles-Edouard Jeanneret), who, in 1923, published his work, *Towards a New Architecture.* In that volume, he set forth, with revolutionary zeal, "the lessons of the *machine,*" which entailed the emphasis of pure forms in simple geometrical relationships. "The house is a machine for living in," Corbusier announced. Turning away from architectural "styles" such as the gothic or baroque, he found inspiration instead, not only in classical projects such as the Athenian Parthenon, but in the unadorned silos and grain elevators of the American landscape. And he paid close attention to the forms of modern transportation—steamships, airplanes, and automobiles. In the West, through the 1950s, it was simply assumed that a modernist philosophy of architecture was a settled matter. In 1966, however, Robert Venturi, a Philadelphia architect, initiated one of many challenges to modernist architectural theory in his *Complexity and Contradiction in Architecture.* Venturi saw decoration on building as a form of communication and as one way to bring architecture back to its contextual, popular, and historical roots. For his own "lessons" Venturi looked not only to traditional building in the cathedrals and palaces of Europe, but also in the more ordinary places of Las Vegas and Main Street, USA.

Another facet of the postmodernist liberation of architecture from the strictures of high modernism involves what is termed "deconstruction." Christopher Norris's discussion with the French philosopher Jacques Derrida helps to explain what a "deconstructive reading" of architecture might be, as illustrated by projects of provocative architects such as Peter Eisenman. In his conversation with Norris, Derrida gives an excellent account of how deconstructive strategies work.

Taking his departure from the work of Eisenman, David Goldblatt offers an account of a type of persona he calls the "architectural self," the self of traditional architectural practice. Goldblatt uses the Greek idea of *ecstasis* or "being outside" or "beside oneself" to explain Eisenman's controversial attempts at breaking free of an architectural self in order to invent an architecture that is liberated from the agendas of the powerful business of construction and from the architect's own traditional "good" taste.

In the title of his essay "Nolo Contendere," Jeffrey Kipnis uses a legal term that suggests "I do not wish to contend" but is tantamount to an admission of guilt. He uses this motto to explain one of the prominent features of deconstructionist theory, namely, that "the very condition that enables a work to produce any meaning at all guarantees that it must produce many meanings simultaneously— including those that might be regarded as contradictory, unintended and undesirable." According to Kipnis, to put forth *the* meaning of a work is to repress undecidability, whereas to respect undecidability is to pursue meaning without ultimate meaning.

In arguing about the bearing of practical usage on the aesthetics of architecture, we may be tempted to overlook the fact that some of our architecture goes unused simply because it lies in ruins. Donald Crawford examines such cases, as well as the form of art called "earthworks"—as illustrated by the large-scale outdoor projects of Robert Smithson and others. Crawford uses both types in order to illustrate his idea of a dialectical relationship between art and nature.

Art works situated in public places, particularly large-scale works of sculpture, often arouse controversy. This was never clearer than in the critical storm that surrounded Richard Serra's infamous work *Tilted Arc*. This work, at Federal Plaza, although highly regarded by many critics, was widely considered to be an unattractive spatial obstacle by those using the building. Patricia Phillips analyzes the competing pressures that were brought to bear in the decision to remove Serra's piece. The case raises important general issues about the process by which public art is selected.

The Problem of Architecture
■ Roger Scruton ■

Buildings are places where human beings live, work and worship, and a certain form is imposed from the outset by the needs and desires that a building is designed to fulfil. While it is not possible to compose a piece of music without intending that it should be listened to and hence appreciated, it is certainly possible to design a building without intending that it should be looked at—without intending, that is, to create an object of aesthetic interest. Even when there is an attempt to apply 'aesthetic' standards in architecture, we still find a strong asymmetry with other forms of art. For no work of music or literature can have features of which we may say that, because of the function of music, or because of the function of literature, such features are unavoidable. Of course a work of music or literature may *have* a function, as do waltzes, marches and Pindaric odes. But these functions do not stem from the essence of literary or musical art. A Pindaric ode is poetry *put* to a use; and poetry in itself is connected only accidentally with such uses.

'Functionalism' has many forms. Its most popular form is the aesthetic theory, that true beauty in architecture consists in the adapting of form to function. For the sake of argument, however, we might envisage a functionalist theory of exemplary crudeness, which argues that, since architecture is essentially a means to an end, we appreciate buildings as *means*. Hence the value of a building is determined by the extent to which it fulfils its function and not by any purely 'aesthetic' considerations. This theory might naturally seem to have the consequence that the appreciation of architecture is wholly unlike the appreciation of other forms of art, these being valued not as means, but for their own sakes, as ends. However, to put the point in that way is to risk obscurity—for what is the distinction between valuing something as a means and as an end? Even if we feel confident about one term of that distinction (about what is it to value something as a means), we must surely feel considerable doubt about the term with which it is contrasted. What is it to value something as an end? Consider one celebrated attempt to clarify the concept—that of the English philosopher R. G. Collingwood. Collingwood began his exploration of art and the aesthetic from a distinction between art and craft. Initially it seems quite reasonable to distinguish the attitude of the craftsman—who aims at a certain result and does what he can to achieve it—from that of the artist, who knows what he is doing, as it were, only when it is done. But it is precisely the case of architecture which casts doubt on that distinction. For whatever else it is, architecture is certainly, in Collingwood's sense, a craft. The utility of a building is

"The Problem of Architecture" by Roger Scruton is excerpted from *The Aesthetics of Architecture* Princeton University Press (1979), pages 5-17, and is reprinted by permission of the publisher.

not an accidental property; it defines the architect's endeavour. To maintain this sharp distinction between art and craft is simply to ignore the reality of architecture—not because architecture is a *mixture* of art and craft (for, as Collingwood recognized, that is true of all aesthetic activity) but because architecture represents an almost indescribable *synthesis* of the two. The functional qualities of a building are of its essence, and qualify every task to which the architect addresses himself. It is impossible to understand the element of art and the element of craft independently, and in the light of this difficulty the two concepts seem suddenly to possess a formlessness that their application to the 'fine' arts serves generally to obscure.

Moreover, the attempt to treat architecture as a form of 'art' in Collingwood's sense involves taking a step towards expressionism, towards seeing architecture in the way that one might see sculpture or painting, as an expressive activity, deriving its nature and value from a peculiarly artistic aim. For Collingwood 'expression' was the primary aim of art precisely because there could be no *craft* of expression. In the case of expression, there can be no rule or procedure, such as might be followed by a craftsman, with a clear end in view and a clear means to its fulfilment; it was therefore through the concept of 'expression' that he tried to clarify the distinction between art and craft. Collingwood put the point in the following way: Expression is not so much a matter of finding the symbol for a subjective feeling, as of coming to know, through the act of expression, just what the feeling is. Expression is part of the realization of the inner life, the making intelligible what is otherwise ineffable and confused. An artist who could already identify the feeling which he sought to express might indeed approach his work in the spirit of a craftsman, applying some body of techniques which tell him what he must do to express that particular feeling. But then he would not need those techniques, for if he can identify the feeling it is because he has already expressed it. Expression is not, therefore, an activity whose goal can be defined prior to its achievement; it is not an activity that can be described in terms of end and means. So if art is expression, it *cannot* be craft (although its realization may also involve the mastery of many subsidiary crafts).

Those thoughts are complex, and we shall have cause to return to them. But clearly, it would be a gross distortion to assume that architecture is an 'expressive' medium in just the way that sculpture might be, or that the distinction between art and craft applies to architecture with the neatness which such a view supposes. Despite the absurdities of our crude functionalism (a theory which, as Théophile Gautier once pointed out, has the consequence that the perfection of the water closet is the perfection to which all architecture aspires) it is wrong to see architecture in such a way. The value of a building simply cannot be understood independently of its utility. It is of course *possible* to take a merely 'sculptural' view of architecture; but that is to treat buildings as forms whose aesthetic nature is conjoined only accidentally to a certain function. Texture, surface, form, representation and expression now begin to take precedence over those aesthetic aims which we would normally consider to be specifically architectural. The 'decorative' aspect of architecture assumes an unwonted autonomy, and at the same time becomes something more personal than any act of mere decoration would be. Consider, for example, the Chapel of the Colonia Guëll, Santa Coloma de Cervelló, by Gaudì. Such a building tries to represent itself as something other than architecture, as a form of tree-like growth rather than balanced engineering. The strangeness here comes from the attempt to translate a decorative tradition into a structural principle. In the sixteenth-century Portuguese window by J. de Castilho the nature of that tradition is apparent. Structurally and architecturally the window is *not* an organic growth; its charm lies in its being decked out like that. In Gaudì, however, the accidental has become the essential, and what purports to be architecture can no longer be understood as such, but only as a piece of elaborate expressionist sculpture seen from within. It is perhaps the same sculptural view of architecture which finds an architectural significance in the polished geometry of an Egyptian pyramid . . .

The sculptural view of architecture involves the mistaken idea than one can somehow judge the beauty of a thing *in abstracto,* without knowing what *kind* of thing it is; as though I could present you with an object that might be a stone, a sculpture, a box, a fruit or even an animal, and expect you to tell me whether it is beautiful before knowing what it is. In general we might say—in partial opposition to a certain tradition in aesthetics (the tradition which finds expression in eighteenth-century empiricism, and more emphatically in Kant—that our sense of the beauty of an object is always dependent on a conception of that object, just as our sense of the beauty of a human figure is dependent on a conception of that figure. Features that we would regard as beautiful in a horse—developed haunches, a curved back, and so on—we would regard as ugly in a man, and this aesthetic judgement would be determined by our conception of what men are, how they move, and what they achieve through their movements. In a similar way, our sense of the beauty in architectural forms cannot be divorced from our conception of buildings and of the functions that they fulfil.

Functionalism can be seen, then, as part of an attempt to reassert architectural against sculptural values. As such it has sought to extend its explanatory powers through more subtle, and more vague, presuppositions. We are told that in architecture form 'follows', 'expresses' or 'embodies' function, ideas associated with [Eugène] Viollet-le-Duc, with the American pragmatism of [Louis] Sullivan, and with certain aspects of the modern movement. There is also the more subtle functionalism of [Augustus] Pugin and the mediaevalists; according to this view the reference to function is necessary as a standard of taste, a means of distinguishing genuine ornament from idle excrescence. In such diluted forms, functionalism no longer has the ring of necessary truth. Indeed, until we know a little more about the essential features of architectural appreciation we will not even know how the theory of functionalism should be formulated, let alone how it might be proved.

A further distinguishing feature of architecture is its highly localized quality. Works of literature, music and pictorial art can be realized in an infinite number of locations, either through being performed or moved, or even, in the limiting case, reproduced. With certain rare exceptions—frescoes, for example, and monumental sculpture—this change of place need involve no change in aesthetic character. The same cannot be true of architecture. Buildings constitute important features of their own environment, as their environment is an important feature of them; they cannot be reproduced at will without absurd and disastrous consequences. Buildings are also affected to an incalculable extent by changes in their surroundings. Thus the architectural *coup de théâtre* planned by Bernini for the piazza of St Peter's has been partially destroyed by the opening up of the Via Della Conciliazione, as the effect of the spire of St Bride's from the Thames bridges has been destroyed by the saw-like edges of the Barbican. We know of buildings whose effect depends in part on their location, either because they are ingenious solutions to problems of space—such as [Francesco] Borromini's church of S. Carlo alle Quattro Fontane— or because they are built in some striking or commanding position that is essential to their impact—such as the temple at Agrigento in Sicily—or because they involve a grandeur of conception that embraces a whole environment, in the manner of Versailles, where the architectural influence of [André] Le Nôtre's garden is infinite in ambition. This is not to say that buildings cannot be reproduced—there are several neo-classical examples to the contrary, such as the composite souvenir of Athens known as St Pancras' church. However, it must be acknowledged that the point of reproducing buildings is not generally comparable to the point of reproducing or copying paintings, and is certainly unlike the point of performing the same piece of music again. It is a scholarly exercise, playing no part in the natural distribution and enjoyment of a work of art. Indeed, we often feel a certain hostility towards the attempt to translate buildings, in this way, from one part of the world to another. We expect an architect to build in accordance with a sense of place, and not to design his building—as many a modern building is designed—so that it could be placed just anywhere. It is true that the architectural instinct can show itself even in the dwellings of nomadic tribes, but the impulse to which we owe most of the fine architecture that we have inherited is an impulse founded in the sense of place—the desire to mark a sacred spot or place of martyrdom, to build a monument, church or landmark, to claim possession and dominion of the land. This impulse is to be found in all serious architecture, from the antique temple and the martyrium, to the Chapel at Ronchamp and the Sydney Opera House, and it is an impulse which leads us to separate architecture from nature only with a certain considered reluctance.

This sense of place, and the consequent impression of the immovability of architecture, constrains the work of the builder in innumerable ways. Architecture becomes an art of the ensemble. It is intrinsic to architecture that it should be infinitely vulnerable to changes in its surroundings. This is a feature that architecture shares with such pursuits as interior decoration, dress, and the many quasi-moral, quasi-aesthetic activities that fall under the notion of taste. The interest in *ensembles* is partly responsible for the attention paid in architectural theory to style, and to repeatable form. . . .

A further feature of architecture should here be mentioned—the feature of technique. What is possible in architecture is determined by the extent of human competence. In architecture there are changes initiated quite independently of any change in artistic consciousness; the natural evolution of styles is cast aside, interrupted or sent off at a tangent by discoveries that have no aesthetic origin and no aesthetic aim. Consider, for example, the discovery of reinforced concrete, and [Robert] Maillart's use of it in his well-known bridges, which curve through the air across ravines where no straight path would be apt or possible. The aesthetic consequences of that technical discovery have been enormous, and nobody could have envisaged them, still less intended them, in advance. In music, literature and painting evolution has followed more nearly a changing *attitude* to art, and hence a shifting spirit of artistic creation. And while it is true that here, too, there can be technical discoveries, such as that of the piano, which actually interrupt the flow of aesthetic consciousness (as well as others, such as those of the violin, the clarinet, the saxophone and the Wagner tuba, which are more naturally seen as *consequences* of a change in taste); and while there are also engineering achievements (like that of Brunelleschi's dome), which result from aesthetic aspiration, these passing similarities only serve to underline the real distinction between architecture and the other arts. One must greet with a certain scepticism, therefore, those critics who hail the modern movement as a creation of architectural forms more in keeping with the 'spirit of the age', as though the change in these forms were a product only of artistic enterprise, and not of engineering skill.

A more important distinguishing feature of architecture is provided by its character as a public object. A work of architecture imposes itself come what may, and removes from every member of the public the free choice as to whether he is to observe or ignore it. Hence there is no real sense in which an architect creates his public; the case is wholly unlike those of music, literature and painting, which are, or have become, objects of free critical choice. Poetry and music, for example, have become self-consciously 'modern' precisely because they have been able to create for themselves audiences attuned to novelty and active in the pursuit of it. Clearly, the architect may change public taste, but he can do so only by addressing himself to the whole public and not merely to some educated or half-educated part of it. 'Modernism' in architecture therefore raises a special problem which is not raised by modernism in the other forms of art. . . .

For modernism in these other arts has depended upon a certain subjectivity of outlook. By which I mean that modernism has been both self-conscious in its pursuit of an audience, and determinedly individualistic in its expressive aims. Consider the remarkable art of [Arnold] Schoenberg, who argued that he had provided canons of form and structure which were from the auditory point of view equivalent to those of the classical tradition. To the educated ear, the Schoenbergian theme was to be as intelligible and as imbued with musical implications as a melody of Mozart. One can of course doubt that even the most melodious of

Schoenberg's themes (for example, the opening theme of the piano concerto) achieves the immediate intelligibility of Mozart, and one might even doubt that one *ought* to hear a Schoenbergian theme as inflected in the manner of a classical melody (that is to say, as *progressing* towards a conclusion). Be that as it may, it certainly cannot be doubted that the transformation of musical experience which Schoenberg envisaged was a self-conscious affair, in a way that the experience of architecture cannot normally be. . . .

The artist's ability to create his audience, to demand of them a permanent sense of their own modernity, is a necessary precondition not only of the success of such an enterprise but also of its attempt. It is in this way that music, painting and literature continue to survive, even in a state of cultural chaos, through the invention of what are at first (before the successful adoption of a style) arbitrary choices and arbitrary constraints.

Now I doubt that we could freely take up such an attitude to architecture as the one I have sketched. For I doubt that we could consistently view architecture either as a form of personal expression, or as a self-conscious gesture designed for the 'modern consciousness' alone. Architecture is public; it imposes itself whatever our desires and whatever our self-image. Moreover, it takes up space: Either it crushes out of existence what has gone before, or else it attempts to blend and harmonize. . . .

But perhaps the most important feature of architecture, the feature which serves most of all to give it a peculiar status and significance in our lives, is its continuity with the decorative arts, and the corresponding multiplicity of its aims. Even when architects have a definite 'aesthetic' purpose, it may not be more than a desire that their work should 'look right' in just the way that tables and chairs, the lay of places at a table, the folds in a napkin, an arrangement of books, may 'look right' to the casual observer. Architecture is primarily a vernacular art: It exists first and foremost as a process of arrangement in which every normal man may participate, and indeed does participate, to the extent that he builds, decorates or arranges his rooms. It does not normally aim at those 'meanings' ascribed to it by the practitioners of *Kunstgeschichte,* nor does it present itself self-consciously as art. It is a natural extension of common human activities, obeying no forced constraints, and no burden of an 'artistic conception', of anything that might correspond to the romantic's *Kunstwollen,* or to the Hegelian 'Idea'. . . .

One might say that in proposing an aesthetics of architecture, the least one must be proposing is an aesthetics of everyday life. One has moved away from the realm of high art towards that of common practical wisdom. And here one might begin to see just how inappropriate is our post-romantic conception of art to the description of the normal aesthetic judgements of the normal man, and how obscure are all the concepts, such as the concept of expression, which have been used to elucidate it.

Against the background of these differences, we must recognize the immense difficulty that exists in giving any articulate criticism of architecture.

Virtual Space

■ Suzanne K. Langer ■

In the realm of sculpture the role of illusion seems less important than in painting, where a flat surface "creates" a three-dimensional space that is obviously virtual. Sculpture is actually three-dimensional; in what sense does it "create" space for the eye? This is probably the question which led Adolf v. Hildebrand to say that the sculptor's task was to present a three-dimensional object in the two-dimensional picture place of "perceptual space." But the answer, though it satisfies and, in fact, aptly completes his theory, lacks the confirmation of direct experience and artistic intuition. Sculptors themselves rarely think in terms of pictures, and of ideal planes of vision staggered one behind the other to define deep space (except in perfectly flat relief with rectangular cuts, or even mere graven lines, which is really pictorial art, substituting the graving tool for a pencil). Sculpture, even when it is wedded to a background as in true relief, is essentially *volume,* not *scene.*

The volume, however, is not a cubic measure, like the space in a box. It is more than the bulk of the figure; it is a space made visible, and is more than the area which the figure actually occupies. The tangible form has a complement of empty space that it absolutely commands, that is given with it and only with it, and is, in fact, part of the sculptural volume. The figure itself seems to have a sort of continuity with the emptiness around it, however much its solid masses may assert themselves as such. The void enfolds it, and the enfolding space has vital form as a continuation of the figure. . . .

Here we have the primary illusion, virtual space, created in a mode quite different from that of painting, which is *scene,* the field of direct vision. Sculpture creates an equally visual space, but not a space of direct vision; for volume is really given originally to touch, both haptic touch and contact limiting bodily movement, and the business of sculpture is to translate its data into entirely visual terms, i.e. *to make tactual space visible.*

The intimate relationship between touch and sight which is thus effected by the semblance of kinetic volume explains some of the complex sensory reactions which sculptors as well as laymen often have toward it. Many people feel a strong desire to handle every figure. In some persons the wish springs from obviously sentimental motives, anthropomorphizing the statue, imagining a human contact; this was the attitude Rodin expressed, and the knowledge that he would touch cold marble made him wistful, like Pygmalion. But others—among artists, probably the majority—imagine the touch of stone or wood, metal or earth; they wish to feel the substance that is really there, and let their hands pass over its pure form. They know that the sensation will

"Virtual Space" by Suzanne K. Langer is excerpted from *Feeling and Form,* Allyn and Bacon (1953), pages 87–99, 101, and is reprinted by permission of the publisher.

not always bear out the visual suggestion, perhaps will even contradict it. Yet they believe that their perception of the work will somehow be enhanced.

Sculptural form is a powerful abstraction from actual objects and the three-dimensional space which we construe by means of them, through touch and sight. It makes its own construction in three dimensions, namely the *semblance* of kinetic space. Just as one's field of direct vision is organized, in actuality, as a plane at the distance of a natural focus, so the kinetic realm of tangible volumes, or things, and free air spaces between them, is organized in each person's actual experience as his *environment,* i.e. a space whereof he is the center; his body and the range of its free motion, its breathing space and the reach of its limbs, are his own kinetic volume, the point of orientation from which he plots the world of tangible reality—objects, distances, motions, shape and size and mass. . . .

A piece of sculpture is a center of three-dimensional space. It is a virtual kinetic volume, which dominates a surrounding space, and this environment derives all proportions and relations from it, as the actual environment does from one's self. The work is the semblance of a self, and creates the semblance of a tactual space—and, moreover, a visual semblance. It effects the objectification of self and environment for the sense of sight. Sculpture is literally the image of kinetic volume in sensory space.

That is why I say it is a powerful abstraction. And here I have to depart from [Bruno] Adriani; for he, still speaking of the sculptor, continues: "The space of his sculpture is his original world. . . . The 'ideal' beholder . . . transposes the system of coordinated axes, created by the sculptor, into his own organism." On the contrary, it seems to me that just because we do *not* identify the space which centers in a statue with our own environment, the created world remains objective, and can thus become an *image* of our own surrounding space. It is an environment, but not our own; neither is it that of some other person, having points in common with ours, so that the person and his surroundings become 'objects' to us, existing in our space. Though a statue is, actually, an object, we do not treat it as such; we see it as a center of a space all its own; but its kinetic volume and the environment it creates are illusory—they exist for our vision alone, a semblance of the self and its world.

This explains, perhaps, why the tactual encounter with stone or wood, contradicting as it does the organic appearance of sculpture, may nevertheless cause no disappointment, but may really enhance our appreciation of plastic form; it checks the anthropomorphic fancy, and heightens the abstractive power of the work. Yet handling a figure, no matter what it gives us, is always a mere interlude in our perception of the form. We have to step back, and see it unmolested by our hands, that break into the sphere of its spatial influence. . . .

There is a third mode of creating virtual space, more subtle than the construction of illusory scene or even illusory organism, yet just as commandingly artistic, and in its scope the most ambitious of all; that is architecture. Its "illusion" is easily missed because of the obviousness and importance of its actual values: shelter, comfort, safekeeping. Its practical functions are so essential that architects themselves are often confused about its status. Some have regarded it as chiefly utilitarian, and only incidentally aesthetic, except in the case of monuments; others have treated it as "applied art," wherein practical considerations always force some sacrifice of the artist's "vision"; and some have tried to meet the prosaic demands of utility by making function paramount, believing that genuinely appropriate forms are always beautiful. In architecture the problem of appearance and reality comes to a head as in no other art. This makes it a test case in aesthetic theory, for a true general theory has no exceptions, and when it seems to have them it is not properly stated. If architecture is utilitarian *except* in the case of monuments, then utility is not its essence; if it may be treated as sculpture *except* where practical needs interfere as in underground building, or necessities like bulkheads and chicken houses, then sculptural values are not essential to it. If functional interests can ever be adequately served without beauty, then form may follow function with all the happy effect in the world, but functionality is not the measure of beauty. . . .

As *scene* is the basic abstraction of pictorial art, and *kinetic volume* of sculpture, that of architecture is *an ethnic domain*. Actually, of course, a domain is not a "thing" among other "things"; it is the sphere of influence of a function, or functions; it may have physical effects on some geographical locality or it may not. Nomadic cultures, or cultural phenomena like the seafaring life, do not inscribe themselves on any fixed place on earth. Yet a ship, constantly changing its location, is none the less a self-contained place, and so is a Gypsy camp, an Indian camp, or a circus camp, however often it shifts its geodetic bearings. Literally, we say the camp is *in* a place; culturally, it *is* a place. A Gypsy camp is a different place from an Indian camp, though it may be geographically where the Indian camp used to be.

A place, in this non-geographical sense, is a created thing, an ethnic domain made visible, tangible, sensible. As such it is, of course, an illusion. Like any other plastic symbol, it is primarily an illusion of self-contained, self-sufficient, perceptual space. But the principle of organization is its own: for it is organized as a functional realm made visible—the center of a virtual world, the "ethnic domain," and itself a geographical semblance.

Painting creates planes of vision, or "scene" confronting our eyes, on an actual, two-dimensional surface; sculpture makes virtual "kinetic volume" out of actual three-dimensional material, i.e. actual volume; architecture articulates the "ethnic domain," or virtual "place," by treatment of an actual place.

The architectural illusion may be established by a mere array of upright stones defining the magic circle that severs holiness from the profane, even by a single stone that marks a center, i.e. a monument. The outside world, even though not physically shut out, is dominated by the sanctum and becomes its visible context; the horizon, its frame. The Temple of Poseidon at Sounion shows this organizing power of a composed form. On the other hand, a tomb carved out of solid rock may create a complete domain, a world of the dead. It has no outside; its proportions are internally derived—from the stone, from the burial—and define an architectural space that may be deep and high and wide, within but a few cubits of actual measure. The created "place" is essentially a semblance, and whatever effects that semblance is architecturally relevant. . . .

A culture is made up, factually, of the activities of human being; it is a system of interlocking and intersecting actions, a continuous functional pattern. As such it is, of course, intangible and invisible. It has physical ingredients—artifacts; also physical symptoms—the ethnic effects that are stamped on the human face, known as its "expression," and the influence of social condition on the development, posture, and movement of the human body. But all such items are fragments that "mean" the total pattern of life only to those who are acquainted with it and may be reminded of it. They are ingredients in a culture, not its image.

The architect creates its image: a physically present human environment that expresses the characteristic rhythmic functional patterns which constitute a culture. Such patterns are the alternations of sleep and waking, venture and safety, emotion and calm, austerity and abandon; the tempo, and the smoothness or abruptness of life; the simple forms of childhood and the complexities of full moral stature, the sacramental and the capricious moods that mark a social order, and that are repeated, though with characteristic selection, by every personal life springing from that order. . . .

The most familiar product of architecture is, of course, the *house*. Because of its ubiquity it is the most detailed, and yet the most variable general form. It may shelter one person or a hundred families; it may be made of stone or wood, clay, cement or metal, or many materials together—even paper, grass, or snow. People have made houses in the caves of barren mountains, and houses out of animal skins to take along on the march; they have used spreading trees for roofs, anchoring their houses to the live trunks. The imperative need of dwellings under all conditions, from the polar ice, almost as dead as the moon, to the prodigal Mediterranean lands, has caused every means of construction to be exploited; the house has been the builder's elementary school.

But the great architectural ideas have rarely, if ever, arisen from domestic needs. They grew as the temple, the tomb, the fortress, the hall, the theatre. The reason is simple enough: Tribal culture is collective, and its domain therefore essentially public. When it is made visible, its image is a public realm. Most early architecture—Stonehenge, the Mounds, the Temple of the Sun—defines what might be called "religious space." This is a virtual realm; the temple, though oriented by the equinox points, merely symbolizes the "corners of the earth" to simple people who probably did not understand the astronomical scheme at all. The temple really made their greater world of space—nature, the abode of gods and ghosts. The heavenly bodies could be seen to rise and set in the frame it defined; and as it presented this space to popular thought it unified the earth and heaven, men and gods. . . .

In that false assumption lies the error of "functionalism"—lies not very deep, but perhaps as deep as the theory itself goes. Symbolic expression is something miles removed from provident planning or good arrangement. It does not suggest things to do, but embodies the feeling, the rhythm, the passion or sobriety, frivolity or fear with which any things at all are done. That is the image of life which is created in buildings; it is the visible semblance of an "ethnic domain," the symbol of humanity to be found in the strength and interplay of forms. . . .

The most interesting result of the theory, however, is the light it throws on the relation of architecture to sculpture. . . .

The two art forms are, in fact, each other's exact complements: the one, an illusion of kinetic volume, symbolizing the Self, or center of life—the other, an illusion of ethnic domain, or the environment created by Selfhood. Each articulates one half of the life-symbol directly and the other by implication; whichever we start with, the other is its background.

Ornament and Crime
■ Adolf Loos ■

In the womb the human embryo passes through all the development stages of the animal kingdom. At the moment of birth, human sensations are equal to those of a newborn dog. His childhood passes through all the transformations which correspond to the history of mankind. At the age of two, he sees like a Papuan, at four, like a Teuton, at six like Socrates, at eight like Voltaire. When he is eight years old, he becomes aware of violet, the colour which the eighteenth century had discovered, because before that the violet was blue and the purple snail red. Today the physicist points to colours in the sun's spectrum which already bear a name, whose recognition, however, is reserved for the coming generation.

The child is amoral. To us the Papuan is also amoral. The Papuan slaughters his enemies and devours them. He is no criminal. If, however, the modern man slaughters and devours somebody, he is a criminal or a degenerate. The Papuan tattoos his skin, his boat, his oar, in short, everything that is within his reach. He is no criminal. The modern man who tattoos himself is a criminal or a degenerate. There are prisons where eighty percent of the inmates bear tattoos. Those who are tattooed but are not imprisoned are latent criminals or degenerate aristocrats. If a tattooed person dies at liberty, it is only that he died a few years before he committed a murder.

The urge to ornament one's face, and everything within one's reach, is the origin of fine art. It is the babble of painting. All art is erotic.

The first ornament that came into being, the cross, had an erotic origin. The first work of art, the first artistic action of the first artist daubing on the wall, was in order to rid himself of his natural excesses. A horizontal line: the reclining woman. A vertical line: the man who penetrates her. The man who created it felt the same urge as Beethoven, he experienced the same joy that Beethoven felt when he created the Ninth Symphony.

"Ornament and Crime" by Adolf Loos, is excerpted from *Programs and Manifestos in Twentieth Century Architecture,* Ulrich and Conrads eds., Michael Bullock, trans., MIT Press (1970), pages 19–24, and is reprinted by permission of the publisher.

But the man of our time who daubs the walls with erotic symbols to satisfy an inner urge is a criminal or a degenerate. It is obvious that this urge overcomes man; such symptoms of degeneration most forcefully express themselves in public conveniences. One can measure the culture of a country by the degree to which its lavatory walls are daubed. With children it is a natural phenomenon: Their first artistic expression is to scrawl on the walls erotic symbols. But what is natural to the Papuan and the child is a symptom of degeneration in the modern man. I have made the following observation and have announced it to the world:

The evolution of culture is synonymous with the removal of ornament from objects of daily use. I had thought to introduce a new joy into the world: but it has not thanked me for it. Instead the idea was greeted with sadness and despondency. What cast the gloom was the thought that ornament could no longer be produced. What! Are we alone, the people of the nineteenth century, are we no longer capable of doing what any Negro can do, or what people have been able to do before us?

Those objects without ornament, which mankind had created in earlier centuries, had been carelessly discarded and destroyed. We possess no carpenter's benches of the Carolingian period; instead any rubbish which had even the smallest ornament was collected, cleaned and displayed in ostentatious palaces that were built for them, people walked about sadly amongst the display cabinets. Every period had its style: Why was it that our period was the only one to be denied a style? By 'style' was meant ornament. I said, 'Weep not. Behold! What makes our period so important is that it is incapable of producing new ornament. We have out-grown ornament, we have struggled through to a state without ornament. Behold, the time is at hand, fulfilment awaits us. Soon the streets of the cities will glow like white walls! Like Zion, the Holy City, the capital of heaven. It is then that fulfilment will have come.'

But there are hob goblins who will not allow it to happen. Humanity is still to groan under the slavery of ornament. Man had progressed enough for ornament to no longer produce erotic sensations in him, unlike the Papuans, a tattooed face did not increase the aesthetic value, but reduced it. Man had progressed far enough to find pleasure in purchasing a plain cigarette case, even if it cost the same as one that was ornamented. They were happy with their clothes and they were glad that they did not have to walk about in red velvet trousers with gold braids like monkeys at a fun fair. And I said: 'Behold, Goethe's death chamber is more magnificent than all the pomp of the Renaissance, and a plain piece of furniture is more beautiful than all the inlaid and carved museum pieces. Goethe's language is more beautiful than all the ornaments of the shepherds of the Pegnitz.'

This was heard by the hob goblins with displeasure. The state, whose duty it is to impede people in their cultural development, took over the question of development and re-adoption of ornament and made it its own. Woe betide the state, whose revolutions are brought about by its privy councillors!

Soon one was to see a buffet introduced into the Viennese Museum of Applied Arts, which was called 'the properous fish shoal,' there was even a cupboard, which was given the trade name 'the cursed princess' or something similar, which referred to the ornament with which this unfortunate piece of furniture was covered. The Austrian state takes its task so seriously that it ensures that outdated footwear will not disappear from within the boundaries of the Austro-Hungarian Empire. The state forces every cultivated twenty-year old man to wear outdated footwear for three years (after all, every state proceeds on the assumption that a poorly developed population is more easily governed). Well, the epidemic of ornament is recognised by the state and is subsidised with government money. I, however, consider that to be a regressive. I will not subscribe to the argument that ornament increases the pleasures of the life of a cultivated person, or the argument which covers itself with the words: 'But if the ornament is beautiful! . . . ' To me, and to all the cultivated people, ornament does not increase the pleasures of life. If I want to eat a piece of gingerbread I will choose one that is completely plain and not a piece which represents a baby in arms of a horserider, a piece which is covered over and over with decoration. The man of the fifteenth century would not understand me. But modern people will. The supporter of ornament believes that the urge for simplicity is equivalent to self-denial. No, dear professor from the College of Applied Arts, I am not denying myself! To me, it tastes better this way. The dishes of the past centuries which used decoration to make the peacocks, pheasants and lobsters appear more appetising produce the opposite effect on me. I look on such a culinary display with horror when I think of having to eat those stuffed animal corpses. I eat roast beef.

The immense damage and devastation which the revival of ornament has caused to aesthetic development could easily be overcome because nobody, not even the power of the state, can stop the evolution of humanity! It represents a crime against the national economy, and, as a result of it, human labour, money and material are ruined. Time cannot compensate for this kind of damage.

The rate of cultural development is held back by those that cannot cope with the present. I live in the year 1908, but my neighbour lives approximately in the year 1900, and one over there lives in the year 1880. It is a misfortune for any government, if the culture of its people is dominated by the past. The farmer from Kals lives in the twelfth century, and on the occasion of the Jubilee Procession, tribes walked past which even during the period of mass migration were thought to be backward. Happy is the country which does not have such backward-looking inhabitants. Happy is America! Even here we have people in the cities who are survivors from the eighteenth century, and who are appalled by a painting with violet shadows, because they cannot understand why the artist has used violet. To them, the pheasant which the cook has spent days preparing tastes better, and the cigarette case with the Renaissance ornaments is more pleasing. And what is happening in the countryside? Clothes and household utensils belong to previous centuries. The farmer is no Christian, he is still a heathen.

Those who measure everything by the past impede the cultural development of nations and of humanity itself. Ornament is not merely produced by criminals, it commits a crime itself by damaging national economy and therefore its cultural development. Two people living side by side who have the same needs, the same demands on life, and the same income, but belong to different cultures, perceive the national economy differently. The result is that the man of the twentieth century becomes richer and the man of the eighteenth century becomes poorer. I assume that both their lifestyles reflect their different attitudes. The man of the twentieth century can satisfy his needs with a much smaller capital and can, therefore, set aside savings. The vegetable which is appetising to him is simply boiled in water and has butter spread over it. To the other man it will only taste good if honey and nuts are added to it and it has been cooked by someone for hours. Decorated plates are expensive, while white crockery, which is pleasing to the modern individual, is cheap. Whilst one person saves money, the other becomes insolvent. This is what happens to entire nations. Woe betide the nation that remains behind in its cultural development. The English become richer and we become poorer . . .

In a highly productive nation ornament is no longer a natural product of its culture, and therefore represents backwardness or even a degenerative tendency. As a result, those who produce ornament are no longer given their due reward. We are aware of the conditions that exist in the wood carving and turning trades, the very low wages which are paid to the embroiderers and lace makers. The producer of ornament must work for twenty hours to obtain the same income of a modern labourer who works for eight hours. As a rule, ornament increases the price of the object. All the same there are occasions when an ornamented object is offered at half the price, despite the same material cost and production time, which works out to be three times longer as that of a plain unornamented object. The lack of ornament results in reduced working hours and an increased wage. The Chinese carver works sixteen hours, the American labourer works eight hours. If I pay as much for a plain box as I would for an ornamented one, then the difference is in working hours. And if there existed no ornament at all, a condition which might arise in millenia, man would only need to work four instead of eight hours, as the time spent on ornament represents half of today's working day.

Ornament is wasted manpower and therefore wasted health. It has always been like this. But today it also means wasted material, and both mean wasted capital.

As ornament is no longer organically related to our culture, it is also no longer the expression of our culture. The ornament that is produced today bears no relation to us, or to any other human or the world at large. It has no potential for development. What happened to Otto Eckmann's ornaments, and those of [Henry] Van de Velde? The artist always stood at the centre of humanity, full of power and health. The modern producer of ornament is, however, left behind or a pathological phenomenon. He disowns his own products after only three years. Cultivated people find them instantaneously intolerable, others become conscious of their intolerability after many years. Where are Otto Eckmann's products today? Where will Olbrich's work be, ten years from now? Modern ornament has no parents and no offspring, it has no past and no future. Uncultivated people, to whom the significance of our time is a sealed book, welcome it with joy and disown it after a short while.

Today, mankind is healthier than ever before; only a few are ill. These few, however, tyrannise the worker, who is so healthy that he is incapable of inventing ornament. They force him to execute ornament which they have designed, in the most diverse materials.

The change in ornament implies a premature devaluation of labour. The worker's time, the utilised material is capital that has been wasted. I have made the statement: The form of an object should be bearable for as long as the object lasts physically. I would like to try to explain this: A suit will be changed more frequently than a valuable fur coat. A lady's evening dress, intended for one night only, will be changed more rapidly than a writing desk. Woe betide the writing desk that has to be changed as frequently as an evening dress, just because the style has become unbearable. Then the money that was spent on the writing desk will have been wasted.

This fact is well known to the Austrians who promote decoration and try to justify it by saying: 'A consumer who owns furnishings which become unbearable to him, after only ten years, and who is therefore forced to buy furniture every ten years, is preferable to one who only buys an object for himself once the old one can no longer be used. Industry demands it. Millions of people are employed because of this rapid change.' This appears to be the secret of the Austrian national economy; how often does one hear the words uttered on the occasion of the outbreak of a fire: 'Thank God: now there will be some work again.' I know a good remedy! Set a whole city on fire, set the entire Empire alight and everyone will wallow in money and wealth. Let us have furniture made which can be used for firewood after three years; let us have ironmongery which will have to be melted down after four years, as it is impossible to realise even a tenth of the original labour and material costs at the pawn-brokers, and we will become richer and richer.

The loss not only hits the consumer; it hits primarily the producer. Today, decorated objects, which, thanks to progress, have become separated from the realm of ornamentation imply wasted labour and materials. If all objects were to last as long in aesthetic terms as they did physically, the consumer could pay a price for them which would enable the labourer to earn more money and work shorter hours. I would gladly pay forty crowns for my boots even though I could obtain boots for ten crowns at another store. But in every trade which languishes under the tyranny of the ornamentalists, neither good nor bad work is valued. Labour suffers because no one is prepared to pay for its true value.

Thank goodness that this is the case, because these ornamented objects are only bearable in the shabbiest execution. I recover from the news of a fire more rapidly if I hear that only worthless rubbish was burnt. I can be happy about the junk in the Künstlerhaus (the Municipal art gallery in Vienna), as I know that they put on exhibitions in a few days which are pulled down in one. But the flinging of gold coins instead of pebbles, the lighting of a cigarette with a banknote, the pulverisation and drinking of a pearl appear unaesthetic.

Ornamented objects appear truly unaesthetic if they have been executed in the best material, with the highest degree of meticulous detail, and if they have required a long production time. I cannot plead innocence for having been the first to call for quality labour, but not for this kind of work.

The modern man who holds ornament sacred as the sign of artistic achievement of past epochs will immediately recognise the tortured, laboriously extracted and pathological nature of modern ornament. Ornament can no longer be borne by someone who exists at our level of culture.

It is different for people and nations who have not reached this level.

I preach to the aristocrats, I mean the individuals who stand at the pinnacle of humanity and who nevertheless have the deepest understanding for the motivations and privations of those who stand further below. The Kafir who weaves fabric according to a specific order which only appears when one unravels it, the Persian who ties his carpets, the Slovak farmer's wife who embroiders her lace, the old lady who makes beautiful things with glass, beads and silk; all these he understands very well. The aristocrat lets them have their own way; he knows that they are sacred hours in which they work. The revolutionary would come and say 'it is all nonsense.' As he would pull the old lady away from the roadside shrine and say to her: 'There is no God.' But the atheist amongst the aristocrats lifts his hat as he walks past a church.

My shoes are covered all over with ornaments, which result from notches and holes: work which the cobbler carried out and which he was not paid for. I go to the cobbler and say to him: 'For a pair of shoes you are asking thirty crowns. I will pay you forty crowns.' By doing this I have made him happy and he will thank me for it by the work and materials which will not bear any relation in terms of quality to the extra amount. He is happy because rarely does fortune enter his house and he has been given work by a man who understands him, who appreciates his work and who does not doubt his honesty. He already imagines the finished pair in front of him. He knows where the best leather is to be found today, he knows which worker he will entrust with the shoes, and that they will display notches and holes, as many as there is space for on an elegant pair of shoes. And now I say: 'But there is one condition which I have. The shoes must be completely smooth.' By that, I have plunged him from the height of happiness to the depths of Tartarus. He has less work to do, I have robbed him of all pleasures.

I preach to the aristocrats. I allow decoration on my own body, if it provides a source of pleasure for my fellow men. Then they are also my pleasures. I suffer the ornament of the Kafir, that of the Persian, that of the Slovak farmer's wife, the ornaments of my cobbler, because they all have no other means of expressing their full potential. We have our culture which has taken over from ornament. After a day's trouble and pain, we go to hear Beethoven or Wagner. My cobbler cannot do that. I must not rob him of his pleasures as I have nothing else to replace them with. But he who goes to listen to the Ninth Symphony and who then sits down to draw up a wallpaper pattern, is either a rogue or a degenerate.

The absence of ornament has raised the other arts to unknown heights. Beethoven's symphonies would never have been written by a man who walked around in silk, velvet and lace. The person who runs around in a velvet suit is no artist but a buffoon or merely a decorator. We have become more refined, more subtle. Primitive men had to differentiate themselves by various colours, modern man needs his clothes as a mask. His individuality is so strong that it can no longer be expressed in terms of items of clothing. The lack of ornament is a sign of intellectual power. Modern man uses the ornament of past and foreign cultures at his discretion. His own inventions are concentrated on other things.

Towards an Architecture
■ Le Corbusier ■

Architecture has nothing to do with the various "styles."

The styles of Louis XIV, XV, XVI or Gothic, are to architecture what a feather is on a woman's head; it is sometimes pretty, though not always, and never anything more.

Architecture has graver ends; capable of the sublime, it impresses the most brutal instincts by its objectivity; it calls into play the highest faculties by its very abstraction. Architectural abstraction has this about it which is magnificently peculiar to itself, that while it is rooted in hard fact it spiritualizes it, because the naked fact is nothing more than the materialization of a possible idea. The naked fact is a medium for ideas only by reason of the "order" that is applied to it. The emotions that architecture arouses spring from physical conditions which are inevitable, irrefutable and to-day forgotten.

Mass and surface are the elements by which architecture manifests itself.

Mass and surface are determined by the plan. The plan is the generator. So much the worse for those who lack imagination!

Architecture is the masterly, correct and magnificent play of masses brought together in light. Our eyes are made to see forms in light; light and shade reveal these forms; cubes, cones, spheres, cylinders or pyramids are the great primary forms which light reveals to advantage; the image of these is distinct and tangible within us and without ambiguity. It is for that reason that these are *beautiful forms, the most beautiful forms.* Everybody is agreed as to that, the child, the savage and the metaphysician. It is of the very nature of the plastic arts.

Egyptian, Greek or Roman architecture is an architecture of prisms, cubes and cylinders, pyramids or spheres: the Pyramids, the Temple of Luxor, the Parthenon, the Coliseum, Hadrian's Villa.

Gothic architecture is not, fundamentally, based on spheres, cones and cylinders. Only the nave is an expression of a simple form, but of a complex geometry

"Towards an Architecture" by Le Corbusier has been excerpted from *Towards a New Architecture,* Dover Publications Inc. (1931), pages 25–26, 37–41, 47–50, and is reprinted by permission of the publisher.

of the second order (intersecting arches). It is for that reason that a cathedral is not very beautiful and that we search in it for compensations of a subjective kind outside plastic art. A cathedral interests us as the ingenious solution of a difficult problem, but a problem of which the postulates have been badly stated because they do not proceed from the great primary forms. *The cathedral is not a plastic work; it is a drama; a fight against the force of gravity, which is a sensation of a sentimental nature.*

The Pyramids, the Towers of Babylon, the Gates of Samarkand, the Parthenon, the Coliseum, the Pantheon, the Pont du Gard, Santa Sophia, the Mosques of Stamboul, the Tower of Pisa, the Cupolas of Brunelleschi and of Michael Angelo, the Pont-Royal, the Invalides—all these belong to Architecture.

The Gare du Quai d'Orsay, the Grand Palais do not belong to Architecture.

The *architects* of to-day, lost in the sterile backwaters of their plans, their foliage, their pilasters and their lead roofs, have never acquired the conception of primary masses. They were never taught that at the Schools.

Not in pursuit of an architectural idea, but simply guided by the results of calculation (derived from the principles which govern our universe) and the conception of A LIVING ORGANISM, the ENGINEERS of to-day make use of the primary elements and, by co-ordinating them in accordance with the rules, provoke in us architectural emotions and thus make the work of man ring in unison with universal order.

Thus we have the American grain elevators and factories, the magnificent FIRST-FRUITS *of the new age.* THE AMERICAN ENGINEERS OVER-WHELM WITH THEIR CALCULATIONS OUR EXPIRING ARCHITECTURE. . . .

Architecture being the masterly, correct and magnificent play of masses brought together in light, the task of the architect is to vitalize the surfaces which clothe these masses, but in such a way that these surfaces do not become parasitical, eating up the mass and absorbing it to their own advantage: the sad story of our present-day work.

To leave a mass intact in the splendour of its form in light, but, on the other hand, to appropriate its surface for needs which are often utilitarian, is to force oneself to discover in this unavoidable dividing up of the surface the *accusing* and *generating* lines of the form. In other words, an architectural structure is a house, a temple or a factory. The surface of the temple or the factory is in most cases a wall with holes for doors and windows; these holes are often the destruction of form; they must be made an accentuation of form. If the essentials of architecture lie in spheres, cones and cylinders, the generating and accusing lines of these forms are on a basis of pure geometry. But this geometry terrifies the architects of to-day. Architects, to-day, do not dare to construct a Pitti Palace or a *rue de Rivoli;* they construct a *boulevard Raspail.*

Let us base our present observations on the ground of actual needs: what we need is towns laid out in a useful manner whose general mass shall be noble (town planning). We have need of streets in which cleanliness, suitability to the necessities of dwellings, the application of the spirit of mass-production and industrial organization, the grandeur of the idea, the serenity of the whole effect, shall ravish the spirit and bring with them the charm that a happy conception can give.

To model the plain surface of a primary and simple form is to bring into play automatically a rivalry with the mass itself: Here you have a contradiction of intention—the *boulevard Raspail.*

To model the surface of masses which are in themselves complicated and have been brought into harmony is to *modulate* and still remain within the mass: a rare problem—the *Invalides* of Mansard.

A problem of our age and of contemporary æsthetics: Everything tends to the restoration of simple masses: streets, factories, the large stores, all the problems which will present themselves to-morrow under a synthetic form and under general aspects that no other age has even known. Surfaces, pitted by holes in accordance with the necessities of their destined use, should borrow the generating and accusing lines of these simple forms. These accusing lines are in practice the chessboard or grill—American factories. But this geometry is a source of terror.

Not in pursuit of an architectural idea, but guided simply by the necessities of an imperative demand, the tendency of the engineers of to-day is towards the generating and accusing lines of masses; they show us the way and create plastic facts, clear and limpid, giving rest to our eyes and to the mind the pleasure of geometric forms.

Such are the factories, the reassuring first fruits of the new age.

The engineers of to-day find themselves in accord with the principles that Bramante and Raphael had applied a long time ago. . . .

Architecture has nothing to do with the "styles." It brings into play the highest faculties by its very abstraction. Architectural abstraction has this about it which is magnificently peculiar to itself, that while it is rooted in hard fact, it spiritualizes it. The naked fact is a medium for an idea only by reason of the "order" that is applied to it.

Mass and surface are the elements by which architecture manifests itself. Mass and surface are determined by the plan. The plan is the generator. So much the worse for those who lack imagination!

The plan is the generator.

The eye of the spectator finds itself looking at a site composed of streets and houses. It receives the impact of the masses which rise up around it. If these masses are of a formal kind and have not been spoilt by unseemly variations, if the disposition of their grouping expresses a clean rhythm and not an incoherent agglomeration, if the relationship of mass to space is in just proportion, the eye transmits to the brain co-ordinated sensations and the mind derives from these satisfactions of a high order: This is architecture.

The eye observes, in a large interior, the multiple surfaces of walls and vaults; the cupolas determine the large spaces; the vaults display their own surfaces; the pillars and the walls adjust themselves in accordance with comprehensible reasons. The whole structure rises from its base and is developed in accordance with a rule which is written on the ground in the plan: noble forms, variety of form, unity of the geometric principle. A profound projection of harmony: this is architecture.

The plan is at its basis. Without plan there can be neither grandeur of aim and expression, nor rhythm, nor mass, nor coherence. Without plan we have the sensation, so insupportable to man, of shapelessness, of poverty, or disorder, of wilfulness.

A plan calls for the most active imagination. It calls for the most severe discipline also. The plan is what determines everything; it is the decisive moment. A plan is not a pretty thing to be drawn, like a Madonna face; it is an austere abstraction; it is nothing more than an algebrization and a dry-looking thing. The work of the mathematician remains none the less one of the highest activities of the human spirit.

Arrangement is an appreciable rhythm which reacts on every human being in the same way.

The plan bears within itself a primary and pre-determined rhythm: the work is developed in extent and in height following the prescriptions of the plan, with results which can range from the simplest to the most complex, all coming within the same law. Unity of law is the law of a good plan: a simple law capable of infinite modulation.

Architecture as Decorated Shelter
■ Robert Venturi ■

One way to talk about architecture and analyze where you are in it is to define it. Every architect works with a definition in mind even if he or she doesn't know it, or if it is not explicit; every generation of architects has its own definitions. Our current definition is, architecture is shelter with symbols on it. Or, architecture is shelter with decoration on it.

For many architects this may be a shocking definition because definitions in the last seventy-five years have been put in spatial, technological, organic, or linguistic terms. Definitions of Modern architecture never included ornament, nor did they explicitly refer to shelter. Space and process were the essential qualities of architecture in Louis Kahn's definition, "architecture is the thoughtful making of spaces," and in descriptive phrases like Sigfried Giedion's "space-time and architecture," and Frank Lloyd Wright's "in the nature of materials"; space and form predominated in Le Corbusier's "architecture is the masterly, correct, and magnificent

"Architecture as Decorated Shelter" by Robert Venturi is reprinted from *A View from the Campidoglio,* by Robert Venturi and Denise Scott Brown: P. Arnell, T. Bickford, and C. Bergart, eds., Harper and Row (1984), pages 62–67, and is reprinted by permission of the author.

Drawing by Robert Venturi, *The Decorated Shed*, from *Learning from Las Vegas,* Robert Venturi, Denise Scott Brown and Steven Izenour, MIT Press (1972).

Source: Reproduced courtesy of Robert Venturi, Venturi, Scott Brown and Associates, Inc.

play of masses brought together in light." In his definition of a house as a machine for living in, technology and functionalism were the essential elements, although the implication of functionalism in this famous pronouncement is almost unique in Modern architecture despite the emphasis on functionalism in the general theory of the movement. And recently some theorists have attempted semiotic interpretations of architecture, applying in very literal terms some of the complex techniques of that verbal discipline to the perception of architecture. But ornament and symbolism—certainly applied ornament and the simple uses of association—have been ignored in architecture, or condemned. Ornament as equated with crime by Adolf Loos as long ago as 1906, and symbolism was associated with discredited historical eclecticism; appliqué on shelter would have been considered superficial by theorists of the Modern movement and contrary to the industrial techniques integral to Modern architecture.

But we like emphasizing shelter in architecture, thereby including function in our definition; and we like admitting symbolic rhetoric in our definition which is not integral with shelter, thereby expanding the content of architecture beyond itself and freeing function to take care of itself.

To justify our definition of architecture and to clarify how we come to it, I shall use six comparisons—those between Rome and Las Vegas, Abstract Expressionism and Pop Art, Vitruvius and Gropius, Mies van der Rohe and McDonald's hamburger stands, Scarlatti and the Beatles, and plain and fancy styles of architecture.

In the last three comparisons I shall try to justify a particular content for symbolism in architecture, that of the ordinary. For my arguments I shall use material from our book, *Learning from Las Vegas,* because I am elaborating here on a main theme in that book, and because I think hardly anyone has read that book or reads books in general anymore.

Rome and Las Vegas

As architects, we appreciate Rome *and* Las Vegas and we have learned from both sources. (I use Rome to stand for urban tradition—Medieval and Baroque—and Las Vegas to stand for urban sprawl in general.) It is in comparisons between the Roman piazza and the Vegas Strip—illustrating surprising similarities as well as obvious contrasts—that we learned about symbolism in architecture.

Our generation discovered Rome in the fifties. Enclosed exterior space and intimate urban scale were exciting revelations to those of us growing up along wide, ill-defined streets and vast parking lots in amorphous (although not yet hostile) American cities. As post-heroic Moderns reading Sigfried Giedion, we rediscovered history and acknowledged a traditional basis for architecture and urbanism. We had a particular sympathy for the spatial relationships, pedestrian scale, and urban quality of Italian towns exemplified in the piazza. We are now suffering from the results of that enthusiasm—witness the subsequent urban renewal piazzas that disrupt the social fabric and dry up the commercial and visual vitality of the centers of American cities. This is because, as architects of the fifties, we saw the piazza as pure space and we designed our piazzas as dry configurations of compositional elements—forms and textures, patterns and colors, rhythms, accents, and scale—balanced somehow to promote urbanity in space. Historical urban complexes we saw as abstract compositions like those of the Abstract Expressionist paintings of that decade: the symbolism of the building in the piazzas we hardly saw at all. We appreciated the rich evolutionary juxtapositions of historical styles—Baroque palazzo facing Romanesque duomo, for instance—but we limited our observations to the formal relationships of these styles. We ignored the symbolic content of the buildings because of our obsession with the composition of space. We forgot that forms were buildings, texture was sculptural relief, an accent was a statue (and a statue represented a person and ideals), articulation was a portal or decoration, rhythm was composed of pilasters, color and pattern were functions of walls, and that a focus was an obelisk—a sign commemorating an important event. We blotted out the explicit associations evoked by most of the architectural and sculptural elements of the piazza; the ornamentation on the facade of the palazzo symbolizing architectural and structural content and promoting dynastic virtues and civic values, and that of the cathedral, which is like a complex billboard with niches for saintly icons.

We ignored iconography in architecture when we stressed the functional and structural qualities of building in piazzas and idolized their spatial effects, but forgot their symbolic dimensions. We learned inspiring lessons about space in Rome, but the urbanity we were seeking would come from space and signs. We had to go to Las Vegas to learn this lesson about Rome and to acknowledge symbolism in our definition of architecture. On the other hand, we were able to be easy and percep- tive about Las Vegas in the sixties because we loved Rome in the fifties.

We had an exhilarating feeling of revelation in Las Vegas in the sixties, like that which we had in Rome in the previous decade. Our first reaction was that the Strip has a quality and a vitality—a significance—that Modern-designed urban landscapes don't have, and that, ironically, where Modern architecture had won out by supposedly bringing urbanity back to our cities, it didn't. When we ana- lyzed our happy reaction and the peculiar quality and adhesion that exists in com- mercial urban sprawl, we found that their basis was symbolism. As we had learned from the spaces of Rome, we learned from the symbolism of Las Vegas. We soon learned that if you ignore signs as "visual pollution," you are lost. If you look for "spaces between buildings" in Las Vegas, you are lost. If you see the buildings of urban sprawl as forms making space, they are pathetic—mere pimples in an amor- phous landscape. As architecture, urban sprawl is a failure; as space, it is nothing. It is when you see the buildings as symbols in space, not forms in space, that the landscape takes on quality and meaning. And when you see no buildings at all, at night when virtually only the illuminated signs are visible, you see the Strip in its pure state.

This is not to say that the architecture I am describing is without formal con- tent, but to emphasize the predominance of signs over buildings on the Strip and of symbolism over form in the buildings on the Strip as functions of the vast spaces they are seen in and the fast speeds they are seen at. We enumerated, in *Learning from Las Vegas,* the uses of mixed media in architecture, including bold representa- tional kinds of architecture, to create impact and identity—indeed, to be perceived at all—from highways and over parking lots, day and night. In the landscape of the auto age a picture is worth a thousand forms.

In that book we concentrated on the techniques rather than the content of commercial vernacular architecture to help us learn how to design our own archi- tecture. In learning from Las Vegas in this way we were not promoting manipula- tive giant corporatism or even acquiescing to it, as many of our critics—usually ar- chitects of the political left in Europe and those of the aesthetic right in the United States—would have it, any more than our Modern architectural grandfathers pro- moted exploitative free-market capitalism in learning from the industrial vernacu- lar of their day, or than the same critics, if analyzing Versailles or il Gesú, would be advocating a return to absolutism or the Counter-Reformation. Separating tech- nique from content is a traditional and still useful method of analysis and criticism of old or new art, high or low design.

The content of the symbolism of commercial sprawl is different from that of the traditional city, but the commercial messages of the Strip, although bolder to suit our coarser sensibilities and the more gross tempos of our time, are hardly more promotional than the messages on the palaces and cathedral in the piazza promoting civic and religious ideals and power, when you understand the iconogra- phy of these forms. Nor is the popular art of the Strip necessarily more promotional than the high design of the "masterly, correct, and magnificent play of masses" of the corporate headquarters, now that big business has taken over the "progressive" symbolism of orthodox Modern architecture. We ourselves often feel less uncomfortable with the crass commercial advertising on the roadside than we do with some of the subtle and tasteful persuasion inherent in the Modern formalist symbolism that pervades corporate architecture, including that of the industrial-military complex. We think that the sources of many of the visual problems of the roadside commercial environment are more economic, social, and cultural than aesthetic—stemming from the low economic status of some roadside communities, from the bad habits of Americans prone to littering and to "public squalor," and from the varying taste cultures of a multiethnic, heterogeneous society.

Abstract Expressionism and Pop Art

Pop Art in the sixties turned our sensibilities toward the commercial Strip as the painting of the decade before it confirmed our interpretation of the piazza. I have explained how we looked at the piazza in that decade in the same way that we looked at an Abstract Expressionist painting, and how this limited our vision of the urban landscape. The Pop artists opened up our eyes and our minds by showing us again the value of representation in painting, and bringing us thereby to association as an element of architecture. They also showed us the value of familiar and conventional elements by juxtaposing them in new contexts in different scales to achieve new meanings perceived along with their old meanings. Definitions of architecture now included meaning via association as well as expression—a term of the fifties—via perception. And these artists held, we realized later, an ironic view in their love-hate relationship with their vulgar commercial subject matter, paralleling ours toward our ordinary commercial architecture; they made seeing Las Vegas easier, while being still a little uneasy. And now the photorealists of the seventies, whose subject matter is the urban landscape, paint Las Vegas, enhancing the ordinary and beautifying the spectacular.

Vitruvius and Gropius

My third comparison, in my attempt to justify architecture as the decoration of shelter, is between Vitruvius and Gropius. (I use the proper noun Gropius in this comparison to stand for orthodox Modern architecture in general and because of its alliteration.) You will recall the traditional Vitruvian definition of architecture in the words of Sir Henry Wooton: Architecture is firmness, commodity, and delight. The twentieth-century paraphrase of this definition might be: Architecture is structure, program, and expression. (Jean Labatut used to add: shake well before using.) Orthodox Modern architects, if not Walter Gropius then his followers, would significantly alter the Vitruvian juxtaposition of elements. Using the same words, they would have said: Structure and program *are* architecture. When you get structure and program right, expressive architecture will be the automatic result. You shouldn't try for beauty, if you would, indeed, mention that word; architectural quality; the spatial and expressive quality of a building, comes out of the harmonious solution of structural and functional problems. Architecture became frozen process. Certainly the aesthetic element in a Virtuvian triad could not derive from appliqué ornament or from symbolism. Architecture could not represent beauty, it could only be.

It is obvious there is no ornament on Gropius's building of the midtwenties for the Bauhaus in Dessau, but it is hard to believe its form is merely a result of process—of, as Gropius claimed, "our advance from the vagaries of mere architectural caprice to the dictates of structural logic." This building is really a sensitive and effective reworking of an industrial architectural vocabulary of steel frame, glass walls, and flowing space, an adaptation of an existing industrial vernacular architecture of simple geometric forms. It is, indeed, a symbolic building, symbolic of industrial process and advanced technology, whose effect derives in part from the affective properties of its industrial forms. Gropius was doing something different from what he said. There is nothing wrong with this because architects' theories and work often don't correspond; the important thing is that the work be effective. But it is significant, I think, that although Gropius vehemently denied that the Bauhaus could "propagate any 'style,' system, dogma, formula, or vogue," and claimed "a 'Bauhaus Style' would have been a confession of failure and a return to that very stagnation and devitalizing inertia which I had called it into being to combat," he did what architects and artists inevitably do. They intuitively choose a formal vocabulary, an order, a system, a convention, and then adapt it (sometimes avowedly) to their own uses. The Modern movement, whatever was said, picked an existing vocabulary of forms, as the Renaissance master chose the Classical Roman orders, and as we are contemplating the contemporary commercial vernacular.

Of course there were other sources for the forms and symbols of Modern architecture of the heroic period, derived from fine art as well as vernacular art, Cubist painting being an obvious one. Le Corbusier, almost uniquely among the theorists of the Modern movement, admitted to his formalistic adaptation of Cubism and existing mechanical and industrial forms. He was frankly enamored of midwestern American grain elevators which he illustrated in *Towards a New Architecture* in the twenties, he painted Cubist compositions and liked steamships and automobiles. He also illustrated the early Christian basilica of S. Maria in Cosmedin in Rome, focusing on the severe, white, almost Cubist marble furniture in the sanctuary. It is significant that Le Corbusier's architecture of that period looked more like the midwestern grain elevators, steamships, and automobiles illustrated in his book than like the altar of S. Maria in Cosmedin. Why? Because S. Maria was symbolically wrong if formally right, whereas the other precedents were formally and symbolically appropriate. Le Corbusier admittedly employed a formal vocabulary that he adapted and used symbolically to a significant degree, taking existing forms and changing their context. Despite the revolutionary rhetoric of his words, association relying on past experience was part of his architecture.

The main trouble with rejecting a formal system in architecture is that the architects who do so in order to avoid the dangers of formalism, ironically, become more prone to formalism. Late-Modern fundamentalist architects accepted the words of the artists of the heroic period but not the substance of their work. By attempting to exclude symbolism and decoration, and by emphasizing spatial and structural expression, they ended with an architecture of abstract expressionism: pure but limited, it was soon not enough. So they substituted articulation for decoration—articulation through the exaggeration of structural and functional elements: Structure protrudes rhythmically, functions protrude sensitively, clerestories pulsate on the roof. Articulation provides visual richness for form stripped of decoration. In frequent cases, orgies of complex and contradictory articulations produce dramatic expression that becomes expressionism in architecture. Ironically, the exclusion of applied ornament distorts the whole building into *an* ornament. The result is fundamentally more irresponsible than an appliqué of ornament over unarticulated forms would be. We feel that ours is not an era for expressive form and architectural space, but for flat manifestations of symbolism in the landscape—not for the Gallerie des Machines, but for S. Maria in Cosmedin and for the frescoes that were originally applied all over it inside.

There are architects currently working who adopt forms eclectically rather than distort forms expressionistically, but these architects still shun ornamental appliqué. I refer to how the New York Five, sometimes known as the Whites, employ symbolism by quite literally adopting the forms of Le Corbusier's houses of the twenties, and those of De Stijl. Our argument with them is their choice of symbolism: are Cubist industrial forms interesting or relevant for an eclectic style now? Certainly the rather dry abstractions of the houses of the New York Five lack the tension and complexity that was essential to the original houses. We enjoy the unintended irony, however, that these houses are little different in manner from the copies of Norman manor houses and eighteenth-century farmhouses which traditional architects were designing in the twenties and which Le Corbusier and his followers were reacting against at that time. The Italian Rationalists, like the New York Five, are adopting a particular historical style which is minus ornament, and in our context, full of irony; they are a proclaimed Communist-architectural group who are adopting the monumental forms of the Modern, as opposed to the historical-traditional branch of the Italian Fascist style of the twenties and thirties, with meager rationalization on their part for their rather [Giorgio] de Chirico images.

Neither the expressionistic nor the eclectic approaches described above leaves much room for function. It seems that in the end pure functionalism in architecture has been deflected toward something more decorative where function is distorted for the sake of functionalist-structuralist styling or ignored as it is abstracted into pure symbolism. The definition of architecture as shelter with symbols on it presupposes an acceptance of the functional doctrine, not a rejection of it—an augmentation of it for the sake of maintaining it. Why not admit the impossibility of maintaining pure functionalism in architecture and the almost inevitable contradictions between functional and aesthetic requirements in the same building, and then let function and decoration go their own separate ways so that functional requirements need not be distorted for unadmitted decorative aims.

Mies van der Rohe and McDonald's Hamburger Stands

Our fourth comparison, between Mies van der Rohe and McDonald's hamburger stands, is to justify a particular kind of symbolism in architecture. We refer to Mies's work here as representative of the best in Modern architecture and to remind ourselves that Modern architecture went to the industrial vernacular for inspiration for its forms. Mies's work, after he came to the United States, is an even more literal adaptation of an industrial vernacular than Gropius's or Le Corbusier's. His almost Classical orders, derived from the exposed steel I-beams of a certain kind of American factory, were applied, as is well known, with artful contortion, almost as pilasters, to symbolize industrial process and pure order and yet to conform to acceptable standards of fire protection for nonindustrial buildings.

A "factory" of Mies's is vernacular art enhanced as fine art; a McDonald's on the strip is folk art derived from fine art. The history of art reveals many evolutions between low art and high art, back and forth: Third movement themes in the sonata form are scherzo folk tunes, plastic madonnas are Baroque survivals. The parabolic arches of a McDonald's pavilion—illuminated yellow plastic—produce a bold and picturesque image, an effective gestalt from the context of a car driving down the strip, but in the mind they symbolize advanced engineering and good eats.

I refer to the classic version of the pavilion with "structural" arches, rather than the tasteful version with mansard roof, current in our era of roadside beautification. But the iconographic evolution of the McDonald's arch is complex. In its original version it is perhaps derived from Le Corbusier's project, in the twenties, for the Palace of the Soviets, where the arch, in contrast to those of McDonald's, actually supports the roof by cables, and from Eero Saarinen's St. Louis arch, itself a symbol for the "gateway to the West." An original manifestation of the parabolic arch was Eugène Freyssinet's hangars at Orly—an almost pure engineering solution for spanning a great distance at a great height to economically house big dirigibles—whose form made a great impression on Modern architects. The final manifestation of the parabolic arch in these evolutions between high art and low art, form and symbol, and among engineering, architecture, and sculpture, is a commercial sign—the reincarnation of two parabolic arches as siamese twins and a letter of the alphabet—the Big M.

To say that a factory is beautiful was shocking fifty years ago. Since then the paintings of [Charles] Sheeler and [Fernand] Léger, the cover of *Fortune* magazine, the whole repertory and literature of Modern architecture and sculpture have made industrial forms easy to like. But the shock value of this revelation was of tremendous importance at the time. The history of art contains many examples of shock treatment as an aid to the understanding of art. *Épater le bourgeoisie* is a constant theme in the thinking, theorizing, and practice of Modern painters of the nineteenth century. The introduction of pagan Classical orders in fifteenth-century Florence must have had an effect on late Medieval critics akin to the indignation aroused among our orthodox critics by the "crass materialism of our mass society" represented in the commercial vernacular architecture we are looking at now. This kind of outrage does not apply to the exploitative labor practices associated with the beautiful cast-iron fronts of early capitalist loft buildings nor to the harsh realities behind the crafted forms and symbols of primitive villages so admired by the same critics today. And these latter-day Moderns fail to see the ironic parallel between their outrage over the commercial vernacular and that of their Beaux-Arts predecessors over the industrial vernacular as a source for fine art fifty years ago. There was shock value in the Romantic discovery of the natural landscape—of daffodils in fields as a fit subject for poetry, and of peasant architecture—in the Hameau off the allée at Versailles, as there was in the transposition of common speech in the prose and poetry of James Joyce and T. S. Eliot. Returning to the ordinary, looking at the existing again, enhancing the conventional, are old ways of making new art.

My second comparison illustrated the affinity of late Modern architecture to the Abstract Expressionism of the fifties. This fourth comparison connects with the 1850s which were the heyday of the Industrial Revolution. Although we refer to the Machine Aesthetic of the twenties, we tend to forget how much of the symbolism of Modern architecture is based on industrial forms, if not industrial process, and how very obsolete this basis is. Everyone else knows the Industrial Revolution is dead. Why don't the architects? Is it not time for architects to connect with some new revolution, perhaps the electronic one? The existing commercial Strip with moving lights and signs involving representation and symbolism and meaning, and elements far apart in space to accommodate cars moving and parked, is as relevant to us now as were the factories with their industrial processes and functional programs several generations ago. Of course this conclusion is made with hindsight; as artists we found we liked the Strip before we analyzed why it seemed right.

Scarlatti and the Beatles

A connoisseur of music will pride himself on the catholicity of his taste. He will play for his friends, on the same evening, records of Scarlatti *and* the Beatles. Why will this person accept in his own living room, where you would expect him to be not at all tolerant of intrusions on his sensibilities, what he will not accept in the landscape? Why will he be outraged by the local commercial strip at the edge of town, support sign control in the belief that the way to limit bad architecture is to limit the size of signs, and confidently join the local design review board as an architectural connoisseur too? Why will he condemn pop architecture and accept pop music? That Scarlatti will live one thousand years and the Beatles only fifty years is beside the point, and he knows it; there is room for, and need for, a hierarchy of musical forms in our lives. Why not the same thing for architectural forms in our landscapes?

The answer is that our connoisseur clings to outmoded ideas about architecture as a whole. One of these ideas is that there is one dominant and correct canon of taste in our culture and that any art where this canon has not been followed is deviant and inferior. Herbert Gans has effectively countered this idea as a sociologist in his work on the relativity of taste and by his enumeration of the multiple taste cultures in our society; in most fields and media other than those of architecture the heterogeneous quality and ethnic diversity of American culture is accepted and is considered one of the strengths of our culture.

Other ideas which influence our connoisseur are promoted by Modern architects and they concern aesthetic unity: Simple forms and pure order are the only good, and the architect (and later it would be the planner) will lead the community toward these goals. Gropius advocated "total design," but we are ending up with total control—total control through design review boards which promote high design, exclude popular architecture and in the process discourage quality in any architecture and stultify the diversity and hierarchy which have always been part of balanced and vital community architecture.

Plain and Fancy Architecture

As there is room for high design and popular art in the architecture of our communities, there is the need for plain and fancy styles of architecture. The strip, for instance, is the place not only for spectacular symbols, but also for conventional symbols. Most architectural complexes include hierarchies of architectural symbolism. They include original and special elements and conventional and ordinary elements—what we call plain and fancy styles—that are applied with a sense of appropriateness. The palazzo in an Italian town sits among its *contorni*—the name for the vegetables arranged beautifully around the meat in the serving platter at an important meal as well as for the plain architecture at the foot of fancy architecture. I am not advocating hierarchies based on a social caste system, but I am saying that an art school, for instance, is not a cathedral, and that most architecture in a normal context should be plain. Most Modern architects have tended to lose a sense of appropriateness in their urban renewal piazzas and in the often strident college campuses and towns where Modern architecture dominates. This is a plea for a symbolism of the ordinary in the ornament applied to shelter.

We have written, in *Learning from Las Vegas,* of our propensity as architects for modest architecture based at first on necessity, on our experience as a little firm with small jobs and limited budgets, then on an intuition that our situation had a general significance, and finally on a conviction that ours is not an era for heroic or pure architectural statements. Rhetoric for our landscape, when it is appropriate, will come from a less formal and more symbolic medium than pure architecture—perhaps from combinations of signs and sculpture and moving lights which decorate and represent. The source for our fancy architecture is in the conventions of the commercial strip. Its prototype is not the spatial Baroque monument, but the Early Christian basilica, that plain barn smothered in frescoes, the decorated shed par excellence. Ours is also not an era for expensive buildings: Our national budgets do not support the architectural glories of a Parthenon or a Chartres, our collective heart is not in architecture, our collective values direct us in other paths, sometimes social, often military, and our technology and our labor systems promote standard systems of conventional construction.

These are our reasons for advocating and for trying to design shelter with decoration on it: shelter as a manifestation of systems building, conventional in its form and ordinary in its symbolism, always plain and never fancy. But also shelter as a grid for decoration—ordinary in its symbolism if a plain style is appropriate (and it usually is) and heroic in its symbolism if (and only if) a fancy style is appropriate. Function and structure can now go their own ways without regard to rhetoric, and our glories can come perhaps from mass housing, universal and efficient as a structural shelter, but parochial and diverse in its ornamental and symbolic appliqué. This is a way to be sensitive to the practical needs and the expressive wants of the many different people in the world.

A Discussion of Architecture
(with Christopher Norris)
■ Jacques Derrida ■

Of circumstantial detail it is perhaps enough to record that this interview was conducted at Derrida's home near Paris during a two-hour session in March, 1988. . . .

In so far as one can define, explain or summarise the Deconstructionist project, one's account might go very briefly as follows. Deconstruction locates certain crucial oppositions or binary structures of meaning and value that constitute the discourse of 'Western metaphysics.' These include (among many others) the distinctions between form and content, nature and culture, thought and perception, essence and accident, mind and body, theory and practice, male and female, concept and metaphor, speech and writing etc. A Deconstructive reading then goes on to show how these terms are inscribed within a systematic structure of hierarchical privilege, such that one of each pair will always appear to occupy the sovereign or governing position. The aim is then to demonstrate—by way of close reading—how this system is undone, so to speak, from within; how the second or subordinate term in each pair has an equal (maybe a prior) claim to be treated as a *condition of possibility* for the entire system. Thus writing is regularly marginalised, denounced or put in its place—a strictly secondary, 'supplementary' place—by a long line of thinkers in the

"A Discussion of Architecture (with Christopher Norris)" by Jacques Derrida has been excerpted from *Architectural Design*, 59, Number 1–2 (1989), pages 7–11, and is reprinted by permission of the publisher.

Western tradition, from Plato and Aristotle to Rousseau, Husserl, Saussure, Lévi-Strauss and the latter-day structuralist sciences of man. But just as often—as Derrida shows in *Of Grammatology*—writing resurfaces to assert its claim as the repressed other of this whole logocentric tradition, the 'wandering outcast,' scapegoat or exile whose off-stage role is a precondition of the system. And this curious 'logic of supplementarity' operates wherever thinking is motivated by a certain constitutive need to exclude or deny that which makes it possible from the outset.

Now it is not hard to see how such a Deconstructive reading might affect the discourse of current (Post-Modern) architectural thought. Thus Peter Eisenman suggests that: 'the traditional opposition between structure and decoration, abstraction and figuration, figure and ground, form and function could be dissolved. Architecture could begin an exploration of the "between" within these categories. And Derrida has likewise written of an architectural 'supplementarity,' a movement of *différance* between and within concepts that would open up hitherto unthought-of inventive possibilities. The interview has a good deal to say about this in relation to Derrida's collaborative venture with Eisenman and Tschumi. . . .

Christopher Norris:

—Perhaps I could start by asking a perhaps rather naive question: Can there be such a thing as 'Deconstructivist art' or indeed 'Deconstructivist architecture'? That is to say, do these terms refer to a given style, project or body of work? Or do they not rather signify a certain way of looking at various works and projects, a perception that would break with (or at least seek to challenge) established ideas of form, value and aesthetic representation?

Jacques Derrida:

Well, I don't know . . . I must say, when I first met, I won't say 'Deconstructive architecture,' but the Deconstructive discourse on architecture. I was rather puzzled and suspicious. I thought at first that perhaps this was an analogy, a displaced discourse, and something more analogical than rigorous. And then—as I have explained somewhere—then I realised that on the contrary, the most efficient way of putting Deconstruction to work was by going through art and architecture. As you know, Deconstruction is not simply a matter of discourse or a matter of displacing the semantic content of the discourse, its conceptual structure or whatever. Deconstruction goes *through* certain social and political structures, meeting with resistance and displacing institutions as it does so. I think that in these forms of art, and in any architecture, to deconstruct traditional sanctions—theoretical, philosophical, cultural—effectively, you have to displace . . . I would say 'solid' structures, not only in the sense of material structures, but 'solid' in the sense of cultural, pedagogical, political, economic structures. And all the concepts which are, let us say, the target (if I may use this term) of Deconstruction, such as theology, the subordination of the sensible to the intelligible and so forth—these concepts are effectively displaced in order for them to become 'Deconstructive architecture.' That's why I am more and more interested in it, despite the fact that I am technically incompetent.

—Could you say a little more about your work with Bernard Tschumi and Peter Eisenman, and some of the collaborative projects under way in Paris at the moment?

Well, what I could do is just a narration of the way things happened. Once I had a phone call from Bernard Tschumi, who I didn't know at the time, except by reputation. Tschumi told me: 'Some architects today are interested in your work and would you be interested in working with some of them, or one of them, on a project in La Villette?' As you know, Tschumi is responsible for all the architecture at La Villette. Of course I was surprised, but my answer was 'Why not?' And so I had my first encounter with Tschumi and I began to look at those projects and to read some texts by Tschumi and Eisenman. Then I met Eisenman many times in New York. We worked together, we co-ordinated everything in discussion, and now there is a book which is soon to be published on these collaborations. My proposal was that we start with a text that I had recently written on Plato's *Timaeus* because it had to do with space, with Deconstruction, so to speak, 'in the universe.' It also had to do with a problem that I was interested in and that concerned, let us say, the *economic* determination of the way we usually read Plato. This strategic level was extremely important for me. So I gave this text to Peter Eisenman and in his own way he started a project that was correlated with but at the same time independent of my text. That was true collaboration—not 'using' the other's work, not just illustrating or selecting from it . . . and so there is a kind of discrepancy or, I would say, a productive dialogue between the concerns, the styles, the persons too. And so, after about 18 months' or two years' work, the project is now ready to be 'constructed,' you might say . . . to be realised . . .

—So it would be wrong to see this as a new 'turn' in your thinking, a sudden recognition of connections, affinities or common points of interest between Deconstruction and the visual arts? In fact there are many passages in your earlier writing—and I am thinking here of texts like Force and Significance *or* Genesis and Structure—*where the argument turns on certain crucial (let us say) metaphors of an architectural provenance. The context here was your joint reading of the structuralist and phenomenological projects—more specifically, of Saussure and Husserl—as two, equally rigorous but finally incompatible reflections on the character of language and meaning. Thus you write: 'The relief and design of structures appears more clearly when content, which is in the living energy of meaning, is neutralised. Somewhat like the architecture of an uninhabited or deserted city, reduced to its skeleton by some catastrophe of nature or art. A city no longer inhabited, not simply left behind, but haunted by meaning and culture.' And of course these architectural figures and analogies occur more often in your later writings on Kant and the tradition of Classical aesthetics (for instance, 'The Parergon' in* The Truth in Painting). *Thus for Kant,* architectonic *is defined as the 'art of systems,' that which articulates the various orders of truth-claim and ensures their proper (hierarchical) relationship one with another. So in a sense one*

could argue that your work has always been crucially concerned with 'architectural' models and metaphors. Do you perceive a clear continuity there, or am I just imagining all this?

No, not at all. But I would like to say something about the concept of analogy or metaphor you rightly used a moment ago. Of course there is a lot of architectural metaphor, not only in my texts but in the whole philosophical tradition. And Deconstruction—the word Deconstruction—sounds very much like such a metaphor, an architectural metaphor. But I think that it's more complex than that, since the word appeared or was underlined in a certain situation where structuralism was dominant on the scene. So Deconstruction shared certain motifs with the structuralist project while at the same time attacking that project. . . .

But Deconstruction doesn't mean that we have to stay within those architectural metaphors. It doesn't mean, for example, that we have to destroy something which is built—physically built or culturally built or theoretically built—just in order to reveal a naked ground on which something new could be built. Deconstruction is perhaps a way of questioning this architectural model itself—the architectural model which is a general question, even within philosophy, the metaphor of foundations, of superstructures, what Kant calls 'architectonic' etc. as well as the concept of the *arche* . . . So Deconstruction means also the putting into question of architecture in philosophy and perhaps architecture itself.

When I discovered what we now call 'Deconstructive architecture' I was interested in the fact that these architects were in fact deconstructing the essential of tradition, and were criticising everything that subordinated architecture to something else—the value of, let's say, usefulness or beauty or living—'*habite*'—etc.—not in order to build something else that would be useless or ugly or uninhabitable, but to free architecture from all those external finalities, extraneous goals. And not in order to reconstitute some pure and original architecture—on the contrary, just to put architecture in communication with other media, other arts, to *contaminate* architecture . . . And notice that in my way of dealing with Deconstruction I suspect the *concept* of metaphor itself, in so far as it involves a complicated network of philosophemes, a network that would always lead us back at some point into architecture . . .

As you know, I never use the word 'post,' the prefix 'post': and I have many reasons for this. One of those reasons is that this use of the prefix implies a periodisation or an epochalisation which is highly problematic for me. Then again, the word 'post' implies that something is highly finished—that we can get rid of what went *before* Deconstruction, and I don't think anything of the sort. For instance, to go back to the first point of your question. I don't believe that the opposition between concept and metaphor can ever be erased. I have never suggested that all concepts were simply metaphors, or that we couldn't make use of that distinction, because in fact at the end of that essay ['White Mythology'] I deconstruct this argument also, and I say that we need, for scientific reasons and many reasons, to keep this distinction at work. So this is a very complicated gesture.

Now as for architecture, I think that *Deconstruction* comes about—let us carry on using this word to save time—when you have deconstructed some architectural philosophy, some architectural assumptions—for instance, the hegemony of the aesthetic, of beauty, the hegemony of usefulness, of functionality, of living, of dwelling. But then you have to *reinscribe* these motifs within the work. You can't (or you shouldn't) simply dismiss those values of dwelling, functionality, beauty and so on. You have to construct, so to speak a new space and a new form, to shape a new way of building in which those motifs or values are reinscribed, having mean-while lost their external hegemony. The inventiveness of powerful architects consists I think in this reinscription, the economy of this reinscription, which involves also some respect for tradition, for memory. Deconstruction is not simply forgetting the past. What has dominated theology or architecture or anything else is still there, in some way, and the inscriptions, the, let's say, *archive* of these deconstructed structures, the archive should be as readable as possible, as legible as we can make it. That is the way I try to write or to teach. And I think the same is true, to some extent, in architecture. . . .

I wouldn't want to call Deconstruction a critique of modernity. But neither is it 'modern' or in any sense a glorification of modernity. It is very premature to venture these generalisations, these concepts of period. I would say that I just don't know what these categories mean, except that of course I can tell more or less what other people mean them to signify . . . But for me they are not rigorous concepts. Nor is Deconstruction a unitary *concept,* although it is often deployed in that way, a usage that I find very disconcerting . . . Sometimes I prefer to say deconstructions in the plural, just to be careful about the heterogeneity and the multiplicity, the necessary multiplicity of gestures, of fields, of styles. Since it is not a system, not a method, it cannot be homogenised. Since it takes the singularity of every context into account, Deconstruction is different from one context to another. So I should certainly want to reject the idea that 'Deconstruction' denotes any theory, method or univocal concept. Nevertheless it must denote *something,* something that can at least be recognised in its working or its effects . . .

Of course this doesn't mean that Deconstruction *is* that 'something,' or that you can find Deconstruction everywhere. So on the one hand we have to define some working notion, some regulative concept of Deconstruction. But it is very difficult to gather this in a simple formula. I know that the enemies of Deconstruction say: 'Well, since you cannot offer a definition then it must be an obscure concept and you must be an obscurantist thinker.' To which I would respond that Deconstruction is first and foremost a suspicion directed against just that kind of thinking—'what is . . . ?' 'what is the essence of . . . ?' and so on.

—Could we perhaps take that point a bit further? Some theorists of the Post-Modern (Charles Jencks among them) have rejected what they see as the negative, even 'nihilist' implications of the Deconstruction movement in contemporary art. According to Jencks, 'Architecture is essentially constructive. It builds up structures, depends on joint endeavours of mutual confidence, the combination of foresight, goodwill and investment—all of which Deconstruction undermines, if not totally destroys.' I thought you might like to comment on this and similar responses, especially in view of current debates—

*taken up in the American and British press—about the 'politics of Decon-
struction' and its supposed nihilist leanings. I'm sure you would say that they
have misunderstood.*

Absolutely, absolutely . . . There has been much criticism, many objections that we
find in the newspapers, in the bad newspapers . . . Which doesn't just mean that
the people who write such things are jealous. Often they are academics who don't
read the many texts in which not only I but many people insist on the fact that Deconstruction is *not* negative, is not nihilistic. Of course it goes through the experience and the questioning of what nihilism is. Of course, of course. And who knows
what nihilism is or isn't? Even the people who object don't raise the question
'What is nihilism?' Nevertheless, Deconstruction is or should be an affirmation
linked to promises, to involvement, to responsibility. As you know, it has become
more and more concerned with these concepts—even Classical concepts—of responsibility, affirmation and commitment . . . So when people say it's negative, nihilistic and so forth, either they don't read or they are arguing in bad faith. But this
can and should be analysed . . .

> —*In the* Aphorisms *you refer to an 'ageless contract' that has always existed
> between architecture and a certain idea of dwelling or habitation. And of
> course this points toward Heidegger and a whole thematics of building,
> dwelling, and poetic thinking. You also remark—in a slightly different but re-
> lated context—that 'there is no inhabitable place for the aphorism,' that is to
> say, no place within the kind of large-scale conceptual edifice that philoso-
> phy has traditionally taken for its home. Thus: 'The aphorism is neither a
> house, nor a temple, nor a school, nor a parliament, nor an agora, nor a
> tomb. Neither a pyramid nor, above all, a stadium. What else?' Could I ask
> you to pursue this particular line of thought in whatever direction you wish,
> and perhaps suggest also what connections it might have with your latest
> writings on Heidegger?*

Ah, that's a very difficult question . . .

> —*Yes, I'm sorry . . .*

No, no, not at all. Difficult questions are necessary. The fact that architecture has
always been interpreted as dwelling, or the element of dwelling—dwelling for human beings or dwelling for the gods—the place where gods or people are present
or gathering or living or so on. Of course this is a very profound and strong interpretation, but one which first submits architecture, what we call architecture or the
art of building, to a value which can be questioned. In Heidegger such values are
linked with the question of building, with the theme of, let's say, keeping, conserv-
ing, watching over, etc. And I was interested in questioning those assumptions in
Heidegger, asking what this might amount to, an architecture that wouldn't be simply subordinated to those values of habitation, dwelling, sheltering the presence of
gods and human beings. Would it be possible? Would it still be an architecture? I
think that what people like Eisenman and Tschumi have shown me—people who
call themselves Deconstructivist architects—is that this is indeed possible: not
possible as a *fact,* as a matter of simple demonstration, because of course you can

always perceive their architecture as again giving place to dwelling, sheltering, etc: because the question I am asking now is not only the question of what they build, but of how we interpret what they build. Of course we can interpret in a very traditional way—viewing this as simply a 'modern' transformation of the same old kinds of architecture. So Deconstruction is not simply an activity or commitment on the part of the architect; it is also on the part of people who read, who look at these buildings, who enter the space, who move in the space, who experience the space in a different way. For this point of view I think that the architectural experience (let's call it that, rather than talking about 'buildings' as such) . . . what they offer is precisely the chance of experiencing the possibility of these inventions of a different architecture, one that wouldn't be, so to speak, 'Heideggerian' . . .

> —*You have talked about the relationship between 'modernity' in art, architecture, philosophy etc., and a certain idea of the modern university, one that took hold in Germany a couple of centuries back and which still exerts a great influence on the way we think about disciplines, subject-areas, questions of intellectual competence, and so forth. And this would perhaps take us back to what you said previously about Kant's 'architectonic,' his doctrine of the faculties, that which enforces a proper separation of realms between pure and practical reason, theoretical understanding, aesthetic judgment and their various modalities or powers . . . To some extent your work in the International College is a way of deconstructing those relations, showing how they give rise to endless litigation or boundary-disputes, often played out in very practical terms as a matter of institutional politics . . .*

Oh yes, I agree with your definition of what is going on. Deconstructing not only theoretically, not only giving signals of the process at work, but trying to deconstruct in a practical fashion, that is, to set up and build new structures implying this work of Deconstruction. It's not easy, and it is never done in or through a single gesture. It takes a long time and involves some very complicated gestures. It is always unfinished, heterogeneous, and I think there is no such thing as a 'pure' Deconstruction or a deconstructive project that is finished or completed.

> —*Isn't there a risk that Deconstruction might become mixed up with that strain of Post-Modern or neo-pragmatist thought which says that philosophy is just a 'kind of writing,' on a level with poetry, criticism or the 'cultural conversation of mankind'? That these distinctions are merely 'rhetorical' or imposed by an obsolete 'enlightenment' doctrine of the faculties, so that we had best get rid of them and abandon any notion of philosophy as having its own special interests, distinctive truth-claims, conceptual history or whatever? Do you see that as a constant risk?*

There are many risks and this is one of them. Sometimes it is an intersting risk, sometimes it opens doors and spaces in the fields which are trying to protect themselves from Deconstruction. But once the door is open, then you have to make things more specific, and I would say, following your suggestion, that no indeed, philosophy is not *simply* a 'king of writing'; philosophy has a very rigorous specificity which has to be respected, and it is a very hard discipline with its own

152 ■ PART III   ARCHITECTURE AND THE THIRD DIMENSION

requirements, its own autonomy, so that you cannot simply mix philosophy with literature, with painting, with architecture. There is a point you can recognise, some opening of the various contexts (including the philosophical context) that makes Deconstruction possible. But it still requires a rigorous approach, one that would situate this opening in a strict way, that would organise, so to speak, this contamination or this grafting without losing sight of those specific requirements. So I am very suspicious—and this is not just a matter of idiosyncracy or a matter of training—I am very suspicious of the overeasy mixing of discourses to which your question referred. On the contrary, Deconstruction pays the greatest attention to multiplicity, to heterogeneity, to these sharp and irreducible differences. If we don't want to homogenise everything then we have to respect the specificity of discourses, especially that of philosophical discourse.

—*There is one particular essay of yours which I think may help to focus some of these questions. It is called 'Of an Apocalyptic Tone Recently Adopted in Philosophy,' a title that you borrow (or cite) verbatim from Kant, and it strikes me that there are two very different things going on throughout this text. In fact it is often hard to know whether you are writing, as it were, 'in your own voice' or whether the passage in question is* sous rature *or to be read as if placed within quotation-marks. Sometimes you write of the need to maintain 'Enlightenment' values, to preserve what you call the 'lucid vigil' of Enlightenment, critique and truth. In this sense the essay appears to side with Kant against the adepts, the mystagogues, the fake illuminati, those who would claim an immediate or self-present access to truth by virtue of their own 'inner light,' without submitting their claims to the democratic parliament of the faculties. Elsewhere you adopt your own version of the 'apocalyptic tone'—a series of injunctions, apostrophes, speech-acts or performatives of various kinds—as if to defend the right of these characters not to go along with Kant's rules for the proper, self-regulating conduct of philosophic discourse. It does seem to me a profoundly ambivalent essay. On the one hand it is establishing a distance—even an antagonism—between Deconstruction and the discourse of Enlightenment critique. On the other it is saying that the Kantian project is somehow* indispensable, *that it is bound up with the very destiny of thought in our time, that we cannot simply break with it as certain Post-Modernist thinkers would wish—or have I misread your essay in some fairly basic way?*

No, no, you read it very well. I agree with everything you said. It is a very, very ambivalent essay. I tried—as I often do—to achieve and say many things at once. Of course I am 'in favour' of the Enlightenment: I think we shouldn't simply leave it behind us, so I want to keep this tradition alive. But at the same time I know that there are certain historical forms of Enlightenment, certain things in this tradition that we need to criticise or to deconstruct. So it is sometimes in the name of, let us say, a *new* Enlightenment that I deconstruct a given Enlightenment. And this requires some very complex strategies; requires that we should let many voices speak . . . There is nothing monological, no monologue—that's why the responsibility for

Deconstruction is never individual or a matter of the single, self-privileged author-ial voice. It is always a multiplicity of voices, of gestures. . . . And you can take this as a rule: that each time Deconstruction speaks through a single voice, it's wrong, it is not 'Deconstruction' any more. So in this particular essay, as you rightly said a moment ago, not only do I let many voices speak at the same time, but the problem is precisely that multiplicity of voices, that variety of tones, within the *same* utterance or indeed the same word or syllable, and so on. So that's the question. That's one of the questions.

But of course today the political, ideological consequences of the Enlighten-ment are still very much with us—and very much in need of questioning. So a 'new' enlightenment, to be sure, which may mean Deconstruction in its most active or intensive form, and not what we inherited in the name of *Aufklärung,* critique, *siècle des lumières* and so forth. And as you know, these are already very different things. So we have to remember this.

> —*I suppose I'm looking for some kind of equivalence between what we call 'Modernism' in philosophy, let's say Kantian philosophy, and the term 'Mod-ernism' as conventionally applied in architecture and the visual arts. You might compare the attitude that Deconstructivist architects take toward Modernism—not simply one of rejection or supercession, but a critical atti-tude directed toward that particular form of Modernist critique. . . .*

Of course. That's why I'm reluctant to say that Deconstruction is Modern or Post-Modern. But I should also be reluctant to say that it's not Modern, or that it's anti-Modern, or anti-Post-Modern. I wouldn't want to say that what is Deconstructive, if there is such a thing, is specifically Modern or Post-Modern. So we have to be very careful with the use of these epithets.

The Dislocation of the Architectural Self
■ David Goldblatt ■

Enjoying a mild rejuvenation on the contemporary American drug scene, our word 'ecstacy,' like the English words 'derange' and 'delirium,' has its history in spatial terms. The Greek *ecstasis* meaning to put outside, to put out of place, led to the no-tion of being besides oneself, of being transported. In moral theory (I have Kant in mind) the idea of acting against ourselves is often seen as imperative and the prob-lem of distancing, if not removing ourselves from our passions and other inclina-tions, is compounded by our own questionable ability to recognize just when we

"The Dislocation of the Architectural Self" by David Goldblatt has been excerpted from *The Journal of Aesthetics and Art Criticism* (Fall 1991), pages 337–340, 344–347, and is reprinted by per-mission of the publisher.

have succeeded. In art, too, *ecstasis* has had its own place, especially as the self encounters itself as quotidian being. In this paper I will discuss what I believe is the role of *ecstasis* in recent architectural practice, specifically in the work of the American architect Peter Eisenman.

Peter Eisenman's architecture recognizes and reflects a paradox regarding the architectural self: that the architect creates institutions—e.g., the home, the city, but as an inventive force—must also resist the very process of institutionalizing these very commissioned projects. As Eisenman puts it, "In order to be, it must always resist being. . . . This is the paradox of architecture. Thus, in order to reinvent a site . . . the idea of site must be freed from its traditional places, histories, and systems of meaning. This involves the dislocation of the traditional interpretation of its elements." Eisenman's work constitutes an architecture that is somehow removed from an unreinvented architectural milieu, one requiring an architect who will break with architecture's own hierarchical presuppositions.

Under these provisional assumptions rests a deeper difficulty: Breaking with such presuppositions cannot simply be a matter of the architect's choosing to do so. The architect is coimplicated in the tradition of architecture, through schooling, apprenticeship and professional reward as well as by the usual devices of enculturation. The architect comes to understand and to respect architecture as traditionally conceived. And since architecture *qua* artform is also inextricably meshed with everyday life, the impact of culture is also an everyday, ingraining phenomenon. Some, like Alan Colquhoun, appreciate at least part of the negotiated condition of architecture, if only as a matter of degrees of distinction from other arts: "With architecture so bound to the sources of finance and power, it is much more difficult for the architect than for other artists to operate within an apparently autonomous subculture or to retain independence from bourgeois taste that has been the ambition of art since the early nineteenth century." To name oneself as architect is to pose within the context of a tradition, one constituted by expectations, privileges and obligations. I am calling the self that works within the context of a traditional architecture, an architecture of everyday practice, "the architectural self." By definition, the architectural self does not feel the force of Eisenman's paradox. Eisenman's concern is not so much about whether good or interesting work can be produced within architecture's traditional presuppositions; rather, he is skeptical about whether a more "speculative," exploratory architecture, an architecture that investigates its own assumptions, can be designed by a self whose work is an expression of traditional tastes, beliefs and principles.

On the basis of Eisenman's understanding of the architects' situation, the architect ought to attempt to employ a *strategy* that removes that aspect of the coimplicated self from their architecture. It is a matter of the self's not being able to trust the self, in the manner of Kant's heteronymous will being an unreliable trustee for the moral restraint upon desire. Part of the problem, Eisenman has come to suspect, is that there may be "a powerful anthropomorphism operating at the level of the unconscious wish" in entrenched architectural practice. As Jeffrey Kipnis has put it, "Architecture in the service of institution is architecture in the service of man as he wants to see himself and to continue seeing himself. As such, it is a denial of architecture as a, perhaps the, vehicle of becoming." An architectural process that does not privilege those features that assume "man" as the measure of all things architectural may be a way of revealing what the architecture of tradition and the traditional self have repressed, it may be a way, in Derrida's phrase, of "letting other voices speak." A strategy is needed to remove the architect as a source of resistance to non-traditional architecture so that design can begin from a dislocated vantage point. I would like to consider *one* strategy Eisenman employs to achieve this dislocation—the use of a series of architectural moves that center on the notion of "arbitrary text." Eisenman uses the arbitrary text in order to initiate design subsequent to the interruption of the self's usual propensities while doing architecture.

In the course of analyzing what ought to happen to the self of the architect in the context of this strategy, I . . . mention briefly some neglected but provocative ideas from the final chapter of Arthur Danto's *The Transfiguration of the Commonplace*. Danto . . . and Eisenman discuss the dislocation of some version of a *commonplace* self uprooted by a mechanism analytically related to art, with the result in each case being some *extraordinary* self-situation. For Danto and Eisenman the dislocation takes place by means of an "outside" text and can be attributed to some metaphorical aspect of it. Although Danto gives the commonplace/extraordinary dichotomy a central place in his analysis, I want to show that that distinction only instantiates selves that are substantially different from each other. Danto's dislocation is the result of an arbitrary intersection of one "life" metaphorically brought to bear upon some status quo self, e.g., a reader of texts, ordinary or not. Peter Eisenman, on the other hand, seeks the arbitrary in his architecture in order to dislocate the coimplicated self of the traditional architect by virtue of the kind of metaphorical structure recognized by Danto, a metaphorical structure which in its limiting and most arbitrary case, is *catachresis*. The early Nietzsche, like Eisenman, is interested in shaking off the anthrocentric in order to latch onto a power repressed by an externalized quotidian life, a power, according to Nietzsche, internally related to the self of the artist. But first some background and a characterization of the problem at hand must be given.

In the summer of 1988 New York's Museum of Modern Art hosted an exhibit called "Deconstructivist Architecture." "Deconstructivist Architecture" was curated by Philip Johnson and Mark Wigley in Johnson's first major museum project since his 1932 landmark show that introduced the International Style to America. The new exhibit intended to group together seven important architects that by some stretch of the imagination could be called "deconstructivists." (Not merely a variation of "deconstructionist," the term indicates the art born in pre-revolutionary Russia, since they commonly challenged some of the more central traditional aspects of architecture like unity, stability, harmony, comfort and function.) Deconstruction in architecture has come to be seen as a vital response to the historically necessary, but much more facile, architectural postmodernism as well as to a broadly construed notion of classical/modern architecture. But it must be kept in mind that far from being the name of an architectural movement or school, 'decon-structivism' refers at best to the practices of a loose set of diverse members many of whom would justifiably resist that or any other label. Peter Eisenman, one of two Americans in the MOMA show (the other was Frank Gehry), is no exception.

As an example of an attempt to deny the privileging of one or more of the traditional aspects of architecture consider an Eisenman project, his award-winning Guardiola House. Proposed for a site high above the Atlantic on the Spanish Costa de la Luz near Cadiz, it is a startling but also beautiful weekend residence for a single father and his grown son. It has windows in the floor and floors that are unlevel. It is sometimes necessary to go outside to get into another room and the house itself is split by an exterior stairway rising from the sea. The Guardiola House appears fragmented, if not tortured and shaky.

According to Eisenman, the Guardiola design researches the meaning of place or *topos* as part of "the breakdown of the traditional forms of place," and results in something "between place and object, between container and contained." This "simultaneity of two traditionally contradictory states' is to be found in the *Timaeus* in Plato's definition of the receptacle (*chora*), which is, roughly, like a holding place for office (as in political office) but does not exist as a sensible or even intelligible thing itself. Derrida has recently written an essay entitled "Chora," and Eisenman's "research" here exemplifies the usual Derridian breakdown of binary oppositions which Eisenman sometimes expresses as *betweenness.* Working *between* can be characterized as suspending the privilege of one member of a binary opposition at the expense or the devaluation of another. (Eisenman, whose architecture has put into use a network of concepts taken from the writings of Jacques Derrida, has collaborated with Derrida on the design of a garden in Bernard Tschumi's Parc de la Villette in Paris, 1985.) The contemporary philosophical critique of foundational binary oppositions by postmodern thinkers following the lead of Heidegger or Derrida has been given an architectural context by Eisenman: "Traditional opposition between structure and decoration, abstraction and figuration, figure and ground, form and function could be dissolved. Architecture could begin an exploration of the 'between' within these categories." Eisenman's Wexner Center for the Visual Arts at the Ohio State University in Columbus, explores the betweenness of architectural binary opposition. For example, the 516 foot-long, white, uncovered, three-dimensional grid, running almost the entire length of the site, at full-building scale, as "scaffolding" (the temporary, tentative construction apparatus) that remains prominently and permanently there after the structure is completed, falls somewhere between process and product, past and present, shelter and non-shelter, structure and form, structure and ornament, building and non-building, exterior and interior. (More on Wexner later.)

Although Eisenman's projects tend to look significantly different from other architectures, Eisenman neither aims at avant-gardism nor directs his projects towards the manipulation of forms or towards works that please aesthetically. Architecture, according to Eisenman, has the potential to join other artists in a deep exploration of meaning. In the unconcealing or opening of meanings that are often

Peter Eisenman and Richard Trott, *Wexner Center for the Visual Arts and Fine Arts Library,* **The Ohio State University, Columbus (1989) East Elevation.**

Peter Eisenman and Richard Trott, *Wexner Center for the Visual Arts and Fine Arts Library,* **The Ohio State University, Columbus (1989) South Elevation.**

Source: Reproduced by courtesy of Eisenman Architects.

hidden beneath a commonplace traditional surface or among the relationship between traditional objects, that which is not laid bare is often if not always that
which is repressed by traditional forms of meaning. An architecture that is not
merely emblematic of status quo interests or desires, one that can "let other voices
speak," is as capable of engaging in the same tensions between tradition and innovation as painting or literature. A nontraditional architecture can "surgically open
up the Classical and the Modern to find what is repressed."

Indeed for Eisenman the differences between classical and modern architecture are insignificant; in fact, Eisenman often thinks of modernism as merely another form of classicism. Traditional architecture, then, will include the work of
modernists such as Mies, Corbusier and Loos, despite their reputation to the contrary. Eisenman is clear on the reduction of the modern to the classical tradition:

> In trying to reduce architectural form to its essence, to a pure reality, the moderns as-
> sumed they were transforming the field of referential figuration to that of non-
> referential 'objectivity.' In reality, however, their 'objective' forms never left the classi-
> cal tradition. They were simply stripped down classical forms, or forms referring to a
> new set of givens (function, technology). Thus Corbusier's houses that look like modern
> steamships or biplanes exhibit the same referential attitude toward representation as a
> Renaissance or "classical" building.

Eisenman's dislocation from the traditional architectural self in such projects as the
Wexner Center includes dislocation from the self that works in the mode of modern
architecture which Eisenman sees as significantly classical even in the period of its
inception. On his view, differences between the classic and the modern do not run
deep. According to Eisenman, then, the metaphysical presuppositions of architecture, architectural essence as traditionally conceived, are the same for modernism
as they are for classicism.

The Wexner Center and the Guardiola House instantiate one general problem
facing Eisenman: how to make architecture that is unhierarchical, that avoids the
"powerful anthrocentrism" mentioned above. Such an architecture would refuse to
acknowledge the stability of the concept of architecture which is buttressed by a
grounding metaphysics of essentiality and which, in turn, allows for the appearance
of the timeless self-evidence of architecture's "essential" features. "Deconstruction," Derrida has said, "is first and foremost a suspicion directed against just that
kind of thinking—'what is . . . ?' 'what is the essence of?' " The seeming self-
evidence of such features constitute what Kipnis has called, "a resistance, a received
value-structure by which architecture is repressed." Eisenman's aim is to refuse the
privileged status of these anthrocentric features—to deny their centrality, their favored position in the *praxis* of design. But this task is only compounded by the situation of the self when the self is making architecture. The traditional architectural
self is inclined not only to celebrate and express the anthrocentric essentials of traditional architecture but also to make architecture that looks and feels like traditional architecture, i.e., to be pleased and feel perceptually and emotionally satisfied
by what is "designed." The problem at hand is not to be underestimated.

If the quotidian architectural self is itself suspect, it will not do to *express* that self that makes design merely a matter of taste or preference. "A major displacement," Eisenman says, "concerns the role of the architect/ designer and the design process. Something may be designed which can be called displacing, but it may be only an expressionism, a mannerist distortion of an essentially stable language. It may not displace the stable language, but on the contrary further stabilize its normative condition. This can be seen in many examples of current architectural fashion. There is a need for process other than an intuition—'I like this,' or 'I like that.' When the process is intuitive it will already be known, and therefore complicit with the repressions inherent in architectural 'knowledge.' " Architects, then, like to "design," to make buildings that are visually pleasing, to join and further entrench the history of architecture: to make "architecture." Derrida says, "Let us never forget that there is an architecture of architecture. Down even to its archaic foundation, the most fundamental concept of architecture has been constructed." He continues:

> This architecture of architecture has a history, it is historical through and through. Its heritage inaugurates the intimacy of our economy, the law of our hearth (*oikos*), our familial, religious and political 'oikonomy,' all the places of birth and death, temple, school, stadium, agora, square, sepulchre. It goes right through us (*nous transit*) to the point that we forget its very historicity: We take it for nature. It is common sense itself.

According to Derrida then, the commonsensicality of a *certain* metaphysics of architecture has come to present itself as *architecture itself* masking the correct view that the concept of architecture is itself a construct. Once this is understood it is possible, if not yet practical, for the architect to question stability and to explore and initiate other architectures. But practical autonomy in architecture requires something else. "Autonomy . . . depends," Eisenman says in his *Houses of Cards,"* on distancing both the architect from the design process and the object from a traditional history." But since the architect is already coimplicated, perhaps as an unwitting party to the process of design, it cannot *simply* be a matter of choosing to do so. The issue of distancing oneself from the process of architecture is the problem of distancing oneself from oneself, the issue of *ecstasis*. . . .

The dislocation of the architectural self requires a strategy, and one such strategy includes positing a text that will bring into question those architectural assumptions. But such a text cannot be one of the traditional texts of architecture. Instead, Eisenman reaches for an outside text that, relative to some particular current project, is accidental or arbitrary.

The history of the meaning of the word 'arbitrary' seems to have undergone a reversal of sorts with respect to the idea of the will. Once meaning 'that which was a result of the preference *or* will of an arbiter in contrast to being governed or determined by rule or law alone,' 'arbitrary' now seems to designate, at least in some domains, the quality of being selected by preference or impulse only but not really chosen, i.e., not a product of the will. The notion of an arbitrary text continues to include the idea of being generated by an arbiter, a textual arbiter which, like a law, stands *outside* its object of application. Such a textual arbiter may even be selected *more or less* at random and not itself really the product of the will of the selector. This needs certain qualification, but means that although the selector does not know the full consequences of the text for the architectural project beforehand, he or she is nevertheless willing to accept those consequences even if they violate the architect's good, traditional sense: his or her tastes or preferences or those characterstics such as function or harmony, which are traditionally understood to constitute essential architectural conditions.

Wittgenstein said in 1931 that, " 'Arbitrary' as we normally use it always has reference to some practical end: e.g., if I want to make an efficient boiler I *must* fulfill certain specifications, but it is quite arbitrary what colour I paint it." Since willing in traditional architecture tends to be willing toward the constructed metaphysical essentials of entrenched architectural practice, it is possible to say that, by virtue of the arbitrary text, Eisenman, for a specified period during an architectural project, reverses the usual opposition between essence and accident. A reversal of the relationship between traditional architectural essence and accident does not necessarily result in the absence of a traditionally essential quality, say shelter, from an architectural project any more than Wittgenstein's boiler is uncolored. Accidents (in a double sense of that word) are incorporated into the project as practical ends, and traditional essences now become accidents of the project. Acting as the result of some arbitrary text helps remove the architect as a source of resistance toward *establishing* essential/traditional ends as privileged architectural goals including one of a pair of the sets of binary oppositions now held in suspension.

The idea behind an arbitrary text in the context of the dislocation of the self is to remove the hands from the hands of the architect, to eliminate a major motivation from a highly motivated self in order to place the self in a new position regarding its own work. By removing an initiating constituent in the traditional design process the outside text diminishes, but does not eliminate, the architect's role overall in making well-entrenched architecture. The arbitrary text is a text lifted from its own home, its own context, rationale and motivation, its own traditional place and utilized in some materially applicable respect. In a certain sense then, the arbitrary text is context-free, i.e., it is free of the context of the project at hand. Eisenman has used the Derridian notion of *grafting* to express the transplanting of this "other" text onto a particular architectural project.

It seems to me that there are at least two relevant senses in which a text can be context-free. First, a text can be free of or outside architecture as traditionally understood, i.e., a non-architectural text; and second, it can stand outside the traditional subject matter of the project at hand. Eisenman's use of DNA in his BioCentrum research laboratories at the J. W. Goethe University, Frankfurt-am-Main is an example of the former, while his use of scaffolding for the Columbus city grid in the design for the Wexner Center comes at least close to being a example of the latter. Let me call a text that is arbitrary in both of the above senses a *strongly* arbitrary text and a text that is arbitrary in only one of those senses arbitrary in the *weak* sense. It must be said that to the best of my knowledge, Eisenman has never made use of an arbitrary text in the strong sense outside of studio exercises.

The arbitrary text works by the architect's choosing some *materially applicable* aspect of that text, by juxtaposing it to the usual texts of architecture and assigning it more or less equal influence in the final design. In a theoretically limiting case neither will dominate, and the result will be the *betweeness* mentioned earlier. Those aspects then make their appearance in the design as "traces," fragmented signs that indicate but do not image the arbitrary text. The "architect" will also be *between* in a sense: between the architect coimplicated in the institutional history of architecture and an other if noncharacterized self, dislocated but ready to work with design possibilities that intersect the immediate project but are accidental relative to it.

The arbitrary text functions analogically, which implies that only certain of its aspects are contextually transplanted by the architect. The applied aspects of the arbitrary text may surface in the architectural project more or less obviously but in any case are themselves chosen from the text by the architect. There is, then, by virtue of certain shared features, an analogical relationship between the project and the arbitrary text. But the analogy is a peculiar one since the consequences of its use are not entirely worked out. It works, for a time at least, like a metaphor postponed. Since the analogous features of the arbitrary text, now analogue, have not yet been considered, the new insight or vision essential to metaphor is incomplete or open. In the case of the strongly arbitrary text the relationship between new architectural text and arbitrary text may be uninterpretable, the connection not or not yet bearing the metaphorical fruit of novelty or insight. If it does not, *catachresis* takes place, i.e., an abuse of words, a misuse of words, a "forced metaphor" with the structure of metaphor but lacking in metaphorical illustrativeness.

As the result of the imposition of a metaphorical structure on a traditional project by virtue of an arbitrary text, catachresis generates what is traditionally inappropriate. In the practice of architecture it holds before the architect a new value, a polar absence whose possibility of meaning must fall between the initial and the catachretic. Forced metaphor provides a greater "hang time" (to borrow from the sporting life) than ordinary metaphor, where familiarity and propriety lubricate the closure of the activity (the *energeia*) initiated by metaphoric introduction. It is the tension and the possibility for play, along this detour towards and away from meaning, that prompts Derrida to think of catachreses as "*revelation,* unveiling, bringing to light, truth," and why its role is so central for philosophy.

In the case of the strongly arbitrary text there is no guarantee that interesting connections or meaningful relationships will result between new architecture and outside text, although configurational similarities in the form of traces might prevail. Whether these similarities are meaningful at the time of application is out of the control of the no-longer-designing architectural self. But it is precisely this juxtaposition of entities that creates a tension outside the traditional limitations of meaning channeling thought somewhere between the two. Not unlike the Apollonian imposition upon the Dionysian, it is in the words of Eisenman, "a controlled accident." It is metaphor without an end or goal produced by removing the self from its original pursuit of meaning and purpose.

While the architect *chooses* the arbitrary text, the choice is made without deliberation and without knowingly exploiting its potentially metaphorical features for the project. It is an act of conscious disavowal on the part of the self. So that even if the architect chooses the text by the aforementioned tastes and preferences, the arbitrary text replaces the architect in the role of arbiter (worker). In the Wexner Center, for example, which is in part determined by two different sets of intersecting axes (city and campus grids at 12¼ degree angles), a column is allowed to fall on the steps of a major stairway and a dominant enclosed form determined in part by those axes in conjunction with the three-dimensional use of Eisenman's permanent "scaffolding," has no practical function whatsoever, i.e., it is not a space in which anything happens. (Campus lingo has dubbed it "student housing.") A commitment to the arbitrary text on the part of the architect assures that traditional texts are violated. It will sometimes call for compromises with those traditionally essential features of architecture, such as function or shelter, even if the result will be inconvenience or discomfort (or the appearance or representation of such) to the inhabitants of the dwelling.

The employment of the arbitrary text is part of a strategy to undermine the search for origin, to work with "starting points without value," as Eisenman puts it. "'Not-classical' origins," he says, "can be strictly arbitrary." Once the self-evident characteristic of architecture is dismissed, "architecture is seen as having no a priori origins—whether functional, divine or natural—alternative fictions for the origin can be proposed: for example, one that is *arbitrary,* one that has no external values derived from meaning, truth or timelessness." When Eisenman says that the arbitrary is that without origin or value, he has not lost the strong connection with the arbitrary as accidental or unwilled. It is the traditional text that has a place or origin, a meaning that is presupposed by the willer who must know that use or meaning in its proper context. But the unwilled, arbitrary text is outside the tradition, is outside the language-game in which it gains its home or original use. Outside of that, it no longer has its original value, carrying only traces of its "original" or traditional meaning, its function as a sign. With apologies to Aristotle, we see, outside these points of traditional obligation, there is nothing but gods and beasts. And they are untrustworthy and unpredictable.

With respect to the Wexner Center, the completed project is itself what Eisenman calls "a non-building—an archaeological earthwork whose essential elements are scaffolding and landscaping." It instantiates his concept of betweenness. Fractured and looking incomplete, the project nevertheless *functions, shelters* etc., but unlike "modern" architecture, neither *represents,* celebrates nor monumentalizes, function or shelter. It is a Center without a center or an obvious front or back and without some single White House-like gestalt. From one look we have no idea what the rest of it is like.

Eisenman is perfectly comfortable with the idea that he would never want to live in one of his own houses. He is after all, a commonplace dweller, a self replete with resistance and repression, a self seeking traditional comforts. But the issue here is no more one about satisfying human comfort than Kant's concern about morality was the fulfillment of human desire. And while the categorical imperative is anything but arbitrary in that it is a paradigm of logocentric enlightened thinking, it, like the arbitrary text, is *outside* of but applicable within the anthrocentric sphere. In any case, Eisenman's didactic place in contemporary culture should not be evaluated by what I am calling the "manifesto mentality," a belief that in the best of all possible worlds a given kind of art would replace all other artworks. Fortunately for Eisenman there are those persons and institutions who are interested in consuming an architecture that grows out of a suspicion of Enlightenment values. For Eisenman it is an architecture of betweenness; one that refuses to accept the "self-evidence" of the concept of architecture and one that explores extended modes of architectural meaning.

As explained at the outset, I consider this paper an outline that mentions numerous issues without always fully recognizing the problematic nature of those raised. Nevertheless, I hope that the breadth achieved here in drawing together a range of architecturally related items will compensate for this unavoidable omission.

Architecture is usually not the paradigm used by philosophers when dealing with artworks. As was the case for Kant, Ruskin and Loos among others, this probably stems from architecture's role in commonplace life, its questionable status as a pure artwork, its position as hybrid. Unlike the Bacchic festivals or the novels and paintings of contemporary life, architecture in a sense is not merely aberration, a deviance from the everyday that we visit but from which we easily extract ourselves. Wherever architecture is it is enmeshed in forms of life rather than juxtaposed to it. Such a condition simultaneously makes resistance to the hierarchical values of architecture all the more difficult and its overcoming all the more important. Where we no longer ask for feelings of comfort and soothing ideas in other artworks, it still *seems* reasonable to question the need for an architecture that may leave our daily satisfactions shaken or disoriented. But there is also, I suspect, a feeling that architecture lacks a certain philosophical depth that paintings and novels do not. Some recent, important work in architecture, Eisenman's among it, should change all that. In any case, Eisenman's architecture is inseparable from philosophical thinking, for example, thinking about the possibilities of self.

Nolo Contendere
■ Jeffrey Kipnis ■

Jeffrey Kipnis paid ASSEMBLAGE $150.00 to publish this piece.
 I. Plea
   On all charges, I, deconstruction, plea: Nolo Contendere.
 II. Abstract
   1. The meaning of any work is undecidable.
   2. Inasmuch as a work aspires to meaning, it represses undecidability.
   3. It is both possible and desirable to work in such a way as to respect undecidability.
 III. Brief
   1. The meaning of any work is undecidable.

Perhaps the most difficult and virulent aspect of deconstruction is to be found in its many demonstrations of this principle. Every work—written, spoken, performed, drawn, or built—is considered to be decidable in principle, that is, to have an ultimate reason, explanation, meaning, or finite set of meanings (hereafter referred to collectively as "meaning") that could be fully exposed and comprehended. The Western critical and philosophical tradition has been conditioned by this assumption of teleological decidability, conditioned, that is, to a pursuit of the meaning of the underlying work in question, whether a dialogue by Plato, an experiment by Galileo, a play by Shakespeare, or a building by Mies [van der Rohe]. In this tradition, difficulties encountered in the pursuit of the meaning of any particular work are attributed to exigencies of circumstance. Insufficient or incorrect information, bias, prejudice, and so forth distort the ultimate meaning of the work in question, delaying its achievement.

Deconstruction, on the other hand, contends that the very condition that enables a work to produce any meaning at all guarantees that it must produce many meanings simultaneously, including those that are contradictory, unintended, and undesirable. Thus, a work is in its essence undecidable; the difficulties in determining the meaning of a work do not obtain merely from the circumstance of its analysis but are an intrinsic property of the work itself.

To demonstrate undecidability in its most insistent forms, deconstruction has articulated a catalogue of notions such as difference, trace, and supplement, a detailed treatment of which is beyond the scope of this brief. Some sense of the argument can be gathered, however, from the following simplification. In order for there to be meaning at all, one entity must refer to another, a signifier must refer to a signified. For this to be possible, two conditions

"Nolo Contendere" by Jeffrey Kipnis is from *Assemblage* Number 11 (1990), pages 54–57, and is reprinted by permission of the publisher.

are implied: The signifier must be able to refer and the signified must be able to be referred to. Yet every entity—a word, an object, a building, and so on—can both refer to other entities and be referred to by other entities. For example, a black cat can be referred to by the phrase "that is a black cat" and, as well, refer to something else, as then it is taken to be an omen of bad luck.

Every "thing," therefore, is constructed as a "thing" in a field of reference. Before there can be meaning as proper reference there must be reference in general. The conditions of reference in general are primordial and essential, anterior to any thing, origin, or ground. Thus the very conditions that make meaning possible also guarantee its subversion. Inasmuch as the articulation of existence ("that is a black cat") is the fundament of proper referral, it must be concluded that, though the conditions of reference are real, they do not exist. They are the very possibilities of existence, of "things," "presence," "origins," and "grounds," each of which is an aspect of proper reference.

As a consequence, there can be no pure signifier nor any final signified. All "things" are constructed by and construct an interminable web, a textile of referral in which no proper beginning nor authentic end can be located, no privileged path of reference identified. Though the necessary conditions for decidable meaning (origin, linearity, and termination of reference) exist, they are not real. The term text, with its constellation of words such as texture, textile, and context, has come to be used in deconstruction to invoke the undecidable matrix of referral.

2. Inasmuch as a work aspires to meaning, it represses undecidability.

Meaning is wrought from the undecidable text only when a portion of the field of reference has been provisionally and contingently isolated or "framed," that is, when most of the interminable directions of reference are repressed so that one privileged direction of referral emerges, as if from a signifier to a signified. Yet the other threads of reference cannot simply be erased to yield the desired meaning. Framing produces meaning only in and as the violent repression of other strands of meaning, which nevertheless continue to occupy the text, a condition that deconstruction, borrowing from Freud, refers to as the return of the repressed.

Recognizing not only the inevitability but the necessity of meaning, deconstruction does not call for an overthrow of all work aspiring to meaning. Rather, deconstruction operates to keep in motion the contingent and provisional status of meaning, thereby preventing any position, radical or conservative, from gaining absolute privilege. Beyond this, deconstruction has no position.

3. It is both possible and desirable to work in such a way as to respect undecidability.

While all frames are provisional and contingent, always changing and context dependent, frames as such are not optional; there is no such condition as pure, unframed text, present in its naked undecidability. Everything is always already framed text. Thus the concern of deconstruction is not and cannot be to overthrow meaning per se.

Deconstruction does not render works—artistic, political, social, philosophical, etc.—meaningless, despite the relentless efforts to characterize it as doing so. Nor does it dissolve the object. Though it does indeed subvert every analysis, theory, philosophy, or phenomenology of the object, and thus may be said to dissolve the "classical object," insofar as it articulates the inevitability and irrepressibility of framing it also maintains the object.

The concerns of deconstruction are twofold: first, to destabilize the meaning of apparently stable works and, secondly, to produce self-destabilizing works. In the first of its concern, deconstruction displays the contingency of the framing under which any work is held to have canonic meaning by "reframing" that work, that is, by revisiting and respecting it in such a way as to mobilize the many repressed threads of meaning within the work while strictly adhering to the work itself. In so doing, deconstruction not only reads some of the possible but repressed other meanings, but also exposes mechanisms of repression and the agendas that those repressive mechanisms serve.

In the second of its concerns, deconstruction seeks to produce work in respect of undecidability, that is, work that, though not meaningless, does not simply give itself over to meaning. Such works resist, defer, and destabilize meaning by lending themselves to many frames while not allowing any particular frame to gain a foothold from which to narrow and confine the work to one particular meaning.

This aspect of deconstruction aspires to produce a work that is neither meaningful nor meaningless. Hence, strictly speaking, these endeavors cannot be considered as directed toward the development of a new "type" of work in as much as "type" is a concept intimately connected to decidability and therefore to a particular frame. Rather, these works seek to destabilize the order, anteriority, and decidability of type as such.

Nature and Art
■ Donald Crawford ■

This essay explores one general type of relationship between the natural and the artifactual that manifests itself in diverse, aesthetically significant contexts. I believe this relationship is best described as "dialectical," and I shall use that term even though I realize that this raises issues concerning the historical uses of that concept which cannot be fully dealt with here. Let us begin, therefore, with what is a very

"Nature and Art" by Donald Crawford has been excerpted from *The Journal of Aesthetics and Art Criticism* (Fall 1983), pages 49–57, and is reprinted by permission of the publisher.

general and I hope non-controversial concept of the dialectical. In a dialectical relationship, the two terms of the relation designate conflicting forces. It is common, in addition, to apply this relation to cases in which the conflicting interaction brings into being some third object. In the applications we shall consider, this third object is identified with the object of aesthetic attention or appreciation. Thus the two terms designate forces whose conflicting interaction is a determining factor in the constitution of the object of appreciation. In other words, the aesthetic appreciation can be seen as relating to both natural and artifactual elements interacting in other than purely harmonious or straight-forwardly causal ways. I hope the examples provided will make the thesis clearer.

In classical and neoclassical aesthetics, there is nothing dialectical in the relationship between art and nature, nature provides the model for artistic composition and there is, presumably, a harmonious relationship between the two. Conversely, some have suggested that in the aesthetic appreciation of scenery for its pictorial or compositional values, art (especially painting) is the model for an aesthetics of nature, and from the aesthetic standpoint nature is following art. But here, too, nature and art would be in a harmonious relationship, reenforcing one another in a process that leads to a stable, non-dialectical object of aesthetic appreciation.

It might be suggested that these models fail to involve a dialectical relationship between art and nature *not* because of the presence of *harmony,* since the harmony itself might be a resultant of opposing forces, but rather just because these are not cases of art and nature *interacting.* These concepts may not be precise enough to be definitive, but an examination of some varied examples of contemporary environmental sculpture might help determine what is involved in an interactive or dynamic relation. . . .

For a working dialectic between art and nature, one must move outside the physical confines and artistic conventions of the gallery to more obviously environmental creations such as Dennis Oppenheim's *Canceled Crops* (1969), in which two diagonal swaths were cut through a rectangular field of grain. The contrast between the cut and uncut grain draws attention to the fact that the grain is growing and, as such, is part of nature. But since we see a rectangular, planted field we are also visually aware that it is a *crop* and that the normal course of events—that combination of natural forces and human activity known as farming—will leave no trace of Oppenheim's swaths. Another example is Oppenheim's *Annual Rings* (1968), in which semicircular concentric paths were plowed in the snow and ice on either side of a river. Both works were temporary because of nature's course, while only their documentation has been retained; they were executed and presented so that reference to their transience and to the interaction of the artifactual with natural forces was unmistakable.

From the standpoint of artistic intentions, one of the clearest examples of a dialectical interaction between nature and artifact is Smithson's on-site (as opposed to "non-site") earthwork creations, particularly *Spiral Jetty* (1970), a 1500 foot long, 15 foot wide mound of rocks and earth spiraling out into the Great Salt Lake in Utah. Not nearly so transitory as *Canceled Crop,* the dynamic interaction of the artifactual construction with natural forces was truly dialectical, at least in Smithson's judgment:

You are confronted not only with an abstraction but also with physicality of the here and now, and these two things interact in a dialectical method and it's what I call a dialectics of place.

Spiral Jetty emerges as an especially powerful and complicated earthwork even for those not familiar with Smithson's theoretical writings. The site is intentionally inaccessible to the public and the landscape does not fit the paradigms of scenic beauty; it is instead of wasteland site, an expansive backwater portion of a dead sea in the desert adjacent to an abandoned oil drilling operation—useless land and water. Freed from utilitarian and scenic meaning, the present and past natural forces, both geological and climatological, influencing and shaping the site are all the more evident, especially given the incursion of the earthwork artifact:

> It's like the Spiral Jetty is physical enough to be able to withstand all these climate changes, yet it's intimately involved with those climate changes and natural disturbances. That's why I'm not really interested in conceptual art because that seems to avoid physical mass. You're left mainly with an idea. Somehow to have something physical that generates ideas is more interesting to me than just an idea that might generate something physical.

Not all earthworks share this dialectical characteristic. Michael Heizer's monumental earth moving projects appear to be such assertively permanent modifications of the earth's surface that they lack this interactive, dynamic dimension, but they add another—an emphasis on the tremendous difficulty of modifying physical nature on a grand artistic scale, thus drawing attention to the forceful resistance of the earth to our manipulative artistic endeavors. In *Fragmented-Depressed-Replaced Mass* (1969), Heizer had a crane move three blocks of solid rock (30, 52 and 72 tons) sixty miles; in *Double Negative* (1969–70), 240,000 tons of earth were removed by cutting into a desert mesa. Neither of these works were accessible to spectators; elaborate documentation was provided and later displayed.

The role of documentation in environmental works is far from simple. It accentuates the temporary nature of the construction, compounds the issue of what exactly is the *work* of art, and may express an attitude toward the complex artistic/economic institution of the professional artist, gallery and collector. And it uses multiple referential devices to make clear that the intentional object goes beyond the merely physical manipulation of nature or artifacts in becoming conceptual, almost theoretical, in its aesthetic expression.

Ruins similarly involve an interaction between the artifactual and the natural, but differ from earthworks in two important ways. Except in very unusual cases, ruins are aesthetically unintended, even though the partial destruction of the original structure may have been intentional. Second, ruins have a past history usually rich in meaning and associations, while earthworks have no past greatness from which they are in the process of decline, although in some cases attention may be drawn to the natural history of their sites.

Some may find it difficult to take the aesthetics of ruins seriously today, associating it with the Romantic self-indulgent fascination with the past and its decay. This may be especially true for Americans, whose relatively short cultural history

**Robert Smithson, *Spiral Jetty,* Rozel Point,
The Great Salt Lake, Utah, aerial photograph (1970).**
Source: George Steinmetz Photography.

has been future-oriented from the beginning, permeated with a sense of the ever-moving frontier and ideas of progress that, until very recently, left little room for nostalgia. Consciousness of the past has recently increased, revealing itself in many forms, including popular culture. In the environmental arts, the focus has been on restoration and preservation of historic structures and environments, with many attempts to slow down or reverse the hand of time. Within this context, the aesthetic appreciation of a ruined or crumbling structure may be viewed as an inappropriate, if not perverse, anachronism. Most sincerely believe that we must preserve our historic and vernacular architecture, that it would be wrong to allow those structures to decay even if the resulting ruins provided more aesthetic enjoyment than the originals. If aesthetic values here conflict with the cultural and historic, many argue, the aesthetic must give way. We nonetheless must recognize that there is an aesthetic appreciation of fallen and crumbling edifices. Something of their power and fascination is revealed in terms of the dialectical model discussed above.

Ruins, in terms of their material, are only incompletely ruined: They are remains, remnants. This, of course, is a truism, but is has some important implications: First, ruins are material remnants of something past, whose form or material or function has been severely modified. Thus ruins differ from vestiges, tracks and spoors, which provide evidence of something that has passed through without themselves being part of it. An example of an architectural vestige is a foundation depression, without any trace of the foundation itself remaining. Ruins are more than indications of a past structure: They are themselves parts or fragments of the structure itself.

In terms of what we appreciate, however, reference to the past structure is ambiguous. A ruin is not necessarily a fragment of a past *aesthetic* unity, for it may be only a nonaesthetic remnant of the previous structure. For example, the brick ruins now evident at Roman sites originally were plastered and painted; the bricks themselves were not originally visible. Hence we now have only fragments of the material structure but nothing of the aesthetic surface of that structure. Of course, the brick structure is usually the basis of the *form* of the original, so in these cases one can say that we now have a remnant of the aesthetic form. But this is not always the case. We may have only a structural remnant that was never apparent and never meant to be perceived in the original, such as the exposed brick heating systems in Roman baths. Never intended as aesthetic focal points, these are still quite successful as ruins today (e.g., in Trier, West Germany; Bath, England). An aesthetically successful ruin is not necessarily the remnant of an aesthetically successful original.

The exposed material of a ruin may provide one focus for aesthetic interest, but it does not exhaust that interest. The exposed material lacks the naturalness of a natural form, and it does not exhibit the intentionality of a finished artifact. It does not fit comfortably into the natural world, nor does it seem to belong to the world of art or even to the artifactual. It may even lack the compositional unity we usually demand of artistic accomplishments and natural scenery. It hangs suspended, in a state of becoming (as some philosophers might put it), in transition between the artifactual and the natural. The exposed materials reveal the direction of the change implicit in that state of becoming, especially when the ruination of the structure is the result (at least in part) of the incursion of nature (through wind, weather, growth of vegetation, etc.). Ruins possess, for aesthetic perception, an inherent reference to the future, arousing expectations of their continued dissolution, further removal from the artifactual, closer to being absorbed into nature.

We can stop this process of physical decay in some cases if we choose, or slow it down. We can gird up the structure with support, spray the surfaces with polyurethane, or even remove the peristyle to the interior of an atmospherically controlled environment such as a museum. But the object, the ruin, still exemplifies a stage in a process of change, however attenuated the actual change may have become. The appreciation of ruins thus involves awareness of a future state toward which the object is perceived to be moving. Patina appears on the copper, a glaze forms on previously shining surfaces, a wall begins to crumble, weeds start growing in crevices—and the artifact begins to appear more like a thing, untended. This is the forward-leaning aspect of ruins: toward a merging with nature and away from the artifactual.

But ruins simultaneously lean toward the past, since a ruin is literally something that has fallen or crumbled and thus has lost the original structural integrity of the whole. Partial disintegration of structure, material, asthetic surface, etc. is thus necessary for something to be a ruin. Often the partial disintegration brings with it the severance of the functioning of the original. A Roman forum is no longer a forum: A Cistercian abbey is no longer an abbey. But this is not a requirement of ruins. A partially ruined Roman aqueduct may still serve as an aqueduct; a ruined amphitheatre may still be used today for performances.

Some might suggest that what is required is a discontinuity in function resulting from the partial disintegration of structure. Thus it might be said that a Greek theatre, if considered a ruin, may once again be used for performance but only by another culture at a different time, only after the Greeks ceased to use it as such. But even if one believes that a period of disuse is required, it is important to note that the disuse need not be *caused* by the partial disintegration, even in cases of functional discontinuity. Suppose an obsolete lighthouse is simply abandoned and thus falls into disuse and that at some later time it is damaged by an earthquake. We now have a ruin and will continue to have a ruin even if the damage is not severe enough to prevent its subsequent reuse as a lighthouse. But a natural disaster may cause such tragic destruction of human lives and property that we cannot contemporaneously view the remnants without seeing mere devastation. In such cases we might not be able to appreciate the remains aesthetically, either because the destruction is too extensive or because we cannot look at the devastation without becoming occupied with the tragic nature of the specific catastrophe. These considerations allow us to understand the efficacy of the passage of time and the discontinuous use of the ruined structure in the creation of ruins as *actual* objects of aesthetic interest.

In the limited recent literature on the aesthetics of ruins, the distinction has been drawn between the classical and the romantic conception of ruins. On the classical theory, the ruin embodies the past by presenting a fragment of a missing whole, which we then imaginatively reconstruct. The aesthetic enjoyment is said to be in the imaginative apprehension of the past aesthetic unity. As a corollary to the classical view, although I have not found this point in the literature, one might suggest that part of the pleasure arises from the imaginative *activity* of reconstruction and not simply from the imaginative apprehension and contemplation of the original. In any case, the classical conception links the aesthetics of ruins to architectural and archaeological interests in the original construction and site. It is unclear whether the classical view precludes acquiring information through scientific techniques (carbon dating, chemical testing, etc.), but the process of imaginative reconstruction is guided largely by what meets the eye: the physical ruin as perceived by the aesthetic observer.

On the *romantic* conception, the ruin stirs the perceiver's sense of the past and awakens associations of mystery. We are thrilled as we "glimpse the unknown" and as we imaginatively live for a moment in the irretrievable past while simultaneously aware of the power of time to negate the present. The romantic theory may seem a bit old-fashioned and melodramatic, but initially it does appear to provide a moderately plausible explanation of the importance of visible effects of the forces of nature on the ruin. Another wall may fall, lichen appear on the stones, trees begin to grow in the crevices, all making the ruin even more interesting. Since these modifications make the construction of a past unity more difficult, it is initially hard to see how the classical view can accommodate this aesthetic aspect of ruins—the importance of the visible incursion of nature. On the romantic conception, however, incursions of nature serve to emphasize the transience of the present and thus add to the mystery and sense of irretrievability of the past. As dust returns to dust, we are touched by a glimpse backward as the past slips ever further away. As Robert Ginsberg aptly puts the romantic viewpoint, "we stroll about the Acropolis not trying to figure out what stood where or what its exact structure was, but rather glorying in being at the center of Greek greatness."

Common to both conceptions of ruins is the importance of personally apprehending the eroding monuments of the past, exploring their many facets. The experience is thus clearly aesthetic in the sense of direct perceptual satisfaction, and it is environmental by involving a sense of place, of really being at the site and personally exploring it, from the initial approach to being at the site and personally exploring it, from the initial approach to being beside and in front of, within and on top of, and walking through and around it. At the same time, one's attention is not confined to the properties of the material fragments but expands to the ideational level. (Hence, historically, the experience of ruins was linked to that of the sublime, to the reflections on the greatness of the past and the power of natural forces.)

Some suggest that there are new ruins as well. A new highway leaves the old road going nowhere and it quickly falls into ruin after a harsh winter or two. Although usually not raising the issue of past monumentality, one still has a case of the visible effect of nature making incursions on the artifactual, as if reclaiming the materials of the road from their prior status. Ruins can be caused intentionally and found to be interesting immediately without the passage of time or the incursion of nature. The demolition of buildings as it sometimes occurs in urban "renewal" may leave short term ruins which may yield picturesque views or reveal materials and structural forms that provide aesthetic satisfaction for some of the same reasons as classical ruins. They may provide the occasion for the same fascination with decay that is part of the romantic view, a pleasure in perceiving the results of the destruction of mortal edifices. But in most cases the experience does not include an admiration for the original structure itself or projecting oneself into the past.

Returning to the issue of dialectical relationship, on what basis can it be said that the ruin *in situ,* as an object of aesthetic appreciation, is a product of *dialectically* interacting forces?

> Since brass, nor stone, nor earth, nor boundless sea,
> But sad mortality o'ersways their power,
> How with this rage shall beauty hold a plea,
> Whose action is no stronger than a flower?
> (Shakespeare Sonnet #65)
>
> . . .
>
> When I have seen by Time's fell hand defaced
> The rich proud cost of outworn buried age.

When sometime lofty towers I see down razed
And brass eternal slave to mortal rage:
. . .
Ruin hath taught me thus to ruminate,
That Time will come and take my love away.
(Sonnet #64)

That thought might arise in the experience of ruins. But many times, it seems to me, the experience is more complex, that our *perceptual* consciousness shifts back and forth between an awareness of the ruin as the human *resistance* to natural forces and consciousness of the forces of nature as the *destroyer* of the most carefully planned human monuments.

The ruin *in situ* is the dialectical product of this interaction and becomes aesthetically symbolic appropriate to these generalities. Other things being equal, the more monumental the original structure (or what can be imaginatively envisioned of it given the remnants), the better the ruin serves this expressive function. At the same time, both the classical and romantic pleasures in ruins seem dependent upon an awareness of this dialectical process. We experience a peculiar sense of urgency to seize the opportunity to get a glimpse of the past (a variation of *carpe diem*) and feel privileged to be participating in its imaginative reconstruction through personally exploring the remnants. The experience of ruins thus includes affective states based on the complex of physical/temporal status of the ruin as perceived. Ruins have a richly layered aesthetic.

We now turn to the third type of environmental sculpture referred to earlier: non-functional artifacts constructed on scenic sites, as best represented in recent works and projects by Christo (Javacheff), particularly, *Valley Curtain, Running Fence,* and *Surrounded Islands.* In these works synthetic fabric is placed or suspended by structural supports on or over a natural setting. As in the case of ruins, the specific qualities of the materials constitute one focal point; the texture, color and formal qualities of the fabric in place are aesthetically important. But there are several additional points of similarity to the aesthetics of ruins which are worth noting.

First, in both conception and design Christo's works are monumental in scale. We are continually reminded, visually as well as by documentation, of the extensive dimensions and costs of the materials and labor, as well as of the engineering complexity and sometimes the real danger in actual construction. Scale is relative to the comparison class, of course, but in the class of *non-functional* artistic creations, the physicality of these works of Christo are intentionally non-pareil. Just as the monumentality of ruins increases their expressiveness, so the scale of Christo's projects is essential to their heightened visual appeal and to the complex social context of their realization. They are extremely forceful appendages to, if not incursions upon, their natural settings.

Second, there is the similarity with ruins of the importance of the site. A ruin moved inside a museum may retain all of its material properties, but will lose some of its associational and, hence, expressive properties (although it may gain new ones—imagine Tintern Abbey moved to Central Park). Christo, like Smithson, has selected relatively undisturbed sites not already popular as scenic focal points for his projects, although Christo's settings are more accessible to public view given his desire to include an interested (or even antagonistic) public in the realization of his projects. But even more in Christo's work than in Smithson's, the specifics of the construction are influenced by the natural setting, just as the setting itself may have been selected in terms of a vague idea of a type of project. Leaving aside the specifics of the creative process, however, what one perceives is a specific, dynamic interaction between the artifactual and the natural.

Third, Christo's constructions are temporary in nature, not meant to remain in place for more than a week or two; afterwards, their existence is reduced to their extensive documentation (which is intentional and well-planned). In part, legal and economic constraints determine their duration, since the necessary permits to construct the projects have been contingent upon a fixed short lifespan. In addition, the materials themselves partially influence the time period, for the fabric components would deteriorate if exposed to the elements for very long. Christo is well aware of the expressive component to these materials.

> I love [fabric] because it creates temporary, and not permanent relations between things. It is very ephemeral. . . . The fabric lends dynamic form to my projects, because you know very well it's not going to remain forever, and that it will be removed.

It must be remembered, however, that Christo himself *chooses* to design projects that inherently raise the issue of how long they can physically or legally survive. Although Christo promises that the sites will be faithfully restored to their natural condition at the conclusion of the "exhibit," the transience of their physical realization is well publicized and itself becomes an aesthetic aspect of these works. (When this writer recently asked Christo whether he thought that the canyon at Rifle Gap remained unaffected by having hosted *Valley Curtain,* he replied: "Perhaps not. Was Mont-Saint-Victoire ever the same after Cézanne?")

Fourth, the transience of physical construction is a factor in the transformation of Christo's works into something like public performances, which get attention both prior to their physical realization and after their physical demise. The artifact and the natural site are but two elements in this larger work. The work ceases to be the mere physical construction on a natural site, but a project with extended temporal boundaries, whereby the social context of its realization takes on aesthetic import. Christo's projects generate intense controversy and involve legal and political institutions from their earliest planning stages through final construction, maintenance and dismantling. There is no doubt that the public hearing, legal contracts, etc. are part of Christo's intentions. "He insists that the work of art is not merely the physical object finally attained, but the whole process—the surveys, the engineering, the leasing, the fabricating, the assembling, the hearings and the rest of it." If Christo is successful then the experience of the realized work is similar to the experience of ruins in important ways. It can incorporate an awareness of the past (the planning stages and the social interactions required by the developing work, the difficulties in construction and realization), and the object can then be visually apprehended as a stage in an evolving process. At the same time, the experience can incorporate an awareness of the future disintegration of the artifactual components of the construction, after which the work will exist only in imaginative reconstruction on the basis of documentation.

The aesthetic status of Christo's work and his conception of the extended project as a work of art may be theoretically controversial, but in fact the actual controversies surrounding these projects have been confined largely to the environmental implications of the constructions, viewed as incursions on relatively pristine natural settings. Although objections usually take the form of legal recourse through challenging the environmental impact of the construction itself, one cannot help but think that these critics believe Christo is engaged in an *aesthetic* affront to nature that goes deeper than the scientific assessment of environmental implications. This raises the question of whether they are destructive of the natural setting within the aesthetic context. It must be admitted that Christo's constructions are not merely peacefully coexistent artifactual appendages to their sites, living in aesthetic symbiosis with nature (as Frank Lloyd Wright conceived his "natural house"). Christo's artifacts forcibly assert their artifactuality over against nature, by their size, their engineering complexity and their synthetic components. Those who believe he has succeeded aesthetically, however, could argue that he has selected natural sites in which nature is up to the challenge and expresses its own grandeur and power. A dialectics of nature and art is achieved through a synthesis of opposing forces, artifactual and natural, but at the same time both forces retain their identity as separately identifiable components of the completed work.

These are just some of the aesthetically significant interactions of the natural and the artifactual. If I am correct in my analysis, the object of aesthetic appreciation in such cases is quite complex and goes well beyond the perceived physical object. It is in part a product of a dialectic between nature and art, the experience of which incorporates time past and time future into present awareness, but without either the natural or the artifactual losing their identity. Although I cannot endorse the full implications of John Dewey's generalization, his remark in *Art as Experience* seems applicable to the range of examples discussed in this paper: Art celebrates with peculiar intensity the moments in which the past reenforces the present and in which the future is a quickening of what now is.

Something There Is That Doesn't Love A Wall
■ Patricia C. Phillips ■

In the late 1960s and early 1970s the seizures that affected political actions and philosophical positions also changed the production and perception of art. There was an advancing restlessness with the structures, constrictions, and hypocrisy of the commodity-based conventions of art-making and acquisition. An altered and expanded way of thinking about art emerged, one that extended beyond the characteristics of the object to the situations and environments in which art was developed. This climate of agitation generated a context for art outside the regulated contours and operations of galleries and museums—that of unmanaged and unpredictable outdoor spaces. For some artists this new frontier was a way to engage the complexities and ambiguities of public life in a private age; for others it offered a means to reintegrate art and architecture, and art and life.

Finally, it seemed to be a way to investigate the role of the urban artist as a generator of ideas and forms that were vulnerable to change and intervention. Other artists sought desolate, rural sites for an art activity that was the ultimate reclusive gesture of independent pioneers seeking new frontiers. This move from the gallery to the open air led to a rich involvement with site; the hard, resistant edges of the art object yielded to a new pressure to absorb and reflect the conditions of the location. This development of site-oriented art embroiled the roles and responsibilities of both artists and public—an entanglement that was restated most recently by the controversy over Richard Serra's *Tilted Arc* at 26 Federal Plaza, in New York.

The complex tradition of public art in America has for the most part been based on the model of Europe, where every major city and small town has commemorative public sculpture, and where historical, mythological, and inspirational themes are promised perpetuity through the monument's conspicuous placement. However, these monuments offer few lessons applicable to the creation of public art today, when both message and methodology have changed radically. By the 1970s some artists had taken the faltering and increasingly passionless tradition of public art and inserted the idea of the site as an urgent condition, with both observable and psychological effects, in much the same way that earlier environmental artists had done. If being aware of site was a way in which art could confirm its relevance in a transitional world, as well as confirm the meaning derived from context, logically this exploration could and should occur in cities. In the same way that the metropolis had become yet again the new frontier, the populated site offered a messy vitality which intrigued many artists and inspired more than a few.

"Something There Is That Doesn't Love a Wall" by Patricia C. Phillips is reprinted *Art Forum* (Summer, 1985), pages 100–101.

Artists who chose to engage the question of context, in both rural and urban settings, used the site of a work as a source of information for the creative process. The idea of site, treated as concept or as actual raw material (or both), was weighed and interpreted in diverse ways. In the early 20th century [Marcel] Duchamp had begun an inquiry into the relationship of context, object, and content; a snow shovel hanging in a gallery was different from a snow shovel in a garage. In the 1960s artists en masse confirmed that perception influenced content, and some artists—for example, Robert Smithson—sought out industrial wastelands and strip mines in order to generate works that were simultaneously entropic and resurrective. This new interest in site, and often in particular sites, was a phenomenon that was both radical and difficult. Conventional art analysis and classification spawned a new movement called "site-specific art." With a few strokes of the pen a complex and mutable series of actions was condensed into a coherent category. As a device to catalogue the flight from the gallery or a reformed involvement with it, the concept of site-specific work was an embryonic idea which later was inflated into an explanation, an apology, and occasionally a defense. The term "site specific" became so over used that it often codified dissimilar ideas, romanticized some very bad work, and misled serious inquiry.

In a catalogue assembled for an exhibition in 1977 at the Hirshhorn Museum called "Probing the Earth" (an unfortunate title), John Beardsley described site-specific art: "The works elaborate the landscape; the landscape reveals the works. They are site-specific, and provide a focused experience of place." What Beardsley failed to realize was that the kind of specificity he described ends up being ambiguously nonspecific. It was never clearly determined whether site-specificity was a consequence of the artist's intentions or of the characteristics of a place. By injecting the concept of place into the definition of site-specific work, the term was further eroded. The perception of place is unregulated and unanticipated; it is a perceptual phenomenon as much as it is a set of physical characteristics. "Site" is a shifting compound of physical qualities and phenomena; it is also a psychological domain layered with perceptions and associations, individual dreams and shared mythologies. It is what people bring to it; it is subject to creative impulses and initiatives from artists and the public alike.

The magnification of site as an important social as well as formal subject has had great consequences for art in public settings. This new understanding was a creative move, not a predetermined development. When artists began to work creatively with urban sites, this expanded perception extended the boundaries of art and led artworks directly into collaboration, and sometimes confrontation, with architecture. Site became the meeting-ground that forced artists to think about architecture and architects to think more about art. In this new hybrid area, neither art nor architectural criticism proved adequate. Art critics had to wrestle with a complex context that was in many ways alien to the art world, while architecture critics had to face large, ambitious constructions that did not derive from a functional incentive.

The controversy that has swelled around the slash of Cor-ten steel that Serra installed four years ago in Federal Plaza is a vivid example of how the complex interrelations of art, site, architecture, and the public can come to an ugly conflict and create a profound breach between members of the art world and the public. While *Tilted Arc* may be in a public place, it is not public art. Site-specificity and a contract between the artist and the General Services Administration have been the foundations of the argument that Serra's piece should remain in the plaza, while the work is perceived by its detractors as an aggressive obstruction of a public place. Rather than rolling over and playing dead, the sculpture's critics have raised a noisy protest about the location of *Tilted Arc,* and the indignation of the artist and the work's defenders in response has reached righteous proportions. To some Serra has become the new martyred artist. While his significance as an artist is indisputable, his escalation to the status of romantic hero is a little hard to take.

The response that Serra's piece has evoked over the past four years led the General Services Administration to appoint a panel to review the issue; on April 10 the panel recommended that *Tilted Arc* be removed from Federal Plaza. The prelude to this decision included three days of public hearings during which positions and sentiments were publicly confirmed. Whether the panel's decision to remove the work had basically been formulated before these hearings began is a question raised too often to be dismissed. If this was the case, the hearings were simply a charade. They were an important forum, for they allowed artists and others, by speaking for Serra, to protest the creeping repression of our age. The Serra controversy has been selected by some people as a symbol of the current threat to freedom and expression. Several of those who testified recalled the Nazi book-burnings which presaged the Holocaust, but to equate the clashing sentiments surrounding *Tilted Arc* with the horrors of debased and imperiled ideology is unconscionable hyperbole. To misappropriate the Serra event diminishes the urgency of both the general issues and the specific case. The central question is about the role of government in public-art production, and what this sought-after intervention has brought with it. The very real anxieties about this age have compounded the difficulties in distinguishing among government intervention, repression, support of the arts, and the imposition of one individual's will on society. The controversy about Serra's piece, which has to do with government and the arts, and art and the public, has endowed it with a content and potency it would never have had otherwise.

In testimony at the public hearing on March 6, 1985, Serra said: "I don't make portable objects. I don't make works that can be relocated or site-adjusted. I make works that deal with environmental components of given places. Scale, size, location of my site-specific works are determined by the topography of the site, whether it be urban, landscape, or an architectural enclosure." Few can argue that Serra's work is not site-specific. But the significant issue is the degree of sensitivity with which the condition of site as a public place and psychological region was interpreted. While *Tilted Arc* does not psychologically separate the viewer from the art object the way commemorative art on a pedestal does, Serra mended this schism by creating a behavioral autocracy. Everyone who walks through the plaza has been condemned to participate in the artist's investigation of the expectation of passage in an open public space. While the artist's autonomy is an important factor in this controversy, public freedom in the face of art that aggressively limits options merits critical concern as well. Aside from all the things that public art can and should do, the public should have the option to ignore it or avoid participation. In Federal Plaza, though, even the reticent have been forced to participate over and over in the movement laboratory that *Tilted Arc* imposes. Serra's piece has generated outrage because it operates like a demagogue who insistently attacks independent activity. Cities throughout the United States are spotted with public art selected by well-intentioned committees who have failed to consider all the constituencies who become involved when art and environment intersect and converge.

The context that Serra had to work within is as oppressive as the artist's intrusion on the plaza. The buildings surrounding the plaza are foul, faceless, and foreboding. In this context innocence seems like a crime; the atmosphere is punitive. Serra's inclination to critique this sobering setting through his own installation was well-founded; the critical potential of public art has always been subdued in the United States. But the failure of Serra's work as criticism is that it is as awkward and sadistic as the environment he attacks; *Tilted Arc* aggravates rather than illuminates. Smithson's proposed works for tailings and strip-mine sites were provocative critical actions, but their great eloquence was in their cathartic, healing, and informative qualities. Ironically, Serra's arc of condemnation confirms the context by appearing deferential to the vagaries of awful urban design.

Public life is the most variable characteristic of any urban space, and the most vulnerable to idiosyncratic interpretation. In his statement on March 6 Serra also said, "I am interested in a behavioral space in which the viewer interacts with the sculpture in its context." Given this premise, Serra's reported shock and surprise over the negative response his piece has evoked is curious. In a strange inversion, the artist has gotten everything that he hoped for. When one sets up behavioral and perceptual circumstances designed to encourage conceptual confrontation from viewers, the results of the experiment cannot be dismissed simply because they are not all in congruence with the expectations of the originator. Serra clearly wanted to provoke response and activity from the public, but he is said to be outraged because the reaction is so unfriendly and so ungrateful.

In the same statement Serra predicted that his piece would produce a "multitude of readings." It has indeed elicited admiration and respect in certain quarters, but one of the most poignant and pervasive readings of the situation is that the public feels powerless and taken advantage of once again. Another reading is that lack of education and information has provoked such extreme alienation toward the work. But surely Serra's piece, while formally interesting, fails just because it so totally obstructs the potency of public inquiry. The unyielding autocracy of the artwork is its own obstacle, not its sign of uncompromising purity. The work is not in a museum where people can choose to deal with it or not. The *Tilted Arc* controversy has been only partly about freedom of expression; it has also been about whether mistakes can be admitted. *Tilted Arc* is not threatened because the dumb public doesn't get it; if that were the only reason for the opposition, people would have gotten over it by now and learned to live with it. Perhaps the critics understand the work all too well. Individual artistic expression is not always noble, and the public is not always the muscle-bound, pea-brained bully.

While the panel's recommendation that *Tilted Arc* be removed may be secretly welcomed by many (including some of its public supporters), the means by which this decision has been reached have left supporters and dissenters alike in a state of fury or unease. No general postmortem on the process by which public art is selected and occasionally re-evaluated seems likely to occur. Even the urgency of Serra's situation has not forced a reappraisal of the relations between public action and individual freedom, or of government's role in public art. Without this, in an age of neither conviction nor consensus about public art, witch-hunts can be anticipated. In the end, regardless of whether *Tilted Arc* is removed or allowed to stay in its present location, trust on all sides has been eroded.

PART IV

MUSIC

We take for granted the power of music in contemporary life. It takes only an instant to recognize the enormous variety of the world's music available to us through a wide range of musical formats. But music itself has been an object of inquiry and investigation almost since the appearance of civilized life. At least since the time of Pythagoras, music, the art over which the Muses preside, has been closely connected with both mathematics and mysticism. The great quadrivium of the Schoolmen, the "liberal arts" of medieval times, consisted of arithmetic, geometry, astronomy, and music.

We readily recognize a standard role of the graphic arts—sculpture, painting, and photography, for instance—to represent the world through images. We take for granted the capacity of literature to convey thoughts and to express human feelings through words. Should we also assume that music represents and expresses? And if so, would it be in the same ways as other art forms?

Distinguishing between listener-centered and non-listener-centered theories, Jenefer Robinson surveys recent views about expression in music. In developing a view of her own, Robinson argues that sophisticated theories have overlooked the fact that music can relevantly arouse "primitive" emotions. For instance, music can make one feel nervous or tense. This is important if she is right, because she claims that more sophisticated emotional responses to music can be better explained as incorporating these more basic responses.

Contributing to the affective dimensions of music is its multitude of subtle *nuances*. In speaking of these nuances, we are often tempted to say that they are *ineffable*—that is, they cannot be put into words. Diana Raffman argues that this thought reflects a psychological reality. Listening to music is a process in which a sound stream is continuously subjected to an unconscious mental analysis. By embedding the sound in a kind of mental "grid," it gets organized into familiar individual notes and rhythms—A-naturals, eighth notes, etc. Further, we can register differences *among* A-naturals and eighth notes. Some are "good" A-naturals, others are slightly sharp, and still others are slightly flat. However, we are never able to *say* which particular A-natural one is hearing. Such fine-grained nuances, Raffman argues, play important roles in differentiating different performances of the same work.

Even if music can express emotion, it is far from clear that it can depict objects, processes, or events in the way that oil paintings can. True, examples of attempts at musical depiction are familiar. (Consider Wagner's musical renderings of storms, castles, and rushing water.) However, Roger Scruton tries to explain why, in his opinion, we cannot find full-fledged pictures in music. For instance, it is necessary, he states, for a competent viewer to be able to recognize what is depicted in representational visual art. However, with out the aid of extra-musical prompts or cues, we cannot do so with music.

Without making any commitment about the general importance of representation in music, Peter Kivy argues that a consideration of many cases will not support Scruton's arguments. Of special interest in both essays is a consideration of cases in which music seems to represent other music. Kivy tries to demonstrate that Scruton is wrong in claiming that such attempts never succeed.

Regardless of whether music can copy anything in the world, music itself can be copied. With the dawn of the twentieth century, it became common practice to copy music, not simply with musical instruments, but with instruments that record sound. Indeed, the whole point of the recording industry is to make copies of music. But what are recordings? Mere transparent "windows" upon live musical performances? Evan Eisenberg, taking his departure from Walter Benjamin's essay on the aesthetic implications of mechanical reproduction in the visual arts, argues that recording technology makes possible entirely new forms of musical performance and aesthetic experience that would be virtually impossible in live performance.

Lee Brown argues that sound recording has even made possible an entirely new kind of musical artwork—which might be called *works of phonography* or *phonoartworks*. Phonoartworks, unlike works of classical musical, are not performable. (Imagine performing the Beatles' *Sergeant Pepper* album.) What defines such works is not a score, but rather a master recording. However, Brown suggests that sound recording has surprising effects on at least one type of music, namely, music that is improvised. Much of the point of improvised music is that it is created *while* the effect of it is being played, and while you listen to it. But, by pressing the "repeat" button on your CD player, you can transform improvised music into something as expected as a traditional musical work—indeed, as predictable as a work of phonoart.

However, "classical" music, like works of phonography—indeed, like paintings and sculptures—also comes packaged in works, for example, Tchaikovsky's *Serenade for Strings,* or Beethoven's *Symphony No. 7.* Performances, we typically assume, ought to be "true to" those works. But, what *is* a musical work? Some have argued that Beethoven's Seventh is a kind of platonic form with individual performances as its particular instances. Others have said that it is simply the class of its correct performances. In her treatment of the topic, Lydia Goehr argues that the concept of a musical *work* is not built into the general concept of music, but has evolved since the eighteenth century. It functions only as what the philosopher Immanuel Kant termed a *regulative idea*. Arguments attempting to prove that given performances of music either do or do not "belong" to a given work neglect this important fact.

However, not all music is organized into *works*. The concept seems hardly applicable to the African music described by John Chernoff. Addressing the special polyrhythmic features of such music, Chernoff explains its social features—features rarely stressed in European music, except in musical forms derived from Africa, such as jazz. A striking feature of African drumming, Chernoff explains, is that it is inherently conversational. While a single instrumental part in a symphony can be singled out and played separately—in practice, for instance—this is virtually impossible in African drumming, in which one musical line is invariably defined by the others. This mirrors the highly interactive features of African social life.

Since African music and European concert music have such strikingly different features, it might seem difficult to define music cross-culturally. However, Jerrold Levinson attempts to do just this. His view is that music consists of sounds temporally organized for the purpose of enriching or intensifying experience. One merit of the definition, he claims, is that it profiles the fact that music is a human artifact, not simply natural sounds. Another is that creators of music intend the sounds they create to be worth listening to. So, there is some obligation on our part to take them that way.

The Expression and Arousal of Emotion in Music
■ Jenefer Robinson ■

According to some theories of musical expression, the grounds on which we attribute expressive qualities to music have nothing to do with the arousal of emotion in the audience. According to Peter Kivy's account in *The Corded Shell,* a musical element such as a melody, a rhythm, or a chord expresses a feeling not because it arouses that feeling in anyone but for two quite different reasons. (1) It has the same "contour" as expressive human behavior of some kind and thus is "heard as expressive of something or other because heard as appropriate to the expression of something or other" (for example, the "weeping" figure of grief in Arianna's lament from [Claudio] Monteverdi's *Arianna*) or it contributes in a particular context to the forming of such an expressive contour (as the diminished triad in a suitable context can contribute to a *restless* quality in the music, although all by itself it does not express anything). (2) The musical element is expressive by virtue of some custom or convention, which originated in connection with some expressive contour. The minor triad, for example, is "sad" by convention, although it may have started life as part of some expressive contour.

There are many examples of musical expression for which Kivy's argument is convincing. Thus it does seem to be true that Arianna's lament mirrors the passionate speaking voice expressing grief, that Franz Schubert's "Gretchen am Spinnrad" mirrors Gretchen's monotonous, leaden gestures at the spinning wheel and her correspondingly dejected, leaden heart, and that the "Pleni sunt coeli" from Bach's B Minor Mass maps "bodily motion and gesture . . . of tremendous expansiveness, vigor, violent motion," thus mirroring the exuberance of "'leaping' joy." At the same time as Renée Cox, among others, has pointed out, virtually all the musical examples in Kivy's book are examples of music with a text, and it is relatively uncontroversial that a text can specify a particular feeling or object which is characterized by the music. Moreover, when we look closely at Kivy's examples of particular emotions said to be expressed by music we find mainly varieties of joy, sorrow, and restlessness. The vast majority of musical examples in *The Corded Shell* can be characterized as expressions of either positive or negative emotion (joy or sorrow) of various sorts. Thus although what Kivy says seems to be true as far as it goes, it does not go very far, and leaves a great deal of expressiveness in music unexplained.

Kivy holds that music can express particular emotional states such as sorrow and joy, restlessness and serenity. Susanne Langer, while agreeing that emotional

"The Expression and Arousal of Emotion in Music" by Jenefer Robinson has been excerpted from *The Journal of Aesthetics and Art Criticism* (Winter 1994), pages 13–17, 18–21, and is reprinted by permission of the publisher.

qualities are to be found in the *music,* rather than in the *listener,* follows [Eduard] Hanslick in arguing that since only the dynamic qualities of anything (including emotional states) can be expressed by music, no particular emotions can be expressed by music, but only the felt quality of our emotional life and its dynamic development:

> [There] are certain aspects of the so-called "inner life"—physical or mental—which have formal properties similar to those of music—patterns of motion and rest, of tension and release, of agreement and disagreement, preparation, fulfillment, excitation, sudden change, etc.
>
> [Music] reveals the rationale of feelings, the rhythm and pattern of their rise and decline and intertwining, to our minds. . . .

In contrast to Kivy's view that the words of a text supply the "fine shadings" to otherwise only grossly expressive musical meanings, Langer holds that musical meanings are inherently rich and significant yet cannot be linked to any particular words. Langer's theory emphasizes the development of structures of feeling throughout a lengthy piece of music, which Kivy ignores, but she in turn ignores the expression of particular emotional qualities which Kivy emphasizes. Both theorists have insightful things to say about musical expression but neither tells the whole story.

A very different view of musical expression has recently been presented by Kendall Walton in a paper called "What Is Abstract About the Art of Music?" Walton proposes that one important way in which music is expressive is by virtue of the fact that in listening to music we imagine ourselves introspecting, that is being aware of our own feelings. As he puts it, we imagine "of our actual introspective awareness of auditory sensations" that "it is an experience of being aware of our states of mind." Thus the expressiveness of music has to do with its power to *evoke* certain imaginative emotional experiences. Moreover, Walton says that if this is right, then:

> music probably can be said to "portray particulars" in the sense that figurative paintings do, rather than simply properties or concepts. Presumably the listener imagines experiencing and identifying *particular* stabs of pain, *particular* feelings of ecstasy, *particular* sensations of well-being, etc., as in viewing a painting one imagines seeing particular things.

However, whereas one perceives the psychological states of other people, as in figurative paintings, one "introspects one's *own* psychological states."

There are at least two problems I see with Walton's account. (1) First, suppose someone denies that this is what she does when listening to expressive music; we should be able to *explain* to her why this is what she should be doing. What reason is there why we should imagine our awareness of auditory sensations—experienced sequences of musical tones—to be an experience of our feelings and other inner states? True, there are similarities between the two: The experience of auditory sensations is an introspectible state, and so is awareness of our feelings. True, part of what we are aware of in these auditory sensations is, as Langer points out, their ebb and flow, and our feelings too have ebb and flow. But beyond these points of resemblance there seems to be little explanation *why* we should be inclined to imagine our awareness of musical sounds to be an awareness of our feelings. Imagination requires some guidance if it is not to be merely free association: I can imagine the tree at the end of the garden to be a witch because it has a witch-like appearance, but it is unclear what it would mean for me to imagine the snowdrop at my feet to be a witch if there is nothing about the snowdrop to set off my imagination. Similarly, in order for me to imagine my awareness of musical sounds to be awareness of my feelings, something in the musical sounds must guide my imagination. However, if the only points of resemblance between feelings and sounds is introspectibility and ebb and flow, then I would suggest that this is insufficient to ground an imaginative identification between the two. There are, moreover, striking *differences* between the two which would seem to preclude any such imaginative identification. In particular, whereas our feelings clearly rise up inside us (as we say), musical sounds clearly rise up at a distance from us: Even when listening to music over good earphones—when the music is experienced with peculiar immediacy—we still experience the auditory sensations as coming from an external source, such as trombones and the like. That is why although we can perhaps imagine these sounds as feelings welling up inside the *composer,* or perhaps in some *character* described by the music, it is not obvious to me that we can imagine them as feelings welling up inside ourselves.

(2) There is a second problem related to this one. I am willing to grant that there are indeed movements in music which it is appropriate to call "stabbing" or "surging." According to Walton, however, the music induces me to imagine myself feeling a particular ecstatic surge or stab of pain. He says that the music *portrays* these particulars (it picks them out or refers to them). A number of questions need to be distinguished here. (1) Can the stab be identified as a stab of feeling rather than the stab of a dagger or some other kind of stab? (2) If the stab is a stab of feeling, can it be identified as a stab of pain rather than some other feeling such as excitement or jealousy? (3) If the stab is indeed a stab of pain, can it be identified as a stab of pain which I imagine myself experiencing rather than a stab of pain attributed to someone else such as Othello or the composer? If the music *portrays* my imagined stab of pain, as Walton suggests, then the music must be able to distinguish my imagined stab of pain from all these other possible alternatives. Can music do this? Can music portray this particular stab of pain and no other? . . .

Although Walton's theory does not identify musical expression with the straightforward arousal of feelings, he does try to explain expression in terms of the arousal of *imaginary* feelings. I am not actually feeling a stab of pain as I listen to the stabbing music; I am *imagining* experiencing a stab of pain, so it would seem that the pain is an imaginary feeling. In his paper "Music and Negative Emotions," Jerrold Levinson makes a similar point. Levinson's paper deals with the problem of why people enjoy music when it evokes negative emotions such as sadness in them. While the paper does not develop a theory of musical expression, it does make certain assumptions about what often happens when people listen to music which we would characterize as sad. In particular, he assumes that it is a normal response for people to have a sadness-reaction to music.

When a person has a "deep emotional response" to music, this is "generally in virtue of the *recognition* of emotions expressed in music," but recognition then leads to a kind of empathic identification: We "end up feeling as, in imagination, the music does." Such empathic emotional responses to music consist in "something very like experience of the emotion expressed in the music" but not *exactly* like it. In both cases the physiological and affective components of emotion are present and in both cases there is cognitive content, but the "empathic" response lacks *determinate* cognitive content:

> When one hears sad music, begins to feel sad, and imagines that one is actually sad, one must, according to the logic of the concept, be imagining that there is an object for one's sadness and that one maintains certain evaluative beliefs (or attitudes) regarding it. The point, though, is that this latter imagining generally remains indeterminate.

I feel sad but my sadness has no determinate object; it is directed only to "some featureless object posited vaguely by my imagination." Levinson illustrates his view with various kinds of negative emotion: "intense grief, unrequited passion, sobbing melancholy, tragic resolve, and angry despair." Suppose, for example, that the music evokes in me an empathic response of unrequited passion. On Levinson's view, this means that I recognize unrequited passion in the music, I imagine that I am experiencing unrequited passion, and I actually experience the physiological and affective components of unrequited passion. My imagined unrequited passion has a cognitive content which is "etiolated by comparison to that of real-life emotion"; however, I am not really suffering the pangs of unrequited passion, and in particular there is no special person for whom I am languishing.

I am sympathetic to some of Levinson's assumptions: I think he is right to stress that the detection of emotional qualities in music has something to do with the arousal of emotion by music, and I think he is right also to stress the role of the imagination in the appreciation of emotional qualities in music. However, the theory as it stands will not do. First of all, it is far from clear that every emotional state has identifiable physiological and affective components. For example, real-life unrequited passion might on different occasions be accompanied by a great variety of inner feelings (love, grief, longing, jealousy, wretchedness, despair, self-contempt, etc., etc.). For another thing, the particular feelings I experience on a given occasion of unrequited passion may be just the same as I have felt on occasions of angry despair or intense grief. The truth of the matter is that there may be very little difference between the affective and physiological components of very different emotions: I may feel the same mixture of grief and rage when I am jealous or when I am grieving (without jealousy); I may have very similar feelings whether angrily despairing, tragically resolving, or suffering from the pangs of unrequited passion. The difference between these emotions lies not so much in their affective and physiological components as in their cognitive content. The chief difference between unrequited passion, tragic resolve, and angry despair is how I view or conceive of the situation.

But now we come to a second set of difficulties. Levinson argues that I can recognize unrequited passion (say) in the "emotion-laden gestures embodied in musical movement" and by virtue of this recognition respond empathetically with feelings of unrequited passion of my own, since I identify with the music or perhaps "with the person whom we imagine owns the emotions or emotional gestures we hear in the music." However, he fails to tell us how we detect or empathically feel the unrequited passion in the music. Although we all have some idea of what *sad* music is like, I suggest that it is much less clear what a piece of music is like in which we can recognize, and hence empathize with, unrequited passion (always assuming, of course, that there is no accompanying verbal text to help us out). If I am right and there are no distinctive affective or physiological components of unrequited passion, then the obvious way to clarify the nature of music in which we can detect unrequited passion would be to specify its cognitive content. Now, Levinson claims that the cognitive content of an emotional response to music is normally "etiolated." This could mean simply that my imagined feelings of unrequited passion are not directed to any particular individual. While it is a little odd to say that one can feel unrequited passion for someone I know not whom, we can perhaps make sense of this suggestion since on Levinson's view the unrequited passion I feel empathically belongs to the music itself or to someone whom we imagine feels unrequited passion, so that we merely empathize with this imagined person's unrequited passion.

Even if we grant, however, that there need be no specific object for the unrequited passion I detect in the music and empathize with, it would seem that there must be some identifiable cognitive content, however etiolated, which is detectable in the music in order to justify the attribution of this particular emotion. I would suggest that if my response is to count as a response of unrequited passion rather than some other emotion, then I must imagine that there is someone whom I care about deeply, that this person does not care deeply about me, and that I care deeply that this person does not care deeply about me (or something of this sort). It is a serious problem for Levinson's account that he does not tell us how such conceptions can be embodied in music and hence how we can either recognize or empathize with the corresponding emotion. We find the same problem with tragic resolve and angry despair; we cannot clearly distinguish these emotional responses by their affective and physiological components alone, but only by their cognitive content. However, Levinson gives us no clue as to how their cognitive content can be recognized in or induced by music. . . .

Recently Levinson's view has been criticized by Peter Kivy on the grounds that the expression of emotion in music is entirely independent of the arousal of that emotion. Kivy argues that to have one's emotions aroused by a piece of music—in particular, to be moved by a piece of music—is quite distinct from perceiving a particular emotional quality in that piece. Music that is sad or expresses sadness is music with a sad expressive contour or music that is sad by convention, not music that arouses or evokes sadness. Levinson argues that a "deep emotional response" to sad music consists in the arousal of a kind of imaginative but cognitively truncated sadness. Kivy rightly attacks this claim, arguing on the one hand that sad music may or may not make me feel anything, depending on how great the music is (the "yards and yards of mournful music" written by [Georg Philipp] Telemann may fail to make me feel anything much at all), and on the other hand that there are important emotions aroused by music which are full-blown, ordinary, real-life emotions, not "truncated" or "imaginary" in any sense. He illustrates his point by reference to a performance of Josquin [des Pres'] "*Ave verum virginitas*" which, he says *moves* him deeply.

When listening to the "*Ave verum virginitas*" I may simply be moved by "the sheer beauty of the sound as it unfolds in its ebb and flow." If my sophistication increases, however, I may also be moved by "the incomparable beauty and craftsmanship of Josquin's counterpoint" and by the fact that despite its seeming effortlessness, the music is written in a particularly difficult canonic form, "a canon at the fifth, with the voices only one beat apart." This, then, is the cognitive component of the emotion aroused by the music, my being moved by the music. It is not a truncated emotion in any way. It is a genuine emotional experience, arising out of my perception of the music and its qualities. Furthermore, this emotion might be directed at emotional, expressive qualities in the music, such as sadness, but it does not follow that the emotion *aroused by* the music is the emotion *detected in* the music. Part of what I may be moved by in a piece of music may be its sadness, but I can be moved by joyful, by energetic, and by serene music just as well, as well as by music which does not have any marked emotional character. The expressive qualities, if any, which I detect in the music are entirely independent of the emotions I feel as I listen to the music.

Now, Kivy is certainly right to claim that when I am moved by a piece of music, my emotion may be independent of the emotional qualities, if any, that the music happens to have. When I appreciate a piece of music I may indeed be moved in the way Kivy describes. On the other hand, Kivy has not succeeded in showing that the expression of emotion by a piece of music is always and entirely unconnected to the arousal of emotion. Kivy makes this claim based on an analysis of just one emotion, "being moved," and it may well be true that we can be equally moved by music with different emotional qualities, as well as by music which has no marked emotional qualities. However, I believe that music arouses other feelings as well and that some of these may indeed be connected to the expressive qualities that music has. Furthermore, I think Kivy is wrong to insist that *all* the feelings aroused by music have to have a complex cognitive component as in his example from Josquin. It may be true that being moved by music involves complex evaluative judgments, but being moved is not the only emotional or feeling response which music can arouse.

Let me summarize the results of my discussion so far. Walton argues that expressive music evokes the imaginative experience of the emotion expressed: More precisely, music expressive of sadness, say, induces the listener to imagine herself experiencing sad feelings. Levinson similarly claims that sad music has the power to evoke a kind of truncated sadness-response: The listener feels certain symptoms of sadness, has an "indeterminate" idea that there is something or other to be sad about and imagines that she in fact feels sad. Both writers find a connection between the presence of an emotional quality in music and the arousal of that emotion in the listener's imagination. I have urged, however, that neither Walton nor Levinson has shown *how* complex feelings such as unrequited passion, stabs of pain, or even sadness can be aroused by music whether in fact or in imagination. Furthermore, Kivy is clearly right to hold that to have a deep emotional response to music is not necessarily to mirror the feelings that the music expresses.

At the same time, however, I believe that Walton and Levinson are right to stress the connection between the expression and the arousal of emotion in music, and that Kivy is quite wrong to think that his analysis of the one emotion "being moved" demonstrates that no such connection exists. In what remains of this paper I will try to sketch a more adequate account of what this connection really is.

None of the writers I have discussed in this essay has focused on the way in which music can *directly* affect our feelings. For both Walton and Levinson the arousal of feeling is imaginative and it relies on a good deal of cognitive activity on the part of the listener. For Kivy the emotion of being moved is a real emotion, not an imagined one, but it too relies on cognitive activity, such as recognizing the clever part-writing, etc. However, some music has the power to affect our feelings without much, if any cognitive mediation. In particular, music can induce physiological changes and a certain quality of inner feeling (what Levinson calls respectively the "phenomenological" and "sensational" aspects of the "affective" component in emotion). Music can make me feel tense or relaxed; it can disturb, unsettle, and startle me; it can calm me down or excite me; it can get me tapping my foot, singing along, or dancing; it can maybe lift my spirits and mellow me out.

Emotions vary in degree—and perhaps in kind—of cognitive content. At one end of the scale there is the startle response, which is an innate response, found in human neonates as well as throughout the phylogenetic scale. At the other end of the scale there is unrequited passion which, by contrast, is found only in humans with their highly developed cultural norms. What I want to suggest is that in addition to the sophisticated emotions of appreciation, which Kivy identifies as "being moved" by certain perceived aspects of the music, there are more primitive emotions aroused by music, perhaps requiring less developed cognitive mediation. There are, after all, moments in music which make us jump or startle us. Similarly, the perception of certain rhythms may be enough—without any further cognitive mediation—to evoke tension or relaxation, excitement or calm. If the melodic and harmonic elements in a piece of music affect our emotions, this would seem to require familiarity with the stylistic norms of the piece, but no further cognitions need be required in order for us to feel soothed, unsettled, surprised, or excited by developments in the music. Certainly we need not notice that we are listening to a canon at the fifth in order for that canon to soothe us.

We have seen that to feel unrequited passion necessarily involves a certain fairly complicated conception of one's situation. By contrast, to feel disturbed or calm does not require having a conception of one's situation in this way. Music can make me feel disturbed or calm just by perceiving it (listening to it). The feeling is a result of a perception and to this extent it has "cognitive content," but it is not the full-blown cognitive content required for tragic resolve, angry despair or unrequited passion. The sense of relaxation we feel at the end of [Richard Wagner's] "Tristan und Isolde," for example, is the result of the long-awaited resolution, after over four hours of constant modulation without resolution. The feeling is the result of a perception, but we may not even be aware why we feel as we do: The effect of the constantly shifting harmonic pattern affects us "directly" without conscious cognitive mediation (except, of course, what is required by our understanding of Wagner's style). There is some psychological evidence (from [Daniel] Berlyne and others) that people seek high levels of arousal in order to have them drop afterwards: "excitement and complex, conflicting information are sought because of the 'arousal jag.'" The effect of the final Tristan chord may be partly accounted for in these terms.

Now, the feelings evoked "directly" by music explain some of the cases of musical expressiveness that the contour theory finds hard to deal with. Music that disturbs and unsettles us is disturbing, unsettling music. Modulations that surprise us are surprising. Melodies that soothe us are soothing. Furthermore, unexpected harmonic shifts excite us and are exciting; protracted stay in a harmonic area distant from the home key makes us uneasy and produces uneasy music; the return to the home key after a protracted stay in a distant harmonic area relaxes the tension in us and produces relaxing music. And so on. In short, as against Kivy's position, it seems to me that the expression of a feeling by music can sometimes be explained straightforwardly in terms of the arousal of that feeling. However, the feelings aroused "directly" by music are not stabs of pain or feelings of unrequited passion, but more "primitive" feelings of tension, relaxation, surprise, and so on. These feelings do, therefore, in a sense have an "etiolated" cognitive content, in the way that Levinson specifies in "Music and Negative Emotions," but it is not an etiolated, imaginary version of an emotion which normally has a complex cognitive content (such as unrequited passion), but rather a feeling such as surprise, which by its nature just has—or can have—a relatively simple cognitive content. . . .

Now, something that most philosophical theorists of musical expression have either ignored or underemphasized is the fact that the musical expression of complex emotions is not a function of a few isolated measures here and there, as in Kivy's examples in *The Corded Shell;* rather it is very often a function of the large-scale formal structures of the piece as a whole. We cannot understand the expression of complex emotions in music apart from the continuous development of the music itself. None of the philosophical writers I have discussed has fully appreciated this point. . . .

In his celebrated book, *Emotion and Meaning in Music,* Leonard Meyer showed how the formal structure of works in the Classical and Romantic styles could be analyzed in terms of the emotional *responses* of the practiced listener: His was a kind of "Reader-Response" or rather "Listener-Response" theory of musical structure. In order to understand a piece of music, on this view, the listener has to have her feelings aroused in a certain way. If we are experienced in the style of the piece, then we have certain expectations about the way the music will develop; in a meaningful piece of music these expectations will be either frustrated or satisfied in unexpected ways. As we listen new expectations are constantly being aroused and we are just as constantly being *surprised* by novel developments, *relieved* by delayed resolutions, made *tense* by the delays, etc., etc. In short, understanding musical structure, according to Meyer, is not just a matter of detached analysis; rather, it is impossible without the arousal of feeling in the listener. . . .

If a piece of music is heard as successively disturbing and reassuring, or as meandering uncertainly before moving forward confidently, or as full of obstacles which are with difficulty overcome, this is at least in part because of the way the music makes us feel. Disturbing passages disturb us; reassuring ones reassure. Passages that meander uncertainly make us feel uneasy: It is not clear where the music is going. Passages that move forward confidently make us feel satisfied: We know what is happening and seem to be able to predict what will happen next. Passages that are full of obstacles make us feel tense and when the obstacles are overcome, we feel relieved. It is important to notice that the feeling *expressed* is not always the feeling *aroused:* An uncertain, diffident passage may make me uneasy; a confident passage may make me feel reassured or relaxed.

Now, of course we are still a long way from showing how unrequited passion can be expressed by a piece of music, but we can perhaps begin to see how the development of a complex piece of music can mirror the development of a complex emotional experience, and how we can become aware of both the formal development and the corresponding emotional development by means of the relatively "simple" feelings that are *aroused* in the listener as she follows that development. As I listen to a piece which expresses serenity tinged with doubt, I myself do not have to feel serenity tinged with doubt, but the feelings I do experience, such as relaxation or reassurance, interspersed with uneasiness, alert me to the nature of the over-all emotional expressiveness in the piece of music as a whole. Consider, for example, a piece of music in sonata form in which the two chief themes in their initial formulation are respectively lively and ponderous (we can suppose that the contour theory accounts for these characterizations). Now, suppose that the initially lively theme (in the major) gets gradually but relentlessly overwhelmed by the ponderous (minor) theme in such a way that the first theme is never allowed to return to its initial lively formulation but gets increasingly distorted, becomes darker and is finally heard in a truncated form in the same minor key as the ponderous theme. Such music might well make me feel increasingly nervous and tense, even disturbed, as it develops. On the view I am suggesting, the emotional experience aroused by the music is essential to the detection of the emotional expressiveness in the music itself. At the same time, the emotions aroused in me are not the emotions expressed by the music. *I* feel nervous, tense, and disturbed; the *music* expresses cheerful confidence turned to despair, or something of this sort. If this account is correct, then it shows that Kivy is wrong to suppose that expressiveness in music is just a matter of contour and convention, even if some expressive passages in music can be explained in such terms. In my example, it is not enough to spot the respective lively and ponderous contours of the initial statements of the two themes; the expressiveness of the piece as a whole can only be grasped if the listener's feelings are aroused in such a way that they provide a clue to both the formal and the expressive structure of the piece as it develops through time.

A Wealth of Wordless Knowledge
▪ Diana Raffman ▪

[I]t seems peculiarly difficult for our literal minds to grasp the idea that anything can be *known* which cannot be *named*. . . . But this . . . is really the strength of musical expressiveness: that *music articulates the forms that language cannot set forth.* . . . The imagination that responds to music is personal and associative and logical, tinged with affect, tinged with bodily rhythm, tinged with dream, but *concerned* with a wealth of formulations for its wealth of wordless knowledge.

—Susanne Langer 1942, 198, 207

If all meanings could be adequately expressed by words, the [art of] music would not exist. There are values and meanings that can be expressed only by immediately . . . audible qualities, and to ask what they mean in the sense of something that can be put into words is to deny their distinctive existence.

—John Dewey 1934, 74

Langer and Dewey, among many others, join in giving voice to the conviction that our knowledge of music is, in some essential respect, *ineffable: In hearing* a piece of music, we come to know something that cannot be expressed in words. Are these philosophers right? Do we really acquire ineffable knowledge when we hear music,

---

"A Wealth of Wordless Knowledge" by Diana Raffman is published by permission of the author.

and if so, what exactly is it that we know ineffably? In this essay I am going to try to answer these questions.

Some (perhaps most) questions in the philosophy of art are answered by a method called "conceptual analysis." In other words, they are answered simply by reflecting on what we mean by certain words. "What makes something a work of art?" is one such question. "Are the intentions of the artist relevant to an interpretation of his work?" is another. By contrast, questions about ineffable musical knowledge are (at least partly) questions about the nature of musical *experience,* a psychological process: It is supposedly *in hearing* a musical work that we acquire ineffable knowledge. If that's so, then the science of psychology can probably shed some light on our problem. So let's begin by looking at what the psychologists of music have to say.

On at least one popular view, you have unconscious knowledge of a rather fancy set of rules for analyzing pieces of music. When you hear music, you unconsciously make a mental picture of the notes and rhythms, i.e., you make a kind of "mental score" of the piece, and then you analyze it according to those rules. The rules specify where the musical phrases begin and end, where the downbeats and upbeats occur, what the melodies and harmonies are, and so forth. It's because you analyze the music in this way that it "makes sense" to you, rather than sounding like a jumble of nonsense sounds. The thought is that if you didn't analyze the music, it would sound something like the way a foreign language sounds when you don't understand it.

For our purposes here, the most important element of this unconscious musical analysis is its very first step—viz., the formation of a kind of mental picture of the notes and rhythms, a "mental score" if you will. Keep in mind that the sound you hear, the "raw" acoustic signal, does not arrive at your ear already neatly chopped up into notes and rhythms. Rather, the acoustic signal is itself just a more or less continuous stream of undifferentiated sound, and your ear must do the work of organizing it into notes and rhythms. The music psychologists think that your ear does this by "filtering" the acoustic signal through a kind of mental grid that chops it into notes and rhythms, in something like the way cookie dough would be carved into different shapes if you pushed it through a cookie cutter with those shapes cut out of it.

What does all this talk of rules and grids have to do with the question of ineffable knowledge? Well, it turns out that, with the right kind of training, you can learn to say a good deal about what you hear in a piece of music. For instance, you can learn to say (verbalize) what the notes and rhythms are, where the phrases begin and end, what the melodies and harmonies are, and so forth. However—and here is the critical point—it looks very much as if you can verbalize only what your unconscious analysis specifies. Indeed, it is presumably because, and only because, you have generated that analysis that you are able, with proper training, to say what you hear.

The issue of *ineffability,* or verbal inexpressibility, enters in because it turns out that your unconscious analysis doesn't capture everything you hear in the music. In other words, you hear more than you can "analyze." In particular, it doesn't capture the tiny differences in pitch and timing that distinguish the different performances of a given work. These fine-grained differences, often called "nuances," are the expressive tools the performer uses to convey his particular interpretation of the work: One violinist will play a certain A-natural in the [Johannes] Brahms concerto slightly higher than another, or slightly higher on one occasion than on another, while one flutist will hold the opening eighth note of the Bach E-flat sonata slightly longer than another, and so forth. Your unconscious analysis fails to capture these tiny differences because they are "narrower" than the spaces in the grid that makes the notes and rhythms: the difference between those two A-naturals lies *within* the A-natural slot in the grid, the difference between those two eighth notes *within* the eighth-note slot in the grid. What this means is that your unconscious analysis of the music, which begins with your "mental score," will specify the sounds that you hear only as A-naturals and eighth notes; it will not specify them as this or that particular A-natural, this or that particular eighth note.

As a result, if all you can learn to *say* is what your analysis specifies, then you will not be able to learn to say exactly which A-natural you hear at a given time, or exactly which eighth-note length. You will be able to say that you are hearing an A-natural, and that you are hearing an eighth note, but not *which* particular A-natural or eighth note you are hearing. (A number of psychological studies bear this out; if you are interested, see for example Jane A. and William Siegel, "Absolute identification of notes and intervals by musicians," *Perception & Psychophysics* 21, 2 [1977]. 143–152.) But you hear these differences all the same. Indeed, it's precisely these fine-grained nuances that make it interesting to hear different performances of the same work. It's because we hear these differences that we don't get bored!

My answer to our original question, then, is that we do acquire ineffable knowledge when we hear a piece of music. In particular, we acquire ineffable knowledge of its expressive nuances: We hear them but cannot say what we hear. My story accords well with the remarks from Langer and Dewey quoted at the beginning. Langer writes that music's ability to articulate ineffable forms is "the strength of musical *expressiveness*" (my emphasis). In other words, it is the expressive features of music that carry ineffable content. Dewey refers to *meanings* that cannot be expressed in words. Isn't it plausible to suppose that the meaning of a piece of music is what the performer is trying to express when he sculpts the nuances of his performance in such a way as to convey his special interpretation? If that's right, then ineffable knowledge of the nuances comes very close to ineffable knowledge of the meaning of a musical work.

Representation in Music
■ Roger Scruton ■

Music may be used to express emotion, to heighten a drama, to emphasize the meaning of a ceremony; but it is nevertheless an abstract art, with no power to represent the world. Representation, as I understand it, is a property that does not belong to music.

The word 'representation' has many uses, and may often be applied to music. Therefore I shall discuss not the word, but the phenomenon, as it occurs in poetry, drama, sculpture and painting. Being common to both painting and poetry, this phenomenon cannot be identified with the semantic properties of a linguistic system, for painting, unlike poetry, does not belong to such a system. How, then, is it to be characterized? I suggest the following five conditions, not as an analysis, but as a partial description of the aesthetic significance of representation:

1. A man understands a representational work of art only if he gains *some* awareness of what it represents. His awareness may be incomplete, but is must be adequate. He may not see Masaccio's *Tributute Money* as a representation of the scene from the Gospel; but to understand it as a representation he should at least see the fresco as a group of gesturing men. If a man does not see the fresco in some such way—say because he can appreciate it only as an abstract arrangement of colours and lines—then he does not understand it.

2. Representation requires a medium, and is understood only when the distinction between subject and medium has been recognized. Merely to *mistake* a painting for its subject is to misunderstand it; so too is there misunderstanding when a man is unable to extract the features of the subject from the peculiarities and conventions of the medium. (A varnished painting of a man is not a painting of a varnished man, however much it may look as though it were.)

3. Interest in a representation requires an interest in its subject. If an interest in the Masaccio depends in no way upon an interest in the scene portrayed, then the fresco is being treated not as a representation but as a work of abstract art.

4. A representational work of art must express thoughts about its subject, and an interest in the work should involve an understanding of those thoughts. (This is an ingredient in condition 3.) I mean by 'thought' roughly what [Gottlob] Frege meant by *'Gedanke'*: the sense or content of a declarative sentence. In this sense thoughts may be spoken of as true or false, although of course it is not always the truth-value of a thought that is of interest in aesthetic understanding. It is clear

---

"Representation in Music" by Roger Scruton is excerpted from *The Aesthetic Understanding*, Methuen (1983), pages 62–69, 71–72 and is reprinted by permission of Routledge.

that a representational work of art always conveys thoughts, in this Fregean sense, about its subject. Among the thoughts that give rise to my interest in *King Lear,* and which give a reason for that interest, are thoughts about Lear. These thoughts are communicated by the play, and are common property among all who understand it. Something similar occurs in the appreciation of a painting. Even in the most minimal depiction—say, of an apple on a cloth—appreciation depends on determinate thoughts that could be expressed in language without reference to the picture; for example: 'Here is an apple; the apple rests on a cloth; the cloth is chequered and folded at the edge.' Representation, in other words, is essentially propositional.

Sometimes we feel that a work of art is filled with thought, but that the thought cannot be detached from the work. It is impossible to put it into words (or into other words). Such cases, I should like to say, are cases not of representation but of expression. Why I should make such a distinction, and why I should make it in that way, will be apparent later.

5. Interest in representation may involve an interest in its *lifelike* quality; but it is not, for all that, an interest in literal truth. It is irrelevant that the depiction be inaccurate; what matters is that it be convincing. To require accuracy is to ask for a report rather than a representation.

I shall rely on an intuitive understanding of these conditions: They tell us what it is to treat something as a representation, rather than as a report, a copy, or a mere inarticulate sign. On this account, what makes a passage of prose into a representation is not so much its semantic structure as the specific intention with which it is composed. The semantic structure is relevant only because it provides the means whereby that intention is fulfilled. Representational literature is literature written with the intention that conditions 1–5 should be satisfied. Thus one may treat as a representation something that is not a representation; one may achieve representation by novel means; one may create a representation that is never understood, and so on.

Now some philosophers—those who think that music is a language—will give an account of musical representation on the model of description in prose or verse. But such an approach is surely most implausible. Anything that we could envisage as a semantic interpretation of music (a theory of 'musical truth') would deprive music of precisely the aesthetic aims for which we admire it, turning it instead into a clumsy code. Furthermore, all attempts to explain music in such terms end by giving rules of reference without rules of truth. We are told that a certain passage carries a reference to love; but we are not told what the passage is supposed to *say* about love. And to speak of language where there is 'reference,' but no predication, is simply to misuse a word. We are in fact leaving the realm of representation altogether and entering into that of expression. But there is no need to prove that music is a language in order to assign to it the expressive properties that are mentioned, for example, by Deryck Cooke.

A better attempt to prove that music is a representational medium begins by comparing music to painting. It can be said with some truth that music, like painting, may deliberately, 'imitate,' or 'copy' features of an object. Is this not, then, a kind of representation? Examples are familiar: Saint-Saëns' *Carnaval des Animaux*, 'Gretchen am Spinnrade,' *La Mer*. And it is natural to consider such pieces as attempts to 'depict' the objects referred to in their titles. But perhaps what is meant here by 'depiction' is not what is meant when we refer to the visual arts. A few observations about painting will therefore be appropriate.

It is a commonplace that depiction is not simply a matter of resemblance. Nor is it enough that the resemblance be *intended;* nor even that the artist should intend the resemblance to be noticed. No doubt Manet intended us to notice the resemblance between his *Olympia* and Titian's *Venus of Urbino*. But that is certainly not a case of one painting representing another. It is for such reasons that we might wish to lay the burden of our analysis of depiction on the notion of an 'aspect.' The artist intends that the spectator should *see* the painting *as* its subject, not merely that the spectator should notice a resemblance between the two. In other words, the painter intends that we should have the experience of a certain aspect—that we should feel that seeing his painting is importantly *like* seeing its subject—and not merely that we should notice a resemblance. Thus a painter may intend to copy the *Mona Lisa,* but he does not (as a rule) intend that his painting should be seen as Leonardo's; rather, he intends that it should be seen as the woman in Leonardo's painting. On this view, the intention in depicting is not to 'copy' an object, but rather to create a certain visual impression. And surely, it will be argued, precisely the same process, and the same intention, may exist in writing music. Sounds are created which are meant to be *heard as* other things, as the babbling of brooks, the warbling of birds, the roaring and plodding of animals. . . .

However, a difficulty now arises. . . .

Representation can be begun . . . only where it can also be completed. If music is to be representational, then its subject must be not only picked out, but also characterized. But that requires a context, and in music the context seems to add no further precision to the 'representational' parts. A certain passage in *Der Rosenkavalier* 'imitates' the glitter of a silver rose. But what more does this passage say about the glitter, except that it is a glitter (and even that may go unnoticed)? The context adds nothing to the thought, and while there is *musical* development, the development of a *description* seems scarcely to be in point. So too, when the imitation of birdsong in [Olivier] Messiaen is given musical development, there is no thought about the birdsong which is made more determinate by that process. The birdsong is absorbed into the musical structure and takes on a meaning that is purely musical. But, it might be said, does not the music none the less convey a thought about the birdsong, in the sense of a purely *musical* thought? Why should it matter that the thought cannot be put into words? Such a retort gets us nowhere. For whatever is meant by a purely musical thought, we can envisage also a purely painterly thought—a thought that finds its only expression in lines and colours, but which cannot be put into words, and which consequently cannot be regarded as true or false. And it is part of the point of calling painting a representational art that the thoughts involved in its appreciation are *not* all purely painterly, that, on the contrary, an experience of a painting will involve thoughts about its subject, thoughts that could be put into words. This 'narrative' element is an essential feature of the phenomenon of representation. If we insist none the less that there is a type of 'representation' that is purely symbolic (which contains ostension but no description) then we are simply denying the role of representation in aesthetic interest.

It is true, all the same, that I may hear a passage of music as something that I know it not to be. I may hear a passage as forest murmurs, for example, as rushing water, as an approaching or receding horse. Should we lay any emphasis on this phenomenon? One problem is that a man may hear and appreciate 'representational' music *without* hearing the aspect. And while it is true that I may also hear poetry without knowing what it says (as when I listen to the reading of a poem in Chinese), to do so is not to appreciate the poem as poetry. An interest in poetry is not an interest in pure sound; a genuine interest in music, on the other hand, may by-pass its representational pretensions altogether. Therefore we cannot assume that a composer may sit down with the honest intention of creating a piece to be heard as, say, the quarrel between Mr Pickwick and Mrs Bardell's lawyers. For he cannot be sure that it *will* be heard in that way; his intention is vitiated, and must be replaced by what is at best a hope or a wish. If the intention endures none the less, it is because there is available to the composer some independent way of specifying his subject: for instance, through the words of a song, or through action on the stage. Thus, in the more adventurous attempts at representation, such as we find in the symphonic poem, the composer is apt to depend on a specific literary reference in order to secure the hearer's complicity in what is better described as an imaginative endeavour than as an inevitable perception. It is thus with *Don Juan* and *Don Quixote,* with *Taras Bulba* and the anecdotal works of Charles Ives.

The argument is of course by no means conclusive. But certain facts are significant all the same. It is significant, for example, that, while a man may look at an untitled picture and know immediately what it represents, it is most unlikely that he should do the same with an untitled symphonic poem. Significant too is the indefiniteness of the relation between music and its 'subject': the music does not determine some one natural class of interpretations, and can usually be fitted to widely contrasting themes. A quarrel between Mr Pickwick and a lawyer may be 'represented' by music that serves equally well the purpose of 'depicting' a forest fire. We see this ambiguity evidenced in the ballet, where the action is usually left so far indeterminate by the music that several incompatible choreographies may exist side by side as accepted members of the repertoire; as in *The Rite of Spring.* Hence, while the aspect of a painting, and the meaning of a sentence, are publicly recognized facts, which make possible the intention characteristic of representational art, there are no similar facts to enable the intention to be carried over into the realm of music. . . .

When we learn of a piece of music that it *is* supposed to represent something, then its 'auditory aspect' (the way it sounds) may change for us, even when what is 'depicted' is not a sound. On learning of its subject we may come to 'hear it differently,' despite the fact that the subject is not something audible. Consider [Claude] Debussy's prelude, *Voiles,* which may be said to depict the slow drift of sails in a summer breeze. Learning that, I may begin to hear in the musical line a leisurely and day-dreaming quality that I did not hear before, as though I were watching the to-ing and fro-ing of sails on a calm bright sea. But here, of course, what is 'depicted' is not something heard. May we not say, all the same, that we *hear* the music *as* the drifting of sails?

Even if we grant the force of those remarks, however, we find ourselves facing another, and yet more serious objection to the view that there is 'representation' in music. The objection is that one can understand a 'representational' piece of music without treating it as a representation, indeed, without being aware that it is supposed to have such a status. On the other hand, the very suggestion that one might understand—say—Raphael's *St George* (National Gallery of Art, Washington) while being indifferent to, or ignorant of, its representational quality, is absurd. To suggest such a thing is to suggest treating the Raphael as a work of abstract art; it is to ignore the feature of representation altogether, because it is thought to be insignificant, or because it is thought to play no part in aesthetic interest. But to take such a view is simply to dismiss the problem. If I recognize the existence of a problem about music it is partly because I think that there *is* an aesthetically significant notion of representation employed in the discussion and enjoyment of painting.

Now someone might object to the view that one cannot both understand the Raphael and also have no knowledge of its subject. He might claim that at least a *partial* understanding of the painting could be achieved by studying it as a piece of abstract art. One may understand the composition of the painting, he will say, the balance of tensions between ascending and descending lines, the sequence of spatial planes, and so on, and in none of this need one have an awareness of the subject. But such a reply is wholly misguided. For it seems to suggest that these important aesthetic properties of the Raphael—composition, balance, spatial rhythm—are quite independent of the representation; whereas that is clearly not so. For example we perceive the balance between the upward thrust of the horse's hind legs and the downward pressure of the lance only because we see the two lines as filled with the forces of the things depicted—of the horse's muscles and the horseman's lance. Take away the representation and the balance too would dissolve. And the same goes for the composition. Alter the representational meaning of the horse (close its eye, for example, or attach a bangle to its hoof) and the composition would be utterly destroyed. Nothing here is comprehensible until the representation is grasped.

Let us return, then, to our example. When a passage from *Voiles* reminds me of drifting sails I do indeed hear an aspect of the music. But the *important* part of this aspect—the part that seems essential to a full musical understanding—can be perceived by someone who is deaf to the 'representation.' It is possible to hear the relaxed and leisurely quality of the musical line while being unaware that it depicts the movement of sails. The 'reference' to sails does not determine our understanding of the music in the way that representation determines our understanding of the visual arts. . . .

In search for examples of genuine musical representation we may be led by this argument back to the suggestion that the true subject-matter of music is sound. Sounds have properties which music, being itself sound, may share; so music ought to be able to depict *sounds*. For there will be no difficulty here in explaining how it is that the music may lead us *inevitably* to the thought of what is represented. Thoughts of a subject will therefore form an integral part of musical appreciation. But again there is a peculiarity that deserves mention, since it seems to suggest that even here, in the most plausible examples, there is yet another of our five features of understanding representation that fails to belong to music: feature 2. When music attempts the direct 'representation' of sounds it has a tendency to become transparent, as it were, to its subject. Representation gives way to reproduction, and the musical medium drops out of consideration altogether as superfluous. In a sense the first scene of *Die Meistersinger* contains an excellent representation of a Lutheran chorale. But then it *is* a Lutheran chorale. Similarly, the tinkling of teaspoons in Strauss's *Sinfonia Domestica,* and the striking of anvils in *Rheingold,* are not so much sounds represented as sounds reproduced, which in consequence detach themselves from the musical structure and stand out on their own. Nor is this an accident. On the contrary, it is an inevitable consequence of the logical properties of sounds. For sounds . . . may be identified as individuals independently of the objects that possess them. In attempting to represent them, therefore, one need have no regard to the object that produces them: One represents the sound alone. But since there is nothing to music except sound, there ceases to be any *essential* difference between the medium of representation and the subject represented.

Sound and Semblance
■ Peter Kivy ■

In a recent article called "Representation in Music," Roger Scruton argues that "Music . . . is . . . an abstract art, with no power to represent the World." His argument consists in laying out what he takes to be five necessary (but not sufficient) conditions for being an artistic representation, and in claiming that music does not meet some of them. I am interested here only in answering the charge that music

"Sound and Semblance" by Peter Kivy has been excerpted from *Sound and Semblance,* Princeton University Press (1984), pages 146–147, 149–150, 152–155, 157–158, and is reprinted by permission of the publisher.

qua music cannot represent. So I will confine myself only to those criteria of representation adduced by Scruton that bear directly on that charge; and I shall not, therefore, spend time outlining Scruton's position in full.

The first condition on artistic representation, according to Scruton, is that the work be understandable only if the representation be perceived. In other words, the representational part of a truly representational work of art cannot be irrelevant to its aesthetic appreciation: it is a necessary condition. . . .

A corollary of this seems to be, although Scruton does not mention it explicitly, that the representation in representational works be readily recognizable without verbal aids or esoteric knowledge; for one of his reasons for thinking music cannot be representational at all is the familiar claim that musical representation is never apparent, but always needs nonmusical props. "It is significant," he writes, "that, while a man may look at an untitled picture and know immediately what it represents, it is most unlikely that he should do the same with an untitled symphonic poem." However, the major argument against musical representation that emerges from this particular condition is that even what is called "representational" music can be understood, appreciated, or what you will, without ever recognizing the representational aspect. "To understand a representational painting, one must have some knowledge of the subject; but the same has never been honestly claimed for music." And again: "One can understand a 'representational' piece of music without treating it as a representation, indeed, without being aware that it is supposed to be a representation at all."

The claim that musical representation is never apparent and the argument against musical representation that it generates can both, at this point, be dismissed rather peremptorily. If, by "representations," are meant what I have been calling musical "pictures," then the claim is false; and if what I have been calling musical "representations" are intended, the claim is irrelevant. For musical pictures, insignificant though they may be in Western music, are as readily recognizable without verbal aids as any representational painting. (No one fails to recognize the bird songs in Beethoven's *Pastoral,* or, I believe, the steam engine in *Pacific* 231.) And musical representations, like the general's representation of the battle of Balaclava, a circuit diagram of your radio, or, for that matter, Picasso's *Guernica* or [Piet] Mondrian's *Broadway Boogie-woogie,* although they require verbal instructions, are no less *representations* for that.

The argument that what we normally call musical representation is irrelevant to, unnecessary for a proper understanding of music, whereas recognition of representation in representational painting is a necessary condition for painterly understanding, requires careful consideration. Unlike the previous objection, it cannot be summarily dismissed. . . .

I shall [adduce a clear case] where those at least uncommitted to musical purism will readily admit that to be ignorant of the musical representation is not fully to understand (or appreciate) something very important and nontrivial about the *musical* character of the work. An example of this kind occurs in [Karl Maria von] Weber's

Invitation to the Dance. It exhibits, to be sure, a perfect musical form: a slow introduction, a series of waltzes in the form of a rondo, and a brief return of the material of the introduction as a coda. But the musical material of the introduction and its return are completely inexplicable in purely musical terms without Weber's program: "First approach of the dancer (measures 1–5); to whom the lady gives an evasive answer (5–9). His more pressing invitation (9–13); her acceptance of his request (13–16). Now they converse in greater detail; he begins (17–19); she answers (19–21) . . . ," and so on. . . . Anyone familiar with the Western musical tradition will immediately recognize the strangely disjointed thematic material of the introduction as characteristic not of an instrumental composition at all, but of an operatic recitative. It simply does not make any musical sense, does not "hang together" until one knows the program, and can see the alternating melodic fragments of the left and right hands as the conversation of the male and female dancers. (Indeed, had a program not been provided by the composer, it is a safe bet that many would have been by commentators.) It is not that any errors in harmony or counterpoint have been made. It is musically correct: a "well-formed formula." But it is musical hash, bits and pieces, until the program puts them together into a discursive sequence. It seems clear in the Weber . . . that in a very proper sense of "musical," one cannot fully understand the musical structure without knowing the subject of the musical representation. . . .

[I]f I am puzzled by . . . the oddly fragmented thematic structure of the introduction to *Invitation to the Dance,* my puzzlement will perhaps be dispelled, my desire for musical continuity satisfied, when I come to perceive, or it is pointed out to me, . . . that the alternating bass and treble phrases of Weber's introduction represent a conversation between a man and a woman . . . This, it seems to me, is sufficient to defeat Scruton's claim that since we can *always fully understand* representational music without knowing what it represents, music can never be properly representational. . . .

In its weaker form, . . . Scruton's argument seems to be that although we cannot understand a piece of representational music *fully* without knowing the subject of the representation, so little is lost in not knowing, that we cannot fairly call the music representational at all. The problem of course lies with the phrase "so little is lost." How much is "much"? How little "little"? And doesn't it matter at all whether we are talking about a musical composition in which there is a single incidental representation in three hours of music, or one that is built entirely around a program or title? Surely more is lost if—per impossible—I perceive the *Madonna della Sedia* as an abstract design, not a woman's face and figure, than if I fail to perceive that a "growling" figure in the orchestra represents the rolling away of a stone from a cistern in Beethoven's *Fidelio* (the only such piece of representation in the work, so far as I can remember). But to claim that my loss, in failing to perceive the representation in *Invitation to the Dance* . . . , is negligible and musically unimportant, seems to me to be indefensible, however defensible the claim might be in regard to other musical works. Do I lose more or less than if I saw Mondrian's *Broadway Boogie-woogie* without the title? For here is a case of representation in painting where all is *not* lost when the subject is not known. (Compare it with those works of Mondrian in a similar style that are untitled.) I will not belabor this point, for it seems to me clear enough that musical representation of the kind I have been discussing throughout this book cannot in all cases be dismissed as trivial or irrelevant to the *musical* understanding of the music of which it is a part. It would be folly to maintain that . . . I have a full musical understanding of *Invitation to the Dance* while totally ignorant of its title or program . . .

Another condition on artistic representation that Scruton believes music cannot fulfill is the condition that there be, in representation, a *medium:* "Representation requires a medium, and is understood only when the distinction between subject and medium has been recognized." But in musical representation, Scruton insists, no medium can be located, and the distinction between subject and medium dissolves, at least where the subject represented is *sound.*

> When music attempts the direct "representation" of sounds it has a tendency to become transparent, as it were, to its subject. Representation gives way to reproduction, and the musical medium drops out of consideration altogether as superfluous. In a sense the first scene of *Die Meistersinger* contains an excellent representation of a Lutheran chorale. But then it *is* a Lutheran chorale. Similarly, the tinkling of teaspoons in Strauss's *Sinfonia Domestica,* and the striking of anvils in *Rheingold,* are not so much sounds represented as sounds reproduced, which in consequence detach themselves from the musical structure and stand out on their own.

When music attempts to represent sound, "since there is nothing to music except sound, there ceases to be any *essential* difference between the medium of representation and the subject represented.

It is important to notice to start with, that Scruton is talking here only about instances of music representing sounds: more or less what I have been calling musical "pictures," and musical representations of the "sounds like" kind. Nothing he says casts the slightest doubt on instances in which music represents (in my sense of the word) things other than sounds. When Bach represents the imitation of Christ, or Handel the exodus out of Egypt, the distinction between medium and subject is as clear as it is anywhere else. No one takes Bach to be imitating the sound of the imitatio Christi (whatever that would be), or Handel the sound of the children of Israel escaping their Egyptian captivity. They are representing acts, or events, or "things" in sound. These are the subjects, sound—more properly, musical sound—the medium. And since these kinds of musical representations are far and away the most numerous, the most aesthetically interesting, the most musically significant, even if Scruton's argument held good for musical sound pictures and representations of the "sounds like" variety, it still would leave intact the main body of musical representation. However, it does not hold good even for those, as I will now try to show. . . .

To cite an instance, it seems to me that the most felicitous way of describing Mozart's *Musical Joke (Ein musikalischer Spass,* K.522) is as a musical representation of a divertimento composed by a second-rate composer and executed by incompetent musicians. What are the other possibilities? Surely it can't just *be* a divertimento by a second-rate composer, not just for the trivial reason that it was not composed by a second-rate composer, but because it is not second-rate: It has all the marks of Mozart's genius on it. Nor is it an imitation of one, at least not a very good imitation, for the music is splendidly written music and its subject second-rate stuff. A well-made chair cannot be a good imitation of all ill-made one (although it might be a good *representation*).

Furthermore, even if one were to disagree with me that the *Musical Joke* is splendidly written music, a comparison with the real second-rate music of Mozart's time, which he was lampooning, would instantly reveal that the *Musical Joke* is neither an imitation nor just another instance of the second-rate. For like any good satirist, Mozart has exaggerated, distorted, and put into bold relief the object of his raillery for the purpose of casting light on what it is about the music he is lampooning that is inept and clumsy. It is not possible for K.522 to be mistaken for a second-rate eighteenth-century divertimento. There is too much craft and distortion for that. In short, one simply cannot avoid the epithet "representation" in characterizing Mozart's caricature. Nothing else will do, and certainly not "just another example of the very thing pilloried." Where, then, would be the joke, or the art? . . .

The final point I want to consider is Scruton's claim that "representation is . . . essentially propositional," whereas musical "representation" (so-called) cannot be. Scruton writes, of what he takes to be the propositional element in artistic representation:

> A representational work of art must express thoughts about its subject, and an interest in the work should involve an understanding of those thoughts. . . . Even in the most minimal depiction—say, of an apple on a cloth—appreciation depends on determinate thoughts that could be expressed in language without reference to the picture; for example: "Here is an apple; the apple rests on a cloth; the cloth is chequered and folded at the edge."

Representational art, then, makes statements conveying at least minimal information about its subjects. Music, however, even in its so-called representational moments, cannot.

> If music is to be representational, then its subject must be not only picked out, but also characterized. But that requires a context, and in music the context seems to add no further precision to the "representational" parts. A certain passage in *Der Rosenhavalier* "imitates" the glitter of a silver rose. But what more does this passage say about the glitter except that it is a glitter (and even that may go unnoticed)?

In the nineteenth century particularly, extravagant claims were made for the informational content and capabilities of music, perhaps inspired by the claims of [Arthur] Schopenhauer, never matched before or since, which made music out to be nothing less than philosophy in sound, revelatory of the ultimate nature of metaphysical reality. (Extravagant claims were made for *philosophy* as well.) I hardly think anyone is prepared to make such audacious claims today. If representational music is propositional, it is a limiting case; if it conveys information about its subject, the information is minimal. But if Scruton's own account of the propositional in artistic representation is to be credited, still life painting, which is surely a very paradigm of representational art, can only be regarded as a limiting case of the propositional, a minimal conveyor of information about its subject. And if music can come up to the standard of still life painting, it can hardly fall below the standard of representational art. It would seem that a sufficient condition for a representation being propositional is that its subject be describable. A still life of an apple resting on a checkered cloth expresses, according to Scruton, the following propositions: Here is an apple; the apple rests on a cloth; the cloth is checkered, and so on. All these propositions amount to is whatever can be offered as a verbal description of the picture's subject: The subject is an apple; the apple rests on a cloth; the cloth is checkered. And that propositional condition can be fulfilled by any intelligible musical representation or picture as well, for any bona fide, intelligible unproblematic musical representation or picture must, of course, have a subject at least minimally describable in words: "Here is a cuckoo; it sounds a descending major third."

The Recording Angel
■ Evan Eisenberg ■

I

[Walter] Benjamin's 1936 essay "The Work of Art in the Age of Mechanical Reproduction," which started many of us thinking about these matters, deals mainly with the visual arts, and backhandedly sweeps music along. . . .

Photogravure reproduces an art *object,* proliferating it in space. This, as Benjamin says, cheapens its ritual value, which depends less on the observable qualities of the object than on its haecceity or "thisness," its unique identity. Phonography, by contrast, reproduces an art *event,* proliferating it in time. For a moment the analogy wants to keep going. Doesn't an art event, such as a concert, have a ritual value that depends on its uniqueness? . . .

Repetition is essential to ritual, and exact repetition is what it has always striven to attain. According to Hindu scripture, the inaccurate singing of a sacred raga could be fatal to the singer. The same held for off-key Apache shamans. In Polynesia the careless performer might be executed; on the island of Gaua in the New Hebrides (the musicologist Curt Sachs tells us) "old men used to stand by

"The Recording Angel" by Evan Eisenberg has been excerpted from *The Recording Angel,* Penguin Books USA, Inc. (1987), pages 50–55, 150–159, and is reprinted by permission of Francis J. Spieler.

with bows and arrows and shoot at every dancer who made a mistake." The earliest musical notations were designed to preserve sacred formulae; some, such as Babylonian notation, were the secret preserve of priests and cantors. Max Weber ascribed these tendencies, and aesthetic stylization in general, to a concern for magical efficacy. If the death penalty for wrong notes is missing in Christianity, the concern for liturgical accuracy abides. As Henry Raynor writes in his *Social History of Music,* "The history of the development of Western notation is a history of the attempts of ecclesiastical musicians to ensure the accuracy of the rite."

Notation can ensure against lapses of memory, but not against slips of the tongue or the hand. Only recording—above all tape recording, with its absolving splices—can ensure absolute accuracy. Moreover, even an immaculate live performance will differ in some degree from the last immaculate performance. Only a record never varies.

Some people's private phonographic rituals are plainly religious, as when people play *Messiah* on Christmas day. I myself formerly, as an Orthodox Jew who lived in the city but believed that the proper spirit of the Sabbath was pastoral, used to listen on Friday afternoons after my shower to Klemperer's recording of Beethoven's Sixth Symphony, a record most persuasive of the blessedness of leisure. (When the Scherzo was being recorded Walter Legge, the producer, kept calling down from the control booth to ask if the tempo wasn't after all, rather slow? Klemperer, in unusually good humor, would answer: "Don't worry, Walter, you will get used to it.") But most private phonographic ritual is secular. Composers' birthdays are observed in the obvious way. There is the custom of hearing *The Rite of Spring* at the vernal equinox. There is the anticustom of playing The Mothers of Invention on Mother's Day. A critic writes that for him Sunday morning would not be Sunday morning without Thelonious Monk.

People inclined to such observances may also observe taboos. If a record has its special place in your life, you don't cheapen it by playing it at random. If you care deeply about a composer, you don't ask him to accompany you to the bathroom—you take the pickup off for a minute. On the other hand, you don't take a symphony off in the middle, if you can help it; turning the radio off might be excusable, as the show will go on without you, but if you take the record off you boorishly disrupt the performance. (For practical people it's the other way around, because with a record they can always pick up where they left off.)

The physical act of playing a record can itself be ritualistic. My own ancient AR turntable needs to be spun a few times by hand before the pulley and gears will catch, and the tone arm has to be lowered preliminarily beneath the level of the platter to get the damping right. No one else knows to do these things. My Levitical knowledge makes me master of all phonographic rites conducted in my home. But even modern machines want a good deal of attention to their levers and knobs. In fact, the more state-of-the-art the machine, the more attention it wants. No serious discophile will put on an LP without cleaning it, and the most popular cleaning system involves, minimally, squeezing three drops of Hi-Technology Record Cleaning Fluid on a velvety pad with walnut-grained handle, smearing the drops with the bottom of the squeeze bottle, holding the pad perpendicular to the record grooves, pressing the damp side of the convex pad against the surface of the record while making sure that the long axis of the pad is perpendicular to the grooves, turning the pad slowly on its axis so that the dry part is pressed against the record, raking the soiled pad with the bristled DC-1 Pad Cleaner, then wondering what to clean the Pad Cleaner with. The instructions are unctuously dogmatic on the "proper use of 3 drops" in annointing the pad. All this sounds toilsome but soon comes as naturally as laying phylacteries, and then one can hardly bear to put a record on otherwise. There is something soul-satisfying about a ritual that separates music from noise, culture from chaos. . . .

With records, . . . one could make love while listening to the *St. Matthew Passion.* . . . But such things and worse are done. Benjamin Britten complained: "It is one of the unhappiest results of the march of science and commerce that this unique work [the *St. Matthew*], at the turn of a switch is at the mercy of any loud roomful of cocktail drinkers—to be listened to or switched off at will, without ceremony or occasion." Not long ago I heard a late-night classical disk jockey purr, "I suggest that you get out your popcorn, or if you're older and more mature, your martini olives, and sit back and enjoy Bach's *St. Matthew Passion.*" This from a disk jockey, who has taken it upon himself to suggest, if not exactly to construct, a public architecture of time. The private citizen can afford to be even more reckless, and often is. But if his recklessness is not mere callousness, it can be creative. . . .

We have all become like Prospero, able to conjure up invisible musicians who sing and play at our pleasure. Part of the fun is our sense of power. We can manipulate the poker-faced, flawless [Jascha] Heifetz. We can shut up [Barbra] Streisand. We can boost the basses and cellos in the Berlin Philharmonic, defying [Herbert von] Karajan's meticulous balances.

In this the phonograph is rather like the rest of the "home entertainment center," which is a voodoo doll's house full of politicians, movie stars, dangerous romances and world-historical events—all in miniature, all manipulable. These facsimiles assure us that the world makes sense and we can manage it. . . .

II

With [Louis] Armstrong [and Enrico Caruso] the phonograph began to do a job more remarkable than storage. It ceased to be a mimic; if anything, live music and paper-composed music would not mimic records, especially Armstrong's. Anyone could imitate his ballooning cheeks and gravelly voice, and any critic could recognize in him the voice of the phonograph, the voice of invisible man. So it is no accident that when one thinks of a stack of old 78's one thinks first, depending on one's predilections, either of Armstrong or . . . Caruso. . . .

We like to believe that virtuosos of the grand romantic type have a magic in their presence that records can never quite capture. Although it is not the sort of sentiment they tend to express on record jackets, the virtuosos like to believe it, too. Thus Artur Rubinstein speaks, in an interview with Glenn Gould, of the "emanation" that makes an audience "listen like they are in your hand" and that "cannot be done at all by a record." He and Gould are "absolute opposites," he says, for Gould claims that he can influence his listener in a healthier way through the distant, considered intimacy of records. And it is easy to slip from this to a general opposition: the romantic extrovert as recitalist, the cerebral introvert as phonographer. . . . But really the opposition is not so absolute. Gould, too, was a showman, and his preference for doing his show on records, radio, television and film does not disqualify him any more than it disqualifies Stokowski or Cecil B. DeMille. And Rubinstein made plenty of great records, including the Brahms F minor Quintet (with the Guarneri) that Gould professed to be "drunk on."

Still, the extrovert-introvert distinction has its uses. So does the parallel distinction between artists who project and artists who don't. In the early days of phonography, projecting was a necessity. One had physically to project sound into the recording horn, which was not easy. And one had to project emotion into that rearmost of balconies, the living room. Caruso and Armstrong both did both, brilliantly, in the recordings they made before 1925. Of course both played instruments—the voice and the trumpet—that were traditionally projective.

In 1925 electrical recording introduced a second possibility. A musician could make himself the object of the microphone, as great movie actors make themselves objects of the camera; and his inwardness could fascinate. Instead of leaping out at the listener this sort of artist seems to ignore him, and thereby draws him in. *Innigkeit* is a quality much prized by record critics. Concert reviewers, by and large, know better than to demand it; the principle that one who would be heard should whisper is not useful in a hall fifty yards deep. (Unless one means a stage whisper, than which there is nothing stagier.) But in the recording studio it is a very useful principle. Glenn Gould made excellent use of it, and the impression his records give that he is playing only for himself and old Bach is reinforced by his involuntary humming (which used to strike me as comical, but now sounds like the gibbering of a ghost). Projecting, he said, was the bad habit of using rhetorical flourishes to lasso the man in the rear balcony.

Gould's instrument is one that, with the lid up, can be quite projective, but it is also one that people often play for themselves. So inwardness may come more naturally to a pianist. [Arthur] Schnabel, the pianist whom the young Gould most admired, managed to sound inward on acoustic disks and apparently even in concert. My image of *Innigkeit* is Bill Evans hunched over his keyboard at the Village Vanguard; his meditative records bring the image back. But his colleague Miles Davis, whose instrument is the most projective of all—an instrument originally used to signal, to alarm—also sounds as though he were playing for himself. " . . . For myself and for musicians," he told an interviewer. For the rest of us his centripetal solos, which turn the melody around a few hypersensitive notes, are often hard to concentrate on, however taken we may be with the glorious sidemen or the subtle construction of his good records. (We may even feel that he uses the mute to keep his soul inside, away from us. In fact, we may feel that at times a deliberate shutting out of his audience makes his playing something other than inward.)

When we come to the voice we find, in the 1920s, a tradition of projection developed in opera houses and vaudeville palaces and encouraged by acoustic recording; and a quieter tradition surviving in folk music and barely surviving in chamber music. Electric recording brought about a great, creative flowering of this second tradition in popular music and in jazz as Billie Holiday, Bing Crosby, and Fred Astaire taught singers to make themselves objects of the microphone. Louis Armstrong did this when singing, especially when singing scat—those anti-words, with their blithe disregard of all communication theory. His abstraction of tunes and texts makes him seem abstracted himself, as if daydreaming. Lulled, the listener begins, as in "Lazy River," to "dream a dream of me, dream a dream of me." And one secret of Armstrong's formula from 1929 on is the way the projective trumpet reaches out and grabs the listener, the dreamy vocal draws him in, and finally the trumpet pushes him back into his own world, signing off with a high F.

It is not odd for a man with a guitar to sing and play for his own gratification, and the early country bluesmen often give this impression on record. Robert Johnson surely does, confirming the story that when some Mexican musicians came to hear him he first froze, then turned and sang facing the wall. So does his rock descendent Van Morrison (John Cale claims that when recording *Astral Weeks* "Morrison couldn't work with anybody, so finally they just shut him in the studio by himself . . . and later they overdubbed.")

There is another mode, however, which in popular music and jazz may now be the most important of all, and which already has a serviceable name, cool. Neither appealing to the listener nor ignoring him, the cool performer speaks to him from somewhere inside the listener's head. The voice may be Olympian or diabolical, but it is always superior and always calm. It is often ironic. It knows the listener inside out. Cool fascinates, but not the way inwardness fascinates; the listener is not the observer but the observed. I am not sure who invented this mode, but I doubt it could have been done without the microphone; Bing Crosby, Fats Waller and Duke Ellington come to mind. It has been used effectively by T-Bone Walker, Chuck Berry, Miles Davis, Sonny Rollins, Dexter Gordon, Monk, Sinatra, the Beatles (especially Lennon), the Rolling Stones, Dylan, Zappa, Elvis Costello, Talking Heads—in short, by most of the great phonographers in popular music and jazz. In classical music it is much harder to identify. Among composers Satie, Weill, Stockhausen, Partch, Berio and Boulez seem to me cool at least sometimes; among performers Pinza, Richard Stoltzman, Weissenberg, and Teresa Stratas. It is hard to know how much of this is musical, how much mere image, but that conflation is one evidence of cool.

All three modes—the projective, the inward, and the cool—can be seen as responses to one of the paradoxes of the recording situation, namely that the audience is not there. This is just the flip side of the fact that, for the listener, the performer is not there. . . . In general, the paradoxes of making records are mirrored in the paradoxes of listening to them, which is why the artist's responses to the paradoxes are important from the point of view of aesthetics. . . .

The life of the touring blues musician, Charles Kell has observed, furnishes all the loneliness and jealousy he needs to sing the blues authentically. It is a strong extract of modern life. The recording situation is an even stronger and more representative extract. The glass booths and baffles that isolate the musician from his fellow musicians; the abstracted audience; the sense of producing an object and of mass-producing a commodity; the deconstruction of time by takes and its reconstruction by splicing—these are strong metaphors of modern life. Their mirror images in the listener's experience are solitude; the occlusion of the musician; the use of music as an object and a commodity; the collapse of a public architecture of time and the creation of a private interior design of time. Since they contradict everything that music-making once seemed to be, they are paradoxes.

In response to these paradoxes, a set of formal and emotional patterns should by now have emerged that would be characteristic of recorded music as opposed to live music; these would be the modes and archetypes of phonography. Unfortunately, the task of nailing them down is too big for the present book. For now, I will only enlarge a little on a mode I think I can identify, the cool. It can be seen as emerging from several of the paradoxes of phonography. To the abstraction of the audience it responds by speaking as if to a single, utterly known individual, in the manner of a disembodied voice. To the reification of music it responds by creating a curious object. To the hardening of musical language it responds by juxtaposing phrases rather than using them; in place of rhetoric there is irony. (The same irony protects the phonographer from the irony of his unseen listeners, against which he would otherwise be defenseless—like the blind musician of folklore, whose descendant he is.) To the deconstruction of time, the cool mode responds with cyclical rather than linear or dramatic forms. A device that unites several of these responses is that of beginning and ending an album with items that are similar, perhaps similar in having a pointedly antique or naive quality. I find some or all of these responses in the Beatles' *Sgt. Pepper* and the White Album, Zappa's *Burnt Weenie Sandwich*, Lenya's German recording of Weill's *Threepenny Opera*, Thelonious Monk's *Monk's Music*, and Glenn Gould's first recording of the *Goldberg Variations*.

Phonography
■ Lee B. Brown ■

A. *Transparency.* Several years ago, the *New York Times* reported that famed tenor Luciano Pavarotti had lip-synched a taped performance on BBC TV. Such an event jars our assumption that the rationale of recording technology is to provide a transparent window onto the acoustic reality of the living performance—however far it has slipped into the past. The industry has kept this *transparency perspective,* as we might term it, before the public from the earliest days of Thomas Edison's cylinder machines. The recording industry has described each of its technical breakthroughs—from acoustic to electric, from shellac to vinyl, from monophonic to stereophonic, and from analog to digital—in the same glowing terms as the one that came before: Recording technology provides perfect fidelity.

In fact, contrary to the image the recording industry projects, different recording technologies have always had their distinct *styles.* Even in the era of the old 78-rpm technology, different record labels had different sounds. (Experts seem to be able to tell the difference between a Victor and a Brunswick recording, circa 1930, just by listening.) Before the age of "hi-fi," popular recordings made by RCA Victor were "dry" or "dead," in that a listener could register little sense of room "presence." Around 1950, the company began to issue recordings that conveyed the "live" character of the recording hall. Was this merely a difference in fidelity? Or was it no less a difference in *style*?

In the era of vinyl technology, all record labels had a strategy for boosting bass and "rolling-off" the highs to make a more comfortable living room sound. But different companies used different formulas for doing so. The FFRR formula used by Decca-London was quite different from the RIAA curve used by RCA. And there were other differences. Mercury's "living presence" approach, which avoided multiple microphone setups, had its distinctive sound. Later on, those who grew up with stereo probably felt it possessed what Ernst Gombrich—speaking of visual art—called a "neutral naturalism." For many older listeners, however, stereo sound will forever be just that—*stereo* sound. The later digital technology too had its own quality—one that was quite different from analog. Listeners used to their old vinyl typically found the new CD sound to be edgy, or "dehydrated," a quality that reflected the sampling process by which recordings were now made. Further, older technology had always resorted to electronic "compression," by means of which the distance between loud and soft was less extreme than it would be if the music were heard live. This became part of an all-pervasive "living room" sound. In the digital era, some engineers scaled this practice back in the name of "realism."

"Phonography" by Lee B. Brown is published by permission of the author. Revised for this edition.

No wonder, then, that early CD listeners complained that they had to keep turning the volume either up or down, because of the wider dynamic spectrum.

The point is not a question of which sounds best. The point is that different technologies have different acoustic characteristics. The technology leaves its own fingerprint. As a result, one person's realism might be another's unrealism, and vice versa. What one calls "realism" may be a function of one's habituation to a given style.

Philosophical aficionados of high-end sound systems will not give up the transparency ideal easily, particularly given further technological breakthroughs. But there are many conceptual obstacles to the realization of the ideal.

First, consider the difficulty of arranging even the most sophisticated sound equipment in the home so that the music is "imaged" in the right way. In the absence of earphones—which have their own special sound—listeners cannot wander around the room, but need to be located very specifically. High-end aficionados used to call this the "sweet spot." Now consider a parallel situation concerning perspective painting. It might be assumed that, by following the laws of perspective, a painter could, in theory, create pictures that are realistic in some absolute sense. (The bundle of light rays emanating from the object itself would be isomorphic to those radiating from the painting.) Nelson Goodman observes that in order to preserve the isomorphism between looking at a real-world object and looking at the painting, one must view the painting from a single privileged position. The equation is preserved, in other words, only through an artificial restriction on our customary ways of viewing pictures. Does the same not apply to the home sound system?

Second, what is the standard of liveness upon which we would model the canned version? It might seem that the question is answered easily by using the concert hall as the recording studio. But which concert hall? Different halls have different *kinds* of presence due to the different rates at which notes decay in different rooms. And their characteristics change depending on whether they are empty or full of customers. And which of the multitude of positions in the concert hall is the one we are trying to model? One might assume that a place in the hall is superior to others. Presumably, this location won't be a point suspended in air, but a place where someone can sit. However, assuming such a point can be identified, it seems odd to use, as the yardstick for realism, a place hardly any customer ever occupies. It is sometimes said that a well-designed room is one in which there are no "bad" seats. Still, what is heard from one point in the concert hall will not be just the same as what would be heard from another. Which of these many sonic foci should be the measure of fidelity in recording?

These arguments about live as opposed to canned have generated animated discussions in recent academic journals. The *phonophile,* as we might term him, will naturally tend to idealize the canned music experience. To make his point, he will allow his imagination to roam the realm of purely hypothetical possibilities. For instance, *truly* realistic sound would not be stereophonic, but elaborately multiphonic. Performers would appear in holographic images—and so on.

But even these strategies ought not to satisfy the seeker of musical truth. We need to consider performer-audience interaction, an important element in all live music, but conspicuous in some kinds—jazz, for instance, where feedback from the audience, whether hot or cold, has definite effects on performance, which in turn has further effects on the audience, and so on. And there is no good reason to rule out, as irrelevant, the way we coordinate the sight of a performer at work with the sounds she produces. With futuristic technology, of course, we could simulate this interaction. A holographic image of a jazz pianist, for instance, might be programmed to respond to *our* responses to her performance. But, assuming the experience is not simply disconcerting, it would still be very different from actual interaction in a jazz club, for we could hardly ignore our knowledge of how the effects were realized.

It is hard to resist the conclusion that the sonic ideal for home consumption is a specialized construct, rather than a genuine replica of a live music context. Of course, these considerations do not automatically rule in favor of the partisan of live music—the *vivaphile* (or *phonophobe*) as we might call him. The vivaphile is liable to idealize the live music experience in the face of the actual facts. The problem of deciding the ideal live seat—already discussed—is a problem for him as well. Consider the huge range of live-music circumstances—eccentric seat locations, extraneous sounds, etc.

In typical cases, this clash of opinion may really boil down to a conflict between different *communities*. Consider how many music lovers nowadays live more and more within the realm of canned music. Do these listeners really want to hear about how much they are missing by staying at home? Others strongly identify with live music. Does this group really want to hear about the tens of thousands of dollars they should be investing in their home music system? Perhaps the dispute between the phonophiles and the phonophobes may be as much a matter of loyalty to listening communities as of objective facts.

B. *Sonic Manipulation as Art.* An important clarification must be made. Sonic manipulation has often served purely documentary ends. Consider, for instance, the early use of single microphones and the later use of several (non-stereo) mikes for recording bluegrass bands. As Theodor Gracyk has observed, this change did make a *documentary* difference—less overprinting of one instrument by another and more even dynamics, for instance. However, the industry has not made it easy for customers to tell the difference between a purely documentary agenda and a very different one—namely, the creation of a brand new kind of musical work, one that is a sheer artifact of the recording industry—a type to which I now turn.

As early as 1929, long before the invention of magnetic tape, the conductor Leopold Stokowski began cueing the engineer during recording sessions—in effect, making the engineer a member of the Philadelphia Orchestra. In spite of his disclaimer that he was merely "enhancing" the music, Stokowski seemed to have grasped a new idea, namely that phonography—a term we owe to Evan Eisenberg—can be conceived in its *own* terms. The industry gradually fell in with this very different agenda—part of the time. For instance, John Culshaw candidly admitted that in his Decca-London productions of operas (in the early 1960s) by

Richard Wagner and Richard Strauss, he determined to make a record that was "deeply and unabashedly a record." You need only sample the effect of the invisible Alberich ricocheting around the walls of your living room, as he bedevils his miserable brother in the Nibelheim scene of Culshaw's production of *Das Rheingold* to get the point. The defamiliarizing *stereo* effect has only a very tenuous connection with *reproducing* anything. Culshaw's dream of creating purely phonographic music was being even more fully realized in popular music.

But let us turn to even more sharply delineated cases. Consider the grandiose studio productions of the Beatles, for instance, or any number of heavy metal rock recordings of the 1970s. Gracyk has argued that the music embedded in the grooves of those recordings serves purposes that are clearly *non*-documentary. Indeed, he suggested that they deserve their own ontological analysis. (See his *Rhythm and Noise: An Aesthetics of Rock.*) Put simply, the artwork in such cases is the *recording*.

However, in identifying the features of the rock records that concerned him, it seems clear that Gracyk was actually characterizing a much wider sphere of music than he supposed. Indeed, such strategies were known in popular music as far back as the late 1940s, when producer Mitch Miller learned how to use "tracking," as it was then called, in recordings with Mercury and Columbia Records for pop singers such as Frankie Laine. The results of Miller's projects were, as Will Friedwald suggests, a "pop record 'sound' *per se*—an aural texture (usually replete with extramusical sounds) that could be replicated in live performance, instead of the other way around." In such cases, recording technology has created an entirely new category of musical entities—*works of phonography,* or *phonoartworks,* as we might term them. Examples include "serious" compositions generated electronically, or by means of the computer; the musical pastiches of popular groups in the 1980s, such as the Art of Noise; the French experiments in the 1940s known as *musique concrète;* the multilayered pop releases of the 1950s made by Les Paul; countless sample-based hip-hop recordings; and a multitude of techno CDs released almost daily as I write.

Digital information processing has greatly expanded the possibility of exploiting sound for the concoction of phonoartworks. The resources available now for devising works of phonoart could not have been imagined in the early days of tape technology. Hip-hop and "acid jazz" recordings are created by samplings bits of recorded classic jazz. In fact, anyone who hooks a computer keyboard up to a Musical Instrument Digital Interface, or MIDI, has, in the words of journalist Anita Samuels, "access to an extraordinary range of sounds, from drum loops, jackhammers and Indian alto flutes to the soaring notes of an 85-piece orchestra."

These entities, like paintings and symphonies, are full-fledged artworks, where, by "artworks" I mean—as aestheticians tacitly mean by the term—"entities subject to criteria of *reidentification.*" In other words, it is assumed that, once experienced, artworks can be revisited. However, they are different from two paradigmatic classes of artworks. First, although they may have a multitude of instances— e.g., record pressings, or playbacks thereof—they do not have a multitude of *performances* as do traditional musical works. (Try to imagine a performance of the music of the Beatles' *Sergeant Pepper* album.) Second, unlike a painted portrait, they are not representations *of* anything. Rather, they are musical entity unto themselves. For the existence of this category of entities—a kind that really is a new type under the sun—we owe recording technology.

Interesting questions arise about how authentic instances of phonoart are to be identified. An older version of the technology used a metal disk or "matrix"—a metal disk from which physical recordings were pressed like waffles. The analogy with etchings generated from steel or stone plates is striking. Like those artworks, a record matrix could produce a multiplicity of legitimate instances by analogous processes. In more recent terms, the yardsticks for the legitimacy of instances— e.g., tape "dubs," or playbacks therefrom—would be a master tape. However these nice questions play out, works of phonography surely are full-fledged *artworks* in their own right—that is, subject to criteria of reidentification—no less than paintings, symphonies, or sculptures.

C. *Blurred Boundaries.* Parallel with the new perspective represented by such works as the *Sergeant Pepper* album, the older promotional message—framed in terms of the transparency perspective—is alive and well. The putative verisimilitude touted in the days of Edison is morning glory horns has turned up again and again—e.g., in the television ads several years ago showing singers shattering glass with voices captured on Memorex recording tape. The recording industry has not cared to make it clear, by labeling or otherwise, whether a given product is to be understood as a piece of phonoart or a transparent document of a performance.

It might seem easy to distinguish between the use of manipulative strategies for phonoartworks and documentary recordings. But is it? The Victor recording made in 1939 of Coleman Hawkins playing his famous performance of *Body and Soul* is surely a *document* of a musical event. Now consider the albums of "duets" that Frank Sinatra recorded a few years before his death. They *sound* documentary. In fact, though, they were recorded "with" other people, none of whom were actually there in the studio with Frank. Because the other vocalists called in their parts by telephone, the impression of two singers in dialogue with each other is sheer illusion. By such gimmickry, Natalie Cole managed to cross the boundary of mortality and sing duets with her dead father. Are these products works of phonoart? Perhaps they belong to a different, or perhaps subsidiary category, a type we might term "virtual" performances. Perhaps we should say the same of Culshaw's operatic recordings. The very fact that the boundaries are fuzzy is itself culturally and conceptually significant.

D. When we turn to one genre of music, namely music that is *improvised,* reflection shows that sound recording has some curious effects. They concern *time,* and its conceptual relatives, *reidentification* and *repetition.*

Given their close historical and aesthetic connections, the relationship of recording technology to American improvised music—of which jazz is the paradigm—is particularly paradoxical. Phonography is responsible in large measure not merely for our knowledge of the history of jazz but for the dissemination of styles. On the other hand, the technology has always placed temporal constraints on the music. Of course, jazz composers and players showed great ingenuity in the imaginative ways they filled out the time frame allowed by the ten-inch 78-rpm record—which was only about three minutes. This constraint resulted in the "three-minute masterpiece," a type with which we are familiar in the classic jazz catalog. (The 45-rpm "single" had similar temporal boundaries.) But the format would have been incapable of documenting the famous jazz jam sessions of the era, which were radically open-ended. The temporal limitations of the medium do affect the message. (Reflection suggests that different possibilities—but also limitations—were latent in the format of the 33 1/3-rpm vinyl album.)

Repetition is such a familiar phenomenon that its curious effects go unnoticed. Recordings are intended to be played over and over again, under conditions determined by the individual consumer. This freedom to organize one's musical life as one wishes is a principal virtue of the technology. But, again, there is another side to this coin. Consider a specific recorded performance of Beethoven's *opus 111*—by Artur Schnabel, for instance. All its idiosyncrasies and nuances—even if spontaneously generated in the studio—will turn up in exactly the same way every time one plays any reissue of that performance. Each detail is as determinate as the detail in a Pink Floyd album—or in any other work of phonoart. But this has unexpected effects on any recorded performance in which spontaneity plays an important role. And those effects loom particularly large in the context of improvised music.

At leisure, I can go back again and again and examine the unexpected twists and turns of a classical musical composition—*opus* 111 itself, let us say, by playing it again and again, or by listening to others do so. I can go to the Prado Museum and once again examine the optical tricks of Velasquez' painting *Las Meninas*. Likewise, I can return to Hawkins' *Body and Soul* performance again and again and carefully examine its twists and turns—*but only because it was recorded*. The benefits seem obvious. It is only because such performances were recorded that we possess the kind of detailed musical analyses of them that we are able to read in the writing of experts such as André Hodeir, Gunther Schuller, or Martin Williams.

But the coin has another side. Both *opus 111* and *Las Meninas* are similar in one fundamental respect, namely, that they are *reidentifiable* entities. But can the same be said of an improvised performance, considered *as* an improvisation? A request that a pianist, who has just played Beethoven's *opus* 111, play *that* piece again is an intelligible one. By contrast, a request that Sonny Rollins improvise *that* saxophone solo—the one he played in a performance of "Duke of Iron," beginning at 10:32 PM, in Columbus, on October 7, 1994, let's say—makes no sense. True, you could ask Rollins to recall that solo and recreate it as best he can. But that performance would have quite a different status. In short, it seems to be the very essence of a genuinely improvisatory performance that there is no event, object, or sound-structure with which it might elsewhere be *re*identified. With such music, an informed listener understands that the music one is listening to is being created before one's very ears—*as* it is being played. This fact gives improvised music a peculiarly momentous quality. One has to be there at the right time to hear a specific improvisation, yet one cannot plan to hear *that* improvisation. This feature of improvisational performance is not an adventitious feature of it, but part of its *raison d'être*.

But, once recorded, Hawkins' *Body and Soul* performance—an impromptu afterthought of a recording session already completed, as jazz historians tell us—can be visited and *re*visited, as easily as one can return to the Velasquez, indeed, much more easily. Embedded in the grooves or bytes of recording media, such a performance acquires a strange kind of permanence that cannot but have a transforming effect on one's experience of it. It takes only one punch of the "repeat" button to bring home the fact that the music is *not* being created spontaneously as I listen. For this reason alone, there is a gap between the living music and its recorded version. In its recorded form, improvised music loses its *presence*—that is, the palpable sense of its being created *as* it is played.

Without recording technology, it is hard to imagine how we would ever come up with the idea of hearing a specific improvisatory performance again—except in the form of an imitation of it, which is quite a different thing. But with this technology, it is easy to audition multiple "manifestations," so to say, of a *single* improvisation. All one has to do is take the recording off the shelf and play it again.

If we reflect on these matters, we can begin to understand why jazz players such as Stan Getz have sometimes felt their recorded performances to be embalmed. Nowadays, of course, jazz recording sessions, taking advantage of the technology, make fewer attempts to represent real-time options. In much recorded jazz fusion, for example, solos are simply laid on top of tracks already recorded, so that the impression of players reacting to each other's moves is sheer illusion. And, with digital resources, it is possible to tweak the results in any direction one wishes.

In short, the technological medium has worked its way so deeply into the musical message that it has become not merely a means of experiencing kinds of music with which we were already familiar, but kinds of music that possess no reality independent of the technology that brings them to us. Our listening behavior appears to follow suit. Consider the degree to which we live more and more inside private sonic spheres; and the music inside seems less and less connected with human performance.

Being True to the Work
■ Lydia Goehr ■

For most of its history, music was conceived as a practice entirely subject to the constraints of extra-musical occasion and function determined mostly by the church, court, and scientific academy. The changes which took place at the end of the eighteenth century gave rise to a new view of music as an independent practice whose concerns were predominantly musical. This independent practice became a

"Being True to the Work" by Lydia Goehr has been excerpted from *The Journal of Aesthetics and Art Criticism* (Winter 1989), pages 55–60, 63–64, and is reprinted by permission of the publisher.

practice geared towards producing *enduring products* insofar as it was determined by the more general concepts of fine art and the autonomous work of art. Only with the rise of this new view of music did musicians, critics, and the like begin to think predominantly of music in terms of works. Bach did not think centrally in these terms; Beethoven did. Haydn marks the transition.

These claims are supported by a whole series of historical considerations. Thus, in the romantic period, changes took place not only in aesthetic attitudes toward the status of music and composers, but also in the meanings of numerous musical terms. As etymological inquiries reveal, words such as *'Stück,' 'Werk,' 'Oeuvre,'* 'composition,' and related terms such as 'repertoire,' 'performance,' 'rehearsal,' 'transcription,' and 'improvisation,' acquired their modern meanings at the end of the eighteenth century. Each of these terms was reconceptualized with regard to their specific relation to the central regulative concept—the musical work. . . .

I am suggesting that the concept of a musical work is intimately tied to a conception of the complex relationships obtaining between the composer, the score, and the performance, as these are expressed on several levels: within musical and aesthetic literature; and in terms of institutional codes. These relationships came to be sharply defined at a particular time against the background of those theories which first gave to music its autonomy and, indeed, exalted position among the arts. Henceforth, I shall refer to this view as the romantic conception of musical works.

Objectors might claim that my notion of workhood is too closely wedded to a romantic understanding of musical practice. They might suggest that there is an ideologically neutral notion of a work: A work is either a sound pattern *simpliciter;* a work is a sound pattern corresponding to appropriate musical or aesthetic interest. Regarding the former, however, this would mean that any tune or song is also a work, which is going too far. And regarding the latter, as soon as we begin to speak of more complex patterns, perhaps those indicated in scores or embodied in performances, we adopt that conception of music first fully formed in the late eighteenth century. In other words, the very notions of a score, indication, and performance employed in this purportedly neutral description are thick with meaning, as, indeed, is the idea of "appropriate musical or aesthetic interest." It is, therefore, yet to be shown by those who object to the thesis presented here that the concept of a musical work regulates musical practice with something other than a deeply romantic significance.

There are two further objections. The first turns on the claim that even if circumstances of a given sort do not allow at a specific time for conscious or explicit use of a concept, this does not mean that what is produced does not fall under the said concept. The second rests upon the apparent implication of the thesis, that we can speak of music in terms of works only if the music was produced in the period around 1800. If the concept of a musical work is tied to its moment of origin—which was effectively the heyday of romanticism—then its application must similarly be restricted and the boundaries of its extension closed. I shall confine myself in the succeeding sections to forestalling both of these objections by discussing the conditions under which we can and do, in fact, speak about the music, say of Bach, in terms of works.

Of course, the thesis does commit its proponent to a view of meaning and truth as dependent upon the existence of particular conceptual schemes. Given that we have a concept of a musical work, Bach composed works. If the concept had never emerged within musical practice (or, indeed, within any other relevant or re-lated practice) we would speak instead stead of Bach's music in terms perhaps not only more familiar to Bach himself, but also still evident in other existing musical practices which are not regulated by the idea of creating fixed, everlasting musical products.

Nowadays, in fact, there seems to be no form of musical production excluded from being packaged in terms of works. . . . We speak of the works of [John] Cage, [Heinrich] Neuhaus, and [Frederic] Rzewski regardless of the fact that these com-posers do not think of themselves as composing within the romantic tradition. "It's a very deliberate step of mine," Neuhaus writes, "not to record the pieces. These pieces are not musical products; they're meant to be activities."

We often disregard the conceptual differences between a work and an impro-visation or between a work and a transcription. Both improvisation and transcrip-tion (and arrangement) emerged with their modern understanding as concepts sib-ling to that of a work. Undoubtedly they stand in a very intimate relation to the latter concept, but it is not one of identity. The relation seems, however, to be inde-terminate. On occasion, we are content to refer to certain transcriptions as tran-scriptions. Sometimes, however, we speak of them as works in their own right. The same indeterminacy obtains in the case of improvisations and arrangements. . . .

When we speak of works we do not think immediately of jazz, folk, or popu-lar music, nor of music serving as an accompaniment to other art forms, such as film and dance music. Nor do we think immediately of music which is purpose-fully integrated into the everyday world—the music in religious services or other rituals. But this does not exclude the possibility of thinking about these kinds of music in terms of works. . . .

It seems, then, that our contemporary use of the work-concept does not con-fine us to the music of the romantic period. We are, apparently, tempted to under-stand musical practices of many kinds as involving the production of works. But if, as I claim, the work-concept emerged as a result of a specific confluence of aes-thetic, social, and historical conditions, *how* have we been able and *why* have we wanted to extend the employment of the work-concept seemingly so pervasively?

A major part of the answer to the 'why' in this question is that the view of the musical world which romanticism originally provided has continued since 1800, despite much anti-romantic theorizing in the intervening period, to be the dominant view. This view is so entrenched in contemporary musical thought that its constitutive concepts are taken for granted. In fact, we have before us an obvious case of *conceptual imperialism.*

Consider any form of music produced anywhere in the world. Have many musicians, interested in what is generally referred to as classical music, not found good reason to interpret all these musics according to the romantic view? Have they not assumed that the closer all forms of music approximate in their mode of presentation to those determined by romanticism the more civilized they are? The more general concept of a work of art is itself often used as a way of attributing a high value to *any* kind of thing. Consider the pleasure a chef would feel from being told that his Black Forest Gateau is a "work of art," or the satisfaction of a car manufacturer who produces a car deemed a "fine artistic product."

One obvious result of seeing the world's musics—including much of classical music—through romantic-colored spectacles is that many have assumed that these musics can be packaged in terms of works: Ways are sought to assign the 'works' to composers, to represent them in full notational form, thereby allowing them to be regarded as having a fixed structure with a sharply defined beginning and end, thereby allowing them to be performed on numerous occasions as part of a program of works in the fine setting of a concert hall.

Apart from the fact that this way of thinking results in our alienating music from its various socio-cultural contexts, and apart from the fact that most of the world's music is not originally packaged in this way, do we not risk losing something significant when we so interpret it? Do we not lose something when we hear the music of a flamenco or a blues guitarist in a concert hall? For the conventions associated with the concert hall determine that the audience should listen with disinterested respect to the 'work' being performed. The audience cannot even tap its many feet. Do we not lose something—even just an acoustic something—when we hear eighteenth-century chamber music performed, outside of the chamber, in symphonic concert halls? The critic Jonathan Keates, in thinking specifically about eighteenth-century operas, is aware of the tendency for romanticism to dominate. "However much we might pride ourselves on our understanding of the eighteenth century," he writes, "the values of the *Gesamtkunstwerk* continue to be applied with ingenious blindness, to appraising the overall worth of its art-forms."

This conceptual imperialism has not been one-sided. The beliefs associated with the ideal of *Werktreue* have increasingly and sometimes enthusiastically been adopted by those musicians involved in the production of music of many different kinds. Thus, jazz musicians have sought and indeed found respect from 'serious' musicians by dispensing with the smoky and noisy atmosphere of the club and by performing, instead, in tails. Many have willingly adopted the institutional conventions associated with 'serious' music. A Chinese committee, in its bid to produce western-style musical works, acted together as composer to produce, against all Chinese traditions, the *Yellow River Concerto*. [Arnold] Schoenberg, when defending his twelve-tone method, emphasized that "one uses the series and then one composes as before as the great Austro-German composers always have done . . . My works are twelve-note *compositions,* not *twelve-note* compositions." . . .

The assimilation of seemingly alien concepts into a given type of music is not, however, all bad. First, the migration of concepts among different musics is pretty much inevitable given our conceptual or cultural limitations. We can only comprehend the music of cultures to which we do not belong by employing an already familiar conceptual framework. Second, apart from the inevitability of perspectival comprehension, there is sometimes a healthy blurring of the boundaries between different musics, something which can be fostered by conceptual migration. Thus, even given (or despite) imperialistic influence, the adoption of concepts into foreign musics can lead—and has led on occasion—to new and interesting musical styles. . . .

When we use the concept of a musical work we use it with an understanding revealed in our beliefs, ideals, assumptions, expectations, and actions. We can, however, use the concept in different ways. At least two of these ways serve to ground a distinction between paradigm and derivative examples.

Paradigm examples, sometimes more usefully called original examples, are those produced directly and explicitly under the guidance of the relevant concept. We classify examples as derivative, by contrast, when we classify them as being of a certain kind even though these objects were not brought into existence with the relevant kind in mind or within the appropriate practice. Whether an example is paradigm or derivative is not, however, something that is decided independently of how we *use* the concept. Thus, strictly speaking, we should speak of a given concept as having a paradigm and derivative arena of employment and only then of its extension in terms of paradigm and derivative examples.

The paradigm use of a concept, as defined above, tells a familiar story about conceptual use. Derivative use, however, is more complicated. There are in fact different aspects to the derivative use of a concept. Consider the concept of a musical work. We may look first at the extent to which the activities of non-romantic musicians have approximated to the condition of romantic music. We may look at how concepts associated with romantic music have gradually been taken over and thus the extent to which these musicians have begun to speak of their production in terms of works.

When non-romantic musicians borrow romantic concepts they adopt an understanding sufficient to sustain the functioning of these concepts. In romantic eyes, they more or less successfully impose the appropriate categories upon their practice. They act in what the romantic considers to be the right way and in a way they themselves presumably now find satisfactory. The concepts come to be employed in a non-romantic setting in much the same way as natives incorporate into their understanding concepts introduced to them by foreigners. Without exposure to foreign concepts, native musicians remain oblivious to them. It is on this assumption that we say that the use of the concepts is foreign to the native's own practice and, thus, if the concepts are used at all, they are used derivatively. . . .

The view of the concept of a musical work as described here leaves open three important possibilities. First, it is possible that a musician in 1810 and one in 1988 might both be regulated by the work-concept, but because of a possible modification of meaning they might be working with a different understanding and with a different range of paradigm and derivative examples. There is, however, a dynamic and diachronic relation linking together the successive stages of a concept and serving to preserve its identity over time.

Second, to talk of paradigm and derivative examples falling under a given concept does not imply that this is the only way to classify the given instances. It is possible to interpret and perform, say, Beethoven's *Spring Sonata,* in accordance with the ideals implicit in a rain dance. We would then be obliged—in the context of the corresponding practices—to describe the music not as a paradigm example of a work but as a derivative instance of a rain dance. Consider the reconception (and adoption of appropriate evaluative criteria) involved in our listening to originally classical works which have been jazzed up, used in films, or even made into popular hits.

Third, it is possible to speak of pieces of music as falling originally or derivatively under more than one concept. Here, musicians might deliberately produce music which fails to fall neatly under a single concept. Many musicians—especially those of the avant-garde—have recognized the limitations of producing music solely under the dictate of romantic ideals and have chosen instead to employ notions typical of other musics. To what extent, if at all, the work-concept—or the ideal of *Werktreue*—has remained central to their musical production has differed from case to case. . . .

In recent philosophical literature, the concept of a musical work has been treated less in terms of its genealogy than in its role as an ontological category. Accordingly, it has been described in relation to two traditional ontological concerns: a concern to describe the mode of existence of different kinds of objects in terms of categories like universals, types, and classes and a concern to determine the essential properties or the identity conditions for these objects. The idea has been to describe the concept by describing the kind of object a musical work is.

Within these accounts there has usually been an assumption that the concept of a musical work is the sort of concept whose meaning can be given in terms of an unalterable description of its defining characteristics. The objection has then been forwarded that, for any definition of "musical work" formulated in these terms, it is always possible to find an example of what we would in practice call a work which fails to meet these conditions.

With the tension arising from this assumption and the related objection a crucial ambiguity has surfaced concerning the range of examples intended to fall under the concept being defined. This ambiguity has surfaced in the absence of a decisive answer to the question as to whether a definition of "musical work" is designed to determine just the paradigmatic application of the concept of a musical work or the boundaries of its entire extension. It has remained unclear, in other words, whether the concept of a musical work is being treated as open (in which case one cannot close its borders) or as closed (in which case one can).

Theorists have taken different routes. Some have explicitly confined their theories to paradigm examples, thereby engaging in something similar to what was once called monster barring—the exclusion of 'difficult' examples. Others have continued to see their theories as accounting for all examples of musical works. The justification for either *modus operandi* has not, however, been made explicit.

Theorists, furthermore, have apparently had no qualms in using certain examples as paradigm examples of musical works. Their theories—almost without exception—have been formulated on the basis of examples drawn from the repertoire of the early 1800s. Their inquires always begin with the question: "What sort of thing is Beethoven's *Fifth Symphony?*" This should no longer surprise us. But what are we to make of the fact that examples drawn from early pre-1800s and avant-garde music and sometimes from folk, jazz, and popular music, but *never from the 1800s repertoire,* have been appealed to *when and only when* there was an intention to *challenge* a given theory or part thereof?. . . .

The success of a challenge using these kinds of examples—the success of the counterexample method as so employed—depends entirely on whether the examples are *bona fide* examples of works. The challenge rests on the assumption that the work-concept can be employed when speaking about musics other than that of music produced around 1800. But even if it is a worthy assumption it is a big assumption. Yet the fact that this assumption has been made has had almost no recognition, let alone adequate explanation. We should not simply *take it for granted* that any kind of music can be packaged in terms of works. If, however, we do accept that all kinds of music yield examples of musical works, then those who would want to reject a purported definition of the work-concept will have before them an extremely broad range of possible counterexamples. Herein lies the problem. . . .

The counterexample method is called into serious question . . . as soon as we embrace a more complicated account of what it means for something to count as an example of a given kind or what it means for an example to fall under a given concept. Such an account was embraced above when I argued that a given concept is open and thus does not have its borders closed; when a distinction was drawn between paradigm and derivative examples; and when it was suggested that something counts as an example of a kind not directly because it exhibits the appropriate properties but directly because it is brought to fall under the concept by users of that concept within the context of a practice. On this view, what can count as a counterexample turns out to be a complicated matter because a derivative or what otherwise we have called a borderline example cannot anymore be used as a counterexample.

Recall the conceptual dependency that derivative examples have on paradigm examples. Objects come to count as derivative examples in virtue of the relation in which they stand to paradigm examples. Without paradigm examples serving as the standard there could be no conception of the non-standard. In my terms, *derivative instances can only be counted as works if the original instances of works have already been acknowledged as such.* Given this, it makes no sense to think that a derivative example could be used as a counterexample to challenge either a definition confined to paradigm examples or one accommodating, say, all currently existing works. To adapt a Hanslickian principle: No musical practice which is not guided originally by the work-concept can give the lie to a practice which is so guided.

Consider, now, the case of the latest avant-garde work which is brought forward as a paradigm example of a work; it is produced with the work-concept in mind. Nonetheless its creator desires to challenge the traditional notion of a work. Could this example be used as a counterexample? I do not believe so. To see this we need to clarify the difference between using counterexamples to challenge philosophical definitions and using examples—be they paradigm or derivative—to challenge the traditional meaning of a given concept. When one counts X as an example of a work one accepts a given meaning of the concept, a meaning which regulates at least its paradigmatic use. If one subsequently wants X to challenge this meaning, one becomes involved in trying to expand or modify the concept's present meaning. To engage in this process one first acknowledges the present meaning and only then provides a rationale for its suggested expansion or modification. This is not at all the same thing as using X to challenge a philosophical definition of the given concept. It is, rather, an indication of one's real engagement in the dynamic tradition in which the concept functions.

Thus, when, for example, an avant-garde composer produces something which is designed to challenge the romantic conception of the work of music and in turn is designed to expand or modify this conception, there is no suggestion on the part of this composer that Beethoven thereby did not compose musical works. He just composed under a conception of musical practice which is now thought by the composer to be perhaps aesthetically or ideologically unsound. The avant-garde composer at no point thinks that the traditional meaning was 'definitionally' incorrect.

African Music
■ John Miller Chernoff ■

Our approach to rhythm is called divisive because we divide the music into standard units of time. As we mark the time by tapping a foot or clapping our hands, we are separating the music into easily comprehensible units of time and indicating when the next note or chord is likely to come. A Western rhythm marks time at an even pace with a recurrent main beat, generally with a major pulse every two, three, or four beats. What is most noticeable about the rhythm is that it serves to link the different notes to each other. We say, for instance, that a piece of music has a certain rhythm, and as we count out the beats, we will notice certain things. First,

"African Music" by John Miller Chernoff is excerpted from *African Music,* University of Chicago Press (1979), pages 41–42, 46–47, 52–54, 58, 159–162, and is reprinted by permission of the publisher.

most of the instruments play their notes at the same time, and second, if we have a sequence of notes that runs into a phrase or a melody, the whole thing will start when we count "One." It is this fact, that Western musicians count together from the same starting point, which enables a conductor to stand in front of more than a hundred men and women playing in an orchestra and keep them together with his baton. Rhythm is something we *follow,* and it is largely determined in reference to the melody or even actually defined as an aspect of the melody. Our approach to rhythm is obvious in most popular or folk music, but it is no less evident in a fugue in which the melody may start at different points. What is important is that the rhythm is counted evenly and stressed on the main beat, and we have the special word "syncopation" to refer to a shifting of the "normal" accents to produce an uneven or irregular rhythm. Even composers in the Western classical tradition who used complex rhythms, like Beethoven or Brahms, or twentieth-century composers who were influenced by African musical idioms, like Stravinsky, manifest this basic orientation. In the popular or folk idioms of Western music, the more "artistic" complexities rarely arise.

In Western music, then, rhythm is most definitely secondary in emphasis and complexity to harmony and melody. It is the progression of sound through a series of chords or tones that we recognize as beautiful. In African music this sensibility is almost reversed. African melodies are clear enough, even if African conceptions of tonal relationships are sometimes strange to us but more important is the fact that in African music *there are always at least two rhythms going on.* We consider the rhythms complex because often we simply do not know what "the" rhythm of a piece is. There seems to be no unifying or main beat. The situation is uncomfortable because if the basic meter is not evident, we cannot understand how two or more people can play together or, even more uncomfortably, how anyone can play at all. On a superficial level, we might get away with describing the beating as "fanatical" or by referring to the "rhythmic genius" of African people, but such comments explain very little, and they are, of course, inaccurate because they only indicate our sense of what African music seems to require or bring out of us. Since we are used to hearing one set of tones move through "time," we do not expect any distractions from a musician who plays "out of time" or "misses the beat." Exposed to the music of an African drum ensemble, even the most accomplished Western musicians have expressed bafflement. . . .

In such music, the conflicting rhythmic patterns and accents are called *crossrhythms.* The diverse rhythms establish themselves in intricate and changing relationships to each other analogously to the way that tones establish harmony in Western music. The effect of polymetric music is as if the different rhythms were competing for our attention. No sooner do we grasp one rhythm than we lose track of it and hear another. In something like Adzogbo or Zhem it is not easy to find any constant beat at all. The Western conception of a main beat or pulse seems to disappear, and a Westerner who cannot appreciate the rhythmic complications and who maintains his habitual listening orientation quite simply gets lost. . . .

The inadequacy of Western efforts at notation and the clumsiness of Western efforts at participation reflect the basic problem: We can choose any of several rhythmic approaches, yet we have no way to judge the proper one. To a more sensitive ear, the flexible and dynamic relationships of various rhythms actually help distinguish one rhythm from another, and on a basic level, *one rhythm defines another.* One drum played alone gives an impression of a rhythm tripping along clumsily or senselessly accented; however, a second rhythm can make sense of the first. . . .

An interesting illustration of this point occurred while I was trying to record separately the many stylistic variations the lead dondon can play in some of the Dagomba dances because I did not want to forget what I had learned. Ibrahim Abdulai, as the leader of the Takai drummers in Tamale, was to play. . . .

Ibrahim, however, complained that he could not "hear" his variations when he played without a second dondon. He regarded the counter-rhythm which would tend to throw Westerners off the beat as the only thing that kept him on time and enabled him to hear what he was playing and to be creative. It may have been the first time he had ever played the Takai drumming by himself. . . .

We can think about this difference in sensibilities as the difference between perceiving a rhythm as something to "get with" or as something to "respond to." Rhythms which cut across each other are also dynamically coherent. Ibrahim felt that his isolated beating was meaningless without a second rhythm, but more than that, he could not even think of the full range of stylistic variations he might play without the beating of a second drum. There was no *conversation,* and this kind of responsiveness is given another, fuller expression in African musical arrangements. From our discussion of multiple meter and apart-playing, of hand-clapping and "metronome sense," we might tend to conceive of the basic rhythm of a piece of music as the fastest pulse on which all the beats could be located or as the slowest pulse which unites all the patterns. But while certain rhythms may establish a background beat, in almost all African music there is a dominant point of repetition developed from a dominant conversation with a clearly defined alternation, a swinging back and forth from solo to chorus or from solo to an emphatic instrumental reply. *Call-and-response,* as this kind of arrangement is generally known to ethnomusicologists, is a major characteristic of African musical idioms. This characteristic is not particularly difficult to understand, for we are familiar with this standard format in Afro-American music. When James Brown sings "Get up!", Bobby Byrd answers "Get on up!"; when Kool sings "Get down," the Gang's horns answer. In African music, the chorus or response is a rhythmic phrase which recurs regularly; the rhythms of a lead singer or musician vary and are cast against the steady repetition of the response. In essence, if rhythmic complexity is the African alternative to harmonic complexity, the repetition of responsive rhythms is the African alternative to the development of a melodic line. [A.M.] Jones writes that an African "would find our broad changes of melody coarse and inartistic. . . . He knows the artistic value of a good repetitive pattern." . . .

To maintain their poise in their social encounters, Africans bring the same flexibility which characterizes their participation in musical contexts: They expect dialogue, they anticipate movement, and most significantly, they stay very much open to influence. The many ways one can change a rhythm by cutting it with different rhythms is parallel to the many ways one can approach or interpret a situation or a conversation. And there is always an in-between, always a place to add another beat. A musical occasion, like any other social occasion, is therefore beyond any one perspective a person can bring to it, and people in Africa are usually realistic enough not to try to impose a single point of view on the larger context in which they are playing a part. It is not only that one rhythm cannot monopolize all the notes; one rhythm means nothing without another. In a musical context, separation of parts heightens rhythmic dialogue, and in a musical ensemble, singlemindedness of purpose would be equivalent to poverty of expression. And, of course, if a rhythm must be cut by another to be meaningful or interesting, its meaning can be influenced, altered, or defined by another. There are those of us who would feel insecure in a context where who we are is more dependent on other people's perspectives than on our personal self-image, but in Africa a person will generally be prepared to connect his self-image with what others see him doing, and he may hope and expect that people will be steady enough to make sense of him in a complementary way. If you wish to sit alone in a bar, and you politely refuse an African's invitation to join his table, you may be cautioned in a friendly way that someone who sits alone may have crazy and meaningless thoughts, staying too long inside his isolated imagination and misperceiving things: It is better to develop one's thoughts with the open-mindedness ensured by the presence of other people. Their potential to reciprocate or to differ helps provide balance. . . .

In African music, as we know, respect for an established rhythmic framework provides the possibility for comprehensible improvisation, and in daily life as well, people adopt a highly mannered approach in their relationships so that they may act with clarity and relevance. Ibrahim Abdulai could not think of what to do without a second dondon; a master drummer, minding his own improvisations, listens to a "hidden" rhythm, in effect creating another rhythm for his own to engage. In a musical context, the diverse rhythms help people distinguish themselves from each other while they remain profoundly involved; in the discrete encounters of social life, people maintain their boundaries, even in their closest friendships, and a Westerner in Africa may have trouble deciding whether the people he meets are being friendly or circumspect in their approach to him. Though it may seem paradoxical to a Westerner, Africans use stylized social forms and conventions to achieve interpersonal intimacy, but, as at a musical event, Africans impose a formal institutional or social framework on their affairs in order to personalize their behavior and expressions against a specifically limited context of meaning. From an African perspective, once you have brought a structure to bear on your involvements, and made your peace with it, the distinctive gestures and deviant idiosyncrasies of personality can stand out with clarity. You are free to introduce subtle refinements in a dramatic way to focus on the quality or status of your relationship at any moment. Thus, Africans do not so much observe rituals in their lives as they ritualize their lives.

In the model of community presented in an African musical event, integrity is ideally a combination of diverse rhythms which must remain distinct, and the power of the music comes from the conflicts and conversations of the rhythms, from vivid contrasts and complementary movements. . . .

Like a ritual or a musical event, a community too is basically an ordered way of being involved through time. Africans rely on music to build a context for community action, and analogously, many aspects of their community life reflect their musical sensibility. Knowing what we do about artistic realization in African musical events, we should be better able to appreciate the way that, in Africa, the power of community comes from the dramatic coordination and even ritualized opposition of distinct personalities. On a simple level, in a conversation, someone listening will punctuate a speaker's phrases with what a Westerner might consider to be meaningless noises, but without these utterances at the right time, the speaker will stop to wait for encouragement or for an indication of involvement. A speaker may even stop on purpose to elicit such a response, indicating his own need for dialogue. On the broadest level, the African musical sensibility offers a highly sophisticated example of a tendency frequently seen in traditional African political and economic institutions, a tendency toward situating multiple conflicting and opposing forces into a process of mediated and balanced communication.

On the Concept of Music
■ Jerrold Levinson ■

We should at the outset distinguish the question "What is music?" from some others with which it might be confused. One of these is the question of what *kind* of thing a piece of music is—that is to say, what ontological or metaphysical category (e.g., particular, universal, mental, physical) it belongs to and what its identity conditions are. This question . . . can to a large extent be dealt with independently of the distinction between music and nonmusic, and vice versa. We can determine what it is to count something as an instance or occasion of music without deciding precisely what ontological characterization pieces of music should receive.

"On the Concept of Music" by Jerrold Levinson has been excerpted from *Music, Art, and Metaphysics,* Cornell University Press (1990), pages 269–276, and is reprinted by permission of the publisher.

A second question is how we generally *recognize* something to be music—what criteria we employ in making judgments of that sort, by ear, in ordinary situations. It should be apparent that this is more a psychological question than a conceptual one. It asks, in effect, for *typical* features of music which are aurally accessible and prominently noted—e.g., regular meter, definite rhythm, melody, harmony. But something might be a piece of music that lacked almost all typical musical features, and might possess many such features without being a piece of music. There are, furthermore, conditions essential to being a piece of music which are not even directly hearable, and which thus cannot figure as criteria of *recognition*. Nor, since our criteria for recognition are fallible, will everything that satisfies them in fact be an instance of music. A third question asks what it is that makes a piece of music *good,* or *great,* or just *better* than some other piece of music. This question is clearly an evaluative one and should be kept separate from the fundamentally descriptive inquiry into the bounds of music per se, as contrasted with nonmusic.

It has often been suggested that music be defined as *organized sound.* But this is patently inadequate. While sonic organization has some plausibility as a necessary feature of music, it is hardly a sufficient one. The output of a jackhammer, the ticking of a metronome, the shouts of a drill sergeant during a march, the chirping of a sparrow, the roar of a lion, the whine of a police siren, a presidential campaign speech—all are organized sounds but not instances of music.

We can prevent the roar of the lion and the chirping of the sparrow from being counted as music if we amend the initial proposal so as to require that the organized sound be *humanly* produced—or at least produced by intelligent creatures to whom we might accord the status of *persons.* For it seems that one would not strictly consider anything music which was not the outcome of intentional activity on the part of an intelligent being. On the other hand, this may just be indicative of a deeper reason for excluding roars and chirps—that they do not exhibit the appropriate aim or purpose for qualifying as music. I will return to this point later.

Even if we introduce "humanly" as a qualification to "organized sound," we are still left with various sonic items mentioned above which conform to this conception but are not indeed instances of music. We might seek to exclude many of these (e.g., the jackhammer output, the presidential speech) by insisting on those features of music which an elementary textbook of music considers definitive (e.g., *melody, rhythm, harmony*). But that this will not do is brought home to us by early music, contemporary music, and music of non-Western cultures. Gregorian chant and shakuhachi solos are music but lack harmony. [Toru] Takemitsu's *Water Music* (derived from taped raindrop sounds), African drumming, and Webern's pointillistic *Five Pieces,* op. 5, lack melody but are nonetheless music. Certain kinds of atmospheric modern jazz and synthesizer compositions have virtually no rhythms, yet they are music also. Melody, rhythm, and harmony are important features of a lot of music, but they nonetheless remain only typical features for music in general, not necessary ones. In fact, it should be apparent that there are no longer any intrinsic properties of sound that are required for something possibly to be music, and none that absolutely excludes a sonic phenomenon from that category.

It might be thought that what makes African drumming, modern jazz, and Mozart piano concertos music is that they are all organizations of sound which stir the soul or, more soberly, affect the *emotions*. Or perhaps ones that express the emotions of their *creators*. But although emotional evocation and emotional expression are central aspects of most music, they are not definitive ones. The roar of the lion and the whine of the police siren induce emotion in the auditor perhaps more surely than most music does. The orator's speech and the poet's lyric (possibly also the lion's roar) may express their creators' emotions as much as does the *Pathétique* Sonata. On the other hand, some music seems neither the embodiment of a creator's inner state nor a stimulus to emotional response in hearers, but rather an abstract configuration of sounds in motion and/or a reflection of some nonindividual—or even nonhuman—aspect of things. Examples of this might be some Javanese gamelan music, Bach's *Art of the Fugue,* George Crumb's *Makrokosmos,* Conlon Nancarrow's *Studies for Player Piano,* and Tibetan ritual music. So it is clear that music cannot be defined by some special relation to emotional life; no such relation holds for *all* music and *only* for music. Nor can music be understood as humanly organized sound that transmits or communicates *ideas* or the like. For this net is far too wide. Though it may include much music, it also includes sirens, shouts, and messages in Morse code.

It should be fairly obvious that what our preliminary definition lacks, and what is needed to get close to the concept of music, is some sufficiently general notion of the *aim* or *purpose* for which the humanly organized sound in question is produced. Music is such sounds produced (or determined) with a certain *intent.* But what intent is this? Since music in the primary sense is an art (or artistic activity), and the arts are doubtless the foremost arena for aesthetic appreciation, it might seem that music could be defined as "humanly organized sound for the purpose of *aesthetic appreciation.*" Indeed, this is an advance over "organized sound," but there are significant flaws in this formulation which prevent us from resting with it as an acceptable definition.

One flaw is that there are musics in the world which do not seem aimed at what we can comfortably call "aesthetic appreciation." Music for the accompaniment of ritual, music for the intensification of warlike spirit, and music for dancing are all examples of musics whose proper appreciation does not involve contemplative and distanced apprehension of pure patterns of sound, or put otherwise, does not call for specific attention to its beauty or other aesthetic qualities. Another, perhaps more serious, flaw is the failure of the definition to exclude verbal arts such as drama and (especially) poetry. For poetry, at least in its spoken guise, consists of humanly organized sounds for aesthetic appreciation; it so happens that in that case the sounds are words meaningfully arranged.

We can deal with the poetry problem by requiring that the organized sounds in music be intended for listening to primarily *as sounds,* and not primarily as symbols of discursive thought. This is not to say that music cannot contain words—clearly songs, opera, *musique concrète,* and collage musics do—only that to constitute music the verbal component must either be combined with more purely sonorous material or, if not so accompanied, be such that one is to attend to it primarily for its sonic qualities and whatever is supervenient on them.

The other difficulty is that regarding the ultimate *end* of attending to organized sound as sound. We need to find a replacement for "aesthetic appreciation," since this is too narrow an end to comprise all activity that we would count as the making of music. One suggestion would be this: that music, whether absorbed reflectively in a concert hall or reacted to frenetically during a village rite, is engaged in so that a certain *heightening* of life, or of consciousness, is attained. In other words, all sound phenomena that are categorizable as music seem aimed at the *enrichment or intensification of experience* via engagement with organized sounds as such. I claim that this is indeed the central core of the music-making intention. It is this that enables us to construe examples from any number of times and places as examples of the artistic-cultural activity we conceive of as music, despite the absence of any limiting intrinsic sonic characteristics beyond that of mere audibility.

An instructive hypothetical example that we would not count as music, and which our definition in its present state just manages to exclude, is the following. Imagine a sequence of sounds devised by a team of psychological researchers which are such that when subjects are in a semiconscious condition and are exposed to these sounds, the subjects enter psychedelic states of marked pleasurability. Such a sequence is not a piece of music; yet it is humanly organized sound for the purpose (arguably) of enriching experience. It does not, however, seek this enrichment through requiring a person's *attention* to the sounds as such. Sound organized for our own good but which does not ask us to listen to or otherwise actively engage with it is not music.

Now that our definition is approaching adequacy we must add one minor qualification, making explicit something only implicit until now: namely, that the organization of sound must be *temporal* organization if the product is to count as musical. What other sort of organization could there be? Well, one can imagine an art in which the point was to produce colorful instantaneous combinations of sounds—i.e., chords of vanishingly brief duration—which were to be savored independently, each in splendid isolation from the next. My intuition is that we would not regard this art as a type of music (though existing musical knowledge and technique would be relevant to its successful practice). It would be the auditory equivalent of jam tasting or rose smelling—the receiving of a sensory impression, sometimes complex, but one for which temporal development was not an issue. Music as we conceive it seems as essentially an art of time as it is an art of sound.

Our complete definition of music would then go roughly like this:

> *Music* = df sounds temporarily organized by a person for the purpose of enriching or intensifying experience through active engagement (e.g., listening, dancing, performing) with the sounds regarded primarily, or in significant measure as sounds.

I believe this formulation covers all that it should—e.g., classical music, folk music, party music, avant-garde music, opera, the varied phenomena studied by ethnomusicologists—and nothing it should not (including Muzak).

Some brief observations on the analysis, highlighting its salient features: (1) The analysis accords to music certain intrinsic characteristics, albeit limited ones—to wit, soundingness or audibility, and temporal structure. (2) The analysis is intentionalistic and human-centered; it is people (or the near like) who make music in a purposive way, and not unthinking Nature. (3) The analysis purports to be adequate in application cross-culturally, though of course it is not intended as an analysis of any other culture's concept. (4) The analysis explicitly ascribes a normative attitude to the makers or offerers of music: They necessarily conceive or intend their efforts as worth interacting with. (5) The analysis is creator-oriented or creator-driven: Producers make their production music, through their intentional orientation in bringing it forth, and not the receivers or consumers of such production through anything they might do. . . . I now raise [a further point] about the concept of music. The first is that there is a distinction between what *is* music, and what can be *treated* or *regarded* as music. One way to ignore this distinction is to claim, in the spirit of John Cage's Zen-inspired reflections, that any and all sounds are music. This is simply false, and the most cogent of Cage's reflections fails to establish it. What Cage shows perhaps is that any sounds can be listened to *as if* they were music (i.e., attentively, with regard to form, with emotional sensitivity), that one can transform (just about) any sonic environment into an occasion for receptive awareness. It does not follow that all sound events are at present music. The whirr of my blender and the whistling of the wind are not instances of music. They could only be such if they were produced, or proffered, for a certain purpose, as indicated above. But one can *adopt* attitudes toward them which are appropriate for music, with varying degrees of reward.

This Cagean view of music connects to a use of "music" with some currency, in which the word serves as in effect a predicate of experience. The rule of usage is roughly this. If there is a musical experience going on—characterized in some phenomenological fashion or other—then there is music; if not, then the situation is devoid of music. The auditor, through having the right kind of experience, determines whether music is present or is occurring; the source of the sounds experienced in the appropriate way, their raison d'être—or even whether they actually exist—is regarded as irrelevant. It should be clear that from my perspective this is a degenerate notion of music, which obscures more than it illuminates, and denies to music several features that I have argued are central to it, namely, sentient origin, artistic intent, and public character. Furthermore, it is a hopelessly relativistic notion, making the status of anything as music (even Mozart piano concertos) relative to each individual listener and occasion. The concepts of a distinctive musical *experience,* or of the hearing of something *as* music, are useful ones, to be sure, but there is little to be gained by collapsing them into the cultural and objective category of music itself.

PART V

DANCE

Dance historian Curt Sachs conjectures that there is probably no more ancient form of art than dance. "The history of the creative dance," he says, "takes place in pre-history." Arguably, no other art, whether in its "high" art modes, in its ritual types, or in its ordinary social forms, transports its participants so naturally or fully into states of ecstasy. In the ancient Dionysian festival, Friedrich Nietzsche explains, the individual "expresses himself through song and dance as the member of a higher community; he has forgotten how to walk, how to speak, and is on the brink of taking wing as he dances." No wonder its history is so intertwined with magic, or why Suzanne Langer calls the dancing place "the magic circle."

Langer claims that serious attempts to understand dance in its own right are relatively recent in the philosophy of the arts. She explains why, in her opinion, this art cannot be reduced to or derived from any other art form. However, she argues at the same time that dance cannot be equated with any type of everyday behavior. Unlike movements in real life, for instance, dancers are never in the grip of *actual* emotion.

What, then, is the relationship of dance to physical action? Certainly, many feel that Mikhail Baryshnikov's physical power is admirable to behold. However, Langer urges that the purpose of dance is to give us, not examples of *actual* powers, but semblances or symbols of our imagined emotional life. For example, two dancers can appear to affect each other—like magnets tugging each other across a distance—even though there is no actual physical connection between the two. In such cases, dance represents emotional forces as if they were external, magical ones.

With the help of concepts derived from philosophical action theory, Monroe Beardsley addresses the relationship of dance to actual human activity in a different way from the way Langer explains it. He argues that the purpose of dance is to place everyday actions, such as getting on a bus or making a pivot at second base, in high relief—to profile them by stylization or exaggeration.

In their discussion of Beardsley's view, Noël Carroll and Sally Banes maintain that Beardsley cannot account for a recent type of dance in which ordinary, everyday actions are incorporated literally, without any stylization or reference to anything else whatsoever. For Carroll and Banes, postmodernist dance breaks the art form down into its literal mundane elements. In this respect, it shares features with certain trends in contemporary visual art, such as the works of Jasper Johns and Andy Warhol. All are attempts at playing with the task of reducing their art to the very ordinary objects they seem to represent. Such dances represent a studied omission of the qualities we associate with ballet, or even with modern dance.

Philosophical aesthetics tends to focus on dance as witnesses by a detached audience, a pure art form, as is exemplified by European ballet. This focus can give us a distorted picture of what dance is outside Western culture. However, for many cultures, dance is an integral part of social and religious life. This is illustrated by the Indian dance of Śiva. In his essay on the topic, the expert in Indian culture and art, Ananda Coomaraswamy makes clear how dance, in this instance, has a much larger philosophical import. The dance of Śiva, he explains, is an image of cosmic movement in general, the further import of which is to situate the participant at the center of the universe.

Virtual Powers

■ Suzanne K. Langer ■

The most widely accepted view is that the essence of dance is musical: The dancer expresses in gesture what he feels as the emotional content of the music which is the efficient and supporting cause of his dance. He reacts as we all would if we were not inhibited; his dance is self-expression, and is beautiful because the stimulus is beautiful. He may really be said to be "dancing the music."

This view of dance as a gestural rendering of musical forms is not merely a popular one, but is held by a great many dancers, and a few—though, indeed, very few—musicians. The music critic who calls himself Jean D'Udine has written, in his very provocative (not to say maddening) little book, *L'art et le geste:* "The expressive gesticulation of an orchestra conductor is simply a dance. . . . All music is dance—all melody just a series of attitudes, poses." Jacques Dalcroze, too, who was a musician and not a dancer by training, believed that dance could express in bodily movement the same motion-patterns that music creates for the ear. But as a rule it is the dancer, choreographer, or dance critic rather than the musician who regards dance as a musical art. On the assumption that all music could be thus "translated," Fokine undertook to dance Beethoven symphonies; Massine has done the same—both, apparently, with indifferent success.

Alexander Sakharoff, in his *Reflexions sur la musique et sur la danse,* carried the "musical" creed to its full length: "We—Clotilde Sakharoff and I—do not dance *to* music, or with musical accompaniment, we dance *the music.*" He reiterates the point several times. The person who taught him to dance not *with* music, but to dance the music itself, he says, was Isadora Duncan. There can be no doubt that she regarded dance as the visible incarnation of music—that for her there was no "dance music," but only pure music rendered as dance. Sakharoff remarked that many critics maintained Isadora did not really understand the music she danced, that she misinterpreted and violated it; he, on the contrary, found that she understood it so perfectly that she could dare to make free interpretations of it. Now, paradoxically, I believe both Sakharoff and the critics were right. Isadora did not understand the music *musically,* but for her purposes she understood it perfectly; she knew what was balletic, and that was all she knew about it. In fact, it was so absolutely all she knew that she thought it was all there was to know, and that what she danced was really "the music." Her musical taste as such was undeveloped—not simply poor, but utterly unaccountable. She ranked Ethelbert Nevin's "Narcissus" with Beethoven's C# Minor Sonata, and Mendelssohn's "Spring Song" with some very good Chopin *Etudes* her mother played. . . .

"Virtual Powers" by Suzanne K. Langer is excerpted from *Feeling and Form,* Allyn and Bacon (1953), pages 169–178, 184, and is reprinted by permission of the publisher.

There is another interpretation of dance, inspired by the classical ballet, and therefore more generally accepted in the past than in our day: that dance is one of the plastic arts, a spectacle of shifting pictures, or animated design, or even statues in motion. Such was the opinion of the great choreographer [Jean-Georges]Noverre who, of course, had never seen actual moving pictures or mobile sculpture. Since these media have come into existence, the difference between their products and dance is patent. Calder's balanced shapes, moved by the wind, define a truly sculptural volume which they fill with a free and fascinating motion (I am thinking, in particular, of his "Lobster Pot and Fishtail" in the stairwell of the Museum of Modern Art in New York), but they certainly are not dancing. The moving picture has been seriously likened to the dance on the ground that both are "arts of movement"; yet the hypnotic influence of motion is really all they have in common (unless the film happens to be of a dance performance), and a peculiar psychological effect is not the measure of an art form. A screenplay, a newsreel, a documentary film, has no artistic similarity to any sort of dance.

Neither musical rhythm nor physical movement is enough to engender a dance. We speak of gnats "dancing" in the air, or balls "dancing" on a fountain that tosses them; but in reality all such patterned motions are *dance motifs,* not dances.

The same thing may be said of a third medium that has sometimes been regarded as the basic element in dance: pantomime. According to the protagonists of this view, dancing is a dramatic art. And of course they have a widely accepted theory, namely that Greek drama arose from choric dance, to justify their approach. But if one looks candidly at the most elaborate pantomimic dance, it does not appear at all like the action of true drama; one is far more tempted to doubt the venerable origins of acting than to believe in the dramatic ideal of dance motions. For dance that begins in pantomime, as many religious dances do, tends in the course of its subsequent history to become more balletic, not more dramatic. Pantomime, like pure motion patterns, plastic images, and musical forms, is dance material, something that may become a balletic element, but the dance itself is something else.

The true relationship is well stated by [Frank] Thiess, who regards pantomime itself as "a bastard of two different arts," namely dance and comedy, but observes: "To conclude from this fact that it [pantomime] is therefore condemned to eternal sterility, is to misapprehend the nature of some highly important formative processes in art. . . . A true dance pantomime may indeed be evolved, purely within the proper confines of the dance . . . a pantomime that is based entirely, from the first measure to the last, on the intrinsic law of the dance: the law of rhythmic motion." As the first master of such truly balletic miming he names Rudolf von Laban. "In his work," he says, "as in pure music, the content of an event disappears entirely behind its choreographic form. . . . Everything becomes expression, gesture, thrall and liberation of bodies. And by the skillful use of space and color, the balletic pantomime has been evolved, which may underlie the ensemble dance of the future."

What, then, is dance? If it be an independent art, as indeed it seems to be, it must have its own "primary illusion." Rhythmic motion? That is its actual process, not an illusion. The "primary illusion" of an art is something created, and created at the first touch—in this case, with the first motion, performed or even implied. The motion itself, as a physical reality and therefore "material" in the art, must suffer transformation. Into what?—Thiess, in the passage just quoted, has given the answer: "Everything becomes expression, *gesture. . . .*"

All dance motion is gesture, or an element in the exhibition of gesture—perhaps its mechanical contrast and foil, but always motivated by the semblance of an expressive movement. Mary Wigman has said, somewhere: "A meaningless gesture is abhorrent to me." Now a "meaningless gesture" is really a contradiction in terms; but to the great dancer all movement in dance was gesture—that was the only word; a mistake was a "meaningless gesture." The interesting point is that the statement itself might just as well have been made by Isadora Duncan, by Laban, or by Noverre. For, oddly enough, artists who hold the most fantastically diverse theories as to what dancing is—a visible music, a succession of pictures, an unspoken play—all recognize its gestic character. *Gesture* is the basic abstraction whereby the dance illusion is made and organized.

Gesture is vital movement; to the one who performs it, it is known very precisely as a kinetic experience, i.e. as action, and somewhat more vaguely by sight, as an effect. To others it appears as a visible motion, but not a motion of things, sliding or waving or rolling around—it is *seen and understood* as vital movement. So it is always at once subjective and objective, personal and public, willed (or evoked) and perceived.

In actual life, gestures function as signals or symptoms of our desires, intentions, expectations, demands, and feelings. Because they can be consciously controlled, they may also be elaborated, just like vocal sounds, into a system of assigned and combinable *symbols,* a genuine discursive language. People who do not understand each other's speech always resort to this simpler form of discourse to express propositions, questions, judgments. But whether a gesture has linguistic meaning or not, it is always spontaneously expressive, too, by virtue of its form: It is free and big, or nervous and tight, quick or leisurely, etc., according to the psychological condition of the person who makes it. This self-expressive aspect is akin to the tone of voice in speech.

Gesticulation, as part of our actual behavior, is not art. It is simply vital movement. A squirrel, startled, sitting up with its paw against its heart, makes a gesture, and a very expressive one at that. But there is no art in its behavior. It is not dancing. Only when the movement that was a genuine gesture in the squirrel is *imagined,* so it may be performed apart from the squirrel's momentary situation and mentality, it becomes an artistic element, a possible dance-gesture. Then it becomes a free symbolic form, which may be used to convey *ideas* of emotion, of awareness and premonition, or may be combined with or incorporated in other virtual gestures, to express other physical and mental tensions.

Every being that makes natural gestures is a center of vital force, and its expressive movements are seen by others as signals of its will. But virtual gestures are not signals, they are symbols of will. The spontaneously gestic character of dance motions is illusory, and the vital force they express is illusory; the "powers" (i.e. centers of vital force) in dance are created beings—created by the semblance gesture.

The primary illusion of dance is a virtual realm of Power—not actual, physically exerted power, but appearances of influence and agency created by virtual gesture.

In watching a collective dance—say, an artistically successful ballet—one does not see *people running around;* one sees the dance driving this way, drawn that way, gathering here, spreading there—fleeing, resting, rising, and so forth; and all the motion seems to spring from powers beyond the performers. In a *pas de deux* the two dancers appear to magnetize each other; the relation between them is more than a spatial one, it is a relation of forces; but the forces they exercise, that seem to be as physical as those which orient the compass needle toward its pole, really do not exist physically at all. They are dance forces, virtual powers.

The prototype of these purely apparent energies is not the "field of forces" known to physics, but the subjective experience of volition and free agency, and of reluctance to alien, compelling wills. The consciousness of life, the sense of vital power, even of the power to receive impressions, apprehend the environment, and meet changes, is our most immediate self-consciousness. This is the feeling of power; and the play of such "felt" energies is as different from any system of physical forces as psychological time is from clock-time, and psychological space from the space of geometry.

The widely popular doctrine that every work of art takes rise from an emotion which agitates the artist, and which is directly "expressed" in the work, may be found in the literature of every art. That is why scholars delve into each famous artist's life history, to learn by discursive study what emotions he must have had while making this or that piece, so that they may "understand" the message of the work. But there are usually a few philosophical critics—sometimes artists themselves—who realize that the feeling in a work of art is something the artist *conceived* as he created the symbolic form to present it, rather than something he was undergoing and involuntarily venting in an artistic process. There is a Wordsworth who finds that poetry is not a symptom of emotional stress, but an image of it—"emotion recollected in tranquility"; there is a Riemann who recognizes that music *resembles* feeling, and is its objective symbol rather than its physiological effect; a Mozart who knows from experience that emotional disturbance merely interferes with artistic conception. Only in the literature of the dance, the claim to direct self-expression is very nearly unanimous. Not only the sentimental Isadora, but such eminent theorists as Merle Armitage and Rudolf von Laban, and scholars like Curt Sachs, besides countless dancers judging introspectively, accept the naturalistic doctrine that dance is a free discharge either of surplus energy or of emotional excitement.

Confronted with such evidence, one naturally is led to reconsider the whole theory of art as symbolic form. Is dance an exception? Good theories may have special cases, but not exceptions. Does the whole philosophy break down? Does it simply not "work" in the case of dance, and thereby reveal a fundamental weakness that was merely obscurable in other contexts? Surely no one would have the temerity to claim that *all* the experts on a subject are wrong!

Now there is one curious circumstance, which points the way out of this quandary: namely, that the really great experts—choreographers, dancers, aestheticians, and historians—although explicitly they assert the emotive-symptom thesis, implicitly contradict it when they talk about any particular dance or any specified process. No one, to my knowledge, has ever maintained that [Anna] Pavlova's rendering of slowly ebbing life in "The Dying Swan" was most successful when she actually felt faint and sick, or proposed to put Mary Wigman into the proper mood for her tragic "Evening Dances" by giving her a piece of terrible news a few minutes before she entered on the stage. A good ballet master, wanting a ballerina to register dismay, might say: "Imagine that your boy-friend has just eloped with your most trusted chum!" But he would not say, with apparent seriousness, "Your boy-friend told me to tell you goodby from him, he's not coming to see you any more." Or he might suggest to a sylph rehearsing a "dance of joy" that she should fancy herself on a vacation in California, amid palms and orange groves, but he probably would not remind her of an exciting engagement after the rehearsal, because that would distract her from the dance, perhaps even to the point of inducing false motions.

It is *imagined feeling* that governs the dance, not real emotional conditions. If one passes over the spontaneous emotion theory with which almost every modern book on the dance begins, one quickly comes to the evidence for this contention. Dance gesture is not real gesture, but virtual. The bodily movement, of course, is real enough; but *what makes it emotive gesture,* i.e. its spontaneous origin in what Laban calls a "feeling-thought-motion," is illusory, so the movement is "gesture" only within the dance. It is *actual movement,* but *virtual self-expression.*

What Is Going on in a Dance?
■ Monroe C. Beardsley ■

I begin these rather tentative and exploratory reflections by calling upon some provocative remarks by George Beiswanger, from an essay written some years ago and later reprinted:

"What Is Going on in a Dance?" by Monroe C. Beardsley is excerpted from *Dance Research Journal* 15 (1982), pages 31–37, and is reprinted here by permission of *CORD.*

> Muscular capacity is the physical means by which dances are made. But the means be-
> come available to the choreographic imagination only through the operation of a
> metaphor, a metaphor by which a *moving* in the muscular sense takes on the character
> of a *doing* or *goings on*. . . . Strictly speaking, then, dances are not made out of but *upon*
> movement, movement being the poetic bearer, the persistent metaphor, by which mus-
> cular material is made available for the enhanced, meaningful, and designed *goings-on*
> that are dance.

Though this passage summarizes a view that I shall try to defend and articulate, the
attempt to apply the concept of metaphor troubles me: It seems a strained extension
of an otherwise reasonably clear and useful term. So instead of Beiswanger's rather
mysterious "operation of a metaphor," I shall suggest that we employ some concepts and principles borrowed from the philosophical theory of action. But I still
like his favored expression for what we are all trying to understand better—those
special "goings-on" that constitute dance.

A partial, though basic, description of what is going on would be to say, using terms provided by Beiswanger (but I am also borrowing language from legal
theorists such as John Austin and Oliver Wendell Holmes), that there are willed
muscular contractions that cause changes of position in human bodies or parts of
bodies. Such caused changes we may agree to call "bodily motions," or simply
motions, assuming them to be—with surely few exceptions—voluntary. (For even
if push comes to shove in a certain symbolic sense, I take it that no one is actually
knocked off balance. But for a dancer to be lifted up or carried from one location to
another is not a motion, in my sense, of that dancer, though it requires motions by
other dancers.)

Bodily motions are actions; they are, in one sense, basic actions, the foundation of all other actions, at least as far as we are concerned today; for even if there
are such things as purely *mental* actions, in which no muscle is disturbed, these
cannot be the stuff or raw material of dance. But as Beiswanger says, bodily motions are not themselves the goings-on we label *Afternoon of a Faun* or *Jewels.* It is
actions of another sort that we witness and wonder at; how, then, are these related
to bodily motions?

An extremely fruitful discovery of philosophical action theory is that actions
build upon, or grow out of, each other in certain definable ways. The wielding of a
hammer, say, can become, in capable hands, the driving of a nail, and that in turn a
step in the building of a house. One action, in a technical sense, is said to "generate" another action that is its fruition or even its aim. Thus we can analyze and
come to understand certain actions by examining their *generating conditions*—that
is, the conditions that are to be fulfilled in order for act A to generate act B. This is
easy in some cases; clearly it is the presence of the nail and the wood, in proper relationship, that converts the swinging of a hammer into the driving of a nail and
that enables the former action to generate the latter action: *In* or *by* swinging the
hammer, the carpenter drove the nail. Now there is, of course, an endless variety
of such sets of generating conditions; however, they fortunately fall into a limited number of classes, and these classes themselves belong to two fundamental

categories. The first is *causal generation*. Since the swinging of the hammer *causes* the nail to penetrate the two-by-four studding, the swinging of the hammer *generates* the (act of) driving the nail into the wood. If the hammer misses or the nail is balked by a knot, this act-generation does not occur.

In this first category of act-generation, one action generates a second action that is numerically distinct from it: Swinging the hammer is not the same action as driving the nail (or building the house). In the second category, no new action, yet a different kind of action, is generated. If a person mistakenly believes that his or her divorce is final and legal and so marries a second spouse, that person has (unintentionally) committed bigamy; given the generating conditions (the persisting legal bond), the act of marrying generates the act of committing bigamy. The person has not done two things, but two kinds of things: The same action was both an act of marrying and an act of bigamy. This I call *sortal generation:* the act-generation that occurs when an action of one sort becomes also (under the requisite conditions) an action of another sort—without, of course, ceasing to be an action of the first sort as well.

These concepts, simple as they are, can help us clarify idioms sometimes used by dance theorists. Thus when George Beiswanger says that "dances are not made out of but *upon* movement" (and remember he is using the term *movement* the way I am using the term *motion*), we can interpret him, I think, as saying that a dance is not composed of, does not have as its parts or elements, bodily motions, but rather is in some way sortally generated by those motions: under certain conditions, the motion "takes on the character" (as he says) of a dance-movement. And if I may be permitted the license, I should like to take advantage of the dancer's cherished special use of the word *moving* and use it in a nominative form to refer to *actions that have the character of a dance:* I shall call them *movings*. Thus when Beiswanger adds, "Dance does consist of *goings-on* in the act of coming to be," I shall adopt a somewhat more cautious paraphrase: *In a dance, movings are sortally generated by bodily motions.* And this proposition must be supplemented at once to forestall an imminent objection: Certainly there are rests in dance as well as do-ings, and these, however passive, are part and parcel of what is happening (it happens for a time that nothing happens). Muscular contractions may be needed to maintain a position as well as to change one—especially if it is to stand on tiptoe with arm and leg outstretched. So, besides motions we shall have to include *bodily pauses* or cessations of motion; and we can add that just as motions can generate movings, so pauses can generate *posings* (using this term for peculiarly dance states of affairs). Thus we may now propose the following: *Dancing is sortally generating movings by bodily motions and posings by bodily pauses.*

Thus I find myself in disagreement—not wholly verbal, I think—with a recent valuable essay by Haig Khatchadourian. It has been effectively criticized on several points by Julie Van Camp, and I shall not review her objections here but only call attention to a few other matters. According to Khatchadourian, "Dancing consists of movements and not, or not also, of actions of some kind or other." First, although this distinction—which I hope to clarify shortly—may seem oversubtle, I believe (with Beiswanger) that dancing consists not in what Khatchadourian calls movements—that is, motions—but in actions generated by them. And second, I think it is a mistake—and there seems no warrant for this in action theory—to divide bodily motions from actions: They *are* actions of a certain kind, though in themselves generally not as interesting as the actions they generate. However, Khatchadourian's distinction between (as I would say) bodily motions and *other* actions is important; but then the distinguishing features of these other actions need to be spelled out.

Taking off from the first of these two objections to Khatchadourian, I must now try to explain why I say that movings are more than motions: that there is indeed act-generation, a transformation of motions into movings. I have two main reasons.

My first reason rests on two propositions that will probably not be challenged. (1) It seems we do not dance all of the time—not every motion is dancing—so there must be some difference between the motions that generate dancing and those that don't, however difficult it may be to get a fix on. (2) It seems there is nothing in the nature of motions themselves that marks off those that can be dance from those that can't; practically any kind is available. Some insight into the puzzles here may be derived from Marcia Siegel's discussion of Anna Sokolow's *Rooms*. She describes the various motions of the performers—for example:

> Then, drooping across the chair seats, they lower their heads to the floor, lift their arms to the side and let them drop, slapping against the floor with a dead sound. . . . Slowly they lean forward and back in their seats, staring at the audience.
>
> None of this can be called dance movement, but neither is it merely the prosaic activity that it seems to be at first. Sokolow gives these ordinary movements a dancelike character by exaggerating the dynamics and the timing, sometimes beyond "natural" limits. Instead of just raising or lowering a hand, someone might take a very long time to raise it, giving the gesture great importance, then drop it suddenly and heavily, as if, having made all that effort to prepare, there was nothing worth doing with the hand after all. Besides the intensified way everything is carried out, each move or repeated series of moves is a separate gesture that finishes in some way before the next series is undertaken.

I am not sure I fully understand this passage, which is not as clear as Siegel's writing usually is. When she says that "none of this can be called dance movement," she is apparently not denying that what is going on is a dance; I think she means that these motions are not the usual stuff of dance, not conventionally used in dancing. When she adds that "Sokolow gives these ordinary movements a dancelike character," I take this to mean that Sokolow shapes the motions so that they actually *are* dance, not merely *like* dance. Of course this kind of performance is difficult to talk about, but if I understand her, Siegel is marking an important distinction. Of two motions, abstractly classified as, say, "raising an arm," one may be a dance and the other not, depending on some distinguishing feature contributed by the choreographer—so that, more concretely described, they may be somewhat different motions, though they belong to the same shared type. One motion generates moving, in my sense of the term, and the other doesn't. (Some would add that merely transferring an "ordinary" movement to a stage, under a bright spotlight, could give it a quality that makes it a dance.)

My second reason for distinguishing the concept of *motion* from that of *moving* is that this very distinction seems to be deeply embedded in a large special or technical vocabulary that is used for talking about dancing. Take the term *pirouette,* for example. We can explain "how you do" a pirouette, and we can say that in turning rapidly on her toe, the dancer pirouetted. A turning of a certain sort generated a pirouetting, and they were the same event; yet if we first describe the event as a rapid turning on the toe we are adding something to this description when we say that it was also a pirouette, for that is to say it was dancing. So with numerous other familiar terms: *jeté, glissade, demi-plié, sissone fermé, pas de bourrée.* (And, since we must not forget to include posings as well as movings, we should add *arabesque.*) My thesis is that all these terms refer to movings as such, not to the motions that generate them. When the technical terms are supplemented by other words, borrowed from ordinary speech—*leap, lope, skip, run*—these take on a second sense in the context of dance description, though I do not think this is a case of metaphor.

The question that looms next is evidently this: How does it come about that—or what are the generating conditions that make—motions and pauses become the movings and poses of dance? Without pretending to offer much of an argument, I will illustrate some features of action theory by reflecting briefly on a few possible answers to this rather large question.

First, then, let us consider an answer that is not without plausibility and is in fact suggested by Marcia Siegel. You will recall her remark that a dancer in *Rooms* "might take a very long time to raise [his or her hand], giving the gesture great importance, then drop it suddenly and heavily, as if . . . there was nothing worth doing with the hand after all." She speaks of "the intensified way everything is carried out." If we are wary, I think we can make do with the word *expressive* to mark her meaning—and mine. When I use the word in this context, I refer to *regional qualities* of a motion or sequence of motions: It has an air or momentousness or mystery or majesty; it is abrupt, loose, heavy, decisive, or languid. To say that the motion is expressive is just to say that it has some such quality to a fairly intense degree. And this is *all* I mean by "expressive." We might then try formulating our first answer in this way: *When a motion or sequence of motions is expressive, it is dance.*

Selma Jeanne Cohen, . . . apparently holds that expressiveness is present in all true dance—though her defense of this view is, I think, marred by a tendency to confuse expressiveness with other things I shall shortly touch on, such as representation and signalling. Khatchadourian, in reply, says that expressiveness is not a necessary condition of dance but a criterion of *good* dance. An objection to making it a *sufficient* condition is, for example, that an actress in a play might appropriately make exactly the same expressive motion as Sokolow's dancers yet would not be bursting into dance but dramatically revealing a mental state or trait of personality. Thus to make the first answer work we would need to introduce further restrictions on the range of regional qualities that are to be taken into account. If we look about in writings on dance, we find a diversity of terms but some convergence of meaning; take two examples from rather different quarters. As is well known, Susanne Langer speaks of "virtual powers" as the "primary illusion" of dance; and though I don't see the need for talking about illusions, I think "powers" conveys some general truth. Then there is a remark by Merce Cunningham, reported by Calvin Tomkins:

> He has remained firmly committed to dance as dance, although he acknowledges that the concept is difficult to define. "I think it has to do with amplification, with enlargement," he said recently. "Dancing provides something—an amplification of energy—that is not provided any other way, and that's what interests me."

This remark is noteworthy in part because of what it tells about Cunningham's own taste and preferences, but I think "amplification of energy" conveys a general truth.

To put my suggestion briefly, and all too vaguely: In dance the forms and characters of voluntary motion (the generating base) are encouraged to allow the emergence of new regional qualities, which in turn are lifted to a plane of marked perceptibility: They are exhibited or featured. It is the featuring specifically of the qualities of *volition,* of willing to act, that makes movings of motions. This is most obviously true when we see power, energy, force, zest, and other positive qualities of volition; but it also applies to such qualities as droopy exhaustion and mechanical compulsion—weaknesses of the will, as well as strengths. Dances of course may be expressive in other ways, have other qualities besides these volitional qualities. But the first answer to our basic question might be reformulated this way: *When a motion or sequence of motions is expressive in virtue of its fairly intense volitional qualities, it is dance. . . .*

There is also the suggestion that it is somehow the *absence* of practical intent ("no actual work in hand," he says) that distinguishes dance from other actions. This calls for another look, after we have gained a clearer notion of what "actual work" might encompass.

To get to this topic, we may take a short detour by way of another answer to our basic question, one that tries to capture an essence of dance through the concept of representation. Consider an *act-type* (that is, a kind of action, having numerous actual instances): say, snow shovelling. This involves, for effectiveness and efficiency, certain characteristic *motion-types.* If we select certain of these motion-types that distinguish snow shovelling from other activities and perform them for the benefit of someone else, we may enable the other person to recognize the action-type from which the motions have been derived. This, roughly put, is the representation (or depiction) of one action-type by an action of another type—for in representing snow shovelling, we are not actually doing it (the actor smoking a pipe onstage does not represent a man smoking a pipe, for he is one; but he may represent a detective smoking a pipe, which he is not).

Now representation by motions clearly comes in many degrees of abstraction, of which we can perhaps distinguish three degrees in a standard way. In *playacting* (as in drama) we have the most realistic degree: The actor may wield a shovel, and the director may even call for artificial snow for the actor to push about. In *miming,* we dispense with props and verbal utterance, and we allow room for witty exaggeration: The mime would be rushing about the stage, busily moving his arms in shovelling motions, stopping to blow on his fingers or to rub his aching back. In *suggesting,* we merely allude to the original action-type, borrowing a motion or two, sketching or outlining, and mingling these motions with others, such as whirling or leaping. This might be the *Snow-shovelling Dance,* to be performed, of course, after the actual job has been done, by way of celebrating the victory of humankind over one more assault of nature. Playacting, taken quite narrowly, must be comparatively rare in dance, miming much more common, though in short stretches, I should think. Suggesting, on the other hand, is pervasive; it appears in many of the most striking and cogent movings.

Indeed, it is this pervasiveness that prompts another answer to our question: *When a motion, or sequence of motions, represents actions of other types in the mode of suggestion, it is dance.* This will undoubtedly cover a lot of ground, but it will not, of course, be satisfactory to all dancers today. For beyond the third degree of abstraction in representation there lies a fourth degree, where representation disappears; we have loping-back-and-forth and panting dancers, sitting and bending dancers, who don't represent anything. Or pirouetting dancers. Now one could argue that these fragments of moving only become dance when embedded in larger sequences that do represent by suggestion. But I should think many a pas de deux as well as many a contemporary dance episode is utterly nonrepresentational.

Snow shovelling is an example of a class of actions in which we effect a change in the physical world outside our skins; it is causally generated. Many of these actions have their own characteristic, and therefore imitable, forms of motion: corn planting, baby rocking, knitting, hammering. I should like to call such actions *workings,* because they perform work in the physicist's sense—even though some of them would ordinarily be called play: kicking a field goal or sinking a putt. It is plain that dances include many representations of working actions, nearly always at a fairly high degree of abstraction. And this contributes to their expressiveness: Seen as baby rocking, the motions may yield a more intense quality of gentleness.

Besides workings, we may take note of two other broad classes of action that have some bearing upon the subject of this inquiry. In one of these we are concerned, not with physical states of the world, but (indirectly) with mental states of other persons. The actions I refer to, when they are performed with the help of, or by means of, verbal utterances, are called "illocutionary actions," and they are generally of familiar types: asserting, greeting, inviting, thanking, refusing, insisting. These types have subtypes: Insisting on being paid time-and-a-half for last week's overtime, for example, is a subtype that may have numerous instances. Many of these same types of action can also be performed without words; we can greet by gestures as well, or sometimes better. Nodding, shrugging, winking, bowing, kneeling might be called "para-illocutionary actions" when they are done with this sort of significance; so biting the thumb generates insulting, as in act 1, scene 2 of *Romeo and Juliet.* With or without words, such actions can be called *signallings* or *sayings,* in acknowledgment of the messages they carry. I choose the latter term, and the way to put it is: In waving a hand a certain way, the infant is saying good-bye. Sayings, like workings, are representable: In waving his or her hand, the dancer is representing someone saying good-bye. And, like working-representations, saying-representations can contribute much to the expressiveness of motions in dance. The quality of that waving, as a moving, may be intensified by its semantic aspect. The dancer summons up and draws into the texture of his or her moving something of the sorrow or finality of the action-type he or she is representing. Sayings involve a form of sortal generation, what is (very broadly) called "conventional generation." It is the existence of a social convention that enables arm waving to generate good-bying; the dancer does not make use of that convention to say anything, but recalls it to intensify expressiveness.

This raises an important question that there is no time to do more than glance at now: Do dances not only represent, but also constitute sayings? That is, can motions that generate movings also generate sayings? I have read an odd remark attributed to John Cage: "We are not, in these dances, saying something. We are simple-minded enough to think that if we were saying something we would use words." This is indeed simple-minded, given the extraordinary richness of bodily motions as generators of para-illocutionary actions. It might even be argued that representations of para-illocutionary actions can hardly help but be para-illocutionary actions themselves, since by selecting the suggestive elements and giving them a different context we may seem to comment on the sayings we quote. But this claim goes beyond what I am prepared to argue for at the moment.

The third class of actions I shall call attention to consists of motions that are goal-directed, though not necessarily goal-attaining, and that have a point or purpose, even though they move neither other bodies nor other minds. Take, for example, running a race (with the aim of winning), or reaching out, or shrinking away. We might call these actions "strivings." They are generated by the presence of mental states, such as intentions (a form of "circumstantial generation"). Of course strivings, too, can be represented.

Workings, sayings, and strivings seem to belong together at some level of abstraction, as entering into social interactions that have a function, that end in achievement or are so aimed. If it is not too misleading, we may use the label "practical" for them all—and at least we will have tried to delimit the scope of this notorious weasel word somewhat more scrupulously than is usual. With its help, as so defined, we can state St. Augustine's proposal in what seems to be its most plausible form: *When a motion, or sequence of motions, does not generate practical actions, and is intended to give pleasure through perception of rhythmic order, it is dance.* But even at its best the proposal will not serve. Perhaps if we were to add a suitable insistence on expressiveness as another source of the pleasure, we would come close to an adequate characterization of dance as an art. But I assume that we do not wish to limit our concept of dance in this way. Suppose the pueblo corn dance, for example, is not only performed in order to aid the growth of corn but is actually effective; then it is a working, just as much as seed planting or hoeing. Dance shades off into and embraces some part of ritual, which is a kind of saying. If the dance is done at a festival in competition for first prize (although that may be opposed to the true spirit of dance), I suppose it is no less a dance for being at the same time a striving.

Thus we cannot define dance in this negative way as excluding motions that generate practical actions. Yet there is something to this opposition, something about dancing that is different, even if those other actions can be, in their various ways, expressive. Perhaps we can come nearer to it in one final line of thought. If *every* motion of the corn dance is prescribed in detail by magical formulas or religious rules to foster germination, growth, or a fruitful harvest, we might best regard it as pure ritual, however expressive it may be as a *consequence* of its mode of working. Like soldiers on parade or priests officiating at Mass, the participants would verge on dance but they would not really be dancing. But if some part of what goes on in the ritual helps it to achieve expressiveness (of volitional qualities) that is to some degree independent of any practical function, then whatever else it may be, it is also a moving. If, in other words, there is more zest, vigor, fluency, expansiveness, or stateliness than appears necessary for practical purposes, there is an overflow or superfluity of expressiveness to mark it as belonging to its own domain of dance.

Working and Dancing
■ Noël Carroll and Sally Banes ■

Professor Beardsley's paper is distinguished by his customary clarity. Many of the distinctions he draws will undoubtedly be useful not only for dance theoreticians, but for dance critics as well. Nevertheless, the way that these distinctions are placed in the service of a putative characterization of what constitutes a dance "moving" seems to us problematic. This brief note will be devoted to exploring the adequacy of Professor Beardsley's proposal.

Beardsley appears to conclude his paper by stating a condition requisite for a motion to be counted as a dance "moving." He writes,

"Working and Dancing" by Noël Carroll and Sally Banes, is excerpted from *Dance Research Journal,* 15 (1982), pages 37–42, and is reprinted by permission of the authors.

> If, in other words, there is more zest, vigor, fluency, expansiveness, or stateliness than appears necessary for its practical purposes, there is an overflow or superfluity of expressiveness to mark it as belonging to its own domain of dance.

We interpret Beardsley's basic point here as the claim that a superfluity of expressiveness (above the requirements of practical exigencies) is a defining feature of a dance "moving." However, in our opinion, this attribute represents neither a necessary nor a sufficient condition of dance.

First of all, "superfluity of expressiveness" is not exclusive enough to define a dance moving. We often hear of the fervor of socialist volunteers, urbanites, who travel to rural areas to help with a harvest and boost productivity. Imagine a truckload of such patriotic workers arriving at a cane field somewhere in Cuba. Some of them may even be professional dancers. They raise their machetes much higher than necessary, use more force than is required by their task, and perhaps their swinging becomes rhythmic. Their activity is expressive of patriotic zest and revolutionary zeal, but it is not dance. Here we have an overflow of expressiveness, and it is not related to the practical purpose of the event, which is aimed at increasing productivity, not at displaying class solidarity. Of course, a journalist might describe the harvest as a dance, but we would have to understand this as poetic shorthand, meaning "dance-like." To take the term "dance" literally in referring to such an event would commit us to such unlikely ballets as some sweeping infantry maneuvers and the dramatic tantrums of an adolescent. If a dance critic were to review these events, we would be very surprised.

Undoubtedly, a choreographer could take our truckload of harvesters, place them on a proscenium stage, and transform their enthusiasm into a dance. But in such a case, it seems to us that it is the choreographer's act of framing, or recontextualizing, rather than an intrinsic quality of the movement, that is decisive. In general, whether one is speaking about art dance or social dance, the context of the event in which the movement is situated is more salient than the nature of the movement itself in determining whether the action is dance.

Professor Beardsley's definition not only fails to be exclusive enough, but also falters in inclusiveness. There are, we believe, incontestable examples of dance in which there is no superfluity of expressiveness in the movement. One example is *Room Service* by Yvonne Rainer, which was first performed at the Judson Church in 1963 and again the next year at the Institute of Contemporary Art in Philadelphia. Rainer describes it as "a big sprawling piece with three teams of people playing follow-the-leader through an assortment of paraphernalia which is arranged and rearranged by a guy and his two assistants." Part of the dance includes climbing up a ladder to a platform and jumping off. A central segment of the Philadelphia performance (and of particular interest for this paper) was the activity of two dancers carrying a mattress up an aisle in the theater, out one exit, and back in through another.

Although *Room Service* may appear similar to a dance Beardsley discusses—Anna Sokolow's *Rooms*—it differs from it in important ways. The ordinary movement in *Room Service* is not marked by "the intensified way," in which it is carried out. The point of the dance is to make ordinary movement *qua* ordinary movement perceptible. The audience observes the performers navigating a cumbersome object, noting how the working bodies adjust their muscles, weights, and angles. If the dance is performed correctly, there can be no question of superfluity of expression over the requirements of practical purposes, because the *raison d'être* of the piece is to display the practical intelligence of the body in pursuit of a mundane, goal-oriented type of action—moving a mattress. That is, the subject of the dance is the functional economy of a movement in the performance of bodies involved in what Beardsley calls a working. *Room Service* is not a representation of a working; it *is* a working. But it is also a dance—partially because through its aesthetic context it transforms an ordinary working (the sort of thing whose kinetic intricacies usually go unnoticed or ignored) into an object for close scrutiny. Rainer immediately went on to make another dance, *Parts of Some Sextets,* comprising a variety of activities involving ten dancers, twelve mattresses, and gears, string, rope, and buffers. Again, the emphasis in the dance is on the working human body.

Room Service is not an atypical dance. It is an example of a genre of avant-garde performance that might loosely be referred to as task dances, which have been made continuously since the sixties. The roster of task dances includes other works by Rainer, Trisha Brown's Equipment Pieces and her *Rulegame 5* (1964), and Simone Forti's "dance construction" *Slant Board* (1961), in which three or four people move constantly across a wooden ramp slanted against a wall at a 45° angle to the floor, by means of knotted ropes. The existence of this genre is an important motive in writing this reply to Professor Beardsley, because we fear that his definition is unwittingly conservative, operating to exclude prescriptively some of the most exciting work of contemporary choreographers.

Of course, Beardsley may wish to defend his definition by arguing that *Room Service,* and works like it, are not dances. This seems ill-advised for several reasons. First, the dance shares a set of recognized aesthetic preoccupations with contemporary fine art. For example, it is what has been called "anti-illusionist." That is, it attempts to close the conceptual gap between artworks and real things—a major theme of modernist sculpture and painting. In this vein, Jasper Johns reportedly has said that "people should be able to look at a painting 'the same way you look at a radiator.' " John's flag paintings, especially *Flag* (1955, Museum of Modern Art), ingeniously implement this "demystifying" attitude toward artworks, since in certain pertinent respects the painting is a flag (or one side of one), rather than a representation (or "illusion") of one; schoolchildren could pledge to it with no loss of allegiance. John's bronzed beer cans or his Savarin can with paint brushes are sculptures that likewise attempt to narrow the categorical distinction between mundane objects and works of art.

The choice of ordinary working movement as the subject of *Room Service* is on a par with the "demythologizing" tendency toward fine art that one finds in many of Jasper John's pieces. Stated formulaically, we might say that "ordinary object" in art is equivalent to "ordinary movement" in dance. Now, Johns's work is (rightfully, we believe) considered among the major accomplishments of the art of the fifties, sixties, and early seventies. There can be little doubt that it is art or that his patterned canvases are paintings. Why? One answer is that his works are the intelligible products of a century of animated interplay between art making and art theorizing. Since the rise of photography, anti-illusionist arguments for the role and destiny of painting abound. Part of the rhetoric of this theorizing is that a painting is essentially an object (a "real" object), like any other (e.g., a radiator or beer can), rather than a cypher (a virtual object) standing for real objects. The Johns examples, as well as Warhol's Brillo boxes, attempt to literalize this type of theory by proposing masterpieces that in terms of certain relevant features are indistinguishable from everyday objects. *Room Service* bears a *strict genetic resemblance* to the above cases of modernist painting and sculpture. If they are full-blooded examples of painting and sculpture, as we believe their position in the history of twentieth-century art establishes, then *Room Service* is a dance.

Specifically, it is an art dance, since the tradition it directly emerges from is that of the artworld rather than custom, ritual, or popular culture. Indeed, it is an art dance in a triple sense. First, it is presented to the spectator as an object of aesthetic contemplation and not as a social or ritual activity. Second, and more importantly, it mimes (or, less metaphorically, transposes) the theoretical *donnees* of fine art in the medium of dance. And third, in doing this it is also in the domain of art dancing proper, since both the balletic and modern traditions of dance have always made a practice of exploring other arts for inspiration and invention.

In making this argument, we hasten to add that we do not believe that it is necessary for the anti-illusionist theories that form the conceptual background of Johns, of Warhol, or of Rainer to be true or even compelling philosophically in order that the putative paintings, sculptures, and dances be classified as paintings, sculptures, and dances. It is enough that the theories have currency in their appropriate communities of discourse and that the works in question can be seen as their consequences. We are assuming this on the grounds that a genetic link between an evolving artistic tradition (including theory, practice, and the cross-fertilization between the two) and a candidate for inclusion in that tradition is a *prima facie* reason for classifying the candidate as part of the tradition. *Room Service* is both art and art dance because of such genetic links. Indeed, insofar as it is even less ambiguously an ordinary working than painting the design of the Stars and Stripes is a flag, it is perhaps a more effective implementation of modernist concerns than the Johns example. In terms of our use of *Room Service*, and dances like it, as counterexamples to Beardsley's characterization of dance, it is important to iterate that these dances are able to articulate the modernist theme of anti-illusionism precisely because their movements are completely practical—a literal performance of a task—with no superfluity of expressiveness.

A related, though less persuasive reason to believe that *Room Service* is a dance (specifically, an art dance) is that it performs a major (though not essential) function of art in general and art dancing in particular. Namely, it symbolically reflects major values and preoccupations of the culture from which it emerged. In other words, it behaves the way we expect dances to behave. Its anti-illusionist stance and its disavowal of representation, formal decorativeness, and the kinds of expressiveness found in most modern dance (e.g., [Martha] Graham, [Doris] Humphrey, and [José] Limon) evince a reductive bias, a quest to get down to basics, to eschew the layers of convention, coded symbolism, and elaborate structure that "obstruct" the spectator's perception of movement. This search for fundamentals is in many respects utopian. Nevertheless, it does reflect a particular post-war mood—a positivist search for the hard facts of dance, bereft of illusionist "nonsense." Again, whether there are such hard facts is beside the point; it is the quest implied by this dance that reflects the temper of the times. And, to return to Beardsley's definition, *Room Service* reflects the values and prejudices of its cultural context because of the sheer practicality of its movement. (Interestingly, a Laban-analysis of Rainer's non-task dances of this period shows a striking similarity between the efficient motions used in work and those used in the dances: a somewhat narrow and medium level stance, an even flow of energy, and sagittal gestures—in two planes, forward and backward plus up and down—rather than the three-dimensional shaping, gathering, and scattering movements of much modern dance.

Admittedly, *Room Service* is an extremely complex dance, with several levels of symbolic import. It is not our intention to argue that it is not expressive. For example, it communicates a conception of dance, albeit a reductive one, and, as the previous paragraph argues, it espouses identifiable values. However, this sense of expression is different from Beardsley's. It is not a matter of the movement having intensified, nonpractical qualities, but of the movement implying certain polemical commitments, easily statable in propositions, due to the art-historical and cultural contexts in which the dance was produced. Here the propositional import of the dance hinges on the practicality of the movement; this level of expression, in other words, cannot be mapped in terms of an overflow of intensified qualities, above and beyond the functional. Though *Room Service* has propositional meaning, it is not what Beardsley calls a saying, nor is it a representation of a saying. Professor Beardsley's sayings are highly conventionalized signals, e.g., a wave of the hand is regularly associated with "hello." "However, we do not "read" the significance of the movement in *Room Service,* but infer it as the best explanation of Rainer's choreographic choices within a specific historical context.

Room Service might also be called expressive in the sense that the choreography metaphorically possesses certain anthropomorphic qualities; we have already called it "positivist." It might also be called factual or objective. But each of these labels fits the dance specifically because of the theoretically "hard-minded," anti-illusionist position it promotes. That the subject is work in the context of a culture that often identifies art and dance with play also has expressive repercussions: the choreography is "serious" rather than "sentimental" or "frivolous" (in the idiom of the Protestant ethic). Again, it is the choice of unadorned workings as its subject that is the basis of its expressive effect as well as the basis, as previously argued, of its being recognizable as an art dance. Given this, Professor Beardsley's stipulation, identifying dance with a superfluity of expressiveness above practical purposes, does not seem to fit the facts of a major work of postmodern dance and, by extension, a genre of which it is a primary example.

Professor Beardsley's paper also raises issues relevant to postmodern choreography in the section where he argues that the basic constituents of dance are not bodily motions as such. Instead, Beardsley holds that dances are composed of actions that he calls "movings" and "posings." It is interesting to note that in certain postmodern dances and dance theorizing it is presupposed that dance is fundamentally bodily motion and that the function of a dance is to make the spectator see bodily motions as such. The motive behind this enterprise derives from the modernist bias outlined earlier. In brief, in contemporary theoretical discussions of fine art, the conception of a painting as an *ordinary* object easily becomes associated with the idea that it is an object as such. It is a surface. Thus, the role of an artist like Jules Olitski is seen as acknowledging the flat surface of the painting. Painters are cast in a role akin to nuclear physicists, exploring the basic physical constituents of their medium, as if plumbing the mysteries of the atom. The result is paintings "about" paint or, to change media, films "about" celluloid. This anti-illusionist move is also in evidence in postmodern dance. Dances like Trisha Brown's *Accumulation* identify dance as a concatenation of physical motions without any ostensible formal, conventional, expressive, or representational unity. *Accumulation* is a list of abstract gestures—simple rotations, bends, and swings of the joints and limbs—that are accumulated by repeating the first gesture several times, adding the second gesture and repeating gestures one and two several times, and so on. There are no transitions between gestures. *Accumulation* suggests a position about the nature of the basic elements of dance, a position which holds that dance consists of bodily motions.

The philosophical problems raised by dances like *Accumulation* can be quite vexing. But in our opinion, such dances are not counter-examples to Beardsley's claim that dances are made up of actions and never mere bodily motions. Our reasons for believing this are, for the most part, contained in our gloss of *Room Service*. We have admitted that the search for the fundamentals of dance by postmodern choreographers is utopian. Making dances like *Accumulation,* which are designed to *imply* that dance essentially consists of bodily motions, requires that the basic movements chosen for the dance be purposively made so that a) they are not straightforwardly classifiable in terms of traditional categories of dance actions (e.g., Beardsley's "suggestings") and b) they are intelligible, due to their historical context, as rejections of the traditional categories. In meeting the first requirement, each movement is a type of action—namely, a *refraining*. Specifically, each movement is *a studied omission* of the movement qualities found in ballet and modern dance. In the context of the sixties, this sort of refraining implied a commitment to the idea that dance consists primarily of bodily motions. However, the movements used to articulate that position were actually anything but mere bodily motions. They were actions, refrainings whose implicit disavowal of the traditional qualities of dance movements enabled them to be understood as polemical. Thus, though we feel that certain developments in postmodern dance, specifically task dances, threaten Professor Beardsley's concept of dance, we do not believe that the existence of dances like *Accumulation* challenge Beardsley's point that dances consist of actions rather than mere bodily motions.

The Dance of Śiva
■ Ananda K. Coomaraswamy ■

"The Lord of Tillai's Court a mystic dance performs; what's that, my dear?"
—*Tiruvāçagam*, XII, 14.

Amongst the greatest of the names of Śiva is Natarāja, Lord of Dancers, or King of Actors. The cosmos is His theatre, there are many different steps in His repertory, He Himself is actor and audience—

When the Actor beateth the drum,
Everybody cometh to see the show;
When the Actor collecteth the stage properties
He abideth alone in His happiness.

How many various dances of Śiva are known to His worshippers I cannot say. No doubt the root idea behind all of these dances is more or less one and the same, the manifestation of primal rhythmic energy. Śiva is the Eros Protogonos of Lucian, when he wrote:

"It would seem that dancing came into being at the beginning of all things, and was brought to light together with Eros, that ancient one, for we see this primeval dancing clearly set forth in the choral dance of the constellations, and in the planets and fixed stars, their interweaving and interchange and orderly harmony."

I do not mean to say that the most profound interpretation of Śiva's dance was present in the minds of those who first danced in frantic, and perhaps intoxicated energy, in honour of the pre-Aryan hill-god, afterwards merged in Śiva. A great motif in religion or art, any great symbol, becomes all things to all men; age after age it yields to men such treasure as they find in their own hearts. Whatever the origins of Śiva's dance, it became in time the clearest image of the *activity* of God which any art or religion can boast of. Of the various dances of Śiva I shall only speak of three, one of them alone forming the main subject of interpretation. The first is an evening dance in the Himālayas, with a divine chorus, described as follows in the *Śiva Pradosha Stotra:*

"The Dance of Śiva," by Ananda K. Coomaraswamy is published as it appeared in *The Dance of Śiva—Essays on Indian Art and Culture,* Dover Publications (1985).

"Placing the Mother of the Three Worlds upon a golden throne, studded with precious gems, Śūlapīṇi dances on the heights of Kailāsa, and all the gods gather round Him;

"Sarasvatī plays on the *vīṇā,* Indra on the flute, Brahmā holds the time-marking cymbals, Lakshmī begins a song, Vishnu plays on a drum, and all the gods stand round about:

"Gandharvas, Yakshas, Patagas, Uragas, Siddhas, Sadhyas, Vidyādharas, Amaras, Apsarases, and all the beings dwelling in the three worlds assemble there to witness the celestial dance and hear the music of the divine choir at the hour of twilight."

This evening dance is also referred to in the invocation preceding the *Kathā Sarit Sāgara.*

In the pictures of this dance, Śiva is two-handed, and the co-operation of the gods is clearly indicated in their position of chorus. There is no prostrate Asura trampled under Śiva's feet. So far as I know, no special interpretations of this dance occur in Śaiva literature.

The second well known dance of Śiva is called the *Tāṇḍava,* and belongs to His *tāmasic* aspect as Bhairava or Vīra-bhadra. It is performed in cemeteries and burning grounds, where Śiva, usually in ten-armed form, dances wildly with Devī, accompanied by troops of capering imps. Representations of this dance are common amongst ancient sculptures, as at Elūra, Elephanta, and also Bhuvaneśvara. The *tāṇḍava* dance is in origin that of a pre-Aryan divinity, half-god, half-demon, who holds his midnight revels in the burning ground. In later times, this dance in the cremation ground, sometimes of Śiva, sometimes of Devī, is interpreted in Śaiva and Śākta literature in a most touching and profound sense.

Thirdly, we have the Nadānta dance of Naṭarāja before the assembly (*sabhā*) in the golden hall of Chidambaram or Tillai, the centre of the Universe, first revealed to gods and rishis after the submission of the latter in the forest of Tāragam, as related in the *Koyil Purāṇam.* The legend, which has after all, no very close connection with the real meaning of the dance, may be summarised as follows:

In the forest of Tāragam dwelt multitudes of heretical rishis, following of the Mīmāṃsa. Thither proceeded Śiva to confute them, accompanied by Vishnu disguised as a beautiful woman, and Āti-Śeshan. The rishis were at first led to violent dispute amongst themselves, but their anger was soon directed against Śiva, and they endeavoured to destroy Him by means of incantations. A fierce tiger was created in sacrificial fires, and rushed upon Him; but smiling gently, He seized it and, with the nail of His little finger, stripped off its skin, and wrapped it about Himself like a silken cloth. Undiscouraged by failure, the sages renewed their offerings, and produced a monstrous serpent, which however, Śiva seized and wreathed about His neck like a garland. Then He began to dance; but there rushed upon Him a last monster in the shape of a malignant dwarf, Muyalaka. Upon him the God pressed the tip of His foot, and broke the creature's back, so that it writhed upon the ground; and so, His last foe prostrate, Śiva resumed the dance, witnessed by gods and rishis.

Then ĀtiŚeshan worshipped Śiva, and prayed above all things for the boon, once more to behold this mystic dance; Śiva promised that he should behold the dance again in sacred Tillai, the centre of the Universe.

Shiva Ntaraja (Shiva as the King of Dance)
Source: The Cleveland Museum of Art, 2002. Purchase from the T. H. Wade Fund,
1930.

This dance of Śiva in Chidambaram or Tillai forms the motif of the South Indian copper images of Śrī Naṭarājā, the Lord of the Dance. These images vary
amongst themselves in minor details, but all express one fundamental conception.
Before proceeding to enquire what these may be, it will be necessary to describe the
image of Śrī Naṭarājā as typically represented. The images then, represent Śiva
dancing, having four hands, with braided and jewelled hair of which the lower locks
are whirling in the dance. In His hair may be seen a wreathing cobra, a skull, and the
mermaid figure of Gangā; upon it rests the crescent moon, and it is crowned with a
wreath of Cassia leaves. In His right ear He wears a man's earring, a woman's in the
left; He is adorned with necklaces and armlets, a jewelled belt, anklets, bracelets,

finger and toe-rings. The chief part of His dress consists of tightly fitting breeches, and He wears also a fluttering scarf and a sacred thread. One right hand holds a drum, the other is uplifted in the sign of do not fear; one left hand holds fire, the other points down upon the demon Muyalaka, a dwarf holding a cobra; the left foot is raised. There is a lotus pedestal, from which springs an encircling glory (*tiruvāsi*), fringed with flame, and touched within by the hands holding drum and fire. The images are of all sizes, rarely if ever exceeding four feet in total height.

Even without reliance upon literary references, the interpretation of this dance would not be difficult. Fortunately, however, we have the assistance of a copious contemporary literature, which enables us to fully explain not only the general significance of the dance, but equally, the details of its concrete symbolism. Some of the peculiarities of the Naṭarājā images, of course, belong to the conception of Śiva generally, and not to the dance in particular. Such are the braided locks, as of a yogī; the Cassia garland; the skull of Brahmā: the figure of Gangā, (the Ganges fallen from heaven and lost in Śiva's hair); the cobras; the different ear-rings, betokening the dual nature of Mahādev, 'whose half is Umā'; and the four arms. The drum also is a general attribute of Śiva, belonging to his character of Yogī, though in the dance, it has further a special significance. What then is the meaning of Śiva's Nadānta dance, as understood by Śaivas? Its essential significance is given in texts such as the following:

"Our Lord is the Dancer, who, like the heat latent in firewood, diffuses His power in mind and matter, and makes them dance in their turn."

The dance, in fact, represents His five activites *(Pañcakṛitya),* viz: *Śrishṭi* (overlooking, creation, evolution), *Sthiti* (preservation, support), *Samhāra* (destruction, evolution), *Tirobhava* (veiling, embodiment, illusion, and also, giving rest), *Anugraha* (release, salvation, grace). These, separately considered, are the activities of the deities Brahmā, Vishnu, Rudra, Maheśvara and Sadāśiva.

This cosmic activity is the central motif of the dance. Further quotations will illustrate and explain the more detailed symbolisms. *Uṇmai Vilakkam,* verse 36, tells us:

"Creation arises from the drum: protection proceeds from the hand of hope; from fire proceeds destruction; the foot held aloft gives release." It will be observed that the fourth hand points to this lifted foot, the refuge of the soul.

We have also the following from *Chidambara Mummaṇi Kovai:*

"O my Lord, Thy hand holding the sacred drum has made and ordered the heavens and earth and other worlds and innumerable souls. Thy lifted hand protects both the conscious and unconscious order of thy creation. All these worlds are transformed by Thy hand bearing fire. Thy sacred foot, planted on the ground, gives an abode to the tired soul struggling in the toils of causality. It is Thy lifted foot that grants eternal bliss to those that approach Thee. These Five-Actions are indeed Thy Handiwork."

The following verses from the *Tirukūttu Darshana* (Vision of the Sacred Dance), forming the ninth tantra of Tirumūlar's *Tirumantram,* expand the central motif further;

"His form is everywhere: all-pervading in His Śiva-Śakti;
Chidambaram is everywhere, everywhere His dance;
As Śiva is all and omnipresent,
Everywhere is Śiva's gracious dance made manifest.
His five-fold dances are temporal and timeless.
His five-fold dances are His Five Activties.
By His grace He performs the five acts,
This is the sacred dance of Umā-Sahāya.
He dances with Water, Fire, Wind and Ether,
Thus our Lord dances ever in the court.
Visible to those who pass over Māyā and Mahāmāyā (illusion and super-illusion)
Our Lord dances His eternal dance.
The form of the Śakti is all delight—
This united delight is Umā's body;
This form of Śakti arising in time
And uniting the twain is the dance:
His body is Ākāś, the dark cloud therein is Muyalaka,
The eight quarters are His eight arms,
The three lights are His three eyes,
Thus becoming, He dances in our body as the congregation."

This is His dance. Its deepest significance is felt when it is realised that it takes place within the heart and the self. Everywhere is God: that Everywhere is the heart. Thus also we find another verse:

"The dancing foot, the sound of the tinkling bells,
The songs that are sung and the varying steps,
The form assumed by our Dancing Gurupara—
Find out these within yourself, then shall your fetters fall away."

To this end, all else but the thought of God must be cast out of the heart, that He alone may abide and dance therein. In *Uṇmai Vilakkam,* we find:

"The silent sages destroying the threefold bond are established where their selves are destroyed. There they behold the sacred and are filled with bliss. This is the dance of the Lord of the assembly, 'whose very form is Grace'."

With this reference to the 'silent sages' compare the beautiful words of Tirumūlar:

"When resting there they (the yogīs who attain the highest place of peace) lose themselves and become idle. . . . Where the idlers dwell is the pure Space. Where the idlers sport is the Light. What the idlers know is Vedānta. What the idlers find is the deep sleep therein."

Śiva is a destroyer and loves the burning ground. But what does He destroy? Not merely the heavens and earth at the close of a world-cycle, but the fetters that bind each separate soul. Where and what is the burning ground? It is not the place where our earthly bodies are cremated, but the hearts of His lovers, laid waste and desolate. The place where the ego is destroyed signifies the state where illusion and deeds are burnt away; that is the crematorium, the burning-ground where Śri Naṭarāja dances, and whence He is named Sudalaiyādi, Dancer of the burning-ground. In this simile, we recognize the historical connection between Śiva's gracious dance as Naṭarāja and His wild dance as the demon of the cemetery.

This conception of the dance is current also amongst Śāktas, especially in Bengal, where the Mother rather than the Father-aspect of Siva is adored. Kālī is here the dancer, for whose entrance the heart must be purified by fire, made empty by renunciation. A Bengali Hymn to Kālī voices this prayer:

> *"Because Thou lovest the Burning-ground,*
> *I have made a Burning-ground of my heart—*
> *That Thou, Dark One, haunter of the Burning-ground,*
> *Mayest dance Thy eternal dance.*
> *Nought else is within my heart, O Mother;*
> *Day and night blazes the funeral pyre;*
> *The ashes of the dead, strewn all about,*
> *I have preserved against Thy coming,*
> *With death-conquering Mahākāla neath Thy feet*
> *Do Thou enter in, dancing Thy rhythmic dance,*
> *That I may behold Thee with closed eyes."*

Returning to the South, we find that in other Tamil texts the purpose of Śiva's dance is explained. In *Śivajñāna Siddhiyār,* Supaksha, Sūtra V, 5, we find,

"For the purpose of securing both kinds of fruit to the countless souls, our Lord, with actions five, dances His dance." Both kinds of fruit, that is *Iham,* reward in this world, and *Param,* bliss in Mukti.

Again, *Uṇmai Vilakkam,* v. 32, 37, 39 inform us

"The Supreme Intelligence dances in the soul . . . for the purpose of removing our sins. By these means, our Father scatters the darkness of illusion (*māyā*), burns the thread of causality (*karma*), stamps down evil (*mala, āṇava, avidyā*), showers Grace, and lovingly plunges the soul in the ocean of Bliss (*ānanda*). They never see rebirths, who behold this mystic dance."

The conception of the world process as the Lord's pastime or amusement (*līlā*) is also prominent in the Śaiva scriptures. Thus Tirumūlar writes, "The perpetual dance is His play." This spontaneity of Śiva's dance is so clearly expressed in Skryabin's *Poem of Ecstasy* that the extracts following will serve to explain it better than any more formal exposition—what Skryabin wrote is precisely what the Hindu imager moulded:

> *"The Spirit* (purusha) *playing,*
> *The Spirit longing,*
> *The Spirit with fancy* (yoga-māyā) *creating all,*
> *Surrenders himself to the bliss* (ānanda) *of love . . .*
> *Amid the flowers of His creation* (prakṛiti), *He lingers in a kiss. . . .*

Blinded by their beauty, He rushes, He frolics, He dances, He whirls. . . .
He is all rapture, all bliss, in this play (līlā)
Free, divine, in this love struggle.
In the marvellous grandeur of sheer aimlessness,
And in the union of counter-aspirations
In consciousness alone, in love alone,
The Spirit learns the nature (svabhāva) *of His divine being. . . .*
'O, my world, my life, my blossoming, my ecstasy!
Your every moment I create
By negation of all forms previously lived through:
I am eternal negation (neti, neti). *. . .'*
Enjoying this dance, choking in this whirlwind,
Into the domain of ecstasy, He takes swift flight.
In this unceasing change (samsāra, nitya bhava), *in this flight, aimless, di-*
vine
The Spirit comprehends Himself,
In the power of will, alone, free,
Ever-creating, all-irradiating, all-vivifying,
Divinely playing in the multiplicity of forms, He comprehends Himself. . . .
'I already dwell in thee, O, my world,
Thy dream of me—'twas I coming into existence. . . .
And thou art all—one wave of freedom and bliss. . . .'
By a general conflagration (mahā-pralaya) *the universe* (samsāra) *is embraced*
The Spirit is at the height of being, and He feels the tide unending
Of the divine power (śakti) *of free will. He is all-daring;*
What menaced, now is excitement,
What terrified, is now delight. . . .
And the universe resounds with the joyful cry I am."

This aspect of Śiva's immanence appears to have given rise to the objection that he dances as do those who seek to please the eyes of mortals; but it is answered that in fact He dances to maintain the life of the cosmos and to give release to those who seek Him. Moreover, if we understand even the dances of human dancers rightly, we shall see that they too lead to freedom. But it is nearer the truth to answer that the reason of His dance lies in His own nature, all his gestures are own-nature-born (*svabhāva-jaḥ*), spontaneous, and purposeless—for His being is beyond the realm of purposes.

In a much more arbitrary way the dance of Śiva is identified with the *Pañcākshara,* or five syllables of the prayer Śi-va-ya-na-ma, 'Hail to Śiva.' In *Uṇmai Vilakkam* we are told: "If this beautiful Five-Letters be meditated upon, the soul will reach the land where there is neither light nor darkness, and there Śakti will make it One with Śivam."

Another verse of *Uṇmai Vilakkam* explains the fiery arch (*tiruvāsi*): The Pañchākshara and the Dance are identified with the mystic syllable 'Om,' the arch being the *kombu* or hook of the ideograph of the written symbol: "The arch over Śrī Naṭarāja is Omkāra; and the akshara which is never separate from the Omkāra is the contained splendour. This is the Dance of the Lord of Chidambaram."

The *Tiru-Arul-Payan* however (Ch. ix. 3) explains the *tiruvāsi* more naturally as representing the dance of Nature, contrasted with Śiva's dance of wisdom.

"The dance of nature proceeds on one side; the dance of enlightenment on the other. Fix your mind in the centre of the latter."

I am indebted to Mr. Nallasvā,mi Pillai for a commentary on this:

The first dance is the action of matter—material and individual energy. This is the arch, *tiruvāsi,* Omkāra, the dance of Kālī. The other is the Dance of Śiva— the akshara inseparable from the Omkāra—called *ardhamātra* or the fourth letter of the Praṇava—Chaturtam and Turīyam. The first dance is not possible unless Śiva wills it and dances Himself.

The general result of this interpretation of the arch is, then, that it represents matter, nature, Prakṛiti; the contained splendour, Śiva dancing within and touching the arch with head, hands and feet, is the universal omnipresent Spirit (*Purusha*). Between these stands the individual soul, as *ya* is between *Śi-va* and *na-ma*.

Now to summarize the whole interpretation we find that *The Essential Significance of Śiva's Dance is threefold: First, it is the image of his Rhythmic Play as the Source of all Movement within the Cosmos, which is Represented by the Arch: Secondly, the Purpose of his Dance is to Release the Countless souls of men from the Snare of Illusion: Thirdly the Place of the Dance, Chidambaram, the Centre of the Universe, is within the Heart.*

So far I have refrained from all aesthetic criticism and have endeavoured only to translate the central thought of the conception of Śiva's dance from plastic to verbal expression, without reference to the beauty or imperfection of individual works. But it may not be out of place to call attention to the grandeur of this conception itself as a synthesis of science, religion and art. How amazing the range of thought and sympathy of those rishiartists who first conceived such a type as this, affording an image of reality, a key to the complex tissue of life, a theory of nature, not merely satisfactory to a single clique or race, nor acceptable to the thinkers of one century only, but universal in its appeal to the philosopher, the lover, and the artist of all ages and all countries. How supremely great in power and grace this dancing image must appear to all those who have striven in plastic forms to give expression to their intuition of Life!

In these days of specialization, we are not accustomed to such a synthesis of thought; but for those who 'saw' such images as this, there could have been no division of life and thought into water-tight compartments. Nor do we always realize, when we criticise the merits of individual works, the full extent of the creative power which, to borrow a musical analogy, could discover a mode so expressive of fundamental rhythms and so profoundly significant and inevitable.

Every part of such an image as this is directly expressive, not of any mere superstition or dogma, but of evident facts. No artist of today, however great, could more exactly or more wisely create an image of that Energy which science must postulate behind all phenomena. If we would reconcile Time with Eternity, we can scarcely do so otherwise than by the conception of alternations of phase extending over vast regions of space and great tracts of time. Especially significant, then, is the phase alternation implied by the drum, and the fire which 'changes,' not destroys. These are but visual symbols of the theory of the day and night of Brahmā.

In the night of Brahmā, Nature is inert, and cannot dance till Śiva wills it; He rises from His rapture, and dancing sends through inert matter pulsing waves of awakening sound, and lo! matter also dances appearing as a glory round about Him. Dancing, He sustains its manifold phenomena. In the fulness of time, still dancing, he destroys all forms and names by fire and gives new rest. This is poetry; but none the less, science.

It is not strange that the figure of Naṭarāja has commanded the adoration of so many generations past; Familiar with all scepticisms, expert in tracing all beliefs to primitive superstitions, explorers of the infinitely great and infinitely small, we are worshippers of Naṭarāja still.

PART VI

LITERATURE

Literature is typically considered the most imaginative use of language. Although poetry and fiction, for the most part, use the ordinary words of the familiar natural languages, it has seemed to many reflective people that the literary function of language is entirely different from the roles nonliterary language plays.

However, in the article "What Is Literature?" the Marxist literary theorist Terry Eagleton reviews, but rejects, various attempts to demarcate the literary from ordinary usage. In short, Eagleton takes a skeptical position with regard to previous attempts at such definition, for example those of the so-called Russian formalists.

In one attempt to locate the distinctive connection between language and literature, the philosopher R. G. Collingwood argues that literary art has a special relationship to emotion. Poetry, for example, is not *properly* concerned with the *arousal* of emotion. For Collingwood the arousal of emotion is a mere *craft,* not art. However, poetry is the *expression* of emotion. To express emotion for Collingwood is to become *conscious* of it in a clear and individualized manner. For him, we do not really know what we feel until we express those feelings in a properly lucid manner. When that happens, our poetry is artistic in Collingwood's sense of being "art proper."

One of the most controversial topics about literature concerns guidelines for the interpretation of literary texts. A seemingly obvious point of departure is that we need to acknowledge that the meaning of a novel or poem is based upon certain intentions of the author. This view has the advantage of anchoring an interpretation in an apparently objective set of circumstances. Even if we cannot now know the author's actual intentions, the key to the meaning of a literary work is to try to reconstruct them as best we can. However, the philosopher Monroe Beardsley argues that such an approach is guilty of what he calls "the intentional Fallacy." He claims that no appeal to an author's intention can ever be conclusive evidence for a judgment about the meaning of a literary work. Such evidence is never more than a clue. This view greatly influenced the literary movement known as "the New Criticism."

Staking out a more radical position in his essay "What Is an Author?" the French philosopher Michel Foucault suggests that the very idea of an author is a social construct to which the literary critic cannot usefully appeal. Recognizing that the concept of *author* has changed historically, Foucault also argues that actual, real people who write books stand in various kinds of relationships to the authorial voices of their texts and are not the absolute originators of their work. Instead, Foucault recommends that we think of an author as "a certain fundamental principle" operating upon the language of literature, which he calls "the author function."

Richard Wollheim poses two main, incompatible options for an interpretive methodology. On one method, which he calls "scrutiny," an interpreter ought to pay attention to the work in itself, in isolation from its context. Wollheim's sympathies lie with another method, "retrieval," which does try to locate an artwork historically. The artist's intention, as part of this context, cannot be ignored as potentially relevant to a correct understanding of an artwork. Wollheim grants, however, that such intentions may not always be fully conscious in an artist's mind.

It is often held that the interpretation of literature is a bottomless, open-ended affair, and that the possibility of disagreement can never be closed off. Richard Shusterman reviews recent positions on the matter and argues that there are limitations to such a relativist position. Much of our understanding of texts is based upon the simple training we received when we acquired that language.

It is important to recognize that Western ways of appreciating literature may not be suitable for the literary products of other cultures. Richard Bodman makes this clear in his "How to Eat a Chinese Poem," a title he does not intend frivolously. In a traditional Chinese poem, he suggests, look for the "taste," not the message. While a poem may involve abstractions, such as sorrow, truth, and joy, its central "eye" capitalizes upon the more concrete language of sensory experience. A Chinese poem plays upon the basic idea that words do not exhaust meaning. Bodman illustrates this with a detailed discussion of an example.

The study of literature has recently stimulated much philosophical interest in the role of *imagination* in narrative art. As Gregory Currie puts it in his essay, a work authorizes us to imagine various things and to remove the option of imagining others. For instance, *Hamlet* authorizes us to accept that Hamlet lives in Denmark, while proscribing that Hamlet was an orphan. But *Hamlet* also leaves indeterminate certain other things—Hamlet's motives for instance. After drawing a distinction between importantly different kinds of imagination, Currie takes on the important task of showing how the power of imagination supports emotional responses to purely fictional beings and events in a narrative work.

What Is Literature?

■ Terry Eagleton ■

If there is such a thing as literary theory, then it would seem obvious that there is something called literature which it is the theory of. We can begin, then, by raising the question: What is literature?

There have been various attempts to define literature. You can define it, for example, as 'imaginative' writing in the sense of fiction—writing which is not literally true. But even the briefest reflection on what people commonly include under the heading of literature suggests that this will not do. Seventeenth-century English literature includes Shakespeare, Webster, Marvell and Milton; but it also stretches to the essays of Francis Bacon, the sermons of John Donne, Bunyan's spiritual autobiography and whatever it was that Sir Thomas Browne wrote. . . .

A distinction between 'fact' and 'fiction,' then, seems unlikely to get us very far, not least because the distinction itself is often a questionable one. It has been argued, for instance, that our own opposition between 'historical' and 'artistic' truth does not apply at all to the early Icelandic sagas. In the English late sixteenth and early seventeenth centuries, the word 'novel' seems to have been used about both true and fictional events, and even news reports were hardly to be considered factual. Novels and news reports were neither clearly factual nor clearly fictional: Our own sharp discriminations between these categories simply did not apply. . . .

Perhaps literature is definable not according to whether it is fictional or 'imaginative,' but because it uses language in peculiar ways. On this theory, literature is a kind of writing which, in the words of the Russian critic Roman Jakobson, represents an 'organized violence committed on ordinary speech.' Literature transforms and intensifies ordinary language, deviates systematically from everyday speech. If you approach me at a bus stop and murmur 'Thou still unravished bride of quietness,' then I am instantly aware that I am in the presence of the literary. I know this because the texture, rhythm and resonance of your words are in excess of their abstractable meaning—or, as the linguists might more technically put it, there is a disproportion between the signifiers and the signifieds. Your language draws attention to itself, flaunts its material being, as statements like 'Don't you know the drivers are on strike?' do not.

This, in effect, was the definition of the 'literary' advanced by the Russian formalists, who included in their ranks Viktor Shklovsky, Roman Jakobson, Osip Brik, Yury Tynyanov, Boris Eichenbaum and Boris Tomashevsky. The Formalists emerged in Russia in the years before the 1917 Bolshevik revolution, and flourished throughout the 1920s, until they were effectively silenced by Stalinism. . . .

"What Is Literature?" by Terry Eagleton has been excerpted from *Literary Theory: An Introduction,* University of Minnesota Press (1983), pages 1–10, 77–88, and is reprinted by permission of the publisher.

The Formalists started out by seeing the literary work as a more or less arbitrary assemblage of 'devices,' and only later came to see these devices as interrelated elements of 'functions' within a total textual system. 'Devices' included sound, imagery, rhythm, syntax, metre, rhyme, narrative techniques, in fact the whole stock of formal literary elements; and what all of these elements had in common was their 'estranging' or 'defamiliarizing' effect. What was specific to literary language, what distinguished it from other forms of discourse, was that it 'deformed' ordinary language in various ways. Under the pressure of literary devices, ordinary language was intensified, condensed, twisted, telescoped, drawn out, turned on its head. It was language 'made strange'; and because of this estrangement, the everyday world was also suddenly made unfamiliar. In the routines of everyday speech, our perceptions of and responses to reality become stale, blunted, or, as the Formalists would say, 'automatized.' Literature, by forcing us into a dramatic awareness of language, refreshes these habitual responses and renders objects more 'perceptible.' By having to grapple with language in a more strenuous, self-conscious way than usual, the world which that language contains is vividly renewed. The poetry of Gerard Manley Hopkins might provide a particularly graphic example of this. Literary discourse estranges or alienates ordinary speech, but in doing so, paradoxically, brings us into a fuller, more intimate possession of experience. Most of the time we breathe in air without being conscious of it: Like language, it is the very medium in which we move. But if the air is suddenly thickened or infected we are forced to attend to our breathing with new vigilance, and the effect of this may be a heightened experience of our bodily life. We read a scribbled note from a friend without paying much attention to its narrative structure; but if a story breaks off and begins again, switches constantly from one narrative level to another and delays its climax to keep us in suspense, we become freshly conscious of how it is constructed at the same time as our engagement with it may be intensified. The story, as the Formalists would argue, uses 'impeding' or 'retarding' devices to hold our attention; and in literary language, these devices are 'laid bare.' It was this which moved Viktor Shklovsky to remark mischievously of Laurence Sterne's *Tristram Shandy,* a novel which impedes its own story-line so much that it hardly gets off the ground, that it was 'the most typical novel in world literature.'

The Formalists, then, saw literary language as a set of deviations from a norm, a kind of linguistic violence: literature is a 'special' kind of language, in contrast to the 'ordinary' language we commonly use. But to spot a deviation implies being able to identify the norm from which it swerves. . . .

[T]he Russian Formalists recognized that norms and deviations shifted around from one social or historical context to another—that 'poetry' in this sense depends on where you happen to be standing at the time. The fact that a piece of language was 'estranging' did not guarantee that it was always and everywhere so: It was estranging only against a certain normative linguistic background, and if this altered then the writing might cease to be perceptible as literary. If everyone used phrases like 'unravished bride of quietness' in ordinary pub conversation, this kind of language might cease to be poetic. For the Formalists, in other words, 'literariness' was a function of the *differential* relations between one sort of discourse and another; it was not an eternally given property. They were not out to define 'literature,' but 'literariness'—special uses of language, which could be found in 'literary' texts but also in many places outside them. Anyone who believes that 'literature' can be defined by such special uses of language has to face the fact that there is more metaphor in Manchester than there is in Marvell. There is no 'literary' device—metonymy, synecdoche, litotes, chiasmus and so on—which is not quite intensively used in daily discourse.

Nevertheless, the Formalists still presumed that 'making strange' was the essence of the literary. It was just that they relativized this use of language, saw it as a matter of contrast between one type of speech and another. But what if I were to hear someone at the next pub table remark 'This is awfully squiggly handwriting!' Is this 'literary' or 'non-literary' language? As a matter of fact it is 'literary' language, because it comes from Knut Hamsun's novel *Hunger.* But how do I know that it is literary? It doesn't, after all, focus any particular attention on itself as a verbal performance. One answer to the question of how I know that this is literary is that it comes from Knut Hamsun's novel *Hunger.* It is part of a text which I read as 'fictional,' which announces itself as a 'novel,' which may be put on university literature syllabuses and so on. The *context* tells me that it is literary; but the language itself has no inherent properties or qualities which might distinguish it from other kinds of discourse, and someone might well say this in a pub without being admired for their literary dexterity. To think of literature as the Formalists do is really to think of all literature as *poetry.* Significantly, when the Formalists came to consider prose writing, they often simply extended to it the kinds of technique they had used with poetry. But literature is usually judged to contain much besides poetry—to include, for example, realist or naturalistic writing which is not linguistically self-conscious or self-exhibiting in any striking way. People sometimes call writing 'fine' precisely because it *doesn't* draw undue attention to itself: They admire its laconic plainness or low-keyed sobriety. And what about jokes, football chants and slogans, newspaper headlines, advertisements, which are often verbally flamboyant but not generally classified as literature?

Another problem with the 'estrangement' case is that there is no kind of writing which cannot, given sufficient ingenuity, be read as estranging. Consider a prosaic, quite unambiguous statement like the one sometimes seen in the London underground system: 'Dogs must be carried on the escalator.' This is not perhaps quite as unambiguous as it seems at first sight: Does it mean that you *must* carry a dog on the escalator? Are you likely to be banned from the escalator unless you can find some stray mongrel to clutch in your arms on the way up? Many apparently straightforward notices contain such ambiguities: 'Refuse to be put in this basket,' for instance, or the British road-sign 'Way Out' as read by a Californian. But even leaving such troubling ambiguities aside, it is surely obvious that the underground notice could be read as literature. One could let oneself be arrested by the abrupt, minatory *staccato* of the first ponderous monosyllables; find one's mind drifting, by the time it has reached the rich allusiveness of 'carried,' to suggestive resonances of helping lame dogs through life; and perhaps even detect in the very lilt and inflection of the word 'escalator' a miming of the rolling, up-and-down motion of the thing itself. This may well be a fruitless sort of pursuit, but it is not significantly more fruitless than claiming to hear the cut and thrust of the rapiers in some poetic description of a duel, and it at least has the advantage of suggesting that 'literature' may be at least as much a question of what people do to writing as of what writing does to them.

But even if someone were to read the notice in this way, it would still be a matter of reading it as *poetry,* which is only part of what is usually included in literature. Let us therefore consider another way of 'misreading' the sign which might move us a little beyond this. Imagine a late-night drunk doubled over the escalator handrail who reads the notice with laborious attentiveness for several minutes and then mutters to himself 'How true!' What kind of mistake is occurring here? What the drunk is doing, in fact, is taking the sign as some statement of general, even cosmic significance. By applying certain conventions of reading to its words, he pries them loose from their immediate context and generalizes them beyond their pragmatic purpose to something of wider and probably deeper import. This would certainly seem to be one operation involved in what people call literature. When the poet tells us that his love is like a red rose, we know by the very fact that he puts this statement in metre that we are not supposed to ask whether he actually had a lover who for some bizarre reason seemed to him to resemble a rose. He is telling us something about women and love in general. Literature, then, we might say, in 'non-pragmatic' discourse: Unlike biology textbooks and notes to the milkman it serves no immediate practical purpose, but is to be taken as referring to a general state of affairs. Sometimes, though not always, it may employ peculiar language as though to make this fact obvious—to signal that what is at stake is a *way of talking* about a woman, rather than any particular real-life woman. This focusing on the way of talking, rather than on the reality of what is talked about, is sometimes taken to indicate that we mean by literature a kind of *self-referential* language, a language which talks about itself.

There are, however, problems with this way of defining literature too. For one thing, it would probably have come as a surprise to George Orwell to hear that his essays were to be read as though the topics he discussed were less important than the way he discussed them. In much that is classified as literature, the truth-value and practical relevance of what is said *is* considered important to the overall effect. But even if treating discourse 'non-pragmatically' is part of what is meant by 'literature,' then it follows from this 'definition' that literature cannot in fact be 'objectively' defined. It leaves the definition of literature up to how somebody decides to *read,* not to the nature of what is written. There are certain kinds of writing—poems, plays, novels—which are fairly obviously intended to be 'nonpragmatic' in this sense, but this does not guarantee that they will actually be read in this way. I might well read [Edward] Gibbons' account of the Roman empire not because I am misguided enough to believe that it will be reliably informative about ancient Rome but because I enjoy Gibbon's prose style, or revel in images of human corruption whatever their historical source. But I might read Robert Burns's poem because it is not clear to me, as a Japanese horticulturalist, whether or not the red rose flourished in eighteenth-century Britain. . . .

In this sense, one can think of literature less as some inherent quality or set of qualities displayed by certain kinds of writing all the way from *Beowulf* to Virginia Woolf, than as a number of ways in which people *relate themselves* to writing. It would not be easy to isolate, from all that has been variously called 'literature,' some constant set of inherent features. In fact it would be as impossible as trying to identify the single distinguishing feature which all games have in common. There is no 'essence' of literature whatsoever. Any bit of writing may be read 'non-pragmatically,' if that is what reading a text as literature means, just as any writing may be read 'poetically.' If I pore over the railway timetable not to discover a train connection but to stimulate in myself general reflections on the speed and complexity of modern existence, then I might be said to be reading it as literature. John M. Ellis has argued that the term 'literature' operates rather like the word 'weed': Weeds are not particular kinds of plant, but just any kind of plant which for some reason or another a gardener does not want around. Perhaps 'literature' means something like the opposite: any kind of writing which for some reason or another somebody values highly. As the philosophers might say, 'literature' and 'weed' are *functional* rather than *ontological* terms: They tell us about what we do, not about the fixed beings of things. They tell us about the role of a text or a thistle in a social context, its relations with and differences from its surroundings, the ways it behaves, the purposes it may be put to and the human practices clustered around it. 'Literature' is in this sense a purely formal, empty sort of definition. Even if we claim that it is a non-pragmatic treatment of language, we have still not arrived at an 'essence' of literature because this is also so of other linguistic practices such as jokes. In any case, it is far from clear that we can discriminate neatly between 'practical' and 'non-practical' ways of relating ourselves to language. Reading a novel for pleasure obviously differs from reading a road sign for information, but how about reading a biology textbook to improve your mind? Is that a 'pragmatic' treatment of language or not? In many societies, 'literature' has served highly practical functions such as religious ones; distinguishing sharply between 'practical' and 'non-practical' may only be possible in a society like ours, where literature has ceased to have much practical function at all. We may be offering as a general definition a sense of the 'literary' which is in fact historically specific.

The Poetic Expression of Emotion
■ R. G. Collingwood ■

Our first question is this: Since the artist proper has something to do with emotion, and what he does with it is not to arouse it, what is it that he does? It will be remembered that the kind of answer we expect to this question is an answer derived from what we all know and all habitually say; nothing original or recondite, but something entirely commonplace.

Nothing could be more entirely commonplace than to say he expresses them. The idea is familiar to every artist, and to every one else who has any acquaintance with the arts. To state it is not to state a philosophical theory or definition of art; it is to state a fact or supposed fact about which, when we have sufficiently identified it, we shall have later to theorize philosophically. For the present it does not matter whether the fact that is alleged, when it is said that the artist expresses emotion, is really a fact or only supposed to be one. Whichever it is, we have to identify it, that is, to decide what it is that people are saying when they use the phrase. Later on, we shall have to see whether it will fit into a coherent theory.

They are referring to a situation, real or supposed, of a definite kind. When a man is said to express emotion, what is being said about him comes to this. At first, he is conscious of having an emotion, but not conscious of what this emotion is. All he is conscious of is a perturbation or excitement, which he feels going on within him, but of whose nature he is ignorant. While in this state, all he can say about his emotion is: 'I feel . . . I don't know what I feel.' From this helpless and oppressed condition he extricates himself by doing something which we call expressing himself. This is an activity which has something to do with the thing we call language: He expresses himself by speaking. It has also something to do with consciousness: The emotion expressed is an emotion of whose nature the person who feels it is no longer unconscious. It has also something to do with the way in which he feels the emotion. As unexpressed, he feels it in what we have called a helpless and oppressed way; as expressed, he feels it in a way from which this sense of oppression has vanished. His mind is somehow lightened and eased.

This lightening of emotions which is somehow connected with the expression of them has a certain resemblance to the 'catharsis' by which emotions are earthed through being discharged into a make-believe situation; but the two things are not the same. Suppose the emotion is one of anger. If it is effectively earthed, for example by fancying oneself kicking someone down stairs, it is thereafter no longer present in the mind as anger at all: We have worked it off and

"The Poetic Expression of Emotion" by R. G. Collingwood has been excerpted from *The Principles of Art,* Oxford University Press (1938), pages 109–115, 121–122, and is reprinted by permission of the publisher.

are rid of it. If it is expressed, for example by putting it into hot and bitter words, it does not disappear from the mind; we remain angry; but instead of the sense of oppression which accompanies an emotion of anger not yet recognized as such, we have that sense of alleviation which comes when we are conscious of our own emotion as anger, instead of being conscious of it only as an unidentified perturbation. This is what we refer to when we say that it 'does us good' to express our emotions.

The expression of an emotion by speech may be addressed to some one; but if so it is not done with the intention of arousing a like emotion in him. If there is any effect which we wish to produce in the hearer, it is only the effect which we call making him understand how we feel. But, as we have already seen, this is just the effect which expressing our emotions has on ourselves. It makes us, as well as the people to whom we talk, understand how we feel. A person arousing emotion sets out to affect his audience in a way in which he himself is not necessarily affected. He and his audience stand in quite different relations to the act, very much as physician and patient stand in quite different relations towards a drug administered by the one and taken by the other. A person expressing emotion, on the contrary, is treating himself and his audience in the same kind of way; he is making his emotions clear to his audience, and that is what he is doing to himself.

It follows from this that the expression of emotion, simply as expression, is not addressed to any particular audience. It is addressed primarily to the speaker himself, and secondarily to any one who can understand. Here again, the speaker's attitude towards his audience is quite unlike that of a person desiring to arouse in his audience a certain emotion. If that is what he wishes to do, he must know the audience he is addressing. He must know what type of stimulus will produce the desired kind of reaction in people of that particular sort; and he must adapt his language to his audience in the sense of making sure that it contains stimuli appropriate to their peculiarities. If what he wishes to do is express his emotions intelligibly, he has to express them in such a way as to be intelligible to himself; his audience is then in the position of persons who overhear him doing this. Thus the stimulus-and-reaction terminology has no applicability to the situation.

The means-and-end, or technique, terminology too is inapplicable. Until a man has expressed his emotion, he does not yet know what emotion it is. The act of expressing it is therefore an exploration of his own emotions. He is trying to find out what these emotions are. There is certainly here a directed process: an effort, that is, directed upon a certain end; but the end is not something foreseen and preconceived, to which appropriate means can be thought out in the light of our knowledge of its special character. Expression is an activity of which there can be no technique.

Expressing an emotion is not the same thing as describing it. To say 'I am angry' is to describe one's emotion, not to express it. The words in which it is expressed need not contain any reference to anger as such at all. Indeed, so far as they simply and solely express it, they cannot contain any such reference. The curse of Ernulphus, as invoked by Dr. Slop on the unknown person who tied certain knots, is a classical and supreme expression of anger; but it does not contain a single word descriptive of the emotion it expresses.*

This is why, as literary critics well know, the use of epithets in poetry, or even in prose where expressiveness is aimed at, is a danger. If you want to express the terror which something causes, you must not give it an epithet like 'dreadful.' For that describes the emotion instead of expressing it, and your language becomes frigid, that is inexpressive, at once. A genuine poet, in his moments of genuine poetry, never mentions by name the emotions he is expressing.

Some people have thought that a poet who wishes to express a great variety of subtly differentiated emotions might be hampered by the lack of a vocabulary rich in words referring to the distinctions between them; and that psychology, by working out such a vocabulary, might render a valuable service to poetry. This is the opposite of the truth. The poet needs no such words at all; the existence or nonexistence of a scientific terminology describing the emotions he wishes to express is to him a matter of perfect indifference. If such a terminology, where it exists, is allowed to affect his own use of language, it affects it for the worse.

The reason why description, so far from helping expression, actually damages it, is that description generalizes. To describe a thing is to call it a thing of such and such a kind: to bring it under a conception, to classify it. Expression, on the contrary, individualizes. The anger which I feel here and now, with a certain person, for a certain cause, is no doubt an instance of anger, and in describing it as anger one is telling truth about it; but it is much more than mere anger: It is a peculiar anger, not quite like any anger that I ever felt before, and probably not quite like any anger I shall ever feel again. To become fully conscious of it means becoming conscious of it not merely as an instance of anger, but as this quite peculiar anger. Expressing it, we saw, has something to do with becoming conscious of it; therefore, if being fully conscious of it means being conscious of all its peculiarities, fully expressing it means expressing all its peculiarities. The poet, therefore, in proportion as he understands his business, gets as far away as possible from merely labelling his emotions as instances of this or that general kind, and takes enormous pains to individualize them by expressing them in terms which reveal their difference from any other emotion of the same sort.

This is a point in which art proper, as the expression of emotion, differs sharply and obviously from any craft whose aim it is to arouse emotion. The end which a craft sets out to realize is always conceived in general terms, never individualized. However accurately defined it may be, it is always defined as the production of a thing having characteristics that could be shared by other things. A joiner, making a table out of these pieces of wood and no others, makes it to measurements and specifications which, even if actually shared by no other table, might in principle be shared by other tables. A physician treating a patient for a certain complaint is trying to produce in him a condition which might be, and probably has been, often produced in others, namely, the condition of recovering from that

*The reference is to the irascible physician in Lawrence Sterne's *Tristram Shandy*.

complaint. So an 'artist' setting out to produce a certain emotion in his audience is setting out to produce not an individual emotion, but an emotion of a certain kind. It follows that the means appropriate to its production will be not individual means but means of a certain kind: that is to say, means which are always in principle replaceable by other similar means. As every good craftsman insists, there is always a 'right way' of performing any operation. A 'way' of acting is a general pattern to which various individual actions may conform. In order that the 'work of art' should produce its intended psychological effect, therefore, whether this effect be magical or merely amusing, what is necessary is that it should satisfy certain conditions, possess certain characteristics: in other words be, not this work and no other, but a work of this kind and of no other.

This explains the meaning of the generalization which Aristotle and others have ascribed to art. Aristotle's *Poetics* is concerned not with art proper but with representative art, and representative art of one definite kind. He is not analysing the religious drama of a hundred years before, he is analysing the amusement literature of the fourth century, and giving rules for its composition. The end being not individual but general (the production of an emotion of a certain kind) the means too are general (the portrayal, not of this individual act, but of an act of this sort; not, as he himself puts it, what Alcibiades did, but what anybody of a certain kind would do). Sir Joshua Reynolds's idea of generalization is in principle the same; he expounds it in connexion with what he calls 'the grand style,' which means a style intended to produce emotions of a certain type. He is quite right; if you want to produce a typical case of a certain emotion, the way to do it is to put before your audience a representation of the typical features belonging to the kind of thing that produces it: Make your kings very royal, your soldiers very soldierly, your women very feminine, your cottages very cottagesque, your oak-trees very oakish, and so on.

Art proper, as expression of emotion, has nothing to do with all this. The artist proper is a person who, grappling with the problem of expressing a certain emotion, says, 'I want to get this clear.' It is no use to him to get something else clear, however like it this other thing may be. Nothing will serve as a substitute. He does not want a thing of a certain kind, he wants a certain thing. This is why the kind of person who takes his literature as psychology, saying 'How admirably this writer depicts the feelings of women, or busdrivers, or homosexuals . . .', necessarily misunderstands every real work of art with which he comes into contact, and takes for good art, with infallible precision, what is not art at all. . . .

Finally, the expressing of emotion must not be confused with what may be called the betraying of it, that is, exhibiting symptoms of it. When it is said that the artist in the proper sense of that word is a person who expresses his emotions, this does not mean that if he is afraid he turns pale and stammers; if he is angry he turns red and bellows; and so forth. These things are no doubt called expressions; but just as we distinguish proper and improper senses of the word 'art,' so we must distinguish proper and improper senses of the word 'expression,' and in the context of a discussion about art this sense of expression is an improper sense. The characteristic mark of expression proper is lucidity or intelligibility; a person who expresses something thereby becomes conscious of what it is that he is expressing, and enables others to become conscious of it in himself and in them. Turning pale and stammering is a natural accompaniment of fear, but a person who in addition to being afraid also turns pale and stammers does not thereby become conscious of the precise quality of his emotion. About that he is as much in the dark as he would be if (were that possible) he could feel fear without also exhibiting these symptoms of it.

Confusion between these two senses of the word 'expression' may easily lead to false critical estimates, and so to false aesthetic theory. It is sometimes thought a merit in an actress that when she is acting a pathetic scene she can work herself up to such an extent as to weep real tears. There may be some ground for that opinion if acting is not an art but a craft, and if the actress's object in that scene is to produce grief in her audience; and even then the conclusion would follow only if it were true that grief cannot be produced in the audience unless symptoms of grief are exhibited by the performer. And no doubt this is how most people think of the actor's work. But if his business is not amusement but art, the object at which he is aiming is not to produce a preconceived emotional effect on his audience but by means of a system of expressions, or language, composed partly of speech and partly of gesture, to explore his own emotions: to discover emotions in himself of which he was unaware, and, by permitting the audience to witness the discovery, enable them to make a similar discovery about themselves. In that case it is not her ability to weep real tears that would mark out a good actress; it is her ability to make it clear to herself and her audience what the tears are about.

The Intention of the Author
■ Monroe Beardsley ■

The things that naturally come to mind when we think of works of art are the products of deliberate human activity, sometimes long and arduous—think of the Ceiling of the Sistine Chapel, *Elegy in a Country Churchyard, Wozzeck,* and the Cathedral at Chartres. To put it another way, these things were *intended* by someone, and no doubt they are largely what they were intended to be by those who made them.

The artist's intention is a series of psychological states or events in his mind: what he wanted to do, how he imagined or projected the work before he began to make it and while he was in the process of making it. Something was going on in

"The Intention of the Author" by Monroe Beardsley has been excerpted from *Aesthetics,* Hackett Publishing Company (1981), pages 23–26, and is reprinted by permission of the publisher.

Chaucer's mind when he was planning *The Canterbury Tales* and in Beethoven's mind when he was considering various possible melodies for the choral finale of his *D Minor Symphony (No. 9)*. And these happenings were no doubt among the factors that caused those works to come into being. One of the questions we can ask about any work, but probably not with much hope of a conclusive answer, is: What was its *cause?* And of course a good deal of writing about works of art consists in describing the historical situation, the social, economic and political conditions, under which they were produced—including the domestic affairs and physical health of the artist—in an attempt to explain, if possible, why they were created, and why they turned out the way they did.

Let us not stop to discuss the general metaphysical problems that might be raised at this point. Can a work of art be accounted for as the effect of some set of antecedent conditions? Philosophers who believe in freedom of the will, in the sense in which this theory denies that all psychological events are causally determined, would, I suppose, argue that there is an element of spontaneity, or indeterminism, in the creative act, and therefore that even *in principle* it is impossible to explain any work of art in sociological, historical, or psychological terms. Other philosophers—and I believe them to be sound—cannot see why *Tristan and Isolde,* the Hermes of Praxiteles, *Swan Lake* or the Pyramids are necessarily different in this respect from, say, Hurricane Hazel of 1954, the Second Punic War, the outcome of this year's World Series, or the first hydrogen bomb explosion. Like *Tristan and Isolde,* hurricanes and wars are extremely complicated, and to give a complete account of all their causal factors might not be practically feasible, but there seems to be no good reason for saying that it is *in principle* impossible.

Those who practice what they call "historical criticism" or "sociological criticism" of the arts are engaged in the same explanatory enterprise. And though I think there are good reasons to be doubtful of many explanations of particular works of art, or of general movements such as Romanticism, Impressionism, or the Baroque, this is presumably due to the complexity of the thing to be explained and to the scarcity of available evidence. It is a great field for half-baked speculation, which can often not be disproved and is thus allowed to stand. And perhaps this is why more critics concern themselves, not with the remoter antecedents of the work, but with its proximate or immediate cause in the mind of the artist. These are the critics who are fond of inquiring after the artist's *intention*. . . .

Two sets of problems appear when we consider the connection between the aesthetic object and the artist's intention. One set of problems concerns the role of intention in *evaluating* the object. . . . The other concerns the role of intention in *describing* and *interpreting* the object: These we shall consider here. It is the simple thesis of this section that we must distinguish between the aesthetic object and the intention in the mind of its creator.

When you state the distinction that way, it seems harmless enough, and perfectly acceptable. Yet there are some rather serious and interesting difficulties about it, and we shall have to look into them. First, however, it is worth noting that even critics who would perhaps grant the distinction verbally are quite often not able to see the implications of it, both in their critical theory and in their critical practice. Here is part of a paragraph, for example, from a literary critic who generally blurs the distinction in his writing. He is discussing André Malraux's novel *La Condition Humaine:*

> The handling of this huge and complicated subject must have given the author a good deal of trouble. He evidently sat down like an engineer to the problem of designing a structure that would meet a new set of conditions; and *an occasional clumsiness of mechanics appears. The device of presenting in dramatic scenes the exposition of political events,* to which we owe Garin in *Les Conquerants* and his eternal dispatches, *here appears as a series of conversations so exhaustive and so perfectly to the point in their function of political analysis as*—in spite of the author's efforts to particularize the characters—*occasionally to lack plausibility.*

The clauses in italics are about the novel, the rest are about the novelist; and the paragraph passes from one to the other as though there were no change of subject. But, not to be invidious, we must add that equally good examples of the shift back and forth could be found in numerous critics of all the arts.

The consequences that follow from making a distinction between aesthetic objects and artists' intentions are very important, but they are not all obvious, because they depend upon a general principle of philosophy that is often not kept steadily in mind. If two things are distinct, that is, if they are indeed two, and not one thing under two names (like the Vice President of the United States and the Presiding Officer of the Senate), then the evidence for the existence and nature of one cannot be exactly the same as the evidence for the existence and nature of the other. Any evidence, for example, that the Vice President is tall will automatically be evidence that the Presiding Officer of the Senate is tall, and vice versa. But evidence that the Vice President is tall will have no bearing on the height of the President.

This point is obscured where the two things, though distinct, are causally connected, as are presumably the intention and the aesthetic object. For if Jones, Sr., is the father of Jones, Jr., then any evidence about the height of either of them will be *indirect* evidence about the height of the other, in virtue of certain laws of genetics, according to which the tallness of the father at least affects the probability that the son will be tall, though it does not, of course, render it certain.

Thus, in the case of aesthetic object and intention, we have direct evidence of each: We discover the nature of the object by looking, listening, reading, etc., and we discover the intention by biographical inquiry, through letters, diaries, workbooks—or, if the artist is alive, by asking him. But also what we learn about the nature of the object itself is indirect evidence of what the artist intended it to be, and what we learn about the artist's intention is indirect evidence of what the object became. Thus, when we are concerned with the object itself, we should distinguish between internal and external evidence of its nature. Internal evidence is evidence from direct inspection of the object; external evidence is evidence from the psychological and social background of the object, from which we may infer something about the object itself.

Where internal and external evidence go hand in hand—for example, the painter writes in an exhibition catalogue that his painting is balanced in a precise and complicated way, and we go to the painting and see that it *is* so balanced—there is no problem. But where internal and external evidence conflict, as when a painter tells us one thing and our eyes tell us another, there *is* a problem, for we must decide between them. The problem is how to make this decision. If we consider the "real" painting to be that which the painter projected in his mind, we shall go at it one way; if we consider the "real" painting to be the one that is before us, open to public observation, we shall go at it another way.

We generally do not hesitate between these alternatives. As long as we stick to the simplest descriptive level, we are in no doubt; if a sculptor tells us that his statue was intended to be smooth and blue, but our senses tell us it is rough and pink, we go by our senses. We might, however, be puzzled by more subtle qualities of the statue. Suppose the sculptor tells us his statue was intended to be graceful and airy. We might look at it carefully and long, and not find it so. If the sculptor insists, we will give it a second look. But if we still cannot see those qualities, we conclude that they are not there; it would not occur to us to say they must be there, merely because the sculptor is convinced that he has put them there. Yet it is well known that our perceptions can be influenced by what we expect or hope to see, and especially by what we may be socially stigmatized for not seeing. Though no doubt the sculptor cannot talk us into perceiving red as blue, if his words have prestige—if we are already disposed to regard his intention as a final court of appeal—his words may be able to make us see grace where we would otherwise not see it, or a greater airiness than we would otherwise see. If this works on everyone, then everyone will see these qualities in the statue, and for all practical purposes they will be in the statue. Thus the intention, or the announcement of it, actually brings something to pass; what the statue is cannot be distinguished from what it is intended to be. So the argument might go.

But it is precisely this argument that presents a strong reason for not making intention the final court of appeal. Suppose there is an experimental physicist who becomes so emotionally involved in any hypothesis that he cannot help seeing the outcome of his experiments as confirming the hypotheses: He even sees red litmus paper as blue if that is predicted from his hypothesis. No doubt his prospects for a scientific future are dim, but if he is handy around a laboratory, we can still find a way to use him. Let him test other people's hypotheses by performing the experiments called for, but don't tell him until afterward what the hypothesis is. The scientist is wholly imaginary, but the principle is sound. And we shall adopt an analogous rule: If a quality can be seen in a statue *only* by someone who already believes that it was intended by the sculptor to be there, then that quality is not in the statue at all. For what can be seen only by one who expects and hopes to see it is what we would call illusory by ordinary standards—like the strange woman in the crowd who momentarily looks like your wife.

When it comes to *interpreting* the statue, the situation is more complicated. Suppose the sculptor says his statue symbolizes Human Destiny. It is a large, twisted, cruller-shaped object of polished teak, mounted at an oblique angle to the floor. We look at it, and see in it no such symbolic meaning, even after we have the hint. Should we say that we have simply missed the symbolism, but that it must be there, since what a statue symbolizes is precisely what its maker makes it symbolize? Or should we say, in the spirit of Alice confronting the extreme semantical conventionalism of Humpty Dumpty, that the question is whether that object can be made to mean Human Destiny? If we take the former course, we are in effect saying that the nature of the object, as far as its meaning goes, cannot be distinguished from the artist's intention; if we take the latter course, we are saying it can. But the former course leads in the end to the wildest absurdity: Anyone can make anything symbolize anything just by saying it does, for another sculptor could copy the same object and label it "Spirit of Palm Beach, 1938." . . .

This distinction may seem oversubtle, but we shall find it of the highest importance, especially for those arts in which the distinction between object and intention seems most difficult, that is, the verbal arts. In literature, the distinction is most often erased by a principle that is explicitly defended by many critics, and tacitly assumed by many more: Since a poem, in a sense, is what it means, to discover what the *poem* means is to discover what the *poet* meant. This principle implies that the dramatic speaker, the "I" in the poem, is always the author of the poem, so that any evidence about the nature of either of them is automatically evidence about the other. In

When I consider how my light is spent,

we have [John] Milton talking about his blindness, a fragment of autobiography. The problems involved in this notion are many and interesting, but we shall have set them aside. . . . At present we are concerned only with the possibility of the distinction between what words mean and what people mean.

Suppose someone utters a sentence. We can ask two questions: (1) What does the *speaker* mean? (2) What does the *sentence* mean? Now, if the speaker is awake and competent, no doubt the answers to these two questions will turn out to be the same. And for practical purposes, on occasions when we are not interested in the sentence except as a clue to what is going on in the mind of the speaker, we do not bother to distinguish the two questions. But suppose someone utters a particularly confused sentence that we can't puzzle out at all—he is trying to explain income tax exemptions, or the theory of games and economic behavior, and is doing a bad job. We ask him what he meant, and after a while he tells us in different words. Now we can reply, "Maybe that's what you meant but it's not what you said," that is, it's not what the sentence meant. And here we clearly make the distinction.

For what the sentence means depends not on the whim of the individual, and his mental vagaries, but upon public conventions of usage that are tied up with habit patterns in the whole speaking community. It is perhaps easy to see this in the case of an ambiguous sentence. A man says, "I like my secretary better than my wife"; we raise our eyebrows, and inquire: "Do you mean that you like her better than you like your wife?" And he replies, "No, you misunderstand me; I mean I like her better than my wife does." Now, in one sense he has cleared up the misunderstanding, he has told us what he meant. Since what he meant is still not what the first sentence succeeded in meaning, he hasn't made the original sentence any less ambiguous than it was; he has merely substituted for it a better, because unambiguous, one.

Now let us apply this distinction to a specific problem in literary criticism. On the occasion of Queen Victoria's Golden Jubilee, A. E. Houseman published his poem "1887." The poem refers to celebrations going on all over England. "From Clee to Heaven the beacon burns," because "God has saved the Queen." It recalls that there were many lads who went off to fight for the Empire, who "shared the work with God," but "themselves they could not save," and ends with the words,

> Get you the sons your fathers got,
> And God will save the Queen.

Frank Harris quoted the last stanza to Houseman, in a bitterly sarcastic tone, and praised the poem highly: "You have poked fun at the whole thing and made splendid mockery of it." But this reading of the poem, especially coming from a radical like Harris, made Houseman angry:

> I never intended to poke fun, as you call it, at patriotism, and I can find nothing in the sentiment to make mockery of: I meant it sincerely; if Englishmen breed as good men as their fathers, then God will save the Queen. I can only reject and resent your—your truculent praise.

We may put the question, then, in this form: Is Houseman's poem, and particularly its last stanza, ironic? The issue can be made fairly sharp. There are two choices: (1) We can say that the meaning of the poem, including its irony or lack of it, is precisely what the author intended it to be. Then any evidence of the intention will automatically be evidence of what the poem is: The poem is ironic if Houseman says so. He is the last court of appeal, for it is his poem. (2) Or we can distinguish between the meaning of the poem and the author's intention. Of course, we must admit that in many cases an author may be a good reader of his own poem, and he may help us to see things in it that we have overlooked. But at the same time, he is not necessarily the best reader of his poem, and indeed he misconstrues it when, as perhaps in Houseman's case, his unconscious guides his pen more than his consciousness can admit. And if his report of what the poem is intended to mean conflicts with the evidence of the poem itself, we cannot allow him to *make* the poem mean what he wants it to mean, just by fiat. So in this case we would have the poem read by competent critics, and if they found irony in it, we should conclude that it is ironical, no matter what Houseman says.

What Is an Author?

■ Michel Foucault ■

The coming into being of the notion of "author" constitutes the privileged moment of *individualization* in the history of ideas, knowledge, literature, philosophy, and the sciences. . . .

I shall not offer here a sociohistorical analysis of the author's persona. Certainly it would be worth examining how the author became individualized in a culture like ours, what status he has been given, at what moment studies of authenticity and attribution began, in what kind of system of valorization the author was involved, at what point we began to recount the lives of authors rather than of heroes, and how this fundamental category of "the-man-and-his-work criticism" began. For the moment, however, I want to deal solely with the relationship between text and author and with the manner in which the text points to this "figure" that, at least in appearance, is outside it and antecedes it.

[Samuel] Beckett nicely formulates the theme with which I would like to begin: " 'What does it matter who is speaking,' someone said, 'what does it matter who is speaking.' " In this indifference appears one of the fundamental ethical principles of contemporary writing [*écriture*], I say "ethical" because this indifference is not really a trait characterizing the manner in which one speaks and writes, but rather a kind of immanent rule, taken up over and over again, never fully applied, not designating writing as something completed, but dominating it as a practice. Since it is too familiar to require a lengthy analysis, this immanent rule can be adequately illustrated here by tracing two of its major themes.

First of all, we can say that today's writing has freed itself from the dimension of expression. Referring only to itself, but without being restricted to the confines of its interiority, writing is identified with its own unfolded exteriority. This means that it is an interplay of signs arranged less according to its signified content than according to the very nature of the signifier. Writing unfolds like a game [*jeu*] that invariably goes beyond its own rules and transgresses its limits. In writing, the point is not to manifest or exalt the act of writing, nor it is to pin a subject within language; it is rather a question of creating a space into which the writing subject constantly disappears.

The second theme, writing's relationship with death, is even more familiar. This link subverts an old tradition exemplified by the Greek epic, which was intended to perpetuate the immortality of the hero: If he was willing to die young, it was so that his life, consecrated and magnified by death, might pass into immortal-

"What Is an Author?" by Michel Foucault has been excerpted from *Textual Strategies*, Josué V. Harari, ed., Cornell University Press (1979), pages 141–154, 159, and is reprinted by permission of the publisher.

ity; the narrative then redeemed this accepted death. In another way, the motivation, as well as the theme and the pretext of Arabian narratives—such as *The Thousand and One Nights*—was also the eluding of death: One spoke, telling stories into the early morning, in order to forestall death, to postpone the day of reckoning that would silence the narrator. Scheherazade's narrative is an effort, renewed each night, to keep death outside the circle of life.

Our culture has metamorphosed this idea of narrative, or writing, as something designed to ward off death. Writing has become linked to sacrifice, even to the sacrifice of life: It is now a voluntary effacement which does not need to be represented in books, since it is brought about in the writer's very existence. The work, which once had the duty of providing immortality, now possesses the right to kill, to be its author's murderer, as in the cases of Flaubert, Proust, and Kafka. That is not all, however: This relationship between writing and death is also manifested in the effacement of the writing subject's individual characteristics. Using all the contrivances that he sets up between himself and what he writes, the writing subject cancels out the signs of his particular individuality. As a result, the mark of the writer is reduced to nothing more than the singularity of his absence: He must assume the role of the dead man in the game of writing.

None of this is recent; criticism and philosophy took note of the disappearance—or death—of the author some time ago. But the consequences of their discovery of it have not been sufficiently examined, nor has its import been accurately measured. A certain number of notions that are intended to replace the privileged position of the author actually seem to preserve that privilege and suppress the real meaning of his disappearance. I shall examine two of these notions, both of great importance today.

The first is the idea of the work. It is a very familiar thesis that the task of criticism is not to bring out the work's relationship with the author, nor to reconstruct through the text a thought or experience, but rather, to analyze the work through its structure, its architecture, its intrinsic form, and the play of its internal relationships. At this point, however, a problem arises: "What is a work? What is this curious unity which we designate as a work? Of what elements is it composed? Is it not what an author has written?" Difficulties appear immediately. If an individual were not an author, could we say that what he wrote, said, left behind in his papers, or what has been collected of his remarks, could be called a "work"? When Sade was not considered an author, what was the status of his papers? Were they simply rolls of paper onto which he ceaselessly uncoiled his fantasies during his imprisonment?

Even when an individual has been accepted as an author, we must still ask whether everything that he wrote, said, or left behind is part of his work. The problem is both theoretical and technical. When undertaking the publication of Nietzsche's works, for example, where should one stop? Surely everything must be published, but what is "everything"? Everything that Nietzsche himself published, certainly. And what about the rough drafts for his works? Obviously. The plans for his aphorisms? Yes. The deleted passages and the notes at the bottom of the page?

Yes. What if, within a workbook filled with aphorisms, one finds a reference, the notation of a meeting or of an address, or a laundry list; is it a work, or not? Why not? And so on, ad infinitum. How can one define a work amid the millions of traces left by someone after his death? A theory of the work does not exist, and the empirical task of those who naively undertake the editing of works often suffers in the absence of such a theory. . . .

[We] need to clarify briefly the problems arising from the use of the author's name. What is an author's name? How does it function? Far from offering a solution, I shall only indicate some of the difficulties that it presents.

The author's name is a proper name, and therefore it raises the problems common to all proper names. (Here I refer to [John] Searle's analyses, among others.) Obviously, one cannot turn a proper name into a pure and simple reference. It has other than indicative functions: More than an indication, a gesture, a finger pointed at someone, it is the equivalent of a description. When one says "Aristotle," one employs a word that is the equivalent of one, or a series of, definite descriptions, such as "the author of the *Analytics*," "the founder of ontology," and so forth. One cannot stop there, however, because a proper name does not have just one signification. When we discover that Rimbaud did not write *La Chasse spirituelle,* we cannot pretend that the meaning of this proper name, or that of the author, has been altered. The proper name and the author's name are situated between the two poles of description and designation: They must have a certain link with what they name, but one that is neither entirely in the mode of designation nor in that of description; it must be a *specific* link. However—and it is here that the particular difficulties of the author's name arise—the links between the proper name and the individual named and between the author's name and what it names are not isomorphic and do not function in the same way. There are several differences.

If, for example, Pierre Dupont does not have blue eyes, or was not born in Paris, or is not a doctor, the name Pierre Dupont will still always refer to the same person: Such things do not modify the link of designation. The problems raised by the author's name are much more complex, however. If I discover that Shakespeare was not born in the house that we visit today, this is a modification which, obviously, will not alter the functioning of the author's name. But if we proved that Shakespeare did not write those sonnets which pass for his, that would constitute a significant change and affect the manner in which the author's name functions. If we proved that Shakespeare wrote [Francis] Bacon's *Organon* by showing that the same author wrote both the works of Bacon and those of Shakespeare, that would be a third type of change which would entirely modify the functioning of the author's name. The author's name is not, therefore, just a proper name like the rest.

Many other facts point out the paradoxical singularity of the author's name. To say that Pierre Dupont does not exist is not at all the same as saying that Homer or Hermes Trismegistus did not exist. In the first case, it means that no one has the name Pierre Dupont; in the second, it means that several people were mixed together under one name, or that the true author had none of the traits traditionally ascribed to the personae of Homer or Hermes. To say that X's real name is actually Jacques Durand instead of Pierre Dupont is not the same as saying that Stendhal's name was Henri Beyle. One could also question the meaning and functioning of propositions like "Bourbaki is so-and-so, so-and-so, etc." and "Victor Eremita, Climacus, Anticlimacus, Frater Taciturnus, Constantine Constantius, all of these are Kierkegaard." . . .

It would seem that the author's name, unlike other proper names, does not pass from the interior of a discourse to the real and exterior individual who produced it; instead, the name seems always to be present, marking off the edges of the text, revealing, or at least characterizing, its mode of being. The author's name manifests the appearance of a certain discursive set and indicates the status of this discourse within a society and a culture. It has no legal status, nor is it located in the fiction of the work; rather, it is located in the break that founds a certain discursive construct and its very particular mode of being. As a result, we could say that in a civilization like our own there are a certain number of discourses that are endowed with the "author-function," while others are deprived of it. A private letter may well have a signer—it does not have an author; a contract may well have a guarantor—it does not have an author. An anonymous text posted on a wall probably has a writer—but not an author. The author-function is therefore characteristic of the mode of existence, circulation, and functioning of certain discourses within a society. . . .

If we limit our remarks to the author of a book or a text, we can isolate four different characteristics.

First of all, discourses are objects of appropriation. The form of ownership from which they spring is of a rather particular type, one that has been codified for many years. We should note that, historically, this type of ownership has always been subsequent to what one might call penal appropriation. Texts, books, and discourses really began to have authors (other than mythical, "sacralized" and "sacralizing" figures) to the extent that authors became subject to punishment, that is, to the extent that discourses could be transgressive. In our culture (and doubtless in many others), discourse was not originally a product, a thing, a kind of goods; it was essentially an act—an act placed in the bipolar field of the sacred and the profane, the licit and the illicit, the religious and the blasphemous. Historically, it was a gesture fraught with risks before becoming goods caught up in a circuit of ownership.

Once a system of ownership for texts came into being, once strict rules concerning author's rights, author-publisher relations, right of reproduction, and related matters were enacted—at the end of the eighteenth and the beginning of the nineteenth century—the possibility of transgression attached to the act of writing took on, more and more, the form of an imperative peculiar to literature. It is as if the author, beginning with the moment at which he was placed in the system of property that characterizes our society, compensated for the status that he thus acquired by rediscovering the old bipolar field of discourse, systematically practicing transgression and thereby restoring danger to a writing which was not guaranteed the benefits of ownership.

The author-function does not affect all discourses in a universal and constant way, however. This is its second characteristic. In our civilization, it has not always been the same types of texts which have required attribution to an author. There was a time when the texts that we today call "literary" (narratives, stories, epics, tragedies, comedies) were accepted, put into circulation, and valorized without any question about the identity of their author; their anonymity caused no difficulties since their ancientness, whether real or imagined, was regarded as a sufficient guarantee of their status. On the other hand, those texts that we now would call scientific—those dealing with cosmology and the heavens, medicine and illnesses, natural sciences and geography—were accepted in the Middle Ages, and accepted as "true," only when marked with the name of their author. "Hippocrates said," "Pliny recounts," were not really formulas of an argument based on authority; they were the markers inserted in discourses that were supposed to be received as statements of demonstrated truth. . . .

The third characteristic of this author-function is that it does not develop spontaneously as the attribution of a discourse to an individual. It is, rather, the result of a complex operation which constructs a certain rational being that we call "author." Critics doubtless try to give this intelligible being a realistic status, by discerning, in the individual, a "deep" motive, a "creative" power, or a "design," the milieu in which writing originates. Nevertheless, these aspects of an individual which we designate as making him an author are only a projection, in more or less psychologizing terms, of the operations that we force texts to undergo, the connections that we make, the traits that we establish as pertinent, the continuities that we recognize, or the exclusions that we practice. All these operations vary according to periods and types of discourse. We do not construct a "philosophical author" as we do a "poet," just as, in the eighteenth century, one did not construct a novelist as we do today. Still, we can find through the ages certain constants in the rules of author-construction.

It seems, for example, that the manner in which literary criticism once defined the author—or rather constructed the figure of the author beginning with existing texts and discourses—is directly derived from the manner in which Christian tradition authenticated (or rejected) the texts at its disposal. In order to "rediscover" an author in a work, modern criticism uses methods similar to those that Christian exegesis employed when trying to prove the value of a text by its author's saintliness. In *De viris illustribus*, Saint Jerome explains that homonymy is not sufficient to identify legitimately authors of more than one work: Different individuals could have had the same name, or one man could have, illegitimately, borrowed another's patronymic. The name as an individual trademark is not enough when one works within a textual tradition.

How then can one attribute several discourses to one and the same author? How can one use the author-function to determine if one is dealing with one or several individuals? Saint Jerome proposes four criteria: (1) If among several books attributed to an author one is inferior to the others, it must be withdrawn from the list of the author's works (the author is therefore defined as a constant level of value); (2) the same should be done if certain texts contradict the doctrine expounded in the author's other works (the author is thus defined as a field of conceptual or theoretical coherence); (3) one must also exclude works that are written in a different style containing words and expressions not ordinarily found in the writer's production (the author is here conceived as a stylistic unity); (4) finally, passages quoting statements that were made, or mentioning events that occurred after the author's death must be regarded as interpolated texts (the author is here seen as a historical figure at the crossroads of a certain number of events).

Modern literary criticism, even when—as is now customary—it is not concerned with questions of authentication, still defines the author the same way: The author provides the basis for explaining not only the presence of certain events in a work, but also their transformations, distortions, and diverse modifications (through his biography, the determination of his individual perspective, the analysis of his social position, and the revelation of his basic design). The author is also the principle of a certain unity of writing—all differences having to be resolved, at least in part, by the principles of evolution, maturation, or influence. The author also serves to neutralize the contradictions that may emerge in a series of texts: There must be—at a certain level of his thought or desire, of his consciousness or unconscious—a point where contradictions are resolved, where incompatible elements are at last tied together or organized around a fundamental or originating contradiction. Finally, the author is a particular source of expression that, in more or less completed forms, is manifested equally well, and with similar validity, in works, sketches, letters, fragments, and so on. Clearly, Saint Jerome's four criteria of authenticity (criteria which seem totally insufficient for today's exegetes) do define the four modalities according to which modern criticism brings the author-function into play.

But the author-function is not a pure and simple reconstruction made second-hand from a text given as passive material. The text always contains a certain number of signs referring to the author. These signs, well known to grammarians, are personal pronouns, adverbs of time and place, and verb conjugation. Such elements do not play the same role in discourses provided with the author-function as in those lacking it. In the latter, such "shifters" refer to the real speaker and to the spatio-temporal coordinates of his discourse (although certain modifications can occur, as in the operation of relating discourses in the first person). In the former, however, their role is more complex and variable. Everyone knows that, in a novel narrated in the first person, neither the first person pronoun, nor the present indicative refer exactly either to the writer or to the moment in which he writes, but rather to an alter ego whose distance from the author varies, often changing in the course of the work. It would be just as wrong to equate the author with the real writer as to equate him with the fictitious speaker; the author-function is carried out and operates in the scission itself, in this division and this distance.

One might object that this is a characteristic peculiar to novelistic or poetic discourse, a "game" in which only "quasidiscourses" participate. In fact, however, all discourses endowed with the author-function do possess this plurality of self. The self that speaks in the preface to a treatise on mathematics—and that indicates the circumstances of the treatise's composition—is identical neither in its position nor in its functioning to the self that speaks in the course of a demonstration, and that appears in the form of "I conclude" or "I suppose." In the first case, the "I" refers to an individual without an equivalent who, in a determined place and time, completed a certain task; in the second, the "I" indicates an instance and a level of demonstration which any individual could perform provided that he accept the same system of symbols, play of axioms, and set of previous demonstrations. We could also, in the same treatise, locate a third self, one that speaks to tell the work's meaning, the obstacles encountered, the results obtained, and the remaining problems; this self is situated in the field of already existing or yet-to-appear mathematical discourses. The author-function is not assumed by the first of these selves at the expense of the other two, which would then be nothing more than a fictitious splitting in two of the first one. On the contrary, in these discourses the author-function operates so as to effect the dispersion of these three simultaneous selves.

No doubt analysis could discover still more characteristic traits of the author-function. I will limit myself to these four, however, because they seem both the most visible and the most important. They can be summarized as follows: (1) The author-function is linked to the juridical and institutional system that encompasses, determines, and articulates the universe of discourses; (2) it does not affect all discourses in the same way at all times and in all types of civilization; (3) it is not defined by the spontaneous attribution of a discourse to its producer, but rather by a series of specific and complex operations; (4) it does not refer purely and simply to a real individual, since it can give rise simultaneously to several selves, to several subjects—positions that can be occupied by different classes of individuals. . . .

Furthermore, in the course of the nineteenth century, there appeared in Europe another, more uncommon, kind of author, whom one should confuse with neither the "great" literary authors, nor the authors of religious texts, nor the founders of science. In a somewhat arbitrary way we shall call those who belong in this last group "founders of discursivity." They are unique in that they are not just the authors of their own works. They have produced something else: the possibilities and the rules for the formation of other texts. In this sense, they are very different, for example, from a novelist, who is, in fact, nothing more than the author of his own text. Freud is not just the author of *The Interpretation of Dreams* or *Jokes and their Relation to the Unconscious;* Marx is not just the author of the *Communist Manifesto* or *Capital:* They both have established an endless possibility of discourse. . . .

The author is the principle of thrift in the proliferation of meaning. As a result, we must entirely reverse the traditional idea of the author. We are accustomed, as we have seen earlier, to saying that the author is the genial creator of a work in which he deposits, with infinite wealth and generosity, an inexhaustible world of significations. We are used to thinking that the author is so different from all other men, and so transcendent with regard to all languages that, as soon as he speaks, meaning begins to proliferate, to proliferate indefinitely.

The truth is quite the contrary: The author is not an indefinite source of significations which fill a work; the author does not precede the works, he is a certain functional principle by which, in our culture, one limits, excludes, and chooses; in short, by which one impedes the free circulation, the free manipulation, the free composition, decomposition, and recomposition of fiction. In fact, if we are accustomed to presenting the author as a genius, as a perpetual surging of invention, it is because, in reality, we make him function in exactly the opposite fashion. One can say that the author is an ideological product, since we represent him as the opposite of his historically real function. (When a historically given function is represented in a figure that inverts it, one has an ideological production.) The author is therefore the ideological figure by which one marks the manner in which we fear the proliferation of meaning.

Criticism as Retrieval
■ Richard Wollheim ■

It is a deficiency of at least the English language that there is no single word, applicable over all the arts, for the process of coming to understand a particular work of art. To make good this deficiency I shall appropriate the word 'criticism,' but in doing so I know that, though this concurs with the way the word is normally used in connection with, say, literature, it violates usage in, at any rate, the domain of the visual arts, where 'criticism' is the name of a purely evaluative activity.

The central question to be asked of criticism is, What does it do? How is a piece of criticism to be assessed, and what determines whether it is adequate? To my mind the best brief answer, of which this essay will offer an exposition and a limited defence, is, Criticism is *retrieval*. The task of criticism is the reconstruction of the creative process, where the creative process must in turn be thought of as something not stopping short of, but terminating on, the work of art itself. The creative process reconstructed, or retrieval complete, the work is then open to understanding. To the view advanced, that criticism is retrieval, several objections are raised.

The first objection is that, by and large, this view makes criticism impossible: and this is so because, except in exceptional circumstances, it is beyond the bounds of practical possibility to reconstruct the creative process.

"Criticism as Retrieval" by Richard Wollheim has been excerpted from *Art and its Object* Cambridge University Press (1980), pages 185–194 and is reprinted by permission of the publisher.

Any argument to any such conclusion makes use of further premisses—either about the nature of knowledge and its limits, or about the nature of the mind and its inaccessibility—and the character of these further premisses comes out in the precise way the conclusion is formulated or how it is qualified. For, though an extreme form of the objection would be that the creative process can never be reconstructed, the conclusion is likelier to take some such form as that criticism is impossible unless the critic and the artist are one and the same person, or the work was created in the ambience of the critic, or the creative process was fully, unambiguously, and contemporaneously documented by the artist. This is not the place to assess the general philosophical theses of scepticism or solipsism, or their variants, but it is worth observing that these theses ought not to be credited with greater force outside general philosophy than they are inside it. The observation is called for, because traditionally philosophers of art permit the creative process, or, more broadly, the mental life of artists, to give rise to epistemological problems of an order that they would not sanction in inquiry generally.

These difficulties apart, the objection in its present form offers a persuasive rather than a conclusive argument against the retrieval view. For maybe the truth is that criticism *is* a practical impossibility, or is so outside very favoured circumstances. But sometimes the objection is stated to stronger effect, and then an incompatibility is asserted between the sceptical or solipsistic premisses, however framed, and not just the practice of criticism as retrieval but the view that criticism is retrieval.

A step further, and it is asserted that from these same premisses an alternative view of criticism follows. This alternative view may be expressed as, Criticism is *revision,* and it holds that the task of criticism is so to interpret the work that it says most to the critic there and then. Assuming the critical role, we must make the work of art speak 'to us, today.'

It is clear that this derivation too must require further premisses, though less clear what they would be. One thing seems certain, though it is often ignored by adherents of the revisionary view, and that is this: If criticism is justifiably revision when we lack the necessary evidence for reconstructing the creative process, then it must also be revision when we have, if we ever do, adequate evidence for retrieval. We cannot as critics be entitled to make the work of art relate to us when we are in a state of ignorance about its history without our having an obligation to do so, and this obligation must continue to hold in the face of knowledge. Otherwise revision is never a critical undertaking: It is only, sometimes, a *pis-aller,* or a second best to criticism. Indeed, the strongest case for the revisionary view of criticism draws support from a thesis which appears to dispense with scepticism or, at any rate, cuts across it.

The thesis I have in mind, which is generally called 'radical historicism' and is best known through the advocacy of [T.S.] Eliot, holds that works of art actually change their meaning over history. On this thesis the task of the critic at any given historical moment is not so much to impose a new meaning upon, as to extract the new meaning from, the work of art. That works of art are semantically mobile in this way is to be explained not simply—to take the case of a literary work—by reference to linguistic change or to shifts in the meaning of words and idioms, but, more fundamentally, more radically, by appeal to the way in which every new work of art rewrites to some degree or other every related, or maybe every known, work of art in the same tradition. To this central contention the thesis adds the corollary that, as some particular meaning of a work of art becomes invalid or obsolete, it also becomes inaccessible: It ceases to be a possible object of knowledge.

Radical historicism is a doctrine, like the [Benjamin] Whorfian thesis about the non-intertranslatability of natural languages, with which indeed it has much in common, that has its greatest appeal when it gets us to imagine something which on reflection turns out to be just what it asserts is unimaginable. So, for instance, under the influence of radical historicism (or so it seems) we start to imagine how a contemporary of Shakespeare's would find the inherited reading of [Geoffrey] Chaucer's *Troilus* dull or dead, and we find ourselves readily sympathizing with his preference for a new revitalized reading inspired by *Troilus and Cressida*. And then we reflect that, if radical historicism is indeed true, just such a comparison was not open to one of Shakespeare's contemporaries, and is even less so to us. To him only one term to the comparison was accessible: to us neither is.

A second objection to the retrieval view of criticism goes deeper in that it concentrates upon the view itself and not merely upon its consequences. According to this objection, retrieval is, from the critical point of view, on any given occasion either misleading or otiose. From the outset the objection contrasts retrieval with its own favoured view of criticism, which may be expressed as, Criticism is *scrutiny*—scrutiny of the literary text, of the musical score, of the painted surface—and it holds that retrieval is misleading when its results deviate from the findings of scrutiny and it is otiose when its results concur with the findings of scrutiny. In this latter case it is (note) retrieval that is reckoned otiose, not scrutiny, and the reason given is that reliance upon retrieval presupposes scrutiny but not *vice versa*. Scrutiny is presupposed because it is only with the findings of scrutiny also before us that we can be certain that we are dealing with a case where the results of retrieval merely reduplicate those of scrutiny, and hence that retrieval is not misleading. So, overall, retrieval can never do better than scrutiny, sometimes it can do worse, and which is the case cannot be determined without the benefit of scrutiny.

But how does this objection characterize the difference between the cases where retrieval does no worse than, and those where it does worse than, scrutiny? The cases are distinguished in that, given a work of art and the creative process that terminates on it, there are two possibilities. One is that the creative process realizes itself in the work of art: The other is that it fails to. Now it is in the latter case that retrieval is misleading, whereas in the former case it is merely otiose. In the former case, scrutiny will show the critic that the work is as retrieval laboriously allows him to infer that it is: In the latter case, retrieval will lead him to infer that the work is as scrutiny will soon reveal it not to be. This objection to the retrieval view shows itself vulnerable on a number of counts.

In the first place, though it is indubitably true that the creative process either is or is not realized in the work of art, nevertheless, if 'realized' means (as it presumably does) 'fully realized,' this is not, from the point of view of criticism, the best way of setting out the alternatives. For critically it is a highly relevant fact that the creative process may be realized in the work of art to varying degrees. (There are, indeed, theoretical reasons of some strength, which I shall not assess, for thinking that the creative process is never realized in a work of art either to degree 1 or to degree 0: Realization must always be to some intermediate degree.) But, it might be thought, this presents no real problem. For the objection can surely concede that the creative process may be realized to varying degrees, and can then further concede that sometimes, even when the creative process has not been fully realized, retrieval may not be misleading. All that it has to insist upon, surely, is that, if the creative process may be harmlessly, though otiosely, reconstructed up to the point to which it was realized in the work of art, retrieval is misleading if, and as soon as, it is carried beyond this point. However, as we shall see, this concession brings its difficulties in train.

Secondly: Suppose we confine ourselves (as the objection says) to that part of the creative process which is realized in the work of art. It becomes clear that there is something that reconstruction of this part of the process can bring to light which scrutiny of the corresponding part of the work cannot. It can show that that part of the work which came about through design did indeed come about through design and not through accident or error. Scrutiny, which *ex hypothesi* limits itself to the outcome, cannot show this. (A parallel in the philosophy of action: If an action is intentional, then, it might be thought, reconstruction of the agent's mental process will not tell us more about it than we could learn from observation of the action: but we can learn this from observation of the action only if we already or independently know that the action is intentional.) Accordingly—and as yet the point can be made only hypothetically—if criticism is concerned to find out not just what the work of art is like but what the work is like by design, then, contrary to what the objection asserts, scrutiny, to be a source of knowledge, must presuppose retrieval.

Thirdly: The objection, as emended, states that that part of the creative process which is not realized in the work of art is not to be reconstructed. But how is this part of the process to be identified? There are two distinct grounds on which the distinction could be effected, and they give different results. We could exclude from critical consideration any part of the creative process in which the work of art is not . . . more or less directly prefigured: Alternatively, we might exclude only that part of the creative process which has no bearing at all upon the character of the work. Two kinds of case show how crucial it is which way the distinction is effected. The first case is where the artist changes his mind. Rodin's *Monument to Balzac* started off as a nude sculpture. Is the critically relevant part of the creative process only that which includes Rodin's change of mind to, and his subsequent concentration upon, the draped Balzac: or should it also embrace his concentration upon, and his subsequent change of mind from, the naked Balzac? The second case is where an artist sticks to his intention but fails in it. In writing *The Idiot* [Fyodor] Dostoievsky set out to portray a totally good man. Prince Myshkin is not a totally good man, but Dostoievsky's depiction of him is clearly not unaffected by the original aim: It is the failed depiction of a totally good man. Should we, or should we not, regard Dostoievsky's original aim, unsuccessfully realized though it is in the work of art, as a critically relevant part of the creative process?

In the light of the next, or fourth, point, the previous two points can be sharpened. For the objection, in claiming that scrutiny can establish everything that at one and the same time is critically relevant and can be established by retrieval, totally misconceives the nature of the interest that criticism might take in the creative process and, therefore, what it stands to gain from reconstructing it. For the objection appears to assume that, if the critic is interested in the creative process, this is because, or is to be accounted for by the degree to which, it provides him with good evidence for the character of the work. The critic seeks to infer from how the work was brought about how it is. Now, of course, if this were so, then there would, on the face of it at any rate, be reason to think that retrieval was at best a detour to a destination to which scrutiny could be a short cut. But that this is a misconception is revealed by the fact that the critic committed to retrieval is not committed to any assumptions about the likely degree of match between the creative process and the resultant work and he will continue to be interested in the creative process even in the case when he knows that there is a mismatch between the two. The critic who tries to reconstruct the creative process has a quite different aim from that which the objection to the retrieval view assumes. He does so in order to understand the work of art—though it would be wrong to say, as some philosophers of art tend to, that he seeks understanding rather than description. Understanding is reached through description, but through profound description, or description profounder than scrutiny can provide, and such description may be expected to include such issues as how much of the character of the work is by design, how much has come about through changes of intention, and what were the ambitions that went to its making but were not realized in the final product.

But, fifthly, and finally, the objection, in opposing scrutiny to retrieval presents scrutiny as though it were itself quite unproblematic: or as though, given a work of art, there would be no difficulty, or at any rate no theoretical difficulty, in dividing its properties into those which are accessible and those which are inaccessible to scrutiny. In considering the objection I have gone along with this, particularly in the second point I raise. However, in the main body of *Art and its Objects* I rejected this traditional assumption . . . though I preferred to make my point by considering specific properties that resisted the dichotomy. . . . Here I shall consider the matter more directly.

Crucially the view that criticism is scrutiny is seriously under-defined until an answer is given to the question, Scrutiny by whom? The following cases illustrate the problem: The listener who is ignorant of the mission of Christ will miss much of the pathos in the St Matthew Passion; a viewer who has not gathered that [Giovanni Lorenzo] Bernini's mature sculpture requires a frontal point of view, as opposed to the multiple viewpoint against which it reacted; will fail to discern the emotional immediacy it aims at; a reader's response to [Thomas] Hardy's 'At Castle Boterel' will be modified when he learns that the poet's wife had just died, and then it will be modified again as he learns how unhappy the marriage had been; the spectator who is made aware that in the relevant panel of the S. Francesco altarpiece [Stefano di Govanni] Sassetta uses to paint the cloak that the Saint discards, thereby renouncing his inheritance, the most expensive and most difficult pigment available will come to recognize a drama first in the gesture, then in the picture as a whole, of which he had been previously ignorant. With any form of perception— and scrutiny is a form of perception—what is perceptible is always dependent not only upon such physical factors as the nature of the stimulus, the state of the organism, and the prevailing local conditions, but also upon cognitive factors. Accordingly, the scrutiny view needs to be filled out by a definition of the person whose scrutiny is authoritative, or 'the ideal critic,' and any such definition must be partly in terms of the cognitive stock upon which the critic can draw. There are a number of possible definitions, for each of which the appeal of the scrutiny view, as well as its right to go by that name, will vary.

A heroic proposal, deriving from Kant, the aim of which is to ensure the democracy of art, is to define the ideal critic as one whose cognitive stock is empty, or who brings to bear upon the work of art zero knowledge, beliefs, and concepts. The proposal has, however, little to recommend it except its aim. It is all but impossible to put into practice, and, if it could be, it would lead to critical judgments that would be universally unacceptable.

Another proposal is to define the cognitive stock on which scrutiny is based as consisting solely of beliefs that could themselves have been derived— though in practice they may not have been derived—from scrutiny of the work of art concerned. But this takes us round in a circle: for what requirement is placed upon the cognitive stock on which the scrutiny that gives rise to these beliefs itself depends?

Beneath Interpretation
■ Richard Shusterman ■

Since our current hermeneutic turn derives in large part from the rejection of foun-dationalism, it is not surprising that the central arguments for hermeneutic univer-salism* turn on rejecting foundationalist ideas of transparent fact, absolute and univocal truth, and mind-independent objectivity. For such ideas underwrite the possibility of attaining some perfect God's-eye grasp of things as they really are, independent of how we differently perceive them, a seeing or understanding that is free from the corrigibility and perspectival pluralities and prejudices that we will-ingly recognize as intrinsic to all interpretation.

I think the universalists are right to reject such foundational understanding, but wrong to conclude from this that all understanding is interpretation. Their mis-take, a grave but simple one, is to equate the non-foundational with the interpre-tive. In other words, what the universalists are successfully arguing is that all un-derstanding is nonfoundational; that it is always corrigible, perspectival, and somehow prejudiced or prestructured; that no meaningful experience is passively neutral and disinterestedly non-selective. But since, in the traditional foundational-ist framework, interpretation is contrasted and designated as *the* form of non-foundational understanding, the inferior foster home of all corrigible, perspectival perception, it is easy to confuse the view that no understanding is foundational with the view that all understanding is interpretive. Yet this confusion of hermeneutic universalism betrays an unseemly residual bond to the foundationalist framework, in the assumption that what is not foundational must be interpretive. It thus prevents the holists from adopting a more liberating pragmatist perspective which (I shall ar-gue) can profitably distinguish between understanding and interpretation without thereby endorsing foundationalism. Such pragmatism more radically recognizes un-interpreted realities, experiences, and understandings as already perspectival, preju-diced, and corrigible—in short, as non-foundationally given.

So much for a general overview of the universalist arguments. I now want to itemize and consider six of them in detail. Though there is some overlap, we can roughly divide them into three groups, respectively based on three ineliminable features of all understanding: (a) corrigibility, (b) perspectival plurality and preju-dice, and (c) mental activity and process.

"Beneath Interpretation" by Richard Shusterman has been excerpted from *Pragmatist Aesthet-ics,* Blackwell Publishers (1992), pages 120–127, and is reprinted by permission of the publisher.
*Hermeneutic universalism is the view that all human experience is the product of interpre-tation.

(1) What we understand, what we grasp as truth or fact, frequently turns out to be wrong, to require correction, revision, and replacement by a different understanding. Moreover, this new understanding is typically achieved by reinterpreting the former understanding and can itself be replaced and shown to be not fact but "mere interpretation" by a subsequent understanding reached through interpretive thought. Since any putative fact or true understanding can be revised or replaced by interpretation, it cannot enjoy an epistemological status higher than interpretation; and interpretation is paradigmatically corrigible and inexhaustive. This is sometimes what is meant by the claim that there are no facts or truths but only interpretations.

The inference, then, is that since understanding is epistemologically no better than interpretation, it is altogether no different from interpretation (as if all meaningful differences had to be differences of apodicticness!). The conclusion is reinforced by the further inference that since all interpretation is corrigible and all understanding is corrigible, then all understanding is interpretation. Once formulated, the inferences are obviously (indeed pathetically) fallacious. But we tend to accept their conclusion, since we assimilate all corrigible and partial understanding to interpretation, as if genuine understanding itself could never be revised or enlarged, as if understanding had to be interpretive to be corrigible. But why make this rigidly demanding assumption? Traditionally, the reason was that understanding (like its cognates truth and fact) was itself defined in contrast to "mere interpretation" as that which *is* incorrigible. But if we abandon foundationalism by denying that any understanding is incorrigible, the idea of corrigible understanding becomes possible and indeed necessary; and once we recognize this idea, there is no need to infer that all understanding must be interpretation simply because it is corrigible. When hermeneutic universalists make this inference, they show an unintended and unbecoming reliance on the foundationalist linkage of uninterpreted understanding with incorrigible, foundational truth.

(2) The second argument for hermeneutic universalism derives from understanding's ineliminable perspectival character and the plurality of perspectives. . . . [Alexander] Nehamas builds . . . [an] argument that all understanding is interpretive on the premise that all understanding, indeed "all our activity is partial and perspectival." I think the premise is perfectly acceptable and can be established by an argument which Nehamas does not supply. All understanding must be perspectival or aspectual, since all thought and perception exhibit intentionality (in the phenomenological sense of being about something) and all intentionality is aspectual, i.e., grasping its object in a certain way. But the very idea of perspective or aspect implies that there are other possible perspectives or aspects which lie (in [Hans-Georg] Gadamer's words) outside "the horizon" of a particular perspectival standpoint and thus outside its "range of vision.". . . Thus there can be no univocal and exclusive understanding of any thing, but rather many partial or perspectival ways of seeing it, none of which provides total and exclusive truth.

So much for the premise; but how does it follow that all understanding is interpretive? Again, in the traditional foundationalist framework, interpretation marks the realm of partial, perspectival, and plural ways of human understanding in essential contrast to some ideal understanding that grasps things as they really are univocally, exhaustively, and absolutely. Rejecting the very possibility and intelligibility of such univocal and complete understanding (as Nehamas and Gadamer rightly do), the universalists infer that all understanding is thereby reduced to interpretation—the foundationalist category for understanding which is not necessarily false or illegitimate (not a *mis*understanding) but which cannot represent true understanding since it is perspectively plural and not necessarily and wholly true. However, again we should realize that once we are free of foundationalism's doctrines, there is no need to accept its categorizations. There is thus no need to deny that true understanding can itself be perspectively partial and plural, and consequently no reason to conclude that since all understanding must be perspectival, it must also be interpretation.

(3) In speaking of understanding as perspectival and hence partial, we have so far meant that it cannot exclude different perspectives and can in principle always be supplemented. But partiality also has the central sense of bias and prejudice. The third argument why understanding must always be interpretation is that it is always prejudiced and never neutrally transparent. This is a key point in the Nietzschean, Gadamerian, and even pragmatist attacks on foundationalist understanding. Any understanding involves the human element which prestructures understanding in terms (and in service) of our interests, drives, and needs, which significantly overlap but also frequently diverge among different societies and individuals. Moreover, for Nietzsche, Gadamer, and the pragmatists, the fact that understanding is always motivated and prejudiced by our needs and values is a very good thing; it is what allows us to thrive and survive so that we can understand anything at all.

From the premise that "all understanding inevitably involves some prejudice," . . . "that every view depends on and manifests specific values" and "antecedent commitments,". . . it is but a short step to the view that all understanding and perception is interpretation. But it is a step where the more canny pragmatist fears to tread, and where she parts company from grand continental hermeneuts like Nietzsche and Gadamer. In rejecting the foundationalist idea and ideal of transparent mirroring perception, she recognizes that understanding is always motivated and prejudiced, just like interpretation. But she wonders why this makes understanding always interpretive. It just does not follow, unless we presume that *only* interpretation could be prejudiced, while (preinterpretive) understanding or experience simply could not be. But to her, this inference is as strange and offensive as a sexist argument that all humans are really women because they all are influenced by emotions, while presumably real men are not.

(4) The fourth argument for hermeneutic universalism inhabits the overlap between understanding's perspectival partiality and its active process. The argument is basically that since all understanding is selective—focused on some things and features but not on others—all understanding must therefore be interpretive. The fact that understanding is perspectively partial (in both senses of incompleteness and

purposive bias) implies that it is always selective. It always grasps some things rather than others, and what it grasps depends in part on its antecedent purposes.

This much seems uncontestable. What I challenge is the inference that since understanding (or indeed any intelligent activity) is always selective, it is therefore always interpretive. Such a conclusion needs the further premise that all purposive selection must be the product of interpretive thinking and decision. But this premise is false, an instance of the philosophical fallacy [John] Dewey dubbed "intellectualism." For most of the selection involved in our ordinary acts of perception and understanding is done automatically and unconsciously (yet still intelligently and not mechanically) on the basis of intelligent habits, without any reflection or deliberation at all. Interpretation, in its standard ordinary usage, certainly implies conscious thought and deliberate reflection; but not all intelligent and purposive selection is conscious or deliberate. Walking down the stairs requires selecting how and where to place one's feet and body; but such selection involves interpreting only in cases of abnormal conditions when descent of the staircase presents a problem (as with an unusually dark or narrow winding staircase, a sprained ankle, or a fit of vertigo).

Just as it is wrong to confuse all purposive intelligent choice with interpretive decisions requiring ratiocination, so we can distinguish perceptions and understandings that are immediately given to us (albeit only corrigibly and based on prior experience) from understandings reached only by interpretive deliberation on the meaning of what is immediately given. When I awake on the beach at Santa Cruz with my eyes pierced by sunlight, I immediately perceive or understand it is daytime; only when I instead wake to a darkish gloom do I need to interpret that it is no longer night but merely another dreary morning in Philadelphia.

In short, I am arguing that although all understanding is selective, not all selective understanding is interpretive. If understanding's selection is neither conscious nor deliberate but prereflective and immediate, we have no reason to regard that selection or the resultant understanding as interpretation, since interpretation standardly implies some deliberate or at least conscious thinking, whereas understanding does not. We can understand something without thinking about it at all; but to interpret something we need to think about it. This distinction may recall a conclusion from [Ludwig] Wittgenstein's famous discussion of seeing-as, where he distinguishes seeing from interpreting: "To interpret is to think, to do something; seeing is a state."

(5) Though insightful, Wittgenstein's remark is also problematic. For it suspiciously suggests that we could see or understand without doing anything; and this suspicion suggests the fifth argument for hermeneutic universalism. Understanding or perceiving, as Nietzscheans, pragmatists, and even Gadamerians insist, is active. It is not a passive mirroring, but an active structuring of what is encountered. To hear or see anything, before we even attempt to interpret it, involves the activity of our bodies, certain motor responses and tensions in the muscles and nerves of our organs of sensation. To characterize seeing or understanding in sharp

contrast to interpretation as an achieved "state" rather than as "doing something" suggests that understanding is static rather than active; and if passively static, then it should be neutral rather than selective and structuring. The fifth argument for hermeneutic universalism therefore rejects this distinction between understanding as passively neutral and interpretation as actively structuring, and then infers that since all understanding is active, all understanding must be interpretive.

My response to this argument should already be clear. As a pragmatist, I fully accept the premise that all perception and understanding involve doing something; but I deny this entails that they always involve interpretation. The inference relies on an implicit premise that all "doings" that are cognitively valuable or significant for thought are themselves already cases of thinking. Hence any active selection and structuring of perception must already be a thoughtful, deliberate selection, one involving an interpretive decision. This is the premise I contest, the assimilating conflation of all active, selective, and structuring intelligence with the active, selective structuring of the interpreting intellect. Understanding can actively structure and select without engaging in interpretation, just as action can be intelligent without engaging thought or the intellect. When, on my way to the beach, I am told that the surf is up, I immediately understand what is said, pre-reflectively selecting and structuring the sounds and meanings I respond to. I do not need to interpret what is said or meant. Only if I were unfamiliar with idiomatic English, or unable to hear the words, or in a situation where the utterance seemed out of place, would I have to interpret it. Only if there were some problem in understanding, some puzzle or doubt or incongruity, would I have to thematize the utterance as something that needed interpretation, something to think about and clarify or resolve.

(6) But this assertion is precisely what is challenged by the sixth argument for universal hermeneutics, an argument which highlights the intimate link between the hermeneutic turn and the linguistic turn in both continental and Anglo-American philosophy. Briefly and roughly, the argument goes as follows. All understanding is linguistic, because all understanding (as indeed all experience) involves concepts that require language. But linguistic understanding is essentially a matter of decoding or interpreting signs which are arbitrary rather than natural and whose translation into meaningful propositions thus requires interpretation. To understand the meaning of a sentence, we need, on the Quinean-Davidsonian model, to supply a translation or interpretation of it in terms already familiar to us (whether those terms be in the interpreted language itself or in another more familiar "home" language). So [Donald] Davidson boldly asserts that "All understanding of the speech of another involves radical interpretation," and firmly equates "the power of thought" with "speaking a language." And from the continental tradition, Gadamer concurs by basing the universal scope of hermeneutics on "the essential linguisticality of all human experience of the world" and on a view of language as "itself the game of interpretation that we are all engaged in every day." Hence, not only all understanding but all experience is interpretive, since both

are ineliminably linguistic—a conclusion endorsed by [Richard] Rorty, [Jacques] Derrida, and a legion of hermeneutic universalists.

Though the consensus for this position is powerful, the argument strikes me as less than persuasive. It warrants challenging on two points at least. First, we can question the idea that linguistic understanding is always the decoding, translation, or interpretation of arbitrary signs through rules of meaning and syntax. This is, I think, an overly formalistic and intellectualized picture of linguistic understanding. Certainly it is not apparent that we always (or ever) interpret, decode, or translate the uncoded and unproblematic utterances we hear in our native tongue simply in order to understand them. That is precisely why ordinary language distinguishes such direct and simple understandings from decodings, translations, and interpretations.

The hermeneutic universalists will object that we must be interpreting here, even if we don't realize it, since no other model can account for our understanding. But an alternative model *is* available in Wittgenstein, where linguistic understanding is a matter of being able to make the right responses or moves in the relevant language-game, and where such ability or language-acquisition is first gained by brute training or drill. Language mastery is (at least in part) the mastery of intelligent habits of gesture and response for engaging effectively in a form of life, rather than the mastery of a system of semiotic rules for interpreting signs.

So I think a case can be made for some distinction between understanding and interpreting language, between an unreflective but intelligent trained habit of response and a thoughtful decision about how to understand or respond. I have to interpret or translate most utterances I hear in German in order to understand them, but I understand most sentences I hear in English without interpreting them; I interpret only those that seem unclear or insufficiently understood. To defend the conflation of understanding with interpretation by arguing that in simply understanding those alleged uninterpreted utterances, I am in fact already interpreting sounds as words—or, perhaps further, that my nervous system is busy interpreting vibrations into sounds—is not only to stretch the meaning of "interpretation" for no productive purpose; it is also to misrepresent our actual experience. Certainly we can make a distinction between the words and the sounds, and between the sounds and the vibrations that cause them. But this does not mean they are really distinct or distinguishable in experience and that I must therefore interpret the sounds in order to understand them as words. On the contrary, when I hear a language I understand, I typically don't hear the sounds at all but only the understood words or message. If any interpretive effort is needed, it is to hear the words as sounds or vibrations, not vice versa.

Secondly, even if we grant that linguistic understanding is always and necessarily interpretation, it still would not follow that all understanding is interpretive. For that requires the further premise that all understanding and meaningful experience is indeed linguistic. And such a premise, though it be the deepest dogma of the linguistic turn in both analytic and continental philosophy, is neither evident nor immune to challenge. Certainly there seem to be forms of bodily awareness or understanding that are not linguistic in nature and that in fact defy adequate linguistic characterization, though they can be somehow referred to through language. As dancers, we understand the sense and rightness of a movement or posture proprioceptively, by feeling it in our spine and muscles, without translating it into conceptual linguistic terms. We can neither learn nor properly understand the movement simply by being talked through it.

How to Eat a Chinese Poem
■ Richard W. Bodman ■

A Chinese poem is like an artichoke: You have to know how to eat it before you can enjoy it. If you discard all the leaves in looking for the center, you will be left with very little, while if you try to eat the whole leaf you will end up with a bitter taste.

Like an artichoke, a Chinese poem has an inside and an outside, and while both parts need to be tasted, the center is the best. The outside and inside of a Chinese poem, its peel and its pith, are two kinds of language: on the one hand, the language of abstractions, such as sorrow, truth, joy and longing; and on the other hand, the language of sensory images, such as the touch of the wind, the taste of wine, the sound of the brook and the color of the mountains. The language of abstractions is readily comprehensible to the non-Chinese reader, but it is not very tasty, while the language of images is tasty but not readily comprehensible. For the language of images has its own vocabulary and grammar, and the new reader of Chinese poetry must learn not only the range of traditional associations belonging to each image but also how to read the images when they are placed in conjunction. Some images or recurring motifs have only one principal association. Thus, climbing to a height and taking a distant view commonly produces a reflection on the passage of time, or man's mortality; while the sound of the stream or the taste of wine suggest a truth that cannot be conveyed in words. But other images are more complex. Pines and chrysanthemums, which both resist the winter cold, may represent either the vitality of life that defies old age or else the virtue of the man who holds on to ethical principles in the face of adversity. Rivers may suggest either the sadness of parting, the exhilaration of travel, or the relentless passage of time. The interpretation of these complex images relies on understanding the context established both by other images in the same poem and by statements in the language of abstraction.

"How to Eat a Chinese Poem" by Richard Bodman is published by permission of the author.

Like an artichoke, a Chinese poem does not have a message. It has a taste. Throughout the history of Chinese philosophy and aesthetics, taste—that internal and most private of experiences—has served as a metaphor for the truth that cannot be put into words. The Chinese have long recognized both the impossibility of fully expressing truth in words as well as the paradoxical necessity of using words to convey this sense of the ineffable. *"True words are not beautiful and beautiful words are not true,"* says Lao Tzu. Chuang Tzu writes, *"He who knows does not speak, and he who speaks does not know."* And the *I Ching* 易经 or *Book of Changes* laconically states that *"words do not exhaust meaning."* While many more such statements could be found, the one that best sums up this paradox comes also from Chuang Tzu. *"The fish net exists to catch the fish; once the fish is caught, the net can be discarded. Words exist to catch meaning; once the meaning is caught, words can be abandoned. Where can I find a man who has forgotten words so that I can have a word with him?"*

To deal with this paradox, poetry often devises its own paradoxes to put to the reader. As we shall see in the case of T'ao Ch'ien 陶潜 below, such paradoxes can be constructed by placing abstract and imagistic language side by side. For the reader who can solve the paradox or who can see the connection between image and abstraction, the poem is no longer the mysterious artichoke that defies attempts at eating. Rather it become a painting that lures the eye inward, or better yet a door that opens into another world.

For his readers throughout the centuries, T'ao Ch'ien [365–427 A.D.], also known as T'ao Yuanming 陶渊明, has exemplified the Confucian gentleman of high principles who retires from the corrupt world to a rural life marked by hardship and poverty interspersed with the joys of drinking wine and writing poetry. He is celebrated as the first writer of bucolic poetry—in Chinese literally "the poetry of fields and gardens."

One of T'ao Ch'ien's best-known poems belongs to a series of twenty poems entitled "On Drinking Wine," of which it is the fifth. It combines many of the features of the poems quoted above and establishes precedents for the poetry of later periods. It deserves close study not only for the beauty of its images but also for the mystery of its verbal paradoxes, the least of which is that there is no wine in the poem. Below are two English versions, first a word-by-word rendering and second a more polished translation:

In comparing the first and second versions, the reader will note a curious fact: In the first version the pronoun "I" is entirely absent; many connecting words which we expect in English are also absent; and nouns are devoid of number, verbs devoid of tense. All these are common features of Chinese classical poetry and to a lesser extent of classical prose. The general absence of the personal pronoun "I" does not forbid the Chinese poet from making a personal statement. We infer his presence in the poem from verbs of thinking and feeling or from abstract terms, and in rendering Chinese poems into English the translator is often forced to supply an "I." But for the Chinese reader, the lack of an "I" makes the poem quieter

On Drinking Wine, No. 5 of 20 饮酒其五

1	build 结	hut 舍	in 在	human 人	world 境
2	yet 而	no 无	cart 车	horse 马	sound 喧
3	ask 问	you 君	how 何	can 能	be so 尔
4	heart 心	far 远	place 地	itself 自	remote 偏
5	pluck 采	mums 菊	east 东	hedge 篱	below 下
6	distantly 悠然		see 见	South 南	Mountain 山
7	mountain 山 air 气		day's 日	end 夕	fine 佳
8	flying 飞	bird[s] 鸟	together 相	with 与	return 还
9	here 此	in 中	there's 有	true 真	meaning 意
10	want to 欲	explain 辩	already 已	forget 忘	words 言

On Drinking Wine, No. 5 of 20

I built my hut in the midst of men,

2　And yet there's no clamor of carriages and horses.

You ask how that can be?

4　If your heart is distant, your place becomes remote of itself.

Picking chrysanthemums by the eastern hedge,

6　Distantly, I see South Mountain.

At sunset, the mountain air is fine

8　And flying birds return together.

In this there is a true meaning

10　I want to explain but have forgotten the words.

and the poet's personality less obtrusive. He finds it easier to place himself in the poem, to imagine himself as the subject of the verbs. And in some Chinese poems, the absence of an "I" permits the poet to create deliberate ambiguities in which we are no longer sure whether it is nature acting or the poet. In Wang Wei's famous line which literally reads: *"Pine wind blow loose sash"* [松风吹解带], we cannot know whether to read it as *"The wind in the pines blows, and I loosen my sash"* or as *"The wind in the pines blows my sash loose"*—which is exactly what the poet intended. In general, translating from Chinese is a tricky business. Some translators are content to give word-by-word renditions as in the first version above; in doing so, they ignore the syntactic connections between the words and give their translation a staccato quality lacking in the original. Others go to the opposite extreme of supplying all the missing elements and solving all the ambiguities, which makes their translation far wordier and more limited in meaning than the original. While there is no possibility of a perfect translation, the ideal strategy of translation lies somewhere between the two extremes.

Most Chinese readers would agree with the twentieth-century Chinese critic Wang Kuo-wei 王国维 who commented on the above poem, saying:

> There is a world with a self, and there is a world without a self. . . . Examples of worlds without a self are present in lines such as "Picking chrysanthemums by the eastern hedge, / Distantly, I see South Mountain."

Since in the original poem there is no "I," no personal pronoun that is, that sees South Mountain, but only the eye of the poet, we could probably agree with Wang Kuo-wei that the above line represents a world without a self. But Chinese critics make frustrating reading for Western readers. They leap to a high point without showing how they got there. In approaching the above poem, the Western reader wants to know in some detail how the "world without a self" is attained. Let us go through the poem slowly, paying attention to specific images and their associations, but most of all to the way in which the poet directs our attention.

> I built my hut in the midst of men,
> 2   And yet there's no clamor of carriages and horses.

Here the poet presents us with his first paradox: How can he live among men and not hear the noises of carriages and horses? This paradox is designed to pique the reader's curiosity and to prompt the question that starts the next couplet. We should note in passing the strong association in the Nineteen Old Poems of the Han dynasty between the image of riding a carriage and the theme of progressing in an official career. In this couplet, T'ao Ch'ien is thus saying indirectly that he is no longer interested in official service. The building of a hut also indicates the commencement of a life of retirement in the country.

> You ask how that can be?
> 4   If your heart is distant, your place becomes remote of itself.

The poet has now drawn the reader into conversation with him. His enigmatic answer prompts us to ask further, *"If his heart is distant, where is it?"* His answer will also remind readers of Chinese philosophy of a statement by Kuo Hsiang 郭向, an early commentator on Chuang Tzu: *"Although the Sage may occupy the chief position in a court, yet in his mind he is in no different case from being among the hills and woods."* Kuo Hsiang is saying that one does not need to live among the mountains to have the mind of a hermit; one can even work for the state. T'ao Ch'ien would not go so far as to work for the state, but even in retirement he does not want to leave the world of men entirely.

> Picking chrysanthemums by the eastern hedge,
> 6   Distantly, I see South Mountain.

In Chinese lore, both chrysanthemums and South Mountain share a similar quality: resistance to time and decay. The chrysanthemum, as a hardy flower that resists the cold and blossoms late into the fall, is thought to have the special power to prolong youthfulness and delay old age. The poet in the poem may be plucking chrysanthemums in order to make chrysanthemum wine; if so, he will use it both as a tonic to restore his vitality and as a stimulant to heighten his perceptions. At the same time, the poet has in mind the chrysanthemum as a symbol for himself, as a man who maintains his principles even in the midst of adversity.

The mountain in Chinese tradition also has a special magic. Mountains serve as a bridge between earth and heaven. They are the abode of hermits and immortals, places where time passes far more slowly than in the dusty world below. They are also the birthplaces of the clouds and of the streams, rain and wind that bring life back to the world in spring. The ancient *Book of Odes* 诗经 includes the phrase: *"Longevity like the Southern Mountain."* For T'ao Ch'ien the Southern Mountain is a source of tremendous vital power, of longevity that defies time and decay. South Mountain also has a further, personal meaning for T'ao Ch'ien. In one of his "Bearer's Songs," or dirges written for himself, he comments that *"In South Mountain I have my old home."* In desiring to be buried on South Mountain, he is thus returning to a source of life far greater than himself.

> At sunset the mountain air is fine,
> 8   And flying birds return together.

The two images of sunset and returning birds both develop the theme of return. Both the sun and the birds are hastening home: the sun to sink behind the mountain, the birds to a comfortable nest. There is an implied comparison with the poet: As he approaches the end of his life, where is he returning to? Homing birds have strong positive connotations, as does the mountain air which the poet feels on his face. As in the two previous poems, the poet enters into a dialogue with nature. He glances at South Mountain, and the mountain replies with a refreshing breeze that touches him and brings the birds home too.

In this there is a true meaning
10 I want to explain but have forgotten the words.

Here the poet presents us with his second paradox: There is a meaning here, but he can't find the words to explain it. For the reader it is a frustrating ending until he realizes that the poet has actually given him several hints. The poet is suggesting that we must forget abstractions such as "true meaning" and search for the wordless meaning "in this"—in the sequence of sensory images just presented. In other words, we're not done with the poem on one reading. We have to reread.

We have come a long way so far in understanding the individual statements and images in this poem. The artichoke has been taken apart and its mystery is gone. Let us now temporarily put this useful metaphor to one side in order to examine another metaphor which suggests how these separate parts can be seen as a whole again.

The poem is a picture surrounded by a frame. The frame, though of little interest in itself, focuses our attention and keeps our eye from straying outside. The picture is a scene of familiar objects: a scholar in his garden with a mountain in the distance. As we look with greater and greater concentration, something strange happens: The scholar bends down to pluck the chrysanthemum, the sun begins to set behind the mountain, a breeze begins to play upon our face. We are standing before an open window.

In this poem, the first four lines and the last two lines are the frame. The central four lines are the window. The first four lines engage the reader's curiosity and draw him into the poem, while the last two lines tease him with the promise of truth and thrust his gaze back into the window to find it. The process of reading is thus cyclical, not linear. The reader enters the poem, reaches the bottom frame, and is thrust back to repeat the cycle until he finds what the poet wants him to look for. The upper and lower borders of the frame are actually verbal paradoxes: How can there be no noise of carts and horses in the world of men? How can you say there is a meaning when you can't express it? Hemmed in by paradoxes in a frame built of verbal abstractions, the reader is compelled to bounce back and forth aimlessly between the borders until he slows down to concentrate on the images. Chung Jung 钟嵘, a Chinese critic of the sixth century, comments appropriately on the process of reading and appreciating poetry:

> Although the text is finished, there is no end to the meaning. . . . Let all those who taste of it never reach satiety, and those who hear it be moved in their hearts.

Within the frame, the language is all of one kind: It is the words of the poet as he is speaking to us. We listen to his voice; we ask a question, and he answers. His words are on a general, abstract level and thus not easily pictured: "in the midst of men," "a distant heart," "true meaning," and so on. This kind of language cannot express truth, but it can draw attention to its own inadequacy through paradox.

Within the window, we no longer hear the poet's voice. Instead, we see and feel. First, we see him bending over to pluck chrysanthemums; there is still a gap between us and the poet. Next, we see South Mountain. Suddenly we are seeing with his eyes, and there is no longer a gap. Though we have identified with the poet in these lines, and lost our own self in the process, there is still a human self expressed through the verbs "pick" [采] and "see" [见] which require a human subject. In the next two lines, however, there is no self at all, only the direct experience of the breeze at sunset and the appreciation of the returning birds. This is the highest level of the poem.

The window also shows us a cycle of movement. First we see the poet close up, picking chrysanthemums. Next we follow his eyes to the distant mountains. Finally we follow the returning birds back to where the poet is standing and feel the breeze on his face. We have also experienced a return, a return which underlines the theme of return implicit throughout the poem—in the poet's return from city life to the country; in the sun's return to the hill; in the birds' return to their nests; and in the suggestion of the poet's eventual return to nature in death. All the other returns have such strong positive connotations that the poet can feel no anxiety about his eventual return to nothingness. Instead we leave him happy with the embrace of the wind, lost in the enjoyment of the only immortality man can have—the immortality of the moment of time made eternal through concentration on the objects of sense.

Within the window, the language is concrete rather than abstract. The chrysanthemum, hedge, mountain, sun and birds are all concrete images, all easily pictured in our minds. Even the verbs "pick" and "see" represent concrete actions. In the last two lines the verbs "fine" [adjectives are verbs in Chinese] and "return" apply directly to the objects of nature. Nature exists and moves without a hint of human presence or perception.

In reading any Chinese poem, native readers and critics are accustomed to look for its best line or couplet and within that line to seek out the most striking word. That word they call the "eye" of the poem [*shih yen* 诗眼], for they conceive of a poem as a living thing, and it is the eye that gives the body life. Always, the "eye" of a poem is a word on which the poem's interpretation hangs. Most often it is a verb, though occasionally adverbs or prepositions substitute; sometimes it is marked by an odd use of syntax. Does T'ao Ch'ien's poem have a best line, and within that line, an "eye"?

Western readers seeing this poem for the first time usually point to the last two lines as the best: *"In this there is a true meaning / I want to explain but have forgotten the words."* This is a good couplet, and it sums up well an experience that is universal. But from what we have said above about the Chinese preference for the sensory image over the abstract statement, we can see that this would not be the couplet chosen by Chinese readers. Indeed, Chinese readers constantly point to the couplet chosen by Wang Kuo-wei above, and particularly to its second line: *"Picking chrysanthemums by the eastern hedge, / Distantly, I see South Mountain."*

The second line of this couplet is singled out because it permits a variety of complementary meanings; one reading or interpretation does not exhaust its possibilities. "Distantly" [*yu jan* 悠然] describes both the mountain and the poet's state of mind. The mountain is far away, but the poet's mind is also far away from the cares of the world and of self. He and the mountain share the same sort of detachment and unconsciousness of self. We have said above that a distant view in earlier poetry usually signals the reader to reflect upon mortality and the meaning of life. Here the act of seeing South Mountain is such a distant view, but it is an act of understanding or insight. The line cleverly emphasizes the suddenness or immediacy of this insight by the contrast between "distantly" [*yu jan*] and "see" [*chien* 见]. The first words suggests separation; the second, closeness. By putting the two words together, it is as if South Mountain itself had jumped suddenly from the distance to right before our eyes. Finally, critics have said that it is significant that T'ao Ch'ien uses the word *chien* "to see" and not the word *wang* [望] "to gaze at" which is more normal in poems about mountains. The latter word implies an emotional yearning and an intentionality that is absent in the neutral word "to see" and if used would have destroyed "the world without a self" that T'ao Ch'ien is creating. The word *chien* "to see" is appropriate precisely because it is necessary for T'ao Ch'ien to see without consciously trying to see, just as later he has to forget words in order to understand the meaning of his experience. For all these reasons, the word *chien* is the "eye" of the poem.

We began by saying that a Chinese poem is like an artichoke. The skilled reader learns to peel away the layers of abstractions, gleaning what he can from them, while always aiming for the heart and the sensuous experience it provides. But in another sense the roles are reversed. The poem operates on us, dismantling our protective shell of intellect, slowing down our constant flow of thought, drawing us gently into an intense world of good sense in which a moment is eternal and the self forgotten. In other words, the poem has eaten us. So the next time you see an artichoke, watch out! It might be a Chinese poem. It might eat you.

Imagination and Make-Believe
■ Gregory Currie ■

We can make a distinction between two kinds of imagining. For imaginings of the first kind, there is an important relation between the imagining and something of which the imagining is what might imperfectly be called a copy, or a counterpart, and in terms of which it seems we have to describe the imagining. But we must not suppose that the imagining need be anything like a replica of this other thing; we should think of it as a copy in the same way that a toy car is a copy of a real car, without it resembling a real car in all or even many respects. A better way to describe the relation would be to say that imagination simulates this other thing, borrowing a term that has recently acquired a special sense in the philosophy of mind. One advantage of this term is that it suggests that the similarities between imagining and what it simulates are similarities of function; we shall see that this is exactly where some of the relevant similarities lie. Imaginings of the second kind are not like this; they are not to be described in terms of something else, which they simulate.

What cases genuinely fall into the first, simulative category is a matter of debate, but obvious candidates would be the modes of mental imagery. Visual imagery is a copy, in our special sense, of visual experience, and it is in terms of visual experience that we must describe that imagery. Imaginings of this simulative kind raise a problem. As Malcolm Budd puts it, "the root of the problem raised by these concepts of the imagination is the nature of their relationship with their apparent counterparts." Understanding this kind of imagination is very largely a matter of understanding this relationship.

We might call this kind of imagination the 'recreative imagination,' not because the imaginative event is always or even usually the literal recreation of some specific actual event, but because it cannot fully be described without reference to the kind of event of which is a copy. I can see in imagination something no one has ever seen or will see, but my act needs to be described in terms of seeing that thing.

The second, nonsimulative, kind of imagining is exemplified when someone puts together ideas in a way which defies expectation or convention: the kind of imaginative 'leap' that leads to the creation of something valuable in art, science or practical life. We may call this the 'creative imagination.' An instance of imagining can belong to both kinds, as when I imagine saying something witty and brilliant. But the recreative imagination need not be creative. People have said that strong

---

"Imagination and Make-Believe" by Gregory Currie has been excerpted from *Routledge Companion to Aesthetics,* Routledge (2000), Berys Gaut and Dominic McIver Lopes, eds., pages 254–256, 258–261, and is reprinted by permission of the publisher.

mental imagery is no proof that the subject is imaginative, a point that we can now put by saying that such a person possesses at least one element of the recreative imagination, but lacks creative imagination.

Both kinds of imagination play an important role in the arts. While the creative imagination is of obvious importance for the production of art works, it can be important for the successful interpretation of complex works as well; symbol and metaphor invite us to create meaning, and to see connections that are far from obvious. The recreative imagination is fundamental to a proper engagement with many art works, particularly where the work has a strong representational content. It is likely also that the recreative imagination subserves the creative imagination of many artists and interpreters, though the exact relations here must be complex, with wide variation between cases. But neither kind of imagining is proprietary to the arts. The recreative imagination has been important for devising thought experiments in science, and hence for creative breakthroughs in scientific theorizing.

The recreative imagination is more amenable to description and analysis than the creative, which [David] Hume understandably called "magical" and "inexplicable." The recreative imagination is also the kind most closely connected with make-believe. So we can afford to devote our attention here to recreative imagination. Unless there is indication to the contrary, that is what I shall mean by 'imagination' hereafter.

That there is an important connection between imagination and representational art has been powerfully argued by Kendall Walton. Walton claims that paintings, plays, films and novels are representational works of art because they are props in games of make-believe; they prompt us to imagine various things. Indeed they are normative with respect to imagining: They authorize certain imaginings and proscribe others, as *The Old Curiosity Shop* authorizes us to imagine that Nell dies, and proscribes our imagining that she lives on into a happy old age. That which a work authorizes us to imagine is what the work makes fictional. Where the work asks us not to imagine something, it makes fictional the negation of that thing, as *The Old Curiosity Shop* makes it fictional that Nell does not live to old age. Where the work does not pronounce one way or the other we are in the realm of the indeterminate, as it is neither fictional that Holmes was born on an even-numbered day of the month, nor fictional that he was not. But indeterminacies need not be trivial; they can be crucial to the work's effect, as it is with Hamlet's motives which, at least in detail, are indeterminate. So now we have explained being fictional (what is sometimes called 'truth in fiction') in terms of imagining.

There are two things worth saying about this proposal. The first is that someone might complain that it is wrong to say that we imagine that Nell dies, when the text plainly says that she does, there is no indication of narrative unreliability in this instance, and the assumption of her death coheres well with the rest of the story. 'Imagining' sounds better in contexts which involve a hermeneutic effort, as when we are struggling to make sense of a story and hit on the idea that the character's motive was so-and-so: Now we can make sense of it, and we do so by imagining something about the character's motive. But this objection confuses the creative and the recreative imagination. Imagining that little Nell dies takes only the latter; imagining that, say, the governess in *The Turn of the Screw* is deluded, would, at least at one time, have required imagination of both kinds. Works of fiction prescribe acts of recreative, and not of creative, imagination.

The second point concerns the claim that we can explain being fictional in terms of imagining. Take the idea that the work makes it fictional that Nell does not live to a ripe old age because it asks us not to imagine that. Arguably, an appropriate (or at least intended) engagement with the work requires one to greet her death with a sense of sorrow and loss; imagining her living to a ripe old age might be a good way of making that loss vivid. It remains true that the work does not prescribe that one imagine her living to old age; no doubt there are appropriate responses to the work that would not involve this. But saying that it is merely optional whether we imagine her living to old age fails to distinguish this case from cases where imagining is optional because it is indeterminate whether the thing to be imagined is part of the story, and Nell's living to a ripe old age is not merely indeterminate so far as the story goes: It is ruled out. It seems that we need to distinguish imagining things as part of the project of imagining what is fictional, and imagining things which are not fictional but the possibility of which informs our response to what is fictional. It is not immediately clear how this can be done in a way that would save the proposed analysis of being fictional in terms of rules of imagining. Perhaps we need to distinguish different 'levels' at which imagining takes place.

We apply the concept fiction to characters as well as to works (to Hamlet as well as to *Hamlet*), and it is not immediately clear how we could account for fictional characters in terms of imagining; to say that fictional characters are imaginary does not explain anything. One response would be to say that the problem is not really a problem about fictional characters. Fictional characters are those that occur in fictions, and they can be real, as Napoleon is a character in *War and Peace*. The problematic cases are where there really is no such person or object as the character in the fiction, as with Pierre Bolkonski. But this problem is not especially a problem about fiction, since we often use terms which appear to be proper names, only to discover that they do not refer to anything, as with 'Vulcan.' So what we need is a semantics for empty names in general, which can then be applied to the case of nonexistent characters in fiction. We should not expect imagination to be useful in solving that problem. . . .

I have said that the recreative imagination is marked by its instances being copies, or counterparts, or simulations of other things. I began by saying that we would focus here on the recreative imagination. But in what sense is imagining the events of a fictional story recreative? What do these imaginings copy or simulate? One answer is that these imaginings are copies of the events which are being imagined and which the story describes. But it is a mistake to think that when I imagine a battle, there is something going on which is a copy of a battle. That mistake leads to the view that mental imagery involves mental pictures of the things imaged, whereas in fact the counterpart of my having a mental image of something is my seeing it, not the thing itself. It also leads to the confused opinion one hears to the effect that while Hamlet does not exist in the real world, he exists 'in the mind.'

In the case of imagery, we said that what is simulated is perceptual experience. But what of the nonimagistic imagining that is going on when I read a novel? The answer is that in such cases our imagining simulates the having of a propositional attitude, and for the time being we can take the attitude of believing to be the case to focus on. So the view being proposed is that there is a kind of imagining which stands to belief as imagery stands to perceptual experience. Indeed, this kind of imagining is often called 'make-believe.' When we 'make as if to believe' something, we do something that is rather like believing it.

That this is so is suggested by the fact that imagining behaves inferentially like belief. If, as part of your engagement with a piece of contemporary fiction, you imagine that a character was in London one day and in Chicago the next, you will also imagine that he flew there, unless there is some strong indication in the work itself that he got there by another means. It will be much more difficult to know what to imagine if this occurs in a Conan Doyle story about Sherlock Holmes; you will probably conclude that there is some mistake of chronology and give up the attempt to match your imagining to this bit of text. In general, we let our imaginings mingle with our beliefs, and further imaginings emerge which, so far as their contents go, are identical with what would emerge from the operation of inference on belief alone. There are occasions where imagination seems to licence inferences that belief would not; one can be much more willing to infer a magical cause within the scope of a fiction than outside it. But when as readers we imagine P, and infer a magical cause for P, this is best explained by supposing that we are operating on the basis of the, perhaps tacit, acceptance of a further, general bit of imagining to the effect that magical causes operate in cases like P. And if we believed that P-events had magical causes, we would make precisely that inference in belief.

There is more to be said about the ways in which imagining copies believing; one further way that will be of significance later is that imagining someone in danger can have some of the affective and emotional consequences that believing they are in danger does. But it is time to consider a contrary proposal: that imagining is really just a species of believing. That would undermine entirely the claim that this kind of imagining is recreative, because it would show that imagining is believing, rather than being a counterpart of believing.

People often say that an engrossing fiction is one we come to believe, and that it is this believing on our part which explains our often intense concern for the story, its character and their fates: a problem to which we shall return. While not many people would argue that imagination is just the same as belief in the strongest or most complete sense, there seems to be support for the idea that imagination is an attenuated kind of belief, a kind of state that occupies one end of a spectrum of belief states. To the objection that few people would go to, or stay in, the theater if they believed that real murders were going to take place there, an attenuated-belief-theorist will respond that arguments like this simply show that imagining is not believing in any of the very demanding senses that philosophers have proposed. For instance, philosophers sometimes say that whether or not one believes that P is a matter of whether one is disposed to act in a way that is appropriate, given that P is true. It is not plausible that we believe fictions in this sense of 'believe.' One the other hand, we might want an account of belief which makes it possible to believe P without being disposed so to act; it might be enough to give sincere verbal assent to P, for example. And then we might be tempted to say that imagining, with its inferential and affective similarity to belief, really is believing in this broader sense. Would it be more than a terminological stipulation to reject this idea?

The similarities between imagining and believing are important, and a significant clue to the nature of imagining, but they are not grounds for classing imagining as a kind of belief, for the following reason. We may well want to take a liberal view of what counts as a belief, but belief, however weakly conceptualized, is normative in the following sense: an agent who has contradictory beliefs (in any sense of belief) is in a less than ideal epistemic situation. Suppose for example that someone has the belief that P, but also has, in some sense or other, the belief that not-P. This latter might be a very marginal case of a belief. Nevertheless, there is something wrong with this agent's epistemic condition; his or her condition would be improved by finding a way to give up either P or not-P, provided that doing so could be motivated by respectable reasons. The agent's situation need not be a desperate one, it is simply not epistemically *ideal.* Also, from other points of view, there might be benefits in being in this state; perhaps people are more interesting when there is some tension in their views. Again this is not the issue; the question is whether the agent's condition is *epistemically* ideal.

This principle does not govern the relations between beliefs, however weak, and imaginings. It is simply no defect in a person's epistemic condition that he or she imagines things contrary to what he or she believes, in any sense of 'believes'; an otherwise consistent and coherent believer who imagines that Desdemona is murdered is not in any way failing to meet constraints of epistemic virtue. In that case we ought to say that, while imagining is like belief in various ways, it is not to be classed with beliefs, even in a weak sense of 'belief.' And given that this is so, we may continue to explore the imagination-as-simulated-belief proposal.

The strength of that theory can really be seen only through its capacity to solve problems. Here is one: the supposed paradox of fiction, that we often care, and care deeply, about the fates of fictional characters when we know that they do not exist and so do not act and suffer. Let us see briefly how this paradox can be resolved.

The problem is that there is an inconsistency in the conjunction of the following three rather plausible propositions:

1. We fear for characters in fictions who are in danger.
2. To fear for someone we must believe they are [sic] in danger.
3. We do not believe in the dangers described in fictions.

(I have stated the paradox in terms of fearing for; it will be see that the paradox arises for a number of other attitudes.) The conjunction of any two of these entails the negation of the remaining one; no one of them alone entails the negation of any other.

Philosophers have taken a variety of positions on this problem. In an influential piece which launched the contemporary debate about fiction and the emotions Colin Radford seems to be taking the view that there are cases where all of (1) to (3) are true, and that this reveals a contradiction or incoherence in our approach to fiction. A number of philosophers have denied (1), some arguing that the real objects of our emotions are not the fictional characters but other things: real people and events ([Peter] McCormick) or real thoughts ([Noël] Carroll, [Peter] Lamarque). These writers seem to accept that we experience fear, but claim that fictional characters are not the objects of our fear. But one might read Carroll and Lamarque instead as saying that unasserted thoughts, rather than beliefs, are required for fear, and hence as denying (2). Others who deny (1) deny that what we experience is genuine fear. Kendall Walton, for example, says that the film viewer does not really fear the slime in the horror movie, though it is fictional that he does. Some philosophers have denied (2), arguing that we can have emotions concerning things we do not believe in.

Someone who adopts the approach to fiction and the imagination outlined here will say that while (3) is true, we can do something like believing in the dangers described in the fiction; we imagine them, and our imaginings are like believings in their internal functional roles. One of the internal function connections of belief is to affect; we are fearful because we know that we are in danger. And imagining, conceived of as simulation of belief, can be expected to have the same effect. It would then be a matter of further decision whether we say that there is a kind of fear which depends not on belief but on imagining (in which case we deny (2)) or whether we say that while we do not fear for characters in fiction we do something very like fearing for them (in which case we deny (1)). The latter option will be favored by the many philosophers and psychologists who hold that emotions are best understood as states which motivate, guide and monitor our actions, since these connections to action are exactly what is lacking in the fictional case. We need not resolve that issue here.

PART VII

PERFORMANCE

In several of his writings, the Greek philosopher Plato expressed serious reservations about the aims and effects of the arts. His dialogue *Ion,* may be the first philosophical work on the performing stage artist. In that text, Plato discusses the peculiar talents of what used to be known as "rhapsodes," that is, people who presented dramatic performances of epic poetry—ancient precursors to today's actors, singers, or stand-up comics. In *Ion,* Plato, through Socrates, argues that in presenting the works of Homer, Ion, the rhapsode, displays only a form of *inspiration,* not real knowledge. He makes the case that Ion is blessed by the gods but "out of his mind" when acting. Because of that, Socrates says, Ion does not know what he is doing and deserves no real credit for his theatrical achievements, award-winning though they be. More generally, Plato believed that the theater was, on the whole, a pernicious institution because of its tendency to stimulate the emotions of its audience and to deviate irresponsibly from a true conception of reality.

In a classic essay on *tragedy,* Plato's student, Aristotle, responds to his teacher's suspicions about at least one form of dramatic art when he attempts to outline the formal features of tragedy. Aristotle suggests that tragedy aims not simply to stimulate the emotions, but to serve as a *catharsis*—or purgation—of them. Aristotle's account of tragedy influenced millennia of generations in their thinking about the topic.

In the nineteenth century, the philosopher Friedrich Nietzsche wrote *The Birth of Tragedy out of the Spirit of Music,* a book, he says, that is "brimming with artists' secrets, its background a metaphysics of art." Nietzsche insists that Greek tragedy had lost much of its former vital powers by the time of the "decadent" period of Socrates and Euripides, partly through the excessive emphasis on rationality. In his view, tragedy once served the human impulse for intoxication and self-forgetfulness. This aesthetic tendency Nietzsche terms "the Dionysian." In order to mollify the terrifying effects of sheer chaos and irrationality, however, tragedy presents human conflict in a dramatically well-structured, and therefore beautiful, way.

This dimension of tragedy Nietzsche terms "the Apollinian" and associates it, physiologically, with the imagery of dreams. Our selection begins with Nietzsche's "A Critical Glance Backwards," written some fifteen years after his original book and published in its 1886 edition, followed by an excerpt from the original 1871 edition.

The famous Viennese psychologist Sigmund Freud, in his seminal discussion of Sophocles and Shakespeare, takes a different but not unrelated tack about the relationship between tragedy and the emotions. The underlying attraction of certain dramatic classics, Freud hypothesizes, is that they appeal to deep-seated but unconscious desires that we nevertheless fear to acknowledge. His argument is carried on in the context of a discussion of his famous theme of the so-called *Oedipal conflict*. For Freud, this psychological conflict provides an answer to a crucial question about Shakespeare's masterpiece *Hamlet*, namely, why the protagonist delays in carrying out the task of revenge assigned him by his father's ghost early in the play.

Music, of course, is another major sphere of performance. In the era of mass media, complicated issues have followed hard on the heels of the development of sophisticated technologies. While "liveness" has been regarded as one of essential features of theatre and music, acoustic and visual recording and transmission devices have radically problematized the assumption that "live" is more authentic. Philip Auslander explores some of the surprising reversals of traditional assumptions about these matters in his contribution to this volume. For instance, he argues that the concept of a *live* performance may not be a fundamental but is rather derivative from the concept of *media*. Consider, for instance, whether we would have called a performance "live" prior to the invention of radio and sound recording.

It may seem odd to consider literature to be an art of performance, until we recall that Homer's epic poems were probably first disseminated in the form of dramatic song. J.O. Urmson divides the arts into those that have an executant or mediating artist, as do the performing arts and those that do not. Urmson makes the case that, in fact, the most natural placement for literature in general is in the category of the performing arts. For Urmson, the physical object, the book, is merely a recipe, or set of instructions for the reader to perform the work in a manner similar to the musical score instructing the various members of an orchestra.

Ion

■ Plato ■

SOCRATES: Welcome, Ion. Are you from your native city of Ephesus?

ION: No, Socrates; but from Epidaurus, where I attended the festival of Asclepius.

SOC: And do the Epidaurians have contests of rhapsodes at the festival?

ION: O yes; and of all sorts of musical performers.

SOC: And were you one of the competitors—and did you succeed?

ION: I obtained the first prize of all, Socrates.

SOC: Well done; and I hope that you will do the same for us at the Panathenaea.

ION: And I will, please heaven.

SOC: I often envy the profession of a rhapsode, Ion; for you have always to wear fine clothes, and to look as beautiful as you can is a part of your art. Then, again, you are obliged to be continually in the company of many good poets; and especially of Homer, who is the best and most divine of them; and to understand him, and not merely learn his words by rote, is a thing greatly to be envied. And no man can be a rhapsode who does not understand the meaning of the poet. For the rhapsode ought to interpret the mind of the poet to his hearers, but how can he interpret him well unless he knows what he means? All this is greatly to be envied.

ION: Very true, Socrates; interpretation has certainly been the most laborious part of my art; and I believe myself able to speak about Homer better than any man; and that neither Metrodorus of Lampsacus, nor Stesimbrotus of Thasos, nor Glaucon, nor any one else who ever was, had as good ideas about Homer as I have, or as many.

SOC: I am glad to hear you say so, Ion; I see that you will not refuse to acquaint me with them.

ION: Certainly, Socrates; and you really ought to hear how exquisitely I render Homer. I think that the Homeridae should give me a golden crown.

SOC: I shall take an opportunity of hearing your embellishments of him at some other time. But just now I should like to ask you a question: Does your art extend to Hesiod and Archilochus, or to Homer only?

ION: To Homer only; he is in himself quite enough.

SOC: Are there any things about which Homer and Hesiod agree?

ION: Yes; in my opinion there are a good many.

SOC: And can you interpret better what Homer says, or what Hesiod says, about these matters in which they agree?

"Ion" by Plato, has been excerpted from *The Dialogues of Plato,* Vol. I, Benjamin Jowett, trans., Random House Inc. (1937), pages 285–297.

318 ■ PART VII PERFORMANCE

ION: I can interpret them equally well, Socrates, where they agree.

SOC: But what about matters in which they do not agree?—for example, about divination, of which both Homer and Hesiod have something to say,—

ION: Very true:

SOC: Would you or a good prophet be a better interpreter of what these two poets say about divination, not only when they agree, but when they disagree?

ION: A prophet.

SOC: And if you were a prophet, would you be able to interpret them when they disagree as well as when they agree?

ION: Clearly.

SOC: But how did you come to have this skill about Homer only, and not about Hesiod or the other poets? Does not Homer speak of the same themes which all other poets handle? Is not war his great argument? and does he not speak of human society and of intercourse of men, good and bad, skilled and unskilled, and of the gods conversing with one another and with mankind, and about what happens in heaven and in the world below, and the generations of gods and heroes? Are not these the themes of which Homer sings?

ION: Very true, Socrates.

SOC: And do not the other poets sing of the same?

ION: Yes, Socrates; but not in the same way as Homer.

SOC: What, in a worse way?

ION: Yes, in a far worse.

SOC: And Homer in a better way?

ION: He is incomparably better.

SOC: And yet surely, my dear friend Ion, in a discussion about arithmetic, where many people are speaking, and one speaks better than the rest, there is somebody who can judge which of them is the good speaker?

ION: Yes.

SOC: And he who judges of the good will be the same as he who judges of the bad speakers?

ION: The same.

SOC: And he will be the arithmetician?

ION: Yes.

SOC: Well, and in discussions about the wholesomeness of food, when many persons are speaking, and one speaks better than the rest, will he who recognizes the better speaker be a different person from him who recognizes the worse, or the same?

ION: Clearly the same.

SOC: And who is he, and what is his name?

ION: The physician.

SOC: And speaking generally, in all discussions in which the subject is the same and many men are speaking, will not he who knows the good know the bad speaker also? For if he does not know the bad, neither will he know the good when the same topic is being discussed.

ION: True.

SOC: Is not the same person skilful in both?

ION: Yes.

SOC: And you say that Homer and the other poets, such as Hesiod and Archilochus, speak of the same things, although not in the same way; but the one speaks well and the other not so well?

ION: Yes; and I am right in saying so.

SOC: And if you knew the good speaker, you would also know the inferior speakers to be inferior?

ION: That is true.

SOC: Then, my dear friend, can I be mistaken in saying that Ion is equally skilled in Homer and in other poets, since he himself acknowledges that the same person will be a good judge of all those who speak of the same things; and that almost all poets do speak of the same things?

ION: Why then, Socrates, do I lose attention and go to sleep and have absolutely no ideas of the least value, when any one speaks of any other poet; but when Homer is mentioned, I wake up at once and am all attention and have plenty to say?

SOC: The reason, my friend, is obvious. No one can fail to see that you speak of Homer without any art of knowledge. If you were able to speak of him by rules of art, you would have been able to speak of all other poets; for poetry is a whole.

ION: Yes.

SOC: And when any one acquires any other art as a whole, the same may be said of them. Would you like me to explain my meaning, Ion?

ION: Yes, indeed, Socrates; I very much wish that you would: for I love to hear you wise men talk. . . .

SOC: I perceive, Ion; and I will proceed to explain to you what I imagine to be the reason of this. The gift which you possess of speaking excellently about Homer is not an art, but, as I was just saying, an inspiration; there is a divinity moving you, like that contained in the stone which Euripides calls a magnet, but which is commonly known as the stone of Heraclea. This stone not only attracts iron rings, but also imparts to them a similar power of attracting other rings; and sometimes you may see a number of pieces of iron and rings suspended from one another so as to form quite a long chain: and all of them derive their power of suspension from the original stone. In like manner the Muse first of all inspires men herself; and from these inspired persons a chain of other persons is suspended, who take the inspiration. For all good poets, epic as well as lyric, compose their beautiful poems not by art, but because they are inspired and possessed. And as the Corybantian revellers when they dance are not in their right mind, so the lyric poets are not in their right mind when they are composing their beautiful strains: but when falling under the power of music and metre they are inspired and possessed; like Bacchic maidens who draw milk and honey from the rivers when they are under the influence of Dionysus but not when they are in their right mind. And the soul of the lyric poet does the same, as they themselves say; for they tell us that they bring songs from honeyed fountains, culling them out of the gardens and dells of the Muses; they, like the bees, winging their way from flower to flower. And this is true. For the poet is a light and winged and holy thing, and there is no invention in him until he has been inspired and is out of his senses, and the mind is no longer in him: when he has not attained to this state, he is powerless and is unable to utter his oracles. Many are the noble words in which poets speak concerning the actions of men; but like yourself when speaking about Homer, they do not speak of them by any rules of art: they are simply inspired to utter that to which the Muse impels them, and that only; and when inspired, one of them will make dithyrambs, another hymns of praise, another choral strains, another epic or iambic verses—and he who is good at one is not good at any other kind of verse: for not by art does the poet sing, but by power divine. Had he learned by rules of art, he would have known how to speak not of one theme only, but of all; and therefore God takes away the minds of poets, and uses them as his ministers, as he also uses diviners and holy prophets, in order that we who hear them may know them to be speaking not of themselves who utter these priceless words in a state of unconsciousness, but that God himself is the speaker, and that through them he is conversing with us. And Tynnichus the Chalcidian afford a striking instance of what I am saying: he wrote nothing that any one would care to remember but the famous paean which is in every one's mouth, one of the finest poems ever written, simply an invention of the Muses, as he himself says. For in this way the God would seem to indicate to us and not allow us to doubt that these beautiful poems are not human, or the work of man, but divine and the work of God; and that the poets are only the interpreters of the Gods by whom they are severally possessed. Was not this the lesson which the God intended to teach when by the mouth of the worst of poets he sang the best of songs? Am I not right, Ion?

ION: Yes, indeed, Socrates, I feel that you are; for your words touch my soul, and I am persuaded that good poets by a divine inspiration interpret the things of the Gods to us.

SOC: And you rhapsodists are the interpreters of the poets?

ION: There again you are right.

SOC: Then you are the interpreters of interpreters?

ION: Precisely.

SOC: I wish you would frankly tell me, Ion, what I am going to ask of you: When you produce the greatest effect upon the audience in the recitation of some striking passage, such as the apparition of Odysseus leaping forth on the floor, recognized by the suitors and casting his arrows at his feet, or the description of Achilles rushing at Hector, or the sorrows of Andromache, Hecuba, or Priam,—are you in your right mind? Are you not carried out of yourself, and does not your soul in an ecstasy seem to be among the persons or places of which you are speaking, whether they are in Ithaca or in Troy or whatever may be the scene of the poem?

ION: That proof strikes home to me, Socrates. For I must frankly confess that at the tale of pity my eyes are filled with tears, and when I speak of horrors, my hair stands on end and my heart throbs.

SOC: Well, Ion, and what are we to say of a man who at a sacrifice or festival, when he is dressed in holiday attire, and has golden crowns upon his head, of which nobody has robbed him, appears weeping or panic-stricken in the presence of more than twenty thousand friendly faces, when there is no one despoiling or wronging him;—is he in his right mind or is he not?

ION: No indeed, Socrates, I must say that, strictly speaking, he is not in his right mind.

SOC: And are you aware that you produce similar effects on most spectators?

ION: Only too well; for I look down upon them from the stage, and behold the various emotions of pity, wonder, sternness, stamped upon their countenances when I am speaking: and I am obliged to give my very best attention to them; for if I make them cry I myself shall laugh, and if I make them laugh I myself shall cry when the time of payment arrives.

SOC: Do you know that the spectator is the last of the rings which, as I am saying, receive the power of the original magnet from one another? The rhapsode like yourself and the actor are intermediate links, and the poet himself is the first of them. Through all these the God sways the souls of men in any direction which he pleases, and makes one man hang down from another. Thus there is a vast chain of dancers and masters and undermasters of choruses, who are suspended, as if from the stone, at the side of the rings which hang down from the Muse. And every poet has some Muse from whom he is suspended, and by whom he is said to be possessed, which is nearly the same thing; for he is taken hold of. And from these first rings, which are the poets, depend others, some deriving their inspiration from Orpheus, others from Musaeus; but the greater number are possessed and held by Homer. Of whom, Ion, you are one, and are possessed by Homer; and when any one repeats the words of another poet you go to sleep, and know not what to say; but when any one recites a strain of Homer you wake up in a moment, and your soul leaps within you, and you have plenty to say; for not by art or knowledge about Homer do you say what you say, but by divine inspiration and by possession; just as the Corybantian revellers too have a quick perception of that strain only which is appropriated to the God by whom they are possessed, and have plenty of dances and words for that, but take no heed of any other. And you, Ion, when the name of Homer is mentioned have plenty to say, and have nothing to say of others. You ask, 'Why is this?' The answer is that you praise Homer not by art but by divine inspiration.

ION: That is good, Socrates; and yet I doubt whether you will ever have eloquence enough to persuade me that I praise Homer only when I am mad and possessed; and if you could hear me speak of him I am sure you would never think this to be the case.

SOC: I should like very much to hear you, but not until you have answered a question which I have to ask. On what part of Homer do you speak well?—not surely about every part.

ION: There is no part, Socrates, about which I do not speak well: of that I can assure you.

SOC: Surely not about things in Homer of which you have no knowledge?

ION: And what is there in Homer of which I have no knowledge?

SOC: Why, does not Homer speak in many passages about arts? For example, about driving; if I can only remember the lines I will repeat them.

ION: I remember, and will repeat them.

SOC: Tell me then, what Nestor says to Antilochus, his son, where he bids him be careful of the turn at the horse-race in honour of Patroclus.

ION: 'Bend gently,' he says, 'in the polished chariot to the left of them, and urge the horse on the right hand with whip and voice; and slacken the rein. And when you are at the goal, let the left horse draw near, yet so that the nave of the well-wrought wheel may not even seem to touch the extremity; and avoid catching the stone.'

SOC: Enough. Now, Ion, will the charioteer or the physician be the better judge of the propriety of these lines?

ION: The charioteer, clearly.

SOC: And will the reason be that this is his art, or will there be any other reason?

ION: No, that will be the reason.

SOC: And every art is appointed by God to have knowledge of a certain work; for that which we know by the art of the pilot we do not know by the art of medicine?

ION: Certainly not.

SOC: Nor do we know by the art of the carpenter that which we know by the art of medicine?

ION: Certainly not.

SOC: And this is true of all the arts;—that which we know with one art we do not know with the other? But let me ask a prior question: You admit that there are differences of arts?

ION: Yes.

SOC: You would argue, as I should, that when one art is of one kind of knowledge and another of another, they are different?

ION: Yes.

Soc: Yes, surely; for if the subject of knowledge were the same, there would be no meaning in saying that the arts were different,—if they both gave the same knowledge. For example, I know that here are five fingers, and you know the same. And if I were to ask whether I and you became acquainted with this fact by the help of the same art of arithmetic, you would acknowledge that we did?

Ion: Yes. . . .

Soc: Yes, Ion, and you are right also. And as I have selected from the Iliad and Odyssee for you passages which describe the office of the prophet and the physician and the fisherman, do you, who know Homer so much better than I do, Ion, select for me passages which relate to the rhapsode and the rhapsode's art, and which the rhapsode ought to examine and judge of better than other men.

Ion: All passages, I should say, Socrates.

Soc: Not all, Ion, surely. Have you already forgotten what you were saying? A rhapsode ought to have a better memory.

Ion: Why, what am I forgetting?

Soc: Do you not remember that you declared the art of the rhapsode to be different from the art of the charioteer?

Ion: Yes, I remember.

Soc: And you admitted that being different they would have different subject of knowledge?

Ion: Yes.

Soc: Then upon your own showing the rhapsode, and the art of the rhapsode, will not know everything?

Ion: I should exclude certain things, Socrates.

Soc: You mean to say that you would exclude pretty much the subjects of the other arts. As he does not know all of them, which of them will he know?

Ion: He will know what a man and what a woman ought to say, and what a freeman and what a slave ought to say, and what a ruler and what a subject.

Soc: Do you mean that a rhapsode will know better than the pilot what the ruler of a sea-tossed vessel ought to say?

Ion: No; the pilot will know best. . . .

Soc: And in judging of the general's art, do you judge of it as a general or a rhapsode?

Ion: To me there appears to be no difference between them.

Soc: What do you mean? Do you mean to say that the art of the rhapsode and of the general is the same?

Ion: Yes, one and the same.

Soc: Then he who is a good rhapsode is also a good general?

Ion: Certainly, Socrates.

Soc: And he who is a good general is also a good rhapsode?

Ion: No; I do not say that.

SOC: But you do say that he who is a good rhapsode is also a good general.

ION: Certainly.

SOC: And you are the best of Hellenic rhapsodes?

ION: Far the best, Socrates.

SOC: And are you the best general, Ion?

ION: To be sure, Socrates; and Homer was my master.

SOC: But then, Ion, what in the name of goodness can be the reason why you, who are the best of generals as well as the best of rhapsodes in all Hellas, go about as a rhapsode when you might be a general? Do you think that the Hellenes want a rhapsode with his golden crown, and do not want a general?

ION: Why, Socrates, the reason is, that my countrymen, the Ephesians, are the servants and soldiers of Athens, and do not need a general; and you and Sparta are not likely to have me, for you think that you have enough generals of your own.

SOC: My good Ion, did you never hear of Apollodorus of Cyzicus?

ION: Who may he be?

SOC: One who, though a foreigner, has often been chosen their general by the Athenians: and there is Phanosthenes of Andros, and Heraclides of Clazomenae, whom they have also appointed to the command of their armies and to other offices, although aliens, after they had shown their merit. And will they not choose Ion the Ephesian to be their general, and honour him, if he prove himself worthy? Were not the Ephesians originally Athenians, and Ephesus is no mean city? But, indeed, Ion, if you are correct in saying that by art and knowledge you are able to praise Homer, you do not deal fairly with me, and after all your professions of knowing many glorious things about Homer, and promises that you would exhibit them, you are only a deceiver, and so far from exhibiting the art of which you are a master, will not, even after my repeated entreaties, explain to me the nature of it. You have literally as many forms as Proteus; and now you go all manner of ways, twisting and turning, and, like Proteus, become all manner of people at once, and at last slip away from me in the disguise of a general, in order that you may escape exhibiting your Homeric lore. And if you have art, then, as I was saying, in falsifying your promise that you would exhibit Homer, you are not dealing fairly with me. But if, as I believe, you have no art, but speak all these beautiful words about Homer unconsciously under his inspiring influence, then I acquit you of dishonesty, and shall only say that you are inspired. Which do you prefer to be thought, dishonest or inspired?

ION: There is a great difference, Socrates, between the two alternatives; and inspiration is by far the nobler.

SOC: Then, Ion, I shall assume the nobler alternative; and attribute to you in your praises of Homer inspiration, and not art.

On Tragedy

■ Aristotle ■

Tragedy . . . is an imitation of an action that is serious, complete, and of a certain magnitude; in language embellished with each kind of artistic ornament, the several kinds being found in separate parts of the play; in the form of action, not of narrative; with incidents arousing pity and fear, wherewith to accomplish its katharsis of such emotions. By "language embellished," I mean language into which rhythm, "harmony," and song enter. By "the several kinds in separate parts," I mean that some parts are rendered through the medium of verse alone, others again with the aid of song.

Now as tragic imitation implies persons acting, it necessarily follows, in the first place, that Spectacular equipment will be a part of Tragedy. Next, Song and Diction, for these are the media of imitation. By Diction, I mean the mere metrical arrangement of the words; as for "Song," it is a term whose sense everyone understands.

Again, Tragedy is the imitation of an action; and an action implies personal agents who necessarily possess certain distinctive qualities both of character and thought; for it is by these what we qualify actions themselves, and these—thought and character—are the two natural causes from which actions spring, and on actions again all success or failure depends. Hence the Plot is the imitation of the action—for by Plot I here mean the arrangement of the incidents. By Character, I mean that in virtue of which we ascribe certain qualities to the agents. Thought is required wherever a statement is proved or, it may be, a general truth enunciated. Every Tragedy, therefore, must have six parts, which parts determine its quality—namely, Plot, Characters, Diction, Thought, Spectacle, Melody. Two of the parts constitute the medium of imitation, one the manner, and three the objects of imitation. And these complete the list. These elements have been employed, we may say, by the poets to a man; in fact, every play contains Spectacular elements as well as Character, Plot, Diction, Melody, and Thought.

But most important of all is the structure of the incidents. For Tragedy is an imitation, not of men, but of action and of life, and life consists in action, and its end is a mode of action, not a quality. Now character determines men's qualities, but it is by their actions that they are happy or the reverse. Dramatic action, therefore, is not with a view to the representation of character: Character comes in as subsidiary to the actions. Hence the incidents and the plot are the end of a tragedy;

"On Tragedy" by Aristotle has been excerpted from "De Poetica" in *The Student's Oxford Aristotle,* Vol. VI, W. D. Ross, trans., Oxford University Press (1942), pp. 1449b–1451a, and is reprinted by permission of the publisher.

and the end is the chief thing of all. Again, without action there cannot be a tragedy; there may be without character. The tragedies of most of our modern poets fail in the rendering of character; and of poets in general this is often true. It is the same in painting; and here lies the difference between Zeuxis and Polygnotus. Polygnotus delineates character well; the style of Zeuxis is devoid of ethical quality. Again, if you string together a set of speeches expressive of character, and well finished in point of diction and thought, you will not produce the essential tragic effect nearly so well as with a play, which, however deficient in these respects, yet has a plot and artistically constructed incidents. Besides which the most powerful elements of emotional interest in Tragedy—*peripeteia* or "reversal of the situation," and "recognition" scenes—are parts of the plot. A further proof is that novices in the art attain to finish of diction and precision of portraiture before they can construct the plot. It is the same with almost all the early poets.

The Plot, then, is the first principle and, as it were, the soul of a tragedy; Character holds the second place. A similar fact is seen in painting. The most beautiful colors, laid on confusedly, will not give as much pleasure as the chalk outline of a portrait. Thus Tragedy is the imitation of an action, and of the agents mainly with a view to the action.

Third in order is Thought—that is, the faculty of saying what is possible and pertinent in given circumstances. In the case of oratory, this is the function of the political art and of the art of rhetoric; and so indeed the older poets make their characters speak the language of civic life; the poets of our time, the language of the rhetoricians. Character is that which reveals moral purpose, showing what kind of things a man chooses or avoids. Speeches, therefore, which do not make this manifest, or in which the speaker does not choose or avoid anything whatever, are not expressive of character. Thought, on the other hand, is found where something is proved to be or not to be, or a general maxim is enunciated.

Fourth among the elements enumerated comes Diction—by which I mean, as has been already said, the expression of the meaning in words, and its essence is the same both in verse and prose.

Of the remaining elements, Melody holds the chief place among the embellishments.

The Spectacle has, indeed, an emotional attraction of its own, but, of all the parts, it is the least artistic and connected least with the art of poetry. For the power of Tragedy, we may be sure, is felt even apart from representation and actors. Besides, the production of spectacular effects depends more on the art of the stage machinist than on that of the poet.

These principles being established, let us now discuss the proper structure of the Plot, since this is the first and most important thing in Tragedy.

Now, according to our definition, Tragedy is an imitation of an action that is complete and whole and of a certain magnitude; for there may be a whole that is wanting in magnitude. A whole is that which has a beginning, a middle, and an end. A beginning is that which does not itself follow anything by causal necessity, but after which something naturally is or comes to be. An end, on the contrary, is that which itself naturally follows some other thing, either by necessity or as a rule, but has nothing following it. A middle is that which follows something as some other thing follows it. A well-constructed plot, therefore, must neither begin nor end at haphazard but conform to these principles.

Again, a beautiful object, whether it be a living organism or any whole composed of parts, must not only have an orderly arrangement of parts, but must also be of a certain magnitude; for beauty depends on magnitude and order. Hence a very small animal organism cannot be beautiful, for the view of it is confused, the object being seen in an almost imperceptible moment of time. Nor, again, can one of vast size be beautiful; for as the eye cannot take it all in at once, the unity and sense of the whole is lost for the spectator, as, for instance, if there were one a thousand miles long. As, therefore, in the case of animate bodies and organisms a certain magnitude is necessary, and a magnitude which may be easily embraced in one view, so in the plot a certain length is necessary, and a length which can be easily embraced by the memory. The limit of length in relation to dramatic competition and sensuous presentment is no part of artistic theory. For had it been the rule for a hundred tragedies to compete together, the performance would have been regulated by the waterclock—as indeed we are told was formerly done. But the limit as fixed by the nature of the drama itself is this: the greater the length, the more beautiful will the piece be by reason of its size, provided that the whole be perspicuous. And to define the matter roughly, we may say that the proper magnitude is comprised within such limits that the sequence of events, according to the law of probability or necessity, will admit of a change from bad fortune to good, or from good fortune to bad.

The Birth of Tragedy
■ Friedrich Nietzsche ■

A Critical Backward Glance

What meaning did the tragic myth have for the Greeks during the period of their greatest power and courage? And what of the Dionysiac spirit, so tremendous in its implications? What of the tragedy that grew out of that spirit?

Or one might look at it the other way round. Those agencies that had proved fatal to tragedy: Socratic ethics, dialectics, the temperance and cheerfulness of the

"The Birth of Tragedy" by Friedrich Nietzsche, has been excerpted from *The Birth of Tragedy*, Francis Golffing, trans., Doubleday (1956), pages 3–11, 19–29, 32–35 and reprinted by permission of the publisher.

pure scholar—couldn't these, rather than their opposites, be viewed as symptoms of decline, fatigue, distemper, of instincts caught in anarchic dissolution? Or the "Greek serenity" of the later period as, simply, the glow of a sun about to set? Or the Epicurean animus against pessimism merely as the sort of precaution a suffering man might use? And as for "disinterested inquiry," so-called: what, in the last analysis, did inquiry come to when judged as a symptom of the life process? What were we to say of the end (or, worse, of the beginning) of all inquiry? Might it be that the "inquiring mind" was simply the human mind terrified by pessimism and trying to escape from it, a clever bulwark erected against the truth? Something craven and false, if one wanted to be moral about it? Or, if one preferred to put it amorally, a dodge? Had this perhaps been your secret, great Socrates? Most secretive of ironists, had *this* been your deepest irony? . . .

Built from precocious, purely personal insights, all but incommunicable; conceived in terms of *art* (for the issue of scholarly inquiry cannot be argued on its own terms), this book addressed itself to artists or, rather, to artists with analytical and retrospective leanings: to a special kind of artist who is far to seek and possibly not worth the seeking. It was a book novel in its psychology, brimming with artists' secrets, its background a metaphysics of art; the work of a young man, written with the unstinted courage and melancholy of youth, defiantly independent even in those places where the author was paying homage to revered models. In short, a "first book," also in the worst sense of that term, and one that exhibited, for all the hoariness of its topic, every conceivable fault of adolescence. It was terribly diffuse and full of unpalatable ferment. All the same, if one examines its impact it may certainly be said to have *proved* itself—in the eyes of the few contemporaries who mattered and most signally in the eyes of that great artist, Richard Wagner, whom it addressed as in a dialogue. . . .

How, then, are we to define the "Dionysiac spirit"? In my book I answered that question with the authority of the adept or disciple. Talking of the matter today, I would doubtless use more discretion and less eloquence; the origin of Greek tragedy is both too tough and too subtle an issue to wax eloquent over. One of the cardinal questions here is that of the Greek attitude to pain. What kind of sensibility did these people have? Was that sensibility constant, or did it change from generation to generation? Should we attribute the ever increasing desire of the Greeks for beauty, in the form of banquets, ritual ceremonies, new cults, to some fundamental *lack*—a melancholy disposition perhaps or an obsession with pain? If this interpretation is correct—there are several suggestions in Pericles' (or Thucydides') great funeral oration which seem to bear it out—how are we to explain the Greek desire, both prior and contrary to the first, for ugliness, or the strict commitment of the earlier Greeks to a pessimistic doctrine? Or their commitment to the tragic myth, image of all that is awful, evil, perplexing, destructive, ominous in human existence? What, in short, made the Greek mind turn to tragedy? A sense of euphoria maybe—sheer exuberance, reckless health, and power? But in that case, what is the significance, physiologically speaking, of that Dionysiac frenzy which gave rise to tragedy and comedy alike? Can frenzy be viewed as something that is *not* a symptom of decay, disorder, overripeness? Is there such a thing—let alienists answer that question—as a neurosis arising from *health,* from the youthful condition of the race? What does the union of god and goat, expressed in the figure of the satyr, really mean? What was it that prompted the Greeks to embody the Dionysiac reveler—primary man—in a shape like that? Turning next to the origin of the tragic chorus: Did those days of superb somatic and psychological health give rise, perhaps, to endemic trances, collective visions, and hallucinations? And are not these the same Greeks who, signally in the early periods, gave every evidence of possessing tragic vision: a will to tragedy, profound pessimism? Was it not Plato who credited frenzy with all the superlative blessings of Greece? Contrariwise, was it not precisely during their period of dissolution and weakness that the Greeks turned to optimism, frivolity, histrionics; that they grew at once "gayer" and "more scientific"? Why, is it possible to assume—in the face of all the up-to-date notions on that subject, in defiance of all the known prejudices of our democratic age—that the great optimist-rationalist-utilitarian victory, together with democracy, its political contemporary, was at the bottom nothing other than a symptom of declining strength, approaching senility, somatic exhaustion—*it,* and not its opposite, pessimism? Could it be that Epicurus was an optimist—precisely because he suffered? . . .

The reader can see now what a heavy pack of questions this book was forced to carry. Let me add here the heaviest question of all, What kind of figure does ethics cut once we decide to view it in the biological perspective?

In the preface I addressed to Richard Wagner I claimed that art, rather than ethics, constituted the essential metaphysical activity of man, while in the body of the book I made several suggestive statements to the effect that existence could be justified only in esthetic terms. As a matter of fact, throughout the book I attributed a purely esthetic meaning—whether implied or overt—to all process: a kind of divinity if you like, God as the supreme artist, amoral, recklessly creating and destroying, realizing himself indifferently in whatever he does or undoes, ridding himself by his acts of the embarrassment of his riches and the strain of his internal contradictions. Thus the world was made to appear, at every instant, as a successful *solution* of God's own tensions, as an ever new vision projected by that grand redemption. That whole esthetic metaphysics might be rejected out of hand as so much prattle or rant. Yet in its essential traits it already prefigured that spirit of deep distrust and defiance which, later on, was to resist to the bitter end any moral interpretation of existence whatsoever. It is here that one could find—perhaps for the first time in history—a pessimism situated "beyond good and evil"; a "perversity of stance" of the kind [Arthur] Schopenhauer spent all his life fulminating against; a philosophy which dared place ethics among the phenomena (and so "demote" it)—or, rather, place it not even among the phenomena in the idealistic sense but among the "deceptions." Morality, on this view, became a mere fabrication for purposes of gulling: at best, an artistic fiction; at worst, an outrageous imposture.

The depth of this anti-moral bias may best be gauged by noting the wary and hostile silence I observed on the subject of Christianity—Christianity being the most extravagant set of variations ever produced on the theme of ethics. No doubt, the purely esthetic interpretation and justification of the world I was propounding in those pages placed them at the opposite pole from Christian doctrine, a doctrine entirely moral in purport, using absolute standards: God's absolute truth, for example, which relegates all art to the realm of falsehood and in so doing condemns it. I had always sensed strongly the furious, vindictive hatred of life implicit in that system of ideas and values; and sensed, too, that in order to be consistent with its premises a system of this sort was forced to abominate art. For both art and life depend wholly on the laws of optics, on perspective and illusion; both, to be blunt, depend on the necessity of error. From the very first, Christianity spelled life loathing itself, and that loathing was simply disguised, tricked out, with notions of an "other" and "better" life. A hatred of the "world," a curse on the affective urges, a fear of beauty and sensuality, a transcendence rigged up to slander mortal existence, a yearning for extinction, cessation of all effort until the great "sabbath of sabbaths"—this whole cluster of distortions, together with the intransigent Christian assertion that nothing counts except moral values, had always struck me as being the most dangerous, most sinister form the will to destruction can take; at all events, as a sign of profound sickness, moroseness, exhaustion, biological etiolation. And since according to ethics (specifically Christian, absolute ethics) life will *always* be in the wrong, it followed quite naturally that one must smother it under a load of contempt and constant negation; must view it as an object not only unworthy of our desire but absolutely worthless in itself.

As for morality, on the other hand, could it be anything but a will to deny life, a secret instinct of destruction, a principle of calumny, a reductive agent—the beginning of the end?—and, for that very reason, the Supreme Danger? Thus it happened that in those days, with this problem book, my vital instincts turned against ethics and founded a radical counterdoctrine, slanted esthetically, to oppose the Christian libel on life. But it still wanted a name. Being a philologist, that is to say a man of *words,* I christened it rather arbitrarily—for who can tell the real name of the Antichrist?—with the name of a Greek god, Dionysos. . . .

Apollo and Dionysos

Much will have been gained for esthetics once we have succeeded in apprehending directly—rather than merely *ascertaining*—that art owes its continuous evolution to the Apollonian-Dionysiac duality, even as the propagation of the species depends on the duality of the sexes, their constant conflict and periodic acts of reconciliation. I have borrowed my adjectives from the Greeks, who developed their mystical doctrines of art through plausible *embodiments,* not through purely conceptual means. It is by those two art-sponsoring deities, Apollo and Dionysos, that we are made to recognize the tremendous split, as regards both origins and objectives, between the plastic, Apollonian arts and the non-visual art of music inspired by Dionysos. The two creative tendencies developed alongside one another, usually in fierce opposition, each by its taunts forcing the other to more energetic production, both perpetuating in a discordant concord that *agon* which the term *art* but feebly denominates: until at last, by the thaumaturgy of an Hellenic act of will, the pair accepted the yoke of marriage and, in this condition, begot Attic tragedy, which exhibits the salient features of both parents.

To reach a closer understanding of both these tendencies, let us begin by viewing them as the separate art realms of *dream* and *intoxication,* two physiological phenomena standing toward one another in much the same relationship as the Apollonian and Dionysiac. It was in a dream, according to Lucretius, that the marvelous gods and goddesses first presented themselves to the minds of men. That great sculptor, Phidias, beheld in a dream the entrancing bodies of more-than-human beings, and likewise, if anyone had asked the Greek poets about the mystery of poetic creation, they too would have referred him to dreams and instructed him much as Hans Sachs instructs us in [Wagner's] *Die Meistersinger:*

> *My friend, it is the poet's work*
> *Dreams to interpret and to mark.*
> *Believe me that man's true conceit*
> *In a dream becomes complete:*
> *All poetry we ever read*
> *Is but true dreams interpreted.*

The fair illusion of the dream sphere, in the production of which every man proves himself an accomplished artist, is a precondition not only of all plastic art, but even, as we shall see presently, of a wide range of poetry. Here we enjoy an immediate apprehension of form, all shapes speak to us directly, nothing seems indifferent or redundant. Despite the high intensity with which these dream realities exist for us, we still have a residual sensation that they are illusions; at least such has been my experience—and the frequency, not to say normality, of the experience is borne out in many passages of the poets. Men of philosophical disposition are known for their constant premonition that our everyday reality, too, is an illusion, hiding another, totally different kind of reality. It was Schopenhauer who considered the ability to view at certain times all men and things as mere phantoms or dream images to be the true mark of philosophic talent. The person who is responsive to the stimuli of art behaves toward the reality of dream much the way the philosopher behaves toward the reality of existence: He observes exactly and enjoys his observations, for it is by these images that he interprets life, by these processes that he rehearses it. Nor is it by pleasant images only that such plausible connections are made: The whole divine comedy of life, including its somber aspects, its sudden balkings, impish accidents, anxious expectations, moves past him, not quite like a shadow play—for it is he himself, after all, who lives and suffers through these scenes—yet never without giving a fleeting sense of illusion; and I imagine that many persons have reassured themselves amidst the perils of dream by calling out, "It is a dream! I want it to go on." I have even heard of people spinning out the causality of one and the same dream over three or more successive nights. All these facts clearly bear witness that our innermost being, the common substratum of humanity, experiences dreams with deep delight and a sense of real necessity. This deep and happy sense of the necessity of dream experiences was expressed by the Greeks in the image of Apollo. Apollo is at once the god of all plastic powers and the soothsaying god. He who is etymologically the "lucent" one, the god of light, reigns also over the fair illusion of our inner world of fantasy. The perfection of these conditions in contrast to our imperfectly understood waking reality, as well as our profound awareness of nature's healing powers during the interval of sleep and dream, furnishes a symbolic analogue to the soothsaying faculty and quite generally to the arts, which make life possible and worth living. But the image of Apollo must incorporate that thin line which the dream image may not cross, under penalty of becoming pathological, of imposing itself on us as crass reality: a discreet limitation, a freedom from all extravagant urges, the sapient tranquillity of the plastic god. His eye must be sunlike, in keeping with his origin. Even at those moments when he is angry and ill-tempered there lies upon him the consecration of fair illusion. In an eccentric way one might say of Apollo what Schopenhauer says, in the first part of *The World as Will and Idea,* of man caught in the veil of Maya: "Even as on an immense, raging sea, assailed by huge wave crests, a man sits in a little rowboat trusting his frail craft, so, amidst the furious torments of this world, the individual sits tranquilly, supported by the *principium individuationis* and relying on it." One might say that the unshakable confidence in that principle has received its most magnificent expression in Apollo, and that Apollo himself may be regarded as the marvelous divine image of the *principium individuationis,* whose looks and gestures radiate the full delight, wisdom, and beauty of "illusion."

In the same context Schopenhauer has described for us the tremendous awe which seizes man when he suddenly begins to doubt the cognitive modes of experience, in other words, when in a given instance the law of causation seems to suspend itself. If we add to this awe the glorious transport which arises in man, even from the very depths of nature, at the shattering of the *principium individuationis,* then we are in a position to apprehend the essence of Dionysiac rapture, whose closest analogy is furnished by physical intoxication. Dionysiac stirrings arise either through the influence of those narcotic potions of which all primitive races speak in their hymns, or through the powerful approach of spring, which penetrates with joy the whole frame of nature. So stirred, the individual forgets himself completely. It is the same Dionysiac power which in medieval Germany drove ever increasing crowds of people singing and dancing from place to place; we recognize in these St. John's and St. Vitus' dancers the bacchic choruses of the Greeks, who had their precursors in Asia Minor and as far back as Babylon and the orgiastic Sacaea. There are people who, either from lack of experience or out of sheer stupidity, turn away from such phenomena, and, strong in the sense of their own sanity, label them either mockingly or pityingly "endemic diseases." These benighted souls have no idea how cadaverous and ghostly their "sanity" appears as the intense throng of Dionysiac revelers sweeps past them.

Not only does the bond between man and man come to be forged once more by the magic of the Dionysiac rite, but nature itself, long alienated or subjugated rises again to celebrate the reconciliation with her prodigal son, man. . . . Now the slave emerges as a freeman; all the rigid, hostile walls which either necessity or despotism has erected between men are shattered. Now that the gospel of universal harmony is sounded, each individual becomes not only reconciled to this fellow but actually at one with him—as though the veil of Maya had been torn apart and there remained only shreds floating before the vision of mystical Oneness. Man now expresses himself through song and dance as the member of a higher community; he has forgotten how to walk, how to speak, and is on the brink of taking wing as he dances. Each of his gestures betokens enchantment; through him sounds a supernatural power, the same power which makes the animals speak and the earth render up milk and honey. He feels himself to be godlike and strides with the same elation and ecstasy as the gods he has seen in his dreams. No longer the *artist,* he has himself become a *work of art:* The productive power of the whole universe is now manifest in his transport, to the glorious satisfaction of the primordial One. The finest clay, the most precious marble—man—is here kneaded and hewn, and the chisel blows of the Dionysiac world artist are accompanied by the cry of the Eleusinian mystagogues: "Do you fall on your knees multitudes, do you divine your creator?"

So far we have examined the Apollonian and Dionysiac states as the product of formative force arising directly from nature without the mediation of the human artist. At this stage artistic urges are satisfied directly, on the one hand through the imagery of dreams, whose perfection is quite independent of the intellectual rank, the artistic development of the individual; on the other hand, through an ecstatic reality which once again takes no account of the individual and may even destroy him, or else redeem him through a mystical experience of the collective. In relation to these immediate creative conditions of nature every artist must appear as "imitator," either as the Apollonian dream artist or the Dionysiac ecstatic artist, or, finally (as in Greek tragedy, for example) as dream and ecstatic artist in one. We might picture to ourselves how the last of these, in a state of Dionysiac intoxication and mystical self-abrogation, wandering apart from the reveling throng, sinks upon the ground, and how there is then revealed to him his own condition—complete oneness with the essence of the universe—in a dream similitude.

Having set down these general premises and distinctions, we now turn to the Greeks in order to realize to what degree the formative forces of nature were developed in them. Such an inquiry will enable us to assess properly the relation of the Greek artist to his prototypes or, to use Aristotle's expression, his "imitation of nature." Of the dreams the Greeks dreamed it is not possible to speak with any certainty, despite the extant dream literature and the large number of dream anecdotes. But considering the incredible accuracy of their eyes, their keen and unabashed delight in colors, one can hardly be wrong in assuming that their dreams too showed a strict consequence of lines and contours, hues and groupings, a progression of scenes similar to their best bas-reliefs. The perfection of these dream scenes might almost tempt us to consider the dreaming Greek as a Homer and Homer as a dreaming Greek; which would be as though the modern man were to compare himself in his dreaming to Shakespeare.

Yet there is another point about which we do not have to conjecture at all: I mean the profound gap separating the Dionysiac Greeks from the Dionysiac barbarians. Throughout the range of ancient civilization (leaving the newer civilizations out of account for the moment) we find evidence of Dionysiac celebrations which stand to the Greek type in much the same relation as the bearded satyr, whose name and attributes are derived from the hegoat, stands to the god Dionysos. The central concern of such celebrations was, almost universally, a complete sexual promiscuity overriding every form of established tribal law; all the savage urges of the mind were unleashed on those occasions until they reached that paroxysm of lust and cruelty which has always struck me as the "witches' cauldron" *par excellence.* It would appear that the Greeks were for a while quite immune from these feverish excesses which must have reached them by every known land or sea route. What kept Greece safe was the proud, imposing image of Apollo, who in holding up the head of the Gorgon to those brutal and grotesque Dionysiac forces subdued them. Doric art has immortalized Apollo's majestic rejection of all license. But resistance became difficult, even impossible, as soon as similar urges began to break forth from the deep substratum of Hellenism itself. Soon the function of the Delphic god developed into something quite different and much more limited: All he could hope to accomplish now was to wrest the destructive weapon, by a timely gesture of pacification, from his opponent's hand. That act of pacification represents the most important event in the history of Greek ritual; every department of life now shows symptoms of a revolutionary change. The two great antagonists have been reconciled. Each feels obliged henceforth to keep to his bounds, each will honor the other by the bestowal of periodic gifts, while the cleavage remains fundamentally the same. And yet, if we examine what happened to the Dionysiac powers under the pressure of that treaty we notice a great difference: in the place of the Babylonian Sacaea, with their throwback of men to the condition of apes and tigers, we now see entirely new rites celebrated: rites of universal redemption, of glorious transfiguration. Only now has it become possible to speak of nature's celebrating an *esthetic* triumph; only now has the abrogation of the *principium individuationis* become an esthetic event. That terrible witches' brew concocted of lust and cruelty has lost all power under the new conditions. Yet the peculiar blending of emotions in the heart of the Dionysiac reveler—his ambiguity if you will—seems still to hark back (as the medicinal drug harks back to the deadly poison) to the days when the infliction of pain was experienced as joy while a sense of supreme triumph elicited cries of anguish from the heart. For now in every exuberant joy there is heard an undertone of terror, or else a wistful lament over an irrecoverable loss. It is as though in these Greek festivals a sentimental trait of nature were coming to the fore, as though nature were bemoaning the fact of her fragmentation, her decomposition into separate individuals. The chants and gestures of these revelers, so ambiguous in their motivation, represented an absolute *novum* in the world of the Homeric Greeks; their Dionysiac music, in especial, spread abroad terror and a deep shudder. It is true: Music had long been familiar to the Greeks as an Apollonian art, as a regular beat like that of waves lapping the shore, a plastic rhythm expressly developed for the portrayal of Apollonian conditions. Apollo's music was a Doric architecture of sound—of barely hinted sounds such as are proper to the cithara. Those very elements which characterize Dionysiac music and, after it, music quite generally: the heart-shaking power of tone, the uniform stream of melody, the incomparable resources of harmony—all those elements had been carefully kept at a distance as being inconsonant with the Apollonian norm. In the Dionysiac dithyramb man is incited to strain his symbolic faculties to the utmost; something quite unheard of is now clamoring to be heard: the desire to tear asunder the veil of Maya, to sink back into the original oneness of nature; the desire to express the very essence of nature symbolically. Thus an entirely new set of symbols springs into being. First, all the symbols pertaining to physical features: mouth, face, the spoken word, the dance movement which coordinates the limbs and bends them to its rhythm. Then suddenly all the rest of the symbolic forces—music and rhythm as such, dynamics, harmony—assert themselves with great energy. In order to comprehend this total emancipation of all the symbolic powers one must have reached the same measure of inner freedom those powers themselves were making manifest; which is to say that the votary of Dionysos could not be understood except by his own kind. It is not difficult to imagine the awed surprise with which the Apollonian Greek must have looked on him. And that surprise would be further increased as the latter realized, with a shudder, that all this was not so alien to him after all, that his Apollonian consciousness was but a thin veil hiding from him the whole Dionysiac realm.

In order to comprehend this we must take down the elaborate edifice of Apollonian culture stone by stone until we discover its foundations. At first the eye is struck by the marvelous shapes of the Olympian gods who stand upon its pediments, and whose exploits, in shining bas-relief, adorn its friezes. The fact that among them we find Apollo as one god among many, making no claim to a privileged position, should not mislead us. The same drive that found its most complete representation in Apollo generated the whole Olympian world, and in this sense we may consider Apollo the father of that world. But what was the radical need out of which that illustrious society of Olympian beings sprang?

Whoever approaches the Olympians with a different religion in his heart, seeking moral elevation, sanctity, spirituality, loving-kindness, will presently be forced to turn away from them in ill-humored disappointment. Nothing in these deities reminds us of asceticism, high intellect, or duty: We are confronted by luxuriant, triumphant *existence,* which deifies the good and the bad indifferently. And the beholder may find himself dismayed in the presence of such overflowing life and ask himself what potion these heady people must have drunk in order to behold, in whatever direction they looked, Helen laughing back at them, the beguiling image of their own existence. But we shall call out to this beholder, who has already turned his back: Don't go! Listen first to what the Greeks themselves have to say of this life, which spreads itself before you with such puzzling serenity. An old legend has it that King Midas hunted a long time in the woods for the wise Silenus, companion of Dionysos, without being able to catch him. When he had finally caught him the king asked him what he considered man's greatest good. The dae- mon remained sullen and uncommunicative until finally, forced by the king, he broke into a shrill laugh and spoke: "Ephemeral wretch, begotten by accident and toil, why do you force me to tell you what it would be your greatest boon not to hear? What would be best for you is quite beyond your reach: not to have been born, not to *be,* to be *nothing*. But the second best is to die soon." . . .

We can learn something about that naïve artist through the analogy of dream. We can imagine the dreamer as he calls out to himself, still caught in the illusion of his dream and without disturbing it, "This is a dream, and I want to go on dream- ing," and we can infer, on the one hand, that he takes deep delight in the contempla- tion of his dream, and, on the other, that he must have forgotten the day, with its horrible importunity, so to enjoy his dream. Apollo, the interpreter of dreams, will furnish the clue to what is happening here. Although of the two halves of life—the waking and the dreaming—the former is generally considered not only the more important but the only one which is truly lived, I would, at the risk of sounding paradoxical, propose the opposite view. The more I have come to realize in nature those omnipotent formative tendencies and, with them, an intense longing for illu- sion, the more I feel inclined to the hypothesis that the original Oneness, the ground of Being, ever-suffering and contradictory, time and again has need of rapt vision and delightful illusion to redeem itself. Since we ourselves are the very stuff of such illusions, we must view ourselves as the truly non-existent, that is to say, as a perpetual unfolding in time, space, and causality—what we label "empiric real- ity." But if, for the moment, we abstract from our own reality, viewing our empiric existence, as well as the existence of the world at large, as the *idea* of the original Oneness, produced anew each instant, then our dreams will appear to us as illu- sions of illusions, hence as a still higher form of satisfaction of the original desire for illusion. It is for this reason that the very core of nature takes such a deep de- light in the naïve artist and the naïve work of art, which likewise is merely the illu- sion of an illusion. Raphael, himself one of those immortal "naïve" artists, in a symbolic canvas has illustrated that reduction of illusion to further illusion which is the original act of the naïve artist and at the same time of all Apollonian culture. In the lower half of his "Transfiguration," through the figures of the possessed boy, the despairing bearers, the helpless, terrified disciples, we see a reflection of origi- nal pain, the sole ground of being: "Illusion" here is a reflection of eternal contra- diction, begetter of all things. From this illusion there rises, like the fragrance of ambrosia, a new illusory world, invisible to those enmeshed in the first: a radiant vision of pure delight, a rapt seeing through wide-open eyes. Here we have, in a great symbol of art, both the fair world of Apollo and its substratum, the terrible wisdom of Silenus, and we can comprehend intuitively how they mutually require one another. But Apollo appears to us once again as the apotheosis of the *principium individuationis,* in whom the eternal goal of the original Oneness, namely its redemption through illusion, accomplishes itself. With august gesture the god shows us how there is need for a whole world of torment in order for the individual to produce the redemptive vision and to sit quietly in his rocking rowboat in mid-sea, absorbed in contemplation.

If this apotheosis of individuation is to be read in normative terms, we may infer that there is one norm only: the individual—or, more precisely, the observance of the limits of the individual: *sophrosyne*. As a moral deity Apollo demands self-control from his people and, in order to observe such self-control, a knowledge of self. And so we find that the esthetic necessity of beauty is accompanied by the imperatives, "Know thyself," and "Nothing too much." Conversely, excess and *hubris* come to be regarded as the hostile spirits of the non-Apollonian sphere, hence as properties of the pre-Apollonian era—the age of Titans—and the extra-Apollonian world, that is to say the world of the barbarians. It was because of his Titanic love of man that Prometheus had to be devoured by vultures; it was because of his extravagant wisdom which succeeded in solving the riddle of the Sphinx that Oedipus had to be cast into a whirlpool of crime: In this fashion does the Delphic god interpret the Greek past.

The effects of the Dionysiac spirit struck the Apollonian Greeks as titanic and barbaric; yet they could not disguise from themselves the fact that they were essentially akin to those deposed Titans and heroes. They felt more than that: Their whole existence, with its temperate beauty, rested upon a base of suffering and *knowledge* which had been hidden from them until the reinstatement of Dionysos uncovered it once more. And lo and behold! Apollo found it impossible to live without Dionysos. The elements of titanism and barbarism turned out to be quite as fundamental as the Apollonian element. And now let us imagine how the ecstatic sounds of the Dionysiac rites penetrated ever more enticingly into that artificially restrained and discreet world of illusion, how this clamor expressed the whole outrageous gamut of nature—delight, grief, knowledge—even to the most piercing cry; and then let us imagine how the Apollonian artist with his thin, monotonous harp music must have sounded beside the demoniac chant of the multitude! The muses presiding over the illusory arts paled before an art which enthusiastically told the truth, and the wisdom of Silenus cried "Woe!" against the serene Olympians. The individual, with his limits and moderations, forgot himself in the Dionysiac vortex and became oblivious to the laws of Apollo. Indiscreet extravagance revealed itself as truth, and contradiction, a delight born of pain, spoke out of the bosom of nature. Wherever the Dionysiac voice was heard, the Apollonian norm seemed suspended or destroyed. Yet it is equally true that, in those places where the first assault was withstood, the prestige and majesty of the Delphic god appeared more rigid and threatening than before. The only way I am able to view Doric art and the Doric state is as a perpetual military encampment of the Apollonian forces. An art so defiantly austere, so ringed about with fortifications—an education so military and exacting—a polity so ruthlessly cruel—could endure only in a continual state of resistance against the titanic and barbaric menace of Dionysos.

On *Oedipus Rex* and *Hamlet*
■ Sigmund Freud ■

Oedipus, the son of Laius, king of Thebes, and Jocasta, is exposed as a suckling, because an oracle had informed the father that his son, who was still unborn, would be his murderer. He is rescued, and grows up as a king's son at a foreign court, until, being uncertain of his origin, he, too, consults the oracle, and is warned to avoid his native place, for he is destined to become the murderer of his father and the husband of his mother. On the road leading away from his supposed home he meets King Laius, and in a sudden quarrel strikes him dead. He comes to Thebes where he solves the riddle of the Sphinx, who is barring the way to the city, whereupon he is elected king by the grateful Thebans, and is rewarded with the hand of Jocasta. He reigns for many years in peace and honour, and begets two sons and two daughters upon his unknown mother, until at last a plague breaks out—which causes the Thebans to consult the oracle anew. Here Sophocles' tragedy begins. The messengers bring the reply that the plague will stop as soon as the murderer of Laius is driven from the country. But where is he?

> *Where shall be found,*
> *Faint, and hard to be known, the trace of the ancient guilt?*

The action of the play consists simply in the disclosure, approached step by step and artistically delayed (and comparable to the work of a psychoanalysis) that Oedipus himself is the murderer of Laius, and that he is the son of the murdered man and Jocasta. Shocked by the abominable crime which he has unwittingly committed, Oedipus blinds himself, and departs from his native city. The prophecy of the oracle has been fulfilled.

The *Oedipus Rex* is a tragedy of fate; its tragic effect depends on the conflict between the all-powerful will of the gods and the vain efforts of human beings threatened with disaster; resignation to the divine will, and the perception of one's own impotence is the lesson which the deeply moved spectator is supposed to learn from the tragedy. Modern authors have therefore sought to achieve a similar tragic effect by expressing the same conflict in stories of their own invention. But the playgoers have looked on unmoved at the unavailing efforts of guiltless men to avert the fulfilment of curse or oracle; the modern tragedies of destiny have failed of their effect.

If the *Oedipus Rex* is capable of moving a modern reader or playgoer no less powerfully than it moved the contemporary Greeks, the only possible explanation is that the effect of the Greek tragedy does not depend upon the conflict between

"On *Oedipus Rex* and *Hamlet*" by Sigmund Freud has been excerpted from *The Basic Writings of Sigmund Freud,* A. A. Brill, trans., Random House Inc. (1938), pages 307–311, and is reprinted by permission of the publisher.

fate and human will, but upon the peculiar nature of the material by which this conflict is revealed. There must be a voice within us which is prepared to acknowledge the compelling power of fate in the *Oedipus,* while we are able to condemn the situations occurring in *Die Ahnfrau** or other tragedies of fate as arbitrary inventions. And there actually is a motive in the story of King Oedipus which explains the verdict of this inner voice. His fate moves us only because it might have been our own, because the oracle laid upon us before our birth the very curse which rested upon him. It may be that we were all destined to direct our first sexual impulses toward our mothers, and our first impulses of hatred and violence toward our fathers; our dreams convince us that we were. King Oedipus, who slew his father Laius and wedded his mother Jocasta, is nothing more or less than a wish-fulfilment—the fulfilment of the wish of our childhood. But we, more fortunate than he, in so far as we have not become psychoneurotics, have since our childhood succeeded in withdrawing our sexual impulses from our mothers, and in forgetting our jealousy of our fathers. We recoil from the person for whom this primitive wish of our childhood has been fulfilled with all the force of the repression which these wishes have undergone in our minds since childhood. As the poet brings the guilt of Oedipus to light by his investigation, he forces us to become aware of our own inner selves, in which the same impulses are still extant, even though they are suppressed. The antithesis with which the chorus departs:—

> . . . *Behold, this is Oedipus,*
> *Who unravelled the great riddle, and was first in power,*
> *Whose fortune all the townsmen praised and envied;*
> *See in what dread adversity he sank!*

—this admonition touches us and our own pride, us who since the years of our childhood have grown so wise and so powerful in our own estimation. Like Oedipus, we live in ignorance of the desires that offend morality, the desires that nature has forced upon us and after their unveiling we may well prefer to avert our gaze from the scenes of our childhood.

In the very text of Sophocles' tragedy there is an unmistakable reference to the fact that the Oedipus legend had its source in dream-material of immemorial antiquity, the content of which was the painful disturbance of the child's relations to its parents caused by the first impulses of sexuality. Jocasta comforts Oedipus—who is not yet enlightened, but is troubled by the recollection of the oracle—by an allusion to a dream which is often dreamed, though it cannot, in her opinion, mean anything:—

> *For many a man hath seen himself in dreams*
> *His mother's mate, but he who gives no heed*
> *To suchlike matters bears the easier life.*

The dream of having sexual intercourse with one's mother was as common then as it is to-day with many people, who tell it with indignation and astonishment. As may

---

*Drama by Franz Grillparzer.

well be imagined, it is the key to the tragedy and the complement to the dream of the death of the father. The Oedipus fable is the reaction of fantasy to these two typical dreams, and just as such a dream, when occurring to an adult, is experienced with feelings of aversion, so the content of the fable must include terror and self-chastisement. The form which it subsequently assumed was the result of an uncomprehending secondary elaboration of the material, which sought to make it serve a theological intention. The attempt to reconcile divine omnipotence with human responsibility must, of course, fail with this material as with any other.

Another of the great poetic tragedies, Shakespeare's *Hamlet,* is rooted in the same soil as *Oedipus Rex.* But the whole difference in the psychic life of the two widely separated periods of civilization, and the progress, during the course of time, of repression in the emotional life of humanity, is manifested in the differing treatment of the same material. In *Oedipus Rex* the basic wish-phantasy of the child is brought to light and realized as it is in dreams; in *Hamlet* it remains repressed, and we learn of its existence—as we discover the relevant facts in a neurosis—only through the inhibitory effects which proceed from it. In the more modern drama, the curious fact that it is possible to remain in complete uncertainty as to the character of the hero has proved to be quite consistent with the overpowering effect of the tragedy. The play is based upon Hamlet's hesitation in accomplishing the task of revenge assigned to him; the text does not give the cause or the motive of this hesitation, nor have the manifold attempts at interpretation succeeded in doing so. According to the still prevailing conception, a conception for which Goethe was first responsible, Hamlet represents the type of man whose active energy is paralysed by excessive intellectual activity: "Sicklied o'er with the pale cast of thought." According to another conception, the poet has endeavoured to portray a morbid, irresolute character, on the verge of neurasthenia. The plot of the drama, however, shows us that Hamlet is by no means intended to appear as a character wholly incapable of action. On two separate occasions we see him assert himself: once in a sudden outburst of rage, when he stabs the eavesdropper behind the arras, and on the other occasion when he deliberately, and even craftily, with the complete unscrupulousness of a prince of the Renaissance, sends the two courtiers to the death which was intended for himself. What is it, then, that inhibits him in accomplishing the task which his father's ghost has laid upon him? Here the explanation offers itself that it is the peculiar nature of this task. Hamlet is able to do anything but take vengeance upon the man who did away with his father and has taken his father's place with his mother—the man who shows him in realization the repressed desires of his own childhood. The loathing which should have driven him to revenge is thus replaced by self-reproach, by concientious scruples, which tell him that he himself is no better than the murderer whom he is required to punish. I have here translated into consciousness what had to remain unconscious in the mind of the hero; if anyone wishes to call Hamlet an hysterical subject I cannot but admit that this is the deduction to be drawn from my interpretation. The sexual aversion which Hamlet expresses in conversation with Ophelia is perfectly consistent with this deduction—the same sexual aversion which during the next few years was increasingly to take possession of the poet's soul, until it found its supreme utterance in *Timon of Athens*. It can, of course, be only the poet's own psychology with which we are confronted in *Hamlet;* and in a work on Shakespeare by Georg Brandes (1896) I find the statement that the drama was composed immediately after the death of Shakespeare's father (1601)—that is to say, when he was still mourning his loss, and during a revival, as we may fairly assume, of his own childish feelings in respect of his father. It is known, too, that Shakespeare's son, who died in childhood, bore the name of Hamnet (identical with Hamlet). Just as *Hamlet* treats of the relation of the son to his parents, so *Macbeth,* which was written about the same period, is based upon the theme of childlessness. Just as all neurotic symptoms, like dreams themselves, are capable of hyper-interpretation, and even require such hyper-interpretation before they become perfectly intelligible, so every genuine poetical creation must have proceeded from more than one motive, more than one impulse in the mind of the poet, and must admit of more than one interpretation. I have here attempted to interpret only the deepest stratum of impulses in the mind of the creative poet.

Live Performance in a Mediatized Culture
■ Philip Auslander ■

In the spring of 1990, the Franco-German pop singing and dancing duo Milli Vanilli was awarded the Best New Artist Grammy for 1989. The award prompted a spate of newspaper articles with titles like "That Syncing Feeling" (*Detroit News,* July 31, 1990) and other media commentary concerning various performers, including Milli Vanilli, who allegedly lip-synched to prerecorded vocals in concert. (Madonna, Michael Jackson, Paula Abdul, and many others were similarly accused.) Most of the commentary was adamantly opposed to the practice, though virtually all of it also admitted that the main audiences for the performers in question, mostly young teenagers, did not seem to care whether their idols actually sang or not. In November, Milli Vanilli's producer created fresh controversy when he admitted that not only had the duo lip-synched their concerts, they had not even sung on the recording for which they were awarded the Grammy, which was then rescinded, much to the embarrassment of the National Academy of Recording Arts and Sciences (NARAS), the Grammys' institutional sponsor. . . .

"Live Performance in a Mediatized Culture" by Philip Auslander has been excerpted with the help of the author from *Liveness: Performance in a Mediatized Culture,* Routledge (1999), pages 42–43, 50–52, 54–57..

At one level, the anxiety of critics who champion live performance is understandable, given the way our cultural economy privileges the mediatized and marginalizes the live. In the economy of repetition, live performance is little more than a vestigial remnant of the previous historical order of representation, a holdover that can claim little in the way of cultural presence or power. Perhaps making a virtue of necessity, Peggy Phelan* claims that live performance's inability to participate in the economy of repetition "gives performance art its distinctive oppositional edge. . . ."

My purpose here is to destabilize such theoretical oppositions of the live and the mediatized somewhat. . . . Consider Walter Benjamin's observation on what he called "contemporary perception" and its hunger for reproductions. To pry an object from its shell, he writes, "to destroy its aura, is the mark of a perception whose 'sense of the universal equality of all things' has increased to such a degree that it extracts it even from a unique object by means of reproduction." I . . . suggest . . . that this is exactly the state in which live performance now finds itself: Its traditional status as auratic and unique has been wrested from it by an ever-accelerating incursion of reproduction into the live event. Following Benjamin, I might argue that live performance has indeed been pried from its shell and that all performance modes, live or mediatized, are now equal: None is perceived as auratic or authentic; the live performance is just one more reproduction of a given text or one more reproducible text. (To say that no performance in any medium can be perceived as auratic is not to say that all such performances are experienced in the same way—just that no one of them is experienced as the auratic, authentic original.) Live performance could now be said to partake of the ontology that Benjamin ascribes to photography: "From a photographic negative . . . one can make any number of prints; to ask for the 'authentic' print makes no sense." Similarly, it makes little sense to ask which of the many identical live productions of . . . Disney's *Beauty and the Beast* is the "authentic" one. It does not even make much sense to ask which of the many iterations of that *Beauty and the Beast*—as animated film, video cassette, CD, book, or theatrical performance—is the "authentic" iteration. This situation represents the historical triumph of mechanical (and electronic) reproduction (what I am calling *mediatization*) that Benjamin implies: Aura, authenticity, and cult value have been definitively routed, even in live performance, the site that once seemed the last refuge of the auratic.

I am suggesting further that thinking about the relationship between live and mediatized forms in terms of ontological oppositions is not especially productive, because there are few grounds on which to make significant ontological distinctions. Like live performance, electronic and photographic media can be described meaningfully as partaking of the ontology of disappearance ascribed to live performance, and they can also be used to provide an experience of evanescence. Like film and television, theater can be used as a mass medium. Half jokingly, I might

*Phelan is a noted theorist of performance art.

cite Patrice Pavis's* observation that "theatre repeated too often deteriorates" as evidence that the theatrical object degenerates with repeated use in a manner akin to a recorded object! I am not proposing, however, that live performance and mediatization partake of a shared ontology. . . . I am suggesting, rather, that how live and mediatized forms are used is determined not by their ostensibly intrinsic characteristics but by their positions within cultural economy. To understand the relationship between live and mediatized forms, it is necessary to investigate that relationship as historical and contingent, not as ontologically given or technologically determined.

As a starting point for this exploration, I propose that, historically, the live is actually an effect of mediatization, not the other way around. It was the development of recording technologies that made it possible to perceive existing representations as "live." Prior to the advent of those technologies (e.g., sound recording and motion pictures), there was no such thing as "live" performance, for that category has meaning only in relation to an opposing possibility. The ancient Greek theatre, for example, was not live because there was no possibility of recording it. In a special case of Jean Baudrillard's well-known dictum that "the very definition of the real is *that of which it is possible to give an equivalent reproduction*," the "live" can only be defined as *that which can be recorded*. Most dictionary definitions of this usage of the word "live" reflect the necessity of defining it in terms of its opposite: "Of a performance, heard or watched at the time of its occurrence, as distinguished from one recorded on film, tape, etc." (*Oxford English Dictionary,* 2nd edn).

I want to emphasize that reproduction (recording) is the key issue. The Greek theatre may have been technologically mediated, if one subscribes to the theory that the masks acted as megaphones. What concerns me here, however, is technological reproduction, not just technological mediation. Greek theatrical masks may have amplified the actors' voices, but they did not reproduce them, in the manner of electric amplification. Throughout history, performance has employed available technologies and has been mediated in one sense or another. It is only since the advent of mechanical and electric technologies of recording and reproduction, however, that performance has been mediatized. . . .

The im-mediate is not prior to mediation but derives precisely from the mutually defining relationship between the im-mediate and the mediated. Simiarly, live performance cannot be said to have ontological or historical priority over mediatization, since liveness was made visible only by the possibility of technical reproduction. This problematizes Phelan's claim that "to the degree that live performance attempts to enter into the economy of reproduction it betrays and lessens the promise of its own ontology," not just because it is not at all clear that live performance has a distinctive ontology, but also because it is not a question of performance's *entering into* the economy of reproduction, since it has always been there. My argument is that the very concept of live performance presupposes that of reproduction—that the live can exist only *within* an economy of reproduction.

---

*Pavis is a French scholar noted for his work on the semiotics of performance.

In challenging the traditional opposition of the live and the mediatized, I am not suggesting that we cannot make phenomenological distinctions between the respective experiences of live and mediatized representations, distinctions concerning their respective positions within cultural economy, and ideological distinctions among performed representations in all media. What I am suggesting is that any distinctions need to derive from careful consideration of how the relationship between the live and the mediatized is articulated in particular cases, not from a set of assumptions that constructs the relation between live and mediatized representations *a priori* as a relation of essential opposition. . . .

My claim that live performance recapitulates mediatized representations has sometimes been challenged by the demand to know why people still want to see live performances if that is the case. This is an important question usually addressed by recourse to clichés and mystifications concerning aura, presence, the "magic of live theatre," etc. Although any attempt at a general response is bound to be flawed, the single most important point to make with respect to the continued attractiveness of live performance in a mediatized culture is that, like liveness itself, the desire for live experiences is a product of mediatization. . . .

One of the main conventional explanations advanced for the continued appeal of live performance is that it offers a fuller sensory experience than mediatized performances. Whereas mediatized representations appeal primarily to the visual and auditory senses, live performances engage all the senses, including the olfactory, tactile, somatic, and kinesthetic. I would argue that this is not the case, that these other senses *are* engaged by mediatized performances. It certainly can be the case that live performance engages the senses *differently* than mediatized representations, but a difference in kind is not the same thing as a difference in magnitude of sensory experience.

Another conventional argument is that the experience of live performance builds community. It is surely the case that a sense of community may emanate from being part of an audience that clearly values something you value, though the reality of our cultural economy is that the communal bond unifying such an audience is most likely to be little more than the common consumption of a particular performance commodity. Leaving that issue aside, I would argue against the idea that live performance itself somehow generates whatever sense of community one may experience. For one thing, mediatized performance makes just as effective a focal point for the gathering of a social group as live performance. Theodore Gracyk, who discusses this issue as it pertains to popular music, observes that:

> One does not need a live performance to create such a [social] space or its attendant sense of being part of a community engaged with the music: discos, Jamaican sound system trucks, bars and pubs and pool halls with juke boxes, and the British rave scene have created diverse public sites for recorded music.

Gracyk's point can be generalized across performance genres. A parallel example from a different cultural realm would be that of the crowd that gathered in the town square of a small city adjacent to Atlanta to watch a big-screen simulcast of the opening ceremonies of the 1996 Olympic Games. The people gathered around the giant television screen constituted a community in all the same senses as the audience attending the live event a few miles away. Since most of the people gathered in the town square were neighbors, not merely people drawn together to attend an event, their experience was arguably more genuinely communal than that of the audience attending the live performance. My point is simply that, communality is not a function of liveness. The sense of community arises from being part of an audience, and the quality of the experience of community derives from the specific audience situation, not from the spectacle for which that audience has gathered.

Another version of this account of the appeal of live performance proposes that live performance brings performers and spectators together in a community. This view misunderstands the dynamic of performance, which is predicated on the distinction between performers and spectators. Indeed, the effort to eliminate that distinction destroys the very possibility of performance. . . . Those like Jerzy Grotowski and Augusto Boal, for whom bridging this gap has become the primary purpose of their work, albeit for very different reasons, have found themselves constrained to abandon performance as such altogether. Herbert Blau* addresses these issues of performance and communality in his discussion of the theatre audience:

> Desire has always been . . . for the audience as community, similarly enlightened, unified in belief, all the disparities in some way healed by the experience of theater. The very nature of theater reminds us somehow of the original unity even as it implicates us in the common experience of fracture, which produces both what is time-serving and divisive in theater and what is self-serving and subversive in desire. . . . as there is no theater without *separation,* there is no appeasing of desire.

As Blau suggests in this extraordinary passage, the experience of theatre (of live performance generally, I would say) provokes our desire for community but cannot satisfy that desire because performance is founded on difference, on separation and fragmentation, not unity. Live performance places us in the living presence of the performers, other human beings with whom we desire unity and can imagine achieving it, because they are there, in front of us. Yet live performance also inevitably frustrates that desire since its very occurrence presupposes a gap between performer and spectator. Whereas mediatized performance can provide the occasion for a satisfactory experience of community *within* the audience, live performance inevitably yields a sense of the failure to achieve community *between* the audience and the performer. By reasserting the unbridgeable distinction between audience and performance, live performance foregrounds its own fractious nature and the unlikelihood of community in a way that mediatized representations, which never hold out the promise of unity, do not.

---

*Blau, author of many books on theater and performance, has also had a distinguished career in the professional theater.

Literature as a Performing Art
■ J. O. Urmson ■

I wish, in this essay, to raise and suggest answers to two questions about literature. First is the question of the ontological status of a literary work—the question what sort of thing is a poem, a novel, a history. Second is whether or not, when we read a literary work, it is analogous to anything that anybody does in relation to other major arts forms. To pursue these questions I must first make some remarks about these other major art forms, excluding literature, for, since my problem is about what seems, at first sight, to be anomalous features of literature, I must indicate what I take to be normality.

Leaving literature, for the present then, I think that most of the major art forms, in their most common manifestations in Western culture, can be divided into two groups. The reader is asked to note that this is a historical generalization, not a statement of logical or conceptual necessities. First here is the group, which includes painting and sculpture, where the creative artist himself normally fashions the object which is the work of art. We are all, no doubt, aware of imaginative fantasies to the contrary, such as Collingwood's view that all art works are in some way mental, but I assume in this paper that such an art work as a painting or a sculpture is a physical object which can be stolen, or defaced, or stored in a bank and can need to be preserved and restored. This is the common sense view which can be rejected only at the expense of conceptual innovation. Thus it is the work of art as both conceived and made by its creator that spectators typically contemplate in the case of such arts as painting and sculpture. This is no doubt an oversimplified story. There may, for example, be foundry workers involved in the production of a bronze statue, but rightly or wrongly we think of them as living tools of the sculptor, with whom, from beginning to end, all artistic decisions rest.

Then a second group of arts exists, including music, theater, ballet, and opera in their standard forms, in which the audience or spectators do not witness, without any intermediaries, the work made by the creative artist. There is a need for executant artists, with a serious aesthetic role as interpreters. We see and listen to dancers, instrumentalists, and actors, not to choreographers, composers, and playwrights. That the creative artist may from time to time be his own interpreter in performance does not in any way invalidate this distinction.

Now it is only in the case of the performing arts that serious doubts about the identity of the work of art arises, at least at the common sense level. It requires philosophical sophistication even to understand the suggestion that the *Mona Lisa*

"Literature as a Performing Art" by J. O. Urmson has been excerpted from *Aesthetics: A Critical Anthology,* George Dickie and Frank Sclafani, eds., St. Martin's Press (1977), pages 334–341, and is reprinted by permission of the publisher.

is not something that usually can be found hanging on a wall of the Louvre. But the case is quite different with regard to the performing arts. It is plain common sense to see that a symphony, a ballet, or a play cannot be simply identified with any physical object, such as a book or manuscript, or with any event, such as a performance. We can, indeed, speak of hearing Beethoven's Fifth Symphony, as we can speak of seeing Michaelangelo's *David,* but, if we hear the Fifth Symphony, it is equally correct to say that we hear a performance of it, whereas there is nothing even analogous to a performance of the *David* that we could witness.

I have argued in a paper entitled "The Performing Arts" (in *Contemporary British Philosophy*), that the best account to give of the contribution of the creative artist in the case of those arts, or works of art, which require also a performer or executant is that he provides a recipe or set of performing instructions for the executant-artist. A similar opinion has, of course, been put forward by others. Thus, when Beethoven composed the Fifth Symphony, he thought out and wrote down a set of instructions for an orchestra. Similarly, the playwright provides a set of instructions for the actors and the creator of a ballet a set of instructions for the dancers. This view seems more plausible than others that are current. Thus, to say that a musical work is a class of performances requires one to say that the composer created such a class—a view which becomes especially uncomfortable if we consider an unperformed work. The suggestion of [Richard] Wollheim and others that the creative artist creates a type, and [C.L.]Stevenson's view that he creates a megatype, also cause discomfort. It is hard to see how there can be a type or a megatype before there are any tokens.

What may be called a set of performing instructions in the case of temporal arts such as music and ballet, where what the audience witnesses is a set of events that take time, is more naturally called a recipe in the case of such nontemporal arts as require an executant artist. Such nontemporal arts as painting and sculpture, which typically require no artist beyond the creator, comprise works which, as we have seen, are physical objects. Such art works take time to make, and we may spend time contemplating them, but they do not themselves take time. But, if we may consider cooking as an art, it is one which requires an executant artist, the cook, who may be, but need not be, the creator of the recipe he follows. The pecan pie or the hamburger has a status problematic in the same way as that of symphony or ballet. In my view, to create *the* pecan pie is to provide a recipe which, if followed by the executant cook, will result in *a* pecan pie.

So I say that a creative artist may do one of two things. He may himself produce the work of art which the spectator witnesses and which will be a physical object, or he may produce a set of instructions for execution by others. It is rather obvious why, if one wishes to have permanent works of art in the temporal arts, such as music, the creative artist should produce only a set of instructions. There do not have to be permanent works of music; one could have a music which consisted entirely of free improvisation and in which there were no permanent works. It would also be theoretically possible to devise a painting notation so that a creative artist could give a set of instructions for executant painters to follow and produce a set of equally valid interpretations of the painting, analogous to musical performances. It is not difficult to see why we in fact do not do this, except in the case of some rudimentary children's painting games. I have neither claimed that any art form must include performing artists as well as creators nor claimed that any art form cannot do so. I merely observe that the standard classics of painting and sculpture conform to one type and that the standard classics of music, theater, and ballet to the other, and I note that one can see good practical reasons why, with traditional techniques, highly organized art works do fall into these two categories. One would not wish to hear a group improvisation of an opera.

Not all arts fit readily into this twofold classification, more particularly not all applied arts, as is clear from the case of architecture. It is quite interesting to consider such cases, though I do not think that they raise very serious philosophical problems. I think it is largely a matter of loose fit to accounts produced for the paradigm cases. There are also novel variations within the arts discussed: What, for example, are we to say of musical composition directly onto tape in an electronic laboratory, and will the account of live theater readily cover the cinematograph? Still, it is not our present task to examine these problems, but to ask whether or not we can give an adequate account of literature in the light of the characterization of the other arts put forward in this paper.

We have distinguished two categories of works of art. First, there are those directly created by the creative artist when there is no executant artist and the identity of the work is unproblematic; second, there are those where the creative artist produces a recipe or set of instructions for performing or for executant artists and where the identity of the work of art is problematic. Now literature appears, at least at first sight, to be anomalous with respect to this classification. On the one hand, there seem to be no executant artists or performers here: who could such artists be? When one, say, reads a novel to oneself, there seems to be only oneself and the novelist involved. Is the reader in fact the executant artist with himself as audience as the pianist who can play to himself as audience and the dancer who can dance for his own satisfaction? But I do not seem to myself to be exhibiting any technical or interpretative skills when I read to myself, and there are other grave objections to this suggestion which we must notice later. Yet, if there is no performing or executant artist, how can I myself be the audience or spectator?

On the other hand, we cannot readily assimilate literature to sculpture and painting. For one thing, the identity of the novel or other literary work seems to be problematic in the same way as that of the musical balletic or theatrical work. In the case of these other arts, we have attempted to explain their problematic status in terms of a recipe or set of instructions for executant artists. But, how can the literary work be a set of instructions for executant artists if there are none such?

So the literature seems to be a counterexample to my theory, for, if the theory will not work when applied to literature, that certainly casts doubt upon its acceptability. We surely need a theory which will account equally for all cases in which the identity of the work of art is problematic, for it would be an act of desperation to claim that the status of, say, *Pride and Prejudice* was radically different from that of the *Sleeping Beauty* ballet or Beethoven's Fifth Symphony.

That then is my problem. For those who find my view of the other arts unacceptable, in any case the problem does not exist in the specific form in which I see it, but there will still be the old traditional problem of the identity of a literary work.

Now I am not sure how this problem is to be answered, but I am going to suggest an answer in accordance with my general theory. I am going to suggest that, contrary to first appearances, literature is in principle a performing art.

If we are to make this claim, the most natural thing is first to revive the view that, in reading a literary work to oneself, one is simultaneously performer and audience, just as when one plays a piece of music to oneself. I have already raised the objection to this view that one does not seem to oneself, when so reading, to be utilizing any technical or interpretative skills, but this appeal to subjective feelings is, no doubt, of little weight, so we must notice a more serious objection to it.

If we consider a musical score as a set of instructions to the performer, then, for example, the musical notation of the first bar of the first violin's line in the score of Beethoven's Fifth Symphony must be regarded as a shorthand instruction to the players to play three consecutive G naturals, each a quarter of the total time of a bar, the total duration of which is indicated by the metronome mark at the top of the page. Similarly, if in his script an actor reads

Tom (looking out of the window): It is beginning to rain.

He will, if he is playing the part of Tom, take it as an instruction to look out of the window of the stage set and say "It is beginning to rain." Thus we can distinguish quite clearly the performer's reading of the instructions from his action in accordance with them, and it is in his act of complying with the instructions, not the reading of them, that he shows his technical and interpretative skill. That I can read and understand the instruction to the violinist just as well as he can gives me neither his skill nor his interpretative insight.

But, in the case of the solitary novel reader, the situation is not similar. Not only do we have to make him simultaneously performer and audience, we have to collapse into one act his reading of the instructions and his compliance with them. This explains one's initial uneasiness at the suggestion and is surely too implausible in itself. This horse will not run.

If we are to separate the reading of instructions from the act of complying with them, we must claim, I think, that literature is essentially an oral act. Moreover, this move is not made simply in an attempt to save a theory, for with regard to some literature it has an immediate plausibility. If we consider such a work as the *Iliad,* there is good reason to believe that before writing was known to the Greeks there were bards who had learned the poem by heart and who went around giving performances of it, or of excerpts from it. They, the performers, were taught it orally, that is, by example, just as performers in other arts may still be taught their parts other than by studying the score. It is not implausible to think of the *Iliad* as having been written down, probably in the seventh century B.C., as a set of instructions, as a score, for bards. It is fairly certain that Herodotus wrote his *Histories* as a score and that people first got to know them by hearing public performances. No doubt the first performances, *epideixis,* as the Greeks called them, were given by Herodotus himself, but the distinction of creator and performer is not obliterated by the same man's undertaking both roles. Further, in cultures less generously supplied with printing presses than we are, the tradition of purely oral poetry still survives.

It is clear also that even in Western civilization many poets today think of poetry as essentially an oral art; poetry for them is essentially something to be listened to, and so a performer is required. If you now read it aloud to yourself, attempting to equal the skills of the professional poetry reader, this, rather than silent novel reading, would be like playing the piano to oneself as a performance. Also, we must not forget that he gave readings from his novels in public and that reading aloud within the family group is an activity once common and not yet dead.

But this account will certainly not cover the bulk of modern literature. If much ancient and some modern literature was designed by its creators primarily, to be heard, the written word being primarily a score for the performer, this is certainly not true of the great bulk of modern literature. While much of the best literature of all ages can with advantage be read aloud, it is more than doubtful that Dickens's novels, let alone *The Decline and Fall of the Roman Empire,* were ever intended primarily for oral performance.

Faced with this difficulty, let us go back to the case of music. Music is essentially sound; the performer produces sounds in accordance with the instructions of the composer. But there is such a thing as the skill of silent score reading, a skill which some very proficient performers have only to a slight extent. But a reasonably musical person can, after instruction and practice, look at a simple melodic line in a score and recognize what it would sound like if it were performed; he knows what musical sounds would be heard if the instructions were obeyed. Very gifted musicians, after elaborate training, can acquire the same facility in reading complex scores with transposed parts, unusual clefs, and the like. Musical score reading of this kind is neither original creation nor performance, the two factors we originally considered, nor even the sort of reading required of the performer. It is the reading of a recipe or set of instructions with the ability to recognize what would result from following them. I am reliably informed that experienced cooks may acquire the same skill; they may be able to read the recipe and recognize what the confection would taste like.

It would be implausible to say that musical score readers are giving a performance to themselves or that readers of cookery recipes are preparing a private and immaterial feast. Apart from the fact that they need hear no sound (they may or may not hum to themselves), considered, absurdly, as performances, what the best score readers normally do would be intolerably bad. They habitually read through the slower bits far faster than they perfectly well know that the music should go, and, for many reasons, nobody can read a fast complex piece at a speed that he recognizes to be that of the music. Score reading is something quite distinct from composition or performance. The music critic, Ernest Newman, who went blind in old age, expressed the wish that he had become deaf instead, since he preferred to read a score and imagine an ideal performance than to hear what he usually heard. And some music is probably intended primarily for score readers. Some of the puzzle canons at the beginning of Bach's *Musical Offering* were surely intended primarily for the score reader, and it has been known for composers to attempt to make the notes they wrote visual representations of the cross or some other symbol.

Now I suggest that learning to read an ordinary language is like learning to read a score silently to oneself. It is probably easier, and more of us get a thorough training in it and, consequently, mastery of it. There is therefore a large potential market of verbal score readers.

My claim is that the vast literature primarily intended for private reading in silence should be regarded as analogous to a set of musical scores intended primarily for score reading rather than for performance. So reading *Hamlet* to oneself will not be so unlike reading *War and Peace.* But, whereas the text of *Hamlet* was certainly primarily a score or set of instructions for actors and, thus, like a normal musical score, *War and Peace,* like some vast poetic dramas, is left to the score reader. Reading the text of *Hamlet* is surely not a performance, yet it is equally surely not very unlike reading the text of *War and Peace.*

So my claim is that literature is in logical character a performing art, but one in which in practice we frequently, though far from invariably, confine ourselves to score reading. We read to find out how the performance will go and are then content. This view is, I believe, somewhat confirmed by some of the critical remarks we make about literary style. Even in the case of works which would not normally be read aloud it is a commonplace to speak of assonance, dissonance, sonority, rhythm; we reject as unstylish conjunctions of consonants which would be awkward to say aloud, though we easily read them. We criticize the writing in terms of how it would sound, if it were spoken. Contrast the case of logical notation which is not literature and for which we have only a makeshift oral rendering: who would think of criticizing a piece of writing in formal logic as unstylish because our conventional oral reading of it was awkward in sound?

It is certainly not the case that all literature can be covered without remainder by this account. Sometimes its character as written is important, and not merely in the way that we prefer elegantly printed literature as we like elegantly printed musical scores. The poems of e. e. cummings are a very clear case. Again, it is essential that Lewis Carroll's mouse's tale should be printed in the shape of a mouse's tail in the way it regularly is unless we are to miss a pun which could not be brought out orally. At a level of, no doubt, very lightweight literary art, but still literary art, we have such poems as

> While cycling downhill Lord Fermanagh
> Broke his bike, and he hadn't a spanagh,
> But the pieces Lord Crichton
> Was able to tichton
> In quite a professional managh.

Whatever interest this jingle has, the aberrational spelling no doubt is an important part of it.

I cannot account for these cases within my theory, but I do not think they need disturb me, any more than that the notation of [Robert] Schumann's music is full of cryptograms that need to be accounted for in a general discussion of music and its notation. I think that the simple fact is that the notation of a piece of music may also be a code, that a jingle with audible rhyme may be written in a way which is a jest about English spelling, and that, in the case of e. e. cummings, typography may be used, rather like dynamic marks in a musical score, as a hint to a correct reading.

So I can now formally give answers to the two questions with which I started. I resolve the problem of the ontological status of a literary work by saying that for a literary work to exist it is a necessary and sufficient condition that a set of instructions should exist such that any oral performance which complies with that set of instructions is a performance of the work in question. I resolve the problem of the relation of reading a literary work to what we find in other art forms by saying that is analogous to reading the score of a musical work, of a play, or of a ballet. In each of these cases we neither create the work nor perform the work when we read the score, but we become aware of what we would witness if we were to witness a performance.

That there are other questions about literature than those I have attempted to answer is obvious. That one can find problems about my answers is also obvious. It is possible to write at length about the notion of compliance with a set of instructions of which I have made unelucidated use. But one thing at a time is usually enough, so attempting even a sketch of answers to two questions is, for me, sufficiently ambitious.

PART VIII

∎∎

POPULAR AND MASS ARTS

Consider the long lines waiting to enter retrospective shows by the likes of Vermeer, Rembrandt, Picasso, and Mondrian. In one obvious sense, paintings by these painters are *popular*. However, the philosophical study of the arts has typically employed a concept of "popular" according to which the popular arts, for example, "rock" music, are ignored or otherwise treated unfavorably by contrast with the "high" or "fine" arts. In this book, the popular arts, which we believe are deserving of serious theoretical attention, are moved closer to center stage.

The refusal to draw the sharp boundary between "high" and "low" arts is reflected in what Jean-François Lyotard calls "the postmodern condition." In postmodernism, presumably closed borders are opened to embrace a wider range of subjects, including those of the popular arts. Stressing the *eclecticism* of contemporary culture, Lyotard argues against global rules for art, thereby opening the door to a more anti-elitist view of the arts than is traditionally defended or taken for granted. Lyotard sees the postmodernist era as suspicious of grand meta-narratives and asks that we be "witnesses to the *unpresentable*," a concept akin to the eighteenth-century concept of the sublime.

Like Lyotard, Umberto Eco is interested in a postmodern aesthetics, "revisiting" what he calls the *iterative* or *repetitive* aspects of contemporary culture, especially those of television and other products of the mass media. At one time, "serial production" belonged only to industry, but was regarded as alien to art because of the latter's stress on the original and the innovative. A postmodern approach, Eco argues, will take a more inclusive approach to cultural material formerly regarded as lying outside the sphere of art. For example, consider our response to television as an acceptance of *sameness*. That is, we greet television programs as we would greet a familiar friend. Indeed, we feel good about our ability to guess the nearly obvious endings.

In the same spirit, Jean Baudrillard argues that in the postmodernist era, traditional conceptualizations associated with the "high" or "fine" arts are inevitably eroded. In a world saturated with media information, he argues, *signs* of the real become systematically substituted for the real *itself.* The resulting situation— where we fail to distinguish between the real and the imaginary—Baudrillard terms the *hyperreal.* Baudrillard believes that the phenomenon of the hyperreal goes hand in hand with the diminished importance of originality in the postmodernist age.

In this section, the reader will find selections that are *critical* of the popular arts alongside essays that come to their *defense.* Alexander Nehamas, for example, returns to Book X of the *Republic,* in which Plato gave an extended critique of the arts of his time. On the whole, Plato thought that contemporary Greek drama and poetry very likely did more harm than good to the minds' of their audiences. The problem, on Nehamas' interpretation, was that these arts tended to provide simplistic and all-too-quick solutions to complex and difficult personal and social issues. What is timely about Nehamas' essay is that he sees powerful connections between Plato's critique of the arts of Athenian antiquity and contemporary criticisms of prime-time television.

The Marxist philosopher, Theodor Adorno, whose arguments are critically reviewed here in the essay by Lee Brown, defends a strongly dismissive view about the popular arts. American popular music, in Adorno's opinion, consists of formulaic artifacts composed of replaceable parts. Making minimum cognitive demands upon the listener, it is designed to generate mainly standardized reactions. Its larger goal, in his opinion, is to regiment the masses and reconcile them to the world created by the culture industry by selling them the very products that drug the mind in the way he describes. Brown reviews these arguments sympathetically, but provides his own critical evaluation.

Richard Shusterman also takes issue with Adorno, along with other aesthetic elitists, in an essay defending the virtues of the popular arts. He claims, for instance, that the widespread charge that they create a merely passive audience is indefensible and that much of the elitist opposition to the popular arts is based on an objectionable privileging of the mind over the body as well as on confused views about the relationship between form and content in art.

Also taking her departure from Adorno, Anita Waters argues that at least one well-established form of popular music escapes Adorno's critique, namely, Jamaican reggae music. Hostile critics objected to the music's "gun lyrics" and sexual "slackness," particularly in its later "dancehall" form. Waters defends the music against these objections, claiming that it had not abdicated any sense of social responsibility.

"Why is rock music so noisy?" Ted Gracyk poses this question quite seriously and answers it by arguing that what is dismissed as mere noise in rock is really an entirely new sphere of acoustic possibility. The switch to electronic instruments, he claims, allows musicians to paint with a much larger palette.

Joel Rudinow addresses another timely controversy about popular music, namely, whether certain musical forms properly "belong" to specific ethnic cultural groups. It is often suggested, for instance, that white people simply cannot sing blues music with real authenticity. Rudinow teases out reasons one might hold such a view, concluding that in order to avoid both ethnocentrism and racism in these matters, we should say that the authenticity of a blues performance turns fundamentally on the performer's mastery of the idiom and his or her integrity in using the idiom in performance.

If modernist avant-garde art lies at one end of a spectrum of degrees of originality, *kitsch* would seem to lie at the other end. "Kitsch" is a Viennese word originally translated as "trash." Typical examples are quaint figurines, the *Saturday Evening Post* illustrations by Norman Rockwell, and television soap operas. Indeed, modernist theoreticians and critics such as Adorno and Clement Greenberg have often defined their position by taking a strong stand against the addiction of contemporary culture to kitsch. Robert Solomon argues that the stock elitist dismissal of kitsch as too sentimental is simply based on a general but unwarranted suspicion of the emotions. He also regards as highbrow prejudice the moral charge that a preference for kitsch betrays a flaw of character.

Ted Cohen does some serious thinking about jokes in his essay on the topic, thereby opening up an aesthetic sphere that not even typical discussions of the popular arts have often, if ever, addressed. Jokes, he argues, can be considered a kind of performance that taps human *understanding* in interesting ways. In one kind of joke, knowing too much or too little may disqualify someone from thinking the joke is funny. Cohen calls these "conditional" jokes. On the other hand, Cohen thinks, some jokes anyone can "get," which leads to the interesting question whether having a sense of humor is as universal as having a sense of taste or sight. (Eventually, Cohen later came to the conclusion that all narrative jokes are conditional in some respect or other.)

Another familiar source of pleasure is the comic strip. The very medium of this popular art form poses interesting questions. Comics are obviously graphic in character. But they typically, make use of words. What, exactly, *are* comics? Reviewing the available theories about the matter, and an array of curious examples, Henry Pratt and Greg Hayman argue that a comic is a special kind of visual narrative composed of discrete pictures separated by a "gutter" and combined with a text.

Still another source of humor, from vaudeville to television, is the low-tech, lowbrow art of the ventriloquist. David Goldblatt sees this art form as a specific case of the ancient Greek notion of *ecstasis,* or being "outside" oneself. After giving an account of what he calls the "complex-logic of ventriloquism," Goldblatt shows how ventriloquism, a form of illusion without deception, can be used as a general *metaphor* for the interpretation of artworks, as well as for the role of their artists. We ask, "What does this work *say?*" in calling for an interpretation, while knowing it is only the artist who has spoken in an extraordinary voice.

Any reference to the popular arts that did not take into consideration the sphere of pornography would be narrow indeed. Whatever its aesthetic value, much of the current concern about such material is moral and legal. Some have argued, not just that pornography is aesthetically worthless, but that there ought to be legal sanctions against it.

On this issue, Joel Feinberg takes the familiar "liberal" point of view that we are justified in adopting legal restrictions on the freedom of expression only if a case can be made that it is very likely to have *specific* dangerous social effects—that it causes particular acts of rape, for instance. And such conclusions, he insists, can only be established by hard empirical inquiry. In short, the case for criminalizing pornography has not yet been made.

Taking a feminist point of view on the matter, Catharine MacKinnon argues that the liberal demand for evidence about *specific* harms putatively caused by pornography is precisely what is wrong with that point of view. The pernicious effects of pornography cannot be evaluated in a simple "John hit Mary" fashion. Its effects are insidiously pervasive. Like carbon monoxide, pornography is deadly even though unnoticeable. Hence, for MacKinnon, there are good reasons for allowing people who can show they are harmed by pornography to sue for civil rights violations of their sex equality rights.

Thus far in this section, we have made no distinction between *mass art* and *popular* art, one that critics of both kinds of art often fail to distinguish. The impact of the writings of Walter Benjamin has helped to establish mass art as an entirely new category of art. Noël Carroll attempts to analyze this concept and to explain its relationship to the concepts upon which it depends, such as the concepts of *accessibility* and *mass delivery system*. He goes on to explain the relationship of the concept of *mass art* to the traditional concept of *art* and to characterize the kinds of principles by which mass art might be evaluated.

The Postmodern Condition
■ Jean-François Lyotard ■

Eclecticism is the degree zero of contemporary general culture: One listens to reggae, watches a western, eats McDonald's food for lunch and local cuisine for dinner, wears Paris perfume in Tokyo and "retro" clothes in Hong Kong; knowledge is a matter for TV games. It is easy to find a public for eclectic works. By becoming kitsch, art panders to the confusion which reigns in the "taste" of the patrons. Artists, gallery owners, critics, and public wallow together in the "anything goes," and the epoch is one of slackening. But this realism of the "anything goes" is in fact that of money; in the absence of aesthetic criteria, it remains possible and useful to assess the value of works of art according to the profits they yield. Such realism accommodates all tendencies, just as capital accommodates all "needs," providing that the tendencies and needs have purchasing power. As for taste, there is no need to be delicate when one speculates or entertains oneself.

Artistic and literary research is doubly threatened, once by the "cultural policy" and once by the art and book market. What is advised, sometimes through one channel, sometimes through the other, is to offer works which, first, are relative to subjects which exist in the eyes of the public they address, and second, works so made ("well made") that the public will recognize what they are about, will understand what is signified, will be able to give or refuse its approval knowingly, and if possible, even to derive from such work a certain amount of comfort.

The interpretation which has just been given of the contact between the industrial and mechanical arts, and literature and the fine arts is correct in its outline, but it remains narrowly sociologizing and historicizing—in other words, one-sided. Stepping over [Walter] Benjamin's and [Theodor] Adorno's reticences, it must be recalled that science and industry are no more free of the suspicion which concerns reality than are art and writing. To believe otherwise would be to entertain an excessively humanistic notion of the mephistophelian functionalism of sciences and technologies. There is no denying the dominant existence today of techno-science, that is, the massive subordination of cognitive statements to the finality of the best possible performance, which is the technological criterion. But the mechanical and the industrial, especially when they enter fields traditionally reserved for artists, are carrying with them much more than power effects. The objects and the thoughts which originate in scientific knowledge and the capitalist economy convey with them one of the rules which supports their possibility: the rule that there is no reality unless testified by a consensus between partners over a certain knowledge and certain commitments.

_____

"The Postmodern Condition" by Jean-François Lyotard has been excerpted from *The Postmodern Condition,* University of Minnesota Press (1984), pages 76–82, and is reprinted by permission of the publisher.

This rule is of no little consequence. It is the imprint left on the politics or the scientist and the trustee of capital by a kind of flight of reality out of the metaphysical, religious, and political certainties that the mind believed it held. This withdrawal is absolutely necessary to the emergence of science and capitalism. No industry is possible without a suspicion of the Aristotelian theory of motion, no industry without a refutation of corporatism, of mercantilism, and of physiocracy. Modernity, in whatever age it appears, cannot exist without a shattering of belief and without discovery of the "lack of reality" of reality, together with the invention of other realities.

What does this "lack of reality" signify if one tries to free it from a narrowly historicized interpretation? The phrase is of course akin to what Nietzsche calls nihilism. But I see a much earlier modulation of Nietzschean perspectivism in the Kantian theme of the sublime. I think in particular that it is in the aesthetic of the sublime that modern art (including literature) finds its impetus and the logic of avant-gardes finds its axioms.

The sublime sentiment, which is also the sentiment of the sublime, is, according to Kant, a strong and equivocal emotion: It carries with it both pleasure and pain. Better still, in it pleasure derives from pain. Within the tradition of the subject, which comes from Augustine and Descartes and which Kant does not radically challenge, this contradiction, which some would call neurosis or masochism, develops as a conflict between the faculties of a subject, the faculty to conceive of something and the faculty to "present" something. Knowledge exists if, first, the statement is intelligible, and second, if "cases" can be derived from the experience which "corresponds" to it. Beauty exists if a certain "case" (the work of art), given first by the sensibility without any conceptual determination, the sentiment of pleasure independent of any interest the work may elicit, appeals to the principle of a universal consensus (which may never be attained).

Taste, therefore, testifies that between the capacity to conceive and the capacity to present an object corresponding to the concept, an undetermined agreement, without rules, giving rise to a judgment which Kant calls reflective, may be experienced as pleasure. The sublime is a different sentiment. It takes place, on the contrary, when the imagination fails to present an object which might, if only in principle, come to match a concept. We have the Idea of the world (the totality of what is), but we do not have the capacity to show an example of it. We have the Idea of the simple (that which cannot be broken down, decomposed), but we cannot illustrate it with a sensible object which would be a "case" of it. We can conceive the infinitely great, the infinitely powerful, but every presentation of an object destined to "make visible" this absolute greatness or power appears to us painfully inadequate. Those are Ideas of which no presentation is possible. Therefore, they impart no knowledge about reality (experience); they also prevent the free union of the faculties which gives rise to the sentiment of the beautiful; and they prevent the formation and the stabilization of taste. They can be said to be unpresentable.

I shall call modern the art which devotes its "little technical expertise" (*son "petit technique"*), as Diderot used to say, to present the fact that the unpresentable exists. To make visible that there is something which can be conceived and which can neither be seen nor made visible: This is what is at stake in modern painting. But how to make visible that there is something which cannot be seen? Kant himself shows the way when he names "formlessness, the absence of form," as a possible index to the unpresentable. He also says of the empty "abstraction" which the imagination experiences when in search for a presentation of the infinite (another unpresentable): This abstraction itself is like a presentation of the infinite, its "negative presentation." He cites the commandment, "Thou shalt not make graven images" (*Exodus*), as the most sublime passage in the Bible in that it forbids all presentation of the Absolute. Little needs to be added to those observations to outline an aesthetic of sublime paintings. As painting, it will of course "present" something though negatively; it will therefore avoid figuration or representation. It will be "white" like one of Malevitch's squares; it will enable us to see only by making it impossible to see; it will please only by causing pain. One recognizes in those instructions the axioms of avant-gardes in painting, inasmuch as they devote themselves to making an allusion to the unpresentable by means of visible presentations. The systems in the name of which, or with which, this task has been able to support or to justify itself deserve the greatest attention; but they can originate only in the vocation of the sublime in order to legitimize it, that is, to conceal it. They remain inexplicable without the incommensurability of reality to concept which is implied in the Kantian philosophy of the sublime.

It is not my intention to analyze here in detail the manner in which the various avant-gardes have, so to speak, humbled and disqualified reality by examining the pictorial techniques which are so many devices to make us believe in it. Local tone, drawing, the mixing of colors, linear perspective, the nature of the support and that of the instrument, the treatment, the display, the museum: The avant-gardes are perpetually flushing out artifices of presentation which make it possible to subordinate thought to the gaze and to turn it away from the unpresentable. If [Jürgen] Habermas, like [Herbert] Marcuse, understands this task of derealization as an aspect of the (repressive) "desublimation" which characterizes the avant-garde, it is because he confuses the Kantian sublime with Freudian sublimation, and because aesthetics has remained for him that of the beautiful.

The Postmodern

What, then, is the postmodern? What place does it or does it not occupy in the vertiginous work of the questions hurled at the rules of image and narration? It is undoubtedly a part of the modern. All that has been received, if only yesterday (*modo, modo,* Petronius used to say), must be suspected. What space does Cézanne challenge? The Impressionists'. What object do Picasso and Braque attack? Cézanne's. What presupposition does Duchamp break with in 1912? That which says one must make a painting, be it cubist. And Buren* questions that other

*Daniel Buren, French writer on visual art.

presupposition which he believes had survived untouched by the work of Duchamp: the place of presentation of the work. In an amazing acceleration, the generations precipitate themselves. A work can become modern only if it is first postmodern. Postmodernism thus understood is not modernism at its end but in the nascent state, and this state is constant.

Yet I would like not to remain with this slightly mechanistic meaning of the word. If it is true that modernity takes place in the withdrawal of the real and according to the sublime relation between the presentable and the conceivable, it is possible, within this relation, to distinguish two modes (to use the musician's language). The emphasis can be placed on the powerlessness of the faculty of presentation, on the nostalgia for presence felt by the human subject, on the obscure and futile will which inhabits him in spite of everything. The emphasis can be placed, rather, on the power of the faculty to conceive, on its "inhumanity" so to speak (it was the quality Appolinaire demanded of modern artists), since it is not the business of our understanding whether or not human sensibility or imagination can match what it conceives. The emphasis can also be placed on the increase of being and the jubilation which result from the invention of new rules of the game, be it pictorial, artistic, or any other. What I have in mind will become clear if we dispose very schematically a few names on the chessboard of the history of avant-gardes: on the side of melancholia, the German Expressionists, and on the side of *novatio,* Braque and Picasso, on the former Malevitch and on the latter Lissitsky, on the one Chirico and on the other Duchamp. The nuance which distinguishes these two modes may be infinitesimal; they often coexist in the same piece, are almost indistinguishable; and yet they testify to a difference (*un différend*) on which the fate of thought depends and will depend for a long time, between regret and assay.

The work of Proust and that of Joyce both allude to something which does not allow itself to be made present. Allusion, to which Paolo Fabbri recently called my attention, is perhaps a form of expression indispensable to the works which belong to an aesthetic of the sublime. In Proust, what is being eluded as the price to pay for this allusion is the identity of consciousness, a victim to the excess of time (*au trop de temps*). But in Joyce, it is the identity of writing which is the victim of an excess of the book (*au trop de livre*) or of literature.

Proust calls forth the unpresentable by means of a language unaltered in its syntax and vocabulary and of a writing which in many of its operators still belongs to the genre of novelistic narration. The literary institution, as Proust inherits it from Balzac and Flaubert, is admittedly subverted in that the hero is no longer a character but the inner consciousness of time, and in that the diegetic diachrony, already damaged by Flaubert, is here put in question because of the narrative voice. Nevertheless, the unity of the book, the odyssey of that consciousness, even if it is deferred from chapter to chapter, is not seriously challenged: The identity of the writing with itself throughout the labyrinth of the interminable narration is enough to connote such unity, which has been compared to that of [Hegel's] *The Phenomenology of Mind.*

Joyce allows the unpresentable to become perceptible in his writing itself, in the signifier. The whole range of available narrative and even stylistic operators is put into play without concern for the unity of the whole, and new operators are tried. The grammar and vocabulary of literary language are no longer accepted as given; rather, they appear as academic forms, as rituals originating in piety (as Nietzsche said) which prevent the unpresentable from being put forward.

Here, then, lies the difference: Modern aesthetics is an aesthetic of the sublime, though a nostalgic one. It allows the unpresentable to be put forward only as the missing contents; but the form, because of its recognizable consistency, continues to offer to the reader or viewer matter for solace and pleasure. Yet these sentiments do not constitute the real sublime sentiment, which is in an intrinsic combination of pleasure and pain: the pleasure that reason should exceed all presentation, the pain that imagination or sensibility should not be equal to the concept.

The postmodern would be that which, in the modern, puts forward the unpresentable in presentation itself; that which denies itself the solace of good forms, the consensus of a taste which would make it possible to share collectively the nostalgia for the unattainable; that which searches for new presentations, not in order to enjoy them but in order to impart a stronger sense of the unpresentable. A postmodern artist or writer is in the position of a philosopher: The text he writes, the work he produces are not in principle governed by preestablished rules, and they cannot be judged according to a determining judgment, by applying familiar categories to the text or to the work. Those rules and categories are what the work of art itself is looking for. The artist and the writer, then, are working without rules in order to formulate the rules of what *will have been done.* Hence the fact that work and text have the characters of an *event;* hence also, they always come too late for their author, or, what amounts to the same thing, their being put into work, their realization (*mise en oeuvre*) always begin too soon. *Postmodern* would have to be understood according to the paradox of the future (*post*) anterior (*modo*).

It seems to me that the essay (Montaigne) is postmodern, while the fragment (*The Athaeneum*) is modern.

Finally, it must be clear that it is our business not to supply reality but to invent allusions to the conceivable which cannot be presented. And it is not to be expected that this task will effect the last reconciliation between language games (which, under the name of faculties, Kant knew to be separated by a chasm), and that only the transcendental illusion (that of Hegel) can hope to totalize them into a real unity. But Kant also knew that the price to pay for such an illusion is terror. The nineteenth and twentieth centuries have given us as much terror as we can take. We have paid a high enough price for the nostalgia of the whole and the one, for the reconciliation of the concept and the sensible, of the transparent and the communicable experience. Under the general demand for slackening and for appeasement, we can hear the mutterings of the desire for a return of terror, for the realization of fantasy to seize reality. The answer is: Let us wage a war on totality; let us be witnesses to the unpresentable; let us activate the differences and save the honor of the name.

Television and Aesthetics

▪ Umberto Eco ▪

A popular song, a TV commercial, a comic strip, a detective novel, a Western movie were seen as more or less successful tokens of a given model or type. As such they were judged as pleasurable but non-artistic. Furthermore, this excess of pleasurability, repetition, lack of innovation, was felt as a commercial trick (the product had to meet the expectations of its audience), not as the provocative proposal of a new (and difficult to accept) world vision. The products of mass media were equated with the products of industry insofar as they were produced *in series,* and the "serial" production was considered as alien to the artistic invention.

According to the modern aesthetics, the principal features of the mass-media products were repetition, iteration, obedience to a preestablished schema, and redundancy (as opposed to information).

The device of *iteration* is typical, for instance, of television commercials: One distractedly watches the playing out of a sketch, then focuses one's attention on the punch line that reappears at the end of the episode. It is precisely on this foreseen and awaited reappearance that our modest but irrefutable pleasure is based.

Likewise, the reading of a traditional detective story presumes the enjoyment of a scheme. The scheme is so important that the most famous authors have founded their fortune on its very immutability.

Furthermore, the writer plays upon a continuous series of connotations (for example, the characteristics of the detective and of his immediate "entourage") to such an extent that their reappearance in each story is an essential condition of its reading pleasure. And so we have the by now historical "tics" of Sherlock Holmes, the punctilious vanity of Hercule Poirot, the pipe and the familiar fixes of [Inspector] Maigret, on up to the famous idiosyncrasies of the most unabashed heroes of the hard-boiled novel. Vices, gestures, habits of the character portrayed permit us to recognize an old friend. These familiar features allow us to "enter into" the event. When our favorite author writes a story in which the usual characters do not appear, we are not even aware that the fundamental scheme of the story is still like the others: We read the book with a certain detachment and are immediately prone to judge it a "minor" one. . . .

Vol 114

"Television and Aesthetics" by Umberto Eco has been excerpted from "Innovation and Repetition: Between Modern and Post-Modern Aesthetics," *Daedalus* (Fall 1985), pages 162–163, 166–169, 179–180, and is reprinted by permission of the publisher.

The Era of Repetition

I would like to consider now the case of an historical period (our own) for which iteration and repetition seem to dominate the whole world of artistic creativity, and in which it is difficult to distinguish between the repetition of the media and the repetition of the so-called major arts. In this period one is facing the discussion of a new theory of art, one that I would label *postmodern aesthetics,* which is revisiting the very concepts of repetition and iteration under a different profile. Recently in Italy such a debate has flourished under the standard of a "new aesthetics of seriality." I recommend my readers to take "seriality," in this case, as a very wide category or, if one wants, as another term for repetitive art.

Seriality and repetition are largely inflated concepts. The philosophy of the history of art has accustomed us to some technical meanings of these terms that it would be well to eliminate: I shall not speak of repetition in the sense of Kierkegaard, nor of "répétition différente," in the sense of [Gilles] Deleuze. In the history of contemporary music, series and seriality have been understood in a sense more or less opposite what we are discussing here. The dodecaphonic "series" is the opposite of the repetitive seriality typical of all the media, because there a given succession of twelve sounds is used once and only once within a single composition.

If you open a current dictionary, you will find that for "repeat" the meaning is "to say something or do something the second time or again and again; iteration of the same word, act or idea." For "series" the meaning is "a continued succession of similar things." It is a matter of establishing what it means to say "again" or "the same or similar things."

To serialize means, in some way, *to repeat.* Therefore, we shall have to define a first meaning of "to repeat" by which the term means to make a *replica* of the same *abstract type.* Two sheets of typewriter paper are both *replicas* of the same commercial *type.* In this sense one thing is the same as another when the former exhibits the same properties as the latter, at least under a certain description: Two sheets of typing paper are the same from the point of view of our functional needs, even though they are not the same for a physicist interested in the molecular structure of the objects. From the point of view of industrial mass production, two "tokens" can be considered as "replicas" of the same "type" when for a normal person with normal requirements, in the absence of evident imperfection, it is irrelevant whether one chooses one instead of the other. Two copies of a film or of a book are replicas of the same type.

The repetitiveness and the seriality that interests us here look instead at something that at first glance does not appear the same as (equal to) something else.

Let us now see the case in which (1) something is offered as original and different (according to the requirements of modern aesthetics); (2) we are aware that this something is repeating something else that we already know; and (3) notwithstanding this—better, just because of it—we like it (and we buy it).

The Retake

The first type of repetition is the *retake*. In this case one recycles the characters of a previous successful story in order to exploit them, by telling what happened to them after the end of their first adventure. The most famous example of retake is [Alexandre] Dumas's *Twenty Years Later,* the most recent ones are the "to be continued" versions of *Star Wars* or *Superman*. The retake is dependent on a commercial decision. There is no rule establishing whether the second episode of the story should reproduce, with only slight variations, the first one, or must be a totally different story concerning the same characters. The retake is not strictly condemned to repetition. An illustrious example of retake are the many different stories of the Arthurian cycle, telling again and again the vicissitudes of Lancelot or Perceval.

The Remake

The *remake* consists in telling again a previous successful story. See the innumerable editions of *Dr. Jekyll* or of *Mutiny on the Bounty*. The history of arts and literature is full of pseudo-remakes that were able to tell at every time something different. The whole of Shakespeare is a remake of preceding stories. Therefore "interesting" remakes can escape repetition.

The Series

The *series* works upon a fixed situation and a restricted number of fixed pivotal characters, around whom the secondary and changing ones turn. The secondary characters must give the impression that the new story is different from the preceding ones, while in fact the narrative scheme does not change. . . .

To the same type belong the TV serials such as *All in the Family, Starsky and Hutch, Columbo,* etc. (I put together different TV genres that range from soap opera to situation comedy, and to the detective serial.)

With a series one believes one is enjoying the novelty of the story (which is always the same) while in fact one is enjoying it because of the recurrence of a narrative scheme that remains constant. The series in this sense responds to the infantile need of hearing again always the same story, of being consoled by the "return of the Identical," superficially disguised.

The series consoles us (the consumers) because it rewards our ability to foresee: We are happy because we discover our own ability to guess what will happen. We are satisfied because we find again what we had expected, but we do not attribute this happy result to the obviousness of the narrative structure, but to our own presumed capacities to make forecasts. We do not think, "The author has constructed the story in a way that I could guess the end," but rather, "I was so smart to guess the end in spite of the efforts the author made to deceive me."

We find a variation of the series in the structure of the flashback: We see, for example, some comic-strip stories (such as Superman) in which the character is not followed along in a straight line during the course of his life, but is continually rediscovered at different moments of his life, obsessively revisited in order to discover the new opportunities for new narratives. It seems as if these moments of his life have fled from the narrator out of absent-mindedness, but their rediscovery does not change the psychological profile of the character, which is fixed already, once and for all. In topological terms this sub-type of the series may be defined as a *loop*.

Usually the loop-series comes to be devised for commercial reasons: It is a matter of considering how to keep the series alive, of obviating the natural problem of the aging of the character. Instead of having characters put up with new adventures (that would imply their inexorable march toward death), they are made continually to relive their past. The loop solution produces paradoxes that were already the target of innumerable parodies. Characters have a little future but an enormous past, and in any case, nothing of their past will ever have to change the mythological present in which they have been presented to the reader from the beginning. Ten different lives would not suffice to make Little Orphan Annie undergo what she underwent in the first (and only) ten years of her life.

The spiral is another variation of the series. In the stories of Charlie Brown, apparently nothing happens, and any character is obsessively repeating his/her standard performance. And yet in every strip the character of Charlie Brown or Snoopy is enriched and deepened. This does not happen either with Nero Wolfe, or Starsky or Hutch: We are always interested in their new adventures, but we already know all we need to know about their psychology, their habits, their capacities, their ethical standpoints.

I would add finally that form of seriality that, in cinema and television, is motivated less by the narrative structure than by the nature of the actor himself: The mere presence of John Wayne, or of Jerry Lewis (when they are not directed by a great director, and even in these cases) succeeds in making, always, the *same* film. The author tries to invent different stories, but the public recognizes (with satisfaction) always and ever the same story, under superficial disguises. . . .

When one speaks today of the aesthetics of seriality, one alludes to something more radical, that is, to a notion of aesthetic value that wholly escapes the "modern" idea of art and literature.

It has been observed that with the phenomenon of television serials we find a new concept of "the infinity of the text"; the text takes on the rhythms of that same dailiness in which it is produced, and that it mirrors. The problem is not one of recognizing that the serial text varies indefinitely upon a basic scheme (and in this sense it can be judged from the point of view of the "modern" aesthetics). The real problem is that what is of interest is not so much the single variations as "variability" as a formal principle, the fact that one can make variations to infinity. Variability to infinity has all the characteristics of repetition, and very little of innovation. But it is the "infinity" of the process that gives a new sense to the device of variation. What must be enjoyed—suggest the postmodern aesthetics—is the fact that a series of possible variations is potentially infinite. What becomes celebrated here is a sort of victory of life over art, with the paradoxical result that the era of electronics—instead of emphasizing the phenomena of shock, interruptions, novelty, and frustration of expectations—would produce a return to the continuum, the Cyclical, the Periodical, the Regular.

Omar Calabrese has thoroughly looked into this: From the point of view of the "modern" dialectic between repetition and innovation, one can easily recognize how in the Columbo series, for example, on a basic scheme some of the best names in American cinema have worked in variations. Thus it would be difficult to speak, in such a case, of pure repetition: If the scheme of the detection and the psychology of the protagonist actor remains unchanged, the style of the narrative changes each time. This is no small thing, especially from the point of view of the "modern" aesthetics. But it is exactly on a different idea of style that Calabrese's paper is centered. In these forms of repetition "we are not so much interested in what is repeated as we are in the way the components of the text come to be segmented and then how the segments come to be codified in order to establish a system of invariants: Any component that does not belong to the system, can be defined as an *independent variable*." In the most typical and apparently "degenerated" cases of seriality, the independent variables are not altogether the more visible, but the more microscopic, as in a homeopathic solution where the potion is all the more potent because by further "succussions" the original particles of the medicinal product have almost disappeared. This is what permits Calabrese to speak of the Columbo series as an "exercice de style" à la Queneau. We are, says Calabrese, facing a "neobaroque aesthetics" that is instantiated, not only by the "cultivated" products, but even, and above all, by those that are most degenerated. Apropos of *Dallas,* one can say that "the semantic opposition and the articulation of the elementary narrative structures can migrate in combinations of the highest improbability around the various characters."

Organized differentiations, polycentrism, regulated irregularity—such would be the fundamental aspects of this neo-baroque aesthetic, the principal example of which is musical variations à la Bach. Since in the epoch of mass communications "the condition for listening . . . as in the Kabuki theater, it may then be the most minuscule variant that will produce pleasure in the text, or that form of explicit repetition which is already known."

What results from these reflections is clear. The focus of the theoretical inquiry is displaced. Before, mass mediologists tried to save the dignity of repetition by recognizing in it the possibility of a traditional dialectic between scheme and innovation (but it was still the innovation that accounted for the value, the way of rescuing the product from degradation and promoting it to a value). Now, the emphasis must be placed on the inseparable knot of scheme-variation, where the variation is no longer more appreciable than the scheme. The term neobaroque must not deceive: We are witnessing the birth of a new aesthetic sensibility much more archaic, and truly post-postmodern.

Simulations
■ Jean Baudrillard ■

The simulacrum is never that which conceals the truth—it is the truth which conceals that there is none.
The simulacrum is true.

—Ecclesiastes

If we were able to take as the finest allegory of simulation the Borges tale where the cartographers of the Empire draw up a map so detailed that it ends up exactly covering the territory (but where the decline of the Empire sees this map become frayed and finally ruined, a few shreds still discernible in the deserts—the metaphysical beauty of this ruined abstraction, bearing witness to an Imperial pride and rotting like a carcass, returning to the substance of the soil, rather as an aging double ends up being confused with the real thing)—then this fable has come full circle for us, and now has nothing but the discrete charm of second-order simulacra.

Abstraction today is no longer that of the map, the double, the mirror or the concept. Simulation is no longer that of a territory, a referential being or a substance. It is the generation by models of a real without origin or reality: a hyperreal. The territory no longer precedes the map, nor survives it. Henceforth, it is the map that precedes the territory—**PRECESSION OF SIMULACRA**—it is the map that engenders the territory and if we were to revive the fable today, it would be the territory whose shreds are slowly rotting across the map. It is the real, and not the map, whose vestiges subsist here and there, in the deserts which are no longer those of the Empire, but our own. *The desert of the real itself.*

In fact, even inverted, the fable is useless. Perhaps only the allegory of the Empire remains. For it is with the same Imperialism that present-day simulators try to make the real, all the real, coincide with their simulation models. But it is no longer a question of either maps or territory. Something has disappeared: the sovereign difference between them that was the abstraction's charm. For it is the difference which forms the poetry of the map and the charm of the territory, the magic of the concept and the charm of the real. This representational imaginary, which both culminates in and is engulfed by the cartographer's mad project of an ideal coextensivity between the map and the territory, disappears with simulation—whose operation is nuclear and genetic, and no longer specular and discursive. With it goes all of metaphysics. No more mirror of being and appearances, of the real and

"Simulations" by Jean Baudrillard is excerpted from *Simulations,* Semiotext(e) (1983), pages 1–6, 10–13, and reprinted by permission of the publisher.

its concept. No more imaginary coextensivity: Rather, genetic miniaturisation is the dimension of simulation. The real is produced from miniaturised units, from matrices, memory banks and command models—and with these it can be reproduced an indefinite number of times. It no longer has to be rational, since it is no longer measured against some ideal or negative instance. It is nothing more than operational. In fact, since it is no longer enveloped by an imaginary, it is no longer real at all. It is a hyperreal, the product of an irradiating synthesis of combinatory models in a hyperspace without atmosphere.

In this passage to a space whose curvature is no longer that of the real, nor of truth, the age of simulation thus begins with a liquidation of all referentials— worse: by their artificial resurrection in systems of signs, a more ductile material than meaning, in that it lends itself to all systems of equivalence, all binary oppositions and all combinatory algebra. It is no longer a question of imitation, nor of reduplication, nor even of parody. It is rather a question of substituting signs of the real for the real itself, that is, an operation to deter every real process by its operational double, a metastable, programmatic, perfect descriptive machine which provides all the signs of the real and short-circuits all its vicissitudes. Never again will the real have to be produced—this is the vital function of the model in a system of death, or rather of anticipated resurrection which no longer leaves any chance even in the event of death. A hyperreal henceforth sheltered from the imaginary, and from any distinction between the real and the imaginary, leaving room only for the orbital recurrence of models and the simulated generation of difference.

The Divine Irreference of Images

To dissimulate is to feign not to have what one has. To simulate is to feign to have what one hasn't. One implies a presence, the other an absence. But the matter is more complicated, since to simulate is not simply to feign: "Someone who feigns an illness can simply go to bed and make believe he is ill. Some[one] who simulates an illness produces in himself some of the symptoms" (Littre*) Thus, feigning or dissimulating leaves the reality principle intact: the difference is always clear, it is only masked; whereas simulation threatens the difference between "true" and "false," between "real" and "imaginary." Since the simulator produces "true" symptoms, is he ill or not? He cannot be treated objectively either as ill, or as not-ill. Psychology and medicine stop at this point, before a thereafter undiscoverable truth of the illness. For if any symptom can be "produced," and can no longer be accepted as a fact of nature, then every illness may be considered as simulatable and simulated, and medicine loses its meaning since it only knows how to treat "true" illnesses by their objective causes. Psychosomatics evolves in a dubious way on the edge of the illness principle. As for psychoanalysis, it transfers the symptom from the organic to the unconscious order: Once again, the latter is held to be true, more true than the former—but why should simulation stop at the

*Emile Littre, author of *Dictionaire de Medicine*.

portals of the unconscious? Why couldn't the "work" of the unconscious be "produced" in the same way as any other symptom in classical medicine? Dreams already are.

The alienist, of course, claims that "for each form of the mental alienation there is a particular order in the succession of symptoms, of which the simulator is unaware and in the absence of which the alienist is unlikely to be deceived." This (which dates from 1865) in order to save at all cost the truth principle, and to escape the spectre raised by simulation—namely that truth, reference and objective causes have ceased to exist. What can medicine do with something which floats on either side of illness, on either side of health, or with the reduplication of illness in a discourse that is no longer true or false? . . .

Thus perhaps at stake has always been the murderous capacity of images, murderers of the real, murderers of their own model as the Byzantine icons could murder the divine identity. To this murderous capacity is opposed the dialectical capacity of representations as a visible and intelligible mediation of the Real. All of Western faith and good faith was engaged in this wager on representation: that a sign could refer to the depth of meaning, that a sign could *exchange* for meaning and that something could guarantee this exchange—God, of course. But what if God himself can be simulated, that is to say, reduced to the signs which attest his existence? Then the whole system becomes weightless, it is no longer anything but a gigantic simulacrum—not unreal, but a simulacrum, never again exchanging for what is real, but exchanging in itself, in an uninterrupted circuit without reference or circumference.

So it is with simulation, insofar as it is opposed to representation. The latter starts from the principle that the sign and the real are equivalent (even if this equivalence is utopian, it is a fundamental axiom). Conversely, simulation starts from the *utopia* of this principle of equivalence, *from the radical negation of the sign as value,* from the sign as reversion and death sentence of every reference. Whereas representation tries to absorb simulation by interpreting it as false representation, simulation envelops the whole edifice of representation as itself a simulacrum.

This would be the successive phases of the image:

- it is the reflection of a basic reality
- it masks and perverts a basic reality
- it masks the *absence* of a basic reality
- it bears no relation to any reality whatever: it is its own pure simulacrum.

In the first case, the image is a *good* appearance—the representation is of the order of sacrament. In the second, it is an *evil* appearance—of the order of malefice. In the third, it *plays at being* an appearance—it is of the order of sorcery. In the fourth, it is no longer in the order of appearance at all, but of simulation.

The transition from signs which dissimulate something to signs which dissimulate that there is nothing, marks the decisive turning point. The first implies a theology of truth and secrecy (to which the notion of ideology still belongs). The second inaugurates an age of simulacra and stimulation, in which there is no longer any God to recognise his own, nor any last judgement to separate true from false, the real from its artificial resurrection, since everything is already dead and risen in advance.

When the real is no longer what it used to be, nostalgia assumes its full meaning. There is a proliferation of myths of origin and signs of reality; of second-hand truth, objectivity and authenticity. There is an escalation of the true, of the lived experience; a resurrection of the figurative where the object and substance have disappeared. And there is a panic-stricken production of the real and the referential, above and parallel to the panic of material production: This is how simulation appears in the phase that concerns us—a strategy of the real, neo-real and hyperreal whose universal double is a strategy of deterrence.

Plato and the Mass Media
■ Alexander Nehamas ■

Book X of the *Republic* contains a scathing attack on poetry which is still, by turns, both incomprehensible and disturbing. Plato's banishment of the poets from his model city has always been a cause of interpretive difficulties and philosophical embarrassments, even for some of his greatest admirers. But I am now beginning to believe that the difficulties are not real and that the embarrassments are only apparent, and my purpose in what follows is to offer an outline—I cannot do more than that on this occasion—of my reasons for thinking so. I am convinced that close attention to the philosophical assumptions which underlie Plato's criticisms reveals that his attack on poetry is better understood as a specific social and historical gesture than as an attack on poetry, and especially on art, as such. But placed within their original context, Plato's criticisms, perhaps paradoxically, become immediately relevant to a serious contemporary debate. . . .

Plato clearly allows the young Guardians to be imitators of good characters. But actually he allows them to imitate bad characters, if it is necessary and if they do so not seriously (*spoudēi*) and only in play (*paidias charin*)—that is, in order to satirize and ridicule them (396c5–e8). Plato forbids not imitation, which he considers essential to education, but imitativeness, the desire and ability to imitate anything independently of its moral quality and without the proper attitude of praise or blame toward it (395a2–5, 397a1–b2, 398a1–b4). When Socrates says in Book X that "all mimetic poetry" (*poiēseōs hosē mimētikē*) has been excluded

"Plato and the Mass Media" by Alexander Nehamas has been excerpted from *The Monist* 71, Number 2 (April 1988), pages 214–225, and is reprinted by permission of the publisher.

from the city, he does not refer to all imitation but only, as his own word shows, to poetry which involves and encourages imitativeness: The conflict disappears.

The elimination of these interpretative difficulties may help to show that Book X is an integral part of the *Republic*. But this only adds to the philosophical embarrassments it creates. Why, after all, does a work of moral and political philosophy end with a discussion of aesthetics? The obvious answer is that Plato simply does not distinguish aesthetics from ethics. His argument against poetry depends on ontological principles regarding the status of its objects and on epistemological views about the poets' understanding of their subject-matter, but his concern with poetry is ethical through and through. It is expressed in just such terms both at the very beginning of the argument, when Socrates claims that tragedy and all imitative poetry constitute "a harm to the mind of its audience" (595b5–6) and at its very end, when he concludes that if we allow poetry in the city "pleasure and pain will rule as monarchs . . . instead of the law and that rational principle which is always and by all thought to be the best" (607a5–8).

It is just this obvious answer, however, that causes the greatest philosophical embarrassment by far because it suggests that Plato is utterly blind to the real value of art, that he is unable to see that there is much more than an ethical dimension to art, and that even in its ethical dimension art is by no means as harmful as he is convinced it is.

It is against this embarrassment that I want to defend Plato, though I do not want to have to decide whether he was right or wrong in his denunciation of Homer and Aeschylus. I believe, and hope to convince you as well, that the issue is much too complicated for this sort of easy judgment. But I do think that Plato's view deserves to be reexamined and that it is directly relevant to many contemporary concerns. Plato's attitude toward epic and tragic poetry is in fact embodied in our current thinking about the arts, though not specifically in our thinking about epic and tragedy. Though his views often appear incomprehensible, or reprehensible, or both, we often duplicate them, though without being aware of them as his. If this is right, then either Book X of the *Republic* is more reasonable and more nearly correct than we are ever tempted to suppose or we must ourselves reevaluate our own assumptions and attitudes regarding the arts.

First, a preliminary point. Plato is not in any way concerned with art as such. This is not only because, if Paul Kristeller is correct, the very concept of the fine arts did not emerge in Europe until the eighteenth century. The main reason is quite specific: Plato does not even include painting in his denunciation. His argument does in fact depend on a series of analogies between painting and poetry, and he introduces all the major ideas through which he will eventually banish the poets by means of these analogies. This has led a number of scholars to conclude, and to feel they should explain why, Plato banished the artists from his model city. But a careful reading shows that neither painting nor sculpture is outlawed by Plato. This suggests, as we shall see in more detail below, that no general account of Plato's attitude toward the arts is required. It also implies that we must determine which specific feature of imitative poetry makes it so dangerous that, in contrast to the other arts, it cannot be tolerated in Plato's city.

This feature, on which Plato's argument against poetry crucially depends is that poetry (in telling contrast to painting and, particularly, to sculpture) is as a medium inherently suited to the representation, or imitation, of vulgar subjects and shameful behavior:

> The irritable part of the soul gives many opportunities for all sorts of imitations, while the wise and quiet character which always remains the same is neither easy to imitate nor easy to understand when imitated, especially for a festival crowd, people of all sorts gathered in the theaters. (60e1–5)

Plato makes his "greatest" objection to poetry on the basis of this idea. Not only average people but good people as well, even "the best among us," are vulnerable to its harmful influence (605c6–10). Socrates speaks for these select individuals when he says that, confronted with the excessive and unseemly lamentation that is the staple of tragic and epic poetry, "we enjoy it, surrender ourselves, share [the heroes'] feelings, and earnestly praise as a good poet whoever affects us most in this way" (605d3–5; cf. *Phil.* 48a, *Ion* 535a, *Lg.* 800d). And yet, at least in the case of the best among us if not also among the rest of the people as well, this sort of behavior is exactly what we try to avoid when we meet with misfortunes of our own: In life, Plato claims, we praise the control and not the indulgence of our feelings of sorrow. How is it then that we admire in poetry just the kind of person we would be ashamed to resemble in life (605d7–e6)?

Socrates tries to account for this absurdity by means of the psychological terms provided by the tripartition of the soul in Book IV of the *Republic*. The lowest, appetitive, part of the soul, which is only concerned with immediate gratification and not with the good of the whole agent, delights in shameful behavior as it delights in anything that is not measured. Now poetry depicts the sufferings of others, not our own. The rational part of the soul, accordingly, is in this case indulgent toward the appetite, and allows it free expression. The whole agent, therefore, in the belief that such indulgence is harmless, enjoys the pleasure with which poetry provides the appetite (606a3–b5).

What we fail to realize is that enjoying the expression of sorrow in the case of others is directly transferred to the sorrows of our own. Cultivating our feelings of pity in spectacles disposes us to express them in similar ways in our own case and to enjoy (or at least to find no shame in) doing so: Thus it ultimately leads us to make a spectacle of ourselves (606a3–b8). Plato now generalizes his conclusion from sorrow in particular to all the passions:

> So too with sex, anger, and all the desires, pleasures, and pains which we say follow us in every activity. Poetic imitation fosters these in us. It nurtures and waters them when they ought to wither; it places them in command in our soul when they ought to obey in order that we might become better and happier . . . instead of worse and more miserable. (606d1–7)

In short, Plato accuses poetry of perverting its audience. Poetry is essentially suited to the representation of inferior characters and vulgar subjects: These are easy to imitate and what the crowd, which is already perverted to begin with, wants to see and enjoys. But the trouble is that all of us have an analogue to the crowd within our own soul (cf. 580d2–581a1). This is the appetitive part (the counterpart to the third and largest class, the money-lovers, in Plato's analogy between city and soul), to the desires and pleasures of which we are all more or less sensitive. And since—this is a most crucial assumption to which we shall have to return—our reactions to poetry are transferred directly to, and in fact often determine, our reactions to life, poetry is likely to make us behave in ways of which we should be, and often are, ashamed. Poetry "introduces a bad government in the soul of each individual citizen" (605b7–8). But this is to destroy the soul and to destroy the city. It is precisely the opposite of everything the *Republic* is designed to accomplish. This is why poetry is intolerable.

We must now turn to Plato's deeply controversial assumption that our reactions to life follow on the lines of our reactions to poetry: The whole issue of the sense of Plato's charges against poetry and of their contemporary importance depends just on this idea. On its face, of course, this assumption can be easily dismissed. Enjoying (if that is the proper word) Euripides' *Medea* is not likely to dispose us to admire mothers who murder their children for revenge nor to want to do so ourselves nor even to tend to adopt as our own Medea's ways of lamenting her fate. But this quick reaction misses precisely what is deep and important in Plato's attitude.

To begin to see what that is, we should note that Plato's assumption does not seem so unreasonable in connection with children. Almost everyone today would find something plausible in Plato's prohibition that children imitate bad models "lest from enjoying the imitation they come to enjoy the reality" and something accurate in his suspicion that "imitations, if they last from youth for some time, become part of one's nature and settle into habits of gesture, voice, and thought" (395c7–d3). On this issue, Aristotle, who disagrees on so many issues regarding poetry with Plato, is in complete agreement: "We should also banish pictures and speeches from the stage which are indecent . . . the legislator should not allow youth to be spectators of iambi or of comedy" (*Pol.* VII, 1336b14–21). But, also like Plato, Aristotle does not confine his view to children only: "As we know from our own experience . . . the habit of feeling pleasure or pain at mere representations (*ta homoia*) is not far removed from the same feelings about realities" (*Pol.* VIII, 1340a21–25).

To a great extent, in fact, Aristotle's vindication of tragedy against Plato involves the argument that poetry is actually morally beneficial. And the reason for this is that *katharsis* both excites and purifies emotions which, in Stephen Halliwell's words, "although potent, are properly and justifiably evoked by a portrayal of events which, if encountered in reality, would call for the same emotional response." The assumption that there is some direct connection between our reactions to poetry and our reactions to life is common to both philosophers. The main difference is that Aristotle argues, against Plato, that this parallel tends to benefit rather than to harm the conduct of our life.

The Platonic argument seems plausible in the case of children because many of us think (though this view is itself debatable) that, unclear about the difference between them, children often treat representations simply as parts of and not also as symbols for reality. They don't always seem able, for example, to distinguish a fictional danger from a real one. But Plato, as we have seen, believed that the case is similar with adults. Their reactions to poetry, too, determine their reactions to life because, to put the point bluntly, they are exactly the same kind of reactions. And the reason for this is that, as he believed, the representations of poetry are, at least superficially, exactly the same kind of objects as the real things they represent. The expression of sorrow in the theater is superficially identical with—exactly the same in appearance as—the expression of sorrow in life. Though actors do not, or need not, feel the sorrow they express on the stage, this underlying difference is necessarily imperceptible and allows the surface behavior of actors and real grievers to be exactly the same. . . . The clear implication is that the poets produce apparent crafts and apparent virtues in their imitations of what people say and do; they duplicate the appearance of people engaged in the practice of a craft or of virtuous activity (600e3–601b1). . . .

The metaphysics of Pygmalion is still in the center of our thinking about the arts. To see that this is so, and why, we must change subjects abruptly and recall Newton Minnow's famous address to the National Association of Broadcasters in 1961. Though Minnow admitted that some television was of high quality, he insisted that if his audience were to watch, from beginning to end, a full day's programming,

> I can assure you that you will observe a vast wasteland. You will see a procession of game shows, violence, audience participation shows, formula comedies about totally unbelievable families, blood and thunder, mayhem, violence, sadism, murder, western badmen, western goodmen, private eyes, gangsters, more violence, and cartoons.

This general view of the vulgarity of television has been given a less extreme expression, and a rationale, by George Gerbner and Larry Gross:

> Unlike the real world, where personalities are complex, motives unclear, and outcomes ambiguous, television presents a world of clarity and simplicity. . . . In order to complete a story entertainingly in only an hour or even half an hour conflicts on TV are usually personal and solved by action. Since violence is dramatic and relatively simple to produce, much of the action tends to be violent.

An extraordinary, almost hysterical version of such a view, but nevertheless a version that is uncannily close to Plato's attitude that the lowest part of the soul is the subject-matter of poetry, is given by Jerry Mander. Television, he writes, is inherently suited for

> expressing hate, fear, jealousy, winning, wanting, and violence . . . hysteria or ebullience of the kind of one-dimensional joyfulness usually associated with some objective victory—the facial expressions and bodily movements of antisocial behavior.

Mander also duplicates, in connection with television, Plato's view that poetry directly influences our life for the worse: "We slowly evolve into the images we carry, we become what we see." This, of course, is the guiding premise of the almost universal debate concerning the portrayal of sex, violence, and other disapproved or antisocial behavior on television on the grounds that it tends to encourage television's audience to engage in such behavior in life. And a very sophisticated version of this Platonic point, making use of the distinction between form and content, has been accepted by Wayne Booth:

> The effects of the medium in shaping the primary experience of the viewer, and thus the quality of the self during the viewing, are radically resistant to any elevation of quality in the program content: as viewer, I become *how* I view, more than *what* I view. . . . Unless we change their characteristic forms, the new media will surely corrupt whatever global village they create; you cannot build a world community out of misshapen souls.

We have seen that Plato's reason for thinking that our reactions to life duplicate our reactions to poetry is that imitations are superficially identical with the objects of which they are imitations. Exactly this explanation is also given by Rudolph Arnheim, who wrote that television "is a mere instrument of transmission, which does not offer any new means for the artistic interpretation of reality." Television, that is, presents us the world just as it is or, rather, it simply duplicates its appearance. Imitations are substitutes for reality. In Mander's words,

> people were believing that an *image* of nature was equal . . . to the experience of nature . . . . that images of historical events or news events were equal to the events . . . the confusion of . . . information with a wider, direct mode of experience was advancing rapidly.

Plato's argument against poetry is repeated in summary form, and without an awareness of its provenance, in connection with television by Neil Postman: "Television," he writes, "offers viewers a variety of subject-matter, requires minimal skills to comprehend it, and is largely aimed at emotional gratification." The inevitable result, strictly parallel to "the bad government in the soul" which Plato would go to all lengths to avert, is according to Postman, an equally dangerous "spiritual devastation."

Parallels between Plato's view and contemporary attitudes such as that expressed in the statement that "daily consumption of 'Three's Company' is not likely to produce a citizenry concerned about, much less committed to, Madisonian self-government," are to be found wherever you look. Simply put, the greatest part of contemporary criticisms of television depends on a moral disapproval which is identical to Plato's attack on epic and tragic poetry in the fourth century B.C. In this respect, at least, we are most of us Platonists. We must therefore reexamine both our grounds for disapproving of Plato's attack on poetry and our reasons for disapproving of television. . . .

My effort to establish a parallel between Plato's deep, complex, and suspicious hostility toward Homer and Aeschylus on the one hand and the obviously well-deserved contempt with which many today regard *Dynasty* or *Dallas* may well appear simply ridiculous. Though classical Greek poetry still determines many of the criteria that underlie the literary canon of our culture, most of television hardly qualifies as entertainment. Yet my position does not amount to a trivialization of Plato's views. On the contrary, I believe, we are bound to miss (and have already missed) the real urgency of Plato's approach if we persist in taking it as an attack against art as such. Plato was neither insensitive to art nor inconsistent in his desire to produce, as he did, artworks of his own in his dialogues; he neither discerned a deep characteristic of art that pits it essentially against philosophy nor did he envisage a higher form of art which he would have allowed in his city. Plato's argument with poetry concerns a practice which is today paradigmatically a fine art, but it is not an argument directed at it as such a fine art. At this point, the history of art becomes essential for an understanding of its philosophy. Though Plato's attack against poetry in the *Republic* may be the originating text of the philosophy of art, his argument, without being any less profound or disturbing, dismisses poetry as what it was in his time: and poetry then was popular entertainment.

The audience of Attic drama, as far as we now know, was "a 'popular' audience in the sense that it was a body fully representative of the great mass of Athenian people" and included a great number of foreign visitors as well. During the Greater Dionysia in classical times no fewer than 17,000 people, perhaps more, were packed into the god's theater. Pericles, according to Plutarch, established the *theorikon,* a subsidy to cover the price of admission and something more, which ended up being distributed to rich and poor alike, and made of the theater a free entertainment.

The plays were not produced in front of a well-behaved audience. The dense crowd was given to whistling (*syringx*) and the theater resounded with its "uneducated noise" (*amousoi boai plÁthous, Lg.* 700c3). Plato expresses profound distaste for the tumult with which audiences, in the theater and elsewhere, voiced their approval or dissatisfaction (*Rep.* 492c). Their preferences were definitely pronounced if not often sophisticated. Since four plays were produced within a single day, the audience arrived at the theater with large quantities of food. Some of it they consumed themselves—hardly a silent activity in its own right, unlikely to produce the quasi-religious attention required of a fine-art audience today and more reminiscent of other sorts of mass entertainments. Some of their food was used to pelt those actors whom they did not like, and whom they often literally shouted off the stage. In particular, and though this may be difficult to imagine today, the drama was considered a realistic representation of the world: We are told, for example, that a number of women were frightened into having miscarriages or into giving premature birth by the entrance of the Furies in Aeschylus' *Eumenides.*

The realistic interpretation of Attic drama is crucial for our purposes. Simon Goldhill, expressing the recent suspiciousness toward certain naive understandings of realism, has written that Electra's entrance as a peasant in the play Euripides named after her "is upsetting not because it represents reality but because it represents reality in a way which transgresses the conventions of dramatic representations, indeed the representations of reality constructed elsewhere in the play." In fact, he continues, "Euripides constantly forces awareness of theatre as theatre." This, along with the general contemporary claim that all art necessarily contains hints pointing toward its artificial nature and undermining whatever naturalistic pretensions it makes, may well be true. But it doesn't alter the fact that it is of the essence of popular entertainment that these hints are not, while the entertainment still remains popular, consciously perceived. Popular entertainment, in theory and practice, is generally taken to be inherently realistic.

To be inherently realistic is to seem to represent reality without artifice, without mediation and convention. Realistic art is, just in the sense in which Plato thought of imitation, transparent. This transparency, I believe, is not real. It is only the result of our often not being aware of the mediated and conventional nature of the representations to which we are most commonly exposed. As Barish* writes in regard to the theater, "it has an unsettling way of being received by its audiences, at least for the moment and with whatever necessary mental reserves, as reality pure and simple." Whether or not we are aware of it, however, mediation and convention are absolutely essential to all representation. But since, in such cases, they cannot be attributed to the representation itself, which, transparent as it is, cannot be seen as an object with its own status and in its own right, they are instead attributed to the represented subject-matter: The slow-moving speech and action patterns of soap operas, for example, are considered (and criticized) as representations of a slow-moving world.

Attributed to subject-matter, mediation and convention appear, almost by necessity, as distortions. And accordingly (from the fifth century B.C. through Renaissance and Puritan England as well as Jansenist France in connection with the theatre, through the eighteenth- and nineteenth-century attacks on the novel, to contemporary denunciations of the cinema and of television) the reality the popular media are supposed to represent has always been considered, while the media in question are still popular, as a distorted, perverted, and dismal reality. And it has regularly involved campaigns to abolish or reform the popular arts or efforts on the part of the few to distance themselves from the arts as far as possible. And insofar as the audience of these media has been supposed, and has often supposed itself, to react directly to that reality, the audience's undisputed enjoyment of the popular arts has been interpreted as the enjoyment of this distorted, perverted, and dismal reality. It has therefore also been believed that this enjoyment both reflects and contributes to a distorted, perverted, and dismal life—a vast wasteland accurately reflected in the medium which mirrors it.

This is the essence of Plato's attack against poetry and, I believe, the essential idea behind a number of attacks against television today. Nothing in Plato's time answered to our concept of the fine arts, especially to the idea that the arts are a province of a small and enlightened part of the population (which may or may not be interested in attracting the rest of the people to them), and Plato holds no views about them. His quarrel with poetry is not disturbing because anyone seriously believes that Plato could have been right about Homer's pernicious influence. Plato's view is disturbing because we are still agreed with him that representation is

---

*Jonas Barrish, the drama theorist.

transparent—at least in the case of those media which, like television, have not yet acquired the status of art and whose own nature, as opposed to what they depict, has not yet become in serious terms a subject in its own right. And because of this view, we may indeed react to life, or think that we do, as we react to its representations: What is often necessary for a similarity between our reactions to life and our reactions to art is not so much the fact that the two are actually similar but only the view that they are. Many do in fact enjoy things on television which, as Plato wrote in regard to poetry, some at least would be ashamed, even horrified, to enjoy in life.

The problem here is with the single word 'things,' which applies both to the contents of television shows and to the situations those represent. What this suggests is that what is presented on television is a duplicate of what occurs in the world. No interpretation seems to be needed in order to reveal and to understand the complex relations that actually obtain between them.

By contrast, no one believes that the fine arts produce such duplications. Though we are perfectly willing to learn about life from literature and painting (a willingness which, in my opinion, requires close scrutiny in its own right), no one would ever project directly the content of a work of fine art onto the world. The fine arts, we believe, bear an indirect, interpretative relationship to the world, and further interpretation on the part of audience and critics is necessary in order to understand it. It is precisely for this sort of interpretation that the popular arts do not seem to call.

Adorno's Case against Popular Music
■ Lee B. Brown ■

Adorno's views about art in general—high and low—are nested within a complex analysis of the history and social function of art. This function, he believes, is subject to historical change. (Compare modern symphonic concert music with music in its earliest forms—when it was bound up with the fabric of human activities such as birth, death, war, marriage, and work.) Adorno also underpins his examination of the arts with a general critical theory of culture. With the rise of capitalism, he maintains, the things humans produce have lost touch with their original value for the sake of a secondary value, which Adorno calls *exchange value.* Put briefly, the capitalist system attempts to treat every effort of human productivity—including the arts—as a marketable commodity.

In response to this condition, art has been gradually forced to turn its back on the world and to cultivate a sphere unto itself. Corresponding with this impulse to-

"Adorno's Case against Popular Music" by Lee B. Brown is published by permission of the author. Revised for this edition.

ward autonomy, art has cultivated the philosophical stance commonly labeled "purist" or "formalist." By these means, art attempts to resist the invasive effects of commodification on all aspects of life, and to serve as a standard against which actual life can be measured. The downside is that in its isolated state, art can all too easily become a plaything of bourgeois culture. So compromised, it becomes a source of escapism, or a purveyor of easy, falsely reassuring views of our lives. The life of high art under capitalism is thus a precarious one. Although suffering from virtually contradictory pressures, genuine art must hold out against the socioeconomic forces that rule our lives.

By contrast, the popular arts—particularly those we nowadays term "mass" arts—thrive contentedly within the commodity system. Indeed, they are commodities *par excellence.*

Theodor Adorno's views on popular music are expressed in many writings, but nowhere more accessibly than in his long essay, "On Popular Music" (1941). The examples Adorno uses there are obviously dated. (His reference to "the King" is not to Elvis but to Benny Goodman, the so-called "King of Swing.") However, if Adorno were still alive, he would no doubt argue that in a hyper-mediatized twenty-first century environment, his position is even more relevant. The following discussion occasionally refers to more recent examples.

The basic concepts of Adorno's analysis are the interrelated ones of *simplicity* and *standardization.* The tunes, rhythms, and harmonies of popular music, he asserts, are built out of simple, repeatable parts.

Consider, first, the hypnotic character of the well-known rhythmic pulse of most American popular music. Nowadays, most listeners to rock, jazz, disco, punk, techno, and country music are unaware of the historical source of this metronomic feature of their favored music. In fact, if one traces back through rock and rhythm 'n' blues, to swing and jazz, and before that to ragtime, one comes to the ancestor of them all—the military marching band. What, Adorno, asks, is the point of a marching band—except to *regiment* people? The rigid beat of popular music has a similarly similar regimenting effect, he believes.

Adorno also analogizes the omnipresent beat of popular music with hypnosis. Alternatively, he sees the relentless beat—which must go on and on . . . and on—as drug-like. Consider the similarities, indeed the literal interaction, between many forms of popular music and drugs. At the same time, the mechanical character of the omnipresent beat of American popular music illustrates Adorno's view of it as an industrial product, like things made on assembly lines, like ordinary appliances.

To understand Adorno's view, we must bear in mind that most American popular music has been embedded in one of two typical forms:

A basic form for pop music—and the chief focus of Adorno's discussion—is the thirty-two-measure show tune. Such a piece is distributed across four eight-bar segments, in which two tunes are organized according to the pattern AABA. This is the basic model for the composers of Broadway music, such as Irving Berlin and George Gershwin, as well as many rock era tunes by such groups as the Beatles. It is the model for thousands of pop standards such as "Body and Soul" and "Stormy Weather."

Although he didn't do so, Adorno could have further supported his case by citing the other fundamental pop music form—the *blues*. The blues is twelve measures long and moves predictably through a standard progression of chords. When set to words, the blues involves two lines, the first sung twice, the second once, as in the following: "I woke up this morning with an awful aching head / [Repeat] / Because my man had left me with nothin' but an empty bed." Much of jazz, rock, and, of course, "rhythm and blues" derive their musical patterns from the blues.

Because of the similarity of such forms, we can think of the creation of popular songs after the analogy of a "cookie cutter." But Adorno's favored analogy is an appliance, such as a washing machine or an automobile with their replaceable parts. If one part is broken or doesn't work well, another can replace it. For example, when Broadway composers found that the B section of a song did not work, they often simply borrowed one from another song.

The subject matter of popular music is equally simplistic. The topics are the standard sentimental ones—fantasy narratives of love, in which all the real trials of life are magically resolved. Even the dark shadows in pop songs, Adorno would probably say, are formulaic. (The singer Lyle Lovett has wittily boiled down the love content of country music as "Boy meets girl, boy shoots girl.")

It is no surprise, given the foregoing, that Adorno regards popular music—both in form and content—as appealing mainly to infantile impulses. He terms the desire for sheer repetition "regressive," a psychoanalytic term connoting an infantile fixation. He regards such obsessive pleasures as masochistic ones—like biting your nails. The activity is partly painful, and you never get full satisfaction from it, but you can't stop doing it. This infantilism is also registered in the music's vocabulary. (Consider how often lovers are addressed as "baby," "mama," or "papa.") No doubt, the music of early twenty-first century rock bands or hip-hop groups is grittier than the popular music Adorno heard. But he would be struck by the way late-century pop music still celebrates adolescent values and attitudes.

Because of its simplicity in form and content, popular music offers little challenge to the mind. Adorno likes to say that the music hears *for* the listener, by which he means that it leaves no mental work for us to do for ourselves. This fits his view that modern listeners are deficient in real musical literacy. (Consider the degree to which stereos have replaced pianos as the chief source of music in the home.) As a result, our relationship to music is nowadays more a matter of passive consumption than of music making.

To illustrate his overall argument, Adorno makes pointed comparisons between examples of "classical" and popular music. A work such as Beethoven's *Fifth Symphony* does not—like a piece of popular music—consist of a few simple parts revolving repetitiously for our passive reception. First, as a totality, it constitutes an elaborate design, within which its subsidiary parts—or "movements"—have complex and subtle relationships to each other. Second, each movement is an elaborate structure involving complex relationships between the parts. Third, the symphony effects elaborate transformations of its musical sources. For instance, the scherzo movement of the *Fifth Symphony* is a form derivative from a relatively simple dance form. But in Beethoven's hands, the simple elements have been transformed almost beyond recognition. Instead of consisting of polite tunes repeated monotonously, Beethoven's scherzo is wonderfully complex. Adorno takes pains to explain how it makes use of a powerful thematic duality, involving—in his words—a "creeping" theme in the strings, contrasted with a "stone-like" response in the woodwinds. As these interact, a tremendous sense of tension and foreboding is set up, which serves, in turn, as a dramatic introduction to the triumphant music of the last movement.

In such "serious" music, what would otherwise be simple is made complex, developmental, and dramatic. We are challenged to "track" what is happening. Further, we could not replace bits of the music of the *Fifth* with alternatives without ruining its overall sense. By contrast, the placement of the bits in a piece of popular music is fortuitous, devoid of a "logic" of musical progression.

Adorno takes it for granted that *standardization* and *individualization* are at odds. Popular music lacks a hallmark of genuine art, which always speaks with an individualized voice. Popular music, by contrast, does not speak with *anyone's* voice, anymore than a sewing machine does. Instead, popular music makes use of what Adorno calls *pseudo-individualization*. A good example is what is known in the industry as a "hook"—a simple but distinctive chordal pattern, beat, or theme, by means of which record producers try to grab our attention.

Through pseudo-individualism, the industry creates music that *sounds* like a genuinely personal expression, even though it really isn't. (Compare the insincere formulae with which we pretend to express genuine feelings to each other in countless social situations.) Likewise, institutions such as "Top Forty" ratings and the "Grammies" only create a pretence that competing pop groups are highly individualized. Adorno believes the comparisons are largely bogus, and that the differences between various pop groups are really superficial. He characterizes these institutions as examples of "plugging the field." In the narrow sense, song "plugging" on American radio and TV is simply the familiar process by which new recordings are marketed by being aired over and over again. By "plugging the field," Adorno is talking about the way a complex system of practices, such as the Grammies, gives the products of the industry *as a whole* an undeserved sense of importance.

Some popular music—jazz, most notably—uses improvisation as a form of pseudo-individualism. Contrary to the idea that the jazz improviser is freely expressing himself, Adorno believes that the possibilities of anything really unique happening in such music are extremely limited. The music, he insists, is always framed within the context of a musical "prison," the walls of which include the ongoing beat, the rigid forms, and the narrow confines of the music's harmonic potentialities. The individualism is superficial.

We have been speaking of the standardization of the music itself. Going hand in hand with this, Adorno believes, is the process by which the audience's *reactions* are standardized. Just as we are programmed to expect the standardized food at McDonald's, we are programmed to *expect* the music we get. (Adorno would reject the widely repeated claim that the commodity industry "only gives people what they want.")

In sum, by means of its network of strategies, e.g., the cheap pleasures and escapist fantasies of freedom and individuality with which the system provides us, the commodity industry realizes several cooperating goals:

(1) Because we become passive consumers of the product, our sales resistance is lowered. We buy the product, in short.

(2) Our acquired need for simplicity and repetition reduces demands on the industry for genuine creativity. Music producers need only make more of the very thing they have already trained us to want—a relatively simple project.

(3) The planned obsolescence of the products of the entertainment industry insures a continual need for more of the same.

(4) We learn to identify with the whole system that produces these commodities. We become "reconciled," as Adorno puts it, to the capitalism in which we live, move, and have our being. (Consider, for instance, how we have learned to *like* going to shopping malls.) Adorno goes so far as to describe popular music as a means by which the system achieves "musical dictatorship" over the masses.

(5) The converse point is that popular music, unlike serious classical music, is not able to *resist* the system. Indeed, one of the functions of popular music is to assimilate consumers *to* the system. One might reply that popular music has often been a basis for protest. However, Adorno would likely point out, first, that the industry has a way of converting social protest into fashion, while leaving a merely superficial impression of resistance. (Consider the way the industry found it easy to turn the revolutionary images of Mao Tse-Tung and Che Guevara into fashion chic.) Idealizing views of jazz have often celebrated it as an expression of rebellion. Adorno claims, however, that the jazz musician lives in a hostile but basically "compliant" relationship to the system that promotes his music. He would not find it remarkable that the cult of pop stardom typically overtakes "underground" bands such as Nirvana. Commercial success is always the real agenda.

The kind of artistic resistance that Adorno takes seriously is exemplified by the modernist music of composers like Arnold Schönberg or Alban Berg. The almost painful abstractness of such music, he believes, is the truly serious means by which we can hold out against the superficial pleasures of popular culture.

(6) General advantages accrue to the commodity industry as a result of the way the foregoing factors interact with each other to insure the system's success. The consumers keep consuming and the music factories keep humming.

In explaining how popular recordings work their way into the consciousness of listeners, Adorno provides a theory about the stages through which the listener passes as she is both figuratively and literally sold on the music:

(1)*Vague remembrance.* A listener hears a record on the radio and says, at first, "I have heard something like this somewhere before."

(2) *Actual identification.* At a second stage, as Adorno puts it, a "light" of recognition goes on. The listener knows that this specific tune is one she's heard before.

(3) *Subsumption by label.* At this stage, she assigns a name to the tune, to the band playing it, the album title, or some of the lyrics.

(4) *Self-reflection on the act of identification.* At this point, Adorno helps himself to a psychoanalytic idea. The listener now *identifies* with the tune. She has the feeling that it is becoming part of her. Amidst the chaotic whirl of cultural commodities, she knows her way with *this* item. In this connection, Adorno would have relished the modern disc jockey practice of playing records by request. When the DJ says, "This one goes out to Bob and Sally," it is as if the airwaves themselves acknowledge Bob and Sally's private connection with that song. Bob and Sally, of course, say, "They're playing our song." The song is made for them—or so it seems.

Adorno might have added that, along with the identification with the tune, the listener is at the same time identifying with other listeners who are also bonding with that piece of music. This now sets her and her friends apart from the others who "haven't a clue." Adorno would probably take note, in this connection, of the way listeners at the same time identify with the pop stars who perform the music. Consider the extremes to which the cult of the pop star has been carried in our time.

(5) *Psychological transfer.* Finally, the identification with the song becomes so tight that it amounts to a two-way relationship. At this point, the music has acquired an apparent glow of *objective* value. It is judged to be good *in itself.* Clearly, Adorno regards this as a kind of illusion.

Adorno does not take the process further, but it would be easy to do so, once we understand his general perspective. Consider two further steps he might appreciate.

(6) *Disillusionment.* The shallowness of the music eventually becomes apparent. Listeners become sick of it, and the love affair is over. A listener and her peer group now begin to feel a growing contempt for people who haven't moved beyond that piece of music. It is now "corny," "uncool," and so are those who still listen to it. But this further stage beautifully caps off the whole process, because it marks the fact that listeners are now ready to consume new music.

(7) *Recycling.* After a sufficient amount of time has passed, a music recording can be recycled as a "golden oldie," thus enabling the industry to sell it to consumers a second time around. The repackaging of the collected music of famous rock bands is just one example.

Adorno's account is challenging, but subject to the following criticisms.

(1) First, Adorno throws all popular music into one bag. He puts the best music of Cole Porter and George Gershwin on the same level as the most cynical products of the music industry. He seems incapable of making the kinds of discriminations that are requisite for making informed aesthetic judgments about such music. There really are stylistic differences between the Rolling Stones and the Beatles—as anyone in the know can tell you.

In the same vein, it seems obvious that Adorno underestimates the degree to which popular music—like classical music—can transcend the pressures of the commodity industry and to create music of enduring value. Who would deny, in all seriousness, that the Duke Ellington, Charlie Parker, or the Beatles did not do so?

(2) A reason for the foregoing mistake is that Adorno refuses—or is unable—to hear forms of nonclassical music in their own terms. He gauges popular music by the parameters of classical music. Consider the matter of tonality, for example.

Much of African American music makes use of so-called "blue" notes that arise because certain notes of the standard European scale are, in the context of popular music, flatted or bent down in pitch. This practice gives much of our blues, jazz, and rock its distinctive sound. Adorno believes that when we listen to these "bent" notes, our ear struggles to correct them back to their "correct" pitch. In other words, we hear them as if they were mistakes in European scales. On this matter, one might charge Adorno with tonal chauvinism. (What, after all, constitutes "right" notes in a world in which European tonality is only one alternative among many?)

The complaint can be generalized. Adorno does not reckon with the fact that much of the music of the world is not governed by the hierarchies taken for granted in European classical music. In such music, for instance, harmonic development is paramount, whereas in African music—and much of the American popular music that derives from it—specialized modes of rhythmic elaboration are paramount. Indeed, on Adorno's own terms, one might flip the order of musical priority around in order to arrive at a conclusion opposite from his. Gauged by standards reflecting the practices of a Latin percussion ensemble, with its complicated polyrhythms, the music of Bach and Beethoven might seem simplistic.

Adorno's failure in this regard is ironic, for he would be the first to fault listeners who are not able or willing to make similarly refined discriminations within the sphere of classical music.

(3) A connected error on Adorno's part is that, in making his contrast between popular and classical music, Adorno unfairly picks the worst examples of the former while focusing on the best examples of the latter. Surely, tedious and banal examples of classical music abound. Operas that were popular in the seventeenth century may please no one today at all.

(4) Classical music and popular music seem to be on all fours in still one further respect. Consider the possibility that not even Beethoven's music can survive the endless replaying it receives on "good music" radio stations. Can even the finest music, by sheer repetition, not become a sophisticated form of Muzak? (How often do even dedicated listeners to "good music" stations actually sit down and *listen?*) Perhaps neither kind of music can survive the kind of replay that is made possible by contemporary communications technology.

(5) Is Adorno right in claiming that popular music never *resists* the system? Contrary to his implicit judgment, "submissive" is hardly a label we would apply to the art of Charlie Mingus, Ornette Coleman, or John Coltrane. The tragic tone of the latter's "Alabama" is surely as resistant as any music by Arnold Schönberg. To toss Coltrane's music into a heap with the most cynical products of the Time-Warner music industry is laughable.

(6) Although Adorno is right about the socioeconomic pressures that bear on popular music, he underestimates the fact that classical music, no less than pop, is

subject to the pressures of the commodity industry. The popularity of trendy opera stars—such as the Three Tenors—no less than that of many rock stars, is the partial result of high-pressure advertising campaigns. The concert music industry, too, has ways of "plugging the field." Indeed, it is arguable that the "serious" music system creates a standardized kind of listener no less than the pop industry.

Form and Funk

■ Richard Shusterman ■

Popular art has not been popular with aestheticians and theorists of culture, at least not in their professional moments. When not altogether ignored as beneath contempt, it is typically villified as mindless, tasteless trash. The denigration of popular art or mass culture (the debate over the proper term is significant and instructive) seems particularly compelling since it is widely endorsed by intellectuals of violently different socio-political views and agendas; indeed it provides a rare instance where right-wing reactionaries and Marxian radicals join hands and make common cause.

It is difficult to oppose such a powerful coalition of thinkers by defending popular art. Yet this is precisely what I wish to do in this paper; and for a variety of reasons. My pragmatism makes me not only critical of the alienating esotericism and totalizing claims of high art, but acutely suspicious of any essential and unbridgeable divide between its products and those of popular culture. Moreover, history clearly shows that the popular entertainment of one culture (e.g., Greek or even Elizabethan drama) can become the high classics of a subsequent age.

But my deepest and most urgent reason for defending popular art is that it provides us (even us intellectuals) with too much aesthetic satisfaction to accept its wholesale denunciation as aesthetically illegitimate. To condemn it as fit only for the barbaric taste and dull wit of the unenlightened, manipulated masses is to divide us not only against the rest of our community but just as painfully against ourselves. We are made to disdain the things which give us pleasure and to feel ashamed of the pleasure they give. The delegitimating critique of popular art, though typically pursued under the banner of safeguarding our aesthetic satisfaction, thus represents an ascetic renunciation, one of many forms that intellectuals since Plato have employed to subordinate the unruly power and appeal of the aesthetic.

"Form and Funk" by Richard Shusterman has been excerpted from "The Aesthetic Challenge of Popular Art," *The British Journal of Aesthetics,* Oxford University Press, 31, Number 3 (1991), pages 203-211, and is reprinted by permission of the publisher.

Four factors make it particularly difficult to defend popular art against its intellectual critics. First, the defence must be waged more or less on enemy territory, since the very attempt to answer the intellectualist critique involves both accepting the power of its claim to require an answer and accepting the terms of its indictment, terms which are hardly neutral. Secondly, even defenders of popular art tend to concede its aesthetic poverty and instead defend it only by appeal to extenuating circumstances of social needs and democratic principles. It is only good for those whose education and leisure allow them no better. Such social apologies for popular art undermine its genuine defence, since they perpetuate the same myth of aesthetic worthlessness as the critiques they oppose, just as they foster the same sort of social and personal fragmentation. A third problem is that we tend to think of high art only in terms of its most celebrated works of genius, while popular art is typically identified with its most mediocre and standardized products. But just as high art is no unblemished collection of masterpieces, so popular art is not an undifferentiated abyss of tastelessness where no aesthetic quality can be discriminated.

Finally, perhaps the greatest problem in the aesthetic defence of popular art is the tendency in intellectual discourse for the term 'aesthetic' to be exclusively appropriated as a term of high art and sophisticated style, as if the very notion of a popular aesthetic were almost a contradiction in terms. This tendency has prevented some who are sympathetic to popular needs for culture and who see through the 'disinterested,' 'non-commercial' ideology of high culture from recognizing the existence of a popular aesthetic that is not wholly negative, dominated, and impoverished. The most striking example of this regrettable bias is Pierre Bourdieu, who rigorously exposes the hidden economy and veiled interests of the so-called disinterested aesthetic of high culture, but none the less remains too enchanted by the myth he demystifies to acknowledge the existence of any legitimate popular aesthetic. He insists on referring to this notion only with disclaiming scare-quotes and repeatedly stresses that so-called 'popular aesthetic' is nothing more than 'a foil or negative reference point' from which any legitimate aesthetic must distance itself to establish legitimacy.

We must admit that the term 'aesthetic' did indeed originate in intellectual discourse and has been most frequently applied to high art and the most refined appreciation of nature. But it is certainly no longer so narrowly confined in application. (One need only consider the many fashion schools and cosmetics salons which are called 'aesthetic institutes' and whose professional staff are termed 'aestheticians.') Moreover, traditional aesthetic predicates such as 'grace,' 'elegance,' 'unity' and 'style' are regularly applied to the products of popular art with no apparent difficulty. Since no one appreciates more than Bourdieu the great sociopolitical stakes of such highly valued classificatory terms as 'art' and 'aesthetic,' it is surprising and troubling that he so readily concedes them to high culture's exclusive possession. It is therefore all the more necessary that we free them from such monopolistic domination by defending the aesthetic legitimacy of popular art. To provide such defence I shall be challenging the major aesthetic indictments made against popular art, and since there is not adequate space here to treat them all, I shall concentrate only on those raised explicitly by Bourdieu. Similarly, since I cannot pretend to treat all the popular arts I shall concentrate, as my title suggests, on rock music, particularly the funky sort inspired by Afro-American culture.

1. One of the most common and unquestioned complaints against popular art is that it involves no aesthetic challenge but instead requires and induces passivity of response. In contrast to high art whose appreciation demands 'aesthetic work' and thus stimulates aesthetic activity and resultant aesthetic satisfaction, popular art both induces and requires a lifeless and unrewarding passivity. Its 'simple and repetitive structure,' says Bourdieu, only 'invite a passive, absent participation.' This effortless passivity is thought to explain not only its wide appeal but its failure to truly satisfy. Its 'effortlessness' easily captivates those of us who are too weary and beaten to seek the challenging. But since enjoyment (as Aristotle realized) is a by-product attendant upon and essentially bound to activity, our lack of active effort ultimately translates into joyless boredom. Rather than energetically and acutely respond to the work (as we can in high art), we lazily and languidly receive it in a passive, listless torpor. Nor could it tolerate more vigorous scrutiny and response. As [Theodor] Adorno and [Max] Horkheimer describe this 'incurable malady':

> Pleasure hardens into boredom because, if it is to remain pleasure, it must not demand any effort and therefore moves rigorously in the worn grooves of association. No independent thinking must be expected from the audience: the product prescribes every reaction: not by its natural form (which collapses under reflection), but by signals. Any logical connection calling for mental effort is painstakingly avoided.

Many of the products and modes of consumption of popular art do indeed conform to this picture, but what also emerges from Adorno and Horkheimer's allegation is their misguided and simplistic conflation of all legitimate activity with serious thinking, of 'any effort' with 'mental effort' of the intellect. Critics of popular culture are loath to recognize that there are humanly worthy and aesthetically rewarding activities other than intellectual exertion. So even if all art and aesthetic enjoyment do indeed require some active effort or the overcoming of some resistance, it does not follow that they require effortful 'independent thinking.' There are other more somatic forms of effort, resistance, and satisfaction.

Rock songs are typically enjoyed through moving, dancing, and singing along with the music. And such efforts, as [John] Dewey realized, involve overcoming resistances such as 'embarrassment, . . . awkwardness, self-consciousness, [and] lack of vitality.' Often our dancing involves such vigorous effort that we break into a sweat and eventually exhaust ourselves. Clearly, on the somatic level, there is much more effortful activity in the appreciation of rock than in that of highbrow music, whose concerts compel us to sit in a motionless silence which often induces not mere torpid passivity but snoring sleep. The term 'funky' used to characterize and commend many rock songs derives from an African word meaning 'positive sweat' and is expressive of an African aesthetic of vigorously active and communally impassioned engagement rather than dispassionate judgemental remoteness. The much more energetic and kinaesthetic aesthetic response evoked by rock thus exposes the fundamental passivity underlying our established appreciation of high art, a passivity expressed in the traditional aesthetic attitude of disinterested, distanced contemplation, which has its roots in the quest for philosophical and theological knowledge rather than pleasure, for individual enlightenment rather than communal interaction or social change. Popular arts such as rock thus suggest a radically revised aesthetic with a joyous and boisterous return of the somatic dimension which philosophy has long repressed to preserve its own hegemony, through that of the intellect, in all realms of human value. No wonder the aesthetic legitimacy of such art is vehemently denied and its embodied and embodying efforts are ignored or rejected as irrational regression from art's true (i.e., intellectual) purpose. The fact that such art and its appreciation has its roots in non-Western civilization renders it even more unacceptably retrograde.

For Adorno, pop music is 'regressive' and aesthetically invalid because 'it is a somatic stimulus'; for Alan Bloom, the problem with rock is its deep appeal to 'sensuality' and 'sexual desire,' which renders it *'alogon.'* 'It is not only not reasonable, it is hostile to reason.' Mark Miller makes the same mistake of inferring aesthetic illegitimacy and intellectual corruption from the mere fact of rock's more immediate sensuous appeal. 'Rock n' Roll music,' he complains in citing John Lennon, 'gets right through to you without having to go through your brain'; and this sensuous immediacy is negatively misconstrued as entailing effortless nullity and passive 'immobility.' In short, since rock can be enjoyed without intellectual 'interpretation,' it is therefore not sufficiently 'cerebral' to be aesthetically legitimate.

Along with their anti-somatic animus, the arguments of Adorno, Bloom, and Miller share two vitiating logical blunders. First, the sensuous appeal of rock does not entail anti-intellectualism (in either its creators or audience). Only if the sensuous were essentially incompatible and with the intellect would this follow; and why should we sensuous intellects suppose this? It is only the presumption of intellectualist exclusiveness, a powerful philosophical prejudice with a platonic pedigree, which leads these thinkers to regard them as mutually exclusive. A second fallacy is to infer that because rock music can be enjoyed without hard thinking and interpretation, its enjoyment therefore cannot sustain or be enhanced by such reflective analysis. If it can be enjoyed on an intellectually shallow level, it still does not follow that it must be so enjoyed and has nothing else to offer.

2. The effortlessness and shallowness of popular art is often linked to its lack of formal complexity. Inadequacy of form is one of the most common and damning indictments of popular art, and one for which Bourdieu provides a powerful argument. Defining the aesthetic attitude as a capacity to regard things as 'form rather than function,' Bourdieu sees this detached, life-distancing attitude as the key to high art's achievement of 'formal complexity.' It is only through this attitude that we can reach ('as the final stage in the conquest of artistic autonomy') 'the production of an open work, intrinsically and deliberately polysemic.' For Bourdieu,

popular art's greater connection with the content of life 'implies the subordination of form to function' and the consequent failure to achieve such formal complexity. In popular art we are more immediately drawn to and involved in the content or substance of the work; and this, Bourdieu argues, is incompatible with aesthetic appreciation, 'given the basic opposition between form and substance.' Aesthetic legitimacy is only achieved 'by displacing the interest from the "content" to the form, to the specifically artistic effects which are only appreciated relationally, through a comparison with other works which is incompatible with immersion in the singularity of the work immediately given.'

Such comparative and differential relationality with other works and styles in the given artistic tradition is undeniably a rich source of formal complexity in high art. But it is also powerfully present in many works of popular art, which self-consciously allude to and quote from each other to produce a variety of aesthetic effects including a complex formal texture of implied art-historical relations. Nor are these allusions lost on the popular art audience, who are generally more literate in their artistic traditions than are the audiences of high art in theirs.

What is more disturbing about Bourdieu's argument is its apparent assumption that form and content are somehow necessarily opposed, so that we cannot properly experience (or create) a work formally unless we distance ourselves from any investment or enthusiasm in content. Not only does this beg a very contested form/content distinction, but it confuses two senses of 'formal': that which displays formality or formalization and that which simply has form, structure or shape. It is only the former which entails a posture of distance, ceremonious restraint, and denial of life's investments. Rather than something essentially opposed to life, form is, as Dewey stressed, an ever present part of the shape and rhythm of living; and aesthetic form (as Bourdieu himself recognizes) has its deep but denied roots in these organic bodily rhythms and the social conditions which help structure them. Form can be discovered in more immediate and enthusiastic bodily investment as well as through intellectual distance; form can be funky as well as austerely formal.

3. Form, function, and funk all lead into the final charge I shall consider: popular art's lack of aesthetic autonomy and resistance. Aestheticians typically regard autonomy as 'an irrevocable aspect of art' which is crucial to its value. Even Adorno and Bourdieu, who recognize that this autonomy is the product of sociohistorical factors and serves a social agenda of class distinction, nevertheless insist that it is essential to artistic legitimacy and the very notion of aesthetic appreciation. For art to be created and appreciated *qua* art and not as something else, requires, says Bourdieu, 'an autonomous field of artistic production capable of imposing its norms on both the production and consumption of its products' and of refusing external functions or 'any necessity other than those inscribed in . . . [its] specific tradition.' The core of such autonomous norms is granting 'primacy to that of which the artist is master, i.e. the form, manner, style, rather than the

subject, the external referent, which involves subordination to functions—even if only the most elementary one, that of representing, signifying, saying something.' Similarly, for Adorno, art's norms are exclusive of any function other than the service of art itself. Art 'will not play a serving role' and should eschew 'even the childish notion of wanting to be a source of pleasure,' so that 'the autonomous work of art . . . is functional only with reference to itself.' In contrast, popular art forfeits aesthetic legitimacy simply by having more than purely artistic functions, by serving also other needs of life. But why does functionality entail artistic and aesthetic illegitimacy?

Ultimately the entailment rests on defining art and the aesthetic as essentially opposed to reality or life. For Adorno art both defines and justifies itself 'by being different from the ungodly reality' of our world and divorced from its practical functional exigencies. Bourdieu similarly maintains that the very notion of the aesthetic attitude 'implies a break with . . . the world' and the concerns of ordinary life. Since popular art affirms 'the continuity between art and life, which implies the subordination of form to function,' Bourdieu concludes it cannot count as legitimate art. It cannot be aesthetically legitimated by any so-called popular aesthetic, because such an aesthetic, Bourdieu argues, is not worthy of the name. First, because this aesthetic is never positively formulated ('for itself'), but merely serves as a negative reference point for the legitimate life-opposing aesthetic to define itself by contrast. But secondly, because by accepting real-life concerns and pleasures (and thus challenging art's pure autonomy), the popular aesthetic is disqualified as essentially opposed to art, and as instead engaged in a 'systematic reduction of the things of art to the things of life.'

These anti-functionalist arguments all hang on the premise that art and real life are and should be essentially opposed and strictly separated. But though a hoary dogma of aesthetic philosophy, why should this view be accepted? Its provenance and motivation should certainly make us suspicious. Originating in Plato's attack on art for its double removal from reality, it has been sustained by a philosophical tradition which was always eager, even in defending art, to endorse its distance from the real so as to ensure philosophy's sovereignty in determining reality, including the real nature of art.

But if we look at matters free from philosophical prejudice and historical parochiality, art can be seen as part of life, just as life forms the substance of art and even constitutes itself artistically in 'the art of living.' Both as objects and experiences works of art inhabit the world and functions in our lives. Certainly in ancient Athenian culture, from which our concept of art first developed, the arts were intimately integrated into everyday life and its ethos.

Bourdieu, of course, knows this well, and his own work insists on the historical evolution of the nineteenth century where art was transformed into *autonomous* art and the aesthetic into a *pure* aesthetic. But his narrow definition of the aesthetic suggests that history's changes are irrevocably permanent, and that once transfigured into pure autonomy, art and the aesthetic can no longer be legitimate in a less pure, less life-denying form. History, however, continues its transformations; and recent developments in postmodern culture suggest the disintegration of the purist ideal and the implosion of the aesthetic into all areas of life. Moreover, though Bourdieu penetratingly exposes the deeper material conditions and unconscious social interests involved in aesthetic purity (which render it far from pure though it be globally misperceived as pure), he seems unwilling to entertain the idea that we can break with this collective misperception of pure autonomy and still maintain a viable aesthetic. He neglects the possibility of an alternative aesthetic where life is given centrality and popular art can be redeemed. But such an aesthetic is not only possible; it is explicitly formulated in John Dewey's pragmatist theory of art, which makes the energies, needs, and pleasures of 'the live creature' central to aesthetic experience.

Bourdieu advances the further argument that popular art cannot be aesthetically legitimate because it essentially denies its own aesthetic validity by implicitly accepting the domination of the high art aesthetic which haughtily denigrates it. Our culture, for Bourdieu, is one where high art's aesthetic of 'the pure disposition . . . is universally recognized.' Hence, simply by existing in this culture, the popular aesthetic (which he links to the working class) must be 'a dominated aesthetic which is constantly obliged to define itself in terms of the dominant aesthetics.' Since by these dominant standards popular art fails to qualify as art, and since it fails to assert or generate its own independent legitimation, Bourdieu concludes that in a sense 'there is no popular art' and that popular culture is 'a paradoxical notion' which implies willy-nilly the dominant definition of culture and hence its own invalidation or 'self-destruction.'

However compelling this argument may be for the French culture Bourdieu studies, it fails as a global argument against popular art. For, at least in America, such art does assert its aesthetic status and provides its own forms of aesthetic legitimation. Not only do many popular artists regard their role as more than mere entertainment, but the artistic status of their art is frequently thematized in their works. Moreover, awards such as Oscars, Emm[ys], and Gramm[ys], which are neither determined by nor reducible to box-office sales, confer, in the eyes of most Americans, not only aesthetic legitimation but a degree of artistic prestige. There is also a large and growing array of aesthetic criticism of the popular arts, including some aesthetically orientated historical studies of their development. Such criticism, disseminated not only in journals and books but in the mass media, is clearly a form of legitimating discourse, and it employs the same sort of aesthetic predicates one applies to high art. Its sharing of these predicates does not entail its subordination to high art, unless we presume from the outset that the high aesthetic has exclusive control of the legitimate use of aesthetic terms; and this already begs the question of exclusive aesthetic legitimacy, which is precisely what popular art is contesting. . . .

The aesthetic message from America, then, is 'get down' and 'get funky.' Will it be heard in the changing but still aristocratic culture of Europe? Will it be heard by the intellectual aristocrats of European culture, including those born, bred, and thriving in America? If the listening habits of today's youth suggest a resounding 'yes' to the first question, the fastidious conservative taste of contemporary philosophical aesthetics makes the second question more problematic and thus more urgent. In the area of popular aesthetics and its relation to our justifiably cherished high art tradition there is a real need and great opportunity for original and socially important theoretical work. In neglecting or marginalizing this area, aesthetic philosophy risks losing closer touch with the cultural world it purports to investigate but which it can also help transform.

Social Consciousness in Dancehall Reggae
■ Anita M. Waters ■

In his writings about popular music, Theodor Adorno leveled a scathing critique against commercially produced songs. He claimed that the commodity industry allowed only the most banal, formulaic and repetitive offerings past its gatekeepers. According to Adorno, such music leaves no scope for raising social-consciousness. However, many theorists in the latter half of the twentieth century—who have come to recognize popular culture as an arena in which conflicting social groups express their contesting views—have challenged Adorno's ideas. One form of popular music that offers a clear challenge to Adorno's formulation is reggae, the Jamaican popular music that originated in the poorer urban neighborhoods in Kingston, and caught on quickly in the rural areas of Jamaica.

Reggae combined Afro-Caribbean folk traditions like *mento* (early Jamaican folk music) with rhythm and blues imported from African American popular culture. Beginning in 1968, when certain reggae songs were associated with protests and riots by disenfranchised urban Jamaicans, reggae offered new ways in which to analyze and discuss social and political issues. Reggae was imbued with politics and packed with political information. It had an ability to frame or define social realities in common texts popularized and shared by masses of Jamaican people, and created communities of taste that were courted by politicians during election periods. New moods were expressed rhythmically while new perspectives on racial and class conflict were offered lyrically.

Reggae is a commercial music, an estimated two billion dollar industry worldwide, whose artists seem consumed with the desire to "bust out" and achieve commercial success. It can certainly be called repetitive; rhythm tracks serve as

---

"Social Consciousness in Dancehall Reggae" by Anita M. Waters is published by permission of the author.

the basis for "versions," and sometimes hundreds of songs are produced using a single rhythm. In addition, certain stock phrases and stylistic nuances surface in many songs.

Yet reggae music offers social analyses that reiterate the conflicts between the rich men and the sufferers, between Europeans and Africans. One legacy of Jamaica's colonial plantation history is the strong coincidence of divisions along the axis of class and that of race, and reggae from its inception was clearly aligned with the poorer and more African segments of society. A combination of its strong association with a politically mobilized working class, the decentralized production process that allows poor youth a chance at the microphone, the social context of sound systems in which reggae is consumed, and the replacement of routinized music with new, harder core music have all enabled reggae to deviate from Adorno's expectations.

Unlike the way much popular music is consumed in industrialized nations, individually and privately, most reggae in Jamaica has been consumed collectively, in public dances arranged by Jamaican entrepreneurs who owned banks of speakers and public address systems, known as *sound systems*. Among the sound system personnel are deejays, who play an interactive role, not just playing records, but adding lyrics and vocal effects over the music on the turntable. Sound systems began in the 1950s when operators like Coxone Dodd set up equipment for local dances, and continue today with sound systems like Stone Love, Metromedia, and Killamanjaro.

Because of the competition between sound system operators who want exclusive recordings, pressing records in back rooms of studios has long been a decentralized, prolific business in Jamaica. It has been estimated that as many as two hundred new singles have been released in Kingston in a single week. In the early days, records were cheap, and people sold them in the street out of brown paper bags. In an interview, Bob Marley spoke of this decentralization:

> Everyone in Jamaica can go and do a record. It's not like America where people don't know how it happens. In Jamaica you can just go ask any man 'pon the street how fi make a record, and they know. They all do it. No more secret.

The proliferation of reggae artists, and the ease with which anyone could add his, if not her, voice, enhanced the ability of reggae as popular music to serve as the voice of a hitherto silenced socioeconomic group.

The main source of moral authority in reggae during the 1970s was its connection with the philosophy and religion of Rastafari. Rastafari is the religious movement that originated in Jamaica in the 1930s that recognizes Haile Selassie (Ras Tafari), Emperor of Ethiopia, as the messiah in fulfillment of Old Testament prophesies, and that views African slavery and postcolonial racial hierarchy as forms of Babylonian captivity. Rastafari is the antithesis of British colonialism in a myriad of ways, from the African Emperor replacing the British throne as rightful leader of the world to a rejection of "Afro-Saxon" Anglophilia in favor of a celebration of African phenotypical and cultural traits.

Ruling class ambivalence about reggae music was palpable in the 1970s. While political candidates running for office used their work, and record sales made a small handful of entrepreneurs wealthy, reggae music and Rastafari were consistently dismissed by the Jamaican upper classes. Hotels that catered to tourists fired musicians who began to grow dreadlocks, and letters to the editor of the *Gleaner,* a Jamaican weekly, expressed embarrassment and disdain about this ghetto music. Rastas were the "Blackheart men" from whom mothers warned their children to stay away.

One reggae singer, Bob Marley, was commercially removed from his roots in the social context of Jamaican music and promoted to an international audience while retaining his popularity at home as well. The enormous success of this project outside Jamaican markets tested the ambivalence of the Jamaican ruling class. Marley's death from cancer in 1981 became an occasion for the elite to ally itself safely with his legacy. An elaborate and bipartisan state funeral, bestowal of an Order of Merit, and the commission of a public statue of the artist all attest to the routinization of Marley and the music he represented.

The years that followed Marley's death reflect this regularization of reggae in the Jamaican mainstream, especially when it comes to attracting visitors to the island. A Bob Marley song serves as background music on Jamaica Tourist Board videos, and smiling Rastafarians are featured prominently in brochures. As the deejay Snaggapuss puts it in a recent song, "Reggae and Rasta used to have a big fight. . . . Now you can hear reggae music on an airline flight."

Recent writings about popular music in Jamaica have recognized, and sometimes emphasized, its vulnerability to cooptation by political and economic elites. Once a music of resistance, reggae has ended up serving elite interests by attracting tourists and bringing in foreign revenue, by enriching the coffers of transnational music distributors and by succumbing to manipulation and commodification. Adorno's harsh analysis seems appropriate.

While the reggae of the 1970s is now a legitimate part of official Jamaican culture, another form of reggae music is receiving the disdain of the elites but is enormously popular in the distressed urban neighborhoods of Kingston. Significantly, it takes its name, "dancehall," from the social context in which the music is usually collectively consumed, that is, in sound system dances. Dancehall emerged around the late 1970s, became more prominent in the 1980s, and reached a peak of international popularity in 1992 when Shabba Ranks became the first Grammy-winning dancehall artist. Around that year, several dancehall artists were offered contracts with international record companies, but very few of these contracts have been fruitful for either the recording company or the artist.

The distinctions drawn between dancehall and "roots" reggae were both musical and ideological. Roots reggae emphasized harmonic trios singing recorded songs, while live performances by deejays are prominent in dance hall, sometimes in "combination style" with a singer alternating with a deejay at the microphone. Unlike "roots" reggae, dancehall makes use of highly repetitive computerized rhythm tracks, thereby fitting Adorno's negative profile of popular music in general. Instead of Rastafari, dancehall artists embraced two types of songs that were especially odious to their middle-class critics: gun lyrics and slackness.

Many "roots" reggae artists recorded songs that celebrated outlaws and "rude boys," such as Marley's "I Shot the Sheriff" and Peter Tosh's "Stepping Razor." The classic 1972 reggae movie *The Harder They Come* takes an outlaw as its hero. However, dancehall artists took the celebration of the gunman style to a new level. In the 1990s deejays like Ninjaman, Bounty Killer, Mad Cobra, and Cutty Ranks released singles with titles like "Press the Trigger," "Instant Death," "My Weapon," and "Limb by Limb." Among the targets of their rage were gay men. Buju Banton caused an uproar when the New York media became aware of his 1993 hit single, "Boom Bye Bye," in which he advocates murder of homosexuals. Ninjaman's own recording company recommended that radio stations censor his song of the same year, "Take Bill Clinton," which recommended assassination of the U.S. president on account of his administration's acceptance of gays in the military.

Second, dancehall songs were known for their sexually explicitness, or "slackness," the most common theme being extraordinary sexual prowess of the deejay performing the song. Among memorable examples of this subgenre are Shabba Ranks' "Wicked in Bed" and "Love Punany Bad," Skanky Dan's "Slow Push It In," and Bajja Jedd's "Bedwork Sensation." Some songs are classics in the double entendre tradition of Afro-Caribbean culture, like General Degree's song "Pianist," in which a girl meets all the members of General Degree's band, but is particularly taken with the pianist, of whom she cannot get enough and who obligingly plays for her all night long.

The most self-righteous critic was probably Morris Cargill, late curmudgeonly columnist of the *Gleaner,* who vilified reggae for decades. He described a dancehall show as "an orgy of decibels, cacophony, howling, and banging amplified beyond the threshold of pain [and designed to appeal to the] coarse-grained, partly deaf and slightly demented." One of a growing category of Jamaicans, "returning residents," and a new columnist at the *Gleaner,* Dwight Whylie, goes so far as to deny that the words of dancehall songs can even be called lyrics:

> Ever since we returned to Jamaica, it has been there as a constant undertone, sometimes exploding to a sustained barrage. We get it from passing cars, the open doors of bars and on weekends from skyscraper speaker systems blasting at each other across the street. Dancehall and deejays. The angry quarrelling so-called lyrics hammering away on top of an overamplified visceral beat.

These sentiments mirror some of the reactions in the United States to rap music. European Americans sometimes complain about boom box music as, in Houston Baker's words, 'the ethnic pollution of public space by the sonic "other."' Baker responds that the complaint is an effort to demonize those who perpetrate the ethnic pollution. Likewise, reports in the *Gleaner* record efforts made to criminalize dancehall music with laws against loud music. Police raids of dancehalls have been a part of the music scene in Jamaica since sound systems began in the 1950s, and they are the subjects of several dancehall songs. In "Operation Ardent" Buju Banton sings about curfews and often fruitless searches being imposed on dancehall patrons:

> Wid hellecopta inna air
> Bright light a shine a ground
> Haffe decide fe run cau me no waan frisk down
> What more what more unnu want de ghetto people do
> When every dance show we keep get curfew . . .
> All de search dat was conducted no gun appear
> A just niceness mek everybody gather here.

In their song "Dance F. Gwan," Junior Reid and Ricky General complain about police wanting to lock up the dancehall at 9:30 P.M., leaving promoters of ghetto dances unable to support their families. The song refers to the ubiquitous threat of police brutality:

> When [police and soldiers] come they don't say a word
> They screw their face and mash up the place
> Put your hands in the air, don't touch your waist
> Cause if you do them ago shoot up the place.

That particular song also denies the distinction between roots reggae and dancehall by asserting continuity between the persecution endured by the older generation of reggae musicians and that of the dancehall artists. For Junior Reid, all "dancehall music deal with progress."

Asked why reggae music lyrics were so often used by politicians, Bob Marley suggested that "Rasta have the conscience of society." Many others would agree that what gave "roots" reggae its moral authority was its connection with Rastafari. However, until around 1993, this connection was very weak in dancehall. With a few notable exceptions such as Tony Rebel and Charlie Chaplin, most dancehall artists did not profess to be Rastafarians, and continued to comb and cut their hair. Around 1994, this began to change when a number of influential dancehall artists set about reviving interest in Rasta and praising King Selassie in the dancehall.

Among those credited with moving dancehall closer to Rasta is the deejay Capleton. His first hit song in Jamaica, "Bumbo Red," was noted for explicit lyrics. But in 1994 and 1995, with his release "Tour," according to Balford Henry in the *Gleaner,* he

> marked his emergence as a Rastafarian artiste who would swing his coattail across the dancehall topography and change, overnight, the whole outlook of the music. After 'Tour,' . . . the whole dancehall agenda changed from its emphasis on sex, strongly influenced by Shabba Ranks' 'sex sells' campaign and the gun, influenced by the lyrics of Ninjaman and Bounti Killa. Since then religion has become basic to the lyrics and Rastafarian, as a religion, the most essential element of current dancehall.

Probably the biggest influence in the move toward Rasta consciousness in the dancehall is Garnett Silk, the singer who died in a 1994 accident at age 28, just after he had signed a major recording contract. His songs were often otherworldly in nature, praising a Ras Tafari who looked on from above. Garnett Silk's influence has grown since his death, and his associates perceive him as a "sacrificial lamb." Tony Rebel described him as "an angel trodding the flesh. He was very spiritual, very loving and kind."

Given the middle class's cooptation of "roots" reggae, the fans who represent the economically disfranchised demanded a more challenging and oppositional music, and found it in dancehall. Gun lyrics expressed their demand for respect, and slackness challenged Anglophilic Jamaican respectability. The added association with Rastafari made the music even more compelling as a moral expression.

One of the clearest ways that dancehall speaks to the lower class in Jamaica is that it shares their language. The lyrics of deejays like Ninjaman, Capleton, Beenie Man, Simpleton, and others are delivered in patois, virtually inaccessible to North American audiences and therefore not particularly conducive to international recording success. "Standard" English is more closely associated with the professional middle-class Jamaican than with the working and rural classes.

Many songs reveal that artists still perceive that their music speaks for the poor in Jamaica. A good direct example is Beenie Man's song "Music a di beat (a di ghetto)." Other dancehall artists use their lyrics to describe the plight of "low-budget people."

Furthermore, contentious lyrics that criticize the ruling class in general and its specific segments are not uncommon in the work of some of the most popular dancehall deejays. A common dancehall theme of anti-government sentiments is the charge in songs by Terror Fabulous, Lady Saw, and Junior Reid, among others, that politicians are responsible for most of the violence in Kingston, a point with which many academics and journalists agree.

The irony of dancehall being criticized when politicians are at fault is expressed by one of the most "slack" women in the dancehall, Lady Saw, in her song "What Is Slackness?" She suggests that only with the arrival of slack lyrics was she able to be successful in the business, and she redefines slack to deflect criticism from herself and her music to those she believes are truly "slack":

Society blame Lady Saw for the system they create
When culture did a chat them never let me through the gate
When me say sex them want fi jump pon me case
Take the beam out a your eye before you chat in me face.
Slackness is when the road want fi fix
Slackness when government break them promise
Slackness when politicians issue all guns
So the two party shot one another down.

Even in slackness, dancehall artists manage to irk ruling class sensibilities as represented at least in the editorial pages of the *Gleaner.* Carolyn Cooper pointed out that slack dancehall music confronts "patriarchal gender ideology and the pious morality of fundamentalist Jamaican society."

Long-lasting and significant financial success is elusive in the business of all reggae music, but especially dancehall. Lucrative contracts with international labels go bad; a next deejay eclipses the success of the last; one's grandmother's rent needs to be paid; unscrupulous lawyers and greedy managers take their percentage. The political economy approach to popular music focuses on the power of the music industry, but that industry remains ignorant of or indifferent to most dancehall music.

Finally, dancehall's most unique social factor is the breadth of participation. It casts a wide net for contribution. Like reggae of the 1970s, whose "energy derived from dozens of tiny labels operating on shoestring budgets," dancehall formats allow anyone with an idea and the nerve to take up the microphone to become a dancehall artist.

One individual close to the reggae scene was quoted anonymously and provided a bitter but telling critique of dancehall:

> You see a little man, you see a man a pushin' cart 'pon the street, this a man tells me him is a deejay. You see a man him a work in a office, him is a deejay. Every little man right now is a deejay. . . . Any little man who get him hand 'pon a riddim is a deejay.

This is virtually what Bob Marley said about the early years of reggae music when anyone in Jamaica knew how to make a record, but Marley saw that as positive.

Paul Gilroy is correct: Deejays *do* appear in "legion" quantities. But this proliferation cannot be anything but healthy for reggae music in general. Dancehall enjoys a wide pool of individuals getting their words out into public discourse, in distinct contrast to rap and pop music in the United States, with their relatively small entertainment oligopolies and severely limited opportunities for new voices. We should also consider how much better still dancehall would be if every woman who pushed a cart or worked in an office could be a deejay too.

Dancehall music not only contradicts many of Adorno's expectations about the superficiality of commercial music and its political effect on the audience, it turns Adorno on his head in several key ways. First, instead of the undifferentiated, atomized masses, dancehall has its "Massive," as its audience calls itself, a community of taste that also shares economic and social interests. Dancehall serves as a focal point in mobilization of this group in opposition to ruling elites. Second, their very drive for profit, the desire to "head to the top" and be the number one deejay, inspires artists to construct messages that engage the attention of a politically mobilized, economically disfranchised working class. Third, reggae in general and dancehall in particular might be some of commercial music's most repetitive, most formulaic music, but it is here that one can also find some of commercial music's most critical analysis of social and political elites.

In contrast to the older "roots" reggae, dancehall is firmly grounded in Afro-Caribbean working class culture, expressing in the street vernacular a distain for ruling class social and economic practices. With its definitive turn toward religious and political consciousness, it seems clear that dancehall is truly Jamaican roots music.

Why Is Rock Music So Noisy?

■ Theodore Gracyk ■

In a recent study of the music of Jimi Hendrix, researcher Sheila Whitely makes a strange claim about "Purple Haze." Its "sheer volume of noise," she says, "works toward the drowning of personal consciousness." While I am not clear on what it means to drown personal consciousness, that is not the part of her claim that I find strange. Whitely conducted her research some two decades after Hendrix's death in 1970, so she must be talking about a recording of "Purple Haze." But the volume of a recording is not one of its essential properties; after all, in this situation it is Whitely and not Hendrix who controls the volume. If I put a Mozart piano sonata into the CD player and pump up the volume, will that also drown personal consciousness? Will I create a sheer volume of noise"? Presumably not.

Two questions arise here. First, why is Whitely playing Hendrix at high volume? And why does it seem appropriate that David Bowie's *The Rise and Fall of Ziggy Stardust* carries the label TO BE PLAYED AT MAXIMUM VOLUME, while the same label would seem ridiculous on New Age music? Second, what does it mean to describe "Purple Haze" as noise, beyond the mere fact that it is loud? That is, why isn't it just volume that's the issue here?

Let's begin with the second question. Volume or loudness is just one of the features of sound that leads us to classify it as noise. In *Noise: The Political Economy of Music,* Jacques Attali notes that "noise is a resonance that interferes with the audition of a message in the process of emission." In other words, noises are sounds that interfere with communication. Actually, they may interfere in at least two other ways. Sounds that disturb or annoy us may communicate perfectly well, yet by interfering count as noise. (Think here of a ringing telephone when one has a headache.) Sounds that interfere more generally, by threatening our physical well-being, also constitute noise. (Think here of Pearl Jam or Nine Inch Nails blasted at top volume while wearing headphones; over time, it contributes to serious hearing loss.)

Attali wants to call attention to a further dimension of sound as noise. Since musical organization is social, its control is inherently political. The decision to

---

"Why Is Rock Music So Noisy?" by Theodore Gracyk is published by permission of the author.

make music with a sampler rather than an oboe is to align oneself with a particular element within the body politic. The music, in turn, helps create and consolidate the social organization of the community that accepts it. To classify music as noise is to identify it as a violation of "the accepted rules of society." To purposely make noise, or even to listen to Hendrix while conscious of it as noise, is to align oneself with the politically marginalized and repressed. In this vein, Tricia Rose chose the title *Black Noise* for her recent study of rap music.

At one point, Rose criticizes a music professor who hates rap music. He complains about people who "ride down the street at 2:00 A.M. with [rap] blasting from car speakers, and wake up my wife and kids." Rose wants us to dismiss this as blind, blatant prejudice. She explains how she could not get the man to recognize the music's innovations. But is it merely a case of blind prejudice? Surely anyone who plays this music, at this volume and at this hour, has *chosen* that volume level. They are engaged in a behavior that disrupts the rules of the dominant culture. Volume is used as noise. However, Attali warns that rock is now so well established within consumer culture that it serves as an empty gesture. With rock entering its fifth decade, its love affair with noise is, as a subversive gesture, pretty empty. Now that a major share of the market for rap is white suburbia, how can it have any more political punch than Hendrix and other mainstays of "classic" rock?

Something more than politics and social identity is at work when Hendrix's "noise" sells more records now than at the time of his death. Keith Richards of the Rolling Stones found early inspiration in acoustic blues guitar. When the group moved on to live performances in London clubs, "it took a while longer to get the electric bit together," Richards said in 1971. "At the time we thought, 'Oh, it just makes it louder,' but it ain't quite as simple as that." The reason it ain't, unknown to Richards at the time, is that amplification changes the quality of the sound in the process of making it louder. And this is particularly true for Richards' signature instrument, the electric guitar.

Crudely summarized, any two musical sounds might differ from one another in terms of four basic *heard* features: volume, pitch, length, and timbre. This last feature is also called tone color. It is what allows you to identify a sound as coming from a piano instead of a clarinet or violin. Singing along with "Purple Haze," one might sing louder than the radio, sing flat on the first syllable (a different pitch), hold the note longer (a different length), and sing in a voice that does not sound at all like Hendrix (a different timbre). These heard differences are due to differences in the physical dimensions of amplitude, frequency, duration, and wave form of the sound waves. Except for isolated cases of relatively pure pitches, sound waves have very complex patterns. The most prominent frequency in the pattern is the fundamental, which serves as the basis for pitch identification. But different instruments, including voices, impart different complications to the pattern. This is particularly true of the attack and decay phases of the sound (how it begins and how it ends), and of *overtones* (additional pitches, some of which harmonize with the fundamental and some which do not).

What Richards discovered when he went electric was that increases in amplitude *change* the tone color. Increased amplitude gives new prominence to the sound's partial tones, particularly during the complex attack and decay phases. Most electronic instruments also provide controls that selectively amplify specific ranges of frequencies, changing the timbre in further ways. Where traditional acoustic instruments and traditional voice training provide musical sounds with precise pitch articulation, electronic music encourages exploration of timbre. Relative to most music, the complex tone colors of rock music constitute noise. But what counts as distortion and interference in traditional music is viewed as musical *richness* in rock. Playing acoustic instruments might be compared to coloring a picture with a pack of 8 crayons; the switch to electronic instruments is then akin to getting to a set of 64 colors! New possibilities arise.

Furthermore, amplification equipment will contribute its own "sound" to the music. Neil Young's electric guitar sound is largely the result of a 1948 Deluxe amplifier with an accordian input. Amplified music offers yet another set of opportunities at the stage of "mixing" the sound, with selective amplification used on different sound inputs. Tricia Rose emphasizes that, like other African-derived traditions in the Americas, African American music gives high priority to low-end frequencies. As with rhythm, bass and drum sound are more important than harmonic complexity in the construction of the music. It is no coincidence that low-end frequencies require the largest investments of energy (i.e., amplitude and thus volume) to boost successfully. To recover the sound of this low end while cruising around at 2:00 A.M., rap fans have to crank the volume to get the music to sound "right" within the expectations of the music's cultural tradition. The sound that wakes the neighbor in the night may be far less an expression of defiance than it is an aesthetic preference for enhanced tone color.

As Hendrix advised Billy Gibbons, guitarist for ZZ Top: "The best thing you can do, brother, is turn it up as loud as it'll go." When Sheila Whitely cranks up "Purple Haze," she's listening appropriately, responding to the musical richness of the recordings. That is because the musical richness of rock is partly in the music's exploration of timbre, and only volume will bring it out.

Can White People Sing the Blues?
■ Joel Rudinow ■

Can white people sing the blues? Can white people play the blues? On the surface, these may seem to be silly questions. Why not? What is Mose Allison, if not a white blues singer? Surely the performances of guitarists Eric Clapton and Stevie Ray Vaughan and pianist Dr. John must count as playing the blues. But the question "Can white people sing (or play) the blues?" is much more persistent, elusive, and deeper than such ready responses acknowledge. . . . (There is) a tradition of criticism which distinguishes between the performances of black and white blues musicians, preferring those of black musicians and refusing to recognize as genuine those of white musicians. This tradition raises questions of race, ethnicity, and expressive authenticity which go to the heart of the contemporary debate over multiculturalism, the canon, and the curriculum. I derive my title, and take my theme, from the late jazz critic Ralph J. Gleason, who raised the issue definitively, at least for white liberals in the late 1960s, saying:

> [T]he blues is black man's music, and whites diminish it at best or steal it at worst. In any case they have no moral right to use it. . . .

In the literature of musical aesthetics the authenticity question has been focused largely on the relation between performances and "the work"—or, because the work is conceived of as a composition, between performances and what the composer intended—and the criteria for authenticity have been understood in terms of accuracy or conformity with performance specifications which constitute the work. As applied to blues performances the authenticity question must be focused somewhat differently, for although we may speak of blues "compositions," what we thereby refer to consist of no more typically than a simple chord progression shared by many other such "compositions," with no definite key signature, no particular prescribed instrumentation, and a lyrical text which itself is open to *ad lib* interruption, interpretation, and elaboration in performance. As a musical genre, the blues is characterized by what we might call "compositional minimalism" and a complementary emphasis on expressive elements. The question of the authenticity of a given blues performance is thus one of stylistic and expressive authenticity, and our question becomes, "Is white blues 'acceptably enough derived' from the original sources of the blues to be stylistically authentic and authentically expressive within the style?" The negative position can now be understood as: White musicians cannot play the blues in an authentic way because they do not

"Can White People Sing the Blues?" by Joel Rudinow has been excerpted from "Race Ethnicity, Expressive Authenticity: Can White People Sing the Blues?" *The Journal of Aesthetics and Art Criticism* (Winter 1994), pages 128–136, and is reprinted by permission of the publisher.

have the requisite relation or proximity to the original sources of the blues. No one has made the case for the negative position more provocatively, eloquently, profoundly, and forcefully than Amiri Baraka (LeRoi Jones). In what follows I will consider that case, which I believe consists of two interrelated arguments, which I will call the "Proprietary Argument" and the "Experiential Access Argument."

The proprietary argument addresses the question of ownership. Who "owns" the blues? Who has legitimate authority to use the blues as an idiom, as a performance style, to interpret it, to draw from it and to contribute to it as a fund of artistic and cultural wealth, to profit from it? The originators and the major innovative elaborators of the blues were in fact members of the African-American community. Women and men like Ma Rainey, Bessie Smith, Charlie Patton, Robert Johnson, Muddy Waters, Howlin' Wolf, John Lee Hooker, T-Bone Walker, Professor Longhair, and so on. The question arises, to whom does this cultural and artistic heritage belong? Who are Robert Johnson's legitimate cultural and artistic heirs and conservators?

The proprietary argument says in effect that the blues as genre and style belongs to the African-American community and that when white people undertake to perform the blues they misappropriate the cultural heritage and intellectual property of African-Americans and of the African-American community—what Baraka refers to as "the Great Music Robbery." Baraka describes a systematic and pervasive pattern throughout the history of black people in America—a pattern of cultural and artistic co-optation and misappropriation in which not just the blues, but every major black artistic innovation, after an initial period of condemnation and rejection as culturally inferior, eventually wins recognition for superior artistic significance and merit, only to be immediately appropriated by white imitators whose imitations are very profitably mass produced and distributed, and accepted in the cultural mainstream as definitive, generally without due credit to their sources. Calling the blues "the basic national voice of the African-American people," he writes:

> ... after each new wave of black innovation, i.e., New Orleans, big band, bebop, rhythm and blues, hard bop, new music, there was a commercial cooptation of the original music and an attempt to replace it with corporate dilution which mainly featured white players and was mainly intended for a white middle-class audience.

This is not an aberrant or accidental phenomenon, nor is it benign. Rather it is part and parcel of a subtle and systematic form of institutionalized racism which reinforces a racist socioeconomic class structure.

> The problem for the Creators of Black Music, the African-American people, is that because they lack Self-Determination, i.e., political power and economic self-sufficiency, various peoples' borrowings and cooptation of the music can be disguised and the beneficiaries of such acts pretend they are creating out of the air.

Let's consider a possible objection, or set of objections, to this argument. The crucial claim is the ownership claim: that the blues as genre and style belongs to the

African-American community. How is this claim warranted? Part of the warrant is the factual claim that the originators and major innovative elaborators of the blues were members of the African-American community like Ma Rainey, Bessie Smith, Charlie Patton, Robert Johnson, Muddy Waters, Howlin' Wolf, John Lee Hooker, T-Bone Walker, Professor Longhair, and so on. There is an interpretive tradition which holds, contrary to this, that the blues is an oral folk form with an ancient and untraceable pre-history, but in spite of this let us take the factual claim as true. But what is the principle or set of principles which connects this factual claim with the ownership claim that the blues belongs to the African-American *community?*

The crucial assumption underlying this as a *critical* question—as the basis for a series of objections—is the modern notion of intellectual property as applied to the blues. On this assumption, an *individual* is understood to have certain rights regarding the product of his or her original creative work, including the right to control access to the work for the purposes of commercial exploitation, etc. So one could say that the musical literature of the blues rightly belongs to *certain members* of the African American community like Ma Rainey, Bessie Smith, Charlie Patton, Robert Johnson, Muddy Waters, Howlin' Wolf, John Lee Hooker, T-Bone Walker, Professor Longhair, or their estates, legitimate heirs and assigns. But this list, even drawn up on the basis of a liberal reading of "legitimate heirs and assigns," even if *padded,* is not coextensive with "the African-American *community.*"

Moreover, these rights can be alienated voluntarily and involuntarily in various ways. They can be purchased, sold, exchanged, wagered, and so on. So for example the rights inherent in Robert Johnson's entire catalogue of recorded compositions now belong to something called King of Spades Music and the rights to the recordings of his performances of them belong to CBS Records, part of the Sony Corporation. In other words, on this assumption a number of individual and corporate ownership claims would seem to follow from the facts, but not the communal ownership claim central to Baraka's case.

Finally, the proprietary argument claims ownership of the blues as genre and style, so that musical and expressive elements as elusive as timbre, diction, vocal inflection, timing, rhythmic "feel," and their imitations become the subjects of dispute. For example, the rock group ZZ Top has obviously imitated or "borrowed from" elements of John Lee Hooker's distinctive style in several of their original compositions. For Baraka this constitutes misappropriation—just another instance of The Great Music Robbery. But where in the notion of music as intellectual property can one find precedent for this? If anything, the history of music provides ample precedent for accepting such borrowings as legitimate forms of tribute and trade in ideas. The modern notion of intellectual property as applied to music can be used to support ownership claims concerning compositions but not musical ideas as ephemeral and problematic for purposes of documentation as these "elements of style."

Arguably this series of objections does very little damage to the proprietary argument. First of all, what the objection grants is important evidence in support of the proprietary argument. The modern notion of intellectual property, insofar as it is applicable to the blues, would seem to warrant at least an indictment of the American music establishment on the offense of Great Music Robbery, just as Baraka maintains. The means whereby the intellectual property rights inherent in the creative work of African-American blues musicians were alienated from the artists, later to turn up in various corporate portfolios at greatly appreciated value, were in many cases questionable, to say the least.

But more important, though it may not be entirely inappropriate to apply an eighteenth-century English legal concept of intellectual property to the blues—after all, the blues *is* modern American music—it's not entirely appropriate either. Approaching the blues via such a conceptual route entails treating the blues as a collection of compositions, discrete pieces of intellectual property, convenient as commodities to the economic apparatus of the twentieth-century American music and entertainment industries, whereas attention and sensitivity to the social context of the music, its production, presentation, and enjoyment disclose phenomena rather more in the nature of real-time event and communally shared experience, in which the roles of performer and audience are nowhere near as sharply delineated as would be suggested by the imposition of the notions of creative artist and consumer upon them. . . .

On balance, the modern notion of intellectual property as applied to the blues seems little more than an elaborate red herring which in effect obscures crucial facts about the social circumstances of the music's production, appreciation, and indeed, *meaning*. This brings me to what I am calling the "experiential access argument."

Where the proprietary argument addresses the question of ownership, the experiential access argument addresses the questions of meaning and understanding as these bear centrally on issues of culture, its identity, evolution, and transmission. What is the significance of the blues? Who can legitimately claim to understand the blues? Or to speak authoritatively about the blues and its interpretation? Who can legitimately claim fluency in the blues as a musical idiolect? Or the authority to pass it on to the next generation? Who are the real bearers of the blues tradition?

The experiential access argument says in effect that one cannot understand the blues or authentically express oneself in the blues unless one knows what it's like to live as a black person in America, and one cannot know this without being one. To put it more elaborately, the meaning of the blues is deep, hidden, and accessible only to those with an adequate grasp of the historically unique experience of the African-American community. Members of other communities may take an interest in this experience and even empathize with it, but they have no direct access to the experience and therefore cannot fully comprehend or express it. Hence their attempts to master the blues or to express themselves in the idiom of the blues will of necessity tend to be relatively shallow and superficial, i.e., in-authentic. . . .

In the context of the kinds of questions raised here about culture, its identity, evolution, and transmission, the appeal to experience functions as a basis upon which to either establish or challenge authority, based on some such principle as this: Other things equal, the more directly one's knowledge claims are grounded in first hand experience, the more unassailable one's authority. Though there is room for debate about the centrality of experience as a ground of knowledge, as for example in current discussions of "feminist epistemology," such a principle as this one seems plausible and reasonable enough.

Nevertheless, stated badly, and understood literally, the experiential access argument seems to invite the objection that it is either a priori or just dubious. The access that most contemporary black Americans have to the experience of slavery or sharecropping or life on the Mississippi delta during the twenties and thirties is every bit as remote, mediated, and indirect as that of any white would-be blues player. Does the argument subscribe to some "Myth of Ethnic Memory" whereby mere membership in the ethnic group confers special access to the lived experience of ancestors and other former members? It would be just as facile and fatuous for a Jewish-American baby boomer (such as myself) to take the position that only Jews can adequately comprehend the experience of the holocaust.

However the argument is susceptible of a more subtle and defensible reading, namely that the blues is essentially a cryptic language, a kind of secret code. Texts composed in this language typically have multiple layers of meaning, some relatively superficial, some deeper. To gain access to the deeper layers of meaning one must have the keys to the code. But the keys to the code presuppose extensive and detailed familiarity with the historically unique body of experience shared within and definitive of the African-American community and are therefore available only to the properly initiated.

There is a certain amount of theoretical and historical material, as well as textual material within the blues, available to support this argument. A general theoretical framework for understanding the development of cryptic devices and systems of communication under repressive circumstances can be found in the work of Leo Strauss. Strauss maintains that where control of the thought and communication of a subjugated population is attempted in order to maintain a political arrangement, even the most violent means of repression are inadequate to the task, for "it is a safe venture to tell the truth one knows to benevolent and trustworthy acquaintances, or . . . to reasonable friends." The human spirit will continue to seek, recognize, and communicate the truth privately in defiance of even the most repressive regimes, which moreover cannot even prevent public communication of forbidden ideas, "for a man of independent thought can utter his views in public and remain unharmed, provided he moves with circumspection. He can even utter them in print without incurring any danger, provided he is capable of writing between the lines." Unjust and repressive regimes thus naturally tend to engender covert communication strategies with "all the advantages of private communication without having its greatest disadvantage—that it reaches only the writer's acquaintances, [and] all the advantages of public communication without having its greatest disadvantage—capital punishment for the author."

Evidence of the employment of such strategies within the African-American community is fairly well documented. For example, the evolution of "Black English," as well as a number of its salient characteristics, such as crucial ambiguity, understatement, irony, and inversion of meaning ("bad" means "good," and so on), may best be explained as the development of cryptic communicative strategies under repression. . . .

Lyrically the blues are rife with more or less covert allusions to the oppressive conditions of black life in America. If Jimmy Reed's "Big Boss Man"

(Big boss man, can't you hear me when I call [twice]
Well you ain't so big, you just tall, that's all)

is overt, it is merely extending a more covert tradition central to the blues. . . .

Similarly, the blues are full of covert and even overt references, both musical and lyrical, to the esoterica of African religions whose practice on this continent was prohibited and systematically repressed. When Muddy Waters sings:

I got a black cat bone
I got a mojo too
I got John the conqueror root
I'm gonna mess wit' you

we understand very little unless we recognize the references to the conjures and charms of the Dahomean religion which migrated to the Americas under slavery as vodun or "voodoo." . . .

Having said all this, it nevertheless remains apparent that neither the proprietary argument nor the experiential access argument quite secures the thesis that white people cannot sing (or play) authentic blues. The experiential access argument has undeniable moral force as a reminder of and warning against the offense of presumptive familiarity, but it distorts the blues in the process by obscuring what is crucially and universally *human* about its central themes. And it leaves open the possibility of the proper initiation of white people and other non-blacks, if not entirely into the African-American ethnic community, then at least in the use of the blues as an expressive idiom and so into the blues community. Obvious examples would include Johnny Otis and Dr. John. Given this, the force of the proprietary argument is also limited, since initiation into the blues community presumably carries with it legitimate access to the blues as a means of artistic expression. . . .

I think that if we wish to avoid ethnocentrism, as we would wish to avoid racism, what we should say is that the authenticity of a blues performance turns not on the ethnicity of the performer but on the degree of mastery of the idiom and the integrity of the performer's use of the idiom in performance. This last is delicate and can be difficult to discern. But what one is looking for is evidence in and around the performance of the performer's recognition and acknowledgement of indebtedness to sources of inspiration and technique (which as a matter of historical fact *do* have an identifiable ethnicity). . . . Paul Oliver estimates the blues' chances of survival through these times of ethnic mingling as "unlikely." This kind of "blues purism" is no way to keep the blues alive either. The blues, like any oral tradition, remains alive to the extent that it continues to evolve and things continue to "grow out of it." The way to keep the blues alive is to celebrate such evolutionary developments.

Kitsch

■ Robert Solomon ■

The term "kitsch" comes from the nineteenth century. One of several suggested etymologies is that the word is German for "smear" or "playing with mud," and, toying with this, we might speculate that the "mud" in question is emotion and mucking around with emotions inevitably makes a person "dirty." The standard opinion seems to be that kitsch and immorality go together and that sentimentality is what is wrong with both of them. For example, [Karsten] Harries: "Kitsch has always been considered immoral." Of course, one culture's or one generation's kitsch may be another's avant garde, and what is obligatory as "compassion" or "sympathy" in one age may be dismissed as mere sentimentality in another. Accordingly, the sentiments that are provoked by and disdained in "sweet" kitsch may vary as well. But whatever the cause or the context, it is sentimentality of kitsch that makes kitsch, kitsch and sentimentality that makes kitsch morally suspect if not immoral. Granted, kitsch may be bad art. Granted, it may show poor taste. But my question here is why it is the sentimentality of kitsch that should be condemned, why it is thought to be an ethical defect and a danger to society. . . .

The strong, shared contempt for kitsch and sentimentality is something of a standard for good taste, but there is all too little agreement about "what is wrong" with kitsch and sentimentality to back it up. We can accept, as simply irrelevant to our concern here, the claim that kitsch represents "bad taste," but this is hardly a concession given the rarely rational vicissitudes of taste in an art market that now celebrates street graffiti, a pile of bricks and an artist's dragging himself across broken glass as art. But culling through the literature in both ethics and aesthetics, I think we can narrow down the leading candidates for an argument to [the following]:

(1) Kitsch and sentimentality provoke *excessive* or *immature* expressions of emotion. It is true that kitsch is calculated to evoke our emotions, especially those emotions that are best expressed by that limp vocabulary that seems embarrassingly restricted to such adjectives as "cute" and "pretty" or that even more humiliating, drawn-out downward intoned "Aaaaah" that seems inappropriate even in Stuckeys. It is also true that the emotions provoked by kitsch tend to be unsophisticated and even child-like (as opposed to childish). But is the charge that kitsch provokes *too much* of these affectionate emotions, or that it provokes them *at all?* And when the critics of sentimentality call an emotion "immature" or "naive" are they really contrasting it with more mature and knowledgeable emotions or are they, again, dismissing emotions as such? Now I would be the first to insist that emotions develop

---

"Kitsch" by Robert Solomon has been excerpted from *The Journal of Aesthetics and Art Criticism* (Winter 1991), pages 4–10, 12 and is reprinted by permission of the publisher.

with experience and are cultivated through education, and there certainly is a world of difference between the emotions of a seven-year-old and the emotions of a seventy-year-old. But are the emotions of the latter necessarily better or even wiser than the emotions of the child? Indeed, don't we often take emotions to be sophisticated precisely when they are cynical, even bitter, not only controlled but suppressed? There is something charming, even virtuous, about an adult who is capable of child-like feelings and something suspiciously wrong if he or she can never be so, even in the intimacy of a private apartment, a theater or an art gallery. To be sure, the ability to be so moved is no sign of aesthetic or artistic maturity, but neither is it evidence to the contrary nor an emotional flaw in character. To be sure, we outgrow some of our emotions, but one of the purposes of art is to remind us of just those tender, outgrown sentiments, perhaps even to disturb us regarding their loss. Better yet, art can help us feel them again, and move us to action on their behalf.

I think that it is worth noting that our limited vocabulary and expressions indicate a cultivated inability to recognize or publicly express the more gentle emotions. (How rich our vocabulary of abuse and disgust, by way of contrast.) How much of an emotion is "too much"? How is this to be measured? Of course, one can condemn the public expression of emotion as "inappropriate" or as "immature," depending on the context and its customs, and we might well agree without argument that the childish expression of even the most sophisticated emotion is inappropriate in the public space of an art museum, but it is not excessive or childish expression that is being criticized here. It is the emotion as such, whether expressed or not, and the idea is that a sophisticated viewer will be mortified at his or her emotional response to a piece of high kitsch. The usual cultivated response, accordingly, is a sneer. So what is "too much" emotion? What is an "immature" emotion? If we are embarrassed by the gentle emotions I suspect that it is because those emotions themselves make us uncomfortable, in any "amount" and remind us of our own residual naiveté. Of course, it may be that good taste requires subtlety (though one might well object that this is a very cold-blooded and whiggish conception of good taste) and it may be that certain emotions are indeed inappropriate and out of place, e.g., getting sexually "turned on" by [William] Bouguereau's [painting of] two little girls—which may in a few troubled souls be difficult to distinguish from more appropriate feelings of affection. (This sort of pathology is hardly "immaturity.") But the bottom line seems to be that feeling "cuddly" just isn't "cool." Feeling our "hearts going out" to a painting of two little girls in the grass makes us uncomfortable and indicates incipient poor taste if it is not also a mark of some sort of degeneracy (sexual overtones quite aside). But why should we feel so guilty about feeling good or feeling for the moment a childlike affection? In real children, of course, such gentle feelings may well coexist with meanness (I am not trying to sentimentalize children here) and they may play poorly in the rough and tumble world of business outside of the museum. But in such a safe, relatively private context, what would it mean to feel an excess of kindness, even "cuteness"? And why should the unsubtle evocation of tenderness be ethically blameworthy, distasteful or dangerous? Bad art, perhaps, but why any more than this?

(2) One obvious suggestion is that kitsch and sentimentality manipulate our emotions. Of course, it must be said immediately that one puts oneself in the position of being so manipulated, by going to the museum, by standing or walking in front of the painting, and so the "blame" is properly placed on the viewer as well as the artist and the object. Indeed, kitsch is manipulative. It utilizes what Kathleen Higgins calls "icons" to guarantee an instant and wholly predictable emotional response. Why else depict little girls, puppies and other subjects guaranteed to tug at our "heart-strings"? The argument, presumably, is that manipulation of emotions, even with the initial acquiescence of the "victim," is a violation of a person's autonomy. Of course, it is just as manipulative to depict the same subjects being beaten to within an inch of their lives, and while we might object to the latter (on moral grounds to be sure) the objection is not of the same sort as our objection to kitsch. But, again, my suspicion is that the objection, while cast in the language of violation, is a covert reaction against the emotions themselves. We do not talk about a violation of autonomy when a person is "reasoned with," so why do we do so when the appeal is not to reason but emotions? The presumption is that our emotions, unlike our reason, are not truly our own, and they are humiliating rather than ennobling. Of course, this may be true of some emotions but it does not follow for all of them. One would think that feelings of tenderness would be ennobling and not humiliating, but then why should we feel "manipulated" by their provocation?

What does it mean, to "manipulate" someone's emotions? I suppose it means to intentionally bring them about. We do this all the time, of course, in our every social gesture, but one does not ordinarily complain when his or her emotion of gratitude, for example, is intentionally brought about by a gift. The accusation of "manipulation" only emerges when the emotion in question is an unwanted one, e.g., if the gift is given by an offender whom one does not (for whatever reason) want to forgive—or at least not yet. But, why should we find even saccharine sentiments so unwanted that we resent their provocation, particularly in the sanctuary of a museum where such feelings would seem to be appropriate. . . .

. . . (3) So, too, kitsch and sentimentality are said to express or evoke "cheap" or "easy" or "superficial" emotions. We should note with considerable suspicion the ambiguity of the word "cheap," which on the one hand means "low quality" but on the other has unmistakable reference to the socioeconomic status of the sentimentalist. "Cheap" means "low-class," and the suggestion is that we should be "above" such sentiments. We are not particularly surprised when class-conscious Oscar Wilde suggests that the feelings which constitute sentimentality are unearned, had on the cheap and come by too easily. ("To be sentimental is to be shallow.") Irony and skepticism are the marks of the educated; sentimentality is the mark of the uneducated. One cannot understand the attack on kitsch, I propose, without a sociological-historical hypothesis about the fact that the "high" class of many societies associate themselves with emotional control and reject sentimentality as an expression of inferior, ill-bred beings, and male society has long used such a view to demean the "emotionality" of women. I am tempted to suggest that the attack on sentimentality also has an ethnic bias. Northern against Southern Europe and West against East, with only a few geographical modifications for ethical and aesthetic prejudice in North America. But such obviously class-based criticism is not restricted to those who would confuse aesthetic taste with political legitimacy. Indeed, much of the contempt for kitsch, I would suggest, is not the product of personal or cultivated taste at all but rather the "superficial" criterion that teaches us that kitsch—immediately recognizable by its play on the tender sentiments—is unacceptable. Those sentiments are "cheap" not just because kitsch is cheap but because the person who feels them is, emotionally speaking, cheap as well. In a society that strives for political equality, can we afford to tolerate such snobbery? ("Some of my best leftist friends . . . ") . . .

(4) [Milan] Kundera argues at some length that kitsch and sentimentality are self-indulgent. Let us repeat his most famous charge:

> Kitsch causes two tears to flow in quick succession. The first tear says: How nice to see children running on the grass!
> The second tear says: How nice to be moved, together with all mankind, by children running on the grass!
> It is the second tear that makes kitsch kitsch.

The idea that kitsch is "false" because it is the emotion and not the object of emotion that is the primary concern is part of the charge that kitsch and sentimentality are not only fraudulent but self-indulgent as well. Harries writes "kitsch creates illusion for the sake of self-employment" and suggests that love is kitsch, for example, "if love has its center not in the beloved but within itself." We all know the phenomenon of being "in love with love," but what is wrong with this, in our social lives, is that we know from experience that the supposed beloved usually gets the short end of it. Where the putative object is a figure in a painting or porcelain, there is no such danger of abandonment or fraud, and the locus of the enjoyment—in the object or in the emotion itself—would not seem to be a matter of concern. Indeed, is the reflectivity of emotion in such cases self-indulgence, or is it what we would call in philosophical circles "reflection"—the enjoyment of the seeing and not just the seen? What is wrong or self-indulgent about enjoying our emotions, even "for their own sakes"? Has any philosopher not suspected that enjoying the games and skills of reason—quite apart from the putative subject of discussion—might be similarly "self-indulgent"? Again, I suspect a deep distrust of and disdain for the emotions as such, and the ethical innocence of kitsch and its enjoyment thus becomes a suspected vice. . . .

(5) The most common charge against emotions in general and against kitsch and sentimentality in particular is that they distort our perceptions and interfere with rational thought and understanding. I want to argue—briefly—that this epistemological critique of emotions in general as "distorting" or "irrational"—a standard bit in the rationalist's repertoire—seriously confuses both the nature of emotion and the nature of perception. The first argument is that sentimentality is

objectionable because it is *distorting*. Mary Midgley, for instance, argues that, "the central offence lies in self-deception, in distorting reality to get a pretext for indulging in *any* feeling." Sentimentality centers around the "flight from, and contempt for, real people." So too, Mark Jefferson argues that "sentimentality involves attachment to a distorted series of beliefs," in particular "the fiction of innocence." But the reply to this objection is, first of all, that all emotions are "distorting" in the sense intended and such "distortion" isn't really distorting at all. In anger one looks only at the offense and fails to take account of the good humor of the antagonist. In jealousy we are aware only of the threat and not of the wit and charms of our rival. In love one celebrates the virtues and not the vices of the beloved, in envy we seek only the coveted object and remain indifferent to questions of general utility and the fairness of the desired redistribution. It is the very nature of an emotion to be engaged, even if only vicariously, to "take sides," sometimes judiciously and sometimes not. Through our emotions we edit a scene or a situation in such a way that it *matters to us,* and in sentimentality we focus on the sweet and innocent aspects of a scene such that we are *moved*. Kitsch is art (whether or not it is good art) that is deliberately designed to so move us, by presenting a well-selected and perhaps much-edited version of some particularly and predictably moving aspect of our shared experience, including, plausibly enough, innocent scenes of small children and our favorite pets playing and religious and other sacred icons. But what must a critic be thinking of the world when she or he condemns these representations as "the fiction of innocence," or worse (according to [Herman] Broch), as "universal hypocrisy"? . . .

Jokes
■ Ted Cohen ■

If it is irrational to fail to be persuaded by a good argument, what is it to fail to be amused by a good joke? Not irrational, I think; certainly not in the same way. It is like being without taste. We will say 'irrational,' I think, not only of someone unpersuaded by a good argument, but also of someone who is unable to see that it *is* a good argument if the form is plainly valid and the premises obviously true. And we will, I think, deny a sense of humor not only in someone who isn't amused by the funniness he sees, but also in someone who can't see the funniness when it is clearly there.

"Jokes" by Ted Cohen has been excerpted from *Pleasure, Preference and Value,* Eva Schaper, ed., Cambridge University Press (1983), pages 131–136, and is reprinted by permission of the publisher.

What is a sense of humor? A capacity to be amused by the amusing, I suppose. What makes this capacity remarkable is that it is not coerced into activity. You don't *have* to laugh. Your response is not compelled in the way that an argument compels belief. Your response is not arbitrary, however. We don't all just happen coincidentally to be laughing when we've heard a joke, as if we'd all simultaneously been tickled under the arms.

If I am correct, then the 'If—then' in 'If you hear a joke, then you laugh' stands for a relation we are poorly equipped to describe, for it is neither sternly logical nor merely contingent. Surely the joke must *cause* you to laugh, but it isn't the same as when tickling makes you laugh. It is exactly the relation Kant is ill-equipped to describe when he undertakes to analyze the judgment of taste. This judgment, he says, exhibits a response (to beauty) which is free but also somehow necessitated.

What is wrong with you if you are not amused, if you are not reached by this non-necessary, non-contingent relation? In escaping the proper response you are not so much wrong as different. It is not a trivial difference. It is a difference which leaves you outside a vital community, the community of those who feel this fun. It is a community which creates and acknowledges itself in the moment, and is powerless to conscript its membership. To fail to laugh at a joke is to remain outside that community. But you cannot will yourself in, any more than you can will yourself out.

A point in telling a joke is the attainment of community. There is special intimacy in shared laughter, and a mastering aim of joke-telling is the purveyance of this intimacy. The intimacy is most purified, refined, and uncluttered when the laughter is bound to the joke by the relation I have just been worrying over, a relation in which the laughter is not exacted but is nonetheless rendered fit. There are derivative forms of intimacy, in which the laughter is not so absolutely free. These obtain when the joke calls upon the background of the audience and uses this as a material condition for securing the effect. I think there are two main forms.

In the first form the joke is *hermetic*. It really makes sense only to those with special information, and the intimacy brought to those who qualify is bound up with a recognition—or re-recognition—that they do constitute an audience more select than humanity in general. The joke occasions the reconstitution of that select community. For an hermetic joke the required background may be very specific and decisive.

> What is Sacramento?
> It is the stuffing in a Catholic olive.

Either you know about pimento and the Church and its sacraments, and you get this joke, or you don't know these things and the joke is opaque. In America a very common device of this kind of joke is the incorporation of words or phrases in Yiddish. Appreciators of these jokes were once nearly restricted to certain Jews, but this has changed as an endless stream of Jewish comics forces more and more elements of Jewish humor, including vocabulary, on more and more of the general public.

Not every hermetic joke offers itself on this all-or-nothing basis. Some have depths which permit appreciation on different, if cumulative, levels.

> One day Toscanini was rehearsing the NBC Symphony. He stopped the playing to correct the trumpet line only to discover that the first-chair trumpet had intended exactly what he had played, and disagreed with Toscanini over how it should go. There ensued a heated argument which ended only when the trumpeter stalked angrily off the stage. As he reached the wings he turned to Toscanini and said 'Schmuck!' The maestro replied, 'It's-a too late to apologize.'

If you know only the word 'Schmuck' you can manage this joke. In fact even if you don't know what it means you can sense enough from its phonetic quality to salvage the joke. But the more you know of professional musicians in New York, of Toscanini's ego and his peculiar approach to non-Roman language, and so on, the more you will make of the joke.

Here is a more intricate example of an hermetic joke.

> A musician was performing a solo recital in Israel. When he ended the last selection, a thunderous response came from the audience, including many cries of 'Play it again.' He stepped forward, bowed, and said, 'What a wonderfully moving response. Of course I shall be delighted to play it again.' And he did. At the end, again there was a roar from the audience, and again many cries of 'Play it again.' This time the soloist came forward smiling and said, 'Thank you. I have never been so touched in all my concert career. I should love to play it again, but there is no time, for I must perform tonight in Tel Aviv. So, thank you from the bottom of my heart—and farewell.' Immediately a voice was heard from the back of the hall saying, 'You will stay here and play it again until you get it right.'

This joke works with nearly any audience, but its total riches are available only to those who know the Jewish religious requirement that on certain occasions the appropriate portion of the Hebrew Bible be read out, that those present make known any errors they detect in the reading, and that the reader not only acknowledge these corrections but that he then go back and read out the text correctly. That audience—those entirely within the community of this joke—will not only be able to find this extra level, but they should also find it a better joke. For them there is a point in the story's being set in Israel, and if there were no point in that, the joke would do better to omit the geography altogether.

In the second derivative form of intimacy the joke is likely to be rather simple, although not necessarily, and the background required is not one of knowledge but one of attitude or prejudice. I call these *affective* jokes. The most common examples are probably what in America are called ethnic jokes. It is not necessary that one actually believe that Jews are immoral, or Poles inept, or Italians lascivious, or whatever: Indeed, most appreciators known to me have the opposite beliefs. What's needed is not a belief but a predisposition to enjoy situations in which Jews, Poles, Blacks, or whoever are singled out. . . .

The little schematism I've sketched divides jokes into two kinds, the pure ones and the conditional ones. The conditional ones, the ones the success of which requires a special background in the audience, are again divisible into two kinds: the hermetic ones, whose presumed background is one of knowledge or belief, and the affective ones, which require of the audience a particular prejudice, or feeling, or disposition, or inclination. (If you have a passion for this you might further divide the affective jokes into those for which the requisite predisposition is affirmative and those for which it is negative. In what Americans call a 'Polish' joke, the prejudice defames Poles. In Warsaw, however, a Polish joke is typically celebratory, and in the story a Pole subdues a Russian or a German or the Polish government.)

I am not saying that pure jokes are *better.* And they do not seem to be more interesting as a subject. Let me note two excellent topics associated with the complexity of conditional jokes.

First is the matter of active complicity. When your special background is called into play, your sensibility is galvanized. Something that sets you apart from just any person is brought into your apprehension and this adds to the quantity and alters the quality of the intimacy achieved. The point is like the one I think Aristotle has in mind when he declares the enthymeme the argument most suitable for certain kinds of persuasion. His idea is this: If you wish to set your audience in motion, especially with an eye toward provoking them to action, then you are well advised to induce them to supply the initial momentum themselves. You can do this by offering them an incomplete argument. They must then undertake a mental scramble in order to locate the premises necessary to render the argument valid. This scramble is a motion of the mind undertaken *before* the legitimate arrival of the conclusion, and that motion augments the persuasion implicit in the validity of the completed argument. So it is, approximately, with conditional jokes. The requirement of a special background is not stated explicitly. The audience discovers that and it also discovers that it can supply what's needed. It is further aware that not everyone can supply the background (unlike an enthymeme's audience which potentially includes everyone because minimal logical acuity is enough to formulate the implicated missing premiss). In doing this the audience collaborates in the success of the joke—the constitution of intimacy—just as the audience for an enthymeme collaborates in the construction of a valid argument, with the difference that the audience of the joke derives additional intensity of feeling from knowing that the success is due to them specifically, that other groups would fail.

A second good topic concerning conditional jokes is the means they afford to a kind of fakery. A conditional joke demands a special contribution from the audience, either cognitive or affective. What if the joke-teller himself cannot supply this special constituent? In the first case, where the implicated background is cognitive, the teller is like a parrot, and he cannot himself know (find) what fun there is in the joke. This charlatan resembles a musician who doesn't divine the sense of a piece but nonetheless bangs it out note for note, or a religious practitioner who reads out texts or prayers in Latin or Hebrew, perhaps even 'with feeling,' but doesn't know what the words mean.

In the second case, where the requisite special contribution is a matter of feeling, the teller is more like a liar. He can, typically, find the fun—recognize it or identify it—but he cannot feel it. Perhaps the plainest examples of this insincerity are jokes told to groups of (say, racially) prejudiced people—genuine bigots, that is—by one who does not share the true depths of the bigotry but means to ingratiate himself with the group. This is a kind of fraudulence, like that of the man who says 'I apologize' without feeling sorry, of the artist who mimics unfelt forms, and of the performer who does not feel the passion in the scores he plays with mindless virtuosity.

The two kinds of fakery are different. The first is, mainly, simply bizarre. The second is more devious, even deceitful. In both, however, there is the fraudulence of emptiness, as both betray the commitment to intimacy I have characterized as a kind of generic aim of joke-telling. The teller of these jokes is inauthentic: He invites and even induces you into a putative community in which he himself has no place. Who is he to be issuing these invitations?

The difference between pure and conditional jokes corresponds to a difference in moral and religious conceptions. The idea of a pure joke rests on a conviction that at some level people are essentially the same and can all be reached by the same device. This is, perhaps, a fundamentally Christian idea. The denial of the possibility of a pure joke rests on a conviction that people are essentially different, or at least that they belong to essentially different groups. The idea that all jokes necessarily are conditional seems to me a kind of Jewish idea (not the only kind).

Those who believe only in conditional jokes will concede that it is possible to appreciate a joke whose community does not include oneself. How is this possible? It must be through an act of imagination which transports one into the relevant community. Thus I can appreciate jokes meant for women, Englishmen, and mathematicians, although I am none of those. There is a point, however, at which it becomes impossible for me to be amused. I reach that point sooner when the joke is anti-Jewish or anti-American than when it is anti-women or anti-English. And there is a point for any type of affective joke beyond which its instances are objectionable. They are in bad taste. If you think that lapses of 'taste' are always relatively innocuous, then I would insist that these jokes are in fact unacceptable—immoral. Why does this happen, and when?

I cannot give a complete answer, even in outline, because there is a fundamental question I do not know how to answer. Suppose that x is some real event, and that it is (morally) unacceptable to laugh at x. The question I cannot answer is, under what conditions is it wrong to laugh at a fictional report of x, and why? It may be that a heavy traffic of amusement in x-jokes creates or reinforces beliefs or attitudes that are themselves objectionable or that lead to intolerable acts. That answer is insufficient, for two reasons. First, there is little evidence to show that it is always true, and some indication that it is sometimes false. Second, it doesn't get to the heart of the evil, even if it is true, for even if it could be demonstrated that these jokes lead to no bad ends the jokes themselves would still be offensive. With no good answer to the question of why (and when) it is wrong to laugh at a story of something you shouldn't laugh at, I shall nevertheless go on to suggest how an answer—if we had one—might lead to an understanding of the unacceptability of some jokes.

Suppose that prejudice against P's is a bad thing, and that to be amused by an x-joke requires a disposition which is related to anti-P prejudice, although that disposition is not itself a prejudice. The joke will be accessible only to those who either have the disposition or can, in imagination, respond as if they had it. The joke is obviously conditional—it is affective; but it will also be fundamentally parochial (essentially conditional, one might say) if there are people who cannot find it accessible. What people will be in this position? P's, I think. Even the imagined possession of the disposition is in conflict with what makes these people P's. To appreciate the joke a P must disfigure himself. He must forsake himself. He should not do that. In fact he cannot do that while remaining a P. The rest of us, who are not P's, *should* not appreciate the joke although we *can* in this sense in which a P cannot. The joke is viciously exclusionary, and it should be resisted.

What this implies depends upon exactly what people essentially are. Are they essentially men or women, of some race, of some age, of some religion, of some profession, of some size? That is a fine question in the metaphysics of morality, and one I do not care to answer here. I offer this account of a kind of unacceptable joke as an explanation and justification of why some people find some jokes intolerable. A currently common exchange begins with a man telling a joke (involving women, typically) which a woman finds offensive. She objects and is told she has no sense of humor. Her reply could be that she cannot bring her sense of humor to that joke without imaginatively taking on a disposition which is incompatible with her conception of herself as a woman or a certain kind of woman. And if she is essentially a woman or a certain kind of woman, then she cannot reach the joke without a hideous cost.

Although the basis for a pure joke has an obvious moral flavor, akin to the idea of a universal human sameness, conditional jokes are also congenial to the serious idea of morality. Conditional jokes are related to the idea that we can respect and even appreciate one another while remaining irreducibly different. They carry a danger, however, for their parochialism easily becomes unbearably sectarian.

A final note about pure jokes. The major question, I suppose, is whether there are any. If there are, they will be jokes whose presumptive success depends on nothing whatever. The audience needs no special background. They bring to the joke only their humanity. Now the question is, When you tell such a joke, upon what basis do you expect anyone else to be moved? The answer must be, Upon the fact that the joke moves you, plus your estimate that it moves you simply as a person and without regard to any idiosyncrasy of yours. The logic here is exactly the same as that which Kant cites in answering the question, By what right do you judge anything to be beautiful (where this means, Upon what basis do you suppose that anyone else should take pleasure in this thing?)? Kant answers: Upon the fact that the object pleases you, plus your estimate that the pleasure is due to nothing about you beyond the fact that you are a person.

But now comes the nasty question, which Kant believes he can answer with regard to the beauty of things, and I am not so sure about with regard to the funniness of jokes. If a thing touches you, so to speak, only in the rudiments of your person—if ever such a thing happens, with all those things dormant which make you more than just a person; why should it be good as well for any other rudimentary person? Isn't there room within even the most elementary, stripped-down, homogenized human sensibility for variation? Couldn't you and I be mere men and nothing more, and yet be pleased by different beauties and laugh at different jokes? No, says Kant, in the first instance, for the capacity to feel this pleasure is identical with the capacity which makes knowledge possible (and knowledge *is* possible, he insists interminably). And so there is an argument, however good.

Is there such an argument for the postulation of a universal sense of humor? I do not know. Is the capacity to find a joke funny a basic, essential feature of our sensibility? It needn't seem entirely implausible that it is if we suppose it to be, minimally—and it is only its minimal presence that matters—the capacity to feel simultaneously the appropriateness and the absurdity of a punch line. It is like feeling the wonderful hopelessness of the world. (Or is it the hopeless wonder of the world?) But must every one of us have within himself the capacity for that feeling, however disfigured it may have become? God knows.

The sudden click at the end of a certain kind of joke is its hallmark. There is an unexpected, an almost-but-not-quite-predicted coincidence of moments. And this is part of a marvelous reflexivity. Earlier I guessed that the whole joke relates to its effect in an enigmatic relation which renders that effect both unforced and fitting. The relation can be found again entirely within the joke. The joke itself has a beginning which leads to an end which is unforced (and so, unpredicted), but altogether right. In laughing we fit ourselves to a joke just as its punch line fits to its body, by this relation of self-warranting propriety. It is a kind of mirroring. We find ourselves reflected in a surface which mirrors our dearest and perhaps most human hope: to do well, but not under compulsion. A joke shows us that and shows us doing that. Anything which can show us that aspect of ourselves deserves fond and serious attention.

What Are Comics?

■ Greg Hayman and Henry John Pratt ■

Everyone knows what comic strips are—*Peanuts* or *Doonesbury,* for instance. But what *is* it to be a comic? Imagine that Charles Schulz had decided one day to paint *Peanuts* on a canvas and display it in an art gallery instead of drawing it with pen and ink and sending it to be published in the newspaper. Would this object created with paint still be a comic? Can something be a comic if it is never published? What about when the object has no dialogue in it? Such are the questions that arise when we try to define the concept *comic,* which is the purpose of this paper.

Comics are one of the most ubiquitous and interesting forms of art today. Nearly every daily or weekly newspaper prints comics of one kind or another. Comic books sell in large quantity and provide fodder for a significant number of films and television programs. However, comics have rarely been taken seriously as an art form. They are regarded only as a lowbrow form of entertainment for children, degenerate teens, and a few adult misfits. Not unnaturally, comics have received little attention from aestheticians. However, the time has passed when aestheticians are happy to restrict themselves only to the "fine" arts. Further, the draftsmanship of some comic strip artists rises to a plane of astonishing excellence. (Consider the work of Winsor McCay, for instance, who created the early strip *Little Nemo.*) Finally, a comparison of comics with other visual arts raises interesting conceptual questions about how visual arts break into their subcategories.

Attempts to classify comics as a unique art form have resulted in at least three types of definition. One possibility is to attempt a definition of comics within the context of the type of medium in which they are presented. A second is an analysis of the concept in terms of the novel interplay between words and images in comics. A third option is to cite the pictorial narrative structure that comics comprise as their essential common feature.

Let us call the first approach a *medium-based* definition. On this view, comics are classified in terms of the material components by which they are typically produced. According to this approach, certain pictures or pictorial sequences are comics because they are produced with ink and newsprint and are found in the newspaper or in comic books. Comics are distinguished from art forms such as illustrated texts and other pictures by being presented in these formats.

Now, we do tend to recognize as comics the pictures in the newspaper that incorporate text and entertaining characters, precisely because this is where we expect to see them. This is how comics are usually presented to us. We do not typically

"What Are Comics?" by Greg Hayman and Henry John Pratt is published by permission of the authors.

see the sorts of objects we find on a comics page in a newspaper produced via other media—say, chiseled into marble or sewn into needlepoint. So, such an approach to a definition of comics seems plausible.

But it may not be. If only objects created from the kind of materials from which newspapers, magazines, and comic books are created can count as comics, then similar visual representations in other media would not qualify. But that seems implausible. Though most comics are created with ink and some type of newsprint, it would seem that they could also be painted on a canvas, inscribed into woodcuts, sewn into tapestries, or even created on computers.

Think again about the hypothetical *Peanuts* described at the beginning of this paper. That canvas artwork would still display Charlie Brown and Snoopy, with all the good-natured humor that we've come to expect. The strip would still comprise four square panels. Surely this painted object would still be a comic.

Or suppose an artist draws a comic with a pen on paper and then scans it into his computer. According to the medium-based definition, the object on paper would count as a comic but the image on the computer screen would not. And yet, the content of each is identical. Imagine further that the example was not the result of scanning into the computer, but had instead been created by using programs within the computer itself. Surely the result would still be a comic. If so, then the medium-based account is too exclusive.

Of course, we might expand our rules about what kind of media qualify so as to allow the computer-generated example to count as a comic. The problem is how to call a halt to this expansion. The more relaxed the rules about the media that qualify, the more a medium-based definition undermines itself. A definition that included all or nearly all media would hardly be a medium-based analysis any longer.

Before pressing on, consider an assumption that a medium-based definition is likely to presuppose, namely, that comics must occur in the context of a *mass* medium. Indeed, they normally turn up in newspapers, magazines, and books, and can all be printed and reproduced on a mass scale.

However, the assumption may be misguided. While comics are usually produced and distributed via mass media, we must bear in mind examples that are never reproduced, such as the works in a cartoonist's private sketchbook. (Or consider the painted *Peanuts* comic once again.) The assumption would imply that such a one-of-a-kind non-mass-produced work would not be a comic. Surely, this is implausible. Even in the case where comics are mass-produced, the original object from which the copies are made, the autograph copy, is surely a comic in its own right—whether or not it was ever mass reproduced. For these reasons, the mass-reproduction requirement ought to be dismissed. This result casts further doubt on the medium-based approach.

Let us now turn to the second type of approach, which we'll call the *word balloon* definition of comics. Word balloons are the bubble- or balloon-shaped figures within a panel that contain text or other images and represent the thoughts or utterances of the characters from which the balloons emanate. Proponents of this approach construe word balloons as the necessary feature of comics. That is, in order for an object to be classified as a comic it must have at least one word balloon.

It is easy to see what motivates the word balloon approach. The majority of comics produced today do contain word balloons, and their presence is indeed striking. Other art forms seem to have no equivalent device. When novels, for instance, interpolate illustrations into their narratives, the result is not usually seamless. The reader must pause to consider a different kind of information. Though an image may enhance the overall story, it has the effect of breaking up the textual narrative. Likewise, a visual artwork, like a painting, seems unable to combine textual dialogue into its pictorial space seamlessly. When painting does incorporate dialogue in its pictorial space, the effect is surprising, if not jarring—even if the object we are viewing clearly does, in other respects, qualify as a painting. In such cases, the results are—perhaps intentionally—unsettling, because the effect is not what we expect in the sphere of painting. Yet we experience no such result when we read comics. Word balloons enable the artist to incorporate text and dialogue into the pictorial space in order to advance her story. They are helpful—indeed, sometimes necessary—to guide our understanding of the comic we are reading.

Philosopher David Carrier is one of the most prominent advocates of the word balloon approach. In his book *The Aesthetics of Comics,* Carrier argues that a comic is a unique pictorial narrative structure that arises from the unification of image and text through the use of the word balloon. To be a comic, he argues, words in the balloons must be fully integrated into the pictures; otherwise, the work is merely an illustrated text.

Although this definition is compelling and well-motivated, we suggest that any definition dependent on word balloons is vulnerable to significant objections. To begin, this view must countenance what seem to be fatal counterexamples. Many comic artists regularly produce works without balloons like the *Adventures of Beaver Buddy*. One of our favorite examples of a wordless comic is Jim Woodring's *Frank.* Pantomime strips in newspapers, such as *Henry* and Otto Soglow's classic *The Little King,* also lack word balloons. And on occasion, so too do more familiar strips including *Peanuts, Pogo, Doonesbury, Frank and Ernest, Zits,* and *9 Chickweed Lane.* In our experience, a regular reader of a typical comics page is likely to see a wordless work pop up every few weeks or so.

We suggest that Carrier's error is symptomatic of a larger problem, namely, relying too heavily on conventional rather than formal features of comics. Conventional features like word balloons are tools that can be used within a medium to facilitate an artist's goals. Word balloons are inessential to comics in part because other conventions can be used in comics to fulfill their function of unifying text and image (or, more importantly, to advance the narrative). For example, the *Critics Ahoy!* comic has no word balloons but uses a convention that works equally well. The speech of the character on the left of this panel appears at the top left of the panel and the speech of the character on the right appears below it. In this convention, as the characters appear from left to right in any given panel, their words or thoughts are displayed in descending order from the top left corner of that panel.

The word balloon approach to defining comics, like the medium-based approach, is inadequate. Although we may often *recognize* when something is a comic on the basis of the medium in which it is presented, or because of the presence of word balloons, these features fail to provide a reasonable definition as each admits of salient counterexamples. Instead, we need to turn from the conventional and the contextual to the formal. The third approach that we now wish to discuss focuses on just that.

Let's call this third type of approach the *pictorial narrative* definition of comics. According to this approach, we can best understand comics as a special kind of visual narrative. In our definition:

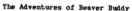

The Adventures of Beaver Buddy, **cartoon by Henry Pratt (2003.)**

Critics Ahoy!, **cartoon by Henry Pratt (2003.)**

Source: Reproduced courtesy of Henry Pratt.

> x is a comic if and only if x is a sequence of discrete, juxtaposed pictures that comprise a narrative, either in their own right or when combined with text.

Other proponents of this type of view include cartoonists Will Eisner and Scott McCloud. (Indeed, the main tenets of our view mirror McCloud's *Understanding Comics*. Where our position diverges somewhat is in the explanation of the details and in drawing out the ramifications of the basic theory.)

One of the primary advantages of this account is that it succeeds where the two other approaches fall short. It allows for a wide variety of conventional features in comics. And as long as they satisfy this definition, comics can be printed in many different media formats, employ inaccessibly avant-garde strategies, or have a total absence of word balloons or other conventions that incorporate text into the pictorial space.

In addition to this notable feature, our definition responds to the problems that motivate its competitors in the first place. Chief among these are how to distinguish comics (qua visual narratives) from other art media that also feature visual narratives, such as film, television, and animated cartoons, as well as how to differentiate them from illustrated texts. It is, to a large degree, the notion of juxtaposition that allows us to make these discriminations. This deserves some explanation.

The term "juxtaposition" is a technical one. In comics, the visual images are distinct, (paradigmatically) side-by-side, and laid out in a way such that they could conceivably be seen all at once. Between each pictorial image is a perceptible space; we'll call this the "gutter." The reader must imagine all of the action that occurs in the gutter. McCloud calls this process, by which we fill in the narrative blanks in the story, "closure." In the experience of comics, the reader *must* engage in closure; filling in the narrative between each and every image is required not only for better or more full understanding, but for any extent of understanding *at all*.

The process of closure in comics is unique to them as a result of the particular *kind* of juxtaposition that they exhibit. In comics, panels are placed next to each other in a way that is *spatial,* not temporal. In this respect, one's experiences of comics are somewhat like one's experiences of a book. Because the images in a comic are juxtaposed like the words of a novel, the comics reader has a great deal of control over how the narrative is presented to her. For instance, she is able to stop and return to panels she read previously, and to jump ahead and skip panels.

Admittedly, filling in analogous narrative gaps is often required of the viewer during scene changes in other visual media such as television and film. For instance, the changes that occur through jump cuts and montage, and indeed between any two film shots, provoke audiences to make the inferences that give the story coherence. (A fade-out on a closing bedroom door following by a scene showing a couple arising in the morning lets us know that an interval of lovemaking has taken place.) Closure may be necessary for understanding here as well, but in a different way than it is for comics. The key is that in such media the human eye does not perceive a space between the image cells. As such, film, television, animation, and the like are laid out side by side only in the *temporal* sense. Since these works are not juxtaposed in our technical, spatial sense, they are excluded by our definition.

Mere illustrated texts are excluded from our definition as well. A comic's images must convey narrative information. But the sequence of images does not merely contribute to the narrative—it contributes necessarily. Without the image sequence, the narrative of a true comic cannot be understood. In contrast, an artwork that consists in a combination of image and text while having a narrative that can be fully understood without the images (like *Alice in Wonderland,* or *Green Eggs and Ham*) is not a comic. Although the pictures therein do provide visual information, their texts taken alone comprise understandable narratives in their own right, independent from the pictures. Illustrated texts are thus distinguished from comics when their image sequence is unnecessary to their identification as narratives.

Of course, the picture sequence in an illustrated text could itself comprise a comic. In such a case, we would have two independent narratives running in parallel. (The classic strip *Prince Valiant* is such a case.) This is not to say that they could not complement each other. Indeed, they probably would, but, again, neither would be necessary in order to comprehend the other. As a matter of practice, however, in most illustrated texts it is unlikely that the pictures taken alone would comprise a comic: the images are simply too disjointed to produce a narrative.

Let us turn now to the features of the pictorial narrative approach that—if properly placed and described—will do justice to the insights that lie behind competing accounts.

The proponent of the media-based account is quite correct to point out that comics often are found in certain media rather than others. It would be worthwhile to provide an explanation of this fact. Indeed, the pictorial narrative approach does not foreclose on such a project. Nor does it foreclose on the typical if not essential importance of the word balloon in comics. Indeed, the pictorial narrative approach illuminates the role of the word balloon, for the obvious reason that this device is an exceptionally ingenious tool for conveying narrative information in an otherwise purely visual context. For instance, word balloons provide important cues about the passage of time within the narrative sequence. In some cases, word balloons—or similarly relevant texts—*are* necessary for understanding the narrative. In other cases, the narrative may even be driven by the text. In such cases, however, the image sequence itself also provides essential information. Indeed, without the imagery, we would not have a comic.

We hope to have shown why and how the pictorial narrative approach to defining comics is preferable to alternatives. Other problems remain, however. For instance, as it stands, our definition remains silent on the status of single-paneled works like *The Far Side* and *The Family Circus.* Intuitively, these works are comics. But the result of including them in the pictorial narrative definition may be troubling. Any construal of pictorial narrative rich enough to encompass single-panel works would also seem to encompass many works that are not comics, such as any paintings with narrative elements. At this point, the most we can say is that we do not think that this problem is intractable. Such problems are only to be expected; after all, philosophical examination of comics is in its infancy. This remains a matter for further philosophical discussion.

Ventriloquism
■ David Goldblatt ■

Ventriloquism is a bizarre practice. Yet a somewhat sober look at its complex logic leads one to see ventriloquism as a vehicle for approaching and understanding two important roles artists play—as interpreters of the world, and as constructors of possible selves. The consideration of ventriloquism in the context of art tends to undermine our general assumption that adults, at least, do not give voice to untalking entities. Ventriloquism, then, extends the domain of our relationships to things ordinarily off-limits to conversation. A look at ventriloquism raises such odd questions as, "What is it like to make things talk?" and "What is it like for things to make us talk?" But at the same time, we understand that we can only ask such questions of ourselves. We ask of artworks not only, "What have you to say about it?" but also "What does it say to you?" The idea here is that being engaged in art, or at least some art, is to will the world vocalities.

It must be one of the ironies of American show business that its most endearing of ventriloquists spent so many celebrated years on radio. Edgar Bergen's talent for appearing not to be speaking while speaking was simply assumed by the visually absent audience—an audience fully aware that Bergen and his dummy, the magnetic Charlie McCarthy, had paid their dues in the presence of vaudeville. And besides, the few members of the studio audience could stand as proxy for the millions of others whose listening was something like an act of faith.

There was something more central to Bergen's talent than motionless speech, however. As I see it, Bergen's success had something to do with what the Greeks called *ecstasis:* a stepping outside of the self that results in a being beside itself, of which ventriloquism is a special case. Even in the dark of radio one could perceive Bergen engaging himself in conversation, phonetically indiscernible from two antithetical personalities going at each other—unless one knew what everyone knew, that the voices came from a single source.

At least since Pythagoras, *ecstasis* (from which our word "ecstasy" can be traced) has played a role in deep thinking. In *The Birth of Tragedy,* Nietzsche writes: "To be a dramatist all one needs is the urge to transform oneself and speak out of strange bodies and souls . . . projecting oneself outside the self and then acting as though one had really entered another body, another character." Ventriloquism took many forms in the ancient world. Usually associated with priests and prophets, ventriloquism promoted the illusion that one person's voice was coming

"Ventriloquism" by David Goldblatt has been excerpted from "Making Things Talk: Ventriloquism and Art," *Art Issues* (March/April 1994), pages 20–25, and is reprinted by permission of the publisher.

Photograph of the dummy Charlie McCarthy and Edgar Bergen.
Source: Reproduced courtesy of Corbis/Bettman.

from another thing—sometimes a river or a stone, sometimes another person. The Greeks called such a person *engastrimanteis,* "a belly prophet," and the modern word is derived from the Latin *venter* (belly) and *loqui* (to speak). Today, ventriloquists are known to each other as "vents" and call their dummies "figures," to which I might add, "figures of speech." Ventriloquism can still be found in a variety of social roles in a diversity of cultural contexts.

During the eighteen nineties, it was not Bergen but an Englishman, Fred Russell, who first performed ventriloquism with the familiar dummy on the knee. Neither was Bergen the first to give his dummy the smart-alecky Irish character it seemed to retain; but he was the one to give a certain surprising reality to it, and to carry ventriloquism into a mass medium.

When ventriloquism, with vaudeville, was on its way out, an unemployed Edgar Bergen dressed Charlie in white tie, tails, and a monocle and brought him to a Chicago supper-club tryout. This event gelled the character that Charlie Mc-Carthy was to approximate until Bergen's death in 1978. In her recent autobiography *Knock Wood,* Candice Bergen (Edgar's daughter) relates the incident in the Chez Paree nightclub: "Coming onstage at three o'clock in the morning . . . before an almost empty club, Charlie suddenly turned on his master, asking, 'Who the hell ever told you you were a good ventriloquist?' Telling Edgar to go back to the farm, the dummy refused to be shushed by a blushing Bergen; Charlie was confident of getting by alone. He then spun on the stunned customers, declaring them a disgrace to civilization, rattling on as Bergen propped him on a chair and slowly backed away. The management was catatonic, but the customers collapsed in laughter, hooting, howling, pounding on the tables. Later, a serene Bergen was found backstage saying, 'I simply had to get that off my chest.' "

The contrast in personalities—with the inanimate dummy active and dominant, and the creator passive and submissive—was also noted by the old *New York Herald Tribune:* "On the one hand, there is the gay, irrepressible Charlie, through whom, by some strange alchemy, the shy and pallid Bergen is transformed into a brilliant comedian. On the other hand, there is an imperious and dominating Charlie, whose almost human personality has so eclipsed his creator that Bergen cannot function as an artist alone. 'Charlie is famous,' says Bergen glumly, 'and I am the forgotten man. I am really jealous of the way Charlie makes friends,' Bergen complains wistfully. 'People are at ease with Charlie. He is so uncomplicated.' "

We can entertain any number of psychological theories either about Edgar Bergen personally, or ventriloquism generally. But here I am not saying that Charlie is Edgar's alter ego, nor that Charlie is a repressed self, a reflection of an overt self, a catharsis, cathexis, regression, death wish, nor any or all of the above. I simply hope to articulate some features of this particular ventriloquial paradigm to shed some light on other, aesthetic issues.

Throwing one's voice is more like throwing a fight than it is like throwing a fastball. The dummy neither emits nor noticeably reflects the thrown voice, but is, rather, made to appear to do so. But while throwing a fight (and here I have professional boxing, not wrestling, in mind) tends to keep the audience in the dark, throwing one's voice in the ventriloquist's act lets them in on the trick. There is, in ventriloquism, illusion without deception. Paraphrasing what Jacques Lacan once said about pictures, the dummy is a trap for the gaze.

Ventriloquism includes speaking in another voice or even in another's voice—a complex and difficult matter in itself. But ventriloquism is not simply speaking in other voices, and hence differs in interesting ways from related performance types. Unlike acting, where the actor may or may not speak in a voice different from his own, the ventriloquist must resort to another voice to facilitate the appearance of conversation. In the role of ventriloquist, he may choose to retain his usual, recognizable voice, but the dummy's voice must be significantly distinct from it—the more radical the contrast, the easier the audience's shift of attention from the body of the ventriloquist to the body of the dummy. This is not to deny that we utilize a wide variety of voices in daily life, but as in Charlie's case, the dummy's voice is somewhat eccentric (as adult voices go), and distinct from any other voice encountered in quotidian life—a difference that cannot be explained by motionless lips alone.

Lip-syncing or puppeteering, like dubbed acting, gets by without the voice source being present to the audience. Unlike puppeteering, in ventriloquism the voice source appears with the figure, is present to it, and is itself a character in the performance. Indeed, the ventriloquist impresses the appearance of the singularity of his role. Ventriloquism requires the thrown voice to take an object—the dummy—so that the ventriloquist and the object may engage each other in smooth and natural conversation. So in ventriloquism, the voice source and the voice object are simultaneously present to the audience and engage in conversation as two distinct characters, as in a play. To succeed, the ventriloquist must not simply speak in another voice, but must efface himself as speaker while simultaneously promoting himself as listener. The key to the act is in the exchange—in the case of Bergen and McCarthy a rapid-fire interplay that displays the ventriloquist's talent for switching between significantly different personalities. Yet on another level, Bergen is talking to himself.

"Talking to oneself," as we seem to use the locution, is talking to oneself aloud, without directing speech to an appropriate or present listener. It is manifested as either the harmless kind that each of us allows ourselves every now and then, or the kind that places one at the margins of society. In either case, talking to oneself is usually talking in a single voice. The ventriloquist's talking to himself, however, is played out in more than one voice, with the dummy functioning as a license of propriety, making talking to oneself or rather talking *with* oneself okay, buttressed, of course, by the institution of show business. (Chevy Chase once reported that New York's Bureau of Tourism, for the sake of appearances, had paired up those citizens talking to themselves.) In Bergen's act, it is not simply talking to oneself that is licensed, but the relatively outrageous and improper content of Charlie's speech in contrast with Bergen's polite demeanor. Charlie's role is similar to the jester's in relationship to the king, as jesters were reputed to have been uniquely frank or abusive to an extent that would have brought others the dungeon. Audiences, of course, knew Bergen was talking with himself, and if they chose to, could have understood his act exactly—or only—that way. But that would have spoiled all the fun. A ventriloquist who actually deceives an audience would undermine his own act.

There are, then, at least two distinct ontological levels in the ventriloquist's act: the mild illusion of Bergen talking to Charlie, and the act of Bergen talking to himself. It is important to note here a phenomenon characteristic of most ventriloquists' acts, especially those that involve comedy, i.e., what I think of as a falling between ontological levels. This kind of slippage recalls Rauschenberg's famous remark that "Painting relates to both art and life (I try to work in the gap between the two)." Though Rauschenberg worked with ordinary objects like mattresses, clocks, and chairs attached or juxtaposed to canvases, his point is more general. It is that painting is neither here nor there—not entirely in the ordinary world, and not entirely outside it.

We have already mentioned Charlie's remark about Edgar's lousy ventriloquism as an example of stepping outside the conversational act. Here is another example from Bergen's radio program, *The Charlie McCarthy Show,* in which the two are joined by W.C. Fields:

> FIELDS (TO CHARLIE): Quiet, you flophouse for termites, or I'll sic a beaver on you.
> BERGEN: Now, Bill . . .
> CHARLIE: Mr. Fields, is that a flame thrower I see or is it your nose?
> FIELDS: Why, you little blockhead, I'll whittle you down to a coat hanger.

Again, we have Charlie as personality and Charlie as shaped wood, and the audience enjoying the free-play, pleased to be in on the joke. The trace of one level is always present even if it is not the one being privileged.

I want to give the name "ventriloquial exchange" to the *ecstatic* relationship that takes place between the aforementioned ontological levels—the exchange between Bergen and McCarthy, and the exchange between Bergen and himself when Bergen is engaged in the project of ventriloquism. This exchange is viewed as conversation on one level and as talking to oneself on another (and may also be understood as a special or deviant form of conversation). But it is important to recognize that the binary opposition between these modes of ventriloquial exchange is continuously being undermined by the act itself. Disbelief is suspended on the part of the audience, deflating the pressure of being caught with one's lips moving, and playing with the ontological levels by vacillating between them in comedic reflexivity.

The idea of a ventriloquial exchange, based on an artistic *ecstasis,* can be seen as well in the problematization of the canonical concepts of "author" and "work" that have grown out of essays by Michel Foucault and others. In his 1968 essay "What Is an Author?" Foucault characterizes the relationship between the author and writer in *ecstatic* terms, as one between a self and an "alter ego whose distance from the author varies, often changing in the course of the work . . . the author-function is carried out and operates in the scisson itself, in this division and this distance." Foucault construes writing as the creation of a space into which the writing subject constantly disappears; in problematizing the idea of an individual work, Foucault attacks the proletarian notion of all work—the work of the plumber and seamstress as well as that of the artist. The artist works too, and while she effaces herself as quotidian self in exchange with her project, she forms herself again—not as a former self but as an author. Making art is work, and it is also the progression of an identity relative to the work. The artist is a product as well as an agent of the work in progress—the ventriloquial exchange is what sets the author off from those that don't go through it. So it might be helpful to think about artistic work as an exchange of voices instead of a one-way ticket from artist to object.

What makes Foucault's work so ripe for ventriloquial analogue is that he sets up the issue as a separation of self from self, an *ecstasis,* and then identifies the place between the two as one in which a multi-voiced exchange or conversation takes place. In art, there is on one level the artist encountering a work—a voice different from her own, with a particular character of its own—and on another level it is just her own voice with which she is engaged.

In Plato's *Phaedrus,* Socrates inveighs a certain silence against painting and writing: "Writing, you know, Phaedrus, has this strange quality about it, which makes it really like painting: The painter's products stand before us quite as though they were alive; but if you question them, they maintain a solemn silence." In contrast, our view opens the door for a garrulous relationship between artworks and artists, and also between artworks and anyone who approaches them with the willingness to resist their silence. But once we undertake the possibility of a vocalized give-and-take with art, it is only one step away from viewing a world that some artists find interesting—one that is rife with meaningful objects that have something to say. And that would just be a special sort of talking to ourselves.

In "The Origin of the Work of Art," Martin Heidegger argues that while the origin of the work of art is the artist, the origin of the artist is the work of art. There is a symbiotic relationship between the two such that without works of art there would be no artists. The artist's identity is in part determined by the work, and, Heidegger adds, both are dependent upon art itself. That Charlie is dependent upon Bergen for what is said is clear enough. But without Charlie, Bergen as ventriloquist would also not exist. If not for Charlie, at least one voice of Bergen's would not be heard; Bergen's identity as a person would be seriously altered. The dummy defines his ventriloquist; in Heideggers' words, "Neither is without the other." And so, ventriloquism is the occasion of letting strange voices speak.

In art, most obviously in a work in progress, the artist will be dealing with something in another voice. Yet the source of this voice is no ordinary other, since it is, in some respect, the voice of the artist herself. During the period of time that an artwork is being created, there is an exchange—sometimes a very complicated one—between artist and material, which results in the completed work of art. Sometimes the artist thinks of the work as an independent voice; sometimes the work says something to the artist, with the artist responding appropriately. At other times, the work just finds the artist talking to herself—but in a different voice from her own.

I am imagining here that during the work in progress, the artist sees her work at one time and asks, "What does *the work* say?" and at another time, "What am *I* saying?" Sometimes it is as if she were dealing with another person, one that speaks to her in a distinct style. Here the work has a character independent of the artist, something in the way that Charlie is taken to have a personality independent of Bergen. When asking "What does this work say (to you)?", any response would be seriously incomplete if it were couched in terms of the artist's voice alone. That would be like mentioning what Bergen was saying during one of his acts without reference to Charlie.

The kind of exchange I am ascribing to the work in progress begins to explain rules by which artists play—both in interpreting artworks and in interpreting aspects of the world by anchoring them with voices. In creating works of art, and in viewing them, one needs the willingness to stand beside or outside oneself. So while I have come to think of ventriloquism as a paradigm for a certain way of organizing artistic phenomena, I also see its possibilities in more deviant pursuits. Without Bergen, Charlie may be silent—but he is not empty. Like any face and body, Charlie is replete with meaning, and ready for voice. Ventriloquial exchange can help us to interpret more freely aspects of a silent world whose voices we are constructing as we pretend to listen to it. Sometimes the voices of others are also our own, and sometimes our own are those of others. Being outside the self, in a Nietzschean manner, is a way of extending and empowering the self, of recognizing other voices in ourselves, and of problematizing the idea that the self is located in the behavior of a single mind or body. I am suggesting that interpreting entities with meaning is something like projecting and engaging voices, and is partly constituted by aesthetic response.

Pornography
■ Joel Feinberg ■

Rape is a harm and a severe one. Harm prevention is definitely a legitimate use of the criminal law. Therefore, if there is a clear enough causal connection to rape, a statute that prohibits violent pornography would be a morally legitimate restriction of liberty. But it is not enough to warrant suppression that pornography as a whole might have some harmful consequences to third parties, even though most specific instances of it do not. "Communications from other human beings are among the most important causes of human behavior," Kent Greenawalt points out, "but criminal law cannot concern itself with every communication that may fortuitously lead to the commission of a crime. It would, for example, be ludicrous to punish a supervisor for criticizing a subordinate, even if it could be shown that the criticism so inflamed the subordinate that he assaulted a fellow worker hours later." An even stronger point can be made. Even where there is statistical evidence that a certain percentage of communications of a given type will predictably lead the second party to harm third parties, so that in a sense the resultant harms are not "fortuitous," that is not sufficient warrant for prohibiting all communications of that

"Pornography" by Joel Feinberg has been excerpted from *Offense to Other: The Moral Limits of the Law,* Vol. II, Oxford University Press (1985), pages 154–157, and is reprinted by permission of the publisher.

kind. It would be even more ludicrous, for example for a legislature to pass a criminal statute against the criticism of subordinates, on the ground that inflamed employees sometimes become aggressive with their fellow workers.

A more relevant example of the same point, and one with an ironic twist, is provided by Fred Berger:

> A journal that has published studies often cited by the radical feminists . . . has also published an article that purports to show that the greater emancipation of women in western societies has led to great increases in criminal activity by women. Such crimes as robbery, larceny, burglary, fraud, and extortion have shown marked increase, as have arson, murder, and aggravated assault. But freedom of expression would mean little if such facts could be taken as a reason to suppress expression that seeks the further liberation of women from their secondary, dependent status with respect to men.

Of course, one can deny that violent porn is a form of valuable free expression analogous to scholarly feminist articles, but the point remains that indirectly produced harms are not by themselves sufficient grounds for criminalizing materials, that some further conditions must be satisfied.

Those instances of sexual violence which may be harmful side-effects of violent pornography are directly produced by criminals (rapists) acting voluntarily on their own. We already have on the statute books a firm prohibition of rape and sexual assault. If, in addition, the harm principle permits the criminalization of actions only indirectly related to the primary harm, such as producing, displaying or selling violent pornography, then there is a danger that the law will be infected with unfairness; for unless certain further conditions are fulfilled, the law will be committed to punishing some parties for the entirely voluntary criminal conduct of other parties. . . . Suppose that *A* wrongfully harms (e.g. rapes) *B* in circumstances such that (1) *A* acts fully voluntarily on his own initiative, and (2) nonetheless, but for what *C* has communicated to him, he would not have done what he did to *B*. Under what further conditions, we must ask, can *C* be rightfully held criminally responsible along with *A* for the harm to *B*? Clearly *C* can be held responsible if the information he communicated was helpful assistance to *A* and intended to be such. In that case *C* becomes a kind of collaborator. Under traditional law, *C* can also incur liability if what he communicated to *A* was some kind of encouragement to commit a crime against *B*. The clearest cases are those in which *C* solicits *A*'s commission of the criminal act by offering inducements to him. "Encouragement" is also criminal when it takes the form of active urging. Sometimes mere advice to commit the act counts as an appropriate sort of encouragement. When the encouragement takes a general form, and the harmful crime is recommended to "the general reader" or an indefinite audience, then the term "advocacy" is often used. Advocating criminal conduct is arguably a way of producing such conduct, and is thus often itself a crime. An article in a pornographic magazine advocating the practice of rape (as opposed to advocating a legislative change of the rape laws) would presumably be a crime if its intent were serious and its audience presumed to be impressionable to an appropriately dangerous degree.

Violent pornography, however, does not seem to fit any of these models. Its authors and vendors do not solicit rapes; nor do they urge or advise rapes; nor do they advocate rape. If some of their customers, some of the time, might yet "find encouragement" in their works to commit rapes because rape has been portrayed in a way that happens to be alluring to them, that is their own affair, the pornographer might insist, and their own responsibility. The form of "encouragement" that is most applicable (if any are) to the pornography case is that which the common law has traditionally called "incitement." Sir Edward Coke wrote in 1628 that "all those that incite . . . set on, or stir up any other" to a crime are themselves acces-sories. Thus, haranguing an angry crowd on the doorsteps of a corn dealer, in [John Stuart] Mill's famous example, might be the spark that incites the mob's violence against the hated merchant, even though the speaker did not explicitly urge, advise, or advocate it. Yet, a similar speech, twenty-four hours earlier, to a calmer audience in a different location, though it may have made a causal contribution to the even-tual violence, would not have borne a close enough relation to the harm to count as an "incitement," or "positive instigation" (Mill's term) of it.

Given that "communication" is a form of expression, and thus has an impor-tant social value, obviously it cannot rightly be made criminal simply on the ground that it may lead some others on their own to act harmfully. Even if works of pure pornography are *not* to be treated as "communication," "expression," or "speech" (in the sense of the first amendment), but as mere symbolic aphrodisiacs or sex aids without further content they may yet have an intimate personal value to those who use them, and a social value derived from the importance we attach to the protection of private erotic experience. By virtue of that significance, one per-son's liberty can be invaded to prevent the harm other parties might cause to *their* victims only when the invaded behavior has a specially direct connection to the harm caused, something perhaps like direct "incitement." Fred Berger suggests three necessary conditions that expected harms must satisfy if they are to justify censorship or prohibition of erotic materials, none of which, he claims, is satisfied by pornography, even violent pornography.

1. There must be strong evidence of a very likely and serious harm. [I would add—"that would not have occurred otherwise."]
2. The harms must be clearly and directly linked with the expression.
3. It must be unlikely that further speech or expression can be used effectively to combat the harm.

Berger suggests that the false shout of "fire" in a crowded theatre is paradigmati-cally the kind of communication that satisfies these conditions. If so, then he must interpret the second condition to be something like the legal standard of incite-ment—setting on, stirring up, inflaming the other party (or mob of parties) to the point of hysteria or panic, so that their own infliction of the subsequent damage is something less than deliberate and fully voluntary. Their inciter in that case is as re-sponsible as they are, perhaps even more so, for the harm that ensues. Surely, the relation between pornographers and rapists is nowhere near that direct and manipulative. If it were, we would punish the pornographers proportionately more severely, and blame the actual rapist (poor chap; he was "inflamed") proportionately less.

It may yet happen that further evidence will show that Berger's conditions, or some criteria similar to them, are satisfied by violent pornography. In that case, a liberal should have no hesitation in using the criminal law to prevent the harm. In the meantime, the appropriate liberal response should be a kind of uneasy skepticism about the harmful effects of pornography on third party victims, conjoined with increasingly energetic use of "further speech or expression" against the cult of macho, "effectively to combat the harm."

The Real Harm of Pornography
■ Catharine A. MacKinnon ■

The fact that pornography, in a feminist view, furthers the idea of the sexual inferiority of women, a political idea, does not make pornography a political idea. That one can express the idea a practice expresses does not make that practice an idea. Pornography is not an idea any more than segregation or lynching are ideas, although both institutionalize the idea of the inferiority of one group to another. The law considers obscenity deviant, antisocial. If it causes harm, it causes antisocial acts, acts against the social order. In a feminist perspective, pornography is the essence of a sexist social order, its quintessential social act.

If pornography is an act of male supremacy, its harm is the harm of male supremacy made difficult to see because of its pervasiveness, potency, and success in making the world a pornographic place. Specifically, the harm cannot be discerned from the objective standpoint because it is so much of "what is." Women live in the world pornography creates, live its lie as reality. As Naomi Scheman has said, "lies are what we have lived, not just what we have told, and no story about correspondence to what is real will enable us to distinguish the truth from the lie." So the issue is not what the harm of pornography is, but how the harm of pornography is to become visible. As compared with what? To the extent pornography succeeds in constructing social reality, it becomes invisible as harm.

The success, therefore the harm, of pornography, is invisible to the male state in its liberal guise and so has been defined out of customary approach taken to, and the dominant values underlying, the First Amendment. The theory of the First Amendment under which most pornography is protected from governmental re-

"The Real Harm of Pornography" by Catharine A. MacKinnon has been excerpted from *Toward a Feminist Theory of the State,* Harvard University Press (1989), pages 204–208, and is reprinted by permission of the publisher.

striction proceeds from liberal assumptions that do not apply to the situation of women. First Amendment theory, like virtually all liberal legal theory, presumes the validity of the distinction between public and private: The "role of law [is] to mark and guard the line between the sphere of social power, organized in the form of the state, and the arena of private right." On this basis, courts distinguish between obscene billboards ("thrust upon the unwilling viewer") and the private possession of obscenity at home. The problem is that not only the public but also the private is a "sphere of social power" of sexism. On paper and in life, pornography is thrust upon unwilling women in their homes. The distinction between public and private does not cut the same for women as for men. As a result, it is men's right to inflict pornography upon women in private that is protected. . . .

In liberalism, speech must never be sacrificed for other social goals. But liberalism has never understood this reality of pornography: The free so-called speech of men silences the free speech of women. It is the same social goal, just other people. This is what a real inequality, a real conflict, a real disparity in social power looks like. First, women do not simply have freedom of speech on a social level. The most basic assumption underlying First Amendment adjudication is that, socially, speech is free. The First Amendment itself says, "Congress shall make no law . . . abridging the freedom of speech." Free speech exists. The problem for government is to avoid constraining that which, if unconstrained by government, is free. This tends to presuppose that whole segments of the population are not systematically silenced socially, prior to government action. Second, the law of the First Amendment comprehends that freedom of expression, in the abstract, is a system but fails to comprehend that sexism (and racism), in the concrete, are also systems. As a result, it cannot grasp that the speech of some silences the speech of others in a way that is not simply a matter of competition for airtime. That pornography chills women's expression is difficult to demonstrate empirically because silence is not eloquent. Yet on no more of the same kind of evidence, the argument that suppressing pornography might chill legitimate speech has supported its protection.

First Amendment logic has difficulty grasping harm that is not linearly caused in the "John hit Mary" sense. The idea is that words or pictures can be harmful only if they produce harm in a form that is considered an action. Words work in the province of attitudes, actions in the realm of behavior. Words cannot constitute harm in themselves—never mind libel, invasion of privacy, blackmail, bribery, conspiracy, most sexual harassment, and most discrimination. What is saying "yes" in Congress—a word or an act? What is saying "Kill" to a trained guard dog? What is its training? What is saying "You're fired" or "We have enough of your kind around here"? What is a sign that reads "Whites Only"? What is a real estate advertisement that reads "Churches Nearby"? What is a "Help Wanted— Male" ad? What is a letter that states: "Constituent interests dictate that the understudy to my administrative assistant be a man"? What is "Sleep with me and I'll give you an 'A' "? These words, printed or spoken, are so far from legally protecting the cycle of events they actualize that they are regarded as evidence that acts occurred, in some cases as actionable in themselves. Is a woman raped by an attitude or a behavior? Which is sexual arousal? Which is cross burning? The difficulty of the distinction in the abstract has not prevented the law from acting when the consequences were seen to matter. When words are tantamount to acts, they are treated as acts. . . .

This notion of causality did not first appear in this law at this time, however. As Judge Jerome Frank said in a footnote in *Roth,* "According to Judge Bok, an obscenity statute may be validly enforced when there is proof of a causal relation between a particular book and undesirable conduct. Almost surely, such proof cannot ever be adduced." Criticizing old ideas of atomic physics in light of Einstein's theory of relativity, Werner Heisenberg stated the conditions that must exist for a causal relation to make sense. "To co-ordinate a definite cause to a definite effect has sense only when both can be observed without introducing a foreign element disturbing their interrelation. The law of causality, because of its very nature, can only be defined for isolated systems." Among the influences that disturb the isolation of systems are observers. . . .

Social systems are not isolated systems. Experimental research, in which it has been scientifically shown that pornography has harmful effects, minimizes what will always be "foreign elements" at some cost of simulating social reality. Yet whenever field experiments are done for verisimilitude, it is said that the interactions are insufficiently isolated to prove pure causality. If pornography is systemic, it may not be isolable from the system in which it exists. This does not mean that no harm exists. It does mean that because the harm is so pervasive, it cannot be sufficiently isolated to be perceived as existing according to this model of causality, a model that is neither the existing legal standard, the only scientific standard, a standard used in other policy areas (like the relation between smoking and cancer or driving drunk and having accidents). Nor is it a social or political standard in which the experiences of victims have any weight. In other words, if pornography's harm cannot be isolated from society's organization itself, its harm will not be perceptible within the episteme.

The dominant view is that pornography must cause harm just as car accidents cause harm, or its effects are not cognizable as harm. The trouble with this individuated, atomistic, linear, exclusive, isolated, narrowly tort-like—in a word, postivistic—conception of injury is that the way pornography targets and defines women for abuse and discrimination does not work like this. It does hurt individuals, just not as individuals in a one-at-a-time sense, but as members of the group women. Individual harm is caused one woman and not another essentially as one number rather than another is caused in roulette; but on a group basis, the harm is absolutely selective and systematic. Its causality is essentially collective and totalistic and contextual. To reassert atomistic linear causality as a sine qua non of injury—you cannot be harmed unless you are harmed through this etiology—is to refuse to respond to the true nature of this specific kind of harm. Such refusals call for explanation. Morton Horowitz has written that the issue of causality in tort law is "one of the pivotal ideas in a system of legal thought that sought to separate private law from politics and to insulate the legal system from the threat of redistribution." Perhaps causality in the law of obscenity is an attempt to privatize the injury pornography does to women in order to insulate the same system from the threat of gender equality.

Defining Mass Art
■ Noël Carroll ■

I have promised to propose a theory of the nature of mass art. By claiming that this theory pertains to the *nature* of mass art, I maintain that my theory is concerned with classifying mass art, rather than with either condemning or commending it. This is meant to distinguish my approach from previous philosophical theories of mass art, which seem preoccupied, at least implicitly, with evaluating mass art either morally, politically, or aesthetically. Dwight MacDonald, [R.G.] Collingwood, [Theodor] Adorno, [Max] Horkheimer, [Clement] Greenberg, and, more recently, Guy Debord and Jean Baudrillard, all appear to me to provide characterizations of mass art primarily in order to condemn it, while Walter Benjamin and Marshall McLuhan present theories meant to valorize it. I, on the other hand, hope merely to say what it is—to classify mass art rather than to judge it morally, politically, or aesthetically.

By identifying my project as classificatory, I mean, among other things, that I intend neither to excoriate nor to defend mass art. This is not because I feel that mass art is indefensible. One can defend it by pointing to mass artworks—such as *Citizen Kane*—that are valuable from both an artistic and a moral perspective. That is, it makes no sense to condemn mass art, as such, if it has produced works of value, including some masterpieces.

But, the task of either condemning or praising mass art in virtue of its very nature seems to me to be quixotic. Like most human practices, mass art involves worthy and unworthy examples (morally, politically, and aesthetically), and it is at the level of particular cases that praise or blame seems appropriate. . . .

My sense of mass art is simply numerical, not evaluative and certainly not pejorative. Mass art is art that is designed to be consumed by lots and lots of people. That is why it is produced on such a large scale and distributed by mass technologies. Thus I am willing to run the risk of calling the phenomenon '*mass art*', despite the potentially, politically incorrect sound of the label because: First, it points to *the* significant feature of the phenomenon—that it is essentially involved

"Defining Mass Art" by Noël Carroll has been excerpted from *A Philosophy of Mass Art,* Oxford University Press (1998), pages 184, 187, 192–193, 195, 197, 199, 205, 209–210, and is reprinted by permission of the publisher.

in production and distribution on a mass scale; and, second, because the alternative way of naming it—calling it 'popular art'—fails to acknowledge the way in which scale is utterly relevant to its nature, and, in consequence, fails to acknowledge its historical specificity as a product of industrial urban mass society. . . .

Vaudeville, as practised in late nineteenth- and early twentieth-century theatres, was a popular art, but not yet a mass art, because the vaudeville performer could only play before one audience of limited size, in one playhouse at a time. On the other hand, when vaudeville and music hall performers, like Charlie Chaplin, Buster Keaton, Harry Langdon, and W. C. Fields, incorporated their stage routines into their films, their performances became mass art, in so far as their performances became available to mass audiences all over the world, at the same time. . . .

Avant-garde art is esoteric; mass art is exoteric. Mass art is meant to command a mass audience. That is its function. Thus it is designed to be user friendly. Ideally, it is structured in such a way that large numbers of people will be able to understand and appreciate it, virtually without effort. It is made in order to capture and to hold the attention of large audiences, while avant-garde art is made to be effortful and to rebuff easy assimilation by large audiences. Insofar as mass art is meant to capture large markets, it gravitates toward the choice of devices that will make it accessible to mass untutored audiences. . . . For example, comic books, commercial movies, and TV tell stories by means of pictorial representation. . . .

Story-telling by pictures, that is, expeditiously satisfies one of the major desiderata of mass art design, since it guarantees virtually immediate pickup by audiences, without those audiences requiring an education in specialized codes of reading or inferential procedures. Since pictorial representation is accessible to anyone, the mass arts that are based upon them have, in principle, unlimited audiences. . . .

Insofar as mass artworks are formulaic, they are easy to follow, i.e., they accord with our expectations. And inasmuch as mass artworks are easy to follow, they are also apt to appeal to more and more people as suitable or appropriate objects with which to occupy one's leisure time. Of course, in order to command large audiences, mass artworks must be more than merely easy to consume. They must also invite or excite our interest. But a precondition, here, of exciting interest, is nevertheless that they be easily comprehended. That is, before mass artworks can be widely enjoyable, they must be widely accessible, at least in terms of comprehensibility.

So once again, in certain respects, critics of mass art, like Clement Greenberg, were right. Mass art is easy, especially when compared to the difficulty—perhaps the self-imposed difficulty–of avant-garde art. However, the ease with which mass art is consumed is not a flaw, but rather a design element, which is predicated on the function of mass art as an instrument for addressing mass audiences. . . .

Gathering together and amplifying some of these observations, then, we may attempt to define the mass artwork in the following way:

X is a mass artwork if and only if 1. x is a multiple instance or type artwork, 2. produced and distributed by a mass technology, 3. which artwork is intentionally designed to gravitate in its structural choices (for example, its narrative forms, symbolism, intended affect, and even its content) toward those choices that promise accessibility with minimum effort, virtually on first contact, for the largest number of untutored (or relatively untutored) audiences.

Here, the parenthetical qualification concerning 'relatively untutored audiences' is meant to accommodate the fact that, to a certain extent, audiences may be tutored by the repetition and formulas of mass art itself.

I have arrived at the first condition by stipulating that my domain of concern is mass *art,* not mass culture, which would represent a broader category. That is, my concern is with those items of mass culture that are more narrowly identifiable as art—such as dramas, stories, and songs—rather than news programmes, cooking shows, sporting events, or talk shows. Since mass artworks are not avant-garde, there should be little problem classifying items in terms of whether or not they fall into already entrenched art-forms—such as drama or song—or in terms of whether they discharge traditionally recognized artistic purposes like representation or expression. Thus, if questioned as to why I suppose that the mass artwork is art, my first impulse is to respond by asking, 'What else could it be?'.

Of course, some readers may not be happy with this. They are apt to challenge the first condition of my definition on the grounds that it is a contested issue as to whether or not what I call mass art is art properly so called. They will object that you just can't stipulate that it is such. In response, I argue that inasmuch as mass art-forms are descended from traditional art-forms, they have a prima-facie claim to art status. That is, inasmuch as many of the genres and forms of mass art are extensions of genres and art-forms that are already regarded as art proper, there seems to be no principled reason to deny that mass art is art. . . .

Mass art is not popular art *simpliciter.* It requires a mass production and delivery technology, where such a technology is defined as one that is capable of simultaneously delivering multiple (at least two) tokens of a mass artwork-type to more than one reception site. The concept of mass art, that is, is derived by drawing a contrast within popular art broadly construed.

By identifying mass art in terms of mass delivery systems, a difference is marked between mass art and the more generic notion of popular art. Mass art is popular art, but a noteworthy subspecies, distinguished by its reliance upon mass delivery systems capable of reaching non-overlapping reception sites simultaneously.

But what exactly is a mass delivery system? Walter Benjamin suggests that it is a technology for the mass reproduction of images and stories. But this is not exactly right. It does a nice job for things like certain photographs, but it does not capture the possibility of such things as one-time, live radio dramas broadcast to multiple reception sites. But such broadcasts should count as examples of mass art, even though they may never be 'reproduced' in Benjamin's sense. So, in contrast to Benjamin's notion of mass reproducibility, I propose to define a mass delivery system as a technology with the capacity to deliver the same performance or the same object to more than one reception site simultaneously.

The frescos on the ceilings of Renaissance cathedrals, though they might be viewed simultaneously by large numbers of people, are not cases of mass art, for such frescos cannot be in two or more places at the same time. On the other hand, the self-same radio performance or live-TV performance has the capacity to be transmitted to many disparate, non-overlapping reception sites; while films and photos are objects that can be reproduced multiply and transported to many different places, thereby affording the possibility that effectively exact tokens of the film-type or the photo-type in question can be consumed simultaneously.

One objection to the emphasis that I place on accessibility in the definition of mass art is that certain forms of mass art may in fact be inaccessible to large groups of people. My students, for example, tell me that heavy metal music is inaccessible to their parents. Indeed, they add, it may even be part of the attraction of heavy metal that it is somehow inaccessible to the older set.

However, I wonder if heavy metal music is really inaccessible, rather than simply distasteful to my students' parents. These oldsters could certainly comprehend it without putting very much mental energy into it, even if they didn't like it. In fact, many of these parents may really comprehend it, and that may be the very reason that they dislike it. But, in any case, the question of whether the Lawrence Welk generation or the folk-song generation can literally understand Guns N'Roses is different from the question of whether they enjoy them, even if old-timers tend to couch their dislike misleadingly in phrases like 'I just can't understand x'. They really mean 'I can't stand x', or 'I can't understand why you (their teenage child) like x.' . . .

Inasmuch as mass art is to be understood functionally, according to my theory, a question arises about evaluation. Should a mass artwork be deemed good just in case it is accessible to large numbers of people? Here I would want to argue that being accessible is a good-making feature of a work *qua* mass artwork—since this realizes a design intention of mass artworks—but that this does not entail that the mass artwork is good, all things considered. There are several reasons for this.

The first is that the mass artwork does not only belong to the category of mass art. Typically, it also falls into some genre. Thus, its evaluation hinges not only on its success as an example of the mass art kind, but also on its success according to the evaluative criteria of the genre to which it belongs—suspense, romance, science fiction, melodrama, horror, and so on. As well, the mass artwork is also an artwork, so its comparative evaluation also involves considering its goodness as an example of one genre *vis-à-vis* the goodness available in other genres. An all-things-considered evaluation of a particular instance of mass art involves an assessment of its virtues or blemishes not only *qua* mass art and *qua* the genre it belongs to, but also in terms of its standing as a work of art.

Moreover, though accessibility is a good-making feature of such a work *qua* mass art, it does not even entail that a candidate is good in any unqualified way as a mass artwork. For accessibility is only a precondition for mass art status. A mass artwork can be accessible but lack-lustre. Simply being accessible does not guarantee that it is enjoyable, appealing, interesting, or possessed of any other quality that might recommend it to a mass audience, or to any audience for that matter. Being accessible is simply *a* good-making feature of a mass artwork, for the reasons already given. However, it does not provide grounds for judging a work to be good overall, nor even good as a mass artwork. For a work that has a good-making feature can still be aesthetically weak. Perhaps in securing accessibility, a given mass artwork can be said to be not altogether bad. It has achieved something. But accessibility does not indicate goodness in any robust sense.

PART IX

❚❙ ❙❚

CLASSIC SOURCES

This group of readings consists of classic essays on the general nature of art and of aesthetic experience.

David Hume's eighteenth-century essay is still a basic port of departure for anyone trying to discover universal rules or principles of taste. Hume argues that there are such standards and this requires him to reply to those skeptics and relativists who point to obvious factual differences in taste to support their claims. Hume says that of several divergent responses to an artwork, not all have equal authority; one must be in the proper position physically and psychologically for one's judgment to be objective. However, Hume grants that this stance is not easy to achieve.

In Hume's century, too, the concept of the *sublime* in nature was a central concept in discussions of aesthetics. Roughly speaking, objects or processes we term "sublime" are those that are mentally or physically overpowering. Indeed, they threaten to overwhelm our very rationality. A frighteningly awesome thunderstorm is a good example, especially when we know we are at a safe distance from its danger. The selection by Edmund Burke is a classic text on the topic.

Writing at the close of that century, Immanuel Kant made the first attempt to isolate and describe genuinely aesthetic experience, and in so doing influenced generations of aestheticians. He boldly argues that judgments of taste—which always have the form "this object is beautiful"—are distinct from judgments that are often confused with them, in particular, judgments about the *agreeable,* as in "this ice cream tastes good to me." Judgments about the beautiful are also distinct from judgments about usefulness, as in "this is a good hammer," as well as moral judgments, e.g., "he is a good man." Kant argues that judgments about the beautiful, even if never demonstrable, have a peculiar kind of universality that reflects the fact that they are grounded in features of the mind that we all have as human beings.

Kant's theory is about aesthetic experience—whether of natural objects or of artworks. G.W.F. Hegel and John Dewey, however, are specifically interested in *art.* A striking feature of the aesthetic theory of Hegel, who wrote not long after Kant, is the way he reverses a traditional view about the relationship between beauty in nature and art. He argues that we find nature beautiful *by analogy with* our experience of works of art, rather than the other way around. Hegel's central idea about art is that it is a sensuous embodiment of fundamental thoughts or perspectives on the universe and our place in it. Art, for Hegel, is intimately tied, from the very beginning, with the rest of human thought, particularly, philosophy and religion.

Dewey's concern is to broaden the concept *art.* His aim is to ensure that the concept applies not merely to a narrow range of objects or art *works,* but rather to the whole range of human experience. What we call artworks are just shining examples of things that are the occasion of experiences that could be called *meaningful,* and he goes on to characterize the relevant sense of "meaning."

Of the Standard of Taste
■ David Hume ■

It is natural for us to seek a *Standard of Taste;* a rule by which the various sentiments of men may be reconciled; at least a decision afforded confirming one sentiment, and condemning another.

There is a species of philosophy, which cuts off all hopes of success in such
an attempt, and represents the impossibility of ever attaining any standard of taste.
The difference, it is said, is very wide between judgment and sentiment. All sentiment is right; because sentiment has a reference to nothing beyond itself, and is always real, wherever a man is conscious of it. But all determinations of the understanding are not right; because they have a reference to something beyond
themselves, to wit, real matter of fact; and are not always conformable to that standard. Among a thousand different opinions which different men may entertain of
the same subject, there is one, and but one, that is just and true: and the only difficulty is to fix and ascertain it. On the contrary, a thousand different sentiments, excited by the same object, are all right; because no sentiment represents what is really in the object. It only marks a certain conformity or relation between the object
and the organs or faculties of the mind; and if that conformity did not really exist,
the sentiment could never possibly have being. Beauty is no quality in things themselves: It exists merely in the mind which contemplates them; and each mind perceives a different beauty. One person may even perceive deformity, where another
is sensible of beauty; and every individual ought to acquiesce in his own sentiment,
without pretending to regulate those of others. To seek the real beauty, or real deformity, is as fruitless an inquiry, as to pretend to ascertain the real sweet or real
bitter. According to the disposition of the organs, the same object may be both
sweet and bitter; and the proverb has justly determined it to be fruitless to dispute
concerning tastes. It is very natural, and even quite necessary, to extend this axiom
to mental, as well as bodily taste; and thus common sense, which is so often at vari-
ance with philosophy, especially with the sceptical kind, is found, in one instance at
least, to agree in pronouncing the same decision.

But though this axiom, by passing into a proverb, seems to have attained the
sanction of common sense; there is certainly a species of common sense, which opposes it, at least serves to modify and restrain it. Whoever would assert an equality
of genius and elegance between Ogilby and Milton, or Bunyan and Addison, would
be thought to defend no less an extravagance, than if he had maintained a mole-hill

---

"Of the Standard of Taste" by David Hume has been excerpted from *Of the Standard of Taste
and Other Essays,* Allyn and Bacon (1918), pages 5–8, 9–13, 16–18, and is reprinted by permission of
the publisher.

to be as high as Teneriffe, or a pond as extensive as the ocean. Though there may be found persons, who give the preference to the former authors; no one pays attention to such a taste; and we pronounce, without scruple, the sentiment of these pretended critics to be absurd and ridiculous. The principle of the natural equality of tastes is then totally forgot, and while we admit it on some occasions, where the objects seem near an equality, it appears an extravagant paradox, or rather a palpable absurdity, where objects so disproportioned are compared together.

It is evident that none of the rules of composition are fixed by reasonings *a priori,* or can be esteemed abstract conclusions of the understanding, from comparing those habitudes and relations of ideas, which are eternal and immutable. Their foundation is the same with that of all the practical sciences, experience; nor are they any thing but general observations, concerning what has been universally found to please in all countries and in all ages. Many of the beauties of poetry, and even of eloquence, are founded on falsehood and fiction, on hyperboles, metaphors, and an abuse or perversion of terms from their natural meaning. To check the sallies of the imagination, and to reduce every expression to geometrical truth and exactness, would be the most contrary to the laws of criticism; because it would produce a work, which, by universal experience, has been found the most insipid and disagreeable. But though poetry can never submit to exact truth, it must be confined by rules of art, discovered to the author either by genius or observation. If some negligent or irregular writers have pleased, they have not pleased by their transgressions of rule or order, but in spite of these transgressions: They have possessed other beauties, which were conformable to just criticism; and the force of these beauties has been able to overpower censure, and give the mind a satisfaction superior to the disgust arising from the blemishes. [Lodovico] Ariosto pleases; but not by his monstrous and improbable fictions, by his bizarre mixture of the serious and comic styles, by the want of coherence in his stories, or by the continual interruptions of his narration. He charms by the force and clearness of his expression, by the readiness and variety of his inventions, and by his natural pictures of the passions, especially those of the gay and amorous kind: and, however his faults may diminish our satisfaction, they are not able entirely to destroy it. Did our pleasure really arise from those parts of his poem, which we denominate faults, this would be no objection to criticism in general: It would only be an objection to those particular rules of criticism, which would establish such circumstances to be faults, and would represent them as universally blamable. If they are found to please, they cannot be faults, let the pleasure which they produce be ever so unexpected and unaccountable. . . .

The same Homer who pleased at Athens and Rome two thousand years ago, is still admired at Paris and at London. All the changes of climate, government, religion, and language, have not been able to obscure his glory. Authority or prejudice may give a temporary vogue to a bad poet or orator; but his reputation will never be durable or general. When his compositions are examined by posterity or by foreigners, the enchantment is dissipated, and his faults appear in their true colors. On the contrary, a real genius, the longer his works endure, and the more wide they are spread, the more sincere is the admiration which he meets with. Envy and jealousy have too much place in a narrow circle; and even familiar acquaintance with his person may diminish the applause due to his performances: but when these obstructions are removed, the beauties, which are naturally fitted to excite agreeable sentiments, immediately display their energy; and while the world endures, they maintain their authority over the minds of men.

It appears, then, that amidst all the variety and caprice of taste, there are certain general principles of approbation or blame, whose influence a careful eye may trace in all operations of the mind. Some particular forms or qualities, from the original structure of the internal fabric are calculated to please, and others to displease; and if they fail of their effect in any particular instance, it is from some apparent defect or imperfection in the organ. A man in a fever would not insist on his palate as able to decide concerning flavors; nor would one affected with the jaundice pretend to give a verdict with regard to colors. In each creature there is a sound and a defective state; and the former alone can be supposed to afford us a true standard of taste and sentiment. If, in the sound state of the organ, there be an entire or a considerable uniformity of sentiment among men, we may thence derive an idea of the perfect beauty; in like manner as the appearance of objects in daylight, to the eye of a man in health, is denominated their true and real color, even while color is allowed to be merely a phantasm of the senses.

Many and frequent are the defects in the internal organs, which prevent or weaken the influence of those general principles, on which depends our sentiment of beauty or deformity. Though some objects, by the structure of the mind, be naturally calculated to give pleasure, it is not to be expected that in every individual the pleasure will be equally felt. Particular incidents and situations occur, which either throw a false light on the objects, or hinder the true from conveying to the imagination the proper sentiment and perception.

One obvious cause why many feel not the proper sentiment of beauty, is the want of that *delicacy* of imagination which is requisite to convey a sensibility of those finer emotions. This delicacy every one pretends to: Every one talks of it; and would reduce every kind of taste or sentiment to its standard. But as our intention in this Essay is to mingle some light of the understanding with the feelings of sentiment, it will be proper to give a more accurate definition of delicacy than has hitherto been attempted. And not to draw our philosophy from too profound a source, we shall have recourse to a noted story in Don Quixote.

It is with good reason, says Sancho to the squire with the great nose, that I pretend to have a judgment in wine: This is a quality hereditary in our family. Two of my kinsmen were once called to give their opinion of a hogshead, which was supposed to be excellent, being old and of a good vintage. One of them tastes it, considers it; and, after mature reflection, pronounces the wine to be good, were it not for a small taste of leather which he perceived in it. The other, after using the same precautions, gives also his verdict in favor of the wine; but with the reserve of a taste of iron, which he could easily distinguish. You cannot imagine how much they were both ridiculed for their judgment. But who laughed in the end? On emptying the hogshead, there was found at the bottom an old key with a leathern thong tied to it.

The great resemblance between mental and bodily taste will easily teach us to apply this story. Though it be certain that beauty and deformity, more than sweet and bitter, are not qualities in objects, but belong entirely to the sentiment, internal or external, it must be allowed, that there are certain qualities in objects which are fitted by nature to produce those particular feelings. Now, as these qualities may be found in a small degree, or may be mixed and confounded with each other, it often happens that the taste is not affected with such minute qualities, or is not able to distinguish all the particular flavors, amidst the disorder in which they are presented. Where the organs are so fine as to allow nothing to escape them, and at the same time so exact as to perceive every ingredient in the composition, this we call delicacy of taste, whether we employ these terms in the literal or metaphorical sense. Here then the general rules of beauty are of use, being drawn from established models, and from the observation of what pleases or displeases, when presented singly and in a high degree; and if the same qualities, in a continued composition, and in a smaller degree, affect not the organs with a sensible delight or uneasiness, we exclude the person from all pretensions to this delicacy. To produce these general rules or avowed patterns of composition, is like finding the key with the leathern thong, which justified the verdict of Sancho's kinsmen, and confounded those pretended judges who had condemned them. Though the hogshead had never been emptied, the taste of the one was still equally delicate, and that of the other equally dull and languid; but it would have been more difficult to have proved the superiority of the former, to the conviction of every bystander. In like manner, though the beauties of writing had never been methodized, or reduced to general principles; though no excellent models had ever been acknowledged, the different degrees of taste would still have subsisted, and the judgment of one man been preferable to that of another; but it would not have been so easy to silence the bad critic, who might always insist upon his particular sentiment, and refuse to submit to his antagonist. But when we show him an avowed principle of art; when we illustrate this principle by examples, whose operation, from his own particular taste, he acknowledges to be conformable to the principle; when we prove that the same principle may be applied to the present case, where he did not perceive or feel its influence: He must conclude, upon the whole, that the fault lies in himself, and that he wants the delicacy which is requisite to make him sensible of every beauty and every blemish in any composition or discourse.

It is acknowledged to be the perfection of every sense or faculty, to perceive with exactness its most minute objects, and allow nothing to escape its notice and observation. The smaller the objects are which become sensible to the eye, the finer is that organ, and the more elaborate its make and composition. A good palate is not tried by strong flavor, but by a mixture of small ingredients, where we are still sensible of each part, notwithstanding its minuteness and its confusion with the rest. In like manner, a quick and acute perception of beauty and deformity must be the perfection of our mental taste; nor can a man be satisfied with himself while he suspects that any excellence or blemish in a discourse has passed him unobserved. In this case, the perfection of the man, and the perfection of the sense of feeling, are found to be united. A very delicate palate, on many occasions, may be a great inconvenience both to a man himself and to his friends. But a delicate taste of wit or beauty must always be a desirable quality, because it is the source of all the finest and most innocent enjoyments of which human nature is susceptible. In this decision the sentiments of all mankind are agreed. Wherever you can ascertain a delicacy of taste, it is sure to meet with approbation; and the best way of ascertaining it is, to appeal to those models and principles which have been established by the uniform consent and experience of nations and ages.

But though there be naturally a wide difference, in point of delicacy, between one person and another, nothing tends further to increase and improve this talent, than *practice* in a particular art, and frequent survey or contemplation of a particular species of beauty. When objects of any kind are first presented to the eye or imagination, the sentiment which attends them is obscure and confused; and the mind is, in a great measure, incapable of pronouncing concerning their merits or defects. The taste cannot perceive the several excellences of the performance, much less distinguish the particular character of each excellency, and ascertain its quality and degree. If it pronounce the whole in general to be beautiful or deformed, it is the utmost that can be expected; and even this judgment, a person so unpractised will be apt to deliver with great hesitation and reserve. But allow him to acquire experience in those objects, his feeling becomes more exact and nice: He not only perceives the beauties and defects of each part, but marks the distinguishing species of each quality, and assigns it suitable praise or blame. A clear and distinct sentiment attends him through the whole survey of the objects; and he discerns that very degree and kind of approbation or displeasure which each part is naturally fitted to produce. The mist dissipates which seemed formerly to hang over the object; the organ acquires greater perfection in its operations, and can pronounce, without danger of mistake, concerning the merits of every performance. In a word, the same address and dexterity which practice gives to the execution of any work, is also acquired by the same means in the judging of it.

So advantageous is practice to the discernment of beauty, that, before we can give judgment on any work of importance, it will even be requisite that that very individual performance be more than once perused by us, and be surveyed in different lights with attention and deliberation. . . .

It is well known, that, in all questions submitted to the understanding, prejudice is destructive of sound judgment, and perverts all operations of the intellectual faculties: It is no less contrary to good taste; nor has it less influence to corrupt our sentiment of beauty. It belongs to *good sense* to check its influence in both cases; and in this respect, as well as in many others, reason, if not an essential part of taste, is at least requisite to the operations of this latter faculty. In all the nobler productions of genius, there is a mutual relation and correspondence of parts; nor can either the beauties or blemishes be perceived by him whose thought is not capacious enough to comprehend all those parts, and compare them with each other, in order to perceive the consistence and uniformity of the whole. Every work of art has also a certain end or purpose for which it is calculated; and is to be deemed more or less perfect, as it is more or less fitted to attain this end. The object of eloquence is to persuade, of history to instruct, of poetry to please, by means of the passions and the imagination. These ends we must carry constantly in our view when we peruse any performance; and we must be able to judge how far the means employed are adapted to their respective purposes. Besides, every kind of composition, even the most poetical, is nothing but a chain of propositions and reasonings; not always, indeed, the justest and most exact, but still plausible and specious, however disguised by the coloring of the imagination. The persons introduced in tragedy and epic poetry must be represented as reasoning, and thinking, and concluding, and acting, suitably to their character and circumstances; and without judgment, as well as taste and invention, a poet can never hope to succeed in so delicate an undertaking. Not to mention, that the same excellence of faculties which contributes to the improvement of reason, the same clearness of conception, the same exactness of distinction, the same vivacity of apprehension, are essential to the operations of true taste, and are its infallible concomitants. It seldom or never happens, that a man of sense, who has experience in any art, cannot judge of its beauty; and it is no less rare to meet with a man who has a just taste without a sound understanding.

[T]hough the principles of taste be universal, and nearly, if not entirely, the same in all men; yet few are qualified to give judgment on any work of art, or establish their own sentiment as the standard of beauty. The organs of internal sensation are seldom so perfect as to allow the general principles their full play, and produce a feeling correspondent to those principles. They either labor under some defect, or are vitiated by some disorder; and by that means excite a sentiment, which may be pronounced erroneous. When the critic has no delicacy, he judges without any distinction, and is only affected by the grosser and more palpable qualities of the object: the finer touches pass unnoticed and disregarded. Where he is not aided by practice, his verdict is attended with confusion and hesitation. Where no comparison has been employed, the most frivolous beauties, such as rather merit the name of defects, are the object of his admiration. Where he lies under the influence of prejudice, all his natural sentiments are perverted. Where good sense is wanting, he is not qualified to discern the beauties of design and reasoning, which are the highest and most excellent. Under some or other of these imperfections, the generality of men labor; and hence a true judge in the finer arts is observed, even during the most polished ages, to be so rare a character: strong sense, united to delicate sentiment, improved by practice, perfected by comparison, and cleared of all prejudice, can alone entitle critics to this valuable character; and the joint verdict of such, wherever they are to be found, is the true standard of taste and beauty.

But where are such critics to be found? By what marks are they to be known? How distinguish them from pretenders? These questions are embarrassing; and seem to throw us back into the same uncertainty from which, during the course of this Essay, we have endeavored to extricate ourselves.

But if we consider the matter aright, these are questions of fact, not of sentiment. Whether any particular person be endowed with good sense and a delicate imagination, free from prejudice, may often be the subject of dispute, and be liable to great discussion and inquiry: but that such a character is valuable and estimable, will be agreed in by all mankind. Where these doubts occur, men can do no more than in other disputable questions which are submitted to the understanding: they must produce the best arguments that their invention suggests to them; they must acknowledge a true and decisive standard to exist somewhere, to wit, real existence and matter of fact; and they must have indulgence to such as differ from them in their appeals to this standard. It is sufficient for our present purpose, if we have proved, that the taste of all individuals is not upon an equal footing, and that some men in general, however difficult to be particularly pitched upon, will be acknowledged by universal sentiment to have a preference above others. . . .

But notwithstanding all our endeavors to fix a standard of taste, and reconcile the discordant apprehensions of men, there still remain two sources of variation, which are not sufficient indeed to confound all the boundaries of beauty and deformity, but will often serve to produce a difference in the degrees of our approbation or blame. The one is the different humors of particular men; the other, the particular manners and opinions of our age and country. The general principles of taste are uniform in human nature: where men vary in their judgments, some defect or perversion in the faculties may commonly be remarked; proceeding either from prejudice, from want of practice, or want of delicacy: and there is just reason for approving one taste, and condemning another. But where there is such a diversity in the internal frame or external situation as is entirely blameless on both sides, and leaves no room to give one the preference above the other; in that case a certain degree of diversity in judgment is unavoidable, and we seek in vain for a standard, by which we can reconcile the contrary sentiments.

A young man, whose passions are warm, will be more sensibly touched with amorous and tender images, than a man more advanced in years, who takes pleasure in wise, philosophical reflections, concerning the conduct of life, and moderation of the passions. At twenty, Ovid may be the favorite author, Horace at forty, and perhaps Tacitus at fifty. Vainly would we, in such cases, endeavor to enter into the sentiments of others, and divest ourselves of those propensities which are natural to us. We choose our favorite author as we do our friend, from a conformity of humor and disposition. Mirth or passion, sentiment or reflection; whichever of these most predominates in our temper, it gives us a peculiar sympathy with the writer who resembles us.

The Sublime
■ Edmund Burke ■

The passion caused by the great and sublime in *nature,* when those causes operate most powerfully, is Astonishment; and astonishment is that state of the soul, in which all its motions are suspended, with some degree of horror. In this case the mind is so entirely filled with its object, that it cannot entertain any other, nor by consequence reason on that object which employs it. Hence arises the great power of the sublime, that far from being produced by them, it anticipates our reasonings, and hurries us on by an irresistible force. Astonishment, as I have said, is the effect of the sublime in its highest degree; the inferior effects are admiration, reverence and respect.

Terror

No passion so effectually robs the mind of all its powers of acting and reasoning as fear. For fear being an apprehension of pain or death, it operates in a manner that resembles actual pain. Whatever, therefore is terrible, with regard to sight, is sublime too, whether this cause of terror, be endued with greatness of dimensions or not; for it is impossible to look on any thing as trifling, or contemptible, that may be dangerous. There are many animals, who though far from being large, are yet capable of raising ideas of the sublime, because they are considered as objects of terror. As serpents and poisonous animals of almost all kinds. And to things of great dimensions, if we annex an adventitious idea of terror, they become without comparison greater. A level plain of a vast extent on land, is certainly no mean idea; the prospect of such a plain may be as extensive as a prospect of the ocean; but can it ever fill the mind with any thing so great as the ocean itself? This is owing to several causes, but it is owing to none more than this, that the ocean is an object of no small terror. Indeed terror is in all cases whatsoever, either more openly or latently the ruling principle of the sublime. Several languages bear a strong testimony to the affinity of these ideas. They frequently use the same word, to signify indifferently the modes of astonishment or admiration and those of terror. . . . The Romans used the verb *stupeo,* a term which strongly marks the state of an astonished mind, to express the effect ei-

"The Sublime" by Edmund Burke has been excerpted from *A Philosophical Inquiry into the Origin of the Sublime and the Beautiful,* Columbia University Press (1958), pages 57–59, and is reprinted by permission of the publishers.

ther of simple fear, or of astonishment; the word *attonitus* (thunder-struck) is equally expressive of the alliance of these ideas; and do not the french *etonnement,* and the english *astonishment* and *amazement,* point out as clearly the kindred emotions which attend fear and wonder? They who have a more general knowledge of languages, could produce, I make no doubt, many other and equally striking examples.

Obscurity

To make any thing very terrible, obscurity seems in general to be necessary. When we know the full extent of any danger, when we can accustom our eyes to it, a great deal of the apprehension vanishes. Every one will be sensible of this, who considers how greatly night adds to our dread, in all cases of danger, and how much the notions of ghosts and goblins, of which none can form clear ideas, affect minds, which give credit to the popular tales concerning such sorts of beings. Those despotic governments, which are founded on the passions of men, and principally upon the passion of fear, keep their chief as much as may be from the public eye. The policy has been the same in many cases of religion. Almost all the heathen temples were dark. Even in the barbarous temples of the Americans at this day, they keep their idol in a dark part of the hut, which is consecrated to his worship. For this purpose too the druids performed all their ceremonies in the bosom of the darkest woods, and in the shade of the oldest and most spreading oaks. No person seems better to have understood the secret of heightening, or of setting terrible things, if I may use the expression, in their strongest light by the force of a judicious obscurity, than Milton. His description of Death in the second book is admirably studied; it is astonishing with what a gloomy pomp, with what a significant and expressive uncertainty of strokes and colouring he has finished the portrait of the king of terrors.

> The other shape,
> If shape it might be called that shape had none
> Distinguishable, in member, joint, or limb;
> Or substance might be called that shadow seemed,
> For each seemed either; black he stood as night;
> Fierce as ten furies; terrible as hell;
> And shook a deadly dart. What seemed his head
> The likeness of a kingly crown had on.

In this description all is dark, uncertain, confused, terrible, and sublime to the last degree.

Judgments about the Beautiful

■ Immanuel Kant ■

Taste **is the faculty of estimating an object or a mode representation by means of a delight or aversion *apart from any interest*. The object of such a delight is called *beautiful*.**

Now, where the question is whether something is beautiful, we do not want to know, whether we, or any one else, are, or even could be, concerned in the real existence of the thing, but rather what estimate we form of it on mere contemplation (intuition or reflection). If any one asks me whether I consider that the palace I see before me is beautiful, I may, perhaps, reply that I do not care for things of that sort that are merely made to be gaped at. Or I may reply in the same strain as that Iroquois *sachem* who said that nothing in Paris pleased him better than the eating-houses. I may even go a step further and inveigh with the vigour of a *Rousseau* against the vanity of the great who spend the sweat of the people on such superfluous things. Or, in fine, I may quite easily persuade myself that if I found myself on an uninhabited island, without hope of ever again coming among men, and could conjure such a palace into existence by a mere wish, I should still not trouble to do so, so long as I had a hut there that was comfortable enough for me. All this may be admitted and approved; only it is not the point now at issue. All one wants to know is whether the mere representation of the object is to my liking, no matter how indifferent I may be to the real existence of the object of this representation. It is quite plain that in order to say that the object *is beautiful,* and to show that I have taste, everything turns on the meaning which I can give to this representation, and not on any factor which makes me dependent on the real existence of the object. Every one must allow that a judgment on the beautiful which is tinged with the slightest interest, is very partial and not a pure judgment of taste. One must not be in the least prepossessed in favour of the real existence of the thing, but must preserve complete indifference in this respect, in order to play the part of judge in matters of taste. . . .

The *beautiful* is that which, apart from a concept, pleases universally.

As regards the *agreeable* every one concedes that his judgment, which he bases on a private feeling, and in which he declares that an object pleases him, is restricted merely to himself personally. Thus he does not take it amiss if, when he says that Canary-wine is agreeable, another corrects the expression and reminds him that he ought to say: It is agreeable *to me*. This applies not only to the taste of the tongue, the palate, and the throat, but to what may with any one be agreeable to eye or ear. A violet colour is to one soft and lovely: to another dull and faded. One

"Judgments about the Beautiful" by Immanuel Kant has been excerpted from *The Critique of Judgement,* James Creed Meredith, trans., Oxford University Press (1952), pages 43, 51–52, 72–73, 82–83, 168–173, and is reprinted by permission of the publisher.

man likes the tone of wind instruments, another prefers that of string instruments. To quarrel over such points with the idea of condemning another's judgment as incorrect when it differs from our own, as if the opposition between the two judgments were logical, would be folly. With the agreeable, therefore, the axiom holds good: *Every one has his own taste* (that of sense).

The beautiful stands on quite a different footing. It would, on the contrary, be ridiculous if any one who plumed himself on his taste were to think of justifying himself by saying: This object (the building we see, the dress that person has on, the concert we hear, the poem submitted to our criticism) is beautiful *for me.* For if it merely pleases *him,* he must not call it *beautiful.* Many things may for him possess charm and agreeableness—no one cares about that; but when he puts a thing on a pedestal and calls it beautiful, he demands the same delight from others. . . .

Beauty is the form of *finality* in an object, so far as perceived in it *apart from the representation of an end.*

THERE are two kinds of beauty: free beauty (*pulchritudo vaga*), or beauty which is merely dependent (*pulchritudo adhaerens*). The first presupposes no concept of what the object should be; the second does presuppose such a concept and, with it, an answering perfection of the object. Those of the first kind are said to be (self-subsisting) beauties of this thing or that thing; the other kind of beauty, being attached to a concept (conditioned beauty), is ascribed to Objects which come under the concept of a particular end.

Flowers are free beauties of nature. Hardly anyone but a botanist knows the true nature of a flower, and even he, while recognizing in the flower the reproductive organ of the plant, pays no attention to this natural end when using his taste to judge of its beauty. Hence no perfection of any kind—no internal finality, as something to which the arrangement of the manifold is related—underlies this judgment. Many birds (the parrot, the humming-bird, the bird of paradise), and a number of crustacea, are self-subsisting beauties which are not appurtenant to any object defined with respect to its end, but please freely and on their own account. So designs *à la grecque,* foliage for framework or on wall-papers, &c., have no intrinsic meaning; they represent nothing—no Object under a definite concept—and are free beauties. We may also rank in the same class what in music are called fantasias (without a theme), and, indeed, all music that is not set to words.

In the estimate of a free beauty (according to mere form) we have the pure judgment of taste. No concept is here presupposed of any end for which the manifold should serve the given Object, and which the latter, therefore, should represent—an incumbrance which would only restrict the freedom of the imagination that, as it were, is at play in the contemplation of the outward form.

But the beauty of man (including under this head that of a man, woman, or child), the beauty of a horse, or of a building (such as a church, palace, arsenal, or summer-house), presupposes a concept of the end that defines what the thing has to be, and consequently a concept of its perfection; and is therefore merely appendant beauty. Now, just as it is a clog on the purity of the judgment of taste to have the agreeable (of sensation) joined with beauty to which properly only the form is relevant, so to combine the good with beauty, (the good, namely, of the manifold to the thing itself according to its end,) mars its purity. . . .

The beautiful is that which, apart from a concept, is cognized as object of a *necessary* delight.

WERE judgments of taste (like cognitive judgments) in possession of a definite objective principle, then one who in his judgment followed such a principle would claim unconditioned necessity for it. Again, were they devoid of any principle, as are those of the mere taste of sense, then no thought of any necessity on their part would enter one's head. Therefore they must have a subjective principle, and one which determines what pleases or displeases, by means of feeling only and not through concepts, but yet with universal validity. Such a principle, however, could only be regarded as a *common sense*. This differs essentially from common understanding, which is also sometimes called common sense (*sensus communis*): for the judgment of the latter is not one by feeling, but always one by concepts, though usually only in the shape of obscurely represented principles.

The judgment of taste, therefore, depends on our presupposing the existence of a common sense. (But this is not to be taken to mean some external sense, but the effect arising from the free play of our powers of cognition.) Only under the presupposition, I repeat, of such a common sense, are we able to lay down a judgment of taste. . . .

■ ■ ■

Fine art is the art of genius. Genius is the talent (natural endowment) which gives the rule to art. Since talent, as an innate productive faculty of the artist, belongs itself to nature, we may put it this way: *Genius* is the innate mental aptitude (*ingenium*) *through which* nature gives the rule to art.

Whatever may be the merits of this definition, and whether it is merely arbitrary, or whether it is adequate or not to the concept usually associated with the word *genius*, it may still be shown at the outset that, according to this acceptation of the word, fine arts must necessarily be regarded as arts of *genius*.

For every art presupposes rules which are laid down as the foundation which first enables a product, if it is to be called one of art, to be represented as possible. The concept of fine art, however, does not permit of the judgment upon the beauty of its product being derived from any rule that has a *concept* for its determining ground, and that depends, consequently, on a concept of the way in which the product is possible. Consequently fine art cannot of its own self excogitate the rule according to which it is to effectuate its product. But since, for all that, a product can never be called art unless there is a preceding rule, it follows that nature in the individual (and by virtue of the harmony of his faculties) must give the rule to art, i.e. fine art is only possible as a product of genius.

From this it may be seen that genius (1) is a *talent* for producing that for which no definite rule can be given: and not an aptitude in the way of cleverness for what can be learned according to some rule; and that consequently *originality* must be its primary property. (2) Since there may also be original nonsense, its products must at the same time be models, i.e. be *exemplary;* and, consequently, though not themselves derived from imitation, they must serve that purpose for others, i.e. as a standard or rule of estimating. (3) It cannot indicate scientifically how it brings about its product, but rather gives the rule as *nature.* Hence, where an author owes a product to his genius, he does not himself know how the *ideas* for it have entered into his head, nor has he it in his power to invent the like at pleasure, or methodically, and communicate the same to others in such precepts as would put them in a position to produce similar products. (Hence, presumably, our word *Genie* is derived from *genius,* as the peculiar guardian and guiding spirit given to a man at his birth, by the inspiration of which those original ideas were obtained.) (4) Nature prescribes the rule through genius not to science but to art, and this also only in so far as it is to be fine art. . . .

All that *Newton* has set forth in his immortal work on the *Principles of Natural Philosophy* may well be learned, however great a mind it took to find it all out, but we cannot learn to write in a true poetic vein, no matter how complete all the precepts of the poetic art may be, or however excellent its models. The reason is that all the steps that Newton had to take from the first elements of geometry to his greatest and most profound discoveries were such as he could make intuitively evident and plain to follow, not only for himself but for everyone else. On the other hand no *Homer* or *Wieland* can show how his ideas, so rich at once in fancy and in thought, enter and assemble themselves in his brain, for the good reason that he does not himself know, and so cannot teach others. In matters of science, therefore, the greatest inventor differs only in degree from the most laborious imitator and apprentice, whereas he differs specifically from one endowed by nature for fine art. No disparagement, however, of those great men, to whom the human race is so deeply indebted, is involved in this comparison of them with those who on the score of their talent for fine art are the elect of nature. The talent for science is formed for the continued advances of greater perfection in knowledge, with all its dependent practical advantages, as also for imparting the same to others. Hence scientists can boast a ground of considerable superiority over those who merit the honour of being called geniuses, since genius reaches a point at which art must make a halt, as there is a limit imposed upon it which it cannot transcend. This limit has in all probability been long since attained. In addition, such skill cannot be communicated, but requires to be bestowed directly from the hand of nature upon each individual, and so with him it dies, awaiting the day when nature once again endows another in the same way—one who needs no more than an example to set the talent of which he is conscious at work on similar lines.

Seeing, then, that the natural endowment of art (as fine art) must furnish the rule, what kind of rule must this be? It cannot be one set down in a formula and serving as a precept—for then the judgment upon the beautiful would be determinable according to concepts. Rather must the rule be gathered from the performance, i.e. from the product, which others may use to put their own talent to the test, so as to let it serve as a model, not for *imitation,* but for *following.* The possibility of this is difficult to explain. The artist's ideas arouse like ideas on the part of his pupil, presuming nature to have visited him with a like proportion of the mental powers. For this reason the models of fine art are the only means of handing down this art to posterity. This is something which cannot be done by mere descriptions (especially not in the line of the arts of speech), and in these arts, furthermore, only those models can become classical of which the ancient, dead languages, preserved as learned, are the medium.

Despite the marked difference that distinguishes mechanical art, as an art merely depending upon industry and learning, from fine art, as that of genius, there is still no fine art in which something mechanical, capable of being at once comprehended and followed in obedience to rules, and consequently something *academic* does not constitute the essential condition of the art. For the thought of something as end must be present, or else its product would not be ascribed to an art at all, but would be a mere product of chance. But the effectuation of an end necessitates determinate rules which we cannot venture to dispense with. Now, seeing that originality of talent is one (though not the sole) essential factor that goes to make up the character of genius, shallow minds fancy that the best evidence they can give of their being full-blown geniuses is by emancipating themselves from all academic constraint of rules, in the belief that one cuts a finer figure on the back of an ill-tempered than of a trained horse. Genius can do no more than furnish rich *material* for products of fine art; its elaboration and its *form* require a talent academically trained, so that it may be employed in such a way as to stand the test of judgment. But, for a person to hold forth and pass sentence like a genius in matters that fall to the province of the most patient rational investigation, is ridiculous in the extreme. One is at a loss to know whether to laugh more at the impostor who envelops himself in such a cloud—in which we are given fuller scope to our imagination at the expense of all use of our critical faculty,—or at the simple-minded public which imagines that its inability clearly to cognize and comprehend this masterpiece of penetration is due to its being invaded by new truths *en masse,* in comparison with which, detail, due to carefully weighed exposition and an academic examination of root-principles, seems to it only the work of a tyro. . . .

For *estimating* beautiful objects, as such, what is required is *taste;* but for fine art, i.e. the *production* of such objects, one needs *genius.*

If we consider genius as the talent for fine art (which the proper signification of the word imports), and if we would analyse it from this point of view into the faculties which must concur to constitute such a talent, it is imperative at the outset accurately to determine the difference between beauty of nature, which it only requires taste to estimate, and beauty of art, which requires genius for its possibility (a possibility to which regard must also be paid in estimating such an object).

A beauty of nature is a *beautiful thing;* beauty of art is a *beautiful representation* of a thing.

To enable me to estimate a beauty of nature, as such, I do not need to be previously possessed of a concept of what sort of a thing the object is intended to be, i.e. I am not obliged to know its material finality (the end), but, rather, in forming an estimate of it apart from any knowledge of the end, the mere form pleases on its own account. If, however, the object is presented as a product of art, and is as such to be declared beautiful, then, seeing that art always presupposes an end in the cause (and its causality), a concept of what the thing is intended to be must first of all be laid at its basis. And, since the agreement of the manifold in a thing with an inner character belonging to it as its end constitutes the perfection of the thing, it follows that in estimating beauty of art the perfection of the thing must be also taken into account—a matter which in estimating a beauty of nature, as beautiful, is quite irrelevant.—It is true that in forming an estimate, especially of animate objects of nature, e.g. of a man or a horse, objective finality is also commonly taken into account with a view to judgment upon their beauty; but then the judgment also ceases to be purely aesthetic, i.e. a mere judgment of taste. Nature is no longer estimated as it appears like art, but rather in so far as it actually *is* art, though superhuman art; and the teleological judgment serves as basis and condition of the aesthetic, and one which the latter must regard. In such a case, where one says, for example, 'that is a beautiful woman,' what one in fact thinks is only this, that in her form nature excellently portrays the ends present in the female figure. For one has to extend one's view beyond the mere form to a concept, to enable the object to be thought in such manner by means of an aesthetic judgment logically conditioned.

The Philosophy of Fine Art
■ G. W. F. Hegel ■

What in the first instance is known to us under current conceptions of a work of art may be subsumed under the three following determinations:

1. A work of art is no product of Nature. It is brought into being through the agency of man.
2. It is created essentially *for* man; and, what is more, it is to a greater or less degree delivered from a sensuous medium, and addressed to his *senses*.
3. It contains an *end* bound up with it.

1. With regard to the first point, that a work of art is a product of human activity, an inference has been drawn from this (a) that such an activity, being the conscious production of an external object can also be *known* and *divulged,* and learned and reproduced by others. For that which one is able to effect, another—such is the notion—is able to effect or to imitate, when he has once simply mastered the way of doing it. In short we have merely to assume an acquaintance with the rules of art-production universally shared, and anybody may then, if he

"The Philosophy of Fine Art" by G. W. F. Hegel is reprinted from *The Philosophy of Fine Art,* F. P. B. Osmaston, trans., Hacker Art Books (1975), pages 33–34, 38–39, 43–44, 57–60, 76–77.

cares to do so, give effect to executive ability of the same type, and produce works of art. It is out of reasoning of this kind that the above-mentioned theories, with their provision of rules, and their prescriptions formulated for practical acceptance, have arisen. Unfortunately that which is capable of being brought into effect in accordance with suggestions of this description can only be something formally regular and mechanical. For only that which is mechanical is of so exterior a type that only an entirely empty effort of will and dexterity is required to accept it among our working conceptions, and forthwith to carry it out; an effort, in fact, which is not under the necessity to contribute out of its own resources anything concrete such as is quite outside the prescriptive power of such general rules. . . .

The natural tendency of ordinary thinking in this respect is to assume that the product of human art is of *subordinate* rank to the works of Nature. The work of art possesses no feeling of its own; it is not through and through a living thing, but regarded as an external object, is a dead thing. It is usual to regard that which is alive of higher worth than what is dead. We may admit, of course, that the work of art is not in itself capable of movement and alive. The living, natural thing is, whether looked at within or without, an organization with the life-purpose of such worked out into the minutest detail. The work of art merely attains to the show of animation on its surface. Below this it is ordinary stone, wood, or canvas, or in the case of poetry idea, the medium of such being speech and letters. But this element of external existence is not that which makes a work a creation of fine art. A work of art is only truly such in so far as originating in the human spirit, it continues to belong to the soil from which it sprang, has received, in short, the baptism of the mind and soul of man, and only presents that which is fashioned in consonance with such a sacrament. An interest vital to man, the spiritual values which the single event, one individual character, one action possesses in its devolution and final issue, is seized in the work of art and emphasized with greater purity and clarity than is possible on the ground of ordinary reality where human art is not. And for this reason the work of art is of higher rank than any product of Nature whatever, which has not submitted to this passage through the mind. In virtue of the emotion and insight, for example, in the atmosphere of which a landscape is portrayed by the art of painting, this creation of the human spirit assumes a higher rank than the purely natural landscape. Everything which partakes of spirit is better than anything begotten of mere Nature. However this may be, the fact remains that no purely natural existence is able, as art is, to represent divine ideals. . . .

2. We have hitherto considered the work of art under the aspect that it is fashioned by man; we will now pass over to the second part of our definition, that it is produced for his *sense-apprehension,* and consequently is to a more or less degree under obligations to a sensuous medium.

This reflection has been responsible for the inference that the function of fine art is to arouse feeling, more precisely the feeling which suits us—that is, pleasant feeling. From such a point of view writers have converted the investigation of fine art into a treatise on the emotions and asked what kind of feelings art ought to excite—take fear, for example, and compassion—with the further question how such can be regarded as pleasant, how, in short, the contemplation of a misfortune can bring satisfaction. This tendency of reflection dates for the most part from the times of Moses Mendelssohn, and many such trains of reasoning may be found in his writings. A discussion of this kind, however, did not carry the problem far. Feeling is the undefined obscure region of spiritual life. What is felt remains cloaked in the form of the separate personal experience under its most abstract persistence; and for this reason the distinctions of feeling are wholly abstract; they are not distinctions which apply to the subject-matter itself. To take examples—fear, anxiety, care, dread, are of course one type of emotion under various modifications; but in part they are purely quantitative degrees of intensity, and in part forms which reflect no light on their content itself, but are indifferent to it. In the case of fear, for instance, an existence is assumed, for which the individual in question possesses an interest, but sees at the same time the negative approach which threatens to destroy this existence, and thereupon discovers in immediate fusion within himself the above interest and the approach of that negative as a contradictory affection of his personal life. A fear of this sort, however, does not on its own account condition any particular content; it may associate with itself subject-matter of the most opposed and varied character. The feeling merely as such is in short a wholly empty form of a subjective state. Such a form may no doubt in certain cases itself be essentially complex, as we find it is with hope, pain, joy, and pleasure; it may also in this very complexity appropriate various modes of content, as, for example, we have a feeling of justice, an ethical feeling, a sublime religious feeling, and so forth; but despite the fact that a content of this kind is present in different modes of feeling, no light whatever is thereby thrown on such content which will disclose its essential and definite character. The feeling throughout remains a purely subjective state which belongs to me, one in which the concrete fact vanishes, as though contracted to a vanishing point in the most abstract of all spheres. . . .

3. There is yet another question to solve, namely, what the interest or the *End* is, which man proposes to himself in the creation of the content embodied by a work of art. This was, in fact, the third point of view, which we propounded relatively to the art-product. Its more detailed discussion will finally introduce us to the true notional concept of art itself.

If we take a glance at our ordinary ideas on this subject, one of the most prevalent is obviously[:]

The principle of the imitation of Nature. According to this view the essential aim or object of art consists in imitation, by which is understood a facility in copying natural forms as present to us in a manner which shall most fully correspond to such facts. The success of such an exact representation of Nature is assumed to afford us complete satisfaction.

Now in this definition there is to start with absolutely nothing but the formal aim to bring about the bare repetition a second time by man, so far as his means will permit of this, of all that was already in the external world, precisely too in the way it is there. A repetition of this sort may at once be set down as[:]

A *superfluous* task for the reason that everything which pictures, theatrical performances represent by way of imitation—animals, natural scenery, incidents of human life—we have already elsewhere before us in our gardens or at home, or in other examples of the more restricted or extended reaches of our personal acquaintance. Looked at, moreover, more closely, such a superfluity of energy can hardly appear otherwise than a presumptuous trifling; it is so because[:]

It lags so far behind Nature. In other words art is limited in its means of representation. It can only produce one-sided illusions, a semblance, to take one example, of real fact addressed exclusively to *one* sense. And, moreover, if it does wholly rely on the bare aim of *mere* imitation, instead of Nature's life all it gives us ever is the mere pretence of its substance. For some such reason the Turks, who are Mohammedans, will not put up with any pictures or copies of men and other objects. When James Bruce, in his travels through Abyssinia, showed a painted fish to a Turk, that worthy was at first astonished; but, quickly recovering himself, he made answer as follows: "If this fish shall rise up against you at the last day, and say, 'You have certainly given me a body, but no living soul,' how are you going to justify yourself against such a complaint?" The prophet himself, moreover, if we may believe the Sunna, said to the two women Ommi Hubiba and Ommi Selma, who told him of certain pictures in the Ethiopian churches: "These pictures will rise up in judgment against their creators on the Last Day." There are, no doubt, no less examples of completely deceptive imitation. The painted grapes of Zeuxis have been accepted from antiquity and long after as an instance of art's triumph, and also of that of the principle of imitation, because, we are told, actual doves pecked at them. We might add to this ancient example that more modern one of Bültner's monkey, which bit to pieces a painted cockchafer in Rösel's "Diversions of Insects," and was consequently forgiven by his master, although he destroyed by this means a fine copy of the precious work, because he proved thus the excellence of its illustrations. But if we will only reflect a moment on such and other instances we can only come to the conclusion that instead of praising works of art, because they have deceived *even* doves and monkeys, the foolish people ought to be condemned who imagine that the quality of a work of art is enhanced if they are able to proclaim an effect of the same so miserable as the supreme and last word they can say for it. In short, to sum up, we may state emphatically that in the mere business of imitation art cannot maintain its rivalry with Nature, and if it makes the attempt it must look like a worm which undertakes to crawl after an elephant.

Having regard, then, to this invariable failure, that is, relative failure of human imitation as contrasted with the natural prototype, we have no end left us but the pleasure offered by sleight of hand in its effort to produce something which resembles Nature. And it is unquestionably a fact that mankind are able to derive enjoyment from the attempt to reproduce with their individual labour, skill, and industry what they find around them. But a delight and admiration of this kind also becomes, if taken alone, indeed just in proportion as the copy follows slavishly the thing copied, so much the more icily null and cold, or brings its reaction of surfeit and repugnance. There are portraits which, as has been drily remarked, are positively

shameless in their likeness; and Kant brings forward a further example of this pleasure in imitation pure and simple to the effect that we are very soon tired of a
man—and there really are such—who is able to imitate the nightingale's song quite
perfectly; for we no sooner find that it is a man who is producing the strain than we
have had enough of it. We then take it to be nothing but a clever trick, neither the
free outpouring of Nature, nor yet a work of art. We expect, in short, from the free
creative power of men something quite other than a music of this kind, which only
retains our interest when, as in the case of the nightingale's note, it breaks forth in
unpremeditated fashion, resembling in this respect the rhythmic flood of human
feeling, from the native springs of its life. And as a general rule this delight we experience in the skill of imitation can only be of a restricted character; it becomes a
man better to derive enjoyment from that which he brings to birth from himself. In
this respect the invention of every insignificant technical product is of higher rank;
and mankind may feel more proud at having invented the hammer, nail, and so
forth, than in making themselves adepts as imitators. For this abstract zest in the
pursuit of imitation is on the same lines as the feat of the man who had taught himself to throw lentils through a small aperture without missing. He made an exhibition of this feat to Alexander, and Alexander merely made him a present as a reward
for this art, empty and useless as it was, of a bushel of lentils. . . .

When discussing moral improvement as the ultimate end accepted for art it
was found that its principle pointed to a higher standpoint. It will be necessary also
to vindicate this standpoint for art.

Thereby the false position to which we have already directed attention vanishes, namely, that art has to serve as a means for moral ends and the moral end of
the world generally by means of its didactive and ameliorating influence, and by
doing so has its essential aim not in itself, but in something else. If we therefore
continue still to speak of an end or goal of art, we must at once remove the perverse
idea, which in the question, "What is the end?" will still make it include the supple-
mental query, "What is the use?" The perverseness consists in this that the work of
art would then have to be regarded as related to something else, which is presented
us as what is essential and ought to be. A work of art would in that case be merely a
useful instrument in the realization of an end which possessed real and independent
importance outside the realm of art. As opposed to this we must maintain that it is
art's function to reveal *truth* under the mode of art's sensuous or material configuration, to display the reconciled antithesis previously described, and by this means to
prove that it possesses its final aim in itself, in this representation in short and self-
revelation. For other ends such as instruction, purification, improvement, procuring
of wealth, struggle after fame and honour have nothing whatever to do with this
work of art as such, still less do they determine the fundamental idea of it.

It is then from this point of view, into which the reflective consideration of
our subject-matter finally issues, that we have to grasp the fundamental idea of art
in terms of its ideal or inward necessity, as it is also from this point of view that historically regarded the true appreciation and acquaintance with art took its origin.
For that antithesis, to which we have drawn attention, did not merely assert its

presence within the general thought of educated men, but equally in philosophy as such. It was only after philosophy was in a position to overcome this opposition absolutely that it grasped the fundamental notion of its own content, and, to the extent it did so, the idea of Nature and of art.

For this reason, as this point of view implies the reawakening of philosophy in the widest connotation of the term, so also it is the re-awakening of the science of art. We may go further and affirm that aesthetic as a science is in a real sense primarily indebted to this re-awakening for its true origination, and art for its higher estimation.

Art as Experience
■ John Dewey ■

Experience occurs continuously, because the interaction of live creature and environing conditions is involved in the very process of living. Under conditions of resistance and conflict, aspects and elements of the self and the world that are implicated in this interaction qualify experience with emotions and ideas so that conscious intent emerges. Oftentimes, however, the experience had is inchoate. Things are experienced but not in such a way that they are composed into *an* experience. There is distraction and dispersion; what we observe and what we think, what we desire and what we get, are at odds with each other. We put our hands to the plow and turn back; we start and then we stop, not because the experience has reached the end for the sake of which it was initiated but because of extraneous interruptions or of inner lethargy.

In contrast with such experience, we have *an* experience when the material experienced runs its course to fulfillment. Then and then only is it integrated within and demarcated in the general stream of experience from other experiences. A piece of work is finished in a way that is satisfactory; a problem receives its solution; a game is played through; a situation, whether that of eating a meal, playing a game of chess, carrying on a conversation, writing a book, or taking part in a political campaign, is so rounded out that its close is a consummation and not a cessation. Such an experience is a whole and carries with it its own ididividualizing quality and self-sufficiency. It is *an* experience.

Philosophers, even empirical philosophers, have spoken for the most part of experience at large. Idiomatic speech, however, refers to experiences each of which is singular, having its own beginning and end. For life is no uniform uninterrupted

---

"Art as Experience" by John Dewey has been excerpted from *Art as Experience,* Putnam Publishing Group (1934), pages 35–38, 43, and is reprinted by permission of the publisher.

march or flow. It is a thing of histories, each with its own plot, its own inception and movement toward its close, each having its own particular rhythmic movement; each with its own unrepeated quality pervading it throughout. A flight of stairs, mechanical as it is, proceeds by individualized steps, not by undifferentiated progression, and an inclined plane is at least marked off from other things by abrupt discreteness.

Experience in this vital sense is defined by those situations and episodes that we spontaneously refer to as being "real experiences"; those things of which we say in recalling them, "that *was* an experience." It may have been something of tremendous importance—a quarrel with one who was once an intimate, a catastrophe finally averted by a hair's breadth. Or it may have been something that in comparison was slight—and which perhaps because of its very slightness illustrates all the better what is to be an experience. There is that meal in a Paris restaurant of which one says "that *was* an experience." It stands out as an enduring memorial of what food may be. Then there is that storm one went through in crossing the Atlantic—the storm that seemed in its fury, as it was experienced, to sum up in itself all that a storm can be, complete in itself, standing out because marked out from what went before and what came after.

In such experiences, every successive part flows freely, without seam and without unfilled blanks, into what ensues. At the same time there is no sacrifice of the self-identity of the parts. A river, as distinct from a pond, flows. But its flow gives a definiteness and interest to its successive portions greater than exist in the homogenous portions of a pond. In an experience, flow is from something to something. As one part leads into another and as one part carries on what went before, each gains distinctness in itself. The enduring whole is diversified by successive phases that are emphases of its varied colors.

Because of continuous merging, there are no holes, mechanical junctions, and dead centers when we have *an* experience. There are pauses, places of rest, but they punctuate and define the quality of movement. They sum up what has been undergone and prevent its dissipation and idle evaporation. Continued acceleration is breathless and prevents parts from gaining distinction. In a work of art, different acts, episodes, occurrences melt and fuse into unity, and yet do not disappear and lose their own character as they do so—just as in a genial conversation there is a continuous interchange and blending, and yet each speaker not only retains his own character but manifests it more clearly than is his wont.

An experience has a unity that gives it its name, *that* meal, that storm, that rupture of friendship. The existence of this unity is constituted by a single *quality* that pervades the entire experience in spite of the variation of its constituent parts. This unity is neither emotional, practical, nor intellectual, for these terms name distinctions that reflection can make within it. In discourse *about* an experience, we must make use of these adjectives of interpretation. In going over an experience in mind *after* its occurrence, we may find that one property rather than another was sufficiently dominant so that it characterizes the experience as a whole. There are absorbing inquiries and speculations which a scientific man and philosopher will recall as "experiences" in the emphatic sense. In final import they are intellectual. But in their actual occurrence they were emotional as well; they were purposive and volitional. Yet the experience was not a sum of these different characters; they were lost in it as distinctive traits. No thinker can ply his occupation save as he is lured and rewarded by total integral experiences that are intrinsically worth while. Without them he would never know what it is really to think and would be completely at a loss in distinguishing real thought from the spurious article. Thinking goes on in trains of ideas, but the ideas form a train only because they are much more than what an analytic psychology calls ideas. They are phases, emotionally and practically distinguished, of a developing underlying quality; they are its moving variations, not separate and independent like Locke's and Hume's so-called ideas and impressions, but are subtle shadings of a pervading and developing hue.

We say of an experience of thinking that we reach or draw a conclusion. Theoretical formulation of the process is often made in such terms as to conceal effectually the similarity of "conclusion" to the consummating phase of every developing integral experience. These formulations apparently take their cue from the separate propositions that are premises and the proposition that is the conclusion as they appear on the printed page. The impression is derived that there are first two independent and ready-made entities that are then manipulated so as to give rise to a third. In fact, in an experience of thinking, premises emerge only as a conclusion becomes manifest. The experience, like that of watching a storm reach its height and gradually subside, is one of continuous movement of subject-matters. Like the ocean in the storm, there are a series of waves; suggestions reaching out and being broken in a clash, or being carried onwards by a coöperative wave. If a conclusion is reached, it is that of a movement of anticipation and cumulation, one that finally comes to completion. A "conclusion" is no separate and independent thing; it is the consummation of a movement.

Hence *an* experience of thinking has its own esthetic quality. It differs from those experiences that are acknowledged to be esthetic, but only in its materials. The material of the fine arts consists of qualities; that of experience having intellectual conclusion are signs or symbols having no intrinsic quality of their own, but standing for things that may in another experience be qualitatively experienced. The difference is enormous. It is one reason why the strictly intellectual art will never be popular as music is popular. Nevertheless, the experience itself has a satisfying emotional quality because it possesses internal integration and fulfillment reached through ordered and organized movement. This artistic structure may be immediately felt. In so far, it is esthetic. What is even more important is that not only is this quality a significant motive in undertaking intellectual inquiry and in keeping it honest, but that no intellectual activity is an integral event (is *an* experience), unless it is rounded out with this quality. Without it, thinking is inconclusive. In short, esthetic cannot be sharply marked off from intellectual experience since the latter must bear an esthetic stamp to be itself complete. . .

Thus the non-esthetic lies within two limits. At one pole is the loose succession that does not begin at any particular place and that ends—in the sense of ceasing—at no particular place. At the other pole is arrest, constriction, proceeding from parts having only a mechanical connection with one another. There exists so much of one and the other of these two kinds of experience that unconsciously they come to be taken as norms of all experience. Then, when the esthetic appears, it so sharply contrasts with the picture that has been formed of experience, that it is impossible to combine its special qualities with the features of the picture and the esthetic is given an outside place and status. The account that has been given of experience dominantly intellectual and practical is intended to show that there is no such contrast involved in having an experience; that, on the contrary, no experience of whatever sort is a unity unless it has esthetic quality.

The enemies of the esthetic are neither the practical nor the intellectual. They are the humdrum; slackness of loose ends; submission to convention in practice and intellectual procedure. Rigid abstinence, coerced submission, tightness on one side and dissipation, incoherence and aimless indulgence on the other, are deviations in opposite directions from the unity of an experience. Some such considerations perhaps induced Aristotle to invoke the "mean proportional" as the proper designation of what is distinctive of both virtue and the esthetic. He was formally correct. "Mean" and "proportion" are, however, not self-explanatory, nor to be taken over in a prior mathematical sense, but are properties belonging to an experience that has a developing movement toward its own consummation.

I have emphasized the fact that every integral experience moves toward a close, an ending, since it ceases only when the energies active in it have done their proper work. This closure of a circuit of energy is the opposite of arrest, of *stasis*. Maturation and fixation are polar opposites. Struggle and conflict may be themselves enjoyed, although they are painful, when they are experienced as means of developing an experience; members in that they carry it forward, not just because they are there. There is, as will appear later, an element of undergoing, of suffering in its large sense, in every experience. Otherwise there would be no taking in of what preceded. For "taking in" in any vital experience is something more than placing something on the top of consciousness over what was previously known. It involves reconstruction which may be painful. Whether the necessary undergoing phase is by itself pleasurable or painful is a matter of particular conditions. It is indifferent to the total esthetic quality, save that there are few intense esthetic experiences that are wholly gleeful. They are certainly not to be characterized as amusing, and as they bear down upon us they involve a suffering that is none the less consistent with, indeed a part of, the complete perception that is enjoyed.

I have spoken of the esthetic quality that rounds out an experience into completeness and unity as emotional. The reference may cause difficulty. We are given to thinking of emotions as things as simple and compact as are the words by which we name them. Joy, sorrow, hope, fear, anger, curiosity, are treated as if each in itself were a sort of entity that enters full-made upon the scene, an entity that may last a long time or a short time, but whose duration, whose growth and career, is irrelevant to its nature. In fact emotions are qualities, when they are significant, of a complex experience that moves and changes. I say, when they are *significant,* for otherwise they are but the outbreaks and eruptions of a disturbed infant. All emotions are qualifications of a drama and they change as the drama develops. Persons are sometimes said to fall in love at first sight. But what they fall into is not a thing of that instant. What would love be were it compressed into a moment in which there is no room for cherishing and for solicitude? The intimate nature of emotion is manifested in the experience of one watching a play on the stage or reading a novel. It attends the development of a plot; and a plot requires a stage, a space, wherein to develop and time in which to unfold. Experience is emotional but there are no separate things called emotions in it.

By the same token, emotions are attached to events and objects in their movement. They are not, save in pathological instances, private. And even an "objectless" emotion demands something beyond itself to which to attach itself, and thus it soon generates a delusion in lack of something real. Emotion belongs of a certainty to the self. But it belongs to the self that is concerned in the movement of events toward an issue that is desired or disliked. We jump instantaneously when we are scared, as we blush on the instant when we are ashamed. But fright and shamed modesty are not in this case emotional states. Of themselves they are but automatic reflexes. In order to become emotional they must become parts of an inclusive and enduring situation that involves concern for objects and their issues. The jump of fright becomes emotional fear when there is found or thought to exist a threatening object that must be dealt with or escaped from. The blush becomes the emotion of shame when a person connects, in thought, an action he has performed with an unfavorable reaction to himself of some other person.

Physical things from far ends of the earth are physically transported and physically caused to act and react upon one another in the construction of a new object. The miracle of mind is that something similar takes place in experience without physical transport and assembling. Emotion is the moving and cementing force. It selects what is congruous and dyes what is selected with its color, thereby giving qualitative unity to materials externally disparate and dissimilar. It thus provides unity in and through the varied parts of an experience. When the unity is of the sort already described, the experience has esthetic character even though it is not, dominantly, an esthetic experience.

PART X

∎
∎

CONTEMPORARY SOURCES

In this section, the reader will find key contemporary sources on a range of general issues in aesthetics that cross the boundaries between different art forms.

Consider the contrast between *aesthetic qualities,* such as "is delicate," "is tightly organized," "is tense," and *descriptive qualities* such as "is square," "is colored red," "is of a house," etc. While the basis for descriptive qualities seems to be relatively unproblematic, it appears that this is not so for aesthetic qualities. Now consider the judgment, "the shape of this vase is delicate." In a famous essay on the matter, Frank Sibley makes a case that judgments of this sort are distinctively "loose," in that no conditions are either necessary or sufficient for these kinds of judgments to hold. What, then, is the basis for such judgments? Sibley says that we make them through an exercise of taste, which is not to be equated with any or all of the standard five senses.

Kendall Walton's important essay argues that our understanding and appreciation of an artwork's aesthetic features is guided by our understanding of what *category* it belongs to. For example, we should not think of Picasso's *Guernica* merely as *art generally,* but as a *painting.* This runs counter to one traditional view that in order to respond adequately to an artwork, we ought to come to it without any preconceptions. An important implication of Walton's view is that it opposes an established tradition that insists that we need not take into consideration an artist's *intention.* He reasons that considering the artist's intention may be crucially relevant to correctly placing an artwork in a given category.

The essay by Morris Weitz explains why, in his opinion, we should be anti-essentialist in our thinking about the concept *art.* In short, the concept *art* cannot be defined. However, he goes on to explain why attempts to do so are nevertheless useful. One reason for these claims, Weitz argues, is that *art* is an open concept—one such that the criteria for applying it are constantly revisable. A related reason is that the descriptive use of the concept *art* is charged with *normative* dimensions. In other words, when we believe we are merely classifying something as art, we are typically praising it as well.

In the essay, "Art as a Social Institution," George Dickie defends an early but straightforward version of his influential *institutional* theory of art. Dickie holds that if we take pains to keep separate the *normative* from the *classificatory* uses of the concept *art,* we ought to be able to circumvent Weitz's skeptical argument about defining *art.* Dickie's definition of *art* depends strongly upon Arthur Danto's concept of an *artworld.* According to Dickie, what makes an object a work of art is not its intrinsic, perceptual features, but its function or role as a candidate for appreciation in an artworld context.

Peg Zeglin Brand's essay "Feminism in Context" is also a critique of a classic position of approaching artworks in isolation from their social, historical, political, and cultural contexts. The classic position, developed by Immanuel Kant, is that our approach to works of art should be *disinterested;* that is, isolated from our desires and needs as practical, ethical, and political beings. Brand argues for a *contextualist* approach, according to which works of art should be apprehended in their larger settings. This approach, she makes clear, will have major implications for a feminist approach to art, in which considerations such as gender become relevant to our experience of and judgments about artworks.

In his essay, "A Different Plea for Disinterest," Theodore Gracyk tries to avoid the classic position of isolating genuinely aesthetic responses from our extra-aesthetic interests. However, he arrives at a result different from Brand's, namely, that *dis*interested attention to artworks can actually enable audiences to identify with works in ways that challenge their previously established interests and social attitudes. Consider the likelihood, for example, that the musical *style* of early Bob Dylan recordings did have something to do with opening previously obdurate racist white audiences to thinking differently about racial matters. Gracyk defends this view by recourse to a range of examples from popular culture.

Maurice Berger addresses a timely and politically charged issue about the possible racial biases built into the policies governing the installation of art in American museums. Although many artworks are private property, most people have access to them only in museums. Since museums play such an important role, we should not overlook several social questions about art: Are African-American artists' works shown only as a form of tokenism? How should ethnic art be presented to the art world? Should forms of affirmative action be applied in that sphere?

Carole Vance weighs certain economic pressures that are often brought to bear on controversial contemporary art. These pressures often reflect negative judgments about such art by conservative political forces. An important effect of these responses has been a reduction of the already weak public funding of the arts in the United States. Vance opposes those conservative forces that believe that tax dollars should not be used to support the arts. Such a policy, she argues, will ensure that only the least threatening, most middle-of-the road art gets funded.

In "Art and Taxes," Paul Mattick traces the broader cultural background of recent controversies about funding the arts. As Mattick views the current scene,

Americans, on the whole, have little concern about recent Supreme Court judgments that rule against the federal funding of contemporary art. The reason for this, he judges, is a great cultural sea change since the days of the New Frontier and Great Society in the 1960s, when the federal support of contemporary art was celebrated. Since then, while there is little thought about the use of public money to support such art, tax dollars are cheerfully earmarked for the promotion of private business interests. In such an atmosphere, according to Mattick, the only art that can thrive is that of well-established high-art institutions.

In his essay on the aesthetics of the natural environment, Allen Carlson attempts to steer between two extremes. On the one hand, some have tried to draw a close analogy between such appreciation and our appreciation of art. Thus, the Grand Canyon might be regarded as a series of *scenes,* as might be presented in landscape painting. Others have reacted by arguing that it is a form of human chauvinism to treat nature as if it were any sort of aesthetic object. Carlson develops what he calls a Natural Environmental Model, which tries to do justice to the ways in which nature is artlike and ways in which it isn't.

Aesthetic Concepts
▪ Frank Sibley ▪

Aesthetic terms span a great range of types and could be grouped into various kinds and sub-species. But it is not my present purpose to attempt any such grouping; I am interested in what they all have in common. Their almost endless variety is adequately displayed in the following list: *unified, balanced, integrated, lifeless, serene, somber, dynamic, powerful, vivid, delicate, moving, trite, sentimental, tragic.* The list of course is not limited to adjectives; expressions in artistic contexts like "telling contrast," "sets up a tension," "conveys a sense of," or "holds it together" are equally good illustrations. It includes terms used by both layman and critic alike, as well as some which are mainly the property of professional critics and specialists . . . .

The expressions I am calling aesthetic terms form no small segment of our discourse. Often, it is true, people with normal intelligence and good eyesight and hearing lack, at least in some measure, the sensitivity required to apply them; a man need not be stupid or have poor eyesight to fail to see that something is graceful. Thus taste or sensitivity is somewhat more rare than certain other human capacities; people who exhibit a sensitivity both wide-ranging and refined are a minority. It is over the application of aesthetic terms too that, notoriously, disputes and differences sometimes go helplessly unsettled. But almost everybody is able to exercise taste to some degree and in some matters . . . .

In order to support our application of an aesthetic term, we often refer to features the mention of which involves other aesthetic terms: "It has an extraordinary vitality because of its free and vigorous style of drawing," "graceful in the smooth flow of its lines," "dainty because of the delicacy and harmony of its coloring." It is as normal to do this as it is to justify one mental epithet by other epithets of the same general type, *intelligent* by *ingenious, inventive, acute,* and so on. But often when we apply aesthetic terms, we explain why by referring to features which do *not* depend for their recognition upon an exercise of taste: "delicate because of its pastel shades and curving lines," or "it lacks balance because one group of figures is so far off to the left and is so brightly illuminated." When no explanation of this kind is offered, it is legitimate to ask or search for one. Finding a satisfactory answer may sometimes be difficult, but one cannot ordinarily reject the question. When we cannot ourselves quite say what non-aesthetic features make something delicate or unbalanced or powerful or moving, the good critic often puts his finger on something which strikes us as the right explanation. In short, aesthetic words apply ultimately because of, and aesthetic qualities ultimately depend upon, the

"Aesthetic Concepts" by Frank Sibley has been excerpted from *The Philosophical Review,* Vol. LXVIII, No. 4, whole number 388 (1959), pages 421–426, 429–432, 442–444, 446–447.

presence of features which, like curving or angular lines, color contrasts, placing of masses, or speed of movement, are visible, audible, or otherwise discernible without any exercise of taste or sensibility. Whatever kind of dependence this is, and there are various relationships between aesthetic qualities and non-aesthetic features, what I want to make clear in this section is that there are no non-aesthetic features which serve as *conditions* for applying aesthetic terms. Aesthetic or taste concepts are not in this respect condition-governed at all . . . .

Being a good chess player can count only *towards* and not *against* intelligence. Whereas mention of it may enter sensibly along with other remarks in expressions like "I say he is intelligent because . . . " or "the reason I call him intelligent is that . . . ," it cannot be used to complete such negative expressions as "I say he is *un*intelligent because . . . " But what I want particularly to emphasize about features which function as conditions for a term is that *some* group or set of them *is* sufficient fully to ensure or warrant the application of that term. An individual characterized by some of these features may not yet qualify to be called lazy or intelligent, and so on, beyond all question, but all that is needed is to add some further (indefinite) number of such characterizations and the point is reached where we have enough. There are individuals possessing a number of such features of whom one cannot deny, cannot but admit, that they are intelligent. We have left necessary-and-sufficient conditions behind, but we are still in the realm of conditions.

But aesthetic concepts are not condition-governed even in this way. There are no sufficient conditions, no non-aesthetic features such that the presence of some set or number of them will beyond question justify or warrant the application of an aesthetic term. It is impossible . . . to make any statements corresponding to those we can make for condition-governed words. We are able to say "If it is true he can do this, and that, and the other, then one just cannot deny that he is intelligent," or "if he does A, B, and C, I don't see how it can be denied that he is lazy," but we cannot make *any* general statement of the form "If the vase is pale pink, somewhat curving, lightly mottled, and so forth, it will be delicate, cannot but be delicate." Nor again can one say *any* such things here as "Being tall and thin is not enough *alone* to ensure that a vase is delicate, but if it is, for example, slightly curving and pale colored (and so forth) as well, it cannot be denied that it is." Things may be described to us in non-aesthetic terms as fully as we please but we are not thereby put in the position of having to admit (or being unable to deny) that they are delicate or graceful or garish or exquisitely balanced . . . .

It is important to observe that I have not merely been claiming that no sufficient conditions can be stated for taste concepts. For if this were all, taste concepts might not be after all really different from one kind of concept recently discussed. They could be accommodated perhaps with those concepts which Professor H. L. A. Hart has called "defeasible"; it is a characteristic of defeasible concepts that we cannot state sufficient conditions for them because, for any sets we offer, there is always an (open) list of defeating conditions any of which might rule out the application of the concept. The most we can say schematically for a defeasible concept is that, for example, A, B, and C together are sufficient for the concept to apply *unless* some feature is present which overrides or voids them. But, I want to emphasize, the very fact that we *can* say this sort of thing shows that we are still to that extent in the realm of conditions. The features governing defeasible concepts can ordinarily count only one way, *either* for *or* against. To take Hart's example, "offer" and "acceptance" can count only towards the existence of a valid contract, and fraudulent misrepresentation, duress, and lunacy can count only against. And even with defeasible concepts, if we are told that there are no voiding features present, we can know that some set of conditions or features, A, B, C, . . . , is enough, in this absence of voiding features, to ensure, for example, that there is a contract. The very notion of a defeasible concept seems to require that some group of features *would* be sufficient in the absence of overriding or voiding features. Defeasible concepts lack *sufficient* conditions then, but they are still, in the sense described, condition-governed. My claim about taste concepts is stronger; that they are not, except negatively, governed by conditions at all. We could not conclude, even if we were told of the absence of all "voiding" or uncharacteristic features (no angularities, and the like), that an object must certainly be graceful, however fully it was described to us as possessing features characteristic of gracefulness . . . .

[I]t is at least noteworthy that in applying words like "lazy" or "intelligent" to new and unique instances we say that we are required to exercise *judgment;* it would be indeed odd to say that we are exercising *taste.* In exercising judgment we are called upon to weigh the pros and cons against each other, and perhaps sometimes to decide whether a quite new feature is to be counted as weighing on one side or on the other. But this goes to show that, though we may learn from and rely upon samples and precedents rather than a set of stated conditions, we are not out of the realm of general conditions and guiding principles . . . .

Nothing like this is possible with aesthetic terms. Examples undoubtedly play a crucial role in giving us a grasp of these concepts; but we do not and cannot derive from these examples conditions and principles, however complex, which will guide us consistently and intelligibly in applying the terms to new cases. When, with a clear case of something which is in fact graceful or balanced or tightly-knit but which I have not seen, someone tells me why it is, what features make it so, it is always possible for me to wonder whether, in spite of these features, it really is graceful, balanced, and so on.

The point I have argued may be reinforced in the following way. A man who failed to realize the nature of taste concepts, or someone who, knowing he lacked sensitivity in aesthetic matters, did not want to reveal this lack might by assiduous application and shrewd observation provide himself with some rules and generalizations; and by inductive procedures and intelligent guessing, he might frequently say the right things. But he could have no great confidence or certainty; a slight change in an object might at any time unpredictably ruin his calculations, and he might as easily have been wrong as right. No matter how careful he has been about working out a set of consistent principles and conditions, he is only in a position to think that the object is very possibly delicate. With concepts like *lazy, intelligent,* or *contract,* someone who intelligently formulated rules that led him aright appreciably often *would* thereby show the beginning of a grasp of those concepts; but the person we are considering is not even beginning to show an awareness of what delicacy is. Though he sometimes says the right thing, he has not seen, but guessed, that the object is delicate. However intelligent he might be, we could easily tell him wrongly that something was delicate and "explain" why without his being able to detect the deception. (I am ignoring complications now about negative conditions.) But if we did the same with, say, "intelligent" he could at least often uncover some incompatibility or other which would need explaining. In a world of beings like himself he would have no use for concepts like delicacy. As it is, these concepts would play a quite different role in his life. He would, for himself, have no more reason to choose tasteful objects, pictures, and so on, than a deaf man would to avoid noisy places. He could not be praised for exercising taste; at best his ingenuity and intelligence might come in for mention. In "appraising" pictures, statuettes, poems, he would be doing something quite different from what other people do when they exercise taste . . . .

To help understand what the critic does, . . . how he supports his judgments and gets his audience to see what he sees, I shall attempt a brief description of the methods we use as critics.

1. We may simply mention or point out non-aesthetic features: "Notice these flecks of color, that dark mass there, those lines." By merely drawing attention to those easily discernible features which make the painting luminous or warm or dynamic, we often succeed in bringing someone to see these aesthetic qualities. We get him to see B by mentioning something different, A. Sometimes in doing this we are drawing attention to features which may have gone unnoticed by an untrained or insufficiently attentive eye or ear: "Just listen for the repeated figure in the left hand," "Did you notice the figure of Icarus in the Breughel? It is very small." Sometimes they are features which have been seen or heard but of which the significance or purpose has been missed in any of a variety of ways: "Notice how much darker he has made the central figure, how much brighter these colors are than the adjacent ones," "Of course, you've observed the ploughman in the foreground; but had you considered how he, like everyone else in the picture, is going about his business without noticing the fall of Icarus?" In mentioning features which may be discerned by anyone with normal eyes, ears, and intelligence, we are singling out what may serve as a kind of key to grasping or seeing something else (and the key may not be the same for each person).

2. On the other hand we often simply mention the very qualities we want people to see. We point to a painting and say, "Notice how nervous and delicate the drawing is," or "See what energy and vitality it has." The use of the aesthetic term itself may do the trick; we say what the quality or character is, and people who had not seen it before see it.

3. Most often, there is a linking of remarks about aesthetic and non-aesthetic features: "Have you noticed this line and that, and the points of bright color here and there . . . don't they give it vitality, energy?"

4. We do, in addition, often make extensive and helpful use of similes and genuine metaphors: "It's as if there are small points of light burning," "as though he had thrown on the paint violently and in anger," "the light shimmers, the lines dance, everything is air, lightness and gaiety," "his canvasses are fires, they crackle, burn, and blaze, even at their most subdued always restlessly flickering, but often bursting into flame, great pyrotechnic displays," and so on.

5. We make use of contrasts, comparisons, and reminiscences: "Suppose he had made that a lighter yellow, moved it to the right, how flat it would have fallen," "Don't you think it has something of the quality of a Rembrandt?", "Hasn't it the same serenity, peace, and quality of light of those summer evenings in Norfolk?" We use what keys we have to the known sensitivity, susceptibilities, and experience of our audience.

Critics and commentators may range, in their methods, from one extreme to the other, from painstaking concentration on points of detail, line and color, vowels and rhymes, to more or less flowery and luxuriant metaphor. Even the enthusiastic biographical sketch decorated with suitable epithet and metaphor may serve. What is best depends on both the audience and the work under discussion. But this would not be a complete sketch unless certain other notes were added.

6. Repetition and reiteration often play an important role. When we are in front of a canvas we may come back time and again to the same points, drawing attention to the same lines and shapes, repeating the same words, "swirling," "balance," "luminosity," or the same similes and metaphors, as if time and familiarity, looking harder, listening more carefully, paying closer attention may help. So again with variation; it often helps to talk round what we have said, to build up, supplement with more talk *of the same kind*. When someone misses the swirling quality, when one epithet or one metaphor does not work, we throw in related ones; we speak of its wild movement, how it twists and turns, writhes and whirls, as though, failing to score a direct hit, we may succeed with a barrage of near-synonyms.

7. Finally, besides our verbal performances, the rest of our behavior is important. We accompany our talk with appropriate tones of voice, expression, nods, looks, and gestures. A critic may sometimes do more with a sweep of the arm than by talking. An appropriate gesture may make us see the violence in a painting or the character of a melodic line . . . .

I shall end by showing that the methods I have outlined are the ones natural for and characteristic of taste concepts from the start. When someone tries to convince me that a painting is delicate or balanced, I have some understanding of these terms already and know in a sense what I am looking for. But if there is puzzlement over how, by talking, he can bring me to see these qualities in this picture, there should be a corresponding puzzlement over how I learned to use aesthetic terms and discern aesthetic qualities in the first place. We may ask, therefore, how we learn to do these things; and this is to inquire (1) what natural potentialities and tendencies people have and (2) how we develop and take advantage of these capacities in training and teaching. Now for the second of these, there is no doubt that our ability to notice and respond to aesthetic qualities is cultivated and developed by our contacts with parents and teachers from quite an early age. What is interesting for my present purpose is that, while we are being taught in the presence of examples what grace, delicacy, and so on are, the methods used, the language and behavior, are of a piece with those of the critic . . . .

When I said at the outset that aesthetic sensitivity was rarer than some other natural endowments, I was not denying that it varies in degree from the rudimentary to the refined. Most people learn easily to make the kinds of remarks I am now considering. But when someone can call bright canvasses gay and lively without being able to spot the one which is really vibrant, or can recognize the obvious outward vigor and energy of a student composition played *con fuoco* while failing to see that it lacks inner fire and drive, we do not regard his aesthetic sensitivity in these as particularly developed. However, once these transitions from common to aesthetic uses are begun in the more obvious cases, the domain of aesthetic concepts may broaden out, become more subtle, and even partly autonomous. The initial steps, however varied the metaphorical shifts and however varied the experiences upon which they are parasitic, are natural and easy.

Categories of Art
■ Kendall L. Walton ■

Paintings and sculptures are to be looked at; sonatas and songs are to be heard. What is important about such works of art is what can be seen or heard in them. This apparent truism has inspired attempts by aesthetic theorists to purge from criticism of works of art supposedly extraneous excursions into matters not available to inspection of the works and to focus attention narrowly on the works themselves. Circumstances connected with a work's origin, in particular, are frequently held to have no essential bearing on an assessment of its aesthetic nature. Thus critics are advised to ignore how and when a work was created, the artist's intentions in creating it, his philosophical views, psychological state and personal life, the artistic traditions and intellectual atmosphere of his society, and so forth. Once produced, it is argued, a work must stand or fall on its own; it must be judged for what it is, regardless of how it came to be as it is . . . .

The view sketched above can easily seem very persuasive. But the tendency of critics to discuss the histories of works of art in the course of justifying aesthetic judgments about them has been remarkably persistent. This is partly because hints derived from facts about a work's history, however dispensable they may be "in

---

"Categories of Art" by Kendall L. Walton has been excerpted from *Art and Philosophy*, St. Martin's Press (1979), W. E. Kennick, ed., pages 594–602, 605–606, 609–614, and is reprinted by permission of the publisher.

principle," are often crucially important in practice. (One might not think to listen for a recurring series of intervals in a piece of music, until he learns that the composer meant the work to be structured around it.) No doubt it is partly due also to genuine confusions on the part of critics. But I will argue that certain facts about the origins of works of art have an *essential* role in criticism, that aesthetic judgments rest on them in an absolutely fundamental way. For this reason, and for another as well, the view that works of art should be judged simply by what can be perceived in them is seriously misleading. Nevertheless there is something right in the idea that what matters aesthetically about a painting or a sonata is just how it looks or sounds.

I will continue to call tension, mystery, energy, coherence, balance, serenity, sentimentality, pallidness, disunity, grotesqueness, and so forth, as well as colors and shapes, pitches and timbres *properties* of works of art, though "property" is to be construed broadly enough not to beg any important questions. I will also, following [Frank] Sibley, call properties of the former sort "aesthetic" properties, but purely for reasons of convenience I will include in this category "representational" and "resemblance" properties, which Sibley excludes—for example, the property of representing Napoleon, that of depicting an old man stooping over a fire, that of resembling, or merely suggesting, a human face, claws (the petals of Van Gogh's sunflowers), or (in music) footsteps or conversation. It is not essential for my purposes to delimit with any exactness the class of aesthetic properties (if indeed any such delimitation is possible), for I am more interested in discussing particular examples of such properties than in making generalizations about the class as a whole. It will be obvious, however, that what I say about the examples I deal with is also applicable to a great many other properties we would want to call aesthetic . . . .

A feature of a work of art is *standard* with respect to a (perceptually distinguishable) category just in case it is among those in virtue of which works in that category belong to that category—that is, just in case the absence of that feature would disqualify, or tend to disqualify, a work from that category. A feature is *variable* with respect to a category just in case it has nothing to do with works belonging to that category; the possession or lack of the feature is irrelevant to whether a work qualifies for the category. Finally, a *contra-standard* feature with respect to a category is the absence of a standard feature with respect to that category—that is, a feature whose presence tends to *disqualify* works as members of the category . . . .

I turn now to my psychological thesis that what aesthetic properties a work seems to have, what aesthetic effect it has on us, how it strikes us aesthetically often depends (in part) on which of its features are standard, which variable, and which contra-standard for us. I offer examples in support of this thesis.

1. Representational and resemblance properties provide perhaps the most obvious illustration of this thesis. Many works of art look like or resemble other objects—people, buildings, mountains, bowls of fruit, and so forth. Rembrandt's *Titus Reading* looks like a boy, and in particular like Rembrandt's son; Picasso's

Les Demoiselles d'Avignon looks like five women, four standing and one sitting (though not *especially* like any particular women). A portrait may even be said to be a *perfect* likeness of the sitter, or to capture his image *exactly.*

An important consideration in determining whether a work *depicts* or *represents* a particular object, or an object of a certain sort (for example, Rembrandt's son, or simply *a* boy), in the sense of being a picture, sculpture, or whatever of it is whether the work resembles that object, or objects of that kind. A significant degree of resemblance is, I suggest, a necessary condition in most contexts for such representation or depiction, though the resemblance need not be obvious at first glance. If we are unable to see a similarity between a painting purportedly of a woman and women, I think we would have to suppose either that there is such a similarity which we have not yet discovered (as one might fail to see a face in a maze of lines), or that it simply is not a picture of a woman. Resemblance is of course not a *sufficient* condition for representation, since a portrait (containing only one figure) might resemble both the sitter and his twin brother equally but is not a portrait of both of them. (The title might determine which of them it depicts.)

It takes only a touch of perversity, however, to find much of our talk about resemblances between works of art and other things preposterous. Paintings and people are *very* different sorts of things. Paintings are pieces of canvas supporting splotches of paint, while people are live, three-dimensional, flesh-and-blood animals. Moreover, except rarely and under special conditions of observation paintings and people *look* very different. Paintings look like pieces of canvas (or anyway flat surfaces) covered with paint and people look like flesh-and-blood animals. There is practically no danger of confusing them. How, then, can anyone seriously hold that a portrait resembles the sitter to any significant extent, let alone that it is a perfect likeness of him? Yet it remains true that many paintings strike us as resembling people, sometimes very much or even exactly—despite the fact that they look so very different!

To resolve this paradox we must recognize that the resemblances we perceive between, for example, portraits and people, those that are relevant in determining what works of art depict or represent, are resemblances of a somewhat special sort, tied up with the categories in which we perceive such works. The properties of a work which are standard for us are ordinarily irrelevant to what we take it to look like or resemble in the relevant sense, and hence to what we take it to depict or represent. The properties of a portrait which make it *so* different from, so easily distinguishable from, a person—such as its flatness and its *painted* look—are standard for us. Hence these properties just do not count with regard to what (or whom) it looks like. It is only the properties which are variable for us, the colors and shapes on the work's surface, that make it look to us like what it does. And these are the ones which are relevant in determining what (if anything) the work represents . . . .

2. The importance of the distinction between standard and variable properties is by no means limited to cases involving representation or resemblance. Imagine a society that does not have an established medium of painting but does produce a kind of work of art called "guernicas." Guernicas are like versions of

Picasso's *Guernica* done in various bas-relief dimensions. All of them are surfaces with the colors and shapes of Picasso's *Guernica,* but the surfaces are molded to protrude from the wall like relief maps of different kinds of terrain. Some guernicas have rolling surfaces, others are sharp and jagged, still others contain several relatively flat planes at various angles to each other, and so forth. If members of this society should come across Picasso's *Guernica,* they would count it as a guernica—a perfectly flat one—rather than as a painting. Its flatness is variable and the figures on its surface are standard relative to the category of guernicas. Thus the flatness, which is standard for us, would be variable for members of the other society, and the figures on the surface, which are variable for us, would be standard for them. This would make for a profound difference between our aesthetic reaction to *Guernica* and theirs. It seems violent, dynamic, vital, disturbing to us. But I imagine it would strike them as cold, stark, lifeless, or serene and restful, or perhaps bland, dull, boring—but in any case *not* violent, dynamic, and vital. We do not pay attention to or take note of *Guernica's* flatness; this is a feature we take for granted in paintings. But for the other society, this is *Guernica's* most striking and noteworthy characteristic—what is *expressive* about it. Conversely, *Guernica's* color patches, which we find noteworthy and expressive, are insignificant to them . . . .

3. I turn now to features which are contra-standard for us—ones which have a tendency to disqualify a work from a category in which we nevertheless perceive it. We are likely to find such features shocking, or disconcerting, or startling, or upsetting, just because they are contra-standard for us. Their presence may be so obtrusive that they obscure the work's variable properties. Three-dimensional objects protruding from a canvas and movement in a sculpture are contra-standard relative to the categories of painting and (traditional) sculpture respectively. These features are contra-standard for us, and probably shocking, if despite them we perceive the works possessing them in the mentioned categories. The monochromatic paintings of Yves Klein are disturbing to us (at least at first) for this reason: We see them as paintings, though they contain the feature contra-standard for paintings of being one solid color. Notice that we find other similarly monochromatic surfaces—walls of living rooms, for example—not in the least disturbing, and indeed quite unnoteworthy.

If we are exposed frequently to works containing a certain kind of feature which is contra-standard for us, we ordinarily adjust our categories to accommodate it, making it contra-standard for us no longer. The first painting with a three-dimensional object glued to it was no doubt shocking. But now that the technique has become commonplace we are not shocked. This is because we no longer see these works as *paintings,* but rather as members of either (*a*) a new category—*collages*—in which case the offending feature has become standard rather than contra-standard for us, or (*b*) an expanded category which includes paintings both with and without attached objects, in which case that feature is variable for us . . . .

How is it to be determined in which categories a work is correctly perceived? There is certainly no very precise or well-defined procedure to be followed. Different criteria are emphasized by different people and in different situations. But there are several fairly definite considerations which typically figure in critical discussions and which fit our intuitions reasonably well. I suggest that the following circumstances count toward its being correct to perceive a work, W, in a given category, C:

(i) The presence in W of a relatively large number of features standard with respect to C. The correct way of perceiving a work is likely to be that in which it has a minimum of contra-standard features for us. I take the relevance of this consideration to be obvious. It cannot be correct to perceive Rembrandt's *Titus Reading* as a kinetic sculpture, if this is possible, just because that work has too few of the features which make kinetic sculptures kinetic sculptures. But of course this does not get us very far. *Guernica,* for example, qualifies equally well on this count for being perceived as a painting and as a guernica.

(ii) The fact that W is better, or more interesting or pleasing aesthetically, or more worth experiencing when perceived in C than it is when perceived in alternative ways. The correct way of perceiving a work is likely to be the way in which it comes off best.

(iii) The fact that the artist who produced W intended or expected it to be perceived in C, or thought of it as a C.

(iv) The fact that C is well established in and recognized by the society in which W was produced. A category is well established in and recognized by a society if the members of the society are familiar with works in that category, consider a work's membership in it a fact worth mentioning, exhibit works of that category together, and so forth—that is, roughly if that category figures importantly in their way of classifying works of art. The categories of impressionist painting and Brahmsian music are well established and recognized in our society; those of guernicas, paintings with diagonal composition containing green crosses, and pieces of music containing between four and eight F-sharps and at least seventeen quarter notes every eight bars are not. The categories in which a work is correctly perceived, according to this condition, are generally the ones in which the artist's contemporaries did perceive or would have perceived it . . . .

What can be said in support of the relevance of conditions (*ii*), (*iii*), and (*iv*)? In the examples mentioned above, the categories in which we consider a work correctly perceived probably meet all of these conditions. I would suppose that *Guernica* is better seen as a painting than it would be seen as a guernica (though this would be hard to prove). In any case, Picasso certainly intended it to be seen as a painting rather than a guernica, and the category of paintings is well established in his (that is, our) society, whereas that of guernicas is not. But this of course does not show that (*ii*), (*iii*), and (*iv*) *each* is relevant. It tends to indicate only that one or other of them, or some combination, is relevant . . . .

I will begin with (*ii*). If we are faced with a choice between two ways of perceiving a work, and the work is very much better perceived in one way than it is perceived in the other, I think that, at least in the absence of contrary considerations, we would be strongly inclined to settle on the former way of perceiving it as the *correct* way. The process of trying to determine what is in a work consists partly in casting around among otherwise plausible ways of perceiving it for one in which the work is good. We feel we are coming to a correct understanding of a work when we begin to like or enjoy it; we are finding what is really there when it seems worth experiencing.

But if (*ii*) is relevant, it is quite clearly not the *only* relevant consideration. Take any work of art we can agree is of fourth- or fifth- or tenth-rate quality. It is very possible that if this work were perceived in some farfetched set of categories that someone might dream up, it would appear to be first-rate, a masterpiece. Finding such *ad hoc* categories obviously would require talent and ingenuity on the order of that necessary to produce a masterpiece in the first place. But we can sketch how one might begin searching for them. (*a*) If the mediocre work suffers from some disturbingly prominent feature that distracts from whatever merits the work has, this feature might be toned down by choosing categories with respect to which it is standard, rather than variable or contra-standard. When the work is perceived in the new way the offending feature may be no more distracting than the flatness of a painting is to us. (*b*) If the work suffers from an overabundance of clichés it might be livened up by choosing categories with respect to which the clichés are variable or contra-standard rather than standard. (*c*) If it needs ingenuity we might devise a set of rules in terms of which the work finds itself in a dilemma from which it ingeniously escapes, and we might build these rules into a set of categories. Surely, however, if there are categories waiting to be discovered which would transform a mediocre work into a masterpiece, it does not follow that the work really is a hitherto unrecognized masterpiece. The fact that when perceived in such categories it would appear exciting, ingenious, and so forth rather than grating, cliché-ridden, pedestrian, does not make it so. It *cannot* be correct, I suggest, to perceive a work in categories which are totally foreign to the artist and his society, even if it comes across as a masterpiece in them.

This brings us to the historical conditions (*iii*) and (*iv*). I see no way of avoiding the conclusion that one or the other of them at least is relevant in determining in what categories a work is correctly perceived. I consider both relevant, but I will not argue here for the independent relevance of (*iv*). (*iii*) merits special attention in light of the prevalence of disputes about the importance of artists' intentions. To test the relevance of (*iii*) we must consider a case in which (*iii*) and (*iv*) diverge. One such instance occurred during the early days of the twelve-tone movement in music. Schoenberg no doubt intended even his earliest twelve-tone works to be heard as such. But this category was certainly not then well established or recognized in his society: Virtually none of his contemporaries (except close associates such as Berg and Webern), even musically sophisticated ones, would have (or could have) heard these works in that category. But it seems to me that even the very first twelve-tone compositions are correctly heard as such, that the judgments one who hears them otherwise would make of them (for example, that they are chaotic, formless) are mistaken. I think this would be so even if Schoenberg had been working entirely alone, if *none* of his contemporaries had any inkling of the twelve-tone system. No doubt the first twelve-tone compositions are much better when heard in the category of twelve-tone works than when they are heard in any other way people might be likely to hear them. But as we have seen this cannot *by itself* account for the correctness of hearing them in the former way. The only other feature of the situation which could be relevant, so far as I can see, is Schoenberg's intention . . . .

I return now to the issues raised [earlier]. If a work's aesthetic properties are those that are to be found in it when it is perceived correctly, and the correct way to perceive it is determined partly by historical facts about the artist's intention and/or his society, no examination of the work itself, however thorough, will by itself reveal those properties. If we are confronted by a work about whose origins we know absolutely nothing (for example, one lifted from the dust at an as yet unexcavated archaeological site on Mars), we would simply not be in a position to judge it aesthetically. We could not possibly tell by staring at it, no matter how intently and intelligently, whether it is coherent, or serene, or dynamic, for by staring we cannot tell whether it is to be seen as a sculpture, a guernica, or some other exotic or mundane kind of work of art. (We could attribute aesthetic properties to it in the way we do to natural objects, which of course does not involve consideration of historical facts about artists or their societies. But to do this would not be to treat the object as a *work* of art.)

The Role of Theory in Aesthetics
■ Morris Weitz ■

Is aesthetic theory, in the sense of a true definition or set of necessary and sufficient properties of art, possible? If nothing else does, the history of aesthetic itself should give one enormous pause here. For, in spite of the many theories, we seem no nearer our goal today than we were in Plato's time. Each age, each art-movement, each philosophy of art, tries over and over again to establish the stated

"The Role of Theory in Aesthetics" by Morris Weitz has been excerpted from *The Journal of Aesthetics and Art Criticism* (September 1956), pages 27–35, and is reprinted by permission of the publisher.

ideal only to be succeeded by a new or revised theory, rooted, at least in part, in the repudiation of preceding ones. Even today, almost everyone interested in aesthetic matters is still deeply wedded to the hope that the correct theory of art is forthcoming. We need only examine the numerous new books on art in which new definitions are proffered; or, in our own country especially, the basic textbooks and anthologies to recognize how strong the priority of a theory of art is.

In this essay I want to plead for the rejection of this problem. I want to show that theory—in the requisite classical sense—is *never* forthcoming in aesthetics, and that we would do much better as philosophers to supplant the question, "What is the nature of art?," by other questions, the answers to which will provide us with all the understanding of the arts there can be. I want to show that the inadequacies of the theories are not primarily occasioned by any legitimate difficulty such as the vast complexity of art, which might be corrected by further probing and research. Their basic inadequacies reside instead in a fundamental misconception of art. Aesthetic theory—all of it—is wrong in principle in thinking that a correct theory is possible because it radically misconstrues the logic of the concept of art. Its main contention that "art" is amenable to real or any kind of true definition is false. Its attempt to discover the necessary and sufficient properties of art is logically misbegotten for the very simple reason that such a set and, consequently, such a formula about it, is never forthcoming. Art, as the logic of the concept shows, has no set of necessary and sufficient properties, hence a theory of it is logically impossible and not merely factually difficult. Aesthetic theory tries to define what cannot be defined in its requisite sense. But in recommending the repudiation of aesthetic theory I shall not argue from this, as too many others have done, that its logical confusions render it meaningless or worthless. On the contrary, I wish to reassess its role and its contribution primarily in order to show that it is of the greatest importance to our understanding of the arts.

Let us now survey briefly some of the more famous extant aesthetic theories in order to see if they do incorporate correct and adequate statements about the nature of art. In each of these there is the assumption that it is the true enumeration of the defining properties of art, with the implication that previous theories have stressed wrong definitions. Thus, to begin with, consider a famous version of Formalist theory, that propounded by [Clive] Bell and [Roger] Fry. It is true that they speak mostly of painting in their writings but both assert that what they find in that art can be generalized for what is "art" in the others as well. The essence of painting, they maintain, is the plastic elements in relation. Its defining property is significant form, i.e., certain combinations of lines, colors, shapes, volumes—everything on the canvas except the representational elements—which evoke a unique response to such combinations. Painting is definable as plastic organization. The nature of art, what it *really* is, so their theory goes, is a unique combination of certain elements (the specifiable plastic ones) in their relations. Anything which is art is an instance of significant form; and anything which is not art has no such form.

To this the Emotionalist replies that the truly essential property of art has been left out. [Leo] Tolstoy, [C.J.] Ducasse, or any of the advocates of this theory, find that the requisite defining property is not significant form but rather the expression of emotion in some sensuous public medium. Without projection of emotion into some piece of stone or words or sounds, etc., there can be no art. Art is really such embodiment. It is this that uniquely characterizes art, and any true, real definition of it, contained in some adequate theory of art, must so state it.

The Intuitionist disclaims both emotion and form as defining properties. In [Benedetto] Croce's version, for example, art is identified not with some physical, public object but with a specific creative, cognitive and spiritual act. Art is really a first stage of knowledge in which certain human beings (artists) bring their images and intuitions into lyrical clarification or expression. As such, it is an awareness, non-conceptual in character, of the unique individuality of things; and since it exists below the level of conceptualization or action, it is without scientific or moral content. Croce singles out as the defining essence of art this first stage of spiritual life and advances its identification with art as a philosophically true theory or definition.

The Organicist says to all of this that art is really a class of organic wholes consisting of distinguishable, albeit inseparable, elements in their causally efficacious relations which are presented in some sensuous medium. In A. C. Bradley, in piece-meal versions of it in literary criticism, or in my own generalized adaptation of it in my *Philosophy of the Arts,* what is claimed is that anything which is a work of art is in its nature a unique complex of interrelated parts—in painting, for example, lines, colors, volumes, subjects, etc., all interacting upon one another on a paint surface of some sort. Certainly, at one time at least it seemed to me that this organic theory constituted the one true and real definition of art.

My final example is the most interesting of all, logically speaking. This is the Voluntarist theory of [DeWitt] Parker. In his writings on art, Parker persistently calls into question the traditional simple-minded definitions of aesthetics. "The assumption underlying every philosophy of art is the existence of some common nature present in all the arts." "All the so popular brief definitions of art—'significant form,' 'expression,' 'intuition,' 'objectified pleasure'—are fallacious, either because, while true of art, they are also true of much that is not art, and hence fail to differentiate art from other things; or else because they neglect some essential aspect of art." But instead of inveighing against the attempt at definition of art itself, Parker insists that what is needed is a complex definition rather than a simple one. "The definition of art must therefore be in terms of a complex of characteristics. Failure to recognize this has been the fault of all the well-known definitions." His own version of Voluntarism is the theory that art is essentially three things: embodiment of wishes and desires imaginatively satisfied, language, which characterizes the public medium of art, and harmony, which unifies the language with the layers of imaginative projections. Thus, for Parker, it is a true definition to say of art that it is " . . . the provision of satisfaction through the imagination, social

significance, and harmony. I am claiming that nothing except works of art possesses all three of these marks."

Now, all of these sample theories are inadequate in many different ways.
Each purports to be a complete statement about the defining features of all works
of art and yet each of them leaves out something which the others take to be central. Some are circular, e.g., the Bell-Fry theory of art as significant form which is
defined in part in terms of our response to significant form. Some of them, in their
search for necessary and sufficient properties, emphasize too few properties, like
(again) the Bell-Fry definition which leaves out subject-representation in painting,
or the Croce theory which omits inclusion of the very important feature of the public, physical character, say, of architecture. Others are too general and cover objects
that are not art as well as works of art. Organicism is surely such a view since it can
be applied to *any* causal unity in the natural world as well as to art. Still others rest
on dubious principles, e.g., Parker's claim that art embodies imaginative satisfactions, rather than real ones; or Croce's assertion that there is nonconceptual knowledge. Consequently, even if art has one set of necessary and sufficient properties,
none of the theories we have noted or, for that matter, no aesthetic theory yet proposed, has enumerated that set to the satisfaction of all concerned.

Then there is a different sort of difficulty. As real definitions, these theories
are supposed to be factual reports on art. If they are, may we not ask, Are they empirical and open to verification or falsification? For example, what would confirm
or disconfirm the theory that art is significant form or embodiment of emotion or
creative synthesis of images? There does not even seem to be a hint of the kind of
evidence which might be forthcoming to test these theories; and indeed one wonders if they are perhaps honorific definitions of "art," that is, proposed redefini-
tions in terms of some *chosen* conditions for applying the concept of art, and not
true or false reports on the essential properties of art at all.

But all these criticisms of traditional aesthetic theories—that they are circular,
incomplete, untestable, pseudo-factual, disguised proposals to change the meaning
of concepts—have been made before. My intention is to go beyond these to make a
much more fundamental criticism, namely, that aesthetic theory is a logically vain
attempt to define what cannot be defined, to state the necessary and sufficient properties of that which has no necessary and sufficient properties, to conceive the concept of art as closed when its very use reveals and demands its openness.

The problem with which we must begin is not "What is art?," but "What sort
of concept is 'art'?" Indeed, the root problem of philosophy itself is to explain the
relation between the employment of certain kinds of concepts and the conditions
under which they can be correctly applied. If I may paraphrase [Ludwig] Wittgenstein, we must not ask, What is the nature of any philosophical x?, or even, according
to the semanticist, What does "x" mean?, a transformation that leads to the disastrous
interpretation of "art" as a name for some specifiable class of objects; but rather,
What is the use or employment of "x"? What does "x" do in the language? This, I
take it, is the initial question, the begin-all if not the end-all of any philosophical

problem and solution. Thus, in aesthetics, our first problem is the elucidation of the actual employment of the concept of art, to give a logical description of the actual functioning of the concept, including a description of the conditions under which we correctly use it or its correlates.

My model in this type of logical description or philosophy derives from Wittgenstein. It is also he who, in his refutation of philosophical theorizing in the sense of constructing definitions of philosophical entities, has furnished contemporary aesthetics with a starting point for, any future progress. In his new work, *Philosophical Investigations,* Wittgenstein raises as an illustrative question, What is a game? The traditional philosophical, theoretical answer would be in terms of some exhaustive set of properties common to all games. To this Wittgenstein says, let us consider what we call "games": "I mean board-games, card-games, ball-games, Olympic games, and so on. What is common to them all?—Don't say: 'there *must* be something common, or they would not be called "games" 'but *look and see* whether there is anything common to all.—For if you look at them you will not see something that is common to *all,* but similarities, relationships, and a whole series of them at that . . . "

Card games are like board games in some respects but not in others. Not all games are amusing, nor is there always winning or losing or competition. Some games resemble others in some respects—that is all. What we find are no necessary and sufficient properties, only "a complicated network of similarities overlapping and crisscrossing," such that we can say of games that they form a family with family resemblances and no common trait. If one asks what a game is, we pick out sample games, describe these, and add, "This and *similar things* are called 'games'." This is all we need to say and indeed all any of us knows about games. Knowing what a game is is not knowing some real definition or theory but being able to recognize and explain games and to decide which among imaginary and new examples would or would not be called "games."

The problem of the nature of art is like that of the nature of games, at least in these respects: If we actually look and see what it is that we call "art," we will also find no common properties—only strands of similarities. Knowing what art is is not apprehending some manifest or latent essence but being able to recognize, describe, and explain those things we call "art" in virtue of these similarities.

But the basic resemblance between these concepts is their open texture. In elucidating them, certain (paradigm) cases can be given, about which there can be no question as to their being correctly described as "art" or "game," but no exhaustive set of cases can be given. I can list some cases and some conditions under which I can apply correctly the concept of art but I cannot list all of them, for the all-important reason that unforeseeable or novel conditions are always forthcoming or envisageable.

A concept is open if its conditions of application are emendable and corrigible; i.e., if a situation or case can be imagined or secured which would call for some sort of *decision* on our part to extend the use of the concept to cover this, or to close the concept and invent a new one to deal with the new case and its new property. If necessary and sufficient conditions for the application of a concept can be stated, the concept is a closed one. But this can happen only in logic or mathematics where concepts are constructed and completely defined. It cannot occur with empirically-descriptive and normative concepts unless we arbitrarily close them by stipulating the ranges of their uses . . . .

"Art," itself, is an open concept. New conditions (cases) have constantly arisen and will undoubtedly constantly arise; new art forms, new movements will emerge, which will demand decisions on the part of those interested, usually professional critics, as to whether the concept should be extended or not. Aestheticians may lay down similarity conditions but never necessary and sufficient ones for the correct application of the concept. With "art" its conditions of application can never be exhaustively enumerated since new cases can always be envisaged or created by artists, or even nature, which would call for a decision on someone's part to extend or to close the old or to invent a new concept. (E.g., "It's not a sculpture, it's a mobile.")

What I am arguing, then, is that the very expansive, adventurous character of art, its ever-present changes and novel creations, makes it logically impossible to ensure any set of defining properties. We can, of course, choose to close the concept. But to do this with "art" or "tragedy" or "portraiture," etc., is ludicrous since it forecloses on the very conditions of creativity in the arts . . . .

As we actually use the concept, "Art" is both descriptive (like "chair") and evaluative (like "good"); i.e., we sometimes say, "This is a work of art," to describe something and we sometimes say it to evaluate something. Neither use surprises anyone . . . .

The elucidation of the descriptive use of "Art" creates little difficulty. But the elucidation of the evaluative use does. For many, especially theorists, "This is a work of art" does more than describe; it also praises. Its conditions of utterance, therefore, include certain preferred properties or characteristics of art. I shall call these "criteria of evaluation." Consider a typical example of this evaluative use, the view according to which to say of something that it is a work of art is to imply that it is a *successful* harmonization of elements. Many of the honorific definitions of art and its subconcepts are of this form. What is at stake here is that "Art" is construed as an evaluative term which is either identified with its criterion or justified in terms of it. "Art" is defined in terms of its evaluative property, e.g., successful harmonization. On such a view, to say "X is a work of art" is (1) to say something which is taken *to mean* "X is a successful harmonization" (e.g., "Art *is* significant form") or (2) to say something praiseworthy *on the basis* of its successful harmonization. Theorists are never clear whether it is (1) or (2) which is being put forward. Most of them, concerned as they are with this evaluative use, formulate (2), i.e., that feature of art that *makes* it art in the praise-sense, and then go on to state (1), i.e., the definition of "Art" in terms of its art-making feature. And this is clearly to confuse the conditions under which we say something evaluatively with the meaning of what we say. "This is a work of art," said evaluatively, cannot mean "This is a successful harmonization of elements"—except by stipulation—but at most is said in virtue of the art-making property, which is taken as a (the) criterion of "Art," when "Art" is employed to assess. "This is a work of art," used evaluatively, serves to praise and not to affirm the reason why it is said.

The evaluative use of "Art," although distinct from the conditions of its use, relates in a very intimate way to these conditions. For, in every instance of "This is a work of art" (used to praise), what happens is that the criterion of evaluation (e.g., successful harmonization) for the employment of the concept of art is converted into a criterion of recognition. This is why, on its evaluative use, "This is a work of art" implies "This has P," where "P" is some chosen art-making property. Thus, if one chooses to employ "Art" evaluatively, as many do, so that "This is a work of art and not (aesthetically) good" makes no sense, he uses "Art" in such a way that he refuses to *call* anything a work of art unless it embodies his criterion of excellence.

There is nothing wrong with the evaluative use; in fact, there is good reason for using "Art" to praise. But what cannot be maintained is that theories of the evaluative use of "Art" are true and real definitions of the necessary and sufficient properties of art. Instead they are honorific definitions, pure and simple, in which "Art" has been redefined in terms of chosen criteria.

But what makes them—these honorific definitions—so supremely valuable is not their disguised linguistic recommendations; rather it is the *debates* over the reasons for changing the criteria of the concept of art which are built into the definitions. In each of the great theories of art, whether correctly understood as honorific definitions or incorrectly accepted as real definitions, what is of the utmost importance are the reasons proffered in the argument for the respective theory, that is, the reasons given for the chosen or preferred criterion of excellence and evaluation. It is this perennial debate over these criteria of evaluation which makes the history of aesthetic theory the important study it is. The value of each of the theories resides in its attempt to state and to justify certain criteria which are either neglected or distorted by previous theories. Look at the Bell-Fry theory again. Of course, "Art is significant form" cannot be accepted as a true, real definition of art; and most certainly it actually functions in their aesthetics as a redefinition of art in terms of the chosen condition of significant form. But what gives it its aesthetic importance is what lies behind the formula: In an age in which literary and representational elements have become paramount in painting, *return* to the plastic ones since these are indigenous to painting. Thus, the role of the theory is not to define anything but to use the definitional form, almost epigrammatically, to pinpoint a crucial recommendation to turn our attention once again to the plastic elements in painting.

Art as a Social Institution
▪ George Dickie ▪

In what follows it is maintained that [Morris] Weitz is wrong and that the generic sense of "art" can be defined, although it is admitted that he may be right to the extent that all or some of the subconcepts of art such as novel, tragedy, ceramics sculpture, painting, etc., may lack necessary conditions *for their application as subconcepts.* For example, there may not be any characteristics common to all tragedies which would distinguish them from comedies, satyr plays, happenings, and the like *within the domain of art,* but it may be that there are characteristics which works of art have which would distinguish them from nonart.

The first obstacle to defining art is Weitz's contention that artifactuality is not a necessary condition for art. Most people assume that there is a sharp distinction between works of art and natural objects, but Weitz has argued that the fact that we sometimes say of natural objects such as driftwood that they are works of art breaks down the distinction. In short, there appear to be works of art which are not artifacts. However, Weitz's argument is inconclusive because he fails to take account of the two senses of "work of art"—the evaluative and classificatory. . . . There is a certain irony here because Weitz makes the distinction in his article, but he does not see that it undercuts his own argument. The evaluative sense of "work of art" is used to praise an object—for example, "That driftwood is a work of art," or "That painting is a work of art." In these examples we are saying that the driftwood and the painting have qualities worthy of notice and praise. In neither case do we mean that the object referred to by the subject of the sentence is a work of art in the classificatory sense: We are speaking evaluatively about the driftwood and the painting. It would be silly to take "That painting is a work of art" as a classificatory statement; ordinarily to utter the expression "That painting" is to commit oneself to meaning that the referent of the expression is a work of art. The classificatory sense is used simply to indicate that a thing belongs to a certain category of artifacts. We rarely utter sentences in which we use the classificatory sense because it is such a basic notion. We are rarely in situations in which it is necessary to raise the question of whether or not an object is a work of art in the classificatory sense. We generally know straight away whether or not an object is a work of art. Generally, no one needs to say, by way of classification, "That is a work of art." However, recent developments in art such as junk sculpture and found art may occasionally force such remarks. For example, I was recently in a room at the Museum of Modern Art in which a work of art consisting of 144 one-foot-square metal plates was spread out

"Art as a Social Institution" by George Dickie has been excerpted from *Aesthetics,* Prentice Hall (1971), pages 98–105, and is reprinted by permission of the author.

on the floor. A man walked thorough the room and right across the work of art, apparently without seeing it. I did not, but I could have said, "Do you know that you are walking across a work of art?" The point is that the classificatory sense of "work of art" is a basic concept which structures and guides our thinking about our world. The whole point can perhaps be made clear by considering what would happen if one tried to understand the sentence "That painting is a work of art" in the classificatory sense. As indicated above, the expression "That painting" already contains the information that the object referred to is a work of art. Consequently, if the expression "That painting" is replaced in the sentence with its approximate equivalent, "That work of art which was created by putting paint on a surface such as canvas," the resulting sentence would be "That work of art which was created by putting paint on a surface such as canvas is a work of art." Thus, if one tries to understand this sentence by taking the last occurrence of "work of art" in the classificatory sense, the whole sentence turns into a tautology; that is, it is redundant. However, one would scarcely utter "That painting is a work of art" meaning to utter a tautology, that is, simply to say that a work of art in the classificatory sense is a work of art in the classificatory sense. It is clear that what would generally be meant by such a sentence about a painting is that a work of art in the classificatory sense is a work of art in the evaluative sense. A parallel analysis could be given for the sentence about the driftwood, except that if one tried to understand "That piece of driftwood is a work of art" by construing "work of art" in the classificatory sense, a contradiction would result rather than a redundancy. It is, however, easy to understand this sentence construing "work of art" in the evaluative sense.

Weitz's conclusion that *being an artifact* is not a necessary condition for being a work of art rests upon a confusion. What his argument proves is that it is not necessary for an object to be an artifact in order to be called (quite correctly) a work of art, when this expression is understood in the evaluative sense. It is, by the way, not at all surprising that the members of the class of objects which we find worthy of notice and praise do not all have a characteristic in common. Such a class would naturally be large and varied. Once we grasp the significance of the *two* senses of "work of art" and see that Weitz's argument is misleading, we are free to reflect clearly on our understanding of the classificatory sense. And surely when we do so reflect, we realize that *part* of what is meant when we think of or assert of something (not in praise) that it is a work of art is that it is an artifact. The remainder of what is meant by the classificatory sense of "work of art" is the concern of the rest of this chapter. However, before going on to that task, it is worth noting that the property of artifactuality is not an *exhibited* property, or at least usually is not. [Maurice] Mandelbaum accused Wittgenstein of neglecting nonexhibited properties and Weitz also neglects them. The point is that artifactuality, unlike such properties as color, shape, and size, is not exhibited when the artifact is observed, except in those infrequent cases in which the act of creation of the artifact is observed. Artifactuality is a relational, nonexhibited property, and perhaps this is also true of the other property or properties which distinguish art from nonart and which are involved in the definition of art.

Although he does not try to formulate a definition of art, Arthur Danto in his provocative article, "The Artworld," draws conclusions which suggest the direction such attempts at definition must take. In reflecting upon art and its history in general and such present-day developments as [Andy] Warhol's "Brillo Carton" and [Robert] Rauschenberg's "Bed" in particular, Danto writes, "To see something as art requires something the eye cannot descry—an atmosphere of artistic theory, a knowledge of history of art: an art-world." Danto seems to agree with [Maurice] Mandelbaum about the importance of nonexhibited properties (what the eye cannot descry), but he perhaps goes further than Mandelbaum by speaking provocatively, if vaguely, of atmosphere and history—of an artworld. Perhaps the substance of Danto's remark can be captured in a formal definition. The definition will first be formulated and then its implications and adequacy will be examined.

> A work of art in the classificatory sense is 1) an artifact 2) upon which some person or persons acting on behalf of a certain social institution (the artworld) has conferred the status of candidate for appreciation.

The definition speaks of conferring status and what is involved in this must be made clear. The most obvious and clear-cut examples of the conferring of status are certain actions of the state in which legal status is involved. A king's conferring of knighthood, a grand jury's indicting someone, the chairman of the election board certifying that someone is a candidate for office, or a minister pronouncing a couple man and wife are examples in which a person acting on behalf of a social institution (the state) confers *legal* status. These examples suggest that pomp and ceremony are required to establish a legal status; but this is not so. For example, in some jurisdictions common-law marriage is possible—a legal status acquired without ceremony.

The conferring of a Ph.D. degree on someone by a university, the election of someone as president of the Rotary, and the declaring of an object as a relic of the church are examples in which a person or persons confer non-legal status. As before, ceremony is not required to establish this kind of status; for example, a person can acquire without ceremony the status of wise man within a community. What the offered definition of a work of art suggests is that just as a person can be certified as a candidate for office or two persons can acquire the status of common-law marriage within a legal system and as a person can be elected president of the Rotary or a person can acquire the status of wise man within a community, an artifact can acquire the status of candidate for appreciation within the social system which Danto has called "the artworld."

Two questions arise about the *conferring* of the status of candidate for appreciation: How does one know when the status has been conferred, and how is it conferred? An artifact's hanging in an art museum as part of a show or a performance at a theater are sure signs that the status has been conferred; these are paradigm cases of knowing that the status has been conferred. There is, of course, no guarantee that one can always know whether something is a candidate for appreciation, just as one cannot always tell that a given person is a knight or is married. The second question of how the status is conferred is the more important of the two questions, however. The examples mentioned—hanging in a museum and a performance in a theater—seems to suggest that a number of persons is required for the actual conferring of the status in question. In one sense, a number of persons is required, and in another sense, only one person is required. A number of persons are required to make up the social institution of the artworld, but only one person is required to act on behalf of or as an agent of the artworld and to confer the status of candidate for appreciation. Many works of art are never seen by anyone but the persons who create them, but they are still works of art. The status in question may be acquired by *a single person's treating an artifact as a candidate for appreciation.* Of course nothing prevents a group of persons conferring the status, but it is usually conferred by a single person, the artist who creates the artifact.

It may be helpful to compare and contrast the notion of conferring the status of candidate for appreciation with a case in which something is simply presented for appreciation; this device may throw light on the notion of conferring the status of candidate. Consider the case of a salesman of plumbing supplies who spreads his wares before us. There is an important difference between "placing before" and "conferring the status of candidate," and this difference can be brought out by comparing the salesman's action with the superficially similar act of Duchamp in entering a urinal which he christened "Fountain" in that now famous art show. The difference is that Duchamp's action took place within the institutional setting of the artworld, and the plumbing salesman's action took place outside of it. The salesman could do what Duchamp did, that is, convert a urinal into a work of art, but such a thing probably would not occur to him. Please remember that calling "Fountain" a work of art does not mean that it is a good one, nor does this qualification insinuate that it is a bad one either.

It may be felt that the notion of conferring status within the artworld is excessively vague. Certainly this notion is not as clear-cut as is the conferring of status within the legal system, where procedures and lines of authority are explicitly defined and incorporated into law. The counterparts in the artworld to specified procedures and lines of authority are nowhere codified, and the artworld carries on its business at the level of customary practice. Still there *is* a practice and this defines a social institution. A social institution need not have a formally established constitution, officers, and bylaws in order to exist and have the capacity to confer status. Some social institutions are formal and some are informal. The artworld could become formalized, but most people who are interested in art would probably consider this a bad thing: Such formality would threaten the freshness and exuberance of art. Every person who sees himself as a member of the artworld is an "officer" of it and is thereby capable of conferring status in its name. One present-day artist has in the case of one of his works even gone through the motions—no doubt as a burlesque—of using a formal procedure characteristic of many legal and some nonlegal institutions. Walter de Maria's "High Energy Bar," which is a stainless-steel bar, is accompanied by a certificate which bears the name of the work and states that the bar is a work of art only when the certificate is present. This amusing example serves to suggest the significance of the act of naming works of art. An object may acquire the status of art without ever being named, but giving it a title makes clear to whomever is interested that an object is a work of art. Specific titles function in a variety of ways—for example, as aids in understanding a work or as a convenient way of identifying a work—but any title at all (even the name "Untitled") is a badge of status.

Let us now pass on to a discussion of the notion of appreciation. Notice that the definition speaks of the conferring of the status of *candidate* for appreciation. Nothing is said about actual appreciation, and this leaves open the possibility for works of art which, for whatever reason, are not appreciated. It is important not to build into the definition of the classificatory sense of "work of art" value properties such as actual appreciation: to do so would make it impossible to speak of unappreciated works of art and of bad works of art, and this is clearly undesirable. Any theory of art must preserve certain central features of the way in which we talk about art, and we do find it necessary sometimes to speak of bad art. It should also be noted that not every aspect of a work of art is included in the candidacy for appreciation. For example, the color of the back of a painting is not ordinarily an object of appreciation.

Feminism in Context
■ Peg Zeglin Brand ■

Years ago, Jerome Stolnitz provided an interesting analysis of art criticism in a text entitled *Aesthetics and Philosophy of Art Criticism: An Introduction.* Stolnitz claimed that criticism—the talk about art—can have different, often interrelated functions; sometimes criticism is used to ascertain reasons for supporting value-judgments (evaluative criticism) and sometimes it is used simply to describe, explain, or clarify a work of art (interpretive criticism). Writing in the 1950s, during the heyday of Abstract Expressionism and Abstract Formalism, Stolnitz was perhaps little aware that he was focusing on an aspect of the artistic enterprise that would become so encompassing and animated. He naively commented on the need for interpretive criticism, explaining that some works of art are difficult to understand immediately or appreciate fully without recourse to the enlightening words of the critic. This was said at a time when John Cage, Robert Rauschenberg, and the Minimalists were just beginning to gain and hold attention. He could hardly

---

"Feminism in Context" by Peg Zeglin Brand has been excerpted from *Contemporary Philosophy of Art: Readings in Analytic Aesthetics,* Prentice-Hall (1993), pages 106–113, 119, and is reprinted by permission of the publisher.

have predicted the role such criticism would play in the various arenas of literary criticism, art criticism, and aesthetics. Interpretive criticism, in the wake of New Criticism and formalist criticism, came to have a life of its own.

Stolnitz would hardly have approved of contemporary critics' emphasis on theory. He believed that one perceived a work aesthetically (grasping only what is immediately given *in* the work) while maintaining an aesthetic attitude: gratefully and submissively accepting and enjoying the work of art "for its own sake," "no questions asked," without challenge or criticism. Such is the substance of an aesthetic experience. Such experiences give rise to appreciation and aesthetic evaluation, embodied in statements like, "This is a good work of art," or "This work is uglier than that work of art." Only when a viewer has given up the aesthetic attitude to adopt a critical attitude does the work become something to be "probed, analyzed, and wrangled over": activities which give rise to the talk about art (i.e., art criticism). As stated earlier, one of the functions of criticism is to provide reasons that support aesthetic value judgments. The interesting aspect to be investigated (for our purposes) is the *interaction* of these two types of activities: aesthetic valuing and the criticism used as reasons for those values. Stolnitz seems to be speaking inconsistently, at times, when he simultaneously holds that criticism can enhance the appreciation of a work of art and criticism is irrelevant to the appreciation of a work of art. Let us review his ideas in order to become clear on this apparent inconsistency.

Stolnitz insists on two requirements for criticism, namely, that it illuminate (via interpretation) our understanding of the work of art and that it provide workable criteria of evaluation. Within the two basic types of criticism differentiated by *function* (interpretive and evaluative), several kinds of criticism are differentiated by means of their emphases on various aspects of the work. For example, some criticism might emphasize the origins of the work (what he calls contextual criticism and a subspecies, intentionalist criticism), some might emphasize the effects of the work (impressionist criticism), and some might emphasize the intrinsic structure of the work (New Criticism).

Among the several kinds of criticism analyzed by Stolnitz, one kind expanded on at length is collectively called contextual criticism. Included among the general category of contextual criticism are Marxian and Freudian criticism, which stress the origins and effects of the work: its social, historical, and psychological contexts. Contextual criticism, it should be noted at the outset, though praised as *sometimes* extremely helpful in providing interpretive criticism, is also highly suspect: "It should not be permitted to swamp or distort aesthetic evaluation." Stolnitz believes that contextual criticism can provide relevant and informative contextual-factual data with regard to subject matter and content but fails in attending to the purely artistic elements (aesthetic data) of form and medium.

Contextual criticism also fails to provide workable criteria of evaluation. Stolnitz takes issue with contextualist critics for failing to stop at the appropriate boundary (i.e., with the task of interpretation) and for presuming to be qualified to move from the activity of interpreting to the activity of evaluating. Here they commit the fallacy of transforming the concepts used to *describe* the work into concepts used to *judge* the work. In Stolnitz's words, "factual-contextual concepts are converted into criteria of evaluation." As a result, Stolnitz holds these judgments to be *moral* and not aesthetic; thus they are useless in assessing the work aesthetically. Contextual criticism only sometimes fulfills Stolnitz's first requirement (that of illuminating our understanding of the work of art) and completely fails to fulfill the second (that of providing workable criteria of evaluation).

Here we come upon the resolution to the apparent inconsistency of Stolnitz's views on the role of critical evaluation: Stolnitz is really claiming that only *some* forms of criticism enhance aesthetic appreciation. Some interpretive criticism can provide knowledge that enables us to see more in a work of art, thereby enhancing one's aesthetic experience, and some can provide knowledge that causes us to devaluate a work. Similarly, some evaluative criticism can sometimes enhance appreciation and, alternatively, some evaluative criticism distorts or obliterates aesthetic evaluation. One type of evaluative criticism that distorts or obliterates aesthetic evaluation is contextual criticism. Thus Stolnitz is arguing that only certain kinds of criticism are acceptable as evaluative criticism—namely, only noncontextual criticism. Stolnitz's argument can be reconstructed as follows:

1. Aesthetic judgments utilize knowledge of internal data.
2. Moral judgments utilize knowledge of external data.
3. Either aesthetic judgments or moral judgments determine aesthetic value.
4. Moral judgments determine only moral value (i.e., they are irrelevant for determining aesthetic value).
5. Therefore, only aesthetic judgments determine aesthetic value.

Premises (1) and (2) list two types of value judgments, each of which requires support from evaluative criticism. They are distinguished by the type of data utilized by the person making the judgment and the function they serve. Stolnitz stipulates in (1) that only knowledge about the intrinsic, noncontextual aspects of the work is used in making an aesthetic judgment. The use of any other type of data (i.e., contextual-factual data that are external to the work of art "on its own" and "for its own sake") is external or extrinsic to the work. He writes,

> The "context" of the work of art includes the circumstances in which the work originated, its effects upon society, and, in general, all of the relations and interactions of the work with other things, apart from its aesthetic life . . . the work considered nonaesthetically, exists in a context.

Contextual criticism (e.g., Freudian criticism) focuses on extrinsic, external factors—"all the elements which point beyond the work to 'life' "—and *excludes* the intrinsic, internal, purely aesthetic considerations. These aesthetic considerations are seen to be the major constuent of the aesthetic object (i.e., they are what give rise to the aesthetic experience and are not to be glossed over, belittled, or ignored by the limited concerns of contextual criticism). Though often providing relevant and necessary factual information, contextual theories help us to understand and appreciate more fully only part of the aesthetic object. The "aesthetic life" of the work of art, on the other hand, is necessarily approached through aesthetic perception: "Aesthetic perception focuses upon the work itself, taken in isolation." Similarly, the aesthetic attitude gives no thought to causes and consequences outside the object; in an aesthetic experience, the intrinsic aspects of the aesthetic object are experienced and appreciated "in isolation"—without recourse to any external considerations—in a vacuum devoid of any contextual air. Another traditionalist, Monroe C. Beardsley, contrasts the isolationist's approach to the contextualist's as follows:

> Isolationism is the view that in order to appreciate a work of art, we need do nothing but look at it, hear it, or read it—sometimes again and again, with the most concentrated attention—and that we need not go outside it to consult the facts of history, biography, or anything else.
>
> Contextualism holds that a work of art should be apprehended in its total context or setting, and that much historical and other knowledge "feeds into" the work of art, making the total experience of it richer than if it were approached without such knowledge.

Beardsley, like Stolnitz, believes that moral judgments are judgments about the "side effects" of a work of art; they are not about a work's "immediate effect" (i.e., the aesthetic experience).

Premise (3) reflects Stolnitz's and Beardsley's traditional view that only one type of judgment is relevant to a work of art's aesthetic value. In other words, one *can* appreciate a work of art fully enough without recourse to any contextual data. Certain contextual data yield moral judgments which are totally irrelevant to the determination or justification of aesthetic value.

Premise (4) embodies the traditional isolationist's reason for excluding moral judgments from the realm of aesthetic valuing: They are judgments that determine so-called moral value only. A basic underlying assumption is that moral value and aesthetic value are totally separate types of value that a work might possess and that traditional aesthetics is concerned primarily with aesthetic value: moral value is a distraction that a conscientious art viewer and theorist can best do without.

The conclusion (5), which states that only aesthetic judgments determine aesthetic value, follows from (3) and (4); it implies by means of (2) that knowledge of external data is not utilized in determining aesthetic value. It is this claim, namely, the conclusion (5), that I wish to argue against. Feminist theory will be the primary contextual theory I will use to argue against (5), but first I would like to point out a weakness in the isolationist's argument, one that I think was anticipated by Stolnitz and Beardsley both. It resides in premise (4)—in the isolationists' claim that moral judgments are irrelevant for determining aesthetic value.

At one point in arguing for (4), Beardsley presents Aestheticism and Moralism as views that point up the dichotomy of the moral and aesthetic aspects of art. Interestingly, he rejects Aestheticism as a fanatical reaction of "those, who, in their eagerness to exalt the arts, forget that they are after all human products of human activities, and must find their value in the whole context of human life." He does not go on to explain the phrase "the whole context of human life." One is left guessing as to precisely what context of human life might be relevant to establishing value, as Beardsley proceeds to reject Moralism as well as Aestheticism.

Moralism is a point of view in which aesthetic objects are judged "solely, or chiefly, with respect to moral standards." Moralists utilize two forms of argument by which they judge works. The first is the Argument from Reduction in which all critical evaluation is reduced to moral evaluation:

> And so the whole, apparently aesthetic, question whether a particular aesthetic object is a good one or not is reduced to the (moral) question whether the feelings it arouses are good or bad.

This argument is rejected because it fails to assess the separate and independent aesthetic value of a work. The second, less severe, form of argument is the Argument from Correlation by which Moralists grant the existence of a separate form of aesthetic value but make it dependent upon or correlated to moral value. In this view, a work of low moral value is necessarily a work of low aesthetic value. Beardsley is quick to reject this approach with regard to music and nonrepresentational visual art but seems less sure for cases of representational visual art, literature, and film. He cites pornography as an example of visual art that is low in both moral value and aesthetic value. He sees neither a *causal* nor a *necessary* connection between moral value and aesthetic value but admits to some "commonsense evidence to support here, in a rough way, the Argument from Correlation."

Beardsley's failure to dismiss the Argument from Correlation implies a weakness in premise (4). If there is a possibility that the Argument from Correlation is at all plausible and that there is a possibility that contextual factors that determine so-called moral value are relevant in assessing the aesthetic value of a work of art, then the repercussion for traditional theories of aesthetic value is obvious: It is false to claim that aesthetic value is determined solely by internal/intrinsic factors by means of contemplation of the work in isolation.

Stolnitz wavers in his support of premise (4) as well. In discussing an example of a moral judgment of Marxist criticism, he claims that the moral evaluation (that the work is poor due to its failure to inspire social revolt) "also has an aesthetic side to it":

> Like some non-Marxist-critics, the Marxists contend that many of [Henrik] Ibsen's symbols are vague and unintelligible. This is a weakness in the aesthetic effectiveness of his plays. If this criticism can be shown to be sound, and if it is supported by the evidence of aesthetic experience, then it is, of course, aesthetically relevant. Again, however, the Marxist does not speak of "purely" aesthetic matters. He holds that Ibsen's symbolism illustrates the artist's "blurred and indefinite" social thinking.

Stolnitz seems to be saying that the value judgment, "Ibsen's symbols are vague and unintelligible," is a value judgment which is based on legitimate internal data for the non-Marxist that becomes a *moral* value judgment when the Marxist extends the data utilized to noninternal, contextual data. Citing the mental state of the author as a reason for the evaluation automatically turns an aesthetic judgment into a moral judgment. But what can Stolnitz mean when he says that this moral judgment "also has an aesthetic side to it"? Could it possibly mean that moral judgments are not so strictly distinguishable from aesthetic judgments? If they are not, this weakens premise (4) in that the possibility is left open for a so-called moral judgment to determine aesthetic value as well as moral value . . . .

Feminists writing about the arts claim that although barely three decades have elapsed, we are well beyond the first phase of feminist theorizing about the arts. This first phase, labelled "the feminist critique" by Elaine Showalter sought to recapture the past by exposing numerous denigrating steretypes of women in works by males, whether works of the visual arts or the literary arts. Another aspect of recapturing the past, what Showalter called "gynocritics," involved (re)discovering female authors and artists previously excluded from the canon and seeking the commonalities of female culture in various artistic modes of expression. In this process of discovery, feminist theorists began to seriously question the dominating ideology of the past which both erected and sustained what feminists regarded as an exclusively male canon (the "Great Masters"). In the process of deconstructing the foundations and myths of this canon, many disciplines, including art history, literature, and philosophy, came under fire. Feminists demanded to know how purportedly universal and objective criteria of aesthetic value could yield such a biased, subjective set of paradigms. Hence the present phase, marked by an obsessive interest in metacriticism and metatheory in which feminists attempt to construct an unprecedented alternative to the dominating male criteria of interpreting and evaluating art. It is nothing less than fitting that aestheticians pay some attention to these challenges to traditional modes of evaluating art, for when feminists dismantle the canon by rejecting what we've come to know as the greatest *master*pieces of all time, the entire notion of aesthetic value is at stake.

What is feminist theory? The answer is not always forthcoming from a feminist theorist since many hold that feminist theory, in virtue of being feminist and consciously attempting to avoid the mistakes of its phallocentric predecessors who thought defining a worthwhile and beneficial activity, is untheorizable. In spite of this push for open-endedness, feminists do fall into the old habit of characterizing—sometimes in intimate and laborious detail—the parameters and goals of a framework for interpreting and judging works of art in a new and unique way.

It might be helpful to piece together a characterization of feminist theory by first looking at the guiding principles of a feminist, in general. There is perhaps less hesitation to generalize what constitutes a feminist today in spite of the many factions that exist than there is in characterizing feminist theory; in 1980, Janet Racliffe Richards proposed the following principles:

> Feminists are, at the very least, supposed to have committed themselves to such things as participation in consciousness-raising groups and nonhierarchical organization, . . . the inherent equality of the sexes (or the superiority of the female) and the enslavement of women as the root of all oppression.

In other words, a feminist consciously strives to undo the wrongs of previous oppression as well as to prevent similar occurrences from happening in the future. Most feminists believe in *active* promotion of these principles and also believe that works of art can be an expressive and effective means of actively communicating such principles. Along the lines suggested by one philosopher, this would make feminist theory (which is based on these principles) *more* than just a theory—a theory is a system of belief or world view shared by its adherents—but once theory goes beyond advancing a world view to *prescribing* a way of life or certain actions, theory becomes ideology. Feminist theory, like Marxist theory or Christianity, is not merely descriptive but also directive. As Lucy Lippard, feminist art critic and theorist, writes, "Feminism is an ideology, a value system, a revolutionary strategy, a way of life."

Without reservation, some art created by women for other women or for men who need to learn the feminists' message about women, has been labelled "propaganda." The term *propaganda* may ordinarily carry a negative connotation but it is defined rather neutrally as the propagation of ideas, doctrines, or practices. Women's art (art created by women) differs from feminist art (art self-consciously created or interpreted along the lines of a feminist ideology), but both can be means of disseminating feminist propaganda by means of typical artistic media.

Feminist theory in its descriptive form, is similar to any other kind of theory; it is a world view or system of beliefs consisting of a formulation of apparent relationships or underlying principles of certain observed phenomena which has been confirmed to some degree. In its prescriptive form, it is not confirmable; ideologies are either practiced or not.

Basically, all works of art are subject to the dictum, "The personal is the political" (i.e., there is no nonpolitical, unbiased perspective). Beardsley might say (as he has said of Marxist principles of interpretation and evaluation) that feminists adhere to the Principle of Nonneutrality:

> The Marxist . . . judges all behavior with repect to a single goal, the advancement of the revolutionary proletariat toward a classless society . . . considerations of aesthetic value are to be subordinated to political ones, for—and this is the basic Marxist principle— aesthetic objects cannot be politically neutral.

For feminists, the single goal might be the advancement of the revolutionary feminist toward a nonsexist, egalitarian, nonhierarchical society. Compare Beardsley's summary of the Marxists' adherence to the Principle of Nonneutrality to a suggestion by feminist theorist Gisela Ecker:

> . . . feminist aesthetic theory must insist that all investigations into art have to be *thoroughly genderised*. . . . A truly genderised perspective would mean that the sex— male *or* female—of both the artist and the critic is taken into account. This also implies their relation to gender-values in the institutions and within the theories they apply.

This, in light of the picture sketched of contextual theories earlier in this paper, is surely a contextual approach grounded in the belief that no work of art is appropriately assessed without paying attention to issues of gender. I will assume that the question of whether feminist *interpretive* criticism is an aesthetically relevant source of information is moot for both Stolnitz and Beardsley, since both have already acknowledged an acceptance of other types of contextual criticism provided it meets their requirements. It is to the unresolved question of utilizing knowledge of contextual-factual data with regard to resultant *evaluative* criticism that we must now address ourselves.

Let us return to the argument presented earlier in order to pursue the task of arguing against the conclusion (5) by means of feminist theory. It is the belief of feminist art theorists that the concept of an isolationist approach to a work of art is not only ludicrous but more importantly, pernicious. Given the feminist approach to a work of art, grounded in what Beardsley calls the Principle of Non-neutrality, women see it as conceptually impossible for a work of art *ever* to be "objectively" created, interpreted, or evaluated. All aesthetic objects are " 'marked' by gender." Consider one summary of this view, as expressed by Janet Wolff in a text entitled, *The Social Production of Art:*

> . . . the ideas, beliefs, attitudes and values expressed in cultural products are ideological, in the sense that they are always related in a systematic way to the social and economic structures in which the artist is situated . . . Ideas and beliefs which are proposed as value-free or non-partisan are merely those ideas which have assumed the guise of universality, perceiving as natural social facts and relations which are in fact historically specific. To this extent, then, art as a product of consciousness is also permeated with ideology, although it is not reducible to ideology.

If all art is permeated with ideology and marked by gender, then there is no possible way to make aesthetic judgments that do not take contextual data, like ideology and gender, into account. . . .

It is appropriate at this point to ask the following two questions: (1) Is what the isolationist claims true, namely, that someone can experience a work of art fully if he or she experiences it solely for its own sake? and (2) If the answer to (1) is yes, how does one separate internal data from external data in order to ignore external data and experience an artwork solely for its own sake? The resolution of the isolationist-contextualist debate lies in the answer to these two questions, particularly the latter. But determining precisely which qualities or properties of an aesthetic object are internal and external and, hence, are relevant or irrelevant to aesthetic evaluation is hardly unproblematic in light of recent challenges to the very notions of aesthetic attitude, aesthetic experience, aesthetic quality, and aesthetic value . . . . Knowledge of external, contextual data is necessarily required to assess a work of art that has been deemed a work of art by means of external, contextual data. . . . Feminist theory is one type of contextual theory available.

In arguing that knowledge of external, contextual data (like that stressed by feminist theory) is relevant to the aesthetic value of a work of art, I have hoped to accomplish two things: to make feminists and philosophers aware of the commonalities of their views and to point out that more work needs to be done in both camps. . . . I am suggesting that gender is one aspect of contextual theories that needs to be investigated. With such changes afoot, feminist theory will take its rightful place as an essential part of aesthetic inquiry.

A Different Plea for Disinterest
■ Theodore Gracyk ■

When I was a college undergraduate, my art and literature teachers insisted on a distinction between intrinsic and extrinsic features of works of art and other cultural artifacts. Whether we were reading Shakespeare's *As You Like It* or viewing a Renaissance fresco or listening to Bach's *Brandenburg Concertos,* we were taught to ignore extrinsic factors and to focus on the work's objective features. Extrinsic factors included biographical facts about the artist, such as Bach's religious affiliation or Beethoven's political sympathies. Anything we needed to understand about the work was to be derived from our interaction with the work itself. Often called *autonomism,* this position teaches that audiences should employ disinterested attention (DA for short) when engaged with art. Disinterest does not imply a lack of interest, but rather interest that is independent of the preferences and prejudices of everyday life. In the well-known words of Clive Bell's *Art* (1914), "to appreciate a work of art we need bring with us nothing from life, no knowledge of its ideas and affairs, no familiarity with its emotions." Autonomism is generally aligned with aesthetic formalism, as in Bell's claim that nothing but a sense of form is needed to appreciate art.

Today, autonomism is as unfashionable as a seersucker suit. We are now urged to consider each work as a reflection of the circumstances of its creation, as a token of a specific time, place, and ideology. Canonical art is scrutinized for previously overlooked meanings. Setting aside debates about specific interpretations, this emphasis on the centrality of meaning is often called *contextualism.* Most contextualists say that audience response is always already governed by interested attention (IA for short), so autonomism is at best an impossible ideal and at worst a dangerously naïve simplification of what really matters about art. Autonomists respond that IA contaminates the art experience. Responses that are limited by our preexisting attitudes are simply subjective. Worse, art cannot challenge or expand us in any way. Furthermore, if we do not interpret artworks as statements by human agents, most seem noticeably inferior to natural beauty and sublimity as objects for aesthetic interest.

"A Different Plea for Disinterest" is published by permission of the author.

We must endorse some kind of contextualism if we are to regard the formal structures of instrumental music and abstract paintings as statements by artists (as opposed to regarding them simply as aesthetically interesting formal structures). If we do not interpret them as statements by artists speaking from specific historical and cultural contexts, it is difficult to see which of their features will reward IA. However, interpreting artistic designs in the light of their originating contexts generally rewards IA. For instance, there is a prominent melody in the last movement of Dmitri Shostakovich's first Violin Concerto (1947). From the position of DA, we do not ask whether Shostakovich *meant* anything in writing that melody. From the position of IA, we will look for the significance of the fact that Shostakovich is quoting a melody used in his opera *The Lady Macbeth of the Mtsensk District* (1936), a work that offended Joseph Stalin and thus threatened to end Shostakovich's career as a composer. Furthermore, we might ask why the melody imitates Russian "gypsy" music, which at that time and place was regarded as a type of "Jewish" music. By inserting this melody into his concerto, Shostakovich seems to be suggesting a parallel between his own experiences in 1936 and the fate of Russian Jews at a time when the Soviet Union was engaged in a campaign of anti-Semitism. Grasping the anti-Stalinist message of the music requires seeing this double context (the earlier opera and its "Jewish" character). Facts about the music's composer and his times provide a context for understanding this work of instrumental music as a criticism of political oppression, permitting the music to reward IA.

Although my outlines of autonomism and contextualism are brief and therefore simplified, the purpose of this essay is to suggest that audiences can reap unexpected benefits by approaching works disinterestedly. One obstacle to recognizing these benefits is that advocates and critics of disinterest have both assumed that DA and IA are mutually exclusive attitudes. It is assumed that successful interaction with DA does not affect interaction with IA, and vice versa. I am interested in cases where DA supports IA by creating an interest that would not arise if the audience starts out with IA.

I propose that DA can encourage interest in subject matter that challenges our existing interests. DA can get us to relax our inhibitions against ideas that clash with our predispositions. DA generates approval for art that confronts our current sense of identity. DA fosters sympathetic engagement with subject matter associated with an unattractive or threatening identity. In this way I offer a very limited defense of the utility of the autonomy of the aesthetic. Some subject matter may limit our capacity to employ disinterest, but disinterest can be the first step in a potentially liberating experience.

I will make my case for DA by focusing on everyday interactions with popular music. Popular music is routinely used to signify and reinforce social differences. Young males generally avoid music categorized as "women's music." The working poor generally prefer hip-hop to jazz. Women's clothing stores generally play background music, but they seldom play either Beethoven or the Sex Pistols. Yet the ubiquity of popular music (in stores, in restaurants, in movies, in bars, in our friends' cars) frequently brings us music that we would never voluntarily hear.

Because it is almost everywhere, popular music frequently comes to us in a thoroughly decontextualized or recontextualized manner, lending that music a degree of autonomy from its creative origins. Moments of disinterested listening can create an interest in, *and an empathy with,* points of view that we would quickly repress when operating with an interested, contextualist response.

I have three additional reasons why popular music is a good test case when discussing disinterest. First, my central point is most readily illustrated with music, but most people are more familiar with popular music than with "art" music. So I will focus on popular music. Besides, a text's status as a work of art is incidental to what's at issue here.

Second, most theories of popular culture deny that popular art rewards DA. Their model assumes that all interpretation is governed by a desire to find characters with whom the audience identifies. In *Understanding Popular Culture,* John Fiske argues that popular "reading" is "selective and spasmodic" as each audience member searches for "the relevance of the text" to her everyday situation. Treating DA and IA as mutually exclusive attitudes, Fiske and other theorists reason that because DA is the proper response to high culture, IA is the proper response to popular culture. Popular art and music do not offer aesthetic pleasure. Pleasure depends on discovering some confirmation of an existing sense of self or community.

But this position cannot explain how or why we ever tolerate books or movies or music that challenges our current identity and social interests. Consider Laura Mulvey's influential thesis that women do not take pleasure in the male voyeurism at the heart of so many Alfred Hitchcock films (e.g., *Psycho* and *Rear Window*). Women do not ordinarily identify with the male gaze that dominates these and other Hollywood movies. Women enjoy them by unconsciously identifying with the misogynist male perspective or by embracing the masculine demand for female masochism. But whether we examine Mulvey's thesis or some variant, it seems wrongheaded to defend the view that there is no pleasure except through some mechanism of personal identification. We get a different story if we consider popular music, where musical pleasure often comes *before* listeners recognize the identity they are invited to identify with.

A third reason to consider popular music is to avoid the opposite tendency, dismissing IA as irrelevant to music. This view arises when we assume that instrumental "classical" music is the paradigm of musical experience. The value of a symphony or piano sonata is divorced from its function as an occasion for dancing and even from its capacity to evoke an emotional response in the audience. This encourages a musical purism that sees disinterested listening as the paradigm of music reception, with listeners concentrating on the music's formal, compositional, and aesthetic properties. The identity, politics, and standpoint of the music's writers and performers are also dismissed as extrinsic to the music. Non-musical interests are to be set aside as irrelevant to appreciation of the music. Unfortunately, the result is that many people avoid such music as difficult and uninviting.

In contrast, interested attention is directed at subject matter, at something that the work is *about.* Peg Zeglin Brand describes IA as interest grounded in personal identification with the artist or with persons portrayed in a work. But this description is too narrow. When my daughter was in kindergarten, she really liked the cowboy song "Old Paint." Old Paint is the cowboy's horse and my daughter loved horses. While this seems to be a case of IA if anything is, I don't think that she *identified* with the horse. Her response was a case of IA because it arose from a predisposition about the song's subject matter. By extension, IA is also at work whenever unpleasant subjects repulse audiences. IA is at work when viewers turn away from Francisco Goya's brutal images of war. Sexual content also spurs IA, because responses to sexual content usually reflect sexualized predispositions. IA explains attempts to censor Robert Mapplethorpe's photographs displaying homosexual sadomasochism, and it explains arousal or embarrassment at the frank presentation of Edouard Manet's *Olympia,* a painting of a naked courtesan. I will soon return to this point by using sexual orientation as a test case in one of my examples.

To summarize, we have identified three positions about DA and IA.

1. Only IA is legitimate. This contextualism treats every work as having some subject matter, however obscure. DA is a myth fostered by high culture to deny that art represents the interests of the privileged.

2. DA and IA are genuine but mutually incompatible approaches. No text is designed to yield pleasure under both approaches. Texts inviting DA are works of art. (Clive Bell endorses this position.) Texts inviting IA belong to popular culture.

3. DA and IA are genuine but mutually incompatible approaches, yet many texts invite both attitudes. Although DA and IA will involve audience focus on different elements of the text, we should employ both modes of attention when dealing with complex texts, such as works of art. (Peg Brand endorses a version that urges audiences to use both DA and IA, learning to "toggle" back and forth between the two attitudes.)

The pleasure offered by some instrumental music and by abstract painting convinces me that the first of these options is mistaken. Defenders of that option must provide an account of how to discover the hidden content of nonrepresentational works, but when it comes down to the details of the process, I do not find any of these accounts to be persuasive. The other two options share a different problem. Options two and three assume that DA and IA are completely independent of one another. Even the third option's concession (that DA and IA might apply to the same text) postulates a fragmented experience. Why should we bother to employ DA and IA with the same text? Elements rewarding DA seem unrelated to elements rewarding IA.

I propose that we endorse a fourth option, *instrumental autonomism,* in which the two attitudes are not treated as mutually exclusive. DA and IA can reinforce one another and they can interfere with one another. It is obvious how IA can interfere with DA, so that preexisting interests interfere with appreciation of both art and popular culture. But DA can also encourage IA. (Hence the name "instrumental autonomism," capturing the idea that autonomism can be valuable as means to something else.) This means/end relationship is too often ignored in the debate about disinterest. But consider the following examples.

I'll begin with two cases of songs featured in television commercials. Advertisements employ catchy music in order to engage our immediate interest, reducing channel switching during commercials. I recently saw a commercial for blue jeans that opened with the image of an American flag, followed by visuals of teens in jeans accompanied by a pounding drumbeat and driving guitars. At the very end of the commercial, a weathered voice sang these lines: "Some folks are born, made to wave the flag, Ooh, they're red, white, and blue." End of commercial. Was I supposed to think that I'm a patriot if I buy these jeans? A second commercial shows an expensive Jaguar car driving in American localities that dissolve into London landmarks. These scenes are set to a military rhythm and slashing guitar chords. A raspy voice barks out, "London calling" several times, then offers, "yes I was there too/And you know what they said—Well some of it was true."

These commercials do not presuppose an interest in these jeans or this car. They attempt to create an interest through their repeated association with music and images. But what interest arises from the songs? We cannot explain their function if we assume that IA requires an existing interest in subject matter. With extremely brief snatches of lyrics, too little information comes to the listener to secure IA. In fact, the jeans commercial delays the lyrics. It grabs us with music of rising tension, with a feeling of building emotion that climaxes with the lyrics at the commercial's finale. The car commercial splices the music so that we repeatedly hear the song's hook (the catchiest, most memorable moment). Either way, the *music* is what grabs our attention, attention that we will get us to notice the visuals and the commercial message. But neither case gives us enough of the song to provide any determinate meaning for it, so IA cannot explain how the songs succeed in hooking us into the commercials. Empirical research demonstrates that virtually everyone likes or dislikes a particular song for its music before understanding the lyrics. Most popular music has lyrics, yet the *music* is designed to reward listening through DA, that is, apart from our grasp of the song's subject matter.

Now consider a slightly more complicated example from the 1992 movie *Wayne's World*. One of its highlights is placed about four minutes into the movie, as Wayne Campbell (Mike Myers) and several friends pack themselves into a small car in order to cruise the streets of Aurora, Illinois. Wayne chooses music for their drive: "I think we'll go with a little 'Bohemian Rhapsody,' gentlemen." The tape begins in the middle of the song, well past the lyrics that provide the song's narrative. They stop to pick up another friend, cramming him into the back seat, and the song resumes. All five gleefully sing along to the lyric, "Beelzebub has a devil put aside for me!" An instrumental passage suddenly unfolds. Dominated by a powerful guitar riff, a wave of music bucks and weaves like a wild stallion. With perfect synchronization, the five friends thrash their heads up and down to the music in euphoric delight. Then the car stops so that Wayne can admire a Fender Stratocaster guitar in a music store window. Back in the car, the song resumes at the coda. A mournful guitar line accompanies the closing lyric, "nothing really matters to me." But we know that this line does not express Wayne's feelings, because it has just been undercut by his longing for a new electric guitar.

If you have seen *Wayne's World,* you will certainly remember the image of the boys rocking their heads to the music. It is the film's one great merger of music and visual image. Like the jeans and car advertisements, this sequence is constructed to create a sense of identification—not with a product, but with Wayne and his sidekick, Garth (Dana Carvey). Up to this point, Wayne and Garth are objects of humor. But because almost everyone who likes popular music will like this music, their unbridled enthusiasm for the instrument passage of "Bohemian Rhapsody" creates empathy for Wayne and Garth. They may be losers, but the rightness of their response shows that they know what's good.

What interests me about this prominent use of Brian May's guitar is that their (and our) delight is independent of our understanding of the song. As with the two commercials, we get only fragments of the song, and from those fragments we cannot tell what the song is actually about. But if its meaning and subject matter are unclear, then preexisting interests cannot explain its attraction. At the same time, the music draws us into a situation, so that our pleasure in the musical design transfers to whatever is associated with that music. In general, aesthetic rewards can create a powerful approval of a text in advance of actually understanding it.

Exposure of popular music in movies and advertisements routinely stimulates interest in that music, stimulating sales. The use of Nick Drake's song "Pink Moon" in a 2000 Volkswagen commercial resulted in more sales in a few months than Drake's three albums had sold in the previous twenty-five years. Thanks to "Bohemian Rhapsody," the soundtrack for *Wayne's World* was a major hit. Similar results may follow for the two songs I described earlier, Creedence Clearwater Revival's "Fortunate Son" and the Clash's "London Calling." (The Clash's biggest hit, "Should I Stay or Should I Go?" resulted from its use in a jeans commercial.) In all three cases, new fans who purchase the songs and listen to them may discover that the object of their pleasure presents challenging and controversial subject matter. "Fortunate Son" (1969) is an angry, first-person, working-class attack on America's draft policy in the Vietnam era. "London Calling" (1979) is a punk anthem. A first person account of London in the wake of nuclear catastrophe and global warming, it criticizes Western military and ecological policies. But new audiences will not discover these themes until after they've embraced the music. As the songwriters no doubt intended, seductive music may translate into receptivity to a song's subject matter. Without the seduction of the music, IA would limit their message to those already disposed to agree, a phenomenon known as preaching to the choir.

In *Wayne's World,* "Bohemian Rhapsody" is heavily edited. Listeners who buy the soundtrack or the collection *Classic Queen* will discover that it is a campy pastiche of styles. As for subject matter, its nihilistic narrator kills a man for no reason and then resigns himself to execution and subsequent damnation. Its over-the-top chorale passage mocks opera and includes a smattering of different languages. It seems to mock everything, including its own nihilism; its chief appeal is not subject matter but its own musical delight. Listeners respond to what Roland Barthes calls *signifiance,* to the text's sheer *intentionality* more than to the artist's intentions. But if listeners do search for the intentions behind "Bohemian Rhapsody," interest will fall on Freddie Mercury, the song's writer, arranger, and vocalist. If the song expresses Mercury's vision, it seems to signify Mercury's refusal to apologize for his own "crime" of bisexuality. (Mercury died from AIDs between the filming of *Wayne's World* and the film's release.) Wayne and Garth might be surprised to find that their cruising ritual centers on an anthem of gay pride. The millions of sports fans who regularly chant Queen's "We Will Rock You" and "We Are the Champions" might be equally surprised about the pleasure they derive from a gay author. My proposal is that when we already take great pleasure in such texts, we are more tolerant of the subject matter if it turns out to be something that IA would reject as an affront to our current sense of identity. (The flip side is the danger that we will also endorse ideas and behaviors that may have a harmful effect, a danger that led Plato to advocate censorship of poetry and music in Books II and X of *The Republic*.)

We might call this the "spoonful-of-sugar-helps-the-medicine-go-down" defense of disinterest. Unless we have an overriding prejudice against political art, we can see that these songs (including the edited versions that disguise their content) are valuable for getting audiences to expose themselves to messages that they would otherwise avoid. DA secures attention to subject matter, but in a way that integrates DA with IA. As Kendall Walton notes in his theory of representational art, music's representational capacities are weak and ambiguous compared with literature, painting, and other art forms. The meaning of a musical design must be clarified by a text. Yet the text's subject matter is not simply an *addition* to the music. Lyrics inform the experience of the music, so the tension created by the interplay of drums and guitar in "Fortunate Son" is transformed into an expression of mounting frustration. "Bohemian Rhapsody" combines outrageous vocalizing with muscular guitars to suggest that masculinity and homosexuality are not incompatible. In each case, musical construction turns out to be part of the message. Popular music is certainly not the only field where aesthetic properties and subject matter interact, and instrumental autonomism extends to many art forms.

Are Art Museums Racist?

■ Maurice Berger ■

Walking through a group exhibition installed last fall at the New Museum of Contemporary Art in New York, I heard the distinctive, albeit muffled, voice of the late Malcolm X. The sounds emanated from a multi-medium installation by the African-American artist David Hammons. The installation itself, titled *A Fan* (1989), was

"Are Art Museums Racist?" by Maurice Berger has been excerpted from *Art in America,* Brant Publications (September 1990), pages 69–72, and is reprinted by permission of the publisher.

almost surreal in its juxtapositions: A funeral bouquet, its flowers dried and decayed, stood next to an antique table on which the head of a white, female mannequin "watched"' one of Malcolm X's early television interviews. The work was powerful, challenging, even painful. Rather than advocating conciliation (as he would later), in this video interview Malcolm X spoke of his distrust of white people and of the inherent foolishness of integration. An understandable sense of frustration echoed in his voice when he said, "There is nothing that the white man will do to bring about true, sincere citizenship or civil rights recognition for black people in this country. . . . They will always talk but they won't practice it."

These words offered an appropriate postscript to my museum experience. The exhibition in question was "Strange Attractors: Signs of Chaos," what the curator called an exploration of "some of the most compelling issues raised by the new science of chaos as they relate to recent works of art." The confluence of Malcolm's ideas and the show's theoretical perspective summarized for me the difficult place of African-American artists in museums—even in ones as ostensibly supportive of racial inclusion as the New Museum. The charismatic presence of Malcolm X's voice in "Strange Attractors" simply underscored how irrelevant both the exhibition and its catalogue were to the issues about which he was speaking—that is, when those words could be heard at all, given the video monitor's subdued volume. The catalogue reverberates with the jargon of "the new chaos science": Words like *period doubling, bifurcation cascade, phase space, limit cycle, hysteresis* appear throughout its pages. As one reads through the catalogue, one recognizes the names of white, male academics. And while curator Laura Trippi maintains that "the discourse of postmodernism sets up within the aesthetic (sometimes to the point of shrillness) a situation of extreme urgency and indeterminacy," nowhere are the systemic, institutionally defined conditions of racism discussed.

Twenty-five years after Malcolm X was assassinated, "his voice is being heard again and his ideology is being reexamined" as many African-Americans search for new social structures for survival and growth in a period of renewed conservatism and indifference. This search contemplates a radical realignment of society that is unthinkable to most white people—a realignment that is not about chaos but about order. Perhaps it is the urgency of this project that made the inclusion of Malcolm X in this art exhibition so striking. Without the Hammons piece the sensibility of "Strange Attractors" would have been very different, more typical of the splashy group shows of contemporary art that simply ignore the issue of race. That one image threw the entire show into question and pointed up the racial bias of its institutional context. Increasingly, across the country, similar catalysts are inserting painful questions into the heretofore complacent space of exhibition as curators with good intentions attempt to "include" the cultural production of people of color.

Having grown up in a predominantly black and Hispanic low-income housing project on Manhattan's Lower East Side—a place that was presumably also about good intentions—I am used to the experience of witnessing social and cultural indifference to people of color as a white person on the inside. It is startling to me, however, that in a nation that has seen at least some effort made by white people to share mainstream cultural venues (and the concomitant social and economic rewards) with African-Americans and other people of color—most notably in the areas of popular music, dance, literature and theater—the visual arts remain, for the most part, stubbornly resistant. My point in this article, then, is to examine the complex institutional conditions that result in the exclusion or misrepresentation of major cultural voices in the United States. These muted voices are complex and varied. There are veteran black artists, such as Al Loving, Faith Ringgold and the late Romare Bearden, who have received considerable art-world attention but are prevented from rising to the superstar status available to white artists of equal (or less than equal) talent. There are the younger African-American artists of the so-called MFA generation, such as Maren Hassinger, Pat Ward Williams and David Hammons, who have had considerable difficulty finding gallery representation. And finally, there is a new generation of "outsiders," artists and collectives that function independently of the gallery system in communities across the country.

Viewed in the broader context of social changes in American race relations—from the advances of the civil rights movement in the 1960s to the reversal of many of these advances in the Reagan era—the question of black cultural disenfranchisement seems daunting. Is the art world merely mirroring social changes or can art institutions actually play a role in challenging the conditions of institutional racism in America? Sad to say, with regard to race, art museums have for the most part behaved like many other businesses in this country—they have sought to preserve the narrow interests of their upperclass patrons and clientele. It is this upper-class, mostly white bias that I want to interrogate in order to find out "what's going on with whiteness" (as the writer bell hooks might say) at one of America's most racially biased cultural institutions—the art museum.

Despite the recent increase in exhibitions devoted to African-American art in major museums, these shows rarely address the underlying resistance of the art world to people of color. Such exhibitions often fall into what the art historian Judith Wilson has called the syndrome of "separate-but-unequal programming": African American shows in February, during Black History Month, white shows the rest of the year. A recent study of "art-world racism" in New York from 1980–87 by artist Howardena Pindell seems to verify that white-identified galleries and museums have little interest in enfranchising African-Americans and other people of color. Based on her statistical overview of the demographics of mainstream art exhibitions, Pindell concludes that "black, Hispanic, Asian, and Native American artists are . . . with a few, very few, exceptions systematically excluded.' PESTS, an anonymous group of New York-based African, Asian, Latino and Native American artists organized in 1986 to combat "art-world apartheid," came to a similar conclusion. In 1987, the *PESTS Newsletter* published a roster of 62 top New York galleries whose stables were all or nearly all white. While the situation would appear to be somewhat better outside of New York (a city where, Wilson claims, "the relative economic powerlessness of the black population . . . keeps displays at the . . . largest, publicly funded museums less integrated"),

African-American and other artists of color remain underrepresented in museums and galleries across the United States.

During the past 25 years a number of institutions devoted to African-American art and culture have opened in the United States, a response to the general problem of institutional racism and the art world's frustrating indifference to people of color. The Studio Museum in Harlem, for example, was founded in 1967 to fill a void left by mainstream institutions; its mission was to support the "study, documentation, collection, preservation and exhibition of art and artifacts of Black America and the African diaspora." The Studio Museum is to the African-American art world as the Museum of Modern Art is to the white art establishment in terms of visibility and prestige. But there are literally hundreds of smaller, lesser-known institutions across the country devoted to the art of African-Americans and other people of color. Such alternative museums raise a number of questions about the relationship between white and black culture in America. Are African-American artists stifled by the segregation by black museums, or do these institutions allow their art to flourish despite the dominant culture's lack of interest? Must African-Americans renounce their own cultural identity in order to be accepted by mainstream institutions? To what extent does the mere existence of African-American museums unintentionally absolve majority institutions of their social responsibility to black Americans?

Kinshasha Holman Conwill, executive director of the Studio Museum in Harlem, maintains that African-American museums are necessary:

> Black artists are segregated by society. If we waited for Romare Bearden, Al Loving or Betye Saar or other black artists to have their retrospectives at the Museum of Modern Art or in some of the wonderful contemporary museums around this country, we would be waiting a long, long time. Many people ask me if the [Studio Museum] perpetuates [this problem]. It's as if racism would end tomorrow if we disbanded the Studio Museum in Harlem, and there would be this great opening of doors and black artists would start pouring in to the mainstream of American art. Well, that's not what is happening.

On the whole, the financial situation for African-American and other minority art institutions remains poor. The American Association of Museums (AAM) in Washington, D.C., has begun to address the needs of these institutions, but their own rigorous accreditation standards, including stringent technical and acquisition guidelines, actually discourage validation of younger and economically poorer institutions. The Studio Museum in Harlem, accredited in 1987, is still the only black or Hispanic museum certified by the AAM. Because most corporate and private sponsors insist on proof of accreditation as part of their grant-giving process, lack of accreditation has serious consequences for institutions seeking outside funding. As a result, alternative spaces devoted to African-American art, a relatively recent programming phenomenon, are often dependent on severely limited funding sources. This problem of accreditation is so serious that the Association of African-American Museums was formed recently to help validate institutions overlooked by the AAM. The Ford Foundation, responding to its own study of 29 black and Hispanic art museums, recently instituted a three-year, $5-million program designed to improve economic conditions in these museums . . . .

Still, few programs are directed toward improving African-American representation in white-identified, mainstream art venues. Even fewer programs press the culture industry to examine its own racism and indifference. A rare instance was the program for this year's annual conference of the College Art Association in New York, where an unprecedented number of presentations were devoted to issues of cultural disenfranchisement and institutional racism. Mainstream support of the interests of the "Other" (when it does occur) generally takes one of two forms. By far the more prevalent approach depends on a pragmatic, statistically calibrated inclusion of artists of color, either as tokens in mostly white group shows or, more likely, in token exhibitions devoted exclusively to people of color. This statistical approach is one way of correcting years of exclusion from the art world. Other institutions take a second approach. Wishing to go beyond mere quotas, they organize exhibitions concerned with exploring and ultimately embracing cultural and social differences. The Dallas Museum of Art, for example, has instituted progressive programming in order to confront the reality that "our museums are devoted almost exclusively to the representation of 'white' culture, our libraries to the Western tradition of literature, our universities to the history of ancient Mediterranean and modern Europe." Significantly, the 1987 appointment of Alvia Wardlaw as the DMA's adjunct curator of African-American art made her the first holder of such a position at a major museum.

But in an art world that remains what Judith Wilson has called "one of the last bastions of white supremacy-by-exclusion," most art museums offer little more than lip service to the concept of racial inclusion. Art that demonstrates its "difference" form the mainstream or that challenges dominant values is rarely acceptable to white curators, administrators and patrons. This cultural elite bases its selections on arbitrary, Eurocentric standards of "taste" and "quality"—the code words of racial indifference and exclusion. "Race has become a trope of ultimate, irreducible difference between cultures, linguistic groups, or adherents of specific belief systems which—more often than not—also have fundamentally opposed economic interests," writes Henry Louis Gates, Jr., in an observation that has searing relevance to the art world. "Race is the ultimate trope of difference because it is so very arbitrary in its application."

These tastemakers, in turn, reflect the interests of the ruling caste of cultural institutions. The boards of art museums, publishers of art magazines and books and owners of galleries rarely hire people of color in policy-making positions. Thus, the task of cultural interpretation—even in instances where artists of color are involved—is usually relegated to "people of European descent, as if their perspective was universal." The very ground of art history, in fact, has proven infertile for most African-American students. As Lowery Sims, associate curator of 20th-century art at the Metropolitan Museum of Art, observes:

Art history was not a career that black middle-class children were taught to aspire to. For one, the Eurocentrism of art history often made it irrelevant to black college students who never heard African-American culture discussed in art-history classes. Museums—the major conduit for teaching young people about art—were not always accessible to blacks. African-Americans were socialized into certain careers after Reconstruction; visual art was not one of them. The economic realities made a career in art even less desirable. You didn't see many black visual artists until the 1920s and '30s, when the black colleges started to establish art departments. Black art historians are an even rarer breed.

While majority museums have not totally ignored the interests of people of color, they have had an extremely difficult time approaching cultures outside of the Anglo-European tradition. The 1969 exhibition "Harlem on My Mind" at the Metropolitan Museum in New York remains the classic example of the deep problems between white institutions and people of color. Twenty years later, the issues surrounding "Harlem on My Mind" offer an interesting model for rethinking our own era of cultural indifference to people of color.

Organized by the white art historian Allon Schoener, then visual-arts director of the New York State Council on the Arts, the exhibition represented an unprecedented effort on the part of an old-line American art museum to sociologically "interpret" African-American culture. The exhibition was not an art show in the traditional sense but an ambitious historical survey of Harlem from 1900 to 1968. Attempting to celebrate Harlem as the "cultural capital of black America," the show consisted of blown-up photographs, photomurals, slide and film projections and audio recordings. As Schoener explained in his introduction to the exhibition's catalogue, the objective of "Harlem on My Mind" was "to demonstrate that the black community in Harlem is a major cultural environment with enormous strength and potential . . . [a] community [that] has made major contributions to the mainstream of American culture in music, theater, and literature." Art was one form of cultural expression not mentioned by Schoener, despite the exhibition's location in a major New York art museum. This omission seemed to reflect Schoener's conviction that "museums should be electronic information centers" and that "paintings have stopped being a vehicle for valid expression in the 20th century." While responding to the ideological inadequacies of elitist art museums, Schoener's view also allowed the Metropolitan to almost completely ignore African-American painting and sculpture. Schoener felt free to construct a sociopolitical profile of Harlem, but he never applied this sociological methodology to his own position or to that of the museum that commissioned him. Rather than engaging Harlem writers, art historians and intellectuals to help interpret the culture of Harlem, a "curious" Schoener felt compelled to conduct his own investigation of the subject because *he* decided "it was time . . . [to find] something out about this other world."

When it opened, the show was widely condemned by African-Americans and others as yet another example of white carpetbagging and well-intentioned meddling.

In a 1969 *Artform* critique, historian Eugene Genovese questioned the proliferation of material related to Malcolm X in the exhibition:

> There are pictures of Malcolm the Muslim minister and the street-corner speaker and of Malcolm the corpse, together with indifferent excerpts from his magnificent autobiography. The exhibit immediately involved political decisions: should you emphasize the early or the late Malcolm? Malcolm the uncompromising black nationalist or Malcolm the man who ended his life edging toward a new position? The exhibition settles these questions in a manner that will not be to everyone's taste, but the real problem lies elsewhere: Who is making the decision to interpret Malcolm? Since the show purports to be a cultural history of Harlem, only that community as a whole or, more realistically, one or more of the clearly identified groups recognized as legitimate by the people of Harlem have the right.

Concluding his discussion of Malcolm X, Genovese suggested a compelling metaphor for the problem with "Harlem on My Mind." Trying to listen to Malcolm's speeches in the exhibition galleries, Genovese realized that he could not hear them because "the loudspeaker in one room drown[ed] out the one in the next." As in "Strange Attractors," the voice of one of America's most influential black leaders had been subjugated by the curatorial apparatus of an art exhibition. In each case, the museum's attempt to deal with African-American culture was in the end simply embarrassing. While Malcolm X can be an engaging, even sympathetic figure for white curators, his complex teachings must be understood first of all in relation to the African-American community to whom he was principally speaking. It is not that white people are incapable of analyzing his ideas but rather that cultural interpretations offered in exhibitions like "Harlem on My Mind" and "Strange Attractors" can never stray too far from the interests of their white, upper-class patrons or their principally white audience.

The War on Culture
■ Carole S. Vance ■

The storm that had been brewing over the National Endowment for the Arts (NEA) funding broke on the Senate floor on May 18, 1989, as Senator Alphonse D'Amato rose to denounce Andres Serrano's photograph *Piss Christ* as "trash." "This so-called piece of art is a deplorable, despicable display of vulgarity," he said. Within minutes over 20 senators rushed to join him in sending a letter to Hugh Southern,

"The War on Culture" by Carole S. Vance has been excerpted from *Art in America,* Brant Publications, 77, Number 9 (September 1989), pages 39, 41–43, and is reprinted by permission of the publisher.

acting chair of the NEA, demanding to know what steps the agency would take to change its grant procedures. "This work is shocking, abhorrent and completely undeserving of any recognition whatsoever," the senators wrote. For emphasis, Senator D'Amato dramatically ripped up a copy of the exhibition catalogue containing Serrano's photograph.

Not to be outdone, Senator Jesse Helms joined in the denunciation: "The Senator from New York is absolutely correct in his indignation and in his description of the blasphemy of the so-called art work. I do not know Mr. Andres Serrano, and I hope I never meet him. Because he is not an artist, he is a jerk." He continued, "Let him be a jerk on his own time and with his own resources. Do not dishonor our Lord."

The object of their wrath was a 60-by-40 inch Cibachrome print depicting a wood-and-plastic crucifix submerged in yellow liquid—the artist's urine. The photograph had been shown in an uneventful three-city exhibit organized by the Southeastern Center for Contemporary Art (SECCA), a recipient of NEA funds. A juried panel appointed by SECCA had selected Serrano and nine others from some 500 applicants to win $15,000 fellowships and appear in the show, "Awards in the Visual Arts 7." How the senators came to know and care about this regional show was not accidental.

Although the show had closed by the end of January 1989, throughout the spring the right-wing American Family Association, based in Tupelo, Mississippi, attacked the photo, the exhibition and its sponsors. The association and its executive director, United Methodist minister Rev. Donald Wildmon, were practiced in fomenting public opposition to allegedly "immoral, anti-Christian" images and had led protests against Martin Scorsese's film *The Last Temptation of Christ* the previous summer. The AFA newsletter, with an estimated circulation of 380,000 including 178,000 churches, according to association spokesmen, urged concerned citizens to protest the art work and demand that responsible NEA officials be fired. The newsletter provided the relevant names and addresses, and letters poured in to congressmen, senators and the NEA. A full-fledged moral panic had begun.

Swept up in the mounting hysteria was another photographic exhibit scheduled to open on July 1 at the Corcoran Gallery of Art in Washington, D.C. The 150-work retrospective, "Robert Mapplethorpe: The Perfect Moment," was organized by the University of Pennsylvania's Institute of Contemporary Art (ICA), which had received $30,000 for the show from the NEA. The show included the range of Mapplethorpe's images: formal portraiture, flowers, children and carefully posed erotic scenes—sexually explicit, gay and sadomasochistic. The show had been well received in Philadelphia and Chicago, but by June 8, Representative Dick Armey (R-Tex) sent Southern a letter signed by over 100 congressmen denouncing grants for Mapplethorpe as well as Serrano, and threatening to seek cuts in the agency's $170-million budget soon up for approval. Armey wanted the NEA to end its sponsorship of "morally reprehensible trash," and he wanted new grant guidelines that would "clearly pay respect to public standards of taste and decency." Armey claimed he could "blow their budget out of the water" by circulating the

Mapplethorpe catalogue to fellow legislators prior to the House vote on the NEA appropriation. Before long, about 50 senators and 150 representatives had contacted the NEA about its funding.

Amid these continuing attacks on the NEA, rumors circulated that the Corcoran would cancel the show. Director Christina Orr-Cahall staunchly rejected such rumors one week, saying, "This is the work of a major American artist who's well known, so we're not doing anything out of the ordinary." But by the next week she had caved in, saying, "We really felt this exhibit was at the wrong place at the wrong time." The director attempted an ingenious argument in a statement issued through a museum spokesperson: Far from being censorship, she claimed, the cancellation actually protected the artist's work. "We decided to err on the side of the artist, who had the right to have his work presented in a non-sensationalized, non-political environment, and who deserves not to be the hostage for larger issues of relevance to us all," Orr-Cahall stated. "If you think about this for a long time, as we did, this is not censorship; in fact, this is the full artistic freedom which we all support." Astounded by the Corcoran decision, artists and art groups mounted protests, lobbied and formed anticensorship organizations, while a local alternative space, The Washington Project for the Arts (WPA), hastily arranged to show the Mapplethorpe exhibition.

The Corcoran cancellation scarcely put an end to the controversy, however. Instead, attacks on NEA funding intensified in the House and Senate, focusing on the 1990 budget appropriations and on new regulations that would limit or possibly end NEA subcontracts to arts organizations. Angry representatives wanted to gut the budget, though they were beaten back in the House by more moderate amendments which indicated disapproval of the Serrano and Mapplethorpe grants by deducting their total cost ($45,000) from next year's allocation. By late July, Sen. Jesse Helms introduced a Senate amendment that would forbid the funding of "offensive," "indecent" and otherwise controversial art and transfer monies previously allocated for visual arts to support "folk art" and local projects. The furor is likely to continue throughout the fall, since the NEA will be up for its mandated, five-year reauthorization, and the right-wing campaign against images has apparently been heartened by its success. In Chicago, for example, protestors assailed an Eric Fischl painting of a fully clothed boy looking at a naked man swinging at a baseball on the grounds that it promotes "child molestation" and is, in any case, not "realistic," and therefore, bad art.

The arts community was astounded by this chain of events—artists personally reviled, exhibitions withdrawn and under attack, the NEA budget threatened, all because of a few images. Ironically, those who specialize in producing and interpreting images were surprised that any images could have such power. But what was new to the art community is, in fact, a staple of contemporary right-wing politics.

In the past ten years, conservative and fundamentalist groups have deployed and perfected techniques of grass-roots and mass mobilization around social issues, usually centering on sexuality, gender and religion. In these campaigns, symbols figure prominently, both as highly condensed statements of moral concern and

as powerful spurs to emotion and action. In moral campaigns, fundamentalists select a negative symbol which is highly arousing to their own constituency and
which is difficult or problematic for their opponents to defend. The symbol, often
taken literally, out of context and always denying the possibility of irony or multiple interpretations, is waved like a red flag before their constituents. The arousing
stimulus could be an "un-Christian" passage from an evolution textbook, explicit
information from a high school sex-education curriculum or "degrading" pornography said to be available in the local adult bookshop. In the antiabortion campaign, activists favor images of late-term fetuses or better yet, dead babies, displayed in jars. Primed with names and addresses of relevant elected and appointed
officials, fundamentalist troops fire off volleys of letters, which cowed politicians
take to be the expression of popular sentiment. Right-wing politicians opportunis-
tically ride the ground swell of outrage, while centrists feel anxious and disempow-
ered to stop it—now a familiar sight in the political landscape. But here, in the
NEA controversy, there is something new.

Fundamentalists and conservatives are now directing mass-based symbolic
mobilizations against "high culture." Previously, their efforts had focused on popular culture—the attack on rock music led by Tipper Gore, the protests against *The
Last Temptation of Christ* and the Meese Commission's war against pornography.
Conservative and neoconservative intellectuals have also lamented the allegedly
liberal bias of the university and the dilution of the classic literary canon by including "inferior" works by minority, female and gay authors, but these complaints have
been made in books, journals and conferences, and have scarcely generated thousands of letters to Congress. Previous efforts to change the direction of the NEA
had been made through institutional and bureaucratic channels—by appointing
more conservative members to its governing body, the National Council on the
Arts, by selecting a more conservative chair and in some cases by overturning grant
decisions made by professional panels. Although antagonism to Eastern elites and
upper-class culture has been a thread within fundamentalism, the NEA controversy
marks the first time that this emotion has been tapped in mass political action.

Conservative columnist Patrick Buchanan sounded the alarm for this populist attack in a *Washington Times* column last June, calling for "a cultural revolution in the '90s as sweeping as the political revolution in the '80s." Here may lie a
clue to this new strategy: The Reagan political revolution has peaked, and with
both legislatures under Democratic control, additional conservative gains on social
issues through electoral channels seem unlikely. Under these conditions, the slower
and more time-consuming—though perhaps more effective—method of changing
public opinion and taste may be the best available option. For conservatives and
fundamentalists, the arts community plays a significant role in setting standards
and shaping public values: Buchanan writes, "The decade has seen an explosion of
anti-American, anti-Christian, and nihilist 'art.' . . . [Many museums] now feature
exhibits that can best be described as cultural trash," and "as in public television
and public radio, a tiny clique, out of touch with America's traditional values, has
wormed its way into control of the arts bureaucracy." In an analogy chillingly

reminiscent of Nazi cultural metaphors, Buchanan writes, "As with our rivers and lakes, we need to clean up our culture: for it is a well from which we must all drink. Just as a poisoned land will yield up poisonous fruits, so a polluted culture, left to fester and stink, can destroy a nation's soul." Let the citizens be warned: "We should not subsidize decadence." Amid such archaic language of moral pollution and degeneracy, it was not surprising that Mapplethorpe's gay and erotic images were at the center of controversy.

The second new element in the right's mass mobilization against the NEA and high culture has been its rhetorical disavowal of censorship per se and the cultivation of an artfully crafted distinction between absolute censorship and the denial of public funding. Senator D'Amato, for example, claimed, "This matter does not involve freedom of artistic expression—it does involve the question whether American taxpayers should be forced to support such trash." In the battle for public opinion, "censorship" is a dirty word to mainstream audiences, and hard for conservatives to shake off because their recent battles to control school books, libraries and curricula have earned them reputations as ignorant book-burners. By using this hairsplitting rhetoric, conservatives can now happily disclaim any interest in censorship, and merely suggest that no public funds be used for "offensive" or "indecent" materials. Conservatives had employed the "no public funds" argument before to deny federal funding for Medicaid abortions since 1976 and explicit safe-sex education for AIDS more recently. Fundamentalists have attempted to modernize their rhetoric in other social campaigns, too—antiabortionists borrow civil rights terms to speak about the "human rights" of the fetus, and antiporn zealots experiment with replacing their language of sin and lust with phrases about the "degradation of women" borrowed from antipornography feminism. In all cases, these incompatible languages have an uneasy coexistence. But modernized rhetoric cannot disguise the basic, censorious impulse which strikes out at NEA public funding precisely because it is a significant source of arts money, not a trivial one.

NEA funding permeates countless art institutions, schools and community groups, often making the difference between survival and going under; it also supports many individual artists. That NEA funds have in recent years been allocated according to formulas designed to achieve more democratic distribution—not limited to elite art centers or well-known artists—makes their impact all the more significant. A requirement that NEA-funded institutions and artists conform to a standard of "public taste," even in the face of available private funds, would have profound impact. One obvious by-product would be installing the fiction of a singular public with a universally shared taste and the displacement of a diverse public composed of many constituencies with different tastes. In addition, the mingling of NEA and private funds, so typical in many institutions and exhibitions, would mean that NEA standards would spill over to the private sector, which is separate more in theory than in practice. Although NEA might fund only part of a project, its standards would prevail, since noncompliance would result in loss of funds.

No doubt the continuous contemplation of the standards of public taste that should obtain in publicly funded projects—continuous, since these can never be known with certainty—will itself increase self-censorship and caution across the board. There has always been considerable self-censorship in the art world when it comes to sexual images, and the evidence indicates that it is increasing: Reports circulate about curators now examining their collections anew with an eye toward "disturbing" material that might arouse public ire, and increased hesitation to mount new exhibitions that contain unconventional material. In all these ways, artists have recognized the damage done by limiting the types of images that can be funded by public monies.

But more importantly, the very distinction between public and private is a false one, because the boundaries between these spheres are very permeable. Feminist scholarship has shown how the most seemingly personal and private decisions—having a baby, for example—are affected by a host of public laws and policies, ranging from available tax benefits to health services to day care. In the past century in America and England, major changes in family form, sexuality and gender arrangements have occurred in a complex web spanning public and private domains, which even historians are hard put to separate. In struggles for social change, both reformers and traditionalists know that changes in personal life are intimately linked to changes in public domains—not only through legal regulation, but also through information, images and even access to physical space available in public arenas.

This is to say that what goes on in the public sphere is of vital importance for both the arts and for political culture. Because American traditions of publicly supported culture are limited by the innate conservatism of corporate sponsors and by the reduction of individual patronage following changes in the tax laws, relegating controversial images and art work to private philanthropy confines them to a frail and easily influenced source of support. Even given the NEA's history of bureaucratic interference, it is paradoxically public funding—insulated from the day-to-day interference of politicians and special-interest groups that the right wing would now impose—that permits the possibility of a heterodox culture. Though we might reject the overly literal connection conservatives like to make between images and action ("When teenagers read sex education, they go out and have sex"), we too know that diversity in images and expression in the public sector nurtures and sustains diversity in private life. When losses are suffered in public arenas, people for whom controversial or minority images are salient and affirming suffer a real defeat. Defending private rights—to behavior, to images, to information—is difficult without a publicly formed and visible community. People deprived of images become demoralized and isolated, and they become increasingly vulnerable to attacks on their private expressions of nonconformity, which are inevitable once sources of public solidarity and resistance have been eliminated.

For these reasons, the desire to eliminate symbols, images and ideas they do not like from public space is basic to contemporary conservatives' and fundamentalists' politics about sexuality, gender and the family. On the one hand, this behavior may signal weakness, in that conservatives no longer have the power to directly control, for example, sexual behavior, and must content themselves with controlling a proxy, images of sexual behavior. The attack on Mapplethorpe's images, some of them gay, some sadomasochistic, can be understood in this light. Indeed, the savage critique of his photographs permitted a temporary revival of a vocabulary—"perverted, filth, trash"—that was customarily used against gays but has become unacceptable in mainstream political discourse, a result of sexual liberalization that conservatives hate. On the other hand, the attack on images, particularly "difficult" images in the public domain, may be the most effective point of cultural intervention now—particularly given the evident difficulty liberals have in mounting a strong and unambivalent response and given the way changes in public climate can be translated back to changes in legal rights—as, for example, in the erosion of support for abortion rights, where the image of the fetus has become central in the debate, erasing the image of the woman.

Because symbolic mobilizations and moral panics often leave in their wake residues of law and policy that remain in force long after the hysteria has subsided, the fundamentalist attack on art and images requires a broad and vigorous response that goes beyond appeals to free speech. Free expression is a necessary principle in these debates, because of the steady protection it offers to all images, but it cannot be the only one. To be effective and not defensive, the art community needs to employ its interpretive skills to unmask the modernized rhetoric conservatives use to justify their traditional agenda, as well as to deconstruct the "difficult" images fundamentalists choose to set their campaigns in motion. Despite their uncanny intuition for culturally disturbing material, their focus on images also contains many sleights of hand (Do photographs of nude children necessarily equal child pornography?), and even displacements, which we need to examine. Images we would allow to remain "disturbing" and unconsidered put us anxiously on the defensive and undermine our own response. In addition to defending free speech, it is essential to address why certain images are being attacked—Serrano's crucifix for mocking the excesses of religious exploitation (a point evidently not lost on the televangelists and syndicated preachers who promptly assailed his "blasphemy") and Mapplethorpe's photographs for making minority sexual subcultures visible. If we are always afraid to offer a public defense of sexual images, then even on religion we have granted the right wing its most basic premise: Sexuality is shameful and discrediting. It is not enough to defend the principle of free speech, while joining in denouncing the image, as some in the art world have done.

The fundamentalist attack on images and the art world must be recognized not as an improbable and silly outburst of Yahoo-ism, but as a systematic part of a right-wing political program to restore traditional social arrangements and reduce diversity. The right wing is deeply committed to symbolic politics, both in using symbols to mobilize public sentiment and in understanding that, because images do stand in for and motivate social change, the arena of representation is a real ground for struggle. A vigorous defense of art and images begins from this insight.

Art and Taxes
■ Paul Mattick ■

On June 25, 1998 the U.S. Supreme Court ruled against the so-called NEA Four, Karen Finley, John Fleck, Holly Hughes, and Tim Miller. (The NEA, or National Endowment for the Arts, is the main federal institution for funding the arts with tax dollars.) These performance artists had sued for the restoration of grants first awarded in 1990 by a panel convened by the federal arts agency and then withdrawn by the NEA's governing National Council on the Arts and the agency chairperson, John Frohnmayer. The high court's decision was for all practical purposes the last act of a drama that had begun in 1989 with Congressional agitation against the NEA in response to complaints orchestrated by right-wing Christian outfits, notably Rev. Donald Wildmon's American Family Association, against supposedly blasphemous and indecent artworks by Andres Serrano and Robert Mapplethorpe which had been exhibited in NEA-supported institutions.

The turn-of-the-decade battles over NEA funding and related events—like the 1990 obscenity trial against the Cincinnati Contemporary Art Center and its director, Dennis Barrie, again for exhibiting Mapplethorpe's photographs—provoked art professionals of all sorts, from artists to museum directors, to express various degrees of outrage at the threat to free expression. The Supreme Court's decision in the NEA Four case, however, passed almost unnoticed. In the years since then, moreover, controversy over the role of the NEA seems to have completely evaporated. While the use of public money for the promotion of private business interests thrives, the lack of funding of contemporary art at the federal level currently shocks almost no one. How has this happened, and what does it tell us about the place of the arts in society at the present time?

Art has long embodied both the spirit of modern market-centered society and a critical attitude toward it. Essential to the eighteenth-century emergence of the modern idea of art, as a distinct domain of activities and objects characterized by "aesthetic" functions, was a new conception of artistic activity as the expression of individual genius. Artistic labor came to be conceptualized, as Immanuel Kant famously put it, as "free"—ruled only by the internal compulsions of its creator.

It is, of course, no accident that this reconception of the arts emerged in a context that involved the replacement of work to the order of a patron, characteristic of the premodern arts, by work for an anonymous market. The premodern artist worked to order, his or her subject matter and even formal means controlled to a large extent by guild (or academic) regulations and by his customer. The modern artist produces to suit him- or herself, albeit with the hope of finding customers.

"Art and Taxes" by Paul Mattick is published by permission of the author.

He or she thus combines a market practice with an aristocratic disdain for trade. On this rests the idea of the bohemian or avant-garde artist—the penniless bourgeois (as the painter, Camille Pissaro put it)—at odds with philistine society, and the modernist orientation of art towards aesthetic autonomy, the foregrounding of artistic materials and methods as the stuff of aesthetic meaning. At the same time, in the course of the nineteenth century the worship of art came to express the claim of capitalist society's higher orders to rise above the confines of commerce as worthy inheritors of the aristocratic culture of the past.

The producer and consumer of art need to be brought together for the fine arts to exist as a social reality. As the manufacturers and financiers of Europe and America bought estates and took up fox hunting, so they filled their houses with old furniture, Old Masters, or the art of their own moment. And they expressed their growing mastery of the political sphere by the development of public art institutions. In the United States, the institutionalization of art was largely the work of private citizens. This was a consequence not only of the absence of the aristocratic establishments but also of the weakness and disunity of the federal state before the Civil War, and of continuing conflict among the industrialists and financiers who were the masters of the nation that war produced. Characteristically, it was not until 1939 that the United States acquired a national gallery, and even this came to begin with as a massive gift from a private individual. Of course, the creation and maintenance of art institutions did not proceed without the aid of public authorities, in the form of concessions, funds, and services from municipal and state governments and, ultimately, federal tax policy.

In addition, American philanthropy, in opposition to European tradition, emphasized, not status differentiation, but public service. Under the conditions of bourgeois democracy cultural philanthropy had both to embody in institutions the membership of outstanding individuals in an elite and to suggest the notion of the potential openness of social advancement to all. Only by being offered to the public could culture—in this way unlike fox hunting—signify superiority without privilege, ideologically basic to modern class relations. Class differences disappear from view within the concept of the "public," as with that of the "citizen" who is the subject of democratic politics and the rule of law.

The acceptance of the principle of the income tax in 1913 by the dominant classes of the United States signaled their recognition of the necessity for some governmental regulation of social relations in a country in which the forces of economic exploitation had been allowed to run quite free. As the turn-of-the-century Progressives were the first to articulate in programmatic terms, such regulation was even in the interest of a developing corporate capitalism. In the 1930s, the New Deal—and its extension into the war economy—further applied this principle by increasing the participation of the state in economic affairs, a natural development in a situation in which the leading role once played by individual barons of industry, commerce, and finance has been taken over by corporations and foundations.

As was dimly sensed by the opponents of a federal arts policy, an important element in the way in which this transformation made itself felt in the domain of culture was the movement of modernism, particularly in the visual arts, to the center of the aesthetic stage. This was due to more than the gradual disappearance of Old Masters form the market. While earlier in this century the promotion of modern art served to differentiate certain scions of wealthy families from their conservative elders, the later engagement with modernism undertaken by social agents ranging from the federal government to the mass media not only proclaimed the glory of capitalism but specifically celebrated the political and economic triumph of the United States after World War II. Art came to be seen not so much as an incarnation of values higher than those of the marketplace but as a distillation of those characteristics—daring, innovation, attunement to unarticulated social desires—that make an individual, company, or nation successful.

It was in these terms that calls were issued for cultural competition with World Communism; that John F. Kennedy, asserting the existence of "a connection, hard to explain logically but easy to feel, between achievement in public life and progress in the arts," linked a "New Frontier in the Arts" to the "surge in economic growth" and "openness toward what is new" he promised; and that Lyndon Johnson established the NEH and NEA as facets of the Great Society. (The NEH, or National Endowment for the Humanities, is the main federal institution for funding programs in the humanities with tax dollars.)

Beyond issues of international political prestige and the aristocratic pretensions of the very rich, the idea was gaining ground among America's upper classes—particularly in the Northeast but also in cities like Chicago and St. Louis—that art is a Good Thing, a glamorous thing, even a fun thing. This attitude rapidly trickled down to the middle ranks, whose self-assertiveness as leading citizens of an affluent and powerful nation was expressed by a new attachment to culture. The 1950s saw galleries in department stores, rising museum and concert attendance, and the commercial distribution of classical LPs and inexpensive reproductions of famous paintings. Studio training and art history departments proliferated in colleges and universities.

In part the new interest in culture reflected the changing nature of the business class: While fewer than 50 percent of top executives had some college education in 1900, 76 percent did by 1950. The postwar rise of the professional manager helped break down the traditional barrier between the worlds of business and culture, affecting the self-image of American society as a whole. To this was joined—with the growth of academia, research institutions, and all levels of government—the emergence of the new professional-intellectual stratum, connected in spirit to the power elite in a way unknown to the alienated intelligentsia of yesteryear. By the 1960s art, and modern art in particular, seemed to the politically dominant forces in the United States to have a part to play in the construction of a nationally authoritative ideology.

The NEA was prefigured, as it was later accompanied, by private efforts, not necessarily oriented towards modernism, such as the Ford Foundation's ballet and orchestra programs. Under the name of a democratization of the arts, a relatively unified national culture came into existence, complementing the increasingly integrated political economy. Executives and professionals could now move from New York to Santa Fe or Portland and find the opera, ballet, and contemporary art waiting for them. While formally open to all, this national culture remained in general practice class-specific, combining a continuing focus for the business elite with an associated participation by the corps of educated professionals and managers that came with postwar economic development.

Most recently, official culture has embraced "cultural pluralism" and "multiculturalism." As in academia, with which this phenomenon is closely connected, multiculturalism in the arts, in responding to demands made by members of formerly excluded groups (women, minorities) for greater participation in officially sanctioned cultural production, bears witness to new ideological conditions. In place of the "general interest" in which it has become increasingly difficult to believe, this art defines itself in terms of variously conceived "communities" that, whatever their real content, obscure class relationships as effectively as did the old idea of the "public"—an idea which makes a contemporary appearance in the phenomenon of "public art," representing in a concentrated form the nexus of academy, corporation, and the state in the production of art. This in turn provided a new dimension for the opposition to federal art programs of congressional conservatives articulating the concerns of a social fraction that feels itself threatened by the continued development of a state-facilitated globalized "multicultural" capitalism.

Interestingly enough, one of the chief arguments opponents of government arts spending made from the 1940s until the creation of the NEA in 1965 was the threat of government censorship or bureaucratic control of art. This concern was voiced by professional organizations representing conservative artists, who saw early on that modernism would be favored by any future arts policy, as it was in the few efforts to sponsor traveling exhibitions of American art. Conservative congressmen, who identified modern art as Communist in its basic orientation, supported their position. Such politicians could be depended on to trace the party affiliation of as many government-exhibited artists as possible. The fact that the congressional distaste for modernism was one they shared with Stalin, while amusing, is beside the point. The underlying ideological structure of the opposition to state arts funding in the United States has always had less to do with art than with the general idea of government deficit spending as a violation of the private-property foundation of the "free enterprise" economy. Concern about links between immorality and abstraction went hand in hand with the wish to drive a stake through the heart of the New Deal.

Communism was, of course, state spending in monstrous form. But from the start communism was accompanied by sexual immorality as the other great threat to the American way of life. The collapse of the Soviet Union in 1991 meant its complete replacement by homosexuality and feminism as ideological bugaboos; in 1999 NEA chairman William Ivey had to promote his organization as pro-family as well as patriotic, just as the arts advocates of the 1950s and 1960s recommended government-sponsored art as a weapon against Soviet propaganda. Fully to unravel the politics of arts policy would require a detailed understanding of party and national political dynamics, but underlying the mobilization of class feeling for partisan purposes seems to be the general issue of relations between state and economy. Art is an easy target because its relative economic insignificance accompanies its nature as a form of what anthropologist Pierre Bourdieu called cultural capital. Congressmen devoted to government aid to peanut farmers or weapons builders can thunder away against using the taxpayers' money to subsidize immoral entertainment for the wealthy, standing up against deficits while keeping the mixed economy going. The issue is evidently not the mixed economy as such, but state spending that does not provide an immediate subsidy to some politically powerful business interest.

Explicit defense of the principle of free enterprise has throughout its history accompanied politicians' populist rhetoric on the theme of "Eastern liberal elites" spending the tax money of the hard working "middle class" on trash. Since one important function of art in the modern world has been as an indicator of class position, it is not surprising that many low-income people see it as a possession of the rich. As noted above, it is in fact true that fine art is by and large an elite pleasure, although this is as true of opera as of sexually daring performance art. It should be remembered, however, that not much of the taxpayers' money is being spent on art: In 1988, the funds at the disposal of the NEA amounted to 68 cents per taxpayer. (By comparison, Western European countries spend from twenty to forty dollars per taxpayer on the arts). The funds spent on other elite interests, such as access to foreign markets or oil supplies, or direct subsidies to large corporations, about which politicians or "pro-family" organizations rarely complain, are disproportionately higher. The total appropriation for the NEA in 1988 was less than $168 million; In 1989, the Pentagon's military band program alone was funded at $193 million.

Interestingly enough, in any case, most working-class Americans have displayed no particular interest in the anti-NEA campaigns of figures like Wildmon and Helms. Strikingly, the completely art-inexperienced jury carefully chosen by prosecutors in the Cincinnati obscenity trial acquitted the Art Center director of the charge against him, accepting expert testimony to the effect that the Mapplethorpe works were genuine art. In fact, the power of the NEA's opponents, like that of the anti-choice forces with which they overlap, was due not so much to wide popular support as to the peculiar mechanics of American electoral politics, in which the need to attract small ideologically motivated blocs within the voting minority gives them political power unmerited by their numbers. In any case, reference to class in the NEA controversy remained covert, always subordinated to appeals to patriotism and family values. For, after all, the religious right, whatever its particular interests, serves the same greater class interest as the promoters of liberal culture. This explains how the same corporation, Philip Morris, can finance both Jesse Helms and the sort of art he fulminates against. It also explains the survival of the NEA alongside the more significant efforts of Keynesian economics. [John Maynard Keynes was a 20th century English economist who theorized that economic downturns could be managed into prosperity by means of government spending.] The mixed economy is here to stay, though budgets may be cut and welfare in particular "reformed" to aid in the general lowering of real wages at a time of increasing global economic instability. And while the privatization of cultural institutions, as of schools, medicine, and other social amenities, is a definite trend and the state subsidization of individual artists has been severely cut, governmental support of the arts continues, since it is necessary for the maintenance of institutions now central to the mode of life of the dominant classes.

The developments I have sketched have naturally had an effect on the conceptualization and practice of art. The post-war rise to near-official status of American modernism made this nation's first avant-garde the world's last. A bohemia that sues for state financing is a contradiction in terms. Among artists, scorn for society's dominant values has been replaced by an ironic sense of the limits of the powers of art and open acceptance of the coexistence of the commercial character of art with its aspiration to transcendence, or even the dominance of the former over the latter. Former NEA chairman Ivey's insistence in a 1998 public talk that the arts "can constitute an urban business strategy," helping to revitalize downtown areas and attracting professionals and corporate headquarters, expresses the same point of view with an administrator's distance from irony.

This is surely part of the explanation of the low level of concern about the defeat of the NEA Four and the ongoing restructuring of the NEA away from funding contemporary art and towards commercial and traditional performance, alongside established high-art institutions. A decade after the crisis of 1990, declining federal arts spending—in particular, the loss of individual artist grants—seems just an aspect of the general turn away from New Frontier and Great Society spending to a nearly unmodulated use of public money for the promotion of private business interests. This trend, opposed by no significant political force, seems to be an ineluctable phenomenon, to which we must simply adapt. And indeed, nonadaptation to the imperatives of our moment would mean going far beyond the politics of state arts policy to question the forces dominating social life, and indeed the basic organization of our society, including the position of art within it.

Aesthetic Appreciation of the Natural Environment
■ Allen Carlson ■

In his classic work, *The Sense of Beauty,* philosopher George Santayana characterizes the natural landscape as follows:

> The natural landscape is an indeterminate object; it almost always contains enough diversity to allow . . . great liberty in selecting, emphasizing, and grouping its elements, and it is furthermore rich in suggestion and in vague emotional stimulus. A landscape to be seen has to be composed. . . . then we feel that the landscape is beautiful. . . . The promiscuous natural landscape cannot be enjoyed in any other way.

"Aesthetic Appreciation of the Natural Environment" by Allen Carlson is published by permission of the author.

With these few words, Santayana poses the central question of aesthetic appreciation of nature. The natural landscape, he says, is indeterminate and promiscuous.
To be appreciated, it must be composed. Yet it is so rich in diversity, suggestion,
and emotional stimulus that it allows great liberty in selecting, emphasizing, and
grouping. Thus, the problem is that of *what* and *how* to select, emphasize, and
group, of what and how to compose, to achieve appropriate appreciation.

It is significant that there is no parallel problem concerning appreciation of
art. With traditional works of art we typically know both the what and the how of
appropriate aesthetic appreciation. We know *what* to appreciate in that we know the
difference between a work and that which is not it nor a part of it and between its
aesthetically relevant qualities and those without such relevance. We know that we
are to appreciate the sound of the piano in the concert hall and not the coughing
that interrupts it; we know that we are to appreciate a painting's delicacy and balance, but not where it happens to hang. Similarly, we know *how* to appreciate
works of art in that we know the modes of appreciation that are appropriate for different kinds of works. We know that we are to listen to the sound of the piano and
look at the surface of the painting.

With art our knowledge of what and how to appreciate is grounded in the fact
that works of art are our creations. We know what are and are not parts of works,
which of their qualities are aesthetically relevant, and how to appreciate them, because we have made them for the purpose of aesthetic appreciation and to fulfill
that purpose this knowledge must be accessible. In making an object we know what
we make and thus its parts, its purposes, and what to do with it. In creating a painting, we know that it ends at its frame, that its colors and lines are aesthetically important, and that we are to look at it rather than listen to it. Moreover, works of different types have different kinds of boundaries, different foci of aesthetic
significance, and demand different acts of aspection.

Nature is not art and it is not our creation. Rather it is our whole natural environment, our natural world. It surrounds us and confronts us, in Santayana's words,
indeterminately and promiscuously, rich in diversity, suggestion, and stimulus. But
what are we to appreciate in all this richness, what are the limits and the proper foci
of appreciation; and how are we to appreciate, what are the appropriate modes of
appreciation and acts of aspection? Moreover, what are the grounds on which we
can justify answers to such questions?

One such approach may be called the Object of Art Model (OAM). Consider
our appreciation of a non-representation sculpture, for example, a work by Con-
stantin Brancusi, such as *Bird in Space* (1919). We appreciate the actual physical
object; the aesthetically relevant features are sensuous and design qualities of the
object and certain abstract expressive qualities. Such sculpture need not relate to
anything external to itself; it is a self-contained aesthetic unit. The Brancusi has no
direct representational ties to the rest of reality and no relational connections with
its immediate surroundings. Yet it has significant aesthetic qualities: It glistens, has
balance and grace, and expresses flight itself. Clearly we can aesthetically appreciate objects of nature in accord with OAM. We can appreciate a rock or a piece of

driftwood as we appreciate a Brancusi: We actually or imaginatively remove the object from its surroundings and dwell on its sensuous and possible expressive qualities. Natural objects are often appreciated in precisely this way: Mantelpieces are littered with rocks and pieces of driftwood. Moreover, the model fits the fact that natural objects, like non-representational sculpture, have no representational ties to the rest of reality.

Nonetheless, OAM is in many ways inappropriate for aesthetic appreciation of nature. Santayana notes the natural environment's indeterminateness. However, he also observes that nature contains objects that have determinate forms, but suggests that when appreciation is directed specifically to such objects, we no longer have genuine aesthetic appreciation of nature. Santayana's observation marks a distinction between appreciating nature and simply appreciating the objects of nature. In fact, on one understanding of OAM, the objects of nature when so appreciated become "readymades" or "found art." Natural objects are granted what is called "artistic enfranchisement," and they, like artifacts such as Marcel Duchamp's famous urinal, which he enfranchised as a work called *Fountain* (1917), become works of art. The questions of what and how to aesthetically appreciate are answered, but for art rather than for nature; the appreciation of nature is lost in the shuffle. Appreciating a sculpture that was once driftwood is no closer to appreciating nature than is appreciating a purse that was once a sow's ear.

However, OAM need not turn natural objects into art objects. It may approach the objects of nature simply by actually or imaginatively removing them from their surroundings. We need not appreciate the rock on our mantel as a readymade sculpture; we can appreciate it only as an aesthetically pleasing object. Our appreciation focuses on the sensuous qualities of the physical object and a few expressive qualities: Our rock has a wonderfully smooth and gracefully curved surface and expresses solidity. Yet OAM is still problematic in involving the removal of natural objects from their surroundings. The model is appropriate for art objects that are self-contained aesthetic units such that neither their environment of creation nor their environment of display is aesthetically relevant. However, natural objects are a part of and have been formed within their environments of creation by means of the natural forces at work within them. Thus, for natural objects, environments of creation are aesthetically relevant and, because of this, environments of display are equally relevant in virtue of being either the same as or different from environments of creation.

A second artistic approach to aesthetic appreciation of nature may be called the Landscape or Scenery Model (LSM). In one of its senses "landscape" means a prospect—usually an imposing prospect—seen from a specific standpoint and distance. Landscape paintings traditionally represent such prospects and LSM is closely tied to this art form. In appreciating a landscape painting the focus is typically not the actual object, the painting, nor the represented object, the prospect, but rather the representation of the object and its represented features. Thus the appreciative emphasis is on qualities that play an essential role in representing a prospect: visual qualities relating to line, color, and overall design. Such features are central in landscape painting and the focus of LSM. The model encourages perceiving and appreciating nature as if it were a landscape painting, as a representation of a prospect viewed from a specific position and distance. It directs appreciation to artistic and scenic qualities of line, color, and design.

There can be no doubt that LSM has been historically significant in aesthetic appreciation of nature. It is the direct descendent of the eighteenth century concept of the picturesque. This term literally means "picture-like" and indicates a mode of appreciation by which the natural world is divided into scenes, each aiming at an ideal dictated by art.

In a similar fashion, modern tourists frequently show a preference for LSM by visiting "scenic viewpoints" where the actual space between tourist and prescribed "view" constitutes "a due distance" that aids the impression of "soft colours of nature, and the most regular perspective the eye can perceive." And the "regularity" of the perspective is enhanced by the position of the viewpoint itself. Moreover, modern tourists also desire "the finished picture, in highest colouring, and just perspective"—whether this be the "scene" framed and balanced in a camera viewfinder, the result of this in the form of a color print, or "artistically" composed postcard and calendar reproductions of the "scene," which often receive more appreciation than that which they "reproduce."

LSM's answers to the what and how questions cause some uneasiness in a number of thinkers. The model dictates appreciation of the natural environment as if it were a series of landscape paintings. It recommends dividing nature into scenes, each to be viewed from a specific position by a viewer separated by appropriate spatial (and emotional?) distance. It reduces a walk in the natural environment to something like a stroll through an art gallery. When seen in this light, some individuals, such as human ecologist Paul Shepard, find LSM so misguided that they doubt the wisdom of any aesthetic approach to nature. Others find the model ethically and environmentally worrisome. For example, after contending that modern tourists are only interested in prospects, Rees concludes that the picturesque:

> . . . simply confirmed our anthropocentrism by suggesting that nature exists to please as well as to serve us. Our ethics . . . have lagged behind our aesthetics. It is an unfortunate lapse which allows us to abuse our local environments and venerate the Alps and the Rockies.

Moreover, LSM is also questionable on purely aesthetic grounds. The model construes the environment as if it were a static, essentially "two dimensional" representation; it reduces it to a scene or view. But the natural environment is not a scene, not a representation, not static, and not two dimensional. In short, the model requires appreciation of the environment not as what it is and with the qualities it has, but as something it is not and with qualities it does not have. The model is unsuited to the actual nature of the object of appreciation. Consequently it not only, as OAM, unduly limits appreciation, in this case to certain artistic and scenic qualities, it also misleads it. Philosopher Ronald Hepburn puts the point in general terms:

> Supposing that a person's aesthetic education . . . instills in him the attitudes, the tactics of approach, the expectations proper to the appreciation of art works only, such a person will either pay very little aesthetic heed to natural objects or else heed them in the wrong way. He will look—and of course look in vain—for what can be found and enjoyed only in art . . . .

One alternative, alive to the problems of picturesque appreciation and of LSM and seemingly skeptical about aesthetic approaches to nature in general, simply denies the possibility of aesthetic appreciation of nature. This position accepts the traditional account of aesthetic appreciation of art, but stresses the fact that nature is natural, not art, and not our creation. It argues that aesthetic appreciation necessarily involves aesthetic evaluation, which entails judging the object of appreciation as the achievement of its creator and, therefore, since nature, unlike art, is not our creation, indeed is not the product of any designing intellect, appreciation of it is not aesthetic. One version of this position is called the Human Chauvinistic Aesthetic (HCA). Environmental philosophers Don Mannison and Robert Elliot have elaborated this view. For example, Elliot claims that our appreciative responses to nature do not "count as aesthetic responses," arguing that a:

> . . . judgemental element in aesthetic evaluation serves to differentiate it from environmental evaluation . . . [for] . . . Evaluating works of art involves explaining them, and judging them, in terms of their author's intentions; . . . locating them in some tradition and in some special *milieu* . . . [but] . . . Nature is not a work of art . . . .

A second alternative approach to appreciation of nature is more troubled by the limitations of OAM and focuses on the environmental dimension of our natural environment. It argues that traditional aesthetic approaches as exemplified by OAM, and to a lesser extent LSM, presuppose a subject/object dichotomy involving an isolating, distancing, and objectifying stance that is inappropriate for aesthetic appreciation not only of nature but of art as well. It is claimed that this stance wrongly abstracts both natural objects and appreciators from the environments in which they properly belong and in which appropriate appreciation is achieved. Thus, this position proposes to replace abstraction with engagement, distance with immersion, and objectivity with subjectivity, calling for a participatory aesthetics of nature.

By highlighting natural and environmental dimensions of the natural environment, HCA and AOE address many of the shortcomings of the traditional artistic models. However, these two approaches have problems of their own. HCA runs counter to both the orthodox view that everything is open to aesthetic appreciation and the common-sense idea that at least some instances of appreciation of natural things, such as fiery sunsets and soaring birds, constitute paradigm cases of aesthetic appreciation. AOE is also problematic. First, since at least some degree of the subject/object dichotomy seems essential to the very nature of aesthetic appreciation, its total rejection may necessitate a rejection of the aesthetic itself, reducing AOE to a version of HCA. Second, AOE seemingly embraces an unacceptable degree of subjectivity in aesthetic appreciation of both nature and art. However, the main problem with both positions is that, in the last analysis, they do not provide adequate answers to the questions of what and how to aesthetically appreciate in nature. Concerning the what question, HCA's answer is quite simply "nothing," while AOE's is seemingly "everything." And, therefore, concerning the how question, the former view has nothing more to say, while the latter apparently recommends "total immersion," an answer offering less guidance than we might wish.

Nonetheless, in spite of the problems inherent in HCA and AOE, both positions, in their respective emphases on the natural and the environmental, point toward a certain kind of paradigm for appreciation of nature. This paradigm is exemplified in the following description by geographer Yi-Fu Tuan:

> An adult must learn to be yielding and careless like a child if he were to enjoy nature polymorphously. He needs to slip into old clothes so that he could feel free to stretch out on the hay beside the brook and bathe in a meld of physical sensations: the smell of the hay and of horse dung; the warmth of the ground, its hard and soft contours; the warmth of the sun tempered by breeze; the tickling of an ant making its way up the calf of his leg; the play of shifting leaf shadows on his face; the sound of water over the pebbles and boulders, the sound of cicadas and distant traffic. Such an environment might break all the formal rules of euphony and aesthetics, substituting confusion for order, and yet be wholly satisfying.

Tuan's characterization of how to appreciate nature accords well with AOE's answer to the question of what to appreciate, that is, everything. This answer, of course, will not do. We cannot appreciate everything; there must be limits and emphases in appreciation of nature as there are in appreciation of art. Without such limits and emphases our experience of the natural environment would be only "a meld of physical sensations" without any meaning or significance, what philosopher William James characterized as a "blooming buzzing confusion." Such experience would indeed substitute "confusion for order" but, contra to both Tuan and AOE, would be neither "wholly satisfying" nor aesthetic.

Consider Tuan's example: We experience a "meld of sensations"—the smell of hay and of horse dung, the feel of the ant, the sound of cicadas and of distant traffic. However, if our response is to be aesthetic appreciation rather than just raw experience, the meld cannot remain a "blooming buzzing confusion." Rather it must become what philosopher John Dewey called a "consummatory experience": one in which knowledge and intelligence transform raw experience by making it determinate, harmonious, and meaningful. For example, we must recognize the smell of hay and that of horse dung and perhaps distinguish between them; we must feel the ant at least as an insect rather than as, say, a twitch. Such recognizing and distinguishing generate foci of aesthetic significance, natural foci appropriate to the particular natural environment. Likewise knowledge of the environment may yield appropriate boundaries and limits; the sound of cicadas may be appreciated as a proper part of the environment, but the sound of distant traffic excluded much as we ignore coughing in the concert hall.

Moreover, common sense and scientific knowledge of natural environments is relevant not only to the question of what to appreciate, but also to that of how to appreciate. Tuan's case may be taken as exemplifying a paradigm of nature appreciation, somewhat of a general environmental act of aspection. However, since natural environments, as works of art, differ in type, different natural environments require different acts of aspection; and as with the question of what to appreciate, knowledge of the environments in question indicates how to appreciate, indicates the appropriate act or acts of aspection. Paul Ziff tells us to look for contours in the Florentine school, for light in a Claude, and for color in a Bonnard, to survey a Tintoretto and to scan a Bosch. Likewise, we must survey a prairie, looking at the subtle contours of the land, feeling the wind blowing across the open space, and smelling the mix of prairie grasses and flowers. But such acts of aspection have little place in a dense forest. Here we must examine and scrutinize, inspecting the detail of the forest floor, listening carefully for the sounds of birds and smelling carefully for the scent of spruce and pine. Similarly, Tuan's description, in addition to characterizing environmental acts of aspection in general, also indicates the act of aspection appropriate for a particular type of environment—perhaps classifiable as pastoral. In appropriate aesthetic appreciation of nature, as in that of art, classification is, as Ziff says, of the essence.

Thus the questions of what and how to aesthetically appreciate concerning the natural environment may be answered analogously to the parallel questions about art. The difference is that with natural environments the relevant knowledge is common sense and scientific knowledge that we have discovered about the environments in question. Such knowledge yields appropriate boundaries of appreciation, particular foci of aesthetic significance, and relevant acts of aspection . . . .

This position, which takes natural and environmental science to be the key to aesthetic appreciation of the natural environment, may be termed the Natural Environmental Model (NEM). Like HCA and AOE, this model stresses the importance of the fact that the natural environment is both natural and an environment and, unlike OAM and LSM, it does not assimilate natural objects to art objects nor natural environments to scenery. Yet, unlike HCA and AOE, NEM does not reject the general and traditional structure of aesthetic appreciation of art as a model for aesthetic appreciation of the natural world. In fact it applies that structure rather directly to nature, making only such adjustments as are necessary in light of the nature of the natural environment. In doing so it avoids the absurdity of deeming appreciation of nature non-aesthetic while yet promoting aesthetic appreciation of nature for what it is and for the qualities it has. Thus, it discourages us from being appreciators who "either pay very little aesthetic heed to natural objects or else heed them in the wrong way," who "look—and of course look in vain—for what can be found and enjoyed only in art."

NEM acknowledges Santayana's assessment of the natural environment as indeterminate and promiscuous, so rich in diversity, suggestion, and vague stimulus that it must be composed to be appreciated. Moreover, NEM suggests that to achieve appropriate aesthetic appreciation, to, as Santayana says, find nature beautiful, the composition must be in terms of common sense and scientific knowledge. In addition to answering the central problem of the aesthetics of nature, this suggestion has a number of other ramifications.

Some of these ramifications are environmental and ethical. As noted, the traditional artistic models, such as OAM and LSM, and by implication other aesthetic approaches to appreciation of nature, are frequently condemned as anthropocentric or as superficial and trivial. They are said to be anti-natural, not appreciative of nature "on its own terms," and arrogantly disdainful of environments not conforming to artistic ideals. The root source of these environmental and ethical concerns is that artistic approaches do not encourage appreciation of nature for what it is and for the qualities it has. However, NEM bases aesthetic appreciation on the scientific view of what nature is and of what qualities it has. NEM thereby endows aesthetic appreciation of nature with a degree of objectivity that helps dispel environmental and moral criticisms, such as that of anthropocentrism or of superficiality.

Further, NEM aids in the alignment of aesthetics with other areas of philosophy, such as ethics, epistemology, and philosophy of mind, in which there is increasingly a rejection of archaic, inappropriate models and a new-found dependence on knowledge relevant to the particular phenomena in question. For example, environmental aesthetics parallels environmental ethics in the latter's rejection of anthropocentric models for the moral assessment of the natural world and the replacement of such models with paradigms drawn from the environmental and natural sciences. The challenge implicit in Santayana's remarks—that *we* confront a natural world that allows great liberty in selecting, emphasizing, and grouping, and that *we* must therefore compose it in order to aesthetically appreciate it— holds out an invitation not simply to find the natural world beautiful, but also to appropriately appreciate it for what it truly is.

CONTRIBUTORS

Aristotle (384–322 B.C.), the great philosopher and scientist of ancient Athens, whose influence on a vast range of topics, including tragedy, has been felt from antiquity to modern times.

Philip Auslander is Professor in the School of Literature, Communication, and Culture of the Georgia Institute of Technology. His books include *Liveness: Performance in a Mediatized Culture;* he is the editor of the four-volume anthology *Performance: Critical Concepts in Literary and Cultural Studies.*

Sally Banes, theorist of avant-garde and postmodern dance, teaches in the University of Wisconsin Dance Program. She is the author of numerous works in the field, including *Democracy's Body, Terpsichore in Sneakers* and *Writing Dance in the Age of Postmodernism.*

Jean Baudrillard, French sociologist and philosopher, is a leading voice in postmodern theory and criticism. He has written many books, including *Le systéme des objets* and *Simulacres et simulation.*

Michael Baxandall is Professor of the History of the Classical Tradition at the Warburg Institute of the University of London. He is the author of a large number of books, including *Giotto and the Orators, Patterns of Intention: On the Historical Explanation of Pictures, Tiepolo and Pictorial Intelligence,* and *Shadows and Enlightenment.*

Monroe C. Beardsley (1915–1985) who taught philosophy at Temple University, is one of the most widely read authors in aesthetics in the Anglo-American world. He is the author of *Aesthetics: Problems in the Philosophy of Criticism.*

Clive Bell (1881–1964), a highly influential critic and member of the famous Bloomsbury group, which included such figures as G. E. Moore and Virginia Woolf, is the author of the widely read book, *Art.*

Walter Benjamin (1892–1940) was a German literary and cultural critic, associated with the Frankfurt School for Social Research. He is the author of *Illuminations,*

The Origin of German Tragic Drama, and *Charles Baudelaire: A Lyrical Poet in the Age of High Capitalism.*

Maurice Berger teaches art history and critical theory at Hunter College and is the author of *Labyrinths: Robert Morris, Minimalism and the 1960s.*

Richard Bodman teaches in the Department of Asian Studies at St. Olaf College in Northfield, Minnesota. He is currently translating the prison diary of a twentieth-century Chinese poet, Huang Wu.

Peg Zeglin Brand is an artist who teaches philosophy and Gender Studies at the Indiana University. Her current project is a book entitled *Beauty Below the Surface: Feminist Visual Parodies.*

Lee B. Brown, who teaches philosophy at The Ohio State University, is the author of numerous articles on a variety of philosophical subjects including popular music, especially jazz.

Edmund Burke (1728–1797) may be known better for his conservative views in his *Reflections on the Revolution in France* than for his ideas on aesthetics. But his *Philosophical Enquiry into the Sublime and the Beautiful* is a major contribution to the philosophy of the arts.

Allen Carlson teaches philosophy at the University of Alberta and has written a number of influential articles on the aesthetics of the natural environment.

Noël Carroll, who teaches philosophy at the University of Wisconsin, is the writer of many essays and books on aesthetics and film theory, including *The Philosophy of Horror and Mystifying Movies.*

Stanley Cavell, who teaches philosophy at Harvard University, has published several influential essays and books on philosophy of language and aesthetics, including *Must We Mean What We Say? The World Viewed* and *Themes out of School.*

John Miller Chernoff, musician and lecturer on the topic of African arts and life, has written several articles on these subjects, including the book *African Rhythm and African Sensibility: Aesthetics and Social Action in African Musical Idiom.*

Ted Cohen, who teaches philosophy at the University of Chicago, is the author of numerous essays in the philosophy of art and a book on the aesthetics of jokes.

R. G. Collingwood (1889–1943), English philosopher and historian, taught at Oxford University and wrote on a variety of subjects, including art. He is the author of *The Principles of Art, The Idea of History,* and *The Idea of Nature.*

Ananda K. Coomaraswamy (1877–1947) was born in Ceylon, raised in England, and is the author of many books and articles on the aesthetics of Indian art. He is credited with having taught the West how to approach, understand, and appreciate the arts of India.

Donald Crawford, presently Vice-Chancellor at the University of California at Santa Barbara, is the author of *Kant's Aesthetic Theory* and many articles on philosophical aesthetics. He was the editor of the *Journal of Aesthetics and Art Criticism* for a number of years.

Gregory Currie teaches philosophy at Nottingham University and is the author of *Meeting of Minds: Thought, Imagination and Perception* and *Image and Moral Philosophy,* as well as many articles in philosophy of literature and film.

Arthur C. Danto, Professor Emeritus at Columbia University, where he was Johnsonian Professor of Philosophy, and art critic for *The Nation,* has published widely in all areas of philosophy including aesthetics. He is the author of the very influential *The Transfiguration of the Commonplace, The Philosophical Disenfranchisement of Art,* and *Playing with the Edge.*

Jacques Derrida, a leading French philosopher and influential exponent of the movement known as *deconstructionism,* is the author of *Of Grammatology, Margins of Philosophy, The Truth in Painting,* and *Speech and Phenomena.*

Mary Devereaux is a philosopher in the Research Ethics Program at the University of California, San Diego. She has published widely in aesthetics, including essays on beauty and evil; artistic autonomy and freedom of expression; feminist aesthetics; and the moral evaluation of narrative art.

John Dewey (1859–1952), one of the most important of American philosophers, is an exponent of pragmatism and a powerful force in theory of education and psychology. He is the author of numerous books, including *Art as Experience, Human Nature and Conduct,* and *The Quest for Certainty.*

George Dickie is Professor Emeritus at the University of Illinois, Chicago Circle Campus. An influential writer on aesthetics, he is the author of several books, including *The Art Circle.*

Denis Dutton is Senior Lecturer in aesthetics at the University of Canterbury, New Zealand, and is co-editor of the *Journal of Philosophy and Literature.* His books include *The Concept of Creativity in Science and Art.*

Terry Eagleton is a fellow of Wadham College, Oxford, and a prolific writer on modern literary theory from a Marxist point of view. His works include *Literary Theory—An Introduction* and *Criticism and Ideology.*

Anne Eaton teaches philosophy at Bucknell University. She specializes in feminist philosophy and the philosophy of art.

Umberto Eco is an Italian semiotician who has held posts at numerous European and American universities. He is the author of *A Theory of Semiotics* and the widely read novels *The Name of the Rose* and *Foucault's Pendulum.*

Evan Eisenberg, a former student of philosophy, writes about culture, technology, and music for a number of publications, including *The Village Voice* and *The Nation.*

Joel Feinberg (1926–2004), Professor Emeritus at the University of Arizona, is the author of numerous essays and books on the philosophy of law such as *The Moral Limits of the Criminal Law,* and *Freedom and Fulfillment: Philosophical Essays.*

Edmund Burke Feldman, who teaches art at the University of Georgia, is the author of several essays and books about art, including *Art as Image and Idea.*

Michel Foucault (1926–1984), a French philosopher of enormous influence, has written many books on a wide range of topics, including *The Order of Things, The History of Sexuality,* and *Madness and Civilization.*

Sigmund Freud (1856–1939) is the Austrian physician and inventor of psychoanalysis, a brilliant writer on a wide range of topics, and the author of *The Interpretation of Dreams, Beyond the Pleasure Principle,* and *Civilization and Its Discontents.*

Lydia Goehr teaches philosophy at Columbia University. She is the author of *The Imaginary Museum of Musical Works: An Essay in the Philosophy of Music.*

David Goldblatt, who teaches philosophy at Denison University, is the author of many articles on the arts, several on architecture, in a variety of philosophical and art theory publications as well as a forthcoming book on ventriloquism and art.

Ernst Gombrich, (1909–2001) a leading theorist of art history, was director of the Warburg Institute (London) and is the author of many influential books, including *Meditations on a Hobby Horse.*

Nelson Goodman, (1906–1998) Professor Emeritus at Harvard University, was the author of some of the most significant books in American analytic philosophy, including *The Structure of Appearance* and *Languages of Art.*

Theodore Gracyk teaches philosophy at Minnesota State University Moorhead and is the author of numerous essays and books in aesthetic theory including, *Rhythm and Noise: An Aesthetics of Rock.*

Clement Greenberg (1909–1994) was an art critic and author of many books, including *Art and Culture, Hans Hofmann,* and *Henri Matisse.* His many essays in *The Partisan Review* and *The Nation,* which are still enormously influential in the artworld, have been published under the title, *Collected Essays in Criticism.*

Garry L. Hagberg teaches philosophy at Bard College. He is author of *Art as Language* and *Meaning and Interpretation* and is co-editor of the *Journal of Philosophy and Literature.*

Greg Hayman is a freelance writer with interests in aesthetics and mass media.

Georg Friedrich Wilhelm Hegel (1770–1831), famous German philosopher and exponent of Absolute Idealism, wrote about virtually every philosophical topic, including art, in a great number of works. Among them are *The Phenomenology of Spirit, The Philosophy of Fine Art,* and *The Philosophy of the Fight.*

Martin Heidegger (1889–1976) is probably the most influential German philosopher of the twentieth century. He helped define the modern philosophical movement that became known as *existentialism* and has authored *Being and Time* and *On the Way to Language.*

David Hume (1711–1776), renowned Scottish empiricist philosopher and essayist, is the author of *A Treatise of Human Nature* and *An Inquiry Concerning Human Understanding.*

Immanuel Kant (1724–1804) is one of the great philosophers of all time whose famous three "critiques" are perennial sources of philosophical inspiration: *Critique* *of Pure Reason, Critique of Practical Reason,* and *Critique of Judgment,* the last of which contains his main writings on aesthetics.

Jeffrey Kipnis, who teaches theory and design in the School of Architecture at The Ohio State University, has written numerous articles on architectural theory and is the author of *In the Manor of Nietzsche.*

Peter Kivy teaches philosophy at Rutgers University, is a scholar of eighteenth-century aesthetics, and is one of the foremost writers in the philosophy of music. His works include *Sound and Semblance* and *The Corded Shell.*

Susanne K. Langer (1895–1985) wrote extensively on aesthetics. She is the author of *Philosophy in a New Key* and *Feeling and Form.*

Le Corbusier (Charles-Édouard Jeanneret) (1887–1965) is one of the most influential theorists and practitioners of modern architecture. He is the author of *Towards a New Architecture, The City of Tomorrow and Its Planning,* and *The Decorative Art of Today.*

Jerrold Levinson, who teaches philosophy at the University of Maryland, has written many books and essays in aesthetics, particularly in the philosophy of music.

Adolf Loos (1870-1933), a Viennese architect influential in architecture's movement toward modernism, wrote extensively on architecture, fashion, and the arts and crafts.

Jean-François Lyotard is noted for his work in the philosophy of culture, and postmodernism. He is the author of *The Postmodern Condition: A Report on Knowledge* and *Lessons on the Analytic of the Sublime.*

Catharine A. MacKinnon is a noted lawyer, political activist, and Elizabeth A. Long Professor of Law the University of Michigan. She is the author of *Toward a Feminist Theory of the State, Feminism Unmodified: Discourses on Life and Law, Only Words,* and *Sex Equality.*

Paul Mattick is Professor of Philosophy at Adelphi University. He is the author of *Art in Its Time* and *Social Knowledge* and has written art criticism for *Arts, Art in America, Artforum,* and other publications.

Laura Mulvey teaches at the British Film Institute in London and is the author of *Visual and Other Pleasures* and *Fetishism and Curiosity.*

Alexander Nehamas, a specialist in ancient philosophy and the philosophy of Nietzsche, teaches at Princeton University. He is the author of *Nietzsche: Life as Literature.*

Friedrich Nietzsche (1844–1900), German philologist and philosopher, is an enormously influential figure in many areas of philosophy. The concept of art played a central role in his many writings on ethics, culture, and metaphysics, including *The Birth of Tragedy, Thus Spake Zarathustra, Beyond Good and Evil, Twilight of the Idols,* and *The Gay Science.*

Linda Nochlin teaches art history at Yale University. Her books include *Realism and Tradition in Art* and *Woman as Sex Object: Studies in Erotic Art.*

Patricia C. Phillips is an art critic and curator and is Dean of the School of Fine and Performing Arts at the State University of New York, New Paltz. She is the Executive Editor of *Art Journal* and a contributor to several art publications.

Plato (427 B.C.–348 B.C.), the Greek thinker, was perhaps the greatest philosopher of the West. His dialogues, *The Republic, Ion,* and *Phaedrus,* discuss a range of metaphysical and ethical problems about art.

Henry John Pratt is completing his doctorate in philosophy at The Ohio State University with a dissertation on the generality of the critical normative principles governing art.

Diana Raffman teaches philosophy at The Ohio State University. She is the author of *Language, Music and Mind* and specializes in philosophy of mind as well as music aesthetics.

Jenefer Robinson teaches philosophy at the University of Cincinnati. She has written many essays and books in aesthetics, particularly in the fields of music and literature.

Joel Rudinow, who teaches philosophy at Sonoma State University and Santa Rosa Junior College, has published widely in the field of aesthetics.

Roger Scruton has held the post of Lecturer in Philosophy at Birbeck College in London. He is the author of numerous essays and books in aesthetics, including *The Aesthetic Understanding, The Aesthetics of Architecture,* and the novel *Francesca.*

Richard Shusterman, who teaches philosophy at Temple University, is the author of several books and essays in aesthetics, including *Pragmatist Aesthetics* and *The Object of Literary Criticism.*

Frank Sibley (1923–1996) taught philosophy at the University of Lancaster, England, and is the author of several influential articles in aesthetics.

Robert Solomon teaches philosophy at the University of Texas, Austin. He is the author and editor of many books and essays on German philosophy, existentialism, aesthetics, and politics, including *On the Spirit of Hegel.*

J. O. Urmson, Fellow of Corpus Christi College, Oxford, is author of *Philosophical Analysis,* a classic in analytic philosophy.

Carole S. Vance teaches anthropology at the School of Public Health at Columbia University and is the editor of *Pleasure and Danger: Exploring Female Sexuality.*

Robert Venturi is a leading practitioner and theorist of postmodern architecture. He is the author of *Complexity and Contradiction in Architecture,* and the co-author of *Learning from Las Vegas* and *A View from the Campidoglio.*

Kendall L. Walton teaches philosophy at the University of Michigan and is the author of *Mimesis as Make-Believe: On the Foundations of the Representational Arts* and many influential essays in philosophy of art.

Anita M. Waters teaches Sociology and Black Studies at Denison University. She is the author of *Race, Class and Political Symbols: Rastafari and Reggae in Jamaican Politics.*

Morris Weitz (1916–1981) taught philosophy at Brandeis and The Ohio State University. He was an "analytic" philosopher who applied Wittgenstein's ideas to aesthetics. He wrote several books in the area of philosophy of literature, including *Hamlet and the Philosophy of Literary Criticism.*

Richard Wollheim (1923–2003) was Grote Professor at the University of London and Mills Professor at the University of California at Berkeley. His books include *The Thread of Life, Painting as an Art,* and *Art and Its Objects.*